Organizational Behavior

Securing Competitive Advantage

Second Edition

John A. Wagner III and
John R. Hollenbeck

Routledge
Taylor & Francis Group

NEW YORK AND LONDON

First published 2015
by Routledge
711 Third Avenue, New York, NY 10017
and by Routledge
2 Park Square, Milton Park, Abingdon, Oxon OX14 4RN

Routledge is an imprint of the Taylor & Francis Group, an informa business

© 2015 Taylor & Francis

Typeset in Galliard by
Swales & Willis Ltd, Exeter, Devon

The right of John A. Wagner III and John R. Hollenbeck to be identified as authors of this work has been asserted by them in accordance with sections 77 and 78 of the Copyright, Designs and Patents Act 1988.

Library of Congress Cataloging in Publication Data
Wagner, John A., 1952–
Organizational behavior : securing competitive advantage / John A. Wagner III & John R. Hollenbeck. — 2nd Edition.
pages cm
Includes bibliographical references and index.
1. Organizational behavior.   I. Hollenbeck, John R.   II. Title.
HD58.7.W24 2014
658.3—dc23
2013051007

ISBN: 978–0–415–82423–1
ISBN: 978–0–415–82424–8
ISBN: 978–0–203–38541–8

Printed and bound in India by Replika Press Pvt. Ltd.

Organizational Behavior

The management of organizational behavior is a critically important source of competitive advantage in today's organizations. Every organization's members share a constellation of skills, abilities, and motivations that differentiates it from every other firm. To gain advantage, managers must be able to capitalize on these individual differences as jobs are designed, teams are formed, work is structured, and change is facilitated. This textbook, now in its second edition, provides its readers with the knowledge required to succeed as managers under these circumstances.

In this book, John Wagner and John Hollenbeck make the key connection between theory and practice to help students excel as managers charged with the task of securing competitive advantage. They present students with a variety of helpful learning tools, including:

- Coverage of the full spectrum of organizational behavior topics
- Managerial models that are based in many instances on hundreds of research studies and decades of management practice
- Introductory mini-cases and current examples throughout the the text to help students contextualize organizational behavior theory and understand its application in today's business world

The ideal book for undergraduate and graduate students of organizational behavior, *Organizational Behavior: Securing Competitive Advantage* is written to motivate exceptional student performance and contribute to their lasting managerial success.

John A. Wagner is Associate Dean for Undergraduate Programs and Professor of Management at Michigan State University, USA. He is an associate editor of the *Administrative Science Quarterly* and has served on the editorial board of the Academy of Management Review, in addition to having published in top-tier journals.

John R. Hollenbeck is University Distinguished Professor and Broad Professor of Management at Michigan State University, USA. He has served as acting editor at *Organizational Behavior and Human Decision Processes*, associate editor of *Decision Sciences*, and editor of *Personnel Psychology*, and has published over 80 articles and book chapters.

To Mary Jane, Allison, Jillian, and Andrew Wagner
To Patty, Jennifer, Marie, Tim, and Jeff Hollenbeck

Brief Contents

Contents

Preface
Competing for Advantage

In today's business environment, competition arises when other organizations seek to do what your company does, only better. Advantage is gained when you can do something your competitors find difficult to duplicate. Competitive advantage is further secured when competitors cannot duplicate your company's special ability at all.

We contend—based on solid research evidence—that an especially strong source of competitive advantage rests in the people who make up an organization. One of the most effective ways to secure competitive advantage is to make the best use of the knowledge, skills, and other human assets possessed by a company's employees. No other firm has the same people. Therefore, no other company can duplicate the range of products and services requiring the particular capabilities of the company's members. Managing organizational behavior is thus essential to the process of gaining and sustaining competitive advantage. This statement is a central theme of our book.

Chapters in the book cover the major topics constituting the field of organizational behavior, and do so with special emphasis on the findings of rigorous organizational research. The models and concepts presented in the following chapters are grounded in literally thousands of studies of behavior in and of organizations. Rather than chasing current fads or fashions, our focus as authors is on surveying and explaining research-based practices that have been proven to work over the long term. Chapters focus on key variables that managers can modify to manage organizational behavior and on relationships among those variables that can help managers determine the likely consequences of managerial action. Managerial tools derived from rigorous research are the means through which managers can secure competitive advantage in the most effective manner. Understanding them and being able to put them to use is critical to managerial effectiveness and organizational success.

Additional instructor resources linked to the book chapters are available on the companion website, **www.routledge.com/cw/wagner**.

An Invitation

By reading our book, you are committing yourself to learn how to manage organizational behavior. We cannot think of anything more important for you to understand. In return for this commitment, we extend a special invitation to you, our newest student. We want to know how you like our book and how you feel about the field of organizational behavior. We encourage you to contact us with your ideas, especially your suggestions for making improvements to future editions. Please write to us at:

Michigan State University, Eli Broad Graduate School of Management
Department of Management, East Lansing, Michigan 48824–1122

John A. Wagner III
John R. Hollenbeck

Part I

Introduction

Chapter 1

Organizational Behavior

Onshoring—bringing work formerly sent to companies located abroad back to its country of origin to be performed in domestic operations—is increasingly common in the United States due to concerns about rising international labor and shipping costs as well as lost control over quality and responsiveness to customer demand. Companies ranging from multinational giants Apple and General Electric to smaller regional firms, such as Multicraft, an automotive parts manufacturer located in Pelahatchie, Mississippi, have onshored manufacturing activities once offshored to parts of the world known for low-cost production. As onshoring has spread among U.S. companies, managers have discovered the critical importance of improving employee productivity so that the effects of higher domestic labor costs are lessened by greater per-worker output.[1]

Imagine that you are a manager in a firm that has recently onshored various production activities and that you seek to influence employee productivity in order to offset related costs. Initial assessments indicate that instances of lower than acceptable productivity in your company are due to poor employee motivation, and your boss tells you to solve this problem. Your future with the company—and, possibly, the future of the company itself—may depend on whether you can find a way to improve employee motivation. To help you decide what to do, you call in four highly recommended management consultants.

After analyzing your company's situation, the first consultant states that many of today's jobs are so simple, monotonous, and uninteresting that they dampen employee motivation and fulfillment. As a result, employees become so bored and resentful that productivity falls off. This consultant recommends that you redesign your firm's jobs in order to make them more complex, stimulating, and fulfilling. Employees challenged by these new jobs will feel motivated to improve performance, leading to higher workforce productivity and reduced production costs.

The second consultant performs her own assessment of your company. As she reviews her findings, she agrees that monotonous work can reduce employee motivation. She says, however, that the absence of clear, challenging goals is an even greater threat to motivation and productivity at your firm. Such goals provide performance targets that draw attention to the work to be done and focus employee effort on achieving success. The second consultant advises you to solve your company's productivity problem by implementing a program of formal goal setting.

The third consultant conducts an investigation and concedes that both job design and goal setting can improve employee motivation. She suggests, however, that you consider establishing a contingent payment program. *Contingent payment* means paying employees according to their performance instead of giving them fixed salaries or hourly wages. For instance, salespeople may be paid commissions on their sales, production employees may be paid piece-rate wages according to their productivity, and executives may be paid bonuses based on the firm's profitability. The consultant points out that contingent payment programs change the way wages are *distributed* but not necessarily the *amount* of wages paid to the workforce as a whole.

Finally, the fourth consultant examines your situation as well as the three approaches proposed by the others. He agrees that any of these approaches might work, but describes another technique that is often used to deal with motivational problems—allowing employees to participate in decision making. He suggests that such participation gives employees a sense of belonging or ownership that energizes productivity. To support his recommendation, he recites an impressive list of companies—among them, General Motors, IBM, and General Electric—that have established well-known participatory programs.

Later, alone in your office, you consider the four consultants' reports and conclude that you should probably recommend all four alternatives—just in case one or more of the consultants are wrong. Unfortunately, you also realize that your company can afford the time and money needed to implement only one of the recommendations. What should you do? Which alternative should you choose?

According to research combining the results of nearly a hundred studies that have compared the effectiveness of these alternatives, if you choose the first option, job redesign, productivity would probably rise by 9 percent.[2] An increase of this size would save your job, keep your company in business, and probably earn you the company president's lasting gratitude. If you choose the second alternative, goal setting, productivity would probably increase by 16 percent.[3] This outcome would save your job and strengthen your company, and it might even put you in the running for a promotion. If you choose the third alternative, contingent payment, productivity could be expected to increase by approximately 30 percent.[4] A gain of this magnitude would certainly gain you the notice of top management and could even lead to a place for you in the company's executive suites.

But what about the fourth alternative, employee participation in decision making? How might this approach affect productivity, where low performance is attributable to poor motivation? Knowing that managers are choosing participatory programs on a regular basis to solve motivation problems, you might think that this alternative should work at least as well as the other three. Surprisingly, however, participation usually has no meaningful effect on productivity problems caused by poor motivation. It can certainly have other positive effects, for example increasing commitment to participatory decisions or facilitating the distribution of information among participants. Despite the fourth consultant's suggestion, however, employee participation is likely to improve motivation and performance only when combined with one or more of the other three alternatives.[5] If you choose participation, then, you might soon be looking for a new job. Perhaps your choice might even cost your company its existence.

How realistic is this story? In fact, the predicament it portrays is an everyday problem, due to onshoring as well as a variety of other organizational challenges. Experts throughout the world have pointed out many instances of low organizational productivity, often identifying "people problems" as an important factor in causing these situations.[6] Solving such problems is critical to company survival and growth in today's competitive environment. Knowing which solutions to choose and how to implement them will differentiate organizations that succeed and thrive from those that fail. Such knowledge is thus a clear source of competitive advantage and success.

More generally, competitive success depends on the ability to produce some product or service that is perceived as valuable by some group of consumers, and to do so in a way that no one else can duplicate.[7] At first glance, there appear to be many ways to accomplish this feat. Most experts agree, however, that an organization's employees are its foremost source of competitive advantage. If your company employs the best people and is able to hold on to them, it enjoys a competitive edge not easily duplicated by other firms. If your company also has the "know-how" to properly manage its employees, it has an advantage that can be sustained and even strengthened over time.[8]

The know-how needed to solve motivational productivity problems, like those focused upon in our opening example, can be found in the field of organizational behavior. Without this knowledge, managers have no solid basis for accepting any one consultant's advice or for choosing one particular way to solve people problems instead of another. With it, managers have the guidance needed to avoid costly or even catastrophic mistakes and instead make effective choices that secure competitive success. *The management of people through the application of knowledge from the field of organizational behavior is a primary means through which competitive advantage can be created and sustained.*

Defining Organizational Behavior

Organizational behavior is a field of study that endeavors to understand, explain, predict, and change human behavior as it occurs in the organizational context. Underlying this definition are three important considerations:

1. Organizational behavior focuses on observable behaviors, such as talking in a meeting, running production equipment, or writing a report. It also deals with the internal states, such as thinking, perceiving, and deciding, that accompany visible actions.
2. Organizational behavior involves the analysis of how people behave both as individuals and as members of groups and organizations.
3. Organizational behavior also assesses the "behavior" of groups and organizations per se. Neither groups nor organizations "behave" in the same sense that people do. Nevertheless, some events occur in organizations that cannot be explained in terms of individual behavior. These events must be examined in terms of group or organizational processes.

Research in organizational behavior traces its roots to the late 1940s, when researchers in psychology, sociology, political science, economics, and other social sciences joined together in an effort to develop a comprehensive body of organizational knowledge.[9] As it has developed, the field of organizational behavior has grown into three distinct subfields, delineated in Table 1.1: micro organizational behavior, meso organizational behavior, and macro organizational behavior.

Table 1.1 Subfields of Organizational Behavior

Subfield	Focus	Origins
Micro organizational behavior	Individuals	Experimental, clinical, and organizational psychology
Meso organizational behavior	Groups	Communication, social psychology, and interactionist sociology, plus the origins of the other two subfields
Macro organizational behavior	Organizations	Sociology, political science, anthropology, and economics

Micro Organizational Behavior

Micro organizational behavior is concerned mainly with the behaviors of individuals working alone.[10] Three subfields of psychology were the principal contributors to the beginnings of micro organizational behavior. *Experimental psychology* provided theories of learning, motivation, perception, and stress. *Clinical psychology* furnished models of personality and human development. *Industrial psychology* offered theories of employee selection, workplace attitudes, and performance assessment. Owing to this heritage, micro organizational behavior has a distinctly psychological orientation. Among the questions it examines are the following: How do differences in ability affect employee productivity? What motivates employees to perform their jobs? How do employees develop perceptions of their workplace, and how do these perceptions in turn influence their behavior?

Meso Organizational Behavior

Meso organizational behavior is a middle ground, bridging the other two subfields of organizational behavior.[11] It focuses primarily on understanding the behaviors of people working together in teams and groups. In addition to sharing the origins of the other two subfields, meso organizational behavior grew out of research in the fields of *communication, social psychology*, and *interactionist sociology*, which provided theories on such topics as socialization, leadership, and group dynamics. Meso organizational behavior seeks answers to questions such as the following: What forms of socialization encourage co-workers to cooperate? What mix of skills among team members increases team performance? How can managers determine which prospective leader will be the most effective?

Macro Organizational Behavior

Macro organizational behavior focuses on understanding the "behaviors" of entire organizations.[12] The origins of macro organizational behavior can be traced to four disciplines. *Sociology* provided theories of structure, social status, and institutional relations. *Political science* offered theories of power, conflict, bargaining, and control. *Anthropology* contributed theories of symbolism, cultural influence, and comparative analysis. *Economics* furnished theories of competition and efficiency. Research on macro organizational behavior considers questions such as the following: How is power acquired and retained? How can conflicts be resolved? What mechanisms can be used to coordinate work activities? How should an organization be structured to best cope with its surrounding environment?

Contemporary Management Issues

Considered both individually and collectively, the three subfields of organizational behavior offer valuable information, insights, and advice to managers facing the challenge of understanding and reacting to a broad range of contemporary management issues.[13] According to various sources, today's managers find five of these issues especially important: workforce diversity, team productivity, organizational adaptability, international growth and development, and ethics.

Workforce Diversity

Within the societal cultures of the United States and Canada, subcultural differences once ignored by many managers now command significant attention and sensitivity. Historically, the North American workforce has consisted primarily of white males. Today, however, white males make up far less than 50 percent of business new hires in the United States, whereas women and African American, Hispanic, and Asian men account for increasingly large segments of the U.S. workforce. Moreover, in the last twenty years the number of women and minorities assuming managerial positions in the U.S. workforce has grown by over 25 percent.[14] It is becoming—and will continue to become—even more important for managers to know about and be ready to respond to the challenges deriving from individual differences in abilities, personalities, and motives. Knowledge about the workplace consequences of these differences, drawn from the subfield of micro organizational behavior, can provide managers with help in this regard.

Team Productivity

Management is becoming less of a process relying on top-down command and control, where managers have all the power and nonmanagerial employees have little say in what they do.[15] For various reasons, organizations now use greater amounts of *empowerment*—the delegation to nonmanagers of the authority to make significant decisions on their jobs. Often, empowerment is accomplished by grouping employees into teams and then giving those teams responsibility for self-management activities such as hiring, firing, and training members, setting production targets, and assessing output quality. Guidance from meso organizational behavior precepts can help managers establish realistic expectations about the implementation difficulties and probable effects of team-based empowerment.

Organizational Adaptability

In today's business world, emphasis is shifting from the mass production of low-cost, interchangeable commodities to the production of high-quality goods and services, made individually or in small batches and geared to meet the specific demands of small groups of consumers. This shift requires greater flexibility than ever before and necessitates that quality receive greater emphasis than it has in the past. Companies are reacting by implementing programs that require new ways of dividing an organization's work into jobs and coordinating the efforts of many employees.[16] Implementations of this sort benefit from insights derived from macro organizational behavior.

International Growth and Development

Fewer firms today limit their operations to a single national or cultural region than was once the case. Instead, multinationalism or even statelessness has become the norm. The resulting globalization is changing the way business is conducted, and it promises to continue to do so at an increasing pace.[17] Managers facing this massive change must develop increased sensitivity to international cultural differences. All three subfields of organizational behavior have valuable advice to offer managers confronted with this challenge.

Ethics

Managing organizational behavior inevitably involves the acquisition and use of power. Thus, managers continually face the issue of determining whether the use of power in a given instance is effective and appropriate. One approach in dealing with this issue is to adopt the *utilitarianist* perspective and judge the appropriateness of the use of power in terms of the consequences of this use. Does using power provide the greatest good for the greatest number of people? If the answer to this question is "yes," then the utilitarian perspective would suggest that power is being used appropriately.

A second perspective, derived from the theory of *moral rights*, suggests that power is used appropriately only when no one's personal rights or freedoms are sacrificed. It is certainly possible for many people to derive great satisfaction from the use of power to accomplish some purpose, thus satisfying utilitarian criteria, while simultaneously causing the rights of a few individuals to be abridged. According to the theory of moral rights, the latter effect is an indication of inappropriateness. Power holders seeking to use their power appropriately must therefore respect the rights and interests of the minority as well as look after the well-being of the majority.

A third perspective, drawn from various theories of *social justice*, suggests that even having respect for the rights of everyone in an organization might not be enough to fully justify the use of power. In addition, those using power must treat people equitably, ensuring that people who are similar in relevant respects are treated similarly, whereas people who are different are treated differently in proportion to those differences. Power holders must also be accountable for injuries caused by their use of power and must be prepared to provide compensation for these injuries.

Obviously, the three perspectives offer conflicting criteria, suggesting that no simple answers exist for questions concerning the appropriateness of using power. Instead, as power holders, managers must seek to balance efficiency, entitlement, and equity concerns as they attempt to influence the behaviors of others.[18]

Putting Organizational Behavior Knowledge to Work

Putting theoretical knowledge from the field of organizational behavior to practical use requires that managers develop skills in using such knowledge to identify and solve problems in an effective manner. To develop your own managerial skills and learn how to put them to work, it is important that you understand the process of problem solving and become proficient at experimenting with ways of becoming a better problem solver. The process of problem solving can be simplified and made more effective by breaking it into the four stages described in Table 1.2: diagnosis, solution, action, and evaluation.[19]

Table 1.2 Four Stages of Problem Solving

Stage	Description
Diagnosis	Collection of information about a troubling organizational situation and summarization of this information in a problem statement.
Solution	Identification of ways to resolve the problem identified during diagnosis.
Action	Stipulation of the activities needed to solve the problem and oversight of the implementation of these activities. Also, identification of the indicators to be used to measure success and collection of data reflecting these measures.
Evaluation	Determination of the extent to which the actions taken to solve the problem had the intended effect, using the indicators and data collected during the action stage.

Diagnosis

Problem solving begins with **diagnosis**, a procedure in which managers gather information about a troublesome situation and try to summarize it in a *problem statement*. Information gathering may require direct observation of events in or around an organization. Experts often praise the practice of "managing by wandering around," in part because it provides a rich source of firsthand information that can be used during problem-solving procedures.

Managers may also conduct interviews to gather facts and opinions, or administer questionnaires to collect others' views. Both approaches lack the immediacy of personal observation, but enable the collection of diverse information and opinions.

Summarizing information in a problem statement requires that managers use the mix of theories, experience, and intuition they have amassed to construct a statement of what is wrong. Often the information placed before a manager looks much like the kind of data that a medical doctor uses to identify the source of an illness. Just as the doctor might have to consider evidence of fever, body pain, and nausea to diagnose a case of influenza, the manager might have to interpret the meanings of numerous *symptoms* to formulate a problem statement.

For example, when the Buick Motor Division of General Motors dropped Plumley Companies as a supplier of hoses and other rubber parts, citing poor product quality, company owner Michael A. Plumley discovered that workers wanted to produce good parts but lacked the knowledge and skills necessary to perform their jobs correctly. After stepping up worker training, the company improved its situation substantially and now holds quality awards from GM, Nissan, Ford, and Chrysler.[20] As indicated in this example, the manager, acting as a diagnostician, often must take responsibility for analyzing the individual symptoms and learning how they fit together to point toward the larger problem.

Solution

Solution is the process of identifying ways to resolve the problem identified during the diagnosis phase. Organizational problems are often multifaceted, and usually more than one way to solve a given problem exists. Effective managers consider several reasonable alternatives before choosing one. In the case of Plumley Companies, Michael Plumley considered but ruled out poor supervision, equipment deficiencies, raw material defects, and employee motivation, and also considered a variety of training approaches before making a final choice. More generally, managers prescribing solutions must resist the urge to *satisfice*—to choose the first alternative that seems workable—and must instead push themselves to consider several potential solutions and choose the best available alternative.[21]

Action

Action is setting a proposed solution into motion. In this stage, managers must first stipulate the specific activities they believe are needed to solve a particular problem and then oversee the implementation of these activities. Sometimes it is possible to implement a step-by-step program that was developed earlier to solve a similar problem encountered previously or in another organization. In other cases, it is necessary to start from scratch, creating a new sequence of activities to be implemented for the first time. In either event, action is the point at which plans developed during the process of formulating a solution are put into play and exert effects intended to reduce or resolve the problem identified in diagnosis.

Evaluation

Problem solving concludes with **evaluation**, the process of determining whether actions taken to solve the problem had the intended effect. To evaluate their solutions properly, managers must identify in advance the indicators they will use to measure success and collect measures of these indicators as the action stage proceeds. For instance, to evaluate a program intended to improve productivity, managers must decide what kinds of measures to use—for example, counts of items produced, questionnaire indices of customer satisfaction, dollar volume of sales, or similar measures. They must then decide how to collect this information and what value or cutoff amount to use as an indication of success (for example, a 5 percent increase in sales, measured as booked transactions).

The evaluation process highlights any differences between the intended results of a particular solution and the actual results. Sometimes the chosen course of action completely resolves the problem. Often, however, additional problems are uncovered and further problem solving becomes necessary. At this point, managers use evaluation information as diagnostic data and the process of problem solving begins again.[22]

Active Problem Solving

As you read this book, you will find yourself thinking about how you might use textbook information to solve real-world problems. To sharpen your skills as a problem solver, we suggest that you study each theory presented in this book to develop a basic understanding of the variables and relationships it describes. As you grow more comfortable with applying the theories, try combining them to develop more comprehensive management tools. For example, you might blend theories of employee motivation, leadership, and job design to develop an enriched explanation of the causes of poor employee performance.

You should also practice following the theories applied during problem definition to their logical conclusions. For instance, the same theory of employee motivation that you use to diagnose a productivity problem in a case might also suggest the actions needed to reduce or eliminate the problem. Similarly, a theory of leadership that helps you begin an exercise on the distribution of power may also provide guidance about how power should be managed later in the exercise. At the same time, you should work on applying several theories simultaneously as you diagnose problems and search for solutions. The more theories you apply during diagnosis, the more comprehensive your final solution is likely to be. As you become a more skillful problem solver, the solutions you devise are likely to become increasingly thorough and more effective.

As part of the process of learning how to apply the material in this book, you should also practice specifying the actions required to implement and assess your proposed solution. Your action plan should include a sequence of steps that indicate what needs to be done, who will do it, and when it will be done. Your evaluation procedure should indicate how you plan to measure the effectiveness of your actions as well as what you expect to do if the evaluation reveals shortcomings in your solution.

Overview of This Book

As we have indicated in this chapter, our book focuses on providing conceptual frameworks that will prove helpful in the future as you solve problems and manage behaviors in organizations. What you learn now will serve later as a valuable source of competitive advantage for you and your firm.

The book consists of five parts. Part I includes two introductory chapters, this one on organizational behavior and a second one on management, that provide a conceptual foundation for later chapters. Part II, on micro organizational behavior, consists of four chapters on diversity and individual differences, decision making and creativity, motivation and work performance, and satisfaction and stress at work. These chapters provide information useful for the management of people as individuals in organizations. Part III, on meso organizational behavior, includes four chapters dealing with work design, socialization and other interpersonal processes, group and team effectiveness, and leadership in groups and organizations. These chapters furnish the information needed to manage interpersonal relations and group processes in organizations. Part IV, on macro organizational behavior, consists of four chapters on the topics of power and conflict, organization structure, organizational design, and culture and organizational development. The information in these chapters concerns organization-level problems and the management of related processes and procedures. Finally, Part V includes two chapters on topics that span the three subfields of organizational behavior. One chapter covers international organizational behavior, and the other focuses on research methods and critical thinking. Both provide information that will help you to adapt and apply what you have learned elsewhere in the book to a wide variety of situations.

Summary

Organizational behavior is a field of research that helps predict, explain, and understand behaviors occurring in and among organizations. Organizational behavior's three subfields—micro organizational behavior, meso organizational behavior, and macro organizational behavior—reflect differences among the scientific disciplines that contributed to the founding of the field. As a consequence, each focuses on a different aspect of organizational behavior. *Micro organizational behavior* is concerned primarily with the attributes and performance of individuals in organizations. *Meso organizational behavior* focuses on the characteristics of groups and the behaviors of people in teams. *Macro organizational behavior* addresses the "behaviors" of organizations as entities.

Effective managers use knowledge from the three subfields during problem solving, which is the process of diagnosis, solution, action, and evaluation. *Diagnosis* involves interpreting symptoms and identifying the problem. *Solution* occurs when one or more ways of resolving the problem are formulated. In *action*, specific activities are enacted and a solution is implemented. *Evaluation*, the final phase of problem solving, involves assessing the effectiveness of the implemented solution and can serve as an input for further problem solving, if required.

Review Questions

1. Define the field of organizational behavior. What kinds of behavior does it examine? Why is knowledge drawn from the field of organizational behavior so important for managers?
2. What are the three subfields of organizational behavior? Why have they developed separately? What kinds of organizational problems does each subfield help managers solve?
3. What are the four stages of the problem-solving process? How can knowing about them help you become a better manager?
4. Why should you refer to textbook theories during the process of problem solving? How will using this textbook make you a better manager?

Notes

1 J. Amy, "Miss. Aims to Lure Factories from other Countries," *Bloomberg Businessweek*, August 21, 2012, http://www.businessweek.com/ap/2012-08-21/miss-dot-aims-to-lure-factories-from-other-countries; H. Sirkin, "Winning the Factory Wars," *Bloomberg Businessweek*, October 1, 2012, http://www.businessweek.com/articles/2012-10-01/winning-the-factory-wars.

2 E. A. Locke, D. B. Feren, V. M. McCaleb, K. N. Shaw, and A. T. Denny, "The Relative Effectiveness of Four Methods of Motivating Employee Performance," in K. D. Duncan, M. M. Gruneberg, and D. Wallis, eds., *Changes in Working Life* (Chichester, UK: Wiley, 1980), 363–388.

3 Ibid.

4 Ibid.; J. A. Wagner III, P. A. Rubin, and T. J. Callahan, "Incentive Payment and Non-managerial Productivity: An Interrupted Time Series Analysis of Magnitude and Trend," *Organizational Behavior and Human Decision Processes* 42 (1988): 47–74; R. D. Banker, S. Y. Lee, G. Potter, and D. Srinivasan, "Contextual Analysis of Performance Impacts of Outcome-Based Incentive Compensation," *Academy of Management Journal* 39 (1996): 920–948.

5 Locke et al., "The Relative Effectiveness"; J. A. Wagner III and R. Z. Gooding, "Shared Influence and Organizational Behavior: A Meta-Analysis of Situational Variables Expected to Moderate Participation-Outcome Relationships," *Academy of Management Journal* 30 (1987): 524–541; J. A. Wagner III and J. A. LePine, "Participation's Effects on Performance and Satisfaction: Additional Evidence from U.S. Research," *Psychological Reports* 84 (1999): 719–725; J. A. Wagner III, "Use Participation to Share Information and Distribute Knowledge," in E. A. Locke, ed., *The Blackwell Handbook of Organizational Behavior*, 2nd ed. (Oxford, UK: Blackwell Publishers, 2008), 304–316.

6 B. Nussbaum, "Needed: Human Capital," *BusinessWeek*, September 19, 1988, 100–103; W. Trueman, "Alternative Visions," *Canadian Business*, March 1991, 28–33; D. Brady, "Wanted: Eclectic Visionary with a Sense of Humor," *BusinessWeek*, August 28, 2000, 143–144; S. S. Kumar, "Motivation as a Strategy to Enhance Organizational Productivity," *Advances in Management* 5 (2012): 142–179.

7 J. Barney, "Strategic Market Factors: Expectation, Luck, and Business Strategy," *Management Science* 32 (1986): 1231–1241; I. Dierickx and K. Cool, "Asset Stock Accumulation and Sustainability of Competitive Advantage," *Management Science* 35 (1989): 1504–1511; J. Nahapiet and S. Ghoshal, "Social Capital, Intellectual Capital, and the Organizational Advantage," *Academy of Management Review* 23 (1998): 242–266; P. M. Wright, G. C. McMahan, and A. McWilliams, "Human Resources and Sustained Competitive Advantage: A Resource-Based Perspective," *International Journal of Human Resource Management* 5 (1994): 301–326; P. De Sa-Perez and J. M. Garcia-Falcon, "A Resource-Based View of Human Resource Management and Organizational Capabilities Development," *International Journal of Human Resource Management* 13 (2002): 123–140.

8 J. Pfeffer, "Producing Sustainable Competitive Advantage through the Effective Management of People," *Academy of Management Executive* 9 (1995): 55–69; P. M. Wright and G. C. McMahan, "Theoretical Perspectives for Strategic Human Resources Management," *Journal of Management* 18 (1992): 295–320.

9 L. L. Greiner, "A Recent History of Organizational Behavior," in S. Kerr, ed., *Organizational Behavior* (Columbus, OH: Grid Publishing, 1979), 3–14.

10 L. L. Cummings, "Toward Organizational Behavior," *Academy of Management Review* 3 (1978): 90–98; D. M. Rousseau, "Reinforcing the Micro/Macro Bridge: Organizational Thinking and Pluralistic Vehicles," *Journal of Management* 37 (2011): 429–442.

11 P. Cappelli and P. D. Sherer, "The Missing Role of Context in OB: The Need for a Meso-Level Approach," in L. L. Cummings and B. M. Staw, eds., *Research in Organizational Behavior* 13 (Greenwich, CT: JAI Press, 1991), 55–110; R. House, D. M. Rousseau, and M. Thomas-Hunt, "The Meso Paradigm: A Framework for the Integration of Micro and Macro Organizational Behavior," in L. L. Cummings and B. M. Staw, eds., *Research in Organizational Behavior* 17 (Greenwich, CT: JAI Press, 1995): 71–114; G. A. Fine, "Group Culture and the Interaction Order: Local Sociology on the Meso-Level," *Annual Review of Sociology* 38 (Palo Alto, CA: Annual Reviews, 2012), 159–179.

12 R. H. Miles, *Macro Organizational Behavior* (Santa Monica, CA: Goodyear, 1980); R. L. Daft and R. M. Steers, *Organizations: A Micro/Macro Approach* (Glenview, IL: Scott, Foresman,

1986); A. Minichilli, A. Zattoni, S. Nielsen, and M. Huse, "Board Task Performance: An Exploration of Micro- and Macro-Level Determinants of Board Effectiveness," *Journal of Organizational Behavior* 33 (2012): 193–215.

13 C. Heath and S. B. Sitkin, "Big-B Versus Big-O: What Is Organizational about Organizational Behavior?" *Journal of Organizational Behavior* 22 (2001): 43–58; J. B. Miner, "The Rated Importance, Scientific Validity, and Practical Usefulness of Organizational Behavior Theories: A Quantitative Review," *Academy of Management Learning & Education* 2 (2003): 250–268.

14 C. Hymowitz, "A Day in the Life of Tomorrow's Manager," *Wall Street Journal*, March 20, 1989, B1; J. Dreyfus, "Get Ready for the New Workforce," *Fortune*, April 23, 1990, 12; R. I. Lerman and S. R. Schmidt, *An Overview of Economic, Social, and Demographic Trends Affecting the Labor Market* (Washington, DC: Urban Institute for the U.S. Department of Labor, 2002); G. M. George and G. R. Jones, *Understanding and Managing Organizational Behavior* (Upper Saddle River, NJ: Pearson Prentice Hall, 2005).

15 G. E. Ledford, Jr., and E. E. Lawler III, "Research on Employee Participation: Beating a Dead Horse," *Academy of Management Review* 19 (1994): 633–636.

16 M. Hammer and J. Champy, *Reengineering the Corporation: A Manifesto for Business Revolution* (New York: Harper Business, 1993); D. Greising, "Quality: How to Make It Pay," *BusinessWeek*, August 8, 1994, 54–59; J. W. Dean, Jr., and D. E. Bowen, "Management Theory and Total Quality: Improving Research and Practice through Theory Development," *Academy of Management Review* 19 (1994): 392–418.

17 W. E. Cascio, "Whither Industrial and Organizational Psychology in a Changing World of Work?" *American Psychologist* 50 (1995): 928–939; G. C. Lodge, *Managing Globalization in the Age of Interdependence* (San Francisco: Pfeiffer, 1995).

18 G. F. Cavanagh, D. Moberg, and M. Velasquez, "The Ethics of Organizational Politics," *Academy of Management Review* 6 (1981): 363–374; D. Vrendenburgh and Y. Brender, "The Hierarchical Abuse of Power in Work Organizations," *Journal of Business Ethics* 17 (1998): 1337–1347.

19 W. L. French, "Organization Development Objectives, Assumptions, and Strategies," *California Management Review* 12 (Winter 1969): 23–34.

20 J. B. Treece, "A Little Bit of Smarts, a Lot of Hard Work," *BusinessWeek*, November 30, 1992, 70–71.

21 H. Simon, *Administrative Behavior*, 3rd ed. (New York: Free Press, 1976).

22 W. L. French and C. H. Bell, Jr., *Organization Development: Behavioral Science Interventions for Organization Improvement*, 6th ed. (Englewood Cliffs, NJ: Prentice Hall, 1999), 76–77.

Chapter 2

Management and Managers

Mark Zuckerberg is well known for his role in launching social networking site Facebook. As captured in the 2010 movie *The Social Network*, Zuckerberg's early efforts consisted of programming parts of the code that enabled the site to become popular among college-student users. Less appreciated, perhaps, is the story of Zuckerberg's self-transformation as his company, through aggressive growth, survived competition from rival Myspace and sought outside investors to expand Facebook further.

Launched in a Harvard dorm room in 2004, Facebook has since moved to Sun Microsystem's former campus in Menlo Park, California, and grown well beyond its original college base to include over a billion users who share photos, comments, and personal history "timelines." In the intervening years, Zuckerberg found his attention increasingly directed away from programming the operations of Facebook, the site, and toward overseeing the details of Facebook, the company. "Monetizing" the site by capturing data about Facebook users for marketers without violating users' privacy expectations has, naturally, challenged Zuckerberg's talents, forcing Facebook's staff to strike a balance between stockholder demands for profitability and user concerns about the disclosure of personal information. Mark Zuckerberg today is less a programmer and entrepreneur, and more a manager.[1]

What does it mean to be a manager like Zuckerberg? Although managers and managerial jobs are ubiquitous in contemporary life, few people really understand what managers do as they perform their jobs. Could you tell someone what management is? What skills and abilities managers need to succeed in their work? How today's management practices have developed? Modern societies depend on the well-being of organizations ranging from giants like Exxon, Goldman Sachs, and IBM to local businesses like the corner grocery store. In turn, all these businesses depend on the expertise of managers. It is therefore important that members of modern societies, including you, know what management is, what managers do, and how contemporary practices have developed.

This chapter introduces management theory and practice. It begins by defining the concept of management in terms of the various functions that managers perform in organizations. Next, it describes the job of a manager in greater detail, focusing on the skills managers use and the roles they fill as they perform their jobs every day. The chapter then examines how modern management theory has evolved, discussing several key schools of thought about management and managers that have developed between the late 1800s and the present.

Defining Management

Management, defined most simply, is the process of influencing behavior in organizations such that common purposes are identified, worked toward, and achieved. To define management in greater detail, we must consider a closely related question: What is an organization?

Three Attributes of Organizations

An **organization** is a collection of people and materials brought together to accomplish purposes not achievable through the efforts of individuals working alone. Three attributes enable an organization to achieve this feat: a mission, division of labor, and a hierarchy of authority.

Mission

Each organization works toward a specific **mission**, which is its purpose or reason for being. As illustrated in Table 2.1, a mission statement identifies the primary goods or services that the organization is intended to produce and the markets that it hopes to serve. An organization's mission helps hold it together by giving members a shared sense of direction.

Division of Labor

In every organization, difficult work is broken into smaller tasks. This **division of labor** can enhance *efficiency* by simplifying tasks and making them easier to perform. A classic example of this effect can be seen in the following analysis of the pin-making process by the eighteenth-century Scottish economist Adam Smith:

> One man draws out the wire, another straightens it, a third cuts it, a fourth points it, a fifth grinds it at the top for receiving a head. To make the head requires two or three more operations. [Using a division of labor such as this,] ten persons could make among them upward of forty-eight thousand pins a day. But if they had all wrought separately and independently they certainly could not each of them have made twenty; perhaps not one pin in a day.[2]

Table 2.1 **Sample Mission Statements**

Company	Mission
Hershey Foods	Hershey Foods' basic business mission is to become a major, diversified food company. . . . A basic principle that Hershey will continue to embrace is to attract and hold customers with products and services of consistently superior quality and value.
Apple	Apple designs Macs, the best personal computers in the world, along with OS X, iLife, iWork and professional software. Apple leads the digital music revolution with its iPods and iTunes online store. Apple has reinvented the mobile phone with its revolutionary iPhone and App Store, and is defining the future of mobile media and computing devices with iPad.

Source: Excerpted from annual stockholder reports.

The division of labor enables organized groups of people to accomplish tasks that would be beyond their physical or mental capacities as individuals. Few people can build a car by themselves, yet companies such as Nissan turn out thousands of cars each year by dividing the complex job of building a car into a series of simple assembly-line tasks.

Hierarchy of Authority

The **hierarchy of authority** is another common organizational attribute. In very small organizations, all members of the organization may share equally the authority to make decisions and initiate actions. In contrast, in larger organizations authority is more often distributed in a pyramidal hierarchical pattern like that shown in Figure 2.1. At the top of this hierarchy, the *chief executive officer* (CEO) has the authority to issue orders to every other member of the organization and to expect these orders to be obeyed. At successively lower levels, managers direct the activities of people beneath them and are constrained by the authority of managers above them.

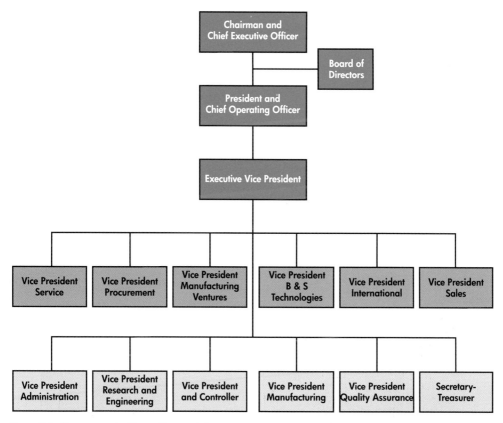

Figure 2.1 Organization Chart (Pyramidal)

An organization chart is a graphic representation of a firm's hierarchy of authority. The organization chart in this figure shows the top and middle management of a manufacturer of small gasoline engines used in lawn mowers, snow blowers, and similar equipment. Note that the company is divided horizontally into various functional departments—such as manufacturing and sales—whose efforts are unified through authority relations that extend vertically between vice presidents and the CEO.

Source: Based on data contained in annual stockholder reports.

Formal Definition of Management

The three attributes of organizations just described help clarify the role of management in organizational life. In a sense, the first two attributes are discordant, as the mission assumes the integration of effort whereas the division of labor produces a differentiation of effort. As a result, an organization's members are simultaneously pushed together and pulled apart. Managerial influence, derived partly from the third attribute of hierarchical authority, reconciles this conflict and balances the two opposing attributes. This balancing act is what managers do and what management is all about.

Management is thus a process of planning, organizing, directing, and controlling organizational behaviors to accomplish a mission through the division of labor. This definition incorporates several important ideas. First, management is a process—an ongoing flow of activities—rather than something that can be accomplished once and for all. Second, managerial activities affect the behaviors of an organization's members *and* the organization itself. Third, to accomplish a firm's mission requires organization. If the mission could be accomplished by individuals working alone, neither the firm nor its management would be necessary. Fourth, the process of management can be further divided into the four functions shown in Figure 2.2: planning, organizing, directing, and controlling.

Planning is a forward-looking process of deciding what to do. Managers who plan try to anticipate the future, setting goals and objectives for a firm's performance and identifying the actions required to attain these goals and objectives. For example, when Robert Iger meets with other Walt Disney Company executives to develop specifications for the attractions and concessions at theme parks under construction, he is engaged in planning. In planning, managers set three types of goals and objectives:

1. *Strategic goals* are the outcomes that the organization as a whole expects to achieve by pursuing its mission.
2. *Functional or divisional objectives* are the outcomes that units within the firm are expected to achieve.
3. *Operational objectives* are the specific, measurable results that the members of an organizational unit are expected to accomplish.[3]

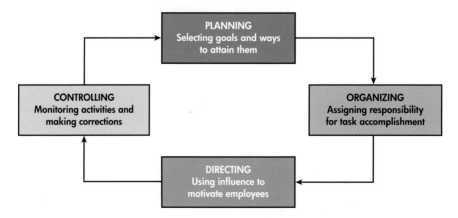

Figure 2.2 The Four Management Functions

As shown in Figure 2.3, these three types of goals and objectives are linked together. The focus of lower-order objectives is shaped by the content of higher-level goals, and achieving higher-level goals depends on the fulfillment of lower-level objectives.

Goals and objectives are performance targets that the members of an organization seek to fulfill by working together—for instance, gaining control over 15 percent of the firm's market, or manufacturing less than one defective product for every thousand produced. Setting such goals and objectives helps managers plan and implement a sequence of actions that will lead to their attainment. For example, financial objectives growing out of Iger's planning meetings at Disney become targets that newly opened theme parks are expected to meet or exceed during their first few years in operation. Goals and objectives also serve as benchmarks of the success or failure of organizational behavior. When they review past performance, managers can judge the company's effectiveness by assessing its goal attainment. For example, Disney theme park managers can assess the success of their operations by comparing actual revenue and cost data with corporate profitability goals.

As part of the **organizing** function, managers develop a structure of interrelated tasks and allocate people and resources within this structure. Organizing begins when managers divide an organization's labor and design tasks that will lead to the achievement of organizational goals and objectives. In companies such as Whirlpool and Boeing, assembly operations are devised and built during this phase. Next, managers decide who will perform these tasks. To make this determination, they analyze the tasks to identify the knowledge, skills, and abilities needed to perform them successfully. They can then select qualified employees or train other employees who lack the necessary qualifications to carry out these tasks.

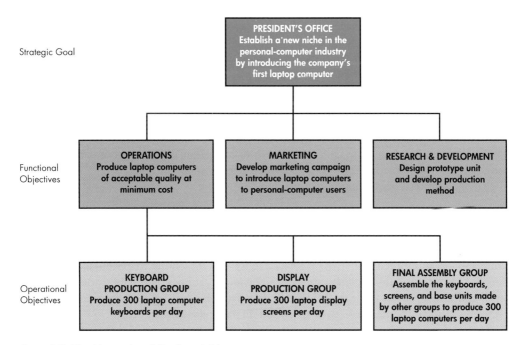

Figure 2.3 The Hierarchy of Goals and Objectives

An organization's strategic goals set boundaries within which functional objectives are established. In turn, functional objectives shape the objectives of operational units. Accomplishing operational objectives therefore contributes to the attainment of functional objectives and strategic goals.

Grouping tasks and the people who perform them into *organizational units* is another step in the organizing process. One type of organizational unit, a *department*, includes people who perform the same type of work. For instance, all employees who market an organization's goods or services can be brought together in a marketing department. Another type of unit, a *division*, includes people who do the company's work in the same geographic territory, who work with similar kinds of clients, or who make or provide the same type of goods or services. For example, Coca-Cola has a European division that does business in Europe. General Electric's financial services division markets only financial services.

The **directing** function encourages member effort and guides it toward the attainment of organizational goals and objectives. Directing is partly a process of communicating goals and objectives to members wherein managers announce, clarify, and promote targets toward which effort should be directed. For example, Jeff Bezos is directing when he meets with other top managers at Amazon.com to announce yearly sales objectives. Directing is also a process of learning employees' desires and interests and of ensuring that these desires and interests are satisfied in return for successful goal-oriented performance. In addition, directing may require managers to use personal expertise or charisma to inspire employees to overcome obstacles that might appear insurmountable.

In sum, directing is a process in which managers *lead* their subordinates, influencing them to work together to achieve organizational goals and related objectives.

Controlling means evaluating the performance of the organization and its units to see whether the firm is progressing in the desired direction. In a typical evaluation, managers compare an organization's actual results with the desired results as described in its goals and objectives. For example, Capital One executives might compare the actual profitability of their Visa card operations with the profitability objectives set during previous planning sessions. To perform this kind of evaluation, members of the organization must collect and assess performance information. A firm's accounting personnel might gather data about the costs and revenues of organizational activities. Marketing representatives might provide additional data about sales volume or the organization's position in the marketplace. Finance specialists might then appraise the firm's organizational performance by determining whether the ratio of costs to revenues meets or surpasses the company's target level.

If the evaluation reveals a significant difference between goals and actual performance, the control process enters a phase of *correction*. In this phase, managers return to the planning stage and redevelop their goals and objectives, indicating how differences between goals and outcomes can be reduced. The process of management then continues anew, as managers engage in additional organizing, directing, and controlling.

What Managers Do

Managers are the people who plan, organize, direct, and control so as to manage organizations and organizational units. Managers establish the directions to be pursued, allocate people and resources among tasks, supervise individual, group, and organizational performance, and assess progress toward goals and objectives. To succeed in these functions, they perform specific jobs, use a variety of skills, and fill particular roles.

Managerial Jobs

Although all managers are responsible for fulfilling the same four functions, not all of them perform exactly the same jobs. Instead, most organizations have three general types of managers: top managers, middle managers, and supervisory managers. Figure 2.4 illustrates the distinctive combination of planning, organizing, directing, and controlling performed by each type of manager.[4]

Top Managers

Top managers, who are responsible for managing the entire organization, include individuals with the title of *chairperson, president, chief executive officer, executive vice president, vice president,* or *chief operating officer.* Managerial work at this level consists mainly of performing the planning activities needed to develop the organization's mission and strategic goals. Top managers also carry out organizing and controlling activities as determined by strategic planning. As part of the controlling function, they assess the firm's progress toward attainment of its strategic goals by monitoring information about activities both within the firm and in its surrounding environment. Top management's responsibilities include adjusting the organization's overall direction on the basis of information reviewed in the controlling procedures. Because strategic planning, organizing, and controlling require a great deal of time, top managers have little time to spend in directing subordinates' activities. Typically, they delegate responsibility for such direction to middle managers lower in the hierarchy of authority.

Middle Managers

Middle managers are usually responsible for managing the performance of a particular organizational unit and for implementing top managers' strategic plans. As they work to transform these strategies into programs that can be implemented at lower levels of the company, middle managers help establish functional or divisional objectives that will guide unit performance toward attainment of the firm's strategic goals. For instance, middle managers in a

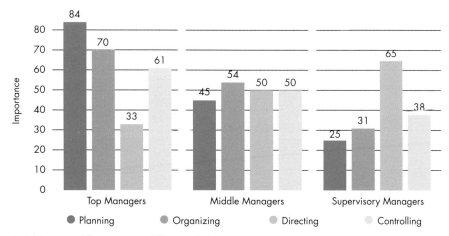

Figure 2.4 Managerial Functions and Types of Managers

Planning is the most important function of top managers. Middle managers fulfill all four management functions about equally. Directing is the most important function of supervisory managers.

Source: Based on information presented in L. R. Gomez-Mejia, J. E. McCann, and R. C. Page, "The Structure of Managerial Behaviors and Rewards," *Industrial Relations* 24 (1985): 147–154.

company's marketing department might transform the strategic goal of attaining control of 35 percent of the company's market into objectives specifying the level of sales to be achieved in each of the company's twelve sales districts. Middle managers are also responsible for ensuring that the managers beneath them implement the unit goals and appropriately direct employees toward their attainment. Terms such as *director* or *manager* are usually a part of a middle manager's title—for example, *director of human resources* or *western regional manager*.

Supervisory Managers

Supervisory managers, often called *superintendents, supervisors*, or *foremen*, are charged with overseeing the nonsupervisory employees who perform the organization's basic work. Of the three types of managers, supervisory managers spend the greatest amount of time actually directing employees. Except for making small, on-the-job adjustments, they seldom perform planning and organizing activities. Instead, supervisory managers initiate the upward flow of information that middle and top managers use to control organizational behavior. They may also distribute many of the rewards or punishments used to influence nonsupervisory employees' behaviors. Their ability to control subordinates' activities is limited, however, to the authority delegated to them by middle management.

Managerial Skills

Not surprisingly, the skills that managers use to succeed in their jobs are largely determined by the combination of planning, organizing, directing, and controlling functions that they must perform. As shown in Figure 2.5, each level of management has its own skill requirements.[5]

Conceptual skills include the ability to perceive an organization or organizational unit as a whole, to understand how its labor is divided into tasks and reintegrated by the pursuit of common goals or objectives, and to recognize important relationships between the organization or unit and the environment that surrounds it. Conceptual skills involve a manager's ability to *think* and are most closely associated with planning and organizing. These skills are used most frequently by top managers, who take responsibility for organization-wide strategic endeavors.

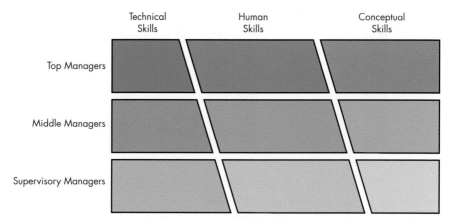

Figure 2.5 **Managerial Skills**

Source: Based on information presented in R. L. Katz, "Skills of an Effective Administrator," *Harvard Business Review* 52 (1974): 90–102.

Included in **human skills** is the ability to work effectively as a group member and build cooperation among the members of an organization or unit. Managers with well-developed human skills can create an atmosphere of trust and security in which people can express themselves without fear of punishment or humiliation. Such managers, who are adept at sensing the aspirations, interests, and viewpoints of others, can often foresee others' likely reactions to prospective courses of action. Because all management functions require that managers interact with other employees to acquire information, make decisions, implement changes, and assess results, it is not surprising that top, middle, and supervisory managers all put human skills to use.

Technical skills involve understanding the specific knowledge, procedures, and tools required to make the goods or services produced by an organization or unit. For example, members of a company's sales force must have skills in selling. Accountants have bookkeeping or auditing skills. Maintenance mechanics may need to have welding skills. For managers at the top or middle of an organization's hierarchy of authority, who are far removed from day-to-day production activities, technical skills are the least important of the three types of skills to have. Such skills are more critical to the success of supervisory managers overseeing employees who use technical skills in performing their jobs.

Managerial Roles

Like skill requirements, **managerial roles** vary from one kind of manager to another. Indeed, the same manager may play more than one role at the same time. As shown in Table 2.2, these roles cluster together in three general categories: interpersonal, informational, and decisional roles.[6]

Table 2.2 **Ten Roles of Managers**

Role	Description
Interpersonal roles:	
Figurehead	Representing the organization or unit in ceremonial and symbolic activities
Leader	Guiding and motivating employee performance
Liaison	Linking the organization or unit with others
Informational roles:	
Monitor	Scanning the environment for information that can enhance organizational or unit performance
Disseminator	Providing information to subordinates
Spokesperson	Distributing information to people outside the organization or unit
Decisional roles:	
Entrepreneur	Initiating changes that improve the organization or unit
Disturbance handler	Adapting the organization or unit to changing conditions
Resource allocator	Distributing resources within the organization or unit
Negotiator	Bargaining or negotiating to sustain organizational or unit survival

Source: Based on information presented in H. Mintzberg, *The Nature of Managerial Work* (Englewood Cliffs, NJ: Prentice Hall, 1980); S. Carlson, *Executive Behavior* (Stockholm: Stromsberg, 1951); and R. Stewart, *Managers and Their Jobs* (London: Macmillan, 1967).

Interpersonal Roles

In fulfilling interpersonal roles, managers create and maintain interpersonal relationships to ensure the well-being of their organizations or units. They represent their organizations or units to other people in the *figurehead role*, which can include such ceremonial and symbolic activities as greeting visitors, attending awards banquets, and cutting ribbons to open new facilities. Managers also function as figureheads when they perform public service duties, including such activities as chairing the yearly fund drive for the United Way or serving on the board of the local Urban League. In the *leader role*, they motivate and guide employees by performing such activities as issuing orders, setting performance goals, and training subordinates. Managers create and maintain links between their organizations or units and others in the *liaison role*. For example, a company president might meet with the presidents of other companies at an industry conference.

Informational Roles

Because they serve as the primary authority figures for the organizations or units they supervise, managers have unique access to internal and external information networks. In informational roles they receive and transmit information within these networks. In the *monitor role*, managers scan the environment surrounding their organizations or units, seeking information to enhance performance. Such activities can range from reading periodicals and reports to trading rumors with managers in other firms or units. In the *disseminator role*, managers pass information to subordinates who would otherwise have no access to it. To share information with subordinates, they may hold meetings, write memoranda, make telephone calls, and so forth. In the *spokesperson role*, managers distribute information to people outside their organizations or units through annual stockholder reports, speeches, memos, and various other means.

Decisional Roles

In decisional roles, managers determine the direction to be taken by their organizations or units. In the *entrepreneur role*, they make decisions about improvements in the organizations or units for which they are responsible. Such decisions often entail initiating change. For example, a manager who hears about a new product opportunity may commit the firm to producing it. She may also delegate the responsibility for managing the resulting project to others. The *disturbance handler role* also requires making change-oriented decisions. Managers acting in this role must often try to adapt to change beyond their personal control. For instance, they might have to handle such problems as conflicts among subordinates, the loss of an important customer, or damage to the firm's building or plant.

In the *resource allocator role*, managers decide which resources will be acquired and who will receive them. Such decisions often demand difficult trade-offs. For instance, if a manager decides to acquire iPads for sales clerks, he might have to deny manufacturing department employees a piece of production equipment. As part of the resource allocation process, priorities may be set, budgets established, and schedules devised. In the *negotiator role*, managers engage in formal bargaining or negotiations to acquire the resources needed for the survival of their organizations or units. For example, they might negotiate with suppliers about delivery dates or bargain with union representatives about employee wages and hours.

Differences in Roles among Managers

Just as the functions managers perform and the skills they use differ from one managerial job to another, so do the roles managers fill. In Figure 2.6, the roles of liaison, spokesperson, and resource allocator are shown as being most important in the jobs of top managers, reflecting top management's responsibilities for planning, organizing, and controlling the strategic direction of the firm. In addition, monitoring activities are more important for top managers than for other types of managers because they must scan the environment for pertinent information.

For middle managers, the leader, liaison, disturbance handler, and resource allocator roles are the most important. These roles reflect the importance of middle management's job of organizing, directing, and controlling the functional or divisional units of the firm. The role of disseminator is also important in middle managers' jobs, as these managers must explain and implement the strategic plans formulated by top management.

For supervisory managers, the leader role is the most important, as they spend most of their time directing nonsupervisory personnel. They also act as spokespeople who disseminate information within their groups and serve as liaisons who connect their groups with the rest of the organization. In addition, they acquire and distribute the resources that their subordinates need to carry out their jobs.

The Nature of Managerial Work

To further analyze the classification of managerial roles just discussed, Henry Mintzberg observed a group of top managers at work for several weeks. After listing these managers' major activities and monitoring the time it took to perform them, Mintzberg found that the managers spent by far the most time in scheduled meetings. When combined with unscheduled meetings, this activity accounted for almost 70 percent of the managers' time. As Table 2.3 shows, the managers were left with barely a fifth of the day for desk work, and

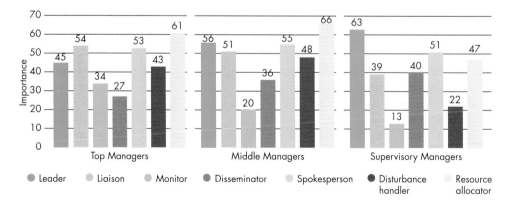

Figure 2.6 **Manager's Jobs and the Roles They Fill**

When researchers asked top, middle, and supervisory managers about the importance of the roles they perform, their answers provided the data illustrated graphically here. Note that the roles of figurehead, entrepreneur, and negotiator were not included in this survey.

Source: Based on data presented in A. I Kraut, P. R. Pedigo, D. D. McKenna, and M. D. Dunnette, "The Role of the Manager: What's Really Important in Different Management Jobs," *Academy of Management Executive* 3 (1989): 286–293.

Table 2.3 Distribution of Managerial Activities

Managerial activity	Percentage of workday consumed	Average duration
Scheduled meetings	59%	61 minutes
Desk work	22%	11 minutes
Unscheduled meetings	10%	12 minutes
Telephone calls	6%	6 minutes
Tours	3%	15 minutes

Source: Based on information presented in H. Mintzberg, *The Nature of Managerial Work* (Englewood Cliffs, NJ: Prentice Hall, 1980).

about a tenth for telephone calls and tours—walking around the company to see what was going on. Mintzberg also recorded the amount of time consumed by each instance of each activity.

As indicated in Table 2.3, scheduled meetings averaged a little more than an hour in length and ranged from less than ten minutes to more than two hours. Unscheduled meetings were generally shorter, lasting from a few minutes to about an hour and averaging approximately twelve minutes each. Periods of desk work and tours to inspect the company averaged from eleven to fifteen minutes each and were fitted in between scheduled meetings and unscheduled interruptions. Telephone calls were almost always quite short, averaging about six minutes each.

Based on his observations, Mintzberg concluded that managers' roles often require them to work in short bursts rather than in long, uninterrupted sessions. Such individuals frequently lack the time to complete rigorous planning, organizing, directing, and controlling. Rather than taking the form of a routine, well-planned course of action, managing can involve making nonroutine *incremental adjustments*.[7] Clearly, managing is a fast-paced, active profession.

A Framework of Management Perspectives

Our discussions thus far are based on management thoughts and practices developed all over the world, many of which are thousands of years old. Consider the following:

1. As early as 3000 BCE, the Sumerians formulated missions and goals for government and commercial enterprises.
2. Between 3000 and 1000 BCE, the Egyptians successfully organized the efforts of thousands of workers to build the pyramids.
3. Between 800 BCE and about 300 CE, the Romans perfected the use of hierarchical authority.
4. Between 450 CE and the late 1400s, Venetian merchants developed commercial laws and invented double-entry bookkeeping.
5. In the early 1500s, Niccolo Machiavelli prepared an analysis of power that is still widely read.
6. At about the same time, the Catholic Church perfected a governance structure built upon the use of standardized procedures.

However, truly modern management practices did not begin to develop until the Industrial Revolution of the 1700s and 1800s. Inventions such as James Watt's steam engine and Eli

Whitney's cotton gin created new forms of mass production that made existing modes of organization obsolete. Mass-assembly operations accelerated the pace of production dramatically and required the employment of large numbers of workers, overwhelming the small administrative staffs then employed by most companies. In addition, expertise became important to maintain production equipment, even though managers had little time to develop this expertise themselves. The field of industrial engineering, which first emerged because of the need to invent and improve workplace machinery, began to address the selection, instruction, and coordination of industrial employees. Toward the end of the Industrial Revolution, managers and engineers throughout North America and Europe focused on developing general theories of management.

1890–1940: The Scientific Management Perspective

Management theories initially took the form of *management principles* intended to provide managers with practical advice about managing their firms. Most of these principles were written by practicing managers or others closely associated with the management profession. Among the first principles to be widely read were those of the **scientific management perspective**.

All principles of scientific management reflected the idea that through proper management an organization could achieve profitability and survive over the long term in the competitive world of business. Theorists sharing the scientific management perspective devoted their attention to describing proper management and determining the best way to achieve it.[8]

Frederick W. Taylor

The founder of scientific management, Frederick W. Taylor (1856–1915), developed his principles of scientific management as he rose from the position of laborer to chief engineer at the Midvale Steel Works in Philadelphia, Pennsylvania. These principles, which appear in Table 2.4, focused on increasing the efficiency of the workplace by differentiating managers from nonsupervisory workers and systematizing the jobs of both types of employees.

According to Taylor, an organization's profitability could be ensured only by finding the "one best way" to perform each job. Managers were charged with teaching workers this technique and implementing a system of rewards and punishments to encourage its use.

Taylor reported that he used this approach to improve the productivity of coal shovelers at the Bethlehem Steel Company. As he observed these workers, he discovered that a shovel load of coal could range from four to thirty pounds, depending on the density of the coal. By experimenting with a group of workers, Taylor discovered that shovelers could move the most coal in one day without suffering undue fatigue if each load of coal weighed twenty-one pounds. He then developed a variety of shovels, each of which would hold approximately twenty-one pounds of coal of a particular density. After Taylor taught workers how to use these shovels, each shoveler's daily yield rose from sixteen tons to fifty-nine tons. At the same time, the average wage per worker increased from $1.15 to $1.88 per day. Bethlehem Steel was able to reduce the number of shovelers in its yard from about 500 to 150, saving the firm about $80,000 per year.[9]

Taylor's ideas influenced management around the world. In a 1918 article for the newspaper *Pravda*, the founder of the Russian Communist Party, Vladimir Lenin, recommended that Taylor's scientific management be used throughout the Soviet Union. In the United States, Taylor's principles had such a dramatic effect on management that in 1912 he was

Table 2.4 Frederick W. Taylor's Principles of Scientific Management

1. Assign all responsibility to managers rather than workers.	Managers should do all the thinking related to the planning and design of work, leaving workers the task of carrying it out.
2. Use scientific methods to determine the one best way of performing each task.	Managers should design each worker's job accordingly, specifying a set of standard methods for completing the task in the right way.
3. Select the person most suited to each job to perform that job.	Managers should match the abilities of each worker to the demands of each job.
4. Train the worker to perform the job correctly.	Managers should train workers to use the standard methods devised for their jobs.
5. Monitor work performance to ensure that specified work procedures are followed correctly and that appropriate results are achieved.	Managers should exercise the control necessary to guarantee that workers under their supervision always perform their jobs in the one best way.
6. Provide further support by planning work assignments and eliminating interruptions.	Managers can help their workers continue to produce at a high level by shielding them from distractions that interfere with job performance.

Source: Adapted from F. W. Taylor, The Principles of Scientific Management (New York: Norton, 1911), 34–40.

called to testify before a special committee of the House of Representatives. Unions and employers both objected to Taylor's idea that employers and employees should share the economic gains of scientific management and wanted Congress to do something about it. Nevertheless, with the newspaper publicity he gained from his appearance, Taylor found even wider support for his ideas and was soon joined in his work by other specialists.

Other Contributors

The husband-and-wife team of Frank (1868–1924) and Lillian (1878–1972) Gilbreth followed in Taylor's footsteps in pursuing the "one best way" to perform any job. The Gilbreths are probably best known for their invention of *motion study*, a procedure in which jobs are reduced to their most basic movements. Table 2.5 lists some of these basic movements, each of which is called a *therblig (Gilbreth* spelled backward without inverting the *th*). The Gilbreths also invented the microchronometer, a clock with a hand capable of measuring time to 1/2000th of a second. Using this instrument, analysts could perform time-and-motion studies to determine the time required by each movement needed to perform a job.

Another contributor to scientific management, Henry Gantt (1861–1919), developed a task-and-bonus wage plan that paid workers a bonus besides their regular wages if they completed their work in an assigned amount of time. Gantt's plan also provided bonuses for supervisors, determined by the number of subordinates who met deadlines.[10] In addition, Gantt invented the *Gantt chart*, a bar chart used by managers to compare actual with planned performance.[11] Present-day scheduling methods such as the *program evaluation and review technique* (PERT) are based on this invention.

Table 2.5 **Therblig Motions**

Search	Transport empty	Transport loaded	Inspect
Find	Position	Disassemble	Assemble
Select	Rest	Preposition	Plan
Grasp	Use	Release load	Avoidable delay

Harrington Emerson (1853–1931), a third contributor to scientific management, applied his own list of twelve principles to the railroad industry in the early 1900s.[12] Among Emerson's principles were recommendations to establish clear objectives, seek advice from competent individuals, manage with justice and fairness, standardize procedures, reduce waste, and reward workers for efficiency. Late in his life, Emerson became interested in the selection and training of employees, stressing the importance of explaining scientific management to employees during their initial training. He reasoned that sound management practices could succeed only if every member of the firm understood them.

1900–1950: The Administrative Principles Perspective

At about the same time that Taylor and his colleagues were formulating their principles of scientific management, another group of theorists was developing the **administrative principles perspective**. In contrast to scientific management's emphasis on reducing the costs of production activities, this perspective focused on increasing the efficiency of administrative procedures.[13]

Henri Fayol

Considered the father of modern management thought, Henri Fayol (1841–1925) developed his principles of administration in the early 1900s while serving as chief executive of a French mining and metallurgy firm, Commentry-Fourchambault-Decazeville, known as "Comambault." Fayol was the first to identify the four functions of management we have already discussed: planning, organizing, directing, and controlling.[14] He also formulated the fourteen principles shown in Table 2.6 to help administrators perform their jobs.

Fayol believed that the number of management principles that might help improve an organization's operation is potentially limitless. He considered his principles to be flexible and adaptable, labeling them principles rather than laws or rules to avoid any idea of rigidity, as there is nothing rigid or absolute in [management] matters; everything is a question of degree. The same principle is hardly ever applied twice in exactly the same way, because we have to allow for different and changing circumstances, for human beings who are equally different and changeable, and for many other variable elements. The principles, too, are flexible, and can be adapted to meet every need; it is just a question of knowing how to use them.[15]

For Fayol, management involved more than mechanically following rules. It required that managers exercise intuition and engage in skillful behavior in deciding how, when, and why to put management principles into action.

Max Weber

Max Weber (1864–1920) was a German sociologist who, although neither a manager nor a management consultant, had a major effect on management thought. Like Fayol, he was

Table 2.6 Fayol's Fourteen Principles of Management

Principle	Description
Division of work	A firm's work should be divided into specialized, simplified tasks. Matching task demands with workforce skills and abilities will improve productivity. The management of work should be separated from its performance.
Authority and responsibility	Authority is the right to give orders, and responsibility is the obligation to accept the consequences of using authority. No one should possess one without having the other as well.
Discipline	Discipline is performing a task with obedience and dedication. It can be expected only when a firm's managers and subordinates agree on the specific behaviors that subordinates will perform.
Unity of command	Each subordinate should receive orders from only one hierarchical superior. The confusion created by having two or more superiors will undermine authority, discipline, order, and stability.
Unity of direction	Each group of activities directed toward the same objective should have only one manager and only one plan.
Individual versus general interests	The interests of individuals and the whole organization must be treated with equal respect. Neither can be allowed to supersede the other.
Remuneration of personnel	The pay received by employees must be fair and satisfactory to both them and the firm. Pay should be distributed in proportion to personal performance, but employees' general welfare must not be threatened by unfair incentive-payment schemes.
Centralization	Centralization is the retention of authority by managers, to be used when managers desire greater control. Decentralization should be used if subordinates' opinions, counsel, and experience are needed.
Scalar chain	The scalar chain is a hierarchical string extending from the uppermost manager to the lowest subordinate. The line of authority follows this chain and is the proper route for organizational communications.
Order	Order, or "everything in its place," should be instilled whenever possible because it reduces wasted materials and efforts. Jobs should be designed and staffed with order in mind.
Equity	Equity means enforcing established rules with a sense of fair play, kindliness, and justice. It should be guaranteed by management, as it increases members' loyalty, devotion, and satisfaction.
Stability of tenure	Properly selected employees should be given the time needed to learn and adjust to their jobs. The absence of such stability undermines organizational performance.
Initiative	Staff members should be given the opportunity to think for themselves. This approach improves the distribution of information and adds to the organization's pool of talent.
Esprit de corps	Managers should harmonize the interests of members by resisting the urge to split up successful teams. They should rely on face-to-face communication to detect and correct misunderstandings immediately.

Table 2.7 Features of Bureaucratic Organizations

Feature	Description
Selection and promotion	Expertise is the primary criterion. Friendship criteria or other favoritism is explicitly rejected.
Hierarchy of authority	Superiors have the authority to direct subordinates' actions. They must ensure that these actions serve the bureaucracy's best interests.
Rules and regulations	Unchanging regulations provide the bureaucracy's members with consistent, impartial guidance.
Division of labor	Work is divided into tasks that can be performed by the bureaucracy's members in an efficient, productive manner.
Written documentation	Records provide consistency and a basis for evaluating bureaucratic procedures.
Separate ownership	Members cannot gain unfair or undeserved advantage through ownership.

Source: Adapted from Max Weber, *From Max Weber: Essays in Sociology*, ed. & trans. H. H. Gerth and C. W. Mills (New York: Oxford University Press, 1946).

interested in the efficiency of different kinds of administrative arrangements. To figure out what makes organizations efficient, Weber analyzed the Egyptian Empire, the Prussian army, the Roman Catholic Church, and other large organizations that had functioned efficiently over long periods of time. Based on the results of these analyses, he developed his model of **bureaucracy**, an idealized description of an efficient organization that is summarized in Table 2.7.

Weber's bureaucratic model provides for both the differentiation (through the division of labor and task specialization) and the integration (by the hierarchy of authority and written rules and regulations) necessary to get a specific job done. Weber believed that any organization with bureaucratic characteristics would be efficient. He noted, however, that work in a bureaucracy could become so simple and undemanding that employees might grow dissatisfied and, as a result, less productive.[16]

Other Contributors

A number of other management experts have contributed to the administrative principles perspective. James Mooney (1884–1957) was vice president and director of General Motors and president of General Motors Overseas Corporation during the late 1920s, when he espoused his principles of organization.[17] Mooney's *coordinative principle* highlighted the importance of organizing the tasks and functions in a firm into a coordinated whole. He defined coordination as the orderly arrangement of group effort to provide unity of action in the pursuit of a common mission. His *scalar principle* identified the importance of scalar—hierarchical—chains of superiors and subordinates as a means of integrating the work of different employees. Finally, Mooney's *functional principle* stressed the importance of functional differences, such as marketing, manufacturing, and accounting. He noted how work in each functional area both differs from and interlocks with the work of other areas as well as how the success of the larger firm requires coordination and scalar linkages among its different functional parts.

Lyndall Urwick (1891–1983), another contributor to the administrative principles perspective, was a British military officer and director of the International Management Institute in Geneva, Switzerland. Urwick made his mark by consolidating the ideas of Fayol and Mooney with those of Taylor.[18] From Taylor, Urwick adopted the idea that systematic, rigorous investigation should inform and support the management of employees. He also used Fayol's fourteen principles to guide managerial planning and control, and Mooney's three principles of organization to structure his discussion of organizing. In this way, Urwick's synthesis bridged Taylor's scientific management and the administrative principles approach, and it integrated the work of others within the framework of the four functions of management identified by Fayol.

Mary Parker Follett (1868–1933), who became interested in industrial management in the 1920s, was among the first proponents of what later became known as *industrial democracy*. In her writings on administrative principles, Follett proposed that every employee should have an ownership interest in his or her company, which would encourage attention to a company's overall mission and goals.[19] In promoting cooperation in the workplace, her work foreshadowed the human relations perspective, which is described next. Follett also suggested that organizational problems tend to resist simple solutions, because they typically stem from a variety of interdependent factors. Here again she anticipated later theorists, contributing to the contingency approach discussed later in this chapter.

1930–1970: The Human Relations Perspective

Although members of the scientific management and administrative principles perspectives advocated the scientific study of management, they rarely evaluated their ideas in any formal way. This omission was corrected in the mid–1920s, when university researchers began to use scientific methods to test existing management thought.

The Hawthorne Studies

The *Hawthorne studies*, which began in 1924 at Western Electric's Hawthorne plant near Chicago, were among the earliest attempts to use scientific techniques to examine human behavior at work.[20] As summarized in Table 2.8, a three-stage series of experiments assessed the effects of varying physical conditions and management practices on workplace efficiency. The first experiment examined the effects of workplace lighting on productivity; it produced the unexpected findings that changes in lighting had little effect but that changes in social conditions seemed to explain significant increases in group productivity. Additional experiments led the researchers to conclude that social factors—in particular, workers' desires to satisfy needs for companionship and support at work—explained the results observed across all of the Hawthorne studies.

Later reanalyses of the Hawthorne experiments not only found weaknesses in the studies' methods and techniques, but also suggested that changes in incentive pay, tasks being performed, rest periods, and working hours led to the productivity improvements attributed by researchers to the effects of social factors.[21] Nonetheless, the Hawthorne studies raised serious questions about the efficiency-oriented focus of the scientific management and administrative principles perspectives. In so doing, they stimulated debate about the importance of human satisfaction and personal development at work. The **human relations perspective** of management thought that grew out of this debate redirected attention away from improving efficiency and toward increasing employee growth, development, and satisfaction.[22]

Table 2.8 **The Hawthorne Studies**

Experiment	Major changes	Results
Stage I:		
Illumination study	Lighting conditions	Improved productivity at nearly all levels of illumination
Stage II:		
First relay-assembly test	Job simplification, shorter work hours, rest breaks, friendly supervision, incentive pay	30 percent productivity improvement
Second relay-assembly test	Incentive pay	12 percent productivity improvement
Mica-splitting test	Shorter work hours, rest breaks, friendly supervision	15 percent productivity improvement
Stage III:		
Interview program	—	Discovery of presence of informal productivity norms
Bank-wiring-room test	Incentive pay	Emergence of productivity norms

Douglas McGregor

Douglas McGregor (1906–1964) played a key role in promoting this redirection, through his efforts at sharpening the philosophical contrast between the human relations approach and the scientific management and administrative principles perspectives.[23] McGregor used the term **Theory X** to describe the key assumptions about human nature, which appear in Table 2.9. He suggested that theorists and managers holding these assumptions would describe management as follows:

1. Managers are responsible for organizing the elements of productive enterprise—money, materials, equipment, people—solely in the interest of economic efficiency.
2. The manager's function is to motivate workers, direct their efforts, control their actions, and modify their behavior to fit the organization's needs.
3. Without such active intervention by managers, people would be passive or even resistant to organizational needs. They must therefore be persuaded, rewarded, and punished for the good of the organization.[24]

According to McGregor, the scientific management and administrative principles perspectives promoted a "hard" version of Theory X. Both perspectives favored overcoming employees' resistance to organizational needs through strict discipline and economic rewards or punishments. McGregor added that a "soft" version of Theory X seemed to underlie the Hawthorne studies, as the Hawthorne researchers appeared to regard satisfaction and social relations mainly as being rewards for employees who followed orders.

Theory Y, a contrasting philosophy of management that McGregor attributed to theorists, researchers, and managers holding the human relations perspective, is based on the second set

Table 2.9 Theory X and Theory Y Assumptions

Theory X assumptions:

1. The average person has an inherent dislike of work and will avoid it if possible.
2. Because they dislike work, most people must be coerced, controlled, directed, or threatened with punishment before they will put forth effort toward the achievement of organizational objectives.
3. The average person prefers to be directed, wishes to avoid responsibility, has relatively little ambition, and desires security above all.

Theory Y assumptions:

1. Expanding physical and mental effort at work is as natural as play and rest. The average person does not inherently dislike work.
2. External control and the threat of punishment are not the only way to direct effort toward organizational objectives. People will exercise self-direction and self-control in the service of objectives to which they feel committed.
3. Commitment to objectives is a function of the rewards associated with their achievement. The most significant rewards—the satisfaction of ego and self-actualization needs—can be direct products of effort directed toward organizational objectives.
4. Avoidance of responsibility, lack of ambition, and emphasis on security are not inherent human characteristics. Under proper conditions, the average person learns not only to accept but also to seek responsibility.
5. Imagination, ingenuity, creativity, and the ability to use these qualities to solve organizational problems are widely distributed among people.

Source: Adapted from D. McGregor, *The Human Side of Enterprise* (New York: McGraw-Hill, 1960), 33–34, 47–48.

of assumptions shown in Table 2.9. According to McGregor, individuals holding Theory Y assumptions would view the task of management as follows:

1. Managers are responsible for organizing the elements of productive enterprise—money, materials, equipment, people—in the interest of economic ends.
2. Because people are motivated to perform, have potential for development, can assume responsibility, and are willing to work toward organizational goals, managers are responsible for enabling people to recognize and develop these basic capacities.
3. The essential task of management is to arrange organizational conditions and methods of operation so that working toward organizational objectives is also the best way for people to achieve their own personal goals.[25]

Unlike Theory X managers, who try to control their employees, Theory Y managers try to help employees learn how to manage themselves.

Other Contributors

Many management theorists, including Abraham Maslow and Frederick Herzberg, embraced the point of view embodied in McGregor's Theory Y and speculated about ways in which personal autonomy and group participation might encourage employee growth, development, and satisfaction. The works of these contributors also served as benchmark theories during the early development of research on micro and meso organizational behavior, as described later in this book.

1960–Present: The Open Systems Perspective

With the emergence in the 1960s of the **open systems perspective**, human relations concerns related to employee satisfaction and development broadened to include a focus on organizational growth and survival. According to the open systems perspective, every organization is a *system*—a unified structure of interrelated subsystems—and it is *open*—subject to the influence of the surrounding environment. Together, these two ideas constitute the central tenet of the open systems approach, which states that organizations whose subsystems can cope with the surrounding environment can continue to do business, whereas organizations whose subsystems cannot cope will not survive.[26]

Daniel Katz and Robert L. Kahn

In one of the seminal works on the open systems perspective, Daniel Katz and Robert Kahn identified the process shown in Figure 2.7 as essential to organizational growth and survival.[27]
   This process consists of the following sequence of events:

1.   Every organization imports *inputs*, such as raw materials, production equipment, human resources, and technical know-how, from the surrounding environment. For instance, Royal Dutch Shell Oil Company hires employees and, from sources around the world, acquires unrefined oil, refinery equipment, and knowledge about how to refine petroleum products.
2.   Some of the inputs are used to transform other inputs during a process of *throughput*. At Shell, employees use refinery equipment and their own know-how to transform unrefined oil into petroleum products such as gasoline, kerosene, and diesel fuel.
3.   The transformed resources are exported as *outputs*—saleable goods or services—to the environment. Petroleum products from Shell's refineries are loaded into tankers and transported to service stations throughout North America.
4.   Outputs are exchanged for new inputs, and the cycle repeats. Shell sells its products and uses the resulting revenues to pay its employees and purchase additional oil, equipment, and know-how.

   According to Katz and Kahn, organizations will continue to grow and survive only as long as they import more material and energy from the environment than they expend in

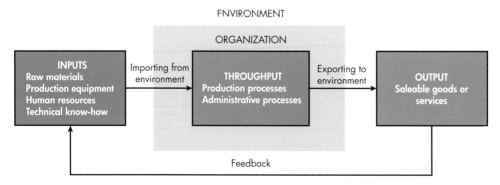

Figure 2.7 **The Open Systems Perspective**

producing the outputs exported back to the environment. *Information inputs* that signal how the environment and organization are functioning can help determine whether the organization will continue to survive. *Negative feedback* indicates a potential for failure and the need to change the way things are being done.

Fred Emery and Eric Trist

In Katz and Kahn's model, the environment surrounding an organization is both the source of needed resources and the recipient of transformed products. Accordingly, organizational survival depends on sensing that environment and adjusting to its demands. Describing environments and their associated demands so as to improve this sensing and adjustment process was the goal of Fred Emery and Eric Trist, two early theorists of the open systems perspective.[28]

After noting that every organization's environment is itself composed of a collection of more or less interconnected organizations—supplier companies, competitors, and customer firms—Emery and Trist proposed the existence of four basic kinds of environments. The first kind, which they labeled the *placid random environment*, is loosely interconnected and relatively unchanging. Organizations in such environments operate independently of one another, and one firm's decision to change the way it does business has little effect on its rivals. These organizations are usually small—for example, landscape maintenance companies, construction firms, and industrial job shops—and can usually ignore each other and still stay in business by catering to local customers.

Placid clustered environments are more tightly interconnected. Under these conditions, firms are grouped together into stable industries. Environments of this sort require organizations to cope with the actions of a *market*—a fairly constant group of suppliers, competitors, and customers. As a result, companies in placid clustered environments develop strategic moves and countermoves that correspond to competitors' actions. Grocery stores in the same geographic region often do business in this type of environment, using coupon discounts, in-store specials, and similar promotions to lure customers away from other stores.

Disturbed reactive environments are as tightly interconnected as placid clustered environments, but are considerably less stable. Changes that occur in the environment itself have forceful effects on every organization. For instance, new competitors from overseas, by increasing automation and changing consumer tastes in the U.S. automobile market, revolutionized the domestic auto industry in the 1970s and 1980s. In response, GM and Ford had to change their way of doing business, Chrysler combined with Germany's Daimler and later with Italy's Fiat, and a fourth long-time manufacturer, American Motors, ceased to exist. In such circumstances, organizations must respond not only to competitors' actions but also to changes in the environment itself. Owing to their unpredictability, it is difficult to plan how to respond to these changes.

Turbulent fields are extremely complex and dynamic environments. Companies operate in multiple markets. Public and governmental actions can alter the nature of an industry virtually overnight. Technologies advance at lightning speed. The amount of information needed to stay abreast of industrial trends is overwhelming. As a result, it is virtually impossible for organizations to do business in any consistent way. Instead, they must remain flexible in the face of such uncertainty, staying poised to adapt themselves to whatever circumstances unfold. Today's computer and communications industries exemplify this sort of environment. Technological change and corporate mergers are creating and destroying entire categories of companies at ever-increasing rates.

Other Contributors

Emery and Trist suggested that organizations must respond in different ways to different environmental conditions. Tighter environmental interconnections require greater awareness about environmental conditions, and more sweeping environmental change necessitates greater flexibility and adaptability. Other open systems theorists, including Paul Lawrence, Robert Duncan, and Jay Galbraith, have similarly stressed the need for organizations to adjust to their environments. Their ideas, and those of other open systems theorists, form the basis of several current models of macro organizational behavior, described in later chapters of this book.

Emerging: The Positive Organizational Behavior Perspective

As we have noted, the field of organizational behavior is rooted in part in the discipline of psychology. For this reason, changes in psychology have influenced thinking in organizational behavior as the two fields have continued to develop. One such area of cross-fertilization involves the area of "positive psychology." Noting that much of the research conducted in psychology during the last half of the twentieth century examined cognitive and behavioral pathologies, that is, negative thoughts and activities, psychologists have recently begun suggesting that more attention be focused on human strengths and potential, thus, on positive psychological processes and outcomes. In introducing a special issue of the *American Psychologist* on the topic of positive psychology, Martin Seligman and Mihaly Csikszentmihalyi described positive psychological results at three levels of operation:[29]

1. The intrapsychic level: well-being, contentment, and satisfaction; hope and optimism; and flow and happiness.
2. The individual level: the capacity for love and vocation, courage, interpersonal skill, aesthetic sensibility, perseverance, forgiveness, originality, future-mindedness, spirituality, high talent, and wisdom.
3. The interpersonal (group) level: the civic virtues and the institutions that move individuals toward better citizenship—responsibility, nurturance, altruism, civility, moderation, tolerance, and work ethic.

Understanding the processes associated with these and similar outcomes, and helping to increase their incidence and prevalence in modern society, is the ultimate aim of positive psychology.[30]

In organizational behavior, the emergence of a "positive organizational behavior" perspective has contributed to renewed interest in and reinterpretation of the basic concepts and models introduced in the four management perspectives that we have just described. Fred Luthans described this emerging perspective as encompassing the study and application of human resource strengths and psychological capacities that can be measured, developed, and managed for performance improvement.[31] Professor Luthans also identified five core areas to be examined in positive organizational behavior, using the acronym CHOSE:[32]

1. **C**onfidence/self-efficacy: one's belief in being able to succeed at a task in a given situation.
2. **H**ope: setting goals, determining how to achieve them, and being self-motivated to pursue their accomplishment.

3.   **O**ptimism: expecting positive outcomes and perception of positive causes linked to happiness, perseverance, and success.
4.   **S**ubjective well-being: positive understanding and evaluation of one's life, and satisfaction with one's accomplishments.
5.   **E**motional adjustment: capacity for recognizing and managing one's emotions and the emotions of others; self-awareness, empathy, and social skills.

Research in positive organization behavior has examined such varied topics as positive emotions and organizational change, finding positive meaning at work, and virtuous organizing and the performance of members and their organizations.[33] Its promise lies in the greater attention paid to human development within the context of organizations and management practices.

A Contingency Framework

Of the five management perspectives just described, none tells the whole story about management and managers. Instead, as indicated in Figure 2.8, each contributes valuable insights that supplement the others' contributions. The scientific management perspective focuses on making a profit in the *external* world by increasing the *efficiency* of production activities. The administrative principles perspective emphasizes improving *internal* operations by increasing the *efficiency* of administration. The human relations perspective stresses the importance of developing the *flexibility* to respond to the individual needs of members *inside* the organization. The open systems perspective focuses on developing the *flexibility* to respond to changes in the *external* environment. The positive organizational behavior perspective represents a refocusing of attention within all four of the quadrants illustrated in the figure toward processes and outcomes that are beneficial to organizations and their members.[34]

Similarities are readily evident among the five perspectives. For example, the scientific management and administrative behavior perspectives both promote attention to efficiency

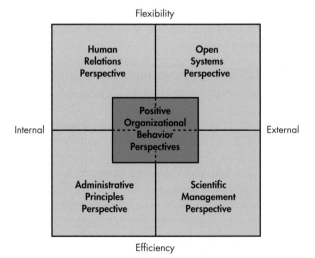

Figure 2.8 **Contingency Framework**
The five management perspectives differ in terms of their emphasis on flexibility or efficiency, and on internal operations or the external environment. Depending on the situation faced by a manager, one or more of the perspectives may provide useful guidance. This contingency relations is summarized in the form of a simple matrix.

and stability. The human relations and open systems perspectives share a common emphasis on flexibility and change. The administrative principles and human relations perspectives focus on procedures within the organization. The open systems and scientific management perspectives emphasize the importance of dealing with demands on the organization from external sources. The positive organizational behavior perspective bridges these differences and thus unites all of the other perspectives in its examination of beneficial processes and outcomes.

Each of the four fundamental perspectives (excluding the positive organizational behavior perspective, which bridges the four) also has an opposite, however. The human relations perspective, with its emphasis on human growth and satisfaction, stands in stark contrast to the scientific management perspective's emphasis on employee efficiency and task simplification. The open systems perspective's focus on adapting to environmental circumstances contrasts sharply with the administrative principles perspective's concern with developing stable, internally efficient operations.

These differences reflect dilemmas that managers face every day. Is it more important to stimulate task performance or employee satisfaction? Should the organization be structured to promote efficiency or flexibility? Should jobs be designed to encourage satisfaction or to maximize profitability? We will address these and other issues in the remaining chapters of this book. For now, we conclude our discussion of management and managers by repeating a key idea: *In dealing with management dilemmas, no single approach is either always right or always wrong*. In recommending this approach, we advocate a **contingency approach** to management—the view that no single theory, procedure, or set of rules is applicable to every situation.[35] Managers must make difficult choices, but the insights offered by all four perspectives can help them weigh the alternatives and decide what to do.

Summary

Management is a process of *planning, organizing, directing*, and *controlling* the behavior of others that makes it possible for an *organization* using a *division of labor* and a *hierarchy of authority* to accomplish a *mission* that would not be achievable through the efforts of individuals working alone. *Managers* differ in terms of where they fit in the organization's hierarchy. These differences influence their use of *conceptual, human*, and *technical skills* and shape the *managerial roles* they fill. The fast-paced job of manager allows little uninterrupted time to devote to any single activity.

Over the years, four perspectives have developed to explain and improve management practices. Supporters of the *scientific management perspective* have tried to increase the efficiency of production processes so as to enhance marketplace profitability. Proponents of the *administrative principles perspective* have focused on enhancing the efficiency of administrative procedures. Researchers in the *human relations perspective* have emphasized nurturing the growth and satisfaction of organization members. Theorists working in the *open systems perspective* have highlighted the importance of coping with the surrounding environment. According to the *contingency approach*, these four perspectives form a framework of alternative ways to view the process of management. This framework provides managers with useful guidance as they manage organizational behavior.

Review Questions

1. How does an organization enable its members to accomplish a goal that might not be achievable by individuals working alone? Why aren't organizations formed to achieve purposes that people can accomplish individually?

2. What is an organization's mission? Its division of labor? Its hierarchy of authority? How do these three organizational attributes fit together to define the nature of management?

3. What are the two key ideas underlying the open systems perspective? What central principle do they support? Explain the cycle of events described by Katz and Kahn's open systems model. Why is it important for managers to be able to diagnose environmental conditions and adapt their organizations to environmental changes as they occur?

4. Explain the contingency model constructed from the five perspectives of management thought described in this chapter. If you were a manager having problems with employee satisfaction, which perspective would you consult for advice? If you were concerned about efficiency, which perspectives could probably help out?

Notes

1   B. Stone, "Sell Your Friends," *Bloomberg Businessweek*, September 27–October 3, 2010, 64–72; B. Stone and D. MacMillan, "How Zuck Hacked the Valley," *Bloomberg Businessweek*, May 21–27, 2012, 60–72; A. Vance, "The Making of 1 Billion," *Bloomberg Businessweek*, October 8–14, 2012, 64–70.

2   A. Smith, *An Inquiry into the Nature and Causes of the Wealth of Nations*, 5th ed. (Edinburgh: Adam and Charles Black, 1859), 3.

3   H. A. Simon, *Administrative Behavior: A Study of Decision Making Processes in Administrative Organizations*, 3rd ed. (New York: Free Press, 1976), 257–278.

4   L. R. Gomez-Mejia, J. E. McCann, and R. C. Page, "The Structure of Managerial Behaviors and Rewards," *Industrial Relations* 24 (1985): 147–154.

5   R. L. Katz, "Skills of an Effective Administrator," *Harvard Business Review* 52 (1974): 90–102.

6   H. Mintzberg, *The Nature of Managerial Work* (Englewood Cliffs, NJ: Prentice Hall, 1980); S. Carlson, *Executive Behavior* (Stockholm: Stromsberg, 1951); R. Stewart, *Managers and Their Jobs* (London: Macmillan, 1967).

7   J. B. Quinn, *Strategies for Change: Logical Incrementalism* (Homewood, IL: Irwin, 1980), 18.

8   R. L. Bell and J. S. Martin, "The Relevance of Scientific Management and Equity Theory in Everyday Managerial Communication Situations," *Journal of Management* 13 (2012): 107–125; M. Tadajewski and D. B. Jones, "Scientific Marketing Management and the Emergence of the Ethical Marketing Concept," *Journal of Marketing Management* 28 (2012): 37–61.

9   The truthfulness of Taylor's accounts of his shovel demonstration and similar industrial experiments has been questioned, as described in R. Kanigel, *The One Best Way* (New York: Viking, 1997) and C. D. Wrenge and R. M. Hodgetts, "Frederick W. Taylor's 1899 Pig Iron Observations: Examining Fact, Fiction, and Lessons for the New Millennium," *Academy of Management Journal* 43 (2000): 1283–1291. Nonetheless, Taylor's descriptions of these experiments, published in F. W. Taylor, *The Principles of Scientific Management* (New York: Norton, 1911) and elsewhere, had an influence on management that was immediate and continues today.

10 H. L. Gantt, "A Bonus System of Rewarding Labor," *ASME Transactions* 23 (1901): 341–372; H. L. Gantt, *Work, Wages, and Profits* (New York: Engineering Magazine Company, 1910), 18–29.

11 H. L. Gantt, *Organizing for Work* (New York: Harcourt, Brace, & Howe, 1919), 74–97.

12 H. Emerson, *The Twelve Principles of Efficiency* (New York: Engineering Magazine Company, 1912), 359–367.

13 L. Schimmoeller, "Henri Fayol and Zero Tolerance Policies," *Review of International Comparative Management* 13 (2012): 31–47.

14 H. Fayol, *General and Industrial Management*, trans. Constance Storrs (London: Pitman & Sons, 1949), 19–43.

15 H. Fayol, *Industrial and General Administration*, trans. J. A. Coubrough (Geneva: International Management Institute, 1930), 19.

16 Max Weber, *From Max Weber: Essays in Sociology*, ed. & trans. H. H. Gerth and C. W. Mills (New York: Oxford University Press, 1946); N. P. Mouzelis, *Organization and Bureaucracy: An Analysis of Modern Theories* (Chicago: Aldine, 1967); Max Weber, *Max Weber: The Theory of Social and Economic Organization*, trans. T. Parsons (New York: Free Press, 1947).

17 J. D. Mooney and A. C. Redev, *Onward Industry: The Principles of Organization and Their Significance to Modern Industry* (New York: Harper & Brothers, 1931); revised and published as J. D. Mooney, *The Principles of Organization* (New York: Harper & Brothers, 1947).

18 L. Urwick, *The Elements of Administration* (New York: Harper & Brothers, 1944).

19 H. C. Metcalf and L. Urwick, eds., *Dynamic Administration: The Collected Papers of Mary Parker Follett* (New York: Harper & Row, 1940). Also see J. Garwood, "A Review of Dynamic Administration: The Collected Papers of Mary Parker Follett," *New Management* 2 (1984): 61–62.

20 A. Carey, "The Hawthorne Studies: A Radical Criticism," *American Sociological Review* 33 (1967): 403–416.

21 Ibid.; R. H. Franke and J. D. Kaul, "The Hawthorne Experiments: First Statistical Interpretation," *American Sociological Review* 43 (1978): 623–643; A. J. M. Sykes, "Economic Interests and the Hawthorne Researchers," *Human Relations* 18 (1965): 253–263.

22 Examples from the body of research stimulated by the Hawthorne studies include L. Coch and J. R. French, Jr., "Overcoming Resistance to Change," *Human Relations* 1 (1948): 512–533; L. Berkowitz, "Group Standards, Cohesiveness, and Productivity," *Human Relations* 7 (1954): 509–514; S. E. Seashore, *Group Cohesiveness in the Industrial Work Group* (Ann Arbor: University of Michigan Survey Research Center, 1954).

23 D. McGregor, "The Human Side of Enterprise," *Management Review* 56 (1957): 22–28, 88–92; D. McGregor, *The Human Side of Enterprise* (New York: McGraw-Hill, 1960).

24 McGregor, "The Human Side of Enterprise," 23.

25 Ibid., 88–89.

26 W. G. Lawrence, ed., *Exploring Individual and Organizational Boundaries: A Tavistock Open Systems Approach* (London, UK: Karnac Books, 2012).

27 D. Katz and R. L. Kahn, *The Social Psychology of Organizations* (New York: Wiley, 1966).

28 F. E. Emery and E. Trist, "The Causal Texture of Organizational Environments," *Human Relations* 18 (1965): 21–32; F. E. Emery and E. Trist, *Towards a Social Ecology* (London: Plenum, 1973).

29 M. E. Seligman and M. Csikszentmihalyi, "Positive Psychology: An Introduction," *American Psychologist* 55 (2000): 5–14.

30 D. M. Buss, "The Evolution of Happiness," *American Psychologist* 55 (2000): 15–23; E. Diener, "Subjective Well-Being: The Science of Happiness and a Proposal for a National Index," *American Psychologist* 55 (2000): 34–43.

31 F. Luthans, "Positive Organizational Behavior: Developing and Managing Psychological Strengths," *Academy of Management Executive* 16 (2002): 57–75.

32 Ibid.; see also F. Luthans, "The Need for and Meaning of Positive Organizational Behavior," *Journal of Organizational Behavior* 23 (2002): 695–706.

33 K. S. Cameron, J. E. Dutton, and R. E. Quinn, eds., *Positive Organizational Scholarship: Foundations of a New Discipline* (San Francisco: Berrett-Koehler, 2003); K. Golden-Biddle and J. E. Dutton, eds., *Using a Positive Lens to Explore Social Change and Organizations: Building a Theoretical and Research Foundation* (New York: Routledge Academic, 2012).

34 Our classification system is based on research conducted by R. E. Quinn and associates. See, for example, R. E. Quinn and J. Rohrbaugh, "A Spatial Model of Effectiveness Criteria: Towards a Competing Values Approach to Organizational Analysis," *Management Science* 29 (1983): 363–377; R. E. Quinn, *Beyond Rational Management: Mastering the Paradoxes and Competing Demands of High Performance* (San Francisco: Jossey-Bass, 1988), 50–54; R. E. Quinn, S. R. Faerman, M. Thompson, and M. R. McGrath, *Becoming a Master Manager: A Competency Framework*, 3rd ed. (New York: Wiley, 2002), 2–12.

35 J. M. Pennings, "Structural Contingency Theory: A Reappraisal," in B. M. Staw and L. L. Cummings, eds., *Research in Organizational Behavior* 14 (Greenwich, CT: JAI Press, 1992), 267–310.

Part II

Micro Organizational Behavior

Chapter 3

Managing Diversity and Individual Differences

In 2012, for the first time in U.S. history, the majority of children born were not whites of European ancestry. In addition, although African Americans represent the largest minority class among adults over 50, among younger Americans, Hispanics represent the largest minority group, followed by Asians, creating a very new and diverse "majority minority." William Frey, a demographer at the Brookings Institute, noted that, "we are moving from a largely white and black population to one which is more diverse and is a big contrast from what baby boomers grew up with."[1]

The ability of managers to adjust to this diversity will be critical, and one might be concerned with evidence that suggests that Americans are still struggling to get past stereotypes associated with race when it comes to African Americans. A **stereotype** presumes that some person possesses or fails to possess certain individual characteristics based on their sex or membership in a racial, ethnic, or age group. Despite electing an African American for president in both 2008 and 2012, however, recent evidence suggests that Americans still have preconceived notions about race differences in leadership abilities and other critical skills. For example, research shows that when successful organizations are led by black managers, people attribute this to broad market factors over which the leader had no control.[2] In contrast, when successful organizations were led by white managers, this success was perceived to be due to leadership effectiveness. Other research shows that banks considering the exact same business loan application are less likely to lend to a black entrepreneur relative to one who is white, because the former is seen as a higher risk.[3]

Stereotyping is certainly not limited to the United States, and recently, there has been a great deal of controversy in France attributed to discrimination against Muslim workers. For example, as part of research study, Clare Adida and her colleagues sent identical résumés to French employers, except that in half the cases the job applicant had a Christian-sounding name (Aurelie Menard), but in the other half of applications the applicant had a name that reflected a Muslim background (Khadjia Diouf). Despite having identical résumés, Aurelie was invited to interview with companies at a rate four times higher than Khadjia—direct evidence of religious bias. Indeed, across the overall French economy, the unemployment rate for Muslims is three times higher than for the rest of the population, and many suspect that the kind of bias shown against Khadjia is widespread in France.[4] In addition, many have attributed recent troubles with the broader European Union to stereotypes within that community that assume that "Northern Europeans are serious, industrious, and efficient, while Southern Europeans are passionate, chaotic, and indolent."[5] Clearly, if one hopes to manage any organization in a fair and efficient manner, one has to get past overly simplistic stereotypes.

Although stereotyping is one major problem, a different but equally important perceptual distortion is the **mirror image fallacy**, where one presumes that all other people are "just like me." In one sense, this is a comforting bias because, if it were true, it would make managing people very easy. If owners of a firm believe that everyone in their company shares their abilities, interests, beliefs, and values, they will consider it an easy task to organize and encourage their employees to pursue a common goal. Because the mirror image fallacy *is* a fallacy, however, the owners soon find that the myriad differences among the people they employ will make their task far from easy. For example, while few readers of this book would probably ever consider lying on a job application, research suggests that 30 percent of résumés submitted to employers contain false or misleading references.[6] This type of fraud is not limited to lower or midlevel positions and has been detected even among CEOs. For example, former Yahoo! CEO Scott Thompson had to resign from the company in 2012 because he falsely claimed that he had a computer science degree from Stonehill College.[7] Thus, for a host of reasons, managers need to take steps to ensure that those they hire actually have the skills and attributes they claim to have and not rely strictly on self-reported information.

The American essayist Ralph Waldo Emerson once wrote that "the wise man shows his wisdom in separation, in gradation, and his scale of creatures and of merits is as wide as nature. . . . The foolish have no range in their scale, but suppose that every man is as every other man." That statement captures the essence of this chapter. It seeks to familiarize you with some of the major occupationally relevant dimensions on which humans vary and to describe the means by which you can use this information to promote human welfare and secure a competitive advantage for your organization. The first section of the chapter discusses how information about individual differences can be used to generate competitive advantage. Next, we describe some of the critical dimensions on which people vary. Although these dimensions are hardly the *only* ways in which people can vary (indeed, later chapters explore others), they serve as a useful starting point for considering the bases of diversity. A manager needs to treat each person as a unique configuration of these characteristics rather than simply categorizing workers by surface characteristics such as race, sex, age, or culture or assuming they are all alike. Managers who think in terms of these characteristics will be able to capitalize on individual differences in a way that promotes the competitiveness of their organizations, while at the same time avoiding prejudicial stereotypes and the mirror image fallacy.

Capitalizing on Individual Differences

Even the most tolerant manager might sometimes wish that individual differences would just go away. If all supervisors, colleagues, and subordinates were alike, managing would be a much easier task. Of course, such homogeneity is highly unlikely to happen. Consequently, successful organizations must try to capitalize on differences in a way that advances their competitiveness. Indeed, research on how firms gain sustainable competitive advantage consistently identifies selectivity in hiring and an emphasis on training as two central characteristics of successful companies.[8] As shown in Figure 3.1, we can derive benefits from individual differences in organizational behavior through selection, training, and reengineering.

Selecting

Selection programs enable managers to assess people and jobs, and then try to match up the two in a way that maximizes the fit between the abilities and traits of the individual and the abilities and traits required for the job. This type of matching allows us to take advantage of

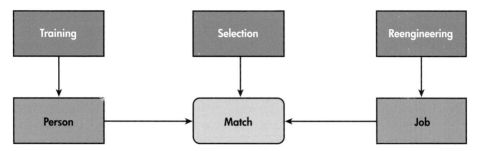

Figure 3.1 Three Ways to Capitalize on Individual Differences

Source: Adapted from K. Birdi, C. Clegg, M. Patterson, A. Robinson, C. B. Stride, and T. B. Wall, "The Impact of Human Resource and Operational Management Practices on Company Productivity," *Personnel Psychology* 61 (2008): 467–501.

individual differences without changing either the person or the job. Personnel selection is the process of choosing some applicants and rejecting others for particular positions.

Personnel selection programs often begin with an analysis of the job, which leads to a written job description, which in turn leads to a list of the various characteristics needed for someone who is likely to be successful in that job. In other cases, jobs may be highly fluid and quick to change, and thus the hiring organization might try to find people who fit with the culture of the organization rather than some specific job.[9] In yet other cases, the organization itself could be going through changes and might simply be looking for a proactive individual who can adapt to a wide variety of different job situations.[10] Regardless, in the end, as one hiring manager notes, "the idea is to define what success looks like for the position you are filling because this helps you determine what questions to ask during the interview and how to screen the applicants."[11]

Once one has laid out the requirements that are critical for success, the next step is to collect information on job applicants. Although almost all organizations rely on some form of interviewing to assess people, it is critical that interviews are structured and that interviewers take notes in order to create a standardized set of questioning and recording of answers. Situational interview questions that require applicants to "think on their feet" with respect to what they would do in critical situations that are likely to come up on the job are often helpful for predicting future behavior. Subjectivity and potential bias can also be reduced by relying on multiple interviewers or standard paper-and-pencil tests or measures. The key is relying on multiple sources and multiple methods when collecting information, because each source or method has its own limitations. For example, although background checks by outside agents are useful, they are not always accurate, and they are no substitutes for a face-to-face interactive exchange with job applicants.[12] In the end, it is critical to see which sources and which measures taken prior to hiring people actually predict the future in terms of work performance and turnover, a process called **test validation**.

Training

A second way to benefit from knowledge of individual differences is to train people so as to compensate for any job-related deficiencies in their current profile of traits or abilities. The beginning of the twenty-first century has been marked by widespread labor shortages in some U.S. industries. Much of this problem can be traced not so much to the scarcity of workers, but rather to shortcomings in the skill levels of those workers who are available. For example, according to surveys conducted by the National Association of Manufacturers, five of six applicants for manufacturing jobs are currently rejected because of gaps between their skills and the job requirements. Of those rejected, two out of five are rejected specifically for lack of basic proficiency in reading and arithmetic.[13] In fact, research has documented that the illiteracy rates associated with the growing segments of the U.S. labor market (young people and immigrants) are among the highest among industrialized nations.[14]

In other cases, rather than a problem with basic skills, labor shortages can be traced to people who lack specific higher-level skills where the demand outstrips the supply. In cases where companies cannot find people with the skills they need, training programs can be employed to help develop the skills. For example, Arcelor-Mittal, the world's largest steelmaker, has initiated a training program called "Steelworker for the Future." This program takes high school graduates and pays them roughly $18 an hour to take part in a three-year training program that provides the skills necessary to take on a wide variety of jobs in the steel industry. The company started this program when it recognized that older steelworkers were retiring and it needed workers with specific skills in mechanical and electrical engineering that were no longer taught in traditional schools.[15]

Of course, training and selection are not mutually exclusive ways of leveraging individual differences. Many organizations find that some people respond better to training initiatives than others, and thus they go out of their way to make sure the people they select in the first place are those who are likely to derive the most out of learning experiences. For example, research shows that people who are high in general intelligence or cognitive ability derive more benefit from training experiences, and so organizations might screen on this characteristic if they engage in a great deal of training.[16]

Reengineering

Assessing individual differences is clearly critical for training purposes because the intent is to change the person. A different approach is to assess individual differences and then respond to any mismatch between person and job by changing the *job* or reengineering work processes. For example, the Americans with Disabilities Act (ADA) requires that employers make "reasonable accommodations" in an effort to employ the disabled. Such accommodations often mean deleting, changing, or moving a job requirement to a different job, so that the lack of a particular ability no longer disqualifies some disabled workers from being considered for a certain position.[17] For example, Walmart was recently successfully sued by one of its employees who had cerebral palsy and was confined to a wheelchair. The employee requested to be able to use a grabber and a shopping cart to help her pick up and hold clothes. Her manager denied the request and then eventually terminated her employment. The court ruled, however, that what she requested was in fact a reasonable accommodation, and the cost of her request was absolutely trivial when compared to the fine they had to pay.[18]

Older workers are another source of valuable talent that sometimes requires reengineered jobs. For example, in the oil industry, there is a serious shortage of petroleum engineers. In order to retain an older workforce whose valuable skills would be difficult to replace, many companies such as ConocoPhillips are reengineering the work to make it less physically demanding. The hope is to stretch out the careers of a set of people who might otherwise retire. Indeed, as one industry expert noted, "this is a graying profession and we are just not ready for the transition."[19] This is not an isolated example, and the Bureau of Labor Statistics data suggests that workers in the 65–69 age range have shown the highest growth in labor force demand in the last five years. Thomas Darrow, a major corporate recruiter, has noted that "this is evolving to be one of the biggest trends in recruiting" and employers are scrambling to make accommodations in work design to attract and retain older workers.[20]

Just as research on training has shown that certain people benefit more from training than others, research also suggests that some people respond better to the redesign of work than others. For example, people who are psychologically open to experience are also more flexible when it comes to reengineered work, and this can be built into selection programs that rely heavily on work redesign initiatives to stay competitive.[21] Thus, work redesign is a useful complement to both selective hiring and training when it comes to deriving competitive advantage from individual differences.

Diversity in Physical Ability

Recent research on individual differences has tended to focus on cognitive abilities and personality traits, and the bulk of this chapter will also focus on human variation on these dimensions. However, a great deal of the early research in the area of organizational behavior examined individual differences in physical abilities. Occupation-oriented studies, taken together with human physiology studies, provide us with a solid foundation for understanding the structure of physical performance (Table 3.1).[22] As noted in this table, physical ability consists of three major dimensions: muscular strength, endurance, and movement quality. Muscular strength comes in three slightly different varieties (tension, power, and endurance); the same is true for movement quality (flexibility, balance, and coordination).

Although a thorough analysis of a job is needed to determine whether it requires a particular physical capacity, the abilities listed in Table 3.1 tend to be needed most frequently in a specific set of industries: the military; protective services, such as police departments, fire departments, and correctional facilities; construction; and other physically demanding industries. If personnel in these industries lack the necessary physical abilities, they or the people they seek to protect may be injured.[23] For example, a recent decision within the U.S. military that allowed women to serve in combat roles was controversial because, as a group, women have less

Table 3.1 **The Three Dimensions of Physical Ability**

1. Muscular strength	Ability to exert muscular force against objects in terms of pushing, pulling, lifting, carrying, or lowering them (muscular tension)
	Exerting muscular force in quick bursts (muscular power)
	Exerting muscular force continuously over time while resisting fatigue (muscular endurance)
2. Endurance	Ability to sustain physical activity that results in increased heart rates for a long period
3. Movement quality	Ability to flex and extend body limbs to work in awkward or contorted positions (flexibility)
	Ability to maintain the body in a stable position and resist forces that cause loss of stability (balance)
	Ability to sequence movement of the fingers, arms, legs, or body to result in skilled action (coordination)

Source: Adapted from N. D. Henderson, M. W. Berry, and T. Matic, "Field Measures of Strength and Fitness Predict Firefighter Performance on Physically Demanding Tasks," *Personnel Psychology* 60 (2007): 431–473.

upper-body strength relative to men. Some considered this a critical attribute to possess for situations where one soldier has to carry another wounded soldier, but others felt that the technological nature of much modern combat, as well as the rigorous physical training that both men and women receive as part of their military experience, mitigated the danger. Indeed, in the two most recent wars waged by U.S. forces, over 280,000 women broke the "brass ceiling" and served in combat zones where there was very little distinction between front lines and rear support.[24]

In jobs that are physically demanding, testing for these kinds of physical abilities is much more common now than in the past for several reasons. First, height and weight criteria were often substituted for specific abilities in the past, but because height and weight measures are considered to discriminate unfairly against women and members of some minority groups, they are rarely used today. Although there tend to be significant differences between men and women on direct measures of physical strength, when one measures endurance or movement quality directly there are few differences between men and women.[25] Second, because of increasingly sedentary lifestyles, the physical abilities of the average person have eroded over time and managers can no longer assume that the people they hire are or will remain fit for physically demanding jobs.[26]

Physical ability tests are also used to select employees for work such as construction, where jobs require both physical strength and agility. Such tests can predict not only a person's level of job performance, but also his or her risk of job-related injuries. This finding is significant because, as many employers pick up the bill for employees' medical costs, tests that predict health problems for a job applicant can prove extremely cost-effective.

Diversity in Cognitive Ability

Although mental abilities are not one-dimensional, we generally find positive relationships between people's performances on different kinds of mental tests. To emphasize the positive relationships among the facets of mental ability while still recognizing their unique features, we discuss each aspect separately. First, we focus on the three traditional aspects of cognitive ability, and then we follow this with two newer dimensions that have received a great deal of interest.

Traditional Dimensions of Cognitive Ability

Because scores across different types of mental tests are related, they are often summed and treated as an index of general intelligence. Specialists tend to prefer the term **general cognitive ability** to *intelligence* because the former term is more precise and because it conjures up less controversy over such issues as the role of genetic factors in mental ability. The term *intelligence* is used imprecisely in the lay community, where the high social value placed on it complicates discussions of things such as age, sex, and racial differences, as well as the means to reduce the impact of such differences.[27] Although general cognitive ability as measured with mental tests has increased significantly over time, so has the variability between individuals, and many organizations go to great lengths to find the most intelligent workers and screen out those who are low in intelligence.[28]

Although cognitive abilities all share some features, certain facets of mental ability are sufficiently distinctive that they are worth assessing in their own right. Because specific jobs may require more of one type of mental ability than of the other types, we might want to home in on gathering data on this particular ability. In this section, we focus our attention on five facets of cognitive or mental ability that stand out in terms of both their generality and their usefulness as predictors of performance in the real world. Table 3.2 defines these abilities.

Table 3.2 Dimensions of Cognitive Ability

1. Verbal ability	The ability to understand and effectively use written and spoken language
2. Quantitative ability	The ability to quickly and accurately solve arithmetic problems of all kinds, including addition, subtraction, multiplication, and division, as well as applying mathematical rules
3. Reasoning ability	The ability to think inductively and deductively to invent solutions to novel problems
4. Emotional intelligence	The ability to generate, recognize, express, understand, and evaluate one's own and others' emotions in order to successfully cope with social demands and pressures
5. Cultural intelligence	The ability to observe, interpret, and act upon unfamiliar social and cultural cues and function effectively in new and foreign environments

The first three dimensions are probably the most familiar to college students who have taken many standardized tests throughout their academic careers. **Verbal ability** reflects the degree to which a person can understand and use written and spoken language. **Quantitative ability** reflects a person's ability to perform all kinds of arithmetic problems— not only problems dealing with addition, subtraction, multiplication, and division, but also those involving square roots, rounding procedures, and the multiplication of positive and negative values.

A different kind of analytical skill is associated with the third dimension of mental ability. **Reasoning ability** is the ability to invent solutions to many different types of problems. Although tests of reasoning ability sometimes employ numbers, they should not be confused with simple measures of quantitative ability. At the heart of a reasoning problem is the need to create a solution or grasp a principle, not a need to make computations. As work in modern organizations has become more complex, the role of problem-solving ability has increased over time, and this is often the most critical attribute that employers look for when making hiring decisions.[29]

The usefulness of traditional cognitive ability tests in predicting task performance has been investigated in both academic and organizational contexts. In academic settings, researchers have found high correlations between tests like the Scholastic Aptitude Test (SAT), and both a person's first-year-college grade-point average (correlations in the .50s) and his or her over-all class rank (correlations in the .60s).[30] The predictive value of these tests is greater for students in the physical sciences or math than it is for students in the humanities or social sciences. The tests are less predictive of success in graduate school (correlations in the .30s) because most applicants for graduate school score relatively high in mental ability and there-fore represent a somewhat homogeneous group.

A great deal of evidence suggests that general cognitive ability is also predictive of success in the work world.[31] Research has shown that, in virtually any job where planning, judgment, and memory are used in day-to-day performance, individuals high in general cognitive ability will generally outperform those who are low in this ability. General cognitive ability is important even for jobs that lack such complexity if these positions expose one to dangerous conditions. Workers high in cognitive ability show much lower on-the-job accident rates.[32] In addition, cognitive ability is important on any job that requires the worker to learn something new. Individuals who are high in general cognitive ability will learn the job quicker than their low-ability counterparts.[33] Finally, individuals high in cognitive ability have also been found to engage in less counterproductive behaviors at work, including destruction of property and engaging in violent acts on the job.[34] Thus, general cognitive ability is important in organizations for a whole host of reasons, and indeed this may be the single most important individual difference variable in work contexts.

For certain jobs, tests of specific mental ability can add significantly to the predictive power of tests of general intelligence.[35] For example, verbal ability and reasoning ability are critical to success in executive, administrative, and professional positions. Quantitative ability is important in jobs such as accountant, payroll clerk, and salesperson and in many types of supervisory positions. Whereas general mental ability tests have relevance for a wide variety of jobs, specific mental ability tests are useful for more job-specific evaluations.

New Dimensions of Cognitive Ability

In addition to these standard measures of cognitive ability, research has also been directed at developing a construct that is referred to as **emotional intelligence**. Emotional intelligence has been defined as a set of abilities, both verbal and nonverbal, that enable a person to generate, recognize, express, understand, and evaluate their own and others' emotions in order to successfully cope with social demands and pressures.[36] People who are high on emotional intelligence have the ability to identify distinct emotions in themselves, as well as in other people, and use this to guide their thinking and actions. This helps them regulate their own moods and manage the emotions of other people who surround them. Like other specific aspects of mental ability, emotional intelligence is correlated modestly, but significantly, with general cognitive ability. Still, the evidence seems to suggest that this variable has unique value in predicting success in jobs that involve interpersonal interaction over and above general cognitive ability and personality traits like those captured by the five factor model.[37] This is especially the case for front-line service jobs in which employees might have to manage the emotions of customers and sense when a customer is becoming upset or angry.[38] Sensing when fellow employees are becoming upset, too, is also necessary in jobs that require teamwork.[39]

Initial treatments of the concept of emotional intelligence conceived of it as an ability, but the concept was quickly picked up in the popular press literature and took on a life of its own, leading to the springing up of a cottage industry of books and seminars on the topic. Many of these treatments strayed from the original conception and increasingly portrayed it as a broad personality-like trait, resulting in a great deal of criticism aimed at the construct in general in the academic literature.[40] However, research that has employed the more narrow, ability-oriented treatment has documented that leaders and managers who score high on this ability tend to be perceived as more effective by their subordinates, peers, and supervisors.[41] Perhaps because of this social effectiveness, high scorers on this ability also tend to show generally higher levels of personal well-being, self-esteem, and life satisfaction.[42]

Just as the perceived need for the concept of emotional intelligence grew out of a general belief that the standard measures of cognitive ability failed to capture all the critical abilities needed for success in contemporary organizations, so too did the concept of **cultural intelligence**. Cultural intelligence has been defined as the ability to observe, interpret, and act upon unfamiliar social and cultural cues and function effectively in new and foreign environments.[43] This includes a cognitive component associated with scanning one's environment and recognizing patterns within cultures, a motivational component that derives satisfaction from adjusting to new situations, and finally a behavioral component that emphasizes practicing new behaviors and developing new habits. Although this ability is related to certain aspects of personality, especially openness to experience, as with emotional intelligence this characteristic is best thought of as ability and not a personality trait.[44]

Cultural intelligence is a critical individual difference for organizations that are trying to move into global product markets. For example, while General Electric has reduced its total workforce in response to recent challenges in the global economy between 2005 and 2010, it reduced its U.S. workforce during that time period by over 28,000, but its non-U.S. workforce by less than 1,000. CEO Jeffrey Immelt stated that "we've globalized around markets, not cheap labor. The era of globalization around cheap labor is over. Today we go to Brazil, we go to China, we go to India because that's where our customers are."[45]

Although one can learn a little about different cultures from reading a book or tourism in general, the behavioral component of cultural intelligence also demands gaining experience working in the novel culture, not going there on a vacation.[46] Many organizations attempt to broaden the cultural experience of their current employees by sending them on international assignments. Many managers struggle with this experience and terminate their assignments early, especially employees who are low in agreeableness, emotional stability, and extroversion.[47]

In addition to competing in product markets, firms have moved into international labor markets to bring in specific types of talent, sometimes at lower cost, that they need in order to compete both domestically and abroad.[48] One aspect of this trend can be seen in the high-skill end of the economy, where U.S. organizations have been forced to search more widely for skilled technicians, engineers, and computer programmers. For example, Central Europe has seen a mass exodus of talent as companies located elsewhere in Europe and in North America raid this region for skilled workers. In Romania alone, an estimated 2.5 million high-skill workers have left the country for more lucrative opportunities abroad.[49]

At the low end of the skill range, an influx of international workers has also entered the United States to perform low-paying jobs that most Americans are unwilling to do—for example, dishwashers, hotel maids, janitors, and construction workers.[50] This labor shortage is especially acute in the summer months because American teens have recently been avoiding the traditional low-skill summer jobs in amusement parks and other recreational areas. As Gene Kijowski, president of Century Pool Management, notes, "There is so much affluence in this whole region, it is hard to find young people who want to hustle." Indeed, to stay in business, Century Pool had to bring in 100 teenagers from Prague to work as lifeguards.[51]

Diversity in Personality

Given the vast number of personality characteristics that are described in the popular press, as well as the scientific literature, we need some type of classification scheme that helps simplify the picture by identifying a small number of the most important individual differences in traits. Fortunately, a great deal of research has been conducted on the dimensionality of personality, which has helped clarify the structure of human traits. Indeed, the current personality literature tends to focus on a consensus group of five dimensions of personality, known as the "Big Five," and occupationally relevant measures of these characteristics have been developed.[52]

The Big Five Framework

The Big Five personality characteristics focus on a person's social reputation, in the sense that they describe what the person is like when viewed by other people. The five characteristics

Table 3.3 Dimensions of Personality

1. Extroversion	Sociable, gregarious, assertive, talkative, expressive
2. Emotional adjustment	Emotionally stable, nondepressed, secure, content
3. Agreeableness	Courteous, trusting, good-natured, tolerant, cooperative, forgiving
4. Conscientiousness	Dependable, organized, persevering, thorough, achievement oriented
5. Openness to experience	Curious, imaginative, artistic, sensitive, broad-minded, playful

Source: Adapted from F. P. Morgeson, M. A. Campion, R. L. Dipboye, J. R. Hollenbeck, K. R. Murphy, and N. Schmitt, "Reconsidering the Use of Personality Tests in Personnel Selection Contexts," *Personnel Psychology* 60 (2007): 683–729.

(Table 3.3) can be used to comprehensively capture what people are like. Because work organizations are social institutions, the fact that these characteristics are expressed in terms of a person's social reputation makes them highly relevant in understanding organizational behavior. The Big Five traits include **extroversion, emotional stability, agreeableness, conscientiousness**, and **openness to experience**.[53]

Many companies, including General Motors, American Cyanamid, JCPenney, and Westinghouse, rely heavily on personality assessment programs to evaluate and promote employees. Many other firms use such programs as screens for initial hiring.[54] Because of the social nature of many of these traits and because companies are increasingly competing on the dimension of quality of service, the importance of the personalities of the people who provide that service has never been more important. These customer-contact people make up one of the fastest-growing segments of the U.S. workforce, and they serve at the front line in the battle among organizations striving for competitive advantage. Many of the most successful firms therefore take great care when hiring people for these jobs.

Despite their widespread adoption by industry, however, the usefulness of such personality measures in explaining and predicting human behavior has been criticized on several counts. Traditionally, the most significant criticism deals with the validity of these measures for actually predicting future job success. Although it is possible to find reliable, commercially available measures of each of the traits shown in Table 3.3, some have suggested that the evidence for their validity and generalizability has traditionally been only mixed.[55]

Conscientiousness is the only dimension of personality that seems to display any validity across a number of different facets of the trait, as well as across different job categories.[56] Conscientiousness is an especially strong predictor of job performance when employees work unsupervised.[57] Although there are many ways of inferring whether or not an individual is high or low in conscientiousness, one way that some employers try to make judgments regarding conscientiousness is whether or not they have been out of work, and if so, for how long. During the recent recession, many employers simply refused to hire people who were unemployed for long durations, and instead filled jobs by recruiting people away from other employers. In particular, research suggested that if an applicant had been unemployed for eight months, it was almost impossible to find a good job because employers attributed long bouts of unemployment with a lack of conscientiousness.[58]

Extroversion is relevant to many jobs such as those involving sales and social influence.[59] Leadership positions tend to attract highly extroverted individuals, and introverts sometimes struggle with being heard and standing out in team contexts. However, there are also advantages at work associated with introversion. Relative to extroverts, introverts are more deliberate, more cautious, and collect more information when making decisions, all of which is helpful when decisions are complex or involve risk. Introverts are also better listeners than extroverts which is certainly a critical aspect of leadership, especially in contexts that want to promote empowerment among lower-level employees.[60]

Emotional stability is also a factor that tends to be associated with leadership, and many organizations put managers who have difficulty controlling their emotions through training programs often referred to as "anger management" sessions. Lockheed Martin, Halliburton, United Parcel Service, and the U.S. Federal Prison System are just a few employers who have used anger management training to ward off lawsuits and high employee turnover caused by perceived abusive supervision.[61] Indeed, many of the positive effects for extroversion highlighted in the previous paragraph are neutralized if the person is also low on emotional stability.[62] Although anger management training is widespread across industries, the medical industry tends to outspend all others by far, for this particular form of training. The stress associated with medical care, particularly in contexts where decision making by physicians is constrained by insurance company policies or countered by lack of compliance by patients, often creates conditions that are not conducive to emotional stability.[63]

The fact that many personality characteristics, such as aggressiveness, sociability, and impulsiveness, are described in everyday language is both good news and bad news for the study of organizational behavior. It is good news because most people can readily perceive individual differences in these qualities and can see how such variations might affect particular situations. It is bad news because terms adopted from everyday language are usually imprecise. This vagueness can create considerable difficulty in understanding, communicating, and using information obtained from scientific measures of personality. We next focus on ways to increase the usefulness of measuring these characteristics in organizational contexts.

Making Personality Tests More Effective

Although the validity of personality tests might never exceed that of cognitive ability tests, organizations can nevertheless take concrete steps to more successfully capitalize on individual differences in personality. First, in many cases, the effects of some trait on performance are revealed only when the person is also high in ability. That is, it is not so much the trait itself, but rather how the trait interacts with ability. For example, one recent study of 703 executives found that highly extroverted executives accumulated more diverse leadership experiences throughout their careers, but this only translated into better strategic thinking and performance when the executive in question was also high in cognitive ability.[64]

Second, the relationship between the trait and performance could be a function of the specific demands of the job. For example, with respect to agreeableness, although it is nice to be around co-workers who are trusting, tolerant, and cooperative, the nature of some jobs demands just the opposite approach. For example, David Duncan, an auditor for Arthur Andersen, was arrested for his part in the Enron disaster. Duncan's job was to monitor Enron's accounting practices to make sure they conformed to the rules laid down by Arthur Andersen. However, many who know him well attribute his downfall to the fact that he was an overly agreeable person who hated conflict and would do anything to keep his clients happy. In fact, he not only avoided conflict with his clients by approving some very questionable practices, he also avoided conflict with co-workers who disapproved of Enron's practices. In a memo that proved significant at his trial, he responded to a concerned co-worker by noting "on your point (i.e., the whole thing is a bad idea), I really couldn't agree more."[65] In this instance, being trusting, tolerant, and cooperative ran counter to actually getting the job done.

Third, even relatively minor wording changes in standard items on personality inventories can help double the predictive ability of scores from such measures if they "contextualize" the questions. For example, rather than just seeking to see if someone is extroverted or conscientious "in general," by making the item more specific to the work context, this can improve one's ability to predict work performance. That is, items should ask if someone is conscientious "at work" or "when filling out paperwork" or "when preparing for a presentation," and so on. Linking the specific trait in question to the specific context that describes the work, also makes the measure seem more job-related to the applicant, and reduces the negative reaction some people have to "generic" items.[66]

Fourth, how one obtains information about the job applicant's personality is also an area where one can take steps to improve the predictive validity of such tests. Unstructured interviews conducted by untrained personnel are unlikely to provide much in the way of valuable information about someone's personality. Standardized paper-and-pencil tests are available for most traits and, although some fear that people will "fake" their responses to these inventories, the evidence suggests that faking is not a large problem in most real-world contexts.[67] Still self-reports of traits tend to be less valid when compared to ratings provided by people who know the person well. In addition, research suggests that structured interviews constructed in the form of judgment tests can often provide much more useful information when making hiring decisions based on personality and interpersonal skills.[68] With a judgment test, applicants are asked to relate either how they would respond to hypothetical events that are likely to occur on the job or actual past experiences they had responding to similar issues in prior jobs. Trained evaluators, often armed with standardized grading forms, then rate the answers provided in terms of what they suggest about the person's personality traits or interpersonal skills. Because of the vast amount of research evidence supporting the validity of situational judgment tests, these are quickly supplanting the use of traditional, unstructured interviews in most organizational hiring contexts.[69] Job applicant's judgment is also increasingly assessed by employers who search for information on people via Google, Facebook, or other social media. In many cases, information obtained in this fashion has uncovered issues (e.g., drug or alcohol problems) that sank the employment chances of otherwise qualified individuals.[70]

Finally, most traditional treatments of individual differences have relied on static conceptions of these traits, with the idea that firms will match people to their work and co-workers. More recent research on individual differences, however, has examined individuals' abilities to display adaptability in their behavior at different times and in different situations.[71] Someone who is adaptive can display one trait in one situation (for example, being agreeable with a customer who has a valid complaint) and the opposite trait in a different situation (for example, being disagreeable with a supplier who is reneging on an established contract). Someone who is adaptive might also be a natural introvert, but can act like an extrovert if the situation demands this latter trait. Thus, adaptability recognizes variance within one person on traits. Highly adaptable people can handle emergencies and deal effectively with uncertain and unpredictable situations. They also tend to be creative problem solvers and quickly learn new tasks, technologies, and procedures. Finally, they demonstrate a sensitivity to interpersonal and cultural differences, and they can work effectively in many different types of groups.[72]

Demographic Diversity

Recent trends related to the labor supply have heightened managers' awareness of individual differences found among workers. Most of this awareness has focused less on differences in physical abilities, cognitive abilities, and personality traits, and more on diversity related to demographic characteristics such as those highlighted in the introduction of this chapter. Indeed, much of the current concern about managing demographic diversity can be traced to studies indicating that an increasingly larger percentage of new entrants into the labor pool tend to be women, minorities, or immigrants. In an effort both to secure the best talent and to market products globally, organizations, industries, and entire nations are often looking across national boundaries when making hiring decisions.

Both developments have forced companies that were once predominantly staffed by white males to rethink their hiring policies. Specifically, the experiences of white males are now seen as too homogeneous to enable them to effectively manage a diverse workforce or to effectively exploit opportunities in the global market. Instead, organizations are looking to hire people with different demographic backgrounds in order to broaden their perspectives.

Legal and Political Aspects of Diversity

In the past, legal and political forces, particularly civil rights activists who tried to increase opportunities for women and minorities in the workplace, drove integration of the workforce. Many of those forces are still in play today, and the Equal Employment Commission (EEC), the federal agency that monitors and deals with discrimination in the workforce, received a record number of complaints—100,000—in 2011 alone.[73] Despite what some might believe, there are still clear vestiges of discrimination in our culture. For example, a recent study that sent out identical résumés of hypothetical job applicants showed that those that came from people with "white-sounding" names, such as Neil, Brett, Emily, or Anne, were 50 percent more likely to be asked for an interview relative to those that came from people with "black-sounding" names, such as Ebony, Tamika, Rasheed, or Khirese.[74]

In the opening of this chapter, we noted how the process of stereotyping can lead to unfair decisions and actions being taken against members of various groups, and the evidence from research studies suggests that these can be powerful. For example, supervisory ratings of subordinate job performance often reflect a bias against racial minorities, even when objective levels of performance seem to be highly similar.[75] These biases also seem to work in the opposite direction, in the sense that subordinate ratings of leadership also seem to be affected by stereotypes that associate leadership of business organizations with white males.[76] These kinds of stereotypes have also been documented with respect to women, who are less likely to be seen either as leaders or as successful entrepreneurs, as well as older workers, who are generally perceived as being less adaptable relative to younger workers.[77] In return, stereotypes of younger workers, dubbed "Millennials," have been documented, suggesting they are perceived as overly demanding, cynical, and lacking in organizational commitment.[78]

Thus, because stereotyping persists, political forces aimed at eliminating discrimination remain alive today. Still, relative to twenty years ago, the strength and breadth of these motivations have waned for several reasons. First, to some extent, many of the affirmative action programs instituted in the 1970s and 1980s have achieved some measure of success. The evidence indicates that the number of African Americans enrolled in colleges and universities has increased 500 percent since 1965, and over the last twenty-five years the share of black families earning more than $50,000 a year rose from 8 percent to 20 percent. In the last five years alone, the ranks of black managers and professionals have increased 30 percent.[79] The enhanced representation of minorities in these kinds of jobs is critical because research shows that higher levels of diversity in the workforce result in less discrimination in terms of wages and promotions. That is, one sees less perceived ethnic and gender-based discrimination and fewer lawsuits in work contexts where there are higher proportions of women and minorities in the workforce.[80] This does not just seem to be a perceptual effect, but instead seems to reflect actual differences in practices. For example, one study in a large sales organization showed that ethnic and gender-based differences in earnings were smaller in teams with proportionately more people of color and women and in organizations that had a higher proportion of ethnic and female managers.[81]

Second, whereas existing affirmative action programs have failed to completely wipe out discrimination or all the differences between races in outcomes, the perception is that these programs no longer target the groups who need the most support. That is, a growing core of poor inner-city black youths are most often the victims of the international competitive forces that are driving down wages and employment levels for low-skilled workers. Manufacturing jobs that used to support this group are increasingly moving overseas, and the types of benefits that come out of current affirmative action programs benefit affluent, middle-class black workers, rather than those in the inner cities who need the support more desperately.

Third, the 1990s witnessed an increase in backlash against affirmative action and other remedial programs aimed at minorities, especially by white males who see such programs as giving preferential treatment to other groups at their expense.[82] This backlash is particularly strong among Generation Xers, who have grown up having no experience with the segregation that drove early civil rights initiatives. The tolerance that many older white workers had with race-based remedial programs, partially fueled by guilt and direct experience, simply does not exist among younger people who grew up in less segregated schools and neighborhoods. Because of this backlash, several legal decisions made it illegal for employers or schools to establish quotas or set aside a specific number of openings for members of minority groups based strictly on race.

Many institutions got around these limitations by basing decisions on factors that were associated only indirectly with race, but still allowed them to integrate the workforce. For example, the University of Texas at Austin used a rule that accepted the top 10 percent of students at any Texas high school, but because many Texas high schools were dominated by one race or the other, this "race-neutral" practice helped integrate the university even though it did not explicitly use race as a factor in admission. However, this practice harmed African American students who *did* happen to be in suburban high schools that were predominantly white, and many minority students at these schools were passed over for admission, despite having academic credentials that were stronger than African Americans at predominantly black schools. When the university tried to reach out to these students, however, a suit was filed that went all the way to the U.S. Supreme Court citing this as an explicit racial preference.[83]

petitive Aspects of Diversity

In addition to being motivated by a sense of social justice or fear of litigation, affirmative action programs in the twenty-first century are also part of a larger strategy that seeks to leverage diverse experience into competitive advantage.[84] Indeed, with respect to the lawsuit filed against the University of Texas described above, it was an interesting sign of the times when a long list of major corporations sent briefs to the Supreme Court explicitly asking that the court not limit them to using race-conscious policies.[85] As these employers know, large-scale studies of organizations have documented the fact that organization-level racial diversity, for the most part, has a positive impact on financial performance, especially in the service sector of the economy.[86] When treated as a legal issue, the goal with respect to diversity is to try to be blind to differences and make sure it does not influence decision making. When treated as a means of gaining competitive advantage, however, the focus for diversity programs shifts from ignoring individual differences to trying to leverage them to enhance profitability.

For example, half of the people in the biggest urban markets for Macy's Department Stores (New York, Los Angeles, and Chicago) are African American or Hispanic. In order to attract more of these customers, Macy's expanded hiring from these groups and reached out to minority vendors to give these new employees new products to sell. The new products were produced by smaller mom-and-pop suppliers owned by minority group members who had been targeting this unexploited sector of the market for a long time but lacked the size or connections to secure space on the shelves of major department stores. Bill Hawthorne, Macy' senior vice president for diversity summed up this competition-enhancing view of diversity when he stated, "When I started down this path, there was a prevailing point of view: That we do not see color, we are all the same. But now we recognize those differences and that is the beauty of diversity. Let's celebrate those, and let's figure out as a retailer how to merchandise that."[87]

As another example, Kaiser Permanente, a large health-care organization headquartered in San Francisco, found that, because its facilities were underrepresented with respect to Asian workers, they often found it difficult to attract Asian patients. Given the demographic makeup of that city, this was an untenable situation, and Kaiser launched an ambitious program to recruit more Asian workers. This program was so successful, in terms of promoting financial performance, that it was later extended to other racial and ethnic groups as well as to women and older workers. By creating an organization that better reflected its community, the organization was better able to serve the community, which in turn fueled growth and profitability.[88]

Once minority workers are hired, firms that value diversity also need to ensure that they can retain the services of members of these groups. Turnover rates among minorities at the managerial level are often two to three times higher than the rates for white males, with the difference often attributable to a perceived lack of opportunities for promotions. Retention of minority representation is enhanced by establishing programs that promote mentoring relationships between new minority employees and more established organizational members.[89] In fact, one study found that the real key in such programs is linking up women and minority members with white male mentors. The benefits that accrue from these cross-race and cross-gender pairings for the new worker seem to be much larger than those realized by women and minorities who have mentors with the same demographic characteristics.[90] Of course, beyond these factors, diversity programs must receive top managerial support if they are to be successful.[91] Indeed, a recent research study involving approximately 800 managers pointed to this factor as the single most important characteristic in predicting the success of these programs. The second most critical factor was the organization's ability to channel this top-level enthusiasm down the hierarchy. The best way to ensure that the effects trickle down is to formally appraise and reward middle- and lower-level managers for creating, maintaining, and profiting from diversity.[92]

In addition to attracting customers, expanding diversity and maintaining a stance of tolerance is critical to help avoid pushing customers away. For example, Chick-fil-A attracted a great deal of unwanted national attention in 2012 when the CEO Dan Cathy weighed in on the same-sex marriage debate and stated, "I think we are inviting God's judgment on our nation when we shake our fist at him and say 'We know better than you as to what constitutes a marriage.'" These comments enraged many activist groups who started a boycott of the stores and used the national press to call attention to the issue. Even though there was never any evidence that Chick-fil-A ever discriminated against gay customers or employees, the bad publicity hindered the company's strategy to expand from the Southern region of the United States to the more Northern regions when the mayors of both Boston and Chicago stated that they would "make it very difficult" for the restaurant to open outlets in those cities.[93]

Although people generally think of race and sex as the major workforce diversity issues, one of the more sweeping demographic forces with which many organizations are attempting to come to grips is the aging of the workforce. Certainly, there are many stereotypes regarding older workers, including those that suggest that as a group they are (1) less motivated, (2) generally less willing to participate in career development, (3) more resistant to change, (4) less trusting, (5) less healthy, and (6) more vulnerable to work–family imbalance. However, a major study of these stereotypes that involved over 200,000 people showed that, with the exception of their rates of participation in development activities, all of these presumptions are false.[94]

Since the majority of the 76 million baby boomers born between 1946 and 1960 are now, or will soon be, 60 years old and because of the "baby bust" that occurred between 1965 and 1976, many have predicted that organizations will eventually face major labor shortages. Thus, firms have to get beyond these false stereotypes and many organizations are seeking to turn these trends into a competitive advantage by hiring and retraining older workers.[95] For example, McDonald's Corporation has recently struggled to find the young workers who once dominated the ranks of its employees. To deal with this problem, the company initiated the ReHIREment Program, which attempts to entice older individuals to work in its restaurants. As part of this program, McDonald's developed specific recruiting materials geared toward the older generation. Whereas its recruiting brochures for young candidates emphasize the learning opportunities and long-term career benefits of McDonald's jobs, the brochures in the ReHIREment Program stress the scheduling flexibility and the fact that part-time earnings do not threaten Social Security earnings.[96] Home Shopping Network (HSN), the Clearwater, Florida based cable network, operates a program for older employees similar to that used at McDonald's. Located in an area well populated by retirees, HSN uses older workers on a part-time basis to answer telephones and take orders for merchandise advertised on its shows. It also maintains a sensitivity program for its managers that gives them valid information about what is fact and what is fiction in the area of aging and job performance.[97]

Indeed, even locations like Florida that are not a traditional haven for retirees are finding access to an increased supply of older workers, partly fueled by the recent financial crisis. That is, since most retirees tend to save for their own retirement via 401(k) plans that are heavily influenced by stock prices, the recent drop in the stock market ravaged the retirement portfolios of many people, sending them back into the labor pool. For example, at Retirementjobs.com, a career site for people over the age of fifty, the number of people who registered for jobs spiked to 600,000 from a previous high of 250,000 in late 2008.[98]

Replacing outdated stereotypes with actual scientific data regarding individual differences is thus a critical skill for today's managers. Consequently, many organizations are trying to train their workers to raise their sensitivity to these kinds of issues. When sensitivity training programs work well, they are able to dispel the mirror image fallacy, yet avoid fostering prejudicial stereotypes about various groups. They achieve their success by helping managers focus on individuals as individuals, each of whom can be seen as a unique constellation of physical abilities, cognitive abilities, personality traits, and experiences. Each personal profile of abilities, traits, and experiences is idiosyncratic, and their differences transcend simple categorization schemes based solely on sex, race, age, or culture.

Summary

Individuals differ on a number of dimensions. Taking advantage of this fact is essential to effective control of organizational behavior. Individuals differ in three primary physical abilities: *muscular strength, endurance*, and *movement quality*. In many job situations, people who lack the necessary physical abilities may perform poorly and put themselves and others at risk for injuries. Individuals may also differ in their cognitive abilities. *General cognitive ability* has important implications for a wide variety of jobs. Indeed, this characteristic is relevant for any job that requires planning and complex decision making on a daily basis. General cognitive ability also affects both a person's ability to learn the job and his or her ability to adapt to new situations. Five specific facets of cognitive ability are *verbal ability, quantitative ability, reasoning ability, emotional intelligence*, and *cultural intelligence*. These characteristics supplement general cognitive ability in affecting performance on certain types of jobs. Individuals may also differ in personality characteristics, which often spill over into job performance differences. The Big Five framework, which focuses on *extroversion, agreeableness, emotional stability, conscientiousness*, and *openness to experience*, can be used to organize these traits and suggest how each might be related to job performance. Finally, the changing nature of the workforce means that the labor pool is also growing more diverse in terms of its demographic and cultural background. In order to gain competitive advantage from demographic and cultural diversity, managers need to move beyond false stereotypes regarding various groups and directly assess the true abilities and traits of each individual person with reliable and valid methods.

Review Questions

1. Is the mirror image fallacy more likely to affect our assessments of others' abilities or our assessments of their personalities? Are particular dimensions of ability or classes of personality characteristics especially susceptible to this kind of mistaken perception? Explain.
2. Think of someone you know who is highly successful in his or her chosen field. What were the important personal characteristics that led to this person's success? Now think of what would have happened if that person had chosen a different line of work. Do you think this person would have been successful in any field, or can you imagine lines of work for which the person was poorly suited? How does your answer to this question relate to the selection-versus-placement distinction?
3. Imagine someone who is turned down for a job because of (a) his or her performance on a paper-and-pencil cognitive ability test, (b) an interviewer's assessment of the person's intelligence and conscientiousness, or (c) his or her responses to a personality inventory. What differential reactions would you expect from this person? Explain your answer.
4. Legal approaches to diversity seek to make organizational decision making "color-blind" and "race-neutral," whereas competitive approaches to diversity seek to leverage individual differences in order to increase profits. Do you see any way to reconcile these two perspectives or are they mutually exclusive alternatives?

Notes

1   C. Dougherty and M. Jordon, "Minority Births Are New Majority," *Wall Street Journal*, May 17, 2012, http://online.wsj.com/article/SB10001424052702303879604577408363003351818.html.
2   C. Rosette, "Race Influences How Leaders Are Assessed," *Wall Street Journal*, January 3, 2012, http://online.wsj.com/article/SB10001424052970203899504577128973024950032.html.

3 D. Brady, "Wanted: More Black Entrepreneurs," *Bloomberg Businessweek*, January 23, 2012, 16–17.

4 C. L. Adida, D. D. Laitin, and M. A. Valfort, "Identifying Barriers to Muslim Integration," *Proceedings from the National Academy of Sciences* 107 (2010): 384–390.

5 A. Reinhardt, "Euro Crises Unleashes Old Stereotypes," *Bloomberg Businessweek*, November 4, 2011, 22.

6 C. Suddath, "Imaginary Friends," *Bloomberg Businessweek*, January 21, 2013, 68.

7 A. Eferati and J. S. Lublin, "Thompson Resigns as CEO of Yahoo," *Wall Street Journal Online*, May 13, 2012, http://online.wsj.com/article/SB100014240527023041927045774022241229006022.html.

8 K. Birdi, C. Clegg, M. Patterson, A. Robinson, C. B. Stride, and T. B. Wall, "The Impact of Human Resource and Operational Management Practices on Company Productivity," *Personnel Psychology* 61 (2008): 467–501.

9 E. A. Amos and B. L. Weathington, "An Analysis of the Relation between Employee–Organization Value Congruence and Employee Attitudes," *Journal of Psychology* 142 (2008): 615–631.

10 M. A. Griffen, A. Neal, and S. K. Parker, "A New Model of Work Role Performance: Positive Behavior in Uncertain and Interdependent Contexts," *Academy of Management Journal* 50 (2007): 327–347.

11 A. Hedger, "Employee Screening: Common Challenges, Smart Solutions," *Workforce Management*, March 17, 2008, 39–46.

12 C. Terhune, "The Trouble with Background Checks," *BusinessWeek*, June 9, 2008, 54–58.

13 J. Smerd, "New Workers Sorely Lacking Literacy Skills," *Workforce Magazine*, December 10, 2007.

14 A. Bernstein, "The Time Bomb in the Workforce: Illiteracy," *BusinessWeek*, February 25, 2002, 122.

15 V. Lou Chen and J. Berman, "Companies Are Hiring—Just Not You," *Bloomberg Businessweek*, August 15, 2011, 10–11.

16 B. S. Bell and S. W. J. Kozlowski, "Active Learning: Effects of Core Training Design Elements on Self-Regulatory Processes, Learning, and Adaptability," *Journal of Applied Psychology* 93 (2008): 296–316.

17 A. Colella, R. L. Paetzold, and M. A. Belliveau, "Factors Affecting Coworkers' Procedural Justice Inferences of the Workplace Accommodations of Employees with Disabilities," *Personnel Psychology* 57 (2004): 1–23.

18 C. Smith, "Manager's Failure to Accommodate Creates Liability for Store," *Compliance Bulletin*, January 15, 2009.

19 M. Herbst, "Big Oils Talent Hunt," *BusinessWeek*, December 14, 2007, 59–62.

20 P. Coy, "Golden Paychecks," *BusinessWeek*, July 2, 2007, 13.

21 F. W. Bond, P. E. Flaxman, and D. Bunce, "The Influence of Psychological Flexibility on Work Redesign: Mediated Moderation of a Work Reorganization Intervention," *Journal of Applied Psychology* 93 (2008): 645–654.

22 J. Hogan, "Structure of Physical Performance in Occupational Tasks," *Journal of Applied Psychology* 76 (1991): 495–507.

23 N. D. Henderson, M. W. Berry, and T. Matic, "Field Measures of Strength and Fitness Predict Firefighter Performance on Physically Demanding Tasks," *Personnel Psychology* 60 (2007): 431–473.

24 L. Browder, "Women in Combat: Listening to Those That Have Been There," *Time Magazine*, January 29, 2013, 32–33.

25 M. Bernekow-Bergkvist, U. Aaus, K. A. Angvuist, and H. Johansson, "Prediction of Development of Fatigue during Simulated Ambulance Work Task from Physical Performance Tests," *Ergonomics* 47 (2004): 1238–1250.

26 J. J. Knapik, "Temporal Changes in the Physical Fitness of U.S. Army Recruits," *Sports Medicine* 36 (2006): 613–634.

27 R. E. Ployhart and B. C. Holtz, "The Diversity–Validity Dilemma: Strategies for Reducing Racio-Ethnic and Sex Sub-Group Differences and Adverse Impact in Selection," *Personnel Psychology* 61 (2008): 153–172.

28 J. R. Flynn, "Are We Really Getting Smarter?" *Wall Street Journal*, September 21, 2012, http://online.wsj.com/article/SB10000872396390444032404578006612858486012.html.

29 M. Korn, "Wealth or Waste: Rethinking the Value of a Business Major," *Wall Street Journal*, April 5, 2012, http://online.wsj.com/article/SB10001424052702304072004577323754019227394.html.

30 R. Sackett, M. J. Borneman, and B. S. Connelly, "High Stakes Testing in Higher Education and Employment: Appraising the Evidence for Validity and Fairness," *American Psychologist* 63 (2008): 215–227.

31 F. L. Schmidt and J. Hunter, "General Mental Ability in the World of Work: Occupational Attainment and Job Performance," *Journal of Personality and Social Psychology* 86 (2004): 162–173.

32 A. Gardner, "Lower IQs in Childhood Linked to Accident-Prone Adulthood," *BusinessWeek*, January 10, 2007, 21.

33 C. G. DeYoung, J. B. Peterson, and D. M. Higgens, "Sources of Openness/Intellect: Cognitive and Neuropsychological Correlates of the Fifth Factor of Personality," *Journal of Personality* 73 (2005): 825–858.

34 S. Dilchert, D. S. Ones, R. D. Davis, and C. D. Rostow, "Cognitive Ability Predicts Objectively Measured Counter-Productive Behavior," *Journal of Applied Psychology* 92 (2007): 616–627.

35 L. G. Humphreys, D. Lubinski, and G. Yao, "Utility in Predicting Group Membership and the Role of Spatial Visualization in Becoming an Engineer, Physical Scientist, or Artist," *Journal of Applied Psychology* 78 (1993): 250–261.

36 D. Goleman, *Working with Emotional Intelligence* (New York: Bantam, 1998).

37 D. L. Van Roy and C. Viswesvaran, "Emotional Intelligence: A Meta-Analytic Investigation of Predictive Validity and Nomological Net," *Journal of Vocational Behavior* 65 (2004): 71–95.

38 D.L. Joseph and D.A. Newman, "Emotional Intelligence: An Integrative Meta-Analysis and Cascading Model," *Journal of Applied Psychology* 95 (2010): 54–78.

39 C. I. C. Chien, M.-G. Seo, and P. E. Tesluk, "Emotional Intelligence, Teamwork Effectiveness, and Job Performance: The Moderating Role of Job Context," *Journal of Applied Psychology* 97 (2012): 890–900.

40 E. A. Locke, "Why Emotional Intelligence Is an Invalid Concept," *Journal of Organizational Behavior* 26 (2005): 425–431.

41 J. D. Mayer, P. Salovey, and D. R. Caruso, "Emotional Intelligence: New Ability or Eclectic Traits?" *American Psychologist* 63 (2008): 503–517.

42 J. D. Mayer, R. D. Roberts, and S. G. Barsade, "Human Abilities: Emotional Intelligence," *Annual Review of Psychology* 59 (2008): 507–536.

43 C. Earley and R. S. Peterson, "The Elusive Cultural Chameleon: Cultural Intelligence as a New Approach to Intercultural Training for the Global Manager," *Academy of Management Learning and Education* 3 (2004): 100–115.

44 S. Ang, L. Van Dyne, and C. Koh, "Personality Correlates of the Four Factor Model of Cultural Intelligence," *Group and Organization Management* 31 (2006): 100–123.

45 D. Wessel, "Big U.S. Firms Shift Hiring Abroad," *Wall Street Journal*, April 19, 2011, B1.

46 R. Takeuchi, P. E. Tesluk, and S. H. Yun, "An Integrative View of International Experience," *Academy of Management Review* 48 (2005): 85–100.

47 M. Caligiuri, "The Big Five Personality Characteristics as Predictors of Expatriates' Desire to Terminate the Assignment and Supervisor-Rated Performance," *Personnel Psychology* 55 (2000): 67–88.

48 L. D. Tyson, "Open the Gates Wide to High Skill Immigrants," *BusinessWeek*, July 9, 2000, 16.

49 J. Ewing, "Desperately Seeking Bulgarian Programmers," *BusinessWeek*, April 9, 2007, 31.

50 W. Zellner, "Keeping the Hive Humming: Immigrants May Prevent the Economy from Overheating," *BusinessWeek*, April 24, 2000, 50–52.

51 R. Sharpe, "Summer Help Wanted: Foreigners Please Apply," *BusinessWeek*, July 24, 2000, 32.

52 C. M. Gill and G. P. Hodgkinson, "Development and Validation of the Five Factor Model Questionnaire: An Adjective-Based Personality Inventory for Use in Occupational Settings," *Personnel Psychology* 60 (2007): 731–766.

53 M. R. Barrick and M. K. Mount, "The Big Five Personality Dimensions and Job Performance: A Meta-Analysis," *Personnel Psychology* 44 (1991): 1–26.

54 F. Wagner, "All Skill, No Finesse," *Workforce*, June 2000, 108–116.

55 F. P. Morgeson, M. A. Campion, R. L. Dipboye, J. R. Hollenbeck, K. R. Murphy, and N. Schmitt, "Reconsidering the Use of Personality Tests in Personnel Selection Contexts," *Personnel Psychology* 60 (2007): 683–729.

56 N. M. Dudley, K. A. Orvis, J. E. Lebiecki, and J. M. Cortina, "A Meta-Analytic Investigation of Conscientiousness in the Prediction of Job Performance: Examining the Inter-Correlations and the Incremental Validity of Narrow Traits," *Journal of Applied Psychology* 91 (2006): 40–57.

57 G. L. Stewart and A. K. Nandkeolyar, "Adaptation and Intraindividual Variation in Sales Outcomes: Exploring the Interactive Effects of Personality and Environmental Opportunity," *Personnel Psychology* 59 (2006): 307–332.

58 D. Akst, "How Employers See Prolonged Joblessness (and Why)," *Wall Street Journal*, September 12, 2012, http://blogs.wsj.com/ideas-market/2012/09/27/how-employers-see-prolonged-joblessness-and-why/.

59 C. J. Thoresen, J. C. Bradley, P. D. Bliese, and J. D. Thoresen, "The Big Five Personality Traits and Individual Job Performance Growth Trajectories in Maintenance and Transitional Job Stages," *Journal of Applied Psychology* 89 (2004): 835–853.

60 B. Walsh, "The Upside of Being an Introvert (and Why Extroverts are Overrated)," *Time Magazine*, February 6, 2012, 40–45.

61 B. Urstadt, "The Sociopath Network," *BusinessWeek*, July 25, 2011, 82–83.

62 T. A. Judge and A. Erez, "Interaction and Intersection: The Constellation of Emotional Stability and Extraversion in Predicting Performance," *Personnel Psychology* 60 (2007): 573–596.

63 E. Spitznagel, "Doctors Without Boundaries," *BusinessWeek*, August 6, 2012, 68–69.

64 L. Dragoni, I. S. Oh, P. Vankatwyk, and P. E. Tesluk, "Developing Executive Leaders: The Relative Contribution of Cognitive Ability, Personality, and the Accumulation of Work Experience in Predicting Strategic Thinking Competency," *Personnel Psychology*, 64 (2011): 829–864.

65 A. Raghavan, "How a Bright Star at Andersen Burned Out along with Enron," *Wall Street Journal*, May 15, 2002, 1–4.

66 J. A. Shaffer and B. E. Postlethwaite, "A Matter of Context: A Meta-analytic Investigation of the Relative Validity of Contextualized and Noncontextualized Personality Measures," *Personnel Psychology* 65 (2012): 445–494.

67 J. E. Ellingson, P. R. Sackett, and B. S. Connelly, "Personality Assessment across Selection and Development Contexts: Insights into Response Distortion," *Journal of Applied Psychology* 92 (2007): 386–395.

68 R. A. Posthuma, F. P. Morgeson, and M. A. Campion, "Beyond Employment Interview Validity: A Comprehensive Narrative Review of Recent Research and Trends over Time," *Personnel Psychology* 55 (2002): 1–81.

69 J. Merritt, "Improv at the Interview," *BusinessWeek*, February 3, 2003, 63.

70 D. Belkin and C. Porter, "Web Profiles Haunt Students," *Wall Street Journal*, October 4, 2012, http://online.wsj.com/article/SB10000872396390443768804578035500956712628.html.

71 E. D. Pulakos, S. Arad, M. Donovan, and K. E. Plamondon, "Adaptability in the Workplace: Development of a Taxonomy of Adaptive Performance," *Journal of Applied Psychology* 85 (2000): 612–624.

72 J. A. LePine, J. A. Colquitt, and A. Erez, "Adaptability to Changing Task Contexts: Effects of General Cognitive Ability, Conscientiousness, and Openness to Experience," *Personnel Psychology* 53 (2000): 563–593.

73 R. Johnson, "Briefing," *Time Magazine*, February 6, 2012, 7.

74 M. Bertrand, "It Helps to Have a 'White' Name," *CNN.com*, January 14, 2003.

75 J. M. Stauffer and M. R. Buckley, "The Existence and Nature of Racial Bias in Supervisory Ratings," *Journal of Applied Psychology* 90 (2005): 586–591.

76 A. S. Rosette, G. J. Leonarelli, and K. W. Phillips, "The White Standard: Racial Bias in Leader Categorization," *Journal of Applied Psychology* 9 (2008): 758–777.

77 S. DeArmond, "Age and Gender Stereotypes: New Challenges in a Changing Workplace and Workforce," *Journal of Applied Social Psychology* 36 (2006): 2184–2214.

78 N. A. Hira, "You Raised Them, Now Manage Them," *Fortune*, May 28, 2007, 38–46.

79 C. Farrell, "Is Black Progress Set to Stall?" *BusinessWeek*, November 6, 2005, 71–73.

80 A. Joshi, H. Liao, and S. E. Jackson, "Cross-Level Effects of Workplace Diversity on Sales Performance and Pay," *Academy of Management Journal* 49 (2006): 459–481.

81 D. R. Avery, P. F. McKay, and D. C. Wilson, "What Are the Odds? How Demographic Similarity Affects the Prevalence of Perceived Employment Discrimination," *Journal of Applied Psychology* 93 (2008): 235–249.

82 G. Shteynberg, L. M, Leslie, A. P. Knight, and D. M Mayer, "But Affirmative Action Hurts Us: Race-related Beliefs Shape Perceptions of White Disadvantage and Policy Unfairness," *Organizational Behavior and Human Decision Processes* 115 (2011): 1–12.

83 J. Bravin, "Justices Clash on Affirmative Action," *Wall Street Journal*, October 12, 2012, http://online.wsj.com/article/SB10000872396390443982904578047192287305354. html.

84 O. C. Richard, "Racial Diversity, Business Strategy, and Firm Performance: A Resource Based View," *Academy of Management Journal* 43 (2000): 164–177.

85 "Race-conscious Admissions in Texas" [editorial], *New York Times*, October 10, 2012, http://www.nytimes.com/2012/10/11/opinion/race-conscious-admissions-in-texas.html.

86 O. C. Richard, B. P. S. Murthi, and K. Ismail, "The Impact of Racial Diversity on Intermediate and Long Term Performance: The Moderating Role of Environmental Context," *Strategic Management Journal* 28 (2007): 1213–1233.

87 C. Timberlake, "At Macy's, the Many Colors of Cash," *Bloomberg Businessweek*, January 16, 2012, 22–23.

88 E. Fraunheim, "Kaiser Permanente," *Workforce Management*, October 20, 2008, 21.

89 S. Mehta, "What Minority Employees Really Want," *Fortune*, July 10, 2000, 181–186.

90 G. F. Dreher and T. H. Cox, "Race, Gender, and Opportunity: A Study of Compensation Attainment and the Establishment of Mentoring Relationships," *Journal of Applied Psychology* 81 (1996): 297–308.

91 G. Bylinsky, "Women Move Up in Manufacturing," *Fortune*, May 15, 2000, 372C–372Z.

92 S. Rynes and B. Rosen, "A Field Survey of Factors Affecting the Adoption and Perceived Success of Diversity Training," *Personnel Psychology* 48 (1995): 247–270.

93 D. Bennett, "Chick-fil-A: Deep Fried Civil War," *Bloomberg Businessweek*, August 2, 2012, 62–64.

94 T. W. C. Ng and D. C. Feldman, "Evaluating Six Common Stereotypes about Older Workers with Meta-Analytical Data," *Personnel Psychology* 65 (2012): 821–858.

95 J. Marquez, "The Would-Be Retirees," *Workforce Management*, November 3, 2008, 25–26.

96 D. Fandray, "Gray Matters: The Tight Job Market Means That Employers Will Increasingly Rely on Older Workers," *Workforce*, July 2000, 32.

97 M. G. Morris, "Age Differences in Technology Adoption Decisions: Implications for a Changing Work Force," *Personnel Psychology* 53 (2000): 375–403.

98 H. Green, "The Unretired," *BusinessWeek*, December 15, 2008, 47–49.

Chapter 4

Perception, Decision Making, and Creativity

In the spring of 2012, Barack Obama considered a series of decisions that could make or break his presidency. The CIA had informed him that its agents had discovered a walled compound in Pakistan believed to be the hiding place of Osama bin Laden. Although this was the best information that the CIA had uncovered on bin Laden in several years, it was by no means a "slam dunk," since there was only a 60 percent chance that the location had been correctly identified. As a matter of politics, to capture or kill bin Laden posed many risks, including a fiasco like that of the failed Iranian hostage rescue, which cost Jimmy Carter his reelection in 1980. Obama, too, had to consider his 2008 campaign promise to hunt down bin Laden and kill him.

At that moment, these and other critical questions and choices confronted the president and his administration. First, when should he act? As hunters know, the toughest choice they face is when to fire. If they fire too soon and from too far away, they may miss the mark, and their prey will escape. If they wait too long, hoping for a cleaner shot, they risk being discovered. Their prey will escape then too. Thus, should he act now, with just 60 percent certainty, or try to collect more information, increasing the level of confidence but also raising the odds that this new information would leak and allow bin Laden to escape?

Second, whose opinions and advice should he seek when considering this decision? On the one hand, adding more people to the decision-making process reduces the chance that some critical piece of information is missed. On the other hand, every additional person added to the decision-making group also increases the chance of a leak. In particular, should the president run the decision by representatives of Pakistan? After all, any attack would occur within its sovereign territory and Pakistan was supposedly a U.S. ally. However, could the Pakistanis be trusted to keep this information secure?

Third, exactly how should any attack be conducted? One sure and safe option, in terms of protecting U.S. lives, would be to drop 2,000-pound bombs from a B-2 bomber. However, this would inflict a great deal of collateral damage, and the CIA also believed that many women and children lived in and near the compound.[1] Unmanned predator drones armed with 500-pound bombs provided a second option. However, such ordnance might be insufficient to guarantee success and, while an airstrike might kill bin Laden, there would be no "friendlies" on the ground to identify his body. Only a commando raid would leave no doubt of the success of the mission and would also allow U.S. forces to retrieve potentially valuable intelligence information kept at the compound. However, if the mission failed, or if bin Laden was not actually at the compound, then U.S. lives would have been sacrificed for no good reason.

Before making his decision, the president took a vote among his closest advisors. Vice President Joe Biden argued against any attack, noting that the 60 percent confidence level was too low to risk such drastic action. He reminded Obama that the CIA had wrongly attached a greater than 60 percent probability that Iraq had weapons of mass destruction, which President George W. Bush used as a premise to justify the Second Gulf War. Secretary of Defense Robert Gates also voted against the mission, stating that any action that did not involve Pakistan would permanently damage the alliance. James Cartwright, chairman of the Joint Chiefs of Staff, felt the best option was a B-2 airstrike in order to mitigate potential U.S. casualties while at the same time ensuring total destruction of the site. Secretary of State Hillary Clinton and CIA Director Leon Panetta were in favor of a commando raid, however, and both believed Pakistan should be left "out of the loop" given the uncertain allegiances of its intelligence service. In the face of this disagreement within his inner circle, the decision was the president's alone to make. In the end, he chose a unilateral commando raid—the option that entailed the highest risk—but also the highest possible reward. On April 30, after months of deliberation, President Obama declared, "It's a go." Fifty-six hours later, Osama bin Laden was dead. Six months later, Barack Obama was reelected to his second term as the president of the United States.[2]

Perception is the process by which individuals select, organize, store, and retrieve information. *Decision making* is the process whereby this perceived information is used to evaluate and choose among possible courses of action. As this example shows, in many cases, important decisions have to be made even though one cannot be totally sure whose perceptions are accurate or inaccurate. Some of those within the President's inner circle thought the 60 percent confidence figure was too low, whereas others felt it was adequate. Some believed our Pakistani allies needed to be consulted regarding any military action that would take place within their country, whereas others believed Pakistan could not be trusted with sensitive information. Some placed the greatest weight on avoiding the loss of U.S. lives, whereas others placed greater emphasis on avoiding collateral damage among women and children. In the end, despite this uncertainty, some decision had to be made and it was clear that history will eventually judge decision makers by the accuracy of their choices.

Indeed, in addition to having accurate perceptions of the present conditions, decision makers also need to be able to envision the future and use their vision to generate *innovative and creative* options. For example, much of the information that helped locate Osama bin Laden came via the use of unmanned aerial vehicles (UAVs), commonly called "drones," an invention that changed the ability to efficiently and unobtrusively observe large stretches of land for extended periods. This innovative technology had not been available to previous U.S. presidents and it created opportunities—and threats—that no previous president had thus far encountered. In addition, post-9/11 changes in the structure of the intelligence community set up the potential for creative collaboration between the CIA and U.S. military that was also historically unprecedented.

These three topics—perception, decision making, and creativity—are examined in this chapter. The first section explores the process of human perception and discusses the keys to developing accurate beliefs about oneself and one's environment. Translating these accurate beliefs into decisions that are rational—or at least satisfactory—is the focus of the second section. Finally, the third section, on creativity, examines the process of going beyond the traditional decision options to uncover new and innovative alternatives.

Figure 4.1 provides an overview of the processes of perception and decision making and serves as a roadmap for the first two sections. We start at the left of Figure 4.1, which shows the environment in which the individual is embedded. Through the perceptual process, the individual uses some portion of the information that exists in that environment to make

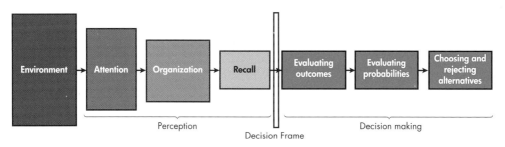

Figure 4.1 The Processes of Perception and Decision Making

decisions. The process of perception will be broken down into three stages: attention, organization, and recall. In Figure 4.1, the boxes become smaller as we move from left to right, indicating that some information is lost at each stage.

At the end of the perceptual process, the decision is framed; that is, the decision maker finishes the process of collecting information and states the decision-making problem in specific terms. At this point, the decision-making process begins. The information collected in the perceptual process is evaluated in terms of what outcomes might result from various decisions and what odds are associated with various outcomes. Using the combined assessment of outcomes and probabilities, the decision maker chooses those alternatives that are most likely to lead to good outcomes and rejects those alternatives that are either unlikely to lead to good outcomes or likely to lead to bad outcomes. We explore each substage of the perception and decision-making processes more closely in the sections that follow.

Perceptual Processes

Humans have five senses through which we experience the world: sight, hearing, touch, smell, and taste. Most of us "trust our senses," but sometimes this blind faith can lead us to believe that our perceptions are a perfect reflection of reality. People react to what they perceive, and their perceptions do not always reflect objective reality. This discrepancy can create major problems because, as the difference between perceived and objective reality increases, so does the opportunity for misunderstanding, frustration, and conflict.

You can begin to appreciate the vast possibilities for perceptual distortion by considering some well-known illusions (Figure 4.2). Obviously, if we can misperceive something as objective as size, shape, and length, then our likelihood of misperceiving something more subjective, such as the intentions or thoughts of other people, is high. For example, the data displayed in Table 4.1 show differences in perceptions between employers and employees from a survey of 13,000 pairs of managers and subordinates.[3]

These kinds of perceptual differences within a work group can lead to trouble and frustration for both the manager and the people with whom that manager works. Consequently, a great deal of research over the past fifty years has focused on reducing the gap between the perceptions of managers and subordinates.

For example, 360-degree feedback programs where managers' self-ratings on various skills are compared to ratings provided by their bosses, peers, and subordinates are now commonplace in organizations. Research suggests that in most cases, similarly to what is documented in Table 4.1, managers' self-perceptions tend to overestimate their skills relative to ratings provided by others.[4] As one recipient of such feedback at HCL Technologies noted, "There was this whole picture of me that emerged suggesting I was a heavy taskmaster. It was very

A. Are there two or three prongs on this object?

B. Ignoring the arrows, which vertical line is longer?

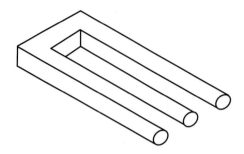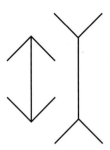

C. Are the four lines of the inner square straight lines?

D. Which dotted circle is larger?

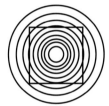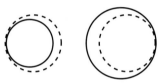

Figure 4.2 Four Common Perceptual Illusions

Table 4.1 Perceptual Differences between Employers and Employees Regarding Rewards

	Employees	*Employers*
Quality of work environment	24%	46%
Cash incentive targets	26%	44%
Merit increases	27%	43%
Recognition programs	21%	42%
Profit sharing	20%	36%
Long-term incentives	15%	29%
Tuition reimbursement	13%	21%
Flexible work schedules	20%	36%
Rotation of assignments	18%	49%
Career development	21%	50%
Training opportunities	26%	58%

Source: Adapted from J. Johnson, "Rewards Disconnect," *Workforce Management*, November 19, (2007): 15.

unsettling the first time."[5] Managers who are armed with this feedback can sometimes improve their ratings over time, but this is not guaranteed, and improvement seems to depend on a number of factors. For example, one sees more improvement when managers accept the feedback, set specific goals for their future performance, and develop concrete action plans for meeting those goals.[6]

Attention

At any given moment in time, our five senses are bombarded with information of all sorts. In the **attention stage**, most of this available information is filtered so that some enters the system but other information does not. Failures to filter this information can result in information overload, destroying concentration, and harming task performance. In the past, managers who needed to concentrate might have just gone into their offices and locked their doors to reduce some of this volume. However, with today's technology, between cell-phone calls, e-mails, text messaging, and social networking interruptions, there is almost nowhere to hide. Research has estimated that non-task-related distractions account for 28 percent of the average U.S. worker's day, sapping over $600 billion from the overall economy.[7] On the other hand, if critical information is never attended to it can never figure into decision making, thus resulting in decision-making errors. Thus, the attention stage is obviously critical in terms of its gatekeeping function, and we need to appreciate how characteristics of the perceiver affect the way in which attention is directed.

For example, the perceiver's expectations of an object will often influence his or her evaluation of that object.[8] This reaction occurs partly because a person's attention is more easily drawn to objects that confirm the individual's expectations. Indeed, in the performance appraisal context, supervisors who are led to anticipate that one group of workers is likely to perform better than another tend to rate subordinates in a way that reflects these expectations, even when the subordinates perform at exactly the same objective level.[9] This bias, which suggests that "believing is seeing," is often referred to as a "Pygmalian effect." This bias is especially pronounced among leaders who are relatively inexperienced. Over time, leaders with more extended experience learn to separate "believing from seeing" by taking note of evidence that disconfirms their expectations.[10]

In addition to expectations, the frequency with which a message is relayed also strongly influences the degree to which one attends to it. This is why repetition is a common element in most advertising campaigns, but the impact of repetition can also be seen when it comes to managerial behavior. For example, research shows that people are more likely to infer that a message is true and popular the more often they hear it—even when the message is simply being repeated by the same person. That is, people sometimes confuse repetition from one single source with consensus from multiple independent sources, even though there might be more validity in the latter relative to the former.[11]

Organization

Although much information is automatically filtered out at the attention stage, the remaining information is still too abundant and too complex to be easily understood and stored. Because human perceivers can process only a few bits of information at a time, in the **organization stage** they further simplify and organize incoming sensory data. For example, humans "chunk" several discrete pieces of information into a single piece of information that can be processed more easily.

To see how effective this kind of chunking can be, imagine your reaction if someone asked you to memorize a string of forty numbers. You might doubt your capacity to memorize so many numbers regardless of how much time you had. Your doubts are probably misplaced, however. If asked to do so, you could probably write down (1) your Social Security number, (2) your telephone number with area code, (3) your license plate number, (4) the month, date, and year of your birth, (5) your current ZIP code, and (6) your height and weight. You might say, "Well, yes, but these are only six numbers." Note, however, that (1) and (2) have nine digits each, (3) and (4) have six digits, and (5) and (6) probably have five; together, the data include a grand total of forty digits. The fact that humans think of these bits of information as six numbers rather than forty digits shows how we mentally chunk things together. In fact, using the chunking process, you can memorize many more than forty numbers (think of all the telephone numbers, ZIP codes, and birthdays that you can recall), which attests to the efficiency of this type of organizing process.

When chunking nonnumerical information, the chunks are called *schemas*. **Schemas** are cognitive structures that group discrete bits of perceptual information in an organized fashion. Schemas are often less complex relative to the actual perceptual object they represent, and thus they create a trade-off between simplicity and understanding on the one hand versus accuracy and detail on the other hand.[12] Two types of schemas are particularly important to understanding the processing of social–interpersonal information: scripts and prototypes.

Schemas that involve sequences of actions are called **scripts** because they resemble the material from movies or plays. Clearly, numerous events in organizations can be conceived of as scripts, such as "taking a client to lunch," "preparing a written report," or "disciplining a subordinate." Each script involves certain sequences of behavior. Thus a request to take a client to lunch is actually a request to engage in hundreds of sequenced behaviors. Although this shorthand is clearly an efficient way of communicating, not everyone will define a script in the same way, with the exact same specific behaviors. For example, some organizations may have informal norms that discourage drinking alcohol at business lunches. A new employee who is told to "take a client to lunch" might not be aware of this specific part of the script, and could get into trouble for "drinking on the job." Thus, while the kind of simplification provided by scripts is vital for efficient information processing, their use might lead to adding things that were not meant to happen or deleting things that were actually supposed to happen. Clarifying these scripts is essential to ensure perceptual accuracy.

While some schemas focus on simplifying descriptions of events, others seek to simplify the descriptions of people. **Prototypes** are schemas that enable us to chunk information about people's characteristics. For example, if one manager asks another manager what a new employee is like, the second person might report that the new hire is spirited, exuberant, outgoing, boisterous, and warm. The manager might then say, "You mean she's an extrovert." In this example, multiple bits of information are chunked into one word that is meant to provide a detailed description of a person. Like scripts, however, prototypes sometimes carry excess baggage and thus might not reflect the person accurately—especially if two people hold different beliefs about the meaning of the word *extrovert*.

One area where this type of chunking creates difficulties is in the area of performance appraisal. When managers are asked to provide subjective ratings of their subordinates' performance, they are often asked many different questions with the idea that each worker has strengths and weaknesses (e.g., efficiency versus creativity), and detailed feedback on each of these can be used by the person being rated to pinpoint areas of improvement. In reality, however, many raters fall victim to the "**halo error**," which means that they categorize their subordinates first into an overall classification of "good" versus "bad," and then base their specific judgments on the overall classification, not the actual dimension. Thus, whereas one might expect a mix of positive and negative ratings, instead one sees an overall picture of good or bad on all dimensions that say more about the person's reputation and the categorization scheme than the person's actual behavior.[13]

This halo error can also be seen at the organizational level, and many organizations go to great lengths to ascertain and manage their overall reputation. For example, studies suggest that companies that enjoy a positive reputation in the media have stock prices that are 3 to 7 percent higher relative to firms matched on size and industry that do not have the same high reputation.[14] In fact, some have suggested that if Walmart, which has generally been found to have a negative reputation, had a similar reputation to Target, this would be worth $9.7 billion in terms of the firm's overall market value.[15]

In the area of organizational behavior, the "leader" prototype is an important one. Most managers want others to perceive them as leaders. What characteristics are likely to cause people to categorize someone in this way? According to a classic study conducted by Robert Lord, the leader prototype consists of the twelve characteristics shown in Table 4.2. People who exhibit most of these characteristics will be seen as leaders.

When prototypes are organized around social categorizations such as gender, race or ethnicity, they revert to **stereotypes**, and when stereotypes fail to match prototypes, this can become a problem. For example, because societal stereotypes suggest that women ought to be nurturing and socially sensitive, but the leader prototype suggests leaders need to be "aggressive" and "determined" some people might believe that women cannot be effective leaders.[16] Beyond this, when expectations are violated, they often lead to even more negative reactions in the sense that women who display "aggressiveness" are often penalized in subordinate ratings of performance for behaviors that are not penalized when manifested by male managers.[17] In fact, rather than fight against these stereotypes, some successful women have come to the conclusion that these expectations are so ingrained that it is better to try to work with them rather than against them. For example, Facebook COO Sheryl Sandberg advises women leaders to be "relentlessly pleasant" and always use the communal "we" instead of "I."[18] Indeed, an examination of the attributes listed in Table 4.2 points to some characteristics that tend to be associated with both the leadership prototype and the female stereotype (such as "caring"). Still, whether they are positive or negative, most stereotypes work against accuracy and managers need to get beyond these when making critical assessments (such as performance appraisals) and decisions (such as promotion decisions). Indeed, even Sheryl Sandberg concludes that "My hope is that we won't have to play to these archaic rules forever and eventually we can all be ourselves."[19] This is exactly the idea that most informed and experienced managers embrace right now.

Another stereotype that is becoming increasingly important due to the aging of the U.S. workforce is the stereotype associated with age. For example, in one recent study, business

Table 4.2 Major Characteristics of the Leader Prototype (in Descending Order of Importance)

1. Intelligent
2. Outgoing
3. Understanding
4. Articulate
5. Aggressive
6. Determined
7. Industrious
8. Caring
9. Decisive
10. Dedicated
11. Educated
12. Well dressed

Source: Adapted from R. G. Lord, R. J. Foti, and D. DeVader, "A Test of Leadership Categorization Theory: Internal Structure, Information Processing, and Leadership Perceptions," *Organizational Behavior and Human Performance* 34 (1984): 343–378.

students displayed a clear stereotype of the elderly. Among other things, they described this group as less creative, less able to do physically demanding work, and less able to change or be innovative. These perceptions led the students to make other negative judgments about elderly workers. For instance, they expressed the belief that these workers would be less likely than younger workers to benefit from training and development. Given the increasing age of our national workforce, such stereotypes need to be reconsidered.[20]

Recall

After information is organized, it next must be stored in memory for later retrieval. Just as raw information is sometimes lost when it is organized into scripts and prototypes, so, too, information can be lost in the storage and retrieval process. To see how this loss can create illusions and lead to decision-making errors, consider the following problem: In a typical passage of English prose, does the letter *k* occur more often as the first or the third letter in a word? When confronted with this problem, twice as many people choose first letter as choose third letter, even though *k* appears in the third spot almost twice as often as in the first. This phenomenon can be explained in terms of the **availability bias**, which means that people tend to judge the likelihood that something will happen by the ease with which they can call examples of it to mind. Most people assume that *k* is more common at the beginning of words simply because humans store words in memory by their first letters—not their third letters. For this reason, it is easier to retrieve and remember words beginning with *k* than words that have *k* as their third letter. The availability bias also manifests itself in a tendency for people to overgeneralize from the recent past to make assumptions about what is going to happen next.

You can see the availability bias at work by considering the way that people think about death, illness, and disasters. In general, people vastly overestimate the number of deaths caused by spectacular events such as airplane crashes and underestimate the number of deaths caused by illnesses such as emphysema or heart disease. Deaths caused by sudden disasters are more easily called to mind because they are so vivid and public, often making the front pages of newspapers across the country. Death caused by illness, on the other hand, is generally private and thus less likely to be recalled. The tendency to confuse the probability that something will happen with the ease with which one can remember it is especially a problem for decision makers who are inexperienced or low in cognitive ability.[21]

Another problem that can arise at the recall stage is hindsight bias. **Hindsight bias** occurs when people feel that they would have predicted the outcome to events better than they actually did or better than they actually would have if they had been asked to make a forecast. For example, a group of students might be asked to read a case that sets up an important decision, such as whether a person should invest in a risky stock. The students would be asked to state the probability of getting a 20 percent return on investment. After the passage of time, the same individuals are told that the company either went out of business or gave a 40 percent return on investment, and they are asked to recall their original probabilities. People who are told about positive outcomes tend to recall their probabilities of reaching the 20 percent return on investment goal as being much higher than they really were. People who are told that the company failed, on the other hand, tend to recall their probabilities of reaching a 20 percent return as being much lower than they really were.[22]

Hindsight bias is particularly problematic in contexts where there is a great deal written about various problems or decisions, because this past written record makes it clear that some people might have been able to predict the future better than others. For example, during the collapse of financial giant Bear Stearns, company officials were clearly victims of perceptual distortion. When asked about how the falling housing market would affect the firm, which was highly leveraged into subprime mortgages, top executive Ralph Cioffi stated that "We're going to make money on this—we don't believe what the markets are telling us."[23] However, at the same time, many state regulation officials were trying to end the practice of selling subprime loans for fear of what it was doing to consumers.[24] Moreover, other financial experts such as Warren Buffett were also decrying the practice, referring to subprime loans as "weapons of mass destruction" as early as 2002.[25] Thus, when Bear Stearns went bankrupt in 2008, a large number of investors sued Cioffi, accusing him of fraud.

Reducing Perceptual Problems

Clearly, a human observer can fail to portray the environment accurately in many ways. Fortunately, one can take many steps to avoid these problems. First, accuracy can be improved by increasing the frequency and representativeness of observations. That is, the observer can be exposed more often to what needs to be observed and be instructed to look for things that he or she did not necessarily expect. This is a direct way of trying to counter expectation effects in rating by making the unexpected more salient and detectable, thus heightening the accuracy of perceptions.[26]

Second, taking care in how and when observations are made can ensure the representativeness of the information. That is, the manner in which observations are obtained should be thoughtfully considered. Random sampling increases the probability that the resulting observations are accurate. If a supervisor observes a group of workers only at a given time on a given day or only when problems develop, the observations might not reflect the group's true behavior. In addition, because the very act of observing someone can cause him or her to alter the normal behavior (and thus destroy representativeness), it is important to make observations as unobtrusively as possible.

The opportunities to observe employee work behaviors frequently, randomly, and unobtrusively have increased rapidly with technological developments in the field of surveillance. The increased use of computerized employee monitoring has been a product of two forces. First, the need to observe employees' work behaviors has long existed and, second, recent developments in surveillance technology have simply made this endeavor easier and less obtrusive. For example, at Christiana Care Hospital, an electronic tracking system that was already used to track every piece of equipment was used to tag every employee and every patient. The use of these radio frequency identification (RFID) systems makes it quicker and easier to find where people are and direct them to where they need to be, speeding up care and service. These systems are especially good for detecting when people are not where they are supposed to be, and, because an increasing number of court cases have held employers liable for the mistakes or crimes of employees, these systems provide some protection from misbehaving employees.[27]

In addition, sociometric badges can even go beyond this, and not only tell the employer where people are, but who they are with, and who is talking and who is listening. That is, sociometric badges contain an infrared device, a Bluetooth signal and a degraded microphone that allow one to detect the frequency and nature of face-to-face conversations, which can then be used to establish an organization's informal communication network. The organization's informal network often differs from the formal organizational chart for a number of different reasons, and mapping out this informal structure often points to people or places that are more central to operations than one would think. For example, with respect to important people, sociometric badges often reveal who is the person everyone goes to for information, and this is not always the formal manager of the unit. In terms of important places, Bank of America learned that its most productive call center workers were often part of very cohesive and close-knit teams that shared information and supported each other during stressful work periods. Much of this cohesiveness was due to socialization, which happened on shared breaks in call center units where group breaks were the norm, but the cohesiveness did not occur in groups where people took breaks on their own. Based on these data, the bank changed how it structured all work breaks so that groups of call center workers took breaks at the same time in the same renovated and upgraded cafeteria space. This resulted in a 10 percent increase in productivity after just six months after the group break policy had been implemented.[28]

Of course, some have noted that electronic monitoring has seriously eroded employees' right to privacy, and finding the right balance between employees' rights and the rights and responsibilities of employers to monitor workers is not a simple process. One critical feature that predicts how employees will react to monitoring is the degree to which they are given advance notice about the practice. People who are given advance warning feel much more positive about the practice and are less likely to turn over than people who learn of it on their own.[29] In addition, if employees are high in organizational commitment, they tend to trust the organization more and thus are more tolerant of electronic surveillance.[30]

The accuracy of perceptions can also be improved by obtaining observations from different people and different perspectives. Having multiple points of view is especially valuable when it comes to self-perceptions of upper-level managers, who often overestimate their interpersonal effectiveness when their perceptions go unchecked.[31] This kind of misperception is based more on ignorance than arrogance because few people are eager to give their boss negative feedback—even if he or she directly asks for it.[32] In order to overcome these problems, as we noted earlier, organizations have increasingly turned to 360-degree feedback programs where managers receive anonymous survey feedback on their strengths and weaknesses from supervisors, peers, and subordinates, and then compare the perceptions of these people to their own self-rated strengths and weaknesses. Managers who tend to overestimate their strengths and underestimate their weaknesses typically perform the worst when it comes to external performance indices, and the purpose of these kinds of feedback programs is to bring perceptions more in line with reality.[33]

Because observers tend to ignore information that does not match their expectations, it is often a good idea to actively seek out information that is inconsistent with or contradicts one's current beliefs.[34] For example, Bell Atlantic uses a team of managers to play the "devil's advocate" role in organizational decision making. This group is explicitly assigned the role of challenging and disputing the key assumptions on which decisions are being made. People are often reluctant to assume this role on their own because they want to be seen as a "team player" and are afraid that dissent is going to be treated as disloyalty. By explicitly saying that someone's role on the team is to engage in counter advocacy, Bell Atlantic ensures that the role is covered and no one becomes alienated from the team.

When a person must work with social groups that differ from his or her own, another method for ensuring perceptual accuracy is to increase that individual's exposure to different social groups in an effort to develop more accurate prototypes. Research shows that experts in all kinds of domains differ from novices not because they ignore prototypes but because they develop more complex, detailed prototypes that are more accurate. By making novices use the same frame of reference as experts, this can speed the development of novice raters.[35]

Decision-Making Processes

At the end of the process of perception depicted in Figure 4.1, the decision has been framed. That is, the decision maker has collected and discarded various pieces of information to arrive at the final set of information that will be used in making the final decision. From this point on, this set of information will be further processed in an effort to choose which course of action to accept and which alternatives to reject. Two general models are employed in understanding the decision-making process: the rational model and the administrative model.

The Rational Decision-Making Model

The rational decision-making model is sometimes referred to as the rational-economic model, reflecting its ties to classic theories of economic behavior. As originally developed, this model included a primary assumption of economic rationality—that is, the notion that people attempt to maximize their individual *economic* outcomes. The system of values consistent with this assumption assesses outcomes based on their current or prospective monetary worth. Values of this type are used in business situations whenever managers weigh alternatives in terms of profitability or loss. They then choose one of the alternatives and implement it as the preferred solution or decision. This choice is determined through a process of utility maximization, in which the alternative with the highest expected worth is selected as the preferred alternative. The expected worth of a particular alternative consists of the sum of the expected values of the costs and benefits of all outcomes associated with that alternative.

Ideally, observers would use this information in a rational way to reach their final decisions. Such is not always the case, however. Our earlier discussion used perceptual illusions to show that perception is not nearly as straightforward as it seems. Here, we will use "decision-making illusions" to show how things can go wrong in the decision-making process.[36]

Evaluating Outcomes

As a prelude to this discussion, read the box titled "Two Strategies for Handling an Environmental Threat" and decide what strategy you would choose if you were the sales executive faced with the situation described. If you perceive strategy one (save the 200 accounts for sure) to be the best approach, you are not alone. Research shows that managers and nonmanagers alike perceive this choice as preferable to strategy two by a margin of roughly three to one.

TWO STRATEGIES FOR HANDLING AN ENVIRONMENTAL THREAT

The development of a new technology by a competitor threatens the viability of your organization, which manages 600 accounts. You have two available strategies to counter this new technology. Your advisors make it clear that if you choose strategy one, 200 of the 600 accounts will be saved. If you choose strategy two, there is a one-third chance that all of the 600 accounts will be saved and a two-thirds chance that none will be saved.

Which strategy will you choose?

Source: Adapted from A. Tversky and D. Kahneman, "The Framing of Decisions and the Psychology of Choice," *Science* 211 (1981): 453–458.

Now turn to a similar decision situation, shown in the box titled "Two More Strategies for Handling an Environmental Threat," and decide which strategy is preferable under these circumstances. If you judge strategy two as being the best option, again you are not alone. Research shows that this choice is preferred by a margin of roughly four to one over strategy one.

TWO MORE STRATEGIES FOR HANDLING AN ENVIRONMENTAL THREAT

The development of a new technology by a competitor threatens the viability of your organization, which manages 600 accounts. You have two available strategies to counter this new technology. Your advisors make it clear that if you choose strategy one, 400 of the 600 accounts will be lost. If you choose strategy two, there is a one-third chance that no accounts will be lost and a two-thirds chance that all will be lost.
   Which strategy will you choose?

Source: Adapted from A. Tversky and D. Kahneman, "The Framing of Decisions and the Psychology of Choice," *Science* 211 (1981): 453–458.

The surprising thing about these results is that the problems described are virtually identical. Reread the paragraphs in the two boxes. Strategy one is the same in both tables. The only difference is that in the first box it is expressed in terms of accounts *saved* (200 out of 600), whereas in the second box it is expressed in terms of accounts *lost* (400 out of 600). Clearly, if 200 accounts are saved, 400 accounts are lost, and vice versa. Why is strategy one preferred in the situation described in the first box and strategy two preferred in the situation outlined in the second box?

Research by Nobel Prize-winning scientist Daniel Kahneman and his colleague Amos Tversky indicates that, in general, people have a slight preference for sure outcomes as opposed to risky ones. However, this research also shows that people hate losing.[37] This **loss-aversion bias** affects their decision making even more strongly than their preference for nonrisky situations. When given a choice between a sure gain and a risky gain, most people will take the sure thing and avoid the risk. When given a choice between a sure loss and a risky loss, however, most people will avoid the sure loss and take a chance on not losing anything.

A real-world example of this can be seen in Arthur Andersen's risky decisions regarding aggressive accounting practices that it employed as part of its work with Enron. For over a decade, Arthur Andersen increasingly derived more of its revenue growth from its consulting contracts as compared to its auditing business. Wanting a larger share of its own success, the consulting side of the business, which brought in close to $10 billion a year in revenue, sought independence. An arbitrator granted them this freedom (creating a new company, Accenture) in return for a one-time $1 billion payment to the parent company. Faced with this huge loss of revenue, Arthur Andersen became highly aggressive in trying to rebuild its consulting business, and many have speculated that an unwarranted level of risk seeking made it overlook problems that were being caused by one of its best-paying new clients—Enron. Former Federal Reserve chairman Paul Volcker stated bluntly, "There is no doubt in my mind that Andersen took its eye off the ball by basing what was acceptable practice on how much revenue it could generate."[38]

In addition to people's asymmetric treatment of losses and gains, evaluating outcomes is also complicated by the fact that often multiple outcomes need to be met, and these may be at odds with each other. For example, we might want decisions to be both timely and correct but, in many contexts, speed and accuracy of decision making are negatively related to each other, and respond differently to managerial actions.[39] Research shows that putting workers in competition with each other generally makes them work faster but with less accuracy, whereas promoting cooperation among workers increases their accuracy but slows them down.[40] Moreover, once a group or organization commits itself to competing on speed or accuracy, this initial decision often persists and forces the group to maintain its current emphasis into the future, even when it might make more sense to change.[41]

Evaluating Probabilities

Irrationality can also enter into the decision-making process through errors made in evaluating the probabilities associated with various outcomes. For example, consider the decision-making problem described in the box titled "Identifying a Hit-and-Run Driver." Most people would conclude that the hit-and-run driver was in the blue cab. In fact, the odds are much better that the cab was green. That is, if a hundred cabs operated in the city, eighty-five would be green and fifteen would be blue. This base rate represents the initial probability given no other piece of information. Using the premise established in the box, which says that the witness (who provides an additional piece of information over and above the base rate) would be right 80 percent of the time, we can analyze what would happen in each possible scenario. If the cab in the accident were actually blue, the witness would identify it correctly as a blue cab twelve times ($.80 \times 15 = 12$) and would incorrectly identify it as a green cab three times ($.20 \times 15 = 3$). If the vehicle were a green cab, however, the witness would correctly identify it sixty-eight times ($.80 \times 85 = 68$) and misidentify it seventeen times ($.20 \times 85 = 17$). Thus the odds are much greater that the witness's identification of the cab as blue was a misidentification of a green cab (which happens 17 out of 100 times) than a correct identification of a blue cab (which happens only 12 out of 100 times).

IDENTIFYING A HIT-AND-RUN DRIVER

A cab is involved in a hit-and-run accident.

Two taxicab companies serve the city. The Green Company operates 85 percent of the cabs, and the Blue Company operates the remaining 15 percent.

A witness describes the hit-and-run cab as blue. When the court tests the witness's reliability under circumstances similar to those on the night of the accident, the witness correctly identifies the color of a cab 80 percent of the time and misidentifies it 20 percent of the time.

Which cab company was most probably involved in the hit-and-run accident?

Source: Adapted from A. Tversky and D. Kahneman, "The Framing of Decisions and the Psychology of Choice," *Science* 211 (1981): 453–458.

The reason why virtually everyone who approaches this problem naively gets it wrong is the tendency to give too much weight to the evidence provided by the witness and not enough weight to the evidence provided by the base rate. Because of **base rate bias**, people tend to ignore the background information in this sort of case and feel that they are dealing with something unique. In this example, decision makers discount the evidence regarding how few cars are actually blue and instead put more confidence in human judgment about the color of the car. Ignoring the base rate can lead to irrational decisions, and this bias is pervasive among decision makers regardless of their level of cognitive ability.[42]

The problem of misplaced confidence is particularly pronounced when more than one probabilistic event is involved. Not surprisingly, actual business ventures frequently face such situations. Suppose, for example, that a house builder contracts to have a house completed by the end of the year. Assume also that the chances of accomplishing four specific tasks in time to meet this deadline are as follows:

Get permits	Excellent (90%)
Get financing	Excellent (90%)
Get materials	Good (75%)
Get subcontractors	Very good (80%)

Reviewing these data, the builder might well conclude that there is a good to excellent chance that the project can be completed in the time specified in the contract. In fact, the odds of this outcome are only 50–50. Multiplying the four probabilities together ($.90 \times .90 \times .75 \times .80 = .49$) gives the builder a less than 50 percent chance to finish on schedule—hardly a good to excellent chance. The axiom, known as Murphy's Law, states that "anything that can go wrong will go wrong." This view may be a tad pessimistic, but in a long series of probabilistic events the odds are quite good that any one event will go wrong, and sometimes a single mishap can destroy an entire venture. Any business executive who is putting together a deal where the ultimate outcome depends on a series of discrete events, none of which is a sure thing, must keep this fact in mind.

Dynamic Influences

The rational model assumes that each decision is made independently of other decisions—that is, each decision is examined on its own merits in terms of outcomes and probabilities. Irrationality can creep into the process, however, because in reality people often see decisions as being related, and because past decisions may "reach forward" and affect future decisions in irrational ways.

For example, in a bias referred to as **escalation of commitment**, people invest more and more heavily in an apparently losing course of action so as to justify their earlier decisions. Usually the investments made once this process gets started are disproportionate to any gain that could conceivably be realized, and the level of irrationality becomes particularly pronounced when the project nears completion.[43] For most decision makers, the regret they anticipate for giving up too early on their decisions is not offset by a corresponding regret to lose even more than they have already lost.[44]

Even when costs clearly outstrip benefits, a decision maker may feel many different kinds of pressure to continue to act in accord with a particular decision.[45] For psychological reasons, the decision maker might not want to appear inconsistent by changing course; that is, the person might not want to admit to an earlier mistake. Moreover, particularly where feedback is ambiguous or complex, perceptual distortions such as the expectation effect can make the picture appear more hopeful than is really the case. Because decision makers cannot make perfect predictions regarding future outcomes, there is always the hope that staying the course will pay off. Moreover, many people have been rewarded in past situations for sticking it out. Although rare, such experiences are usually quite memorable (the availability bias). The experience of giving up when it is the appropriate choice often goes unrewarded, at least in the short run, and thus is something people like to forget. Finally, sometimes cost–benefit analyses are abandoned in favor of a win-at-any-cost mentality. The quest to prove one was right from the start takes over, and obsession overcomes better judgment.

Factors Limiting Rational Decision-Making Models

As the decision-making illusions previously described show, the complexity of real-world decision situations often makes rationality impossible to achieve. This can often lead some decision makers to "freeze up" and attempt to avoid making a decision at all costs. Herbert A. Simon, a cognitive scientist and Nobel laureate in economics, remarks that "the capacity of the human mind for formulating and solving complex problems is very small compared with the size of the problems whose solution is required for objectively rational behavior in the real world."[46] Simon's comment on the limits of human intelligence does not seek to condemn humans, but rather to acknowledge the complexity of the environment in which they must operate. Indeed, according to Simon and to others who have followed his lead, the complexity of the real world often overwhelms the decision maker at each step of the rational decision-making process, making complete rationality impossible.

One issue that may undermine the rational decision-making model is the fact that rational models work only if there is general agreement on the definitions of problems, decisions, and decision-making goals that are framed at the outset. Especially in large organizations, such consensus is difficult to achieve. Different individuals, work groups, and departments are likely to rank outcomes in different ways. For example, many blamed Yahoo!'s recent struggles on slow decision-making processes. Any new product offered at Yahoo! has to go through a long series of meetings and approval processes that delays innovation.[47] Indeed, in large, complex organizations, the only problem definitions likely to be widely shared are those so vague as to be almost meaningless. As an example, the box headed "Generic Corporate Vision Generator" shows a generic formula that seems to be the source of most organizations' "vision statements."[48] Whereas such vision statements may be generally palatable, they provide little in the way of guidance for day-to-day decision making.

Another problem for the rational decision-making model is the difficulty inherent in trying to generate an exhaustive list of alternatives and then select the most promising one. Managers often cannot anticipate which actions will lead to which consequences. Because, as Simon points out, most real-world decisions are characterized by uncertainty, managers cannot even speculate on the odds. Under these conditions, they cannot compute expected values, and thus they lack a common measure with which to compare various alternatives. This problem is especially common with nonroutine decisions—that is, decisions that are out of the ordinary. In making these kinds of decisions, no one ever develops enough experience to easily assess the odds associated with any alternative.

GENERIC CORPORATE VISION GENERATOR

To generate your corporate vision, just circle one entry in each set of brackets.
TO BE A [premier, leading, growing, world-class] COMPANY THAT PROVIDES [innovative, cost-effective, diversified, high-quality] [products, services, products and services] TO [create shareholder value, serve the global marketplace, delight our customers, satisfy our stakeholders] IN THE RAPIDLY CHANGING [information solution, business solution, financial solution, consumer solution] INDUSTRY

Intuitive decision-making processes that result in snap judgments can often be effective when the decision maker has years of experience working with the problem.[49] However, when the decision is unprecedented, one's "gut instincts" can result in decision-making errors that are especially prone to be second-guessed by outsiders who eventually benefit from hindsight bias. For example, in hindsight, many analysts wound up criticizing the $700 billion bailout that President George W. Bush granted financial institutions when it became clear that there were no requirements for how the money was to be spent, and no transparency with respect to what the banks actually did with the money.[50] It also became clear that the companies that made the biggest mistakes wound up benefiting most from the bailout.[51] As one CEO notes, when it comes to crisis decision making, "What you don't do is try to solve a crisis by jumping to the wrong solution too early. Seeing the total landscape and trying to instill the need for that is important."[52]

In addition to overreliance on snap judgments and intuition, rationality is also often precluded because strong emotions intrude on the decision-making process. For example, rather than buying a license from Apple that would have cost only $24 per smartphone, Samsung took a chance and tried to replicate Apple technology itself. Apple successfully sued Samsung for copyright infringement in 2012 and the costs associated with the settlement were close to four times what it would have cost to just purchase the license in the first place. Rather than just paying off the settlement, however, Samsung appealed the case, and in the process incurred even higher litigation costs. As one analyst noted, "tempers have gotten in the way and although Apple and Samsung both have reasons to resolve this, in the near term, this has become a matter of human emotions."[53] Indeed, highly competitive environments tend to trigger biological reactions that result in emotional decision-making and excessive risk taking well beyond what one would expect from a purely rational model.[54]

In addition, to these limits, managers are not free to choose among all the choices they may generate. The term **bounded discretion**, first suggested by Simon, refers to the fact that the list of alternatives generated by any decision maker is restricted by social, legal, moral, and cultural norms. For example, Westinghouse developed a culture of low tolerance for risk because many of its products require a safety-first attitude. When organizational leaders tried to make the company more competitive by developing innovative ideas, they ran into a high level of resistance from many of the company's engineers, who wanted to stick to doing what they knew best. Stephen Tritch, the CEO of Westinghouse Electric, noted that in his division, which builds nuclear power plants, "we don't train people to take risks. We train them not to."[55] Thus, as Figure 4.3 indicates, the discretionary area containing acceptable choices is bounded on many sides. The boundaries between each set of limitations and the discretionary area are not clear cut. As a result, decision makers do not always know whether an alternative is in or out of bounds.

In some cases, social norms and traditions may limit one's options, and the "rational decision" may conflict with these customs. For example, in the high-tech industry, it was customary to offer clients and customers rather large incentives for their businesses. One of the well-known incentives was referred to as "Friends and Family IPO Stock Options," a tradition that often led to initial IPO stock prices that were much too low relative to what rational reasoning would demand. Specifically, friends and family programs allowed companies that were going public for the first time to distribute as much as 5 percent of their offerings early to whomever they chose. These individuals got to purchase the stock at the original IPO price, whereas everyone else had to wait a day. At one point, tech stocks were jumping an average of 65 percent on their first day of trading, guaranteeing a huge payoff to those who were part of the friends and family programs, but a rather large disadvantage to shareholders who were outside the loop. As one commentator noted, "If it weren't for friends and family programs company executives would have pushed for a higher price offering"; and this decision cost these companies more than $60 billion.[56] Although this example shows how the customs of a company or industry can harm the larger society, in other cases the customs and traditions of the larger society can work to harm the interests of companies and industries.

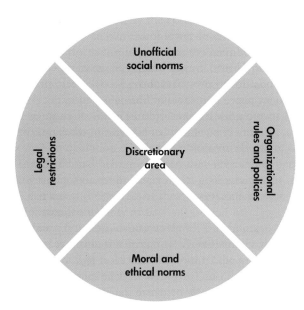

Figure 4.3 The Concept of Bounded Discretion

One step beyond mere social norms are legal restrictions, and when an organization is deal-ing in a global environment, the laws and social norms of one country may conflict with the laws and social norms in others, further complicating the attempt to act rationally. For example, Walmart found itself in a great deal of legal trouble in the United States when an investigative report by the *New York Times* revealed that the giant retailer paid $24 million in bribes to local officials in order to obtain construction permits and sidestep regulations to build new stores in Mexico. Indeed, many of the world's fastest growing markets are rife with corruption, and bribery is not considered a serious crime in some countries such as China, Mexico, and Russia. Indeed, IKEA stopped opening new stores in Russia because of corruption and delayed its expansion into India because it did not believe it could police the local supply chain.[57]

When decision makers choose alternatives that fall outside the legal or ethical boundaries, this often triggers whistleblowers to go public with information that can be highly damaging. Many different factors may motivate such whistleblowers, but, regardless of the motivation, the negative publicity and legal costs associated with organizations that are guilty of these kinds of breaches are significant. Indeed, the passage of the new Sarbanes-Oxley Corporate Reform Act seeks to protect these kinds of whistleblowers, making it illegal for companies to threaten or harass them. This Act requires organizations to establish internal procedures for hearing whistleblower complaints, and any executive who is found to retaliate against a whis-tleblower can be sentenced to up to ten years in a federal prison.[58] In addition, in order to encourage more whistleblowing, the law stipulates that whistleblowers be financially compensated, receiving 15 to 30 percent of damages recovered or punitive damages.

An example of this law in action can be seen in the case of the bicyclist Floyd Landis, a former teammate of Lance Armstrong, who alleged that Armstrong had defrauded the U.S. government when he accepted sponsor money from the U.S. Postal Service. The contract with the Postal Service required that the team refrain from using performance-enhancing drugs, but Landis was able to prove that Armstrong was at the center of a doping ring and therefore knowingly violated the contract. The Postal Service paid a total of $311 million to

Armstrong's team and, if Armstrong was found guilty, Landis could be awarded 30 percent of the funds recovered.[59]

This case highlights the fact that the government tries to support whistleblowing efforts by financially rewarding people who report major violations of ethical misconduct, but this is far from the record. The largest settlement to a whistleblower was given to Bradley Birkenfeld, a former employee of financial institution UBS AG, who was awarded over $100 million when he helped the government prove that his employer engaged in tax evasion. Senator Charles Grassley, a sponsor of the new whistleblowing laws noted that "an award of $104 million is obviously a great deal of money, but billions of dollars in taxes owed will be collected that otherwise would have never been paid."[60]

Although Birkenfeld was identified by the government as part of the UBS AG case, in other instances, the identity of the whistleblower is kept confidential in order to prevent retaliation. For example, the U.S. Internal Revenue Service (IRS) also awarded $38 million to an anonymous whistleblower who helped the agency recover roughly $130 million in unpaid taxes from an unnamed Fortune 500 company. Although the size of these awards is striking, it should be noted that most cases like these take five to seven years to be resolved in court, and whistleblowers do not get paid until after the IRS gets paid. Thus, the decision to blow the whistle is also a high-risk/high-reward decision for anyone who chooses to go this route.[61]

Finally, moving beyond the bounds of discretion, the rational decision-making model assumes that one can evaluate the implemented alternative by checking the actual outcome against the initial intentions. In many contexts, this assumption simply does not hold. Most business situations are complex, and many factors other than the chosen alternative can influence the ultimate outcome. Thus the "right" choice might not invariably lead to the desired outcome. Such decision-making contexts, in which the link between actions and outcomes is tenuous and difficult to predict, are sometimes called noisy environments.

In noisy environments, we can make sense of action–outcome links only by making many observations of the same outcomes after the same actions. If one makes the same decision numerous times, noisy influences factor themselves out, and the true nature of the action–outcome link becomes clearer. Unfortunately, most decision makers in noisy environments fail to stick with one action long enough to sort out the effects of the chosen action from the effects of random influences. This lack of consistency in decision making means that the person moves from one action to another without ever learning much about the action–outcome link associated with any one specific action.[62]

Thus the rational decision-making model can provide helpful guidance in only a limited number of places. It may suggest how to structure routine decision making where everyone agrees on the desired outcomes and the best methods for attaining those outcomes, and where few outcomes and alternatives must be considered. Because the various factors may render the rational decision-making model less useful in many contexts, however, alternatives to the model have been suggested.

The Administrative Decision-Making Model

One of the most influential alternatives to the rational decision-making model is Herbert Simon's administrative decision-making model (Figure 4.4). Simon's model is intended to paint a more realistic picture of the way managers make most decisions.[63] According to Simon, the rational decision-making model may outline what managers *should* do, but the administrative model provides a better picture of what effective managers *actually* do when strict rationality is impossible. Simon's model differs from the rational model in several important ways.

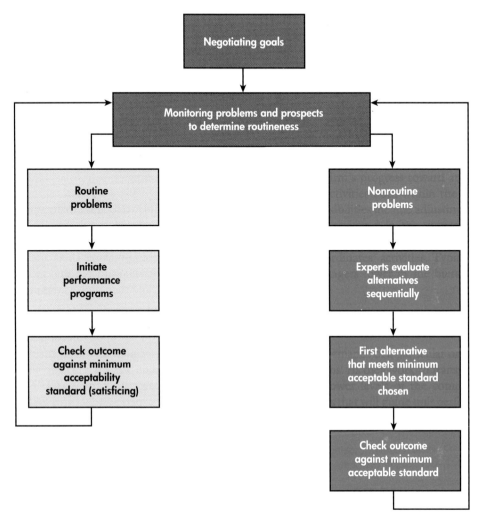

Figure 4.4 The Administrative Decision-Making Model
Source: Adapted from J. G. March and H. A. Simon, *Organizations* (New York: Wiley, 1958).

One difference has to do with satisficing versus optimizing. According to Simon, *optimal* solutions require that the final decision be better than all other possible alternatives. For all the reasons discussed earlier, such optimality is simply not possible most of the time. Instead of striving for this impossible goal, organizations may try to find **satisficing** solutions to their problems. Satisficing means settling for the first alternative that seems to meet some minimum level of acceptability. Needless to say, it is much easier to achieve this goal than to strive for an optimal solution; indeed, Simon evokes the comparison between finding a needle in a haystack (satisficing) and finding the biggest, sharpest needle in the haystack (optimizing).

In searching for satisficing solutions, managers further simplify the process by considering alternatives sequentially rather than simultaneously. Instead of first generating a list of all possible alternatives and then comparing and contrasting each alternative with all the others, the decision makers evaluate each alternative, one at a time, against the criteria for a satisficing outcome. The first satisfactory alternative identified in this way is chosen, and the manager moves on to other problems.[64]

For example, a firm that needs to downsize by reducing its total number of employees faces more than a dozen options for accomplishing this objective. Rather than compare the expected results for every possible downsizing means with every other possible means, the firm's managers might simply consider initiating an early retirement program. If management implements such a program and it achieves the desired results, no further alternatives need be considered. If the plan does not work, some other reasonable alternative, like a hiring freeze, could be tried as well. If this course of action fails, it may be followed by yet another downsizing attempt, such as laying employees off according to seniority.

Reducing Decision-Making Errors

Given our knowledge about the limits to rationality, it is possible to identify many different means of reducing errors in decision making. First, the main problem inherent in many decision-making biases (for example, loss aversion, availability bias, and base rate bias) is that the judges oversimplify information processing and take decision-making shortcuts. One good means of eliminating this problem is to provide decision makers with aids that will force them to ask all the right questions, get all the right information, and then process this information in all the right ways.

Computerized expert systems represent one excellent decision aid. These systems are typically developed by asking a team of experts, "How would you go about making such a decision?" and then recording every piece of information they request as well as the way in which they process those data. The interview findings are then turned into a computer program that performs the same function for a relatively naive decision maker, who is prompted to ask the right questions by the program itself. An expert system turns what was formerly a qualitative, subjective process into a more mechanical, objective process that has higher validity for making personnel selection decisions.[65] The use of these kinds of systems is growing in organizations almost as fast as the adoption of computer technology itself. Although they will never replace the human decision maker, such systems could be instrumental in helping people overcome built-in judgment biases.

For example, Home Depot had a difficult time fairly evaluating female candidates for traditionally masculine jobs. To solve this problem, the company developed an automated hiring and promotion system that helped managers ask the right questions and make decisions that had less adverse impact on women. Now when a Home Depot manager needs to make a hiring or promotion decision, the program offers a list of prescreened candidates as well as a set of interview questions, preferred answers, and advice to give the job seeker if that person lacks the right qualifications. This system has helped Home Depot develop a much more integrated workforce. Since its inception, the number of female managers has increased by 30 percent and the time required for managers to make such decisions has decreased. Similar types of expert systems for personnel selection and promotion have been developed at Target, Publix Supermarkets, and Hollywood Video.[66]

Even though expert systems might help to simplify routine decision making, uncertainty in the environment makes it impossible to develop perfectly detailed scripts that will be applicable everywhere. At the highest level of any field, a need for discretion or individual authority on the part of decision makers persists. Consequently, organizations also need to hire or develop specialized areas of expertise that can be managed by one or more specialized staff members. The range of discretion of such experts tends to be limited to tightly defined areas, and the experts become the decision makers or internal consultants for different subareas.

Using experts in decision making enables people with special expertise in an area to devise more accurate and more detailed scripts. In this way, complexity can be handled more effectively by being broken up into discrete, manageable chunks—jobs—that can be tackled by individuals working alone. The holder of an individual job typically focuses on one very narrow area of organizational problem solving. The ability of the leader to accurately weigh different sources of information when rendering the group's judgment has repeatedly been found to be a critical factor in determining group decision-making accuracy.[67]

As noted earlier in the discussion of the perceptual process, chunking (breaking up jobs into small parts) reduces the burden on any one individual. Of course, each person's contribution must then be integrated with everyone else's contribution. Chunking does not change the fact that organization members are interdependent, and it is unrealistic to think that one expert can operate unaffected by others or that one set of programs can be activated independently of others. In integrating groups, the complexity of planning is greatly simplified by **loosely coupling** the different parts—that is, by weakening the effect that one subgroup has on another so that each subgroup can plan and operate almost as if the other were not present.[68]

The launch of the problem-plagued Boeing 787 "Dreamliner" provides an example of what can happen when a complex system—a jet airliner—becomes too tightly coupled. In order to save costs in the development of this new and innovative carrier, Boeing put half a dozen suppliers in charge of building the big sections of the plane, which were then flown into Boeing's factory in Everett, Washington, where the tightly coupled pieces would then be "snapped together." Lack of coordination among suppliers, however, resulted in costly delays and on numerous occasions, like a faulty jigsaw puzzle, the pieces did not snap together.[69] After seven delays, the plane was finally launched in 2011, but was then grounded by the Federal Aviation Authority in 2013 after fires broke out in the cabins of two of the planes. This was a major setback for Boeing who vowed to never again outsource such a complex task as aviation design and engineering to separate units who had to produce a tightly coupled set of products.[70]

Complexity can also be addressed by **contingency planning** that tries to anticipate some of the major future events that might turn what might have been a good decision into a bad decision due to unforeseen problems. For example, in the case that opened this chapter, the raid on Osama bin Laden's compound in Pakistan, one unforeseen event that might have resulted in a failed mission dealt with the high wall around the compound's perimeter. When the commando team practiced the raid in a simulated compound in the United States, the wall was represented as a chain-link fence. However, when the team actually tried to land helicopters within the compound, the fence turned out to be made of stone. This radically altered the aerodynamics within the small constrained space, and one of the Blackhawk helicopters crashed nose-first into the compound.

Fortunately, the team had developed a contingency plan for this kind of unexpected event should it be impossible to land inside the bin Laden compound or should one of the helicopters be lost. When this happened, Admiral Bill McCraven, the head of the U.S. Special Operations Command, could state calmly, "[W]e will now be amending the mission—my men are prepared for this contingency, and they will deal with it."[71] Plan A had been for the second helicopter to hover over the roof and drop SEALs directly on the bin Laden residence, but now they switched to Plan B, an option in which the raiding force would be dropped into a small open field next to the compound, ensuring that no more helicopters would be lost. In addition, two extra backup helicopters were available in case either or both of the helicopters associated with the primary mission were lost. Finally, even though they were never needed, two additional helicopters packing twenty-four more SEALs were available should the original team get bogged down and have to fight its way out of Pakistan. Contingency planning such as this is another way of dealing with complexity and the potential for unsuspected developments.

With respect to other dynamic influences on decision making, another means of trying to minimize judgment errors caused by escalating commitment is to develop separate project development and project evaluation teams.[72] Because the evaluation team likely will not share the sense of ownership felt by the development team, this structure can eliminate many of the forces that can lead to feelings of psychological entrapment. It is also a good idea to initially set up goals, timetables, and reevaluation parameters that spell out under what conditions the project will be terminated. Establishing these parameters early makes later judgments more rational and coldly calculated. Once a project is begun, however, sunk costs may entice workers to inappropriately reevaluate the level of loss they are willing to risk.

Creativity in Decision Making

One elusive quality essential to all decision making is creativity. Creative decisions consist of choices that are new and unusual but effective. Neither the rational nor the administrative decision-making model deals with the issue of producing creative decisions, nor does guarding against errors in group decision making necessarily guarantee that creativity will result. Indeed, some aspects of everything discussed in this chapter so far will make the generation of creative solutions to problems less—rather than more—likely. For example, strictly adhering to the demands of expert systems will rarely result in innovation. In this last section of the chapter, we emphasize the creativity process and describe how organizations can enhance creativity by selecting appropriate people or by managing in the appropriate fashion.

The Creative Process

Studies of people engaged in the creative process and examinations of the decision-making processes of people who are famous for their creativity suggest that a discernible pattern of events leads up to most innovative solutions. Most creative episodes can be broken down into four distinct stages: preparation, incubation, insight, and verification (Figure 4.5).

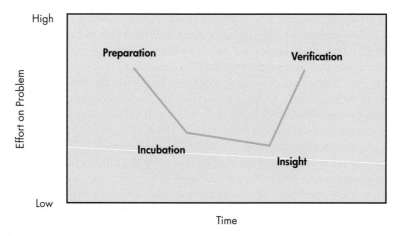

Figure 4.5 **Steps in the Creative Decision-Making Process**

Contrary to what most people think, creative ideas rarely come out of the blue. More often than not, innovations are first sparked by a problem or perceived need for which no current solution or product seems applicable. The current knowledge base or some current product is then stretched or integrated in some way that is so distinctive that the idea takes on a life of its own. For example, digitalized music and flash drives existed before the iPod; however, the iPod, which is a glorified flash drive, is still perceived as being an "invention" that solved the need for easily transportable entertainment.[73]

Because creative decision making resembles other decision-making processes in this way, it should not surprise you to learn that preparation, the first stage in the creative process, requires assembling materials. Analogous to the rational model's stage of generating alternatives, preparation is characterized by plain, old-fashioned hard work. In attempting to solve the problem, the creative person immerses himself or herself in existing solutions to the problem, usually to the point of saturation.

The second stage of creativity, incubation, differs greatly from steps in other decision-making models. Rather than reaching a decision immediately after assembling and evaluating relevant materials, creative decision makers enter a period during which they seem not to expend any visible effort on the problem. Sometimes out of frustration or sheer exhaustion they might stop working on the problem temporarily and turn to other things. Indeed, some have argued that, if such a stage does not evolve naturally, it should be forced on decision-making groups if the goal is to arrive at a creative solution.[74]

After a person spends some time in the incubation stage, the solution to the problem typically manifests itself in a flash of inspiration, or insight. Usually, the person is engaged in some other task when this insight comes, which reinforces the false impression that bold, creative ideas come out of the blue. Without the prior two steps, this flash of inspiration will not be forthcoming; however, it does seem that a state of relaxation, rather than obsession, promotes creative thinking.[75] For example, Arthur Fry, an engineer at 3M Company oversaw what was considered a failed project that produced an adhesive that was so weak that it could barely hold two pieces of paper together. However, Fry also sang in a church choir, and one Sunday when his bookmarks for psalms kept falling out of his hymnal onto the floor, he had an epiphany. The weak glue was perfect for serving as the adhesive for a reusable bookmark, which eventually turned into the Post-It note. The need to step back from focusing too much on a problem in order to gain insight has been found so often in the sciences that Albert Einstein once quipped that "creativity is the residue of wasted time."[76]

The fourth stage of the creative decision-making process is solution verification. In this step, the solution formulated in the insight stage is tested more rigorously to determine its usefulness for solving the problem. This stage in creative decision making closely resembles the rational decision-making model's evaluation stage. Typically, the verification process takes a long time. In fact, it resembles the preparation stage in the amount of hard work it requires. People often resist change, particularly if they have a large investment in traditional ideas and methods. They must be convinced, which is rarely possible without independent verification of the new approach.

Creative People

Certain characteristics of individuals seem to be associated with creative endeavors. First, a modest relationship appears to exist between creativity, general cognitive ability, and the specific capacities of reasoning and deduction. Indeed, some minimum threshold of intelligence seems to be necessary for creative work. Once that minimum threshold is reached, general intelligence becomes less critical and hard work is probably more important.

Personal characteristics such as interests, attitudes, and motivation are more important than intelligence in distinguishing creative people from the general population. Creative people generally set high goals for themselves, which may make them dissatisfied with the status quo and current solutions to problems. Indeed, dissatisfaction seems to be a general precursor to creative activity in that people are much more likely to be creative when they are in a bad mood, relative to a good mood.[77] Their high levels of aspiration might also explain why creative people often do not seem to feel loyalty to a particular employer but instead remain highly mobile, moving from company to company. Like most valued commodities, creative talent is highly sought after, and tends to develop unusual social networks. Thus a company may find it difficult to hold on to its creative people.[78]

Some have suggested that the creative person is unusually persistent and has a high energy level. These characteristics are probably particularly useful in the stages of preparation and verification, which demand hard work carried out over long periods of time. Persistent people will stick with something despite encountering obstacles and setbacks, and people with a lot of energy can continue to work diligently for extended periods. This persistence is often fueled by strong perceptions of creative self-efficacy, and recent research has produced a new measure that specifically taps individual differences in this critical trait.[79]

However, at some point persistence becomes a liability and creative people are often willing to walk away from one idea or product to another. In fact, the willingness to destroy an existing product in favor of a new product is often the key to long-term sustainability and creativity. For example, Steve Jobs was famous for cannibalizing one product in favor of a new product. That is, the iPhone fed off the market for the iPod and iPod touch media players, but Apple now derives close to 40 percent of its revenue from the iPhone. Similarly, the iPad tablet negatively impacted the market for Apple notebooks and PCs, but again, the gain in this case far outweighed the loss. In contrast, many organizations fail when instead of moving on to a new idea, their leaders relentlessly try to defend some old idea, such as Hewlett Packard's insistence on reinvesting in PC technology, long after the margins in that industry ceased to warrant it.[80]

Finally, age seems to be related to creativity. In one classic study of people recognized for their creativity, one consistent finding was that, regardless of the field in which the subjects worked (mathematics, physics, biology, chemistry, medicine, music, painting, and sculpture), creativity peaked between ages 30 and 40.[81]

Creativity-Inducing Situations

Selecting people who have characteristics that seem to be related to creativity is not the only option for organizations that seek to increase their innovativeness. Providing specific and difficult goals and firm deadlines actually seems to stimulate creative achievement, as long as the deadlines are far enough into the future. If the deadlines are set too short, this can create time pressure that stifles creativity, as people begin to look for the simplest and quickest solution rather than a more complex and creative solution.[82]

Some firms even set goals for creativity. For instance, 3M has historically set a goal that 35 percent of its total revenues should come from new products developed in the past four years. Of course, focusing people on coming up with innovative techniques, as opposed to cranking out products with the existing technologies, sometimes comes at the expense of short-term productivity. For example, one of 3M's rules is that each employee should devote 15 percent of his or her time to reading and learning about recent developments that have nothing to do with the employee's primary project.[83]

Certain characteristics of organizational culture (see Chapter 14) may also be related to creativity.[84] First, the degree to which organizations recognize and reward creativity is of paramount importance. Many organizations, either unwittingly or knowingly, place more emphasis on following existing written rules and procedures than on experimenting with new procedures. A culture that promotes creativity must ensure not only that innovativeness is reinforced, but that experimentation leading to failure is not punished. Executives like James Burke, CEO of Johnson & Johnson, attempt to create a climate where the risks of innovation are minimal. Burke, in fact, has even told his employees, "We won't grow unless you take risks. Any successful company is riddled with failures. There's just no other way to do it."[85]

Although they need not reward every failure, companies that seek to encourage innovation must lower the cost of conducting a "failed experiment." Employees need to know that risk taking is perceived as being worth making a few mistakes—especially if the size of the mistake is small and the damage can be contained. Indeed, although we will talk more about this in a subsequent chapter, transformational leaders who employ emotional motivational appeals seem to help promote innovation.[86] This is especially the case when the leader is managing a cross-functional team of narrow specialists who have a tendency to lose the "big picture" perspective required for implementing new ideas.[87]

Because much creativity comes out of collaborative efforts carried out by different individuals, organizations should promote internal diversity and work environments that enhance the opportunity to exchange ideas.[88] If all members of a group share the same interests, experiences, strengths, and weaknesses, they will be less likely to generate new ideas than if they have divergent backgrounds and capabilities. For example, Procter & Gamble (P&G) found that the rate of developing new innovative products decreased when they decentralized research and development (R&D) budgets. One part of this was due to risk aversion on the part of unit heads; the other part, however, was that the stand-alone units, often staffed by people with similar backgrounds, tended to generate incremental changes in existing products instead of major innovations. In the past, many of P&G's major innovations came about when a centralized R&D unit leveraged technologies already in P&G to come up with entirely new products. For example, Crest Whitestrips adapted bleaching methods from P&G's laundry business with film technology from the food wrap business with adhesive techniques gleaned from their paper business in order to create a new category of product. In order to recapture this kind of creativity, P&G restructured R&D so that people with very different backgrounds worked together to come up with new solutions to problems.[89]

Finally, because different organizations do different things in different places, exposing people to varying kinds of experiences, such as foreign assignments, professional development seminars, or extended leaves, may help shake up overly routine decision-making processes. That is, in addition to creating teams that have interpersonal diversity, organizations can also benefit from individuals who have "intra-personal" diversity. For example, Nike sent one of its product development engineers to a sock factory to see if any elements of sock production could be applied to the manufacturing of running shoes. This resulted in Nike's Flyknit technology, where a machine that was formerly used to knit sweaters was reengineered to knit a running shoe. Production of the new running shoe requires a minimum of human labor (one no longer has to sew together thirty-five different parts) and generates much less waste relative to the standard process, all in the service of producing a better-fitting shoe.[90]

Summary

A thorough understanding of the perceptual process by which people encode and make sense out of the complex world around them is critical to those who would manage organizational behavior. At the *attention stage* of the perceptual process, we select a small subset of all information available for subsequent processing. The degree to which any stimulus attracts our attention is a complex function of characteristics of the object and of ourselves. At the *organization stage* of the information-processing cycle, information is simplified. We convert complex behavioral sequences into *scripts* and represent people by *prototypes*. A number of biases, including *stereotyping*, can creep into this complex process. In the decision-making process, we use the information from the perceptual process to evaluate an object, person, or event. This evaluation, once made, affects our decisions, behaviors, and subsequent perceptions. Many features of people and situations need to be considered when trying to increase the accuracy and creativity of decision making.

Review Questions

1. List a set of traits that would make up the prototype for a terrorist, a hippie, an absent-minded professor, and a card-carrying member of the American Civil Liberties Union. Recalling Chapter 3, is your list dominated by ability or personality characteristics? What kinds of abilities or personality characteristics are most heavily represented? What does this exercise tell you about how prototypes are developed and in what ways they are most likely to be accurate?

2. Sometimes the same behavioral episode in an organization—for example, a fight among co-workers, a botched work assignment, or an ineffective meeting—can be organized perceptually along the lines of either a script or a prototype. How might the choice of schema affect what occurs later in the process of interpretation or judgment?

3. Escalation of commitment to a failing course of action has been widely researched, and it is easy to think of many examples of this kind of mistake. The flipside of this mistake, however, is giving up too soon, which has not been studied as much and for which it is more difficult to think of examples. Why can't we recall such events? How might researchers in this area be victims of availability bias?

4. Compare and contrast the decision-making process associated with rational decision making, administrative decision making, and creative decision making. At what points do these three descriptions of decision making diverge most? What implications does this divergence have for decision makers who attempt to follow the wrong model?

Notes

1   P. Bergen, "The Last Days of Osama bin Laden," *Time*, May 7, 2012, 24–33.
2   G. Allison, "How It Went Down," *Time*, May 7, 2012, 32–41.
3   J. Johnson, "Rewards Disconnect," *Workforce Management*, November 19, 2007, 15.
4   L. E. Atwater and J. F. Brett, "Antecedents and Consequences of Reactions to Developmental Feedback," *Journal of Vocational Behavior* 66 (2005): 532–548.
5   J. McGregor, "The Employee Is Always Right," *BusinessWeek*, November 14, 2007, 80–82.
6   J. W. Smither and R. R. Reilly, "Does Performance Improve Following Multisource Feedback? A Theoretical Model, Meta-Analysis, and Review of Empirical Findings," *Personnel Psychology* 58 (2005): 33–66.
7   M. Jackson, "May We Have Your Attention, Please?" *BusinessWeek*, June 23, 2008, 55–56.
8   B. B. Baltes and C. P. Parker, "Reducing the Effects of Performance Expectations on Behavioral Ratings," *Organizational Behavior and Human Decision Processes* 82 (2000): 237–267.
9   O. B. Davidson and D. Eden, "Remedial Self-Fulfilling Prophecy: Two Field Experiments to Prevent Golem Effects among Disadvantaged Women," *Journal of Applied Psychology* 85 (2000): 386–398.

10 P. Whitely, T. Sy, and S.K. Johnson, "Leaders' Conceptions of Followers: Implications for Naturally Occurring Pygmalian Effects," *Leadership Quarterly* 23 (2012): 822–834.

11 K. Weaver, S. M. Garcia, and N. Schwarz, "Inferring the Popularity of an Opinion from Its Familiarity: A Repetitive Voice Can Sound like a Chorus," *Journal of Personality and Social Psychology* 92 (2007): 821–833.

12 M. Kilduff, C. Crossland, and W. Tsai, "Organizational Network Perceptions versus Reality: A Small World after All?" *Organizational Behavior and Human Decision Processes* 107 (2008): 15–28.

13 C. Viswesvaran, F. L. Schmidt, and D. S. Ones, "Is There a General Factor in Ratings of Job Performance? A Meta-Analytic Framework for Disentangling Substantive and Error Influences," *Journal of Applied Psychology* 90 (2005): 108–131.

14 P. Engardio and M. Arndt, "The Value of Perception," *BusinessWeek*, July 9, 2007, 74.

15 M. Arndt and P. Engardio, "Wal-Mart without the Warts," *BusinessWeek*, July 9, 2007, 79.

16 S. Shellenbarger, "Battling Stereotypes, New Moms Face More Stress on the Job," *Wall Street Journal*, March 6, 2013. http://blogs.wsj.com/juggle/2013/03/05/battling-stereotypes-new-moms-face-more-stress-on-the-job/.

17 M. E. Heilman and T. G. Okimoto, "Why Are Women Penalized for Success at Male Tasks? The Implied Communality Deficit," *Journal of Applied Psychology* 92 (2007): 81–92.

18 S. Sandberg, "Why I Want Women to Lean In," *Time*, March 7, 2013, 44–45.

19 A. Pearson, "Waiting for Superwoman," *Bloomberg Businessweek*, March 11, 2013, 6–7.

20 D. Fandray, "Gray Matters," *Workforce*, July 2000, 27–32.

21 C. Ofir, "Ease of Recall versus Recalled Evidence in Judgment: Experts versus Laymen," *Organizational Behavior and Human Decision Processes* 81 (2000): 28–42.

22 T. A. Louie, M. T. Curren, and K. R. Harich, "'I Knew We Would Win': Hindsight Bias for Favorable and Unfavorable Team Decision Outcomes," *Journal of Applied Psychology* 85 (2000): 264–272.

23 M. Goldstein and D. Henry, "Bear Bets Wrong," *BusinessWeek*, October 22, 2007, 50–56.

24 R. Berner and D. Grow, "They Warned Us: The Watchdogs Who Saw the Subprime Disaster Coming—and How They Were Thwarted by the Banks and Washington," *BusinessWeek*, October 20, 2008, 36–42.

25 D. Henry, "None So Blind: How Regulators, Investors and Lenders Failed to See a Crisis Coming," *BusinessWeek*, March 31, 2008, 44.

26 R. F. Martell and D. P. Evans, "Source-Monitoring: Toward Reducing Rater Expectancy Effects in Behavioral Measurement," *Journal of Applied Psychology* 90 (2005): 956–963.

27 L. Landro, "The Hospital Is Watching You," *Wall Street Journal*, November 12, 2008, C1.

28 R.E. Silverman, "Tracking Sensors Invade the Workplace," *Wall Street Journal*, March 7, 2013, http://online.wsj.com/article/SB10001424127887324034804578344303429080678.html.

29 A. D. Hovorka-Mead, W. H. Ross, T. Whipple, and M. B. Renchin, "Watching the Detectives: Seasonal Student Employee Reactions to Electronic Monitoring With and Without Advance Notification," *Personnel Psychology* 55 (2002): 329–361.

30 C. Spitzmueller and J. M. Stanton, "Examining Employee Compliance with Organizational Surveillance and Monitoring," *Journal of Occupational and Organizational Psychology* 79 (2006): 245–272.

31 L. E. Atwater, D. A. Waldman, D. Atwater, and P. Cartier, "An Upward Feedback Field Experiment: Supervisors' Cynicism, Reactions, and Commitment to Subordinates," *Personnel Psychology* 53 (2000): 275–298.

32 T. DeAngelis, "Why We Overestimate Our Competence," *Monitor on Psychology*, February 2003, 60–61.

33 P. W. B. Atkins and R. E. Wood, "Self versus Others' Ratings as Predictors of Assessment Center Ratings: Validation Evidence for 360-Degree Feedback Programs," *Personnel Psychology* 55 (2002): 871–904.

34 S. Alper, D. Tjosvold, and K. S. Law, "Conflict Management Efficacy, and Performance in Organizational Teams," *Personnel Psychology* 53 (2000): 625–642.

35 K. L. Uggerslev and L. M. Sulsky, "Using Frame of Reference Training to Understand the Implications of Rater Idiosyncrasy for Rating Accuracy," *Journal of Applied Psychology* 93 (2008): 711–719.

36 A. Tversky and D. Kahneman, "The Framing of Decisions and the Psychology of Choice," *Science* 211 (1981): 453–458.

37 D. Smith, "Psychologist Wins Nobel Prize," *Psychologist* 15 (2002): 596.

38 J. A. Byrne, "Fall from Grace," *BusinessWeek*, August 12, 2002, 50–55.

39 D. Elliott, W. F. Helsen, and R. Chua, "A Century Later: Woodworth's (1899) Two-Component Model of Goal-Directed Aiming," *Psychological Bulletin* 127 (2001): 342–357.

40 B. Beersma, J. R. Hollenbeck, S. E. Humphrey, H. Moon, D. E. Conlon, and D. R. Ilgen, "Cooperation, Competition and Team Performance: Toward a Contingency Approach," *Academy of Management Journal* 47 (2003): 130–140.

41 L. A. Perlow, G. A. Okhuyson, and N. P. Repenning, "The Speed Trap: Exploring the Relationship between Decision Making and Temporal Context," *Academy of Management Journal* 45 (2002): 931–955.

42 K. E. Stanovich and R. F. West, "On the Relative Independence of Thinking Biases and Cognitive Ability," *Journal of Personality and Social Psychology* 94 (2008): 672–695.

43 D. B. Boehne and P. W. Paese, "Deciding Whether to Complete or Terminate an Unfinished Product: A Strong Test of the Project Completion Hypothesis," *Organizational Behavior and Human Decision Processes* 81 (2000): 178–194.

44 G. Ku, "Learning to De-Escalate: The Effects of Regret in Escalation of Commitment," *Organizational Behavior and Human Decision Processes* 10 (2008): 221–232.

45 D. Sleesman, D. E. Conlon, G. McNamara, and J. E. Miles, "Cleaning Up the Big Muddy: A Meta-analytic Review of the Determinants of Escalation of Commitment," *Academy of Management Journal* 55 (2012): 541–562.

46 G. March and H. A. Simon, *Organizations* (New York: Wiley, 1958), 10.

47 R. Hof, "At Yahoo, a Threat from Within," *BusinessWeek*, July 14, 2008, 36.

48 T. A. Stewart, "A Refreshing Change: Vision Statements that Make Sense," *Fortune*, September 30, 1996, 195–196.

49 C. Arnst, "Why Snap Judgments Work," *BusinessWeek*, August 20, 2007, 110.

50 P. Coy, "$700 Billion, No Strings Attached," *BusinessWeek*, October 6, 2008, 30–32.

51 M. Der Hovanesian, "Helping Those Who Helped Themselves," *BusinessWeek*, October 6, 2008, 33–34.

52 J. A. Byrne, "Judgment: How Winning Leaders Make Great Calls," *BusinessWeek*, November 19, 2007, 68–72.

53 E. Ramstad, "Patent Bet Turns Sour for Korean Behemoth," *Wall Street Journal*, August 26, 2012, http://online.wsj.com/article/SB10000872396390444327204577612951560958304.html.

54 J. Coates, "Risk Factor: How Biology Can Explain What Drives Banks to the Brink of Disaster," *Time*, July 9, 2012, 18.

55 B. Hindo, "Rewiring Westinghouse," *BusinessWeek*, May 19, 2008, 48–49.

56 L. Himelstein and B. Elgin, "Tech's Kickback Culture," *BusinessWeek*, February 10, 2003, 74–77.

57 R. Foroohar, "Walmart's Discounted Ethics," *Time*, May 7, 2012, 19.

58 P. Dwyer and D. Carney, "Year of the Whistleblower," *BusinessWeek*, December 16, 2002, 107–110.

59 R. Albergiotti and V. O'Connell, "Justice Department Poised to Join Armstrong Whistleblower Suit," *The Wall Street Journal Online*, January 15, 2013.

60 L. Saunders and R. Sidel, "Whistleblower Gets $104 Million," *Wall Street Journal*, September 11, 2012, http://online.wsj.com/article/SB10000872396390444017504577645412614237708.html.

61 L. Saunders, "IRS Pays $38 Million in Whistleblower Case," *Wall Street Journal*, October 28, 2012, http://online.wsj.com/article/SB10001424052970204598504578080883203393030.html.

62 B. Brehmer, "Response Consistency in Probabilistic Inference Tasks," *Organizational Behavior and Human Performance* 22 (1978): 103–115.

63 March and Simon, *Organizations*, 10–12.

64 J. N. Bearden and T. Connolly, "Multi-Attribute Sequential Search," *Organizational Behavior and Human Decision Processes* 103 (2007): 147–158.

65 Y. Ganzach, A. N. Kluger, and N. Klayman, "Making Decisions from an Interview: Expert Measurement and Mechanical Combination," *Personnel Psychology* 53 (2000): 1–20.

66 C. Daniels, "To Hire a Lumber Expert, Click Here," *Fortune*, April 3, 2000, 267–270.

67 S. E. Humphrey, J. R. Hollenbeck, C. J. Meyer, and D. R. Ilgen, "Hierarchical Decision-Making Teams," in G. R. Ferris and J. J. Martocchio, eds., *Research in Personnel and Human Resource Management* (Stamford, CT: JAI Press, 2002), 175–213.

68 J. D. Orton and K. E. Weick, "Loosely Coupled Systems: A Reconceptualization," *Academy of Management Review* 15 (1990): 203–223.

69 B. Stone and S. Ray, "Don't Dream It's Over," *Bloomburg Businessweek*, January 28, 2013, 4–5.

70 B. Stone, "It's Not His Mess, Just His to Clean Up," *Bloomburg Businessweek*, January 28, 2013, 14.

71 W. Blitzer, "Admiral McCraven on bin Laden Raid: One of History's Great Intelligence Operations," *CNN Press Room*, July 26, 2012, http://cnnpressroom.blogs.cnn.com/2012/07/26/admiral-mcraven-on-bin-laden-raid-one-of-historys-great-intelligence-operations/.

72 G. McNamara, H. Moon, and P. Bromily, "Banking on Commitment: Intended and Unintended Consequences of an Organization's Attempt to Attenuate Escalation of Commitment," *Academy of Management Journal* 45 (2002): 443–452.

73 J. Carey, "The Science of Aha!" *BusinessWeek*, July 9, 2007, 120.

74 P. B. Paulus, "Idea Generation in Groups: A Basis for Creativity in Organizations," *Organizational Behavior and Human Decision Processes* 82 (2000): 76–87.

75 K. Spors, "Nerf Wars to Scooter Races: Secrets to Making Work Fun," *Wall Street Journal*, November 3, 2008, D1.

76 J. Lerher, "How to Be Creative," *Wall Street Journal*, March 9, 2012, http://online.wsj.com/article/SB10001424052970203370604577265632205015846.html.

77 J. M. George and J. Zhou, "Understanding When Bad Moods Foster Creativity and Good Ones Don't: The Role of Context and Clarity of Feelings," *Journal of Applied Psychology* 87 (2002): 687–697.

78 G. Cattanin and S. Ferriani, "Core/Periphery Perspective on Individual Creative Performance: Social Networks and Cinematic Achievements in the Hollywood Film Industry," *Organization Science* 19 (2008): 824–844.

79 P. Tierney and S. M. Farmer, "Creative Self-Efficacy: Its Potential Antecedents and Relationship to Creative Performance," *Academy of Management Journal* 45 (2002): 1137–1148.

80 S. E. Ante, "Avoiding Innovation's Terrible Toll," *Wall Street Journal*, January 7, 2012, http://online.wsj.com/article/SB10001424052970204331304577144980247499346.html.

81 H. C. Lehman, *Age and Achievement* (Princeton, NJ: Princeton University Press, 1953), 50–61.

82 B. Murray, "A Ticking Clock Means a Creative Drop," *Monitor on Psychology*, November 2002, 24–25.

83 A. Stewart, "3M Fights Back," *Fortune*, February 5, 1996, 94–96.

84 N. Madjar, G. R. Oldham, and M. G. Pratt, "There's No Place Like Home? The Contributions of Work and Nonwork Creativity Support to Employees' Creative Performance," *Academy of Management Journal* 45 (2002): 757–767.

85 G. Hamel, "Reinvent Your Company," *Fortune*, June 12, 2000, 99–118.

86 S. A. Eisenbeiss, D. van Knippenberg, and S. Boerner, "Transformational Leadership and Team Innovation: Integrating Team Climate Principles," *Journal of Applied Psychology* 93 (2008): 1438–1446.

87 S. J. Shin and J. Zhou, "When Is Educational Specialization Heterogeneity Related to Creativity in Research and Development Teams? Transformational Leadership as a Moderator," *Journal of Applied Psychology* 92 (2007): 1709–1721.

88 C. E. Shalley, L. L. Gilson, and T. C. Blum, "Matching Creativity Requirements and the Work Environment: Effects on Satisfaction and Intentions to Leave," *Academy of Management Journal* 43 (2000): 215–223.

89 L. Coleman-Lochner and C. Hymowitz, "At P&G, the Innovation Well Runs Dry," *Bloomburg Businessweek*, September 12, 2012, 24–25.

90 M. Townsend, "Is Nike's Flyknit the Swoosh of the Future," *Bloomburg Businessweek*, March 19, 2012, 31–32.

Chapter 5

Work Motivation and Performance

In 2013, when the unemployment rate fell from 7.7 percent in February to 7.6 percent in April, one might think that this was good news for the U.S. economy. It was not. The problem with this indicator is that the unemployment rate is a ratio that contains a numerator (the number of people working) and a denominator (the number of people looking for work), and the entire change in this case was attributable to the denominator. A vast number of people had stopped looking for work. In fact, in one month alone, roughly 1.5 million unemployed Americans gave up looking for a job despite the fact that the economy showed signs of improvement and the stock market reached an all-time high.

Many experts tried to explain this paradox by suggesting that for most unemployed individuals, there are simply too many government-sponsored disincentives built into the U.S. economy that destroy any motivation for seeking a new job. That is, if one considers jobless insurance, food stamps, Medicaid, tax cuts, and disability insurance, for many unemployed workers, the rewards for doing nothing and staying on the welfare rolls are greater than the rewards associated with going back to work. This is especially the case if the only work available is a low-wage, insecure job that fails to offer health benefits.

For example, let us examine the motivational implications of just one such program—worker disability insurance. Although disability payments are somewhat tied to a worker's actual wages prior to being hurt, on average, someone on disability earns close to $14,000 a year. This is obviously not a great deal of money—just $2,000 more than the federal poverty level. However, this is only $2,000 less than what one would receive if they worked full time at the minimum wage of $7.25 an hour. In addition, many disabled workers can also receive unemployment compensation and this $2,000 deficit attributable to actually working can be quickly wiped out. Finally, after a short period, disabled workers qualify for Medicare health insurance. If the low-wage job they are considering does not offer health insurance, then there is actually more economic value in staying on the disabled list then getting off it. When one examines all the contingencies facing a disabled worker, it is not difficult to see why someone might not be motivated to look for work—even if the alternative is not very lucrative. Indeed, James Ottesen, a former truck driver from Ohio, who has been on disability insurance for over three years, spoke for many when he noted that "the government disability program feels like a blanket covering you and to walk out from it at my age is a little intimidating."[1]

That it is better for individuals to stay out of the job market under these conditions is further exacerbated by other aspects of the reward system that impact employers, regulators, and state governments. For example, the new Affordable Care Act requires employers with fifty or more employees to pay for health benefits or face a penalty. This has motivated many small companies to stay put at forty-nine employees and never hire the fiftieth employee—stunting job growth. In addition, new rules for regulators with respect to what constitutes a disability have made it harder to reject claims. Traditionally, an objective musculoskeletal problem was required to receive benefits, but now it is easier for people to claim back pain, mood disorders, mental problems, and other hard-to-disprove subjective ailments, Finally, many state governments are motivated to shift people out of state-sponsored programs, such as welfare, to federally funded disability programs, making it easier for states to balance their budgets.

Although the motivation for individuals, employers, regulating agencies and states to trim the disabled rolls is very low, the motivation for American society at large is quite high. Between December 2007 and March 2012, the number of Americans receiving disability insurance exploded from 7.1 million to 8.9 million—a full 5.5 percent of the entire civilian workforce. The program costs the government over $10 billion in payments and diminished tax revenues, locks many individuals into poverty, and fails to maximize the utility of human capital toward personal achievement and the betterment of the nation.[2]

Motivation refers to the energy a person is willing to devote to a task. A person who is highly motivated will start work sooner and leave work later, relative to someone who is unmotivated, and may come in on weekends to finish up tasks that were left undone during the week. While engaged at work, a highly motivated person will work faster, take fewer breaks, and be less easily distracted, relative to someone who is unmotivated. A person who is highly motivated will go out of his or her way to learn new things to improve future performance and help co-workers when the workload within the group is unbalanced. Managers who can create high levels of motivation can get more work out of five people than their less inspiring counterparts can get out of ten, and this is a form of competitive advantage that is hard to deny. However, as this opening example shows, in many cases, it is hard to even get people motivated to look for work, let alone work hard at a job once they land it.

One way to try to create motivation is through rewards, and perhaps the easiest thing to say to a manager, *in theory*, is that he or she should "pay for performance" or "link rewards to accomplishment." The most difficult thing to do, *in practice*, is to implement this advice in a manner that does not backfire. For example, although everyone in the U.S. government wants to help people get back to work as soon as they can after being disabled, the set of contingencies created by various programs works to motivate just the opposite goal. Indeed, the history of management is littered with motivational interventions that sound good and simple in theory but get "gamed" by experienced and sophisticated employees who do not always have the best interests of shareholders, co-workers, or management at heart.

The purpose of this chapter is to introduce and discuss the topic of worker motivation and performance. Given the centrality of creating and maintaining high levels of motivation, it should come as no surprise that many, many theories deal with this topic. Indeed, the sheer number of theories of motivation that exist can obscure rather than promote understanding and application. The complexity of this issue drives confused managers toward fads and overly simplistic approaches that promise much and deliver little. In this chapter, we avoid this problem in two ways. First, rather than try to comprehensively cover every theory of motivation, we focus our attention on a subset of five theories: expectancy theory, need theory, learning theory, self-efficacy theory, and goal-setting theory. Second, we will develop an overarching model to clarify how the theories relate to each other and to show how each specific theory is best for describing a certain aspect of the overall motivation process. This model describes four concrete steps that need to be taken in order to motivate people and specifically addresses how to apply what we have learned from research on these theories in real organizational contexts. Managers who learn and apply this model can take four steps forward in their attempts to gain competitive advantage in product and labor markets.

A Model of Motivation and Performance

The model of motivation and performance built in this chapter consists of *five components* put together in *four steps* to explain *three outcomes*. Figure 5.1 presents this model graphically; it serves as a road map for the remainder of this chapter. One component (abilities) was explained in Chapter 3 and will be touched on only briefly here. Three other components defined below—valence, instrumentality, and expectancy—will be elaborated on, using need, learning, and self-efficacy theories. The final component is accuracy of role perceptions, particularly as described via goal-setting theory.

Expectancy Theory

The model of motivation developed in this chapter is an elaboration of *expectancy theory*, particularly as extended by Lyman Porter and Edward Lawler.[3] Expectancy theory is a broad theory of motivation that attempts to explain the determinants of workplace attitudes and behaviors. Three major components underlie expectancy theory: the concepts of *v*alence, *i*nstrumentality, and *e*xpectancy, often called *VIE* theory).

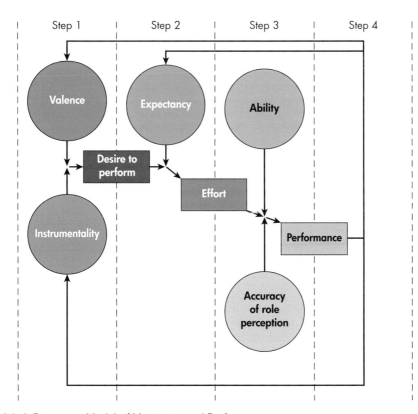

Figure 5.1 **A Diagnostic Model of Motivation and Performance**

The concept of **valence** is based on the assumption that, at any given time, a person prefers certain outcomes to others. Valence measures the satisfaction that the person anticipates receiving from a particular outcome. Outcomes can have positive, negative, or zero valence. An outcome has a positive valence when a person would rather attain it than not attain it. When a person is indifferent to attaining an outcome, that outcome is assigned a valence of zero. If a person prefers *not* to attain the outcome, the outcome is said to have a negative valence. In our earlier example, the thought of potentially losing one's government-sponsored health benefits is an outcome that has negative valence for many unemployed or disabled workers.

In many cases the relative valence between two outcomes is critical for predicting behavior. For example, large employers who fail to provide health care coverage under the Affordable Care Act face penalties, and one might think that being penalized is an outcome with negative valence. However, many employers came to the conclusion that the rising cost of health care was actually worse than the penalties, and hence the penalties failed to motivate them to provide coverage. For example, one employer calculated that the cost of providing coverage for his 100 workers was $500,000 and growing, but his penalty for failing to provide coverage was only $150,000 and fixed—hence, the new law did not motivate any change in behavior.[4]

In other cases, a reward might be too low in valence to motivate one behavior, but high enough in valence to motivate an alternative behavior, and this is the source of many unintended consequences that result from reward programs. For example, in an effort to reduce employee health care costs, Whirlpool offered a special incentive, $500 in the form of nonsmoker discounts. By linking the reward to smoking cessation, the company tried to motivate people to quit smoking. Unfortunately, the company had to fire forty workers at its plant in Evansville, Indiana, who were caught on video smoking in designated locations outside the plant despite having signed forms claiming they were nonsmokers.[5] Thus, the $500 smoking cessation incentive that Whirlpool offered was not high enough to actually motivate people to quit smoking, but it was high enough to get them to falsify documents and lie to the company.[6]

From a motivational perspective, it is important to distinguish between valence and value. *Valence* refers to *anticipated* satisfaction. *Value* represents the *actual* satisfaction a person experiences from attaining a desired outcome. With experience, someone might discover that a discrepancy exists between the anticipated satisfaction from an outcome (its valence) and the actual satisfaction that it provides (its value).[7] When this disparity occurs, a reward might eventually lose its motivational value. For example, if a person comes to believe that "money cannot buy happiness," then the motivational values of financial incentives may quickly wane.

Instrumentality is a person's belief about the relationship between performing an action and experiencing an outcome. It is sometimes referred to as a *performance–outcome expectation*. Determining a person's instrumentalities is important because that individual will likely have a strong desire to perform a particular action only when both valence and instrumentality are perceived as high. Thus, to understand motivation, we need to know more than the satisfaction an individual expects as the consequence of attaining a particular outcome—we need to know what the person believes he or she must do to obtain or avoid that outcome. Thus, from our opening example, if an employer feels that moving from forty-eight to forty-nine employees does not trigger additional costs associated with providing health care benefits, then the employer will feel free to hire another worker. However, if hiring one more worker triggers added costs, then this motivates the employer to stop growing his or her business at that specific point. Thus, avoiding growth beyond fifty employees is instrumental for avoiding certain costs.

The third element of expectancy theory is the concept for which the theory is named: expectancy. **Expectancies** are beliefs about the link between making an effort and actually performing well. Whereas knowledge about valences and instrumentalities tells us what an individual *wants to do*, we cannot anticipate what the individual will *try to do* without knowing the person's expectancies. Thus, even though an unemployed worker might value the benefits that come from obtaining a full time job, if he or she feels that there is no chance they can get a job because they have been unemployed for so long, then there will be no effort directed at finding work. Indeed, the evidence does seem to suggest that employers discriminate against job applicants who have been out of the workforce for an extended period. Although unemployment compensation traditionally lasts for up to forty weeks, someone who has been unemployed for just twenty-seven weeks faces much bleaker job prospects relative to someone who was unemployed for a shorter time.[8] In fact, many employers who are expanding their workforce only search among applicants who already have jobs because there is a social stigma attached to being unemployed.[9] Thus, once one has been out of the workforce for an extended period of time, there is a low expectancy that any amount of effort aimed at job search is going to be successful, and hence motivation drops accordingly.

Thus, expectancy theory defines motivation in terms of desire and effort, whereby the achievement of desired outcomes results from the interaction of valences, instrumentalities, and expectancies. Desire arises only when both valence and instrumentality are high, and effort comes about only when all three aspects are high. If any one of these three factors is missing, then motivation levels are low.

Supplemental Theories

Two primary reasons explain why, to build a model of motivation and performance, we need to supplement expectancy theory with other motivation theories. First, a number of other theories deal in much more detail with certain specific components of motivation. As a consequence, they help to elaborate on expectancy theory. *Need theories* provide important insights into how valences develop and how they might change over time. *Learning theories* explain how perceptions of instrumentality arise. *Self-efficacy theory* describes the origins of effort–performance expectancies and the ways in which they are maintained. Second, expectancy theory must be extended to explain outcomes other than desire and effort. To predict performance, expectancy theory requires information about human ability, goals, and strategies. For these reasons, along with expectancy theory, our model will incorporate ideas from the need, learning, self-efficacy, and goal-setting theories.

Valence: Need Theories

People differ greatly in their personal preferences. For example, a recent study of MBAs found that the relationship between changing jobs and getting higher salaries was strong and positive among white males, but close to zero among women and minorities.[10] White males tended to place a high value on pay and would change employers only if some higher level of compensation was offered. In contrast, women and minorities were more likely to change employers for other reasons; they did not use pay as the single overarching factor driving their mobility. Thus the different valences of these groups can help explain their different behaviors.

The goal for employers is to find exactly what drives each employee and then, as far as possible, build reward systems around these drivers, taking advantage of each person's unique sets of interests and values. In fact, this process is getting so sophisticated that new statistical modeling software is available to track and exploit the different values people have, so that employers can tailor the money spent on human resources in ways that maximize their motivational value. For example, one worker might prefer to receive compensation in the form of retirement support, whereas another might prefer health care coverage; innovative software programs are available that support organizational efforts at customizing their reward systems to the idiosyncratic value systems of each employee.[11] When it comes to understanding how valences originate and why they differ among people, need theories can prove especially informative.

Maslow's Need Hierarchy

Abraham Maslow was a famous clinical psychologist and a pioneer in the development of need theories. Little existed in the way of empirical, scientific studies of motivation when Maslow began work, and hence he based his own theory on twenty-five years of experience in treating individuals with varying degrees of psychological health. Based on this experience, Maslow's need theory proposed the existence of five distinct types of needs: physiological, safety, love, esteem, and self-actualization. These needs, according to Maslow, are genetically based and characteristic of all humans. Moreover, he argued, these five needs are arranged in the hierarchy shown in Figure 5.2 and influence motivation on the basis of need **prepotency**.

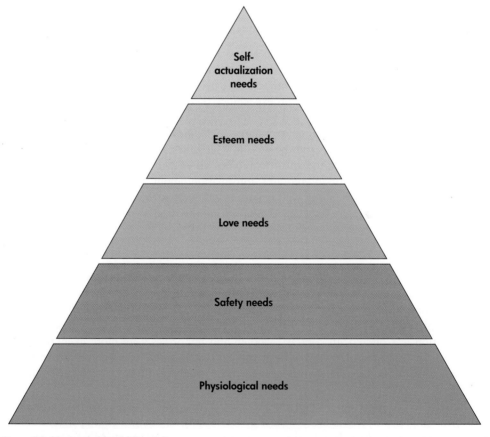

Figure 5.2 Maslow's Need Hierarchy

Source: Adapted from A. H. Maslow, "A Theory of Human Motivation," *Psychological Review* 50, no. 4 (1943): 370–396.

Prepotency means that needs residing higher in the hierarchy can influence motivation only if needs residing lower in the hierarchy are already largely satisfied.

At the lowest level of Maslow's need hierarchy are physiological needs such as hunger and thirst. According to Maslow, these physiological needs possess the greatest initial prepotency, and if these needs are not met they become the sole drivers of motivation. Once these needs have been mostly gratified, however, they no longer serve as strong motivating elements. Under these conditions, second-level safety and security needs increase in importance. Safety and security needs relate to the acquisition of objects and relationships that protect their possessor from future threats, especially threats to the person's ability to satisfy his or her physiological needs. In organizational contexts, the need for job security is often an important motivator, and people are often willing to forgo many other rewards, such as high pay, in return for security. This seems to be especially true of individuals who grew up in families where their parents never secured stable employment histories.[12]

If both physiological and safety needs are mostly fulfilled, love needs become prepotent. Maslow used the term *love* in a broad sense to refer to preferences for affection from others as well as a sense of belongingness and contributing to one's community, broadly defined.

The need for friends, family, and colleagues falls within this category, and in many cases one might be motivated to stay at a company largely because all one's friends work there and hence it serves as a social outlet. The term **prosocial motivation** is often used explicitly to capture the degree to which people are motivated to help other people.[13] When people believe that their work has an important impact on other people, they are much more willing to work longer hours.[14] This prosocial motivation could be directed at co-workers and has been found to relate to helping behavior.[15] This form of motivation can also be triggered by recognizing that one's work has a positive impact on those who benefit from one's service, such as customers or clients.[16] In contrast, when one's social needs are thwarted, people often react negatively and in self-defeating ways that drive others further away from them.[17]

At the fourth level in Maslow's need hierarchy are esteem needs. Maslow grouped two distinct kinds of esteem within this category. Social esteem consists of the respect, recognition, attention, and appreciation of others. Self-esteem reflects an individual's own feelings of personal adequacy. Consequently, esteem needs can be satisfied partly from external sources and partly from internal sources. For many people, pay, income, and acquiring wealth have more to do with satisfying needs for esteem than for meeting physiological or security needs, and this can often trump prosocial motivation. For example, when asked to set a goal for how many hours of prosocial volunteer work they were willing to provide, people who were reminded of their hourly wage (or salaried workers asked to calculate their hourly wage) were less willing to "spend" time volunteering.[18]

The last set of needs, at the top of Maslow's hierarchy, consists of self-actualization needs. According to Maslow, if all needs beneath self-actualization are fulfilled, a person can be considered generally satisfied. In Maslow's words, self-actualization "might be phrased as the desire to become more and more what one is, to become everything that one is capable of becoming."[19] Unlike all the other needs identified by Maslow, self-actualization needs can never be fully satisfied. Hence, the picture of human motivation drawn by this theory emphasizes constant striving as well as constant deprivation of one sort or another.

Perhaps owing to its simplicity, Maslow's need theory has gained wide acceptance among managers and management educators. Maslow failed to provide researchers with clear-cut measures of his concepts, however, and his theory has never received much empirical support.[20] Still, it holds interest for us primarily because of its place in history as one of the earliest motivation models and as a precursor to more modern theories of motivation.

Murray's Theory of Manifest Needs

Henry Murray's theory of manifest needs defines needs as recurrent concerns for particular goals or end states.[21] Each need consists of two components: the object toward which the need is directed (for example, achievement or autonomy) and the intensity or strength of the need for that particular object (for example, strong versus weak). Murray proposed more than twenty needs, several of which are described in Table 5.1.

Because Murray's needs are not arranged in any hierarchical fashion, the theory offers considerable flexibility. Unlike Maslow, Murray held that an individual could be motivated by more than one need simultaneously, and he also suggested that needs could sometimes conflict with each other. Also unlike Maslow, who viewed needs as innate and genetically determined, Murray regarded needs as something people learned from interacting with their environment. Needs are often manifested in the form of personality traits, and in general, people are going to find work that meets their needs as meaningful and hence highly motivating.[22]

Table 5.1 Some of Murray's Manifest Needs

Achievement	To do one's best, to be successful, to accomplish tasks requiring skill and effort, to be a recognized authority, to accomplish something important, to do a difficult job well
Deference	To get suggestions from others, to find out what others think, to follow instructions and do what is expected, to praise others, to accept leadership of others, to conform to custom
Order	To keep things neat and orderly, to make advance plans, to organize details of work, to have things arranged so they run smoothly without change
Autonomy	To be able to come and go as desired, to say what one thinks about things, to be independent of others in making decisions, to do things without regard for what others may think
Affiliation	To be loyal to friends, to participate in friendly groups, to form strong attachments, to share things with friends, to write letters to friends, to make as many friends as possible
Dominance	To argue for one's point of view, to be a leader in groups to which one belongs, to persuade and influence others, to supervise and direct the actions of others
Nurturance	To help friends when they are in trouble, to treat others with kindness and sympathy, to forgive others and do favors for them, to show affection and have others confide in one
Change	To do new and different things, to travel, to meet new people, to have novelty and change in daily routine, to try new and different jobs, to particip-ate in new fads and fashions
Endurance	To keep at a job until it is finished, to work hard at a task, to work at a single job before taking on others, to stick to a problem even though no apparent progress is being made
Aggression	To attack contrary points of view, to tell others off, to get revenge for insults, to blame others when things go wrong, to criticize others publicly, to read accounts of violence

Source: Adapted from H. A. Murray, *Explorations in Personality* (New York: Oxford University Press, 1938), 152–205.

Other researchers later extended and expanded Murray's work on need theories. Most notably, David McClelland developed a theory of motivation that focused particularly on the need for achievement.[23] According to McClelland, people can be characterized as either high or low on the need for achievement, which he abbreviated as "nAch." Those who are high in nAch prefer situations in which they have the opportunity to take personal responsibility. These individuals also prefer to receive personal credit for the consequences of their actions and clear and unambiguous feedback about personal performance. According to McClelland, the key to workplace motivation is to find high-nAch individuals (or raise the levels of low-nAch individuals through training) and expose them to situations conducive to fulfilling the need for achievement.

For example, Microsoft is well known for selecting individuals who have high intelligence and a high need for achievement. To make this strategy truly effective, however, the company must tie the person's perceptions of self-worth and achievement to task accomplishment—often expressed in terms of creating marketable products. As one insider notes, "Creativity is highly regarded at Microsoft for a short period of time, but that is not how people really rank each other. The primary thing is to ship a product. Until you have done that—you're suspect. It involves taking this passion of yours and running it through a humiliating, exhausting process."[24] When people who rate high in their need for achievement are personally challenged in this fashion, they are no longer being driven by the money, but instead are driven by more intrinsic rewards and punishments. The ability to shift away from purely financial inducements is particularly important in an economy where money is tight. Indeed, employers are increasingly trying to lower their costs for labor, which in turn restricts the degree to which they can reward top performers with pay raises. Organizations risk losing their top performers if they cannot come up with alternatives to pay as a means of motivating their workforce.[25]

Instrumentality: Learning Theories

The understanding of valence contributed by need theories provides only one piece of the motivational puzzle—what people want. To understand behavior, we need to know not just what people want but what they believe will lead to the attainment of what they want. As noted earlier, these beliefs are referred to as *instrumentalities*. Learning theories help clarify how relationships between behaviors and rewards come to be perceived. They also provide information that allows us to estimate the character, permanence, and strength of these relationships.

The notion that people generally behave so as to maximize pleasure and minimize pain was first formulated by the ancient Greek philosophers and captured in the concept of **hedonism**. Virtually all modern theories of motivation incorporate this concept. It is especially conspicuous in learning theories, all of which attempt to explain behavior in terms of the associations that people use to link some behavior and some outcome. Two types of learning theories are discussed here: operant learning (reinforcement theory) and social learning.

Reinforcement Theory

Reinforcement theory proposes that a person engages in a specific behavior because that behavior has been reinforced by a specific outcome. A simple example of positive reinforcement can be seen in a recent study that examined ways to reduce absenteeism. In this study, several locations of a garment factory that had been experiencing attendance problems served as the backdrop for an intervention that was designed around public recognition. The idea was to give positive attention to workers who were absent less than three days each quarter. Employees who managed this were given (1) personal attention in the form of a letter from the CEO thanking them for their diligence, (2) a public celebration party where they were wined and dined along with other winners, and (3) small symbolic mementos (a gold necklace for women and a gold penknife for men) to highlight their accomplishments. Within a year, plants that had adopted the recognition program experienced a 50 percent reduction in absenteeism compared to control plants.[26]

Technological enhancements over recent years have offered organizations new ways to try to reinforce certain behaviors. For example, Old Navy and American Eagle Outfitters stores have implemented technology that allows them to detect whenever certain customers walk into any one of their stores. That is, sensors installed in the stores can actually detect the smartphones of shoppers who are enrolled and participating in the program whenever they enter a store. Entering the store then triggers a reinforcing signal to the person, notifying them that they just earned a reward in the form of in-store purchasing credits. Although there are limits, for the most part, the more often you enter the stores, the more credits you get, and the more this behavior is converted into a habit.[27]

Organizations often link rewards to outcomes of their employees in order to reinforce their current culture or signal a change in culture.[28] For example, in terms of reinforcing the existing culture, the online retailer Zappos rates every employee on how well their behavior reflects Zappo's "10 Core Values" including "demonstrating humility," "providing excellent service," "doing more with less," and so on. The performance evaluation system is linked to these ratings and designed to reward employees for embracing and embodying the cultural values that the company believes has been the key for its success.[29] In terms of trying to change a culture, after several fatal accidents, including the mishap that resulted in the worst oil spill in history, BP (formerly British Petroleum) announced in an internal memo to staff that safety would be the sole criterion for rewarding employee performance. BP's CEO, Bob Dudley said the objective of the new reward system was "to ensure that a low probability, high-impact incident such as the Deepwater Horizon tragedy never happens again."[30]

Operant learning is especially good for reinforcing simple or well-learned responses. In some cases, however, managers may want to encourage a complex behavior that might not occur on its own. In this instance, the process of shaping can be helpful. **Shaping** means rewarding successive approximations to a desired behavior, so that "getting close counts." This may mean not only reinforcing high levels of employee performance, but also positive trends in performance that at least reflect the fact that the person may be moving in the right direction, even though they might not be "there" yet.[31]

Shaping is especially useful when trying to reinforce highly complex behaviors. For example, someone who has never played golf is highly unlikely to pick up a club and execute a perfect drive with his or her first swing. Left alone to try repeatedly with no instruction, a novice golfer probably will never exhibit the correct behavior. In shaping, rather than waiting for the correct behavior to occur on its own, close approximations win rewards. Over time, rewards are held back until the person more closely approaches the right behavior. Thus a golf instructor might at first praise a novice golfer for holding the club with the right grip. To obtain a second reward, the novice may be required not only to display the correct grip but also to stand at the appropriate distance from the ball. To obtain additional rewards, the novice may have to do both of these things and execute the backswing correctly, and so on. In this way, simple initial behaviors become shaped into a complex desired behavior. Over time, increasingly difficult behaviors have to be mastered, and this kind of "deliberate practice" can eventually lead to high levels of expertise. Indeed, studies of experts in many different fields suggest that this kind of hard work and dedication directed at learning new details about a specific task is what underlies the success of many great performers in sports, business, science, and medicine. Across many different disciplines, the research seems to suggest that it takes at least ten years to truly develop expertise with any complex task.[32]

Extinction is a second form of reinforcement. In extinction, a weakened response occurs because the desired outcome is no longer paired with some positive reinforcer. Indeed, one problem with reinforcement systems is that they often focus attention so exclusively on the reinforced behavior that other nonreinforced behaviors languish. For example, Washington Mutual (WaMu) was the largest bank failure in American history and the fall of this financial giant can be traced to what values were reinforced and what values were extinguished over the course of the bank's history. Early in the bank's history, the five core values listed in the bank's mission statement were "ethics, respect, teamwork, innovation, and excellence." Over the course of time, these were changed to "dynamic and driven" and this coincided with the bank's aggressive attempts to acquire other banks and focus increasingly on risky sub-prime mortgages. In order to secure a greater quantity of business, bank officers competed against each other and were rewarded for granting NINA loans (no income; no assets) to many borrowers who were poor risks. The values of "excellence," "ethics," and "teamwork" were ignored and behaviors that reflected those values were extinguished. Then, when the housing market crashed, the firm lost over $20 billion in market value.[33] Based upon WaMu's experience, other financial institutions changed their reward polices to reduce the level of risk taking, and Goldman Sachs wrote new policies that stated that bonus payments will be halted if the firm determines that an employee engaged in "materially improper risk analysis or failed sufficiently to raise concerns about risk."[34]

Negative reinforcement and punishment are two other types of reinforcement used to influence behavior. In **negative reinforcement**, the likelihood that a person will engage in a particular behavior increases because the behavior is followed by the removal of something the person dislikes. In **punishment**, the likelihood of a given behavior decreases because it is followed by something that the person dislikes. Figure 5.3 illustrates the distinctions drawn among positive reinforcement, extinction, negative reinforcement, and punishment. As shown in the figure, reinforcement theory can be used to promote or inhibit behaviors, as can employing both positive and negative rewards.

Managers in organizations sometimes contend that they cannot use reinforcement theory because they do not have enough resources to give positive reinforcements. For example, they cannot always raise salaries or award bonuses as they might like. Behavioral management programs that rely on positive reinforcement often need to go beyond money to truly be effective. Moreover, as Figure 5.3 makes clear, positive reinforcement is merely one of a

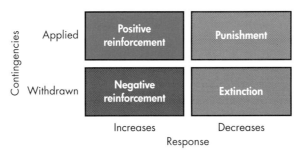

Figure 5.3 **Effects of Methods of Reinforcement on Behavioral Response**

number of possible ways to increase the frequency of a desired behavior. For instance, managers can employ negative reinforcement to increase a response. They can find something about the job that people do not like and, when employees engage in desired behaviors, remove it. A sales manager who wants to increase the quantity and quality of sales might find that salespeople hate to complete paperwork. Based on this knowledge, the manager might offer to shift the responsibility for completing paperwork to others if these employees increase their productivity. The sales force's enthusiasm for selling might increase noticeably as a result.

Although it is sometimes difficult to come up with ideas for positive rewards, most organizations can easily envision a wide variety of ways to punish people. For example, at Michelin North America, in order to reduce the company's health care costs, the tire maker charges workers $1,000 if their waistline exceeds 40 inches for men and 35 inches for women. Similarly, CVS asked staff members to report personal health metrics, including body fat, blood sugar, blood pressure, and cholesterol levels, to the company's insurer or pay a $600 penalty. Many employers feel this kind of punishment reflects a "tough love" culture that saves both lives and money, but many workers see this as an invasion of privacy.[35]

Indeed, managers often instinctively react with punitive measures in this manner when confronted with a behavior that they wish to eliminate. As Figure 5.3 shows, however, by itself punishment can only suppress undesired behaviors but not promote desired behaviors. In many instances, some other undesirable behavior may simply spring up in place of the old, bad behavior. For example, taking away access to the Internet may simply transform a "cyber-slacker" into a "slacker." Moreover, punishment tends to have short-lived effects, and it can produce side effects such as negative emotional reactions among those who are punished.[36] Finally, one important side effect of punishment is that it often leads to cover-ups of information that needs to get out in order to improve systems. For example, the Federal Aviation Authority (FAA) and the airline pilots unions had an agreement on voluntary information sharing that protected any pilot who made an error from prosecution if he or she reported the error within twenty-four hours of the incident. The purpose of this protection was to perfect the entire airline system and make sure no other pilot made the same mistake. However, owing to strained labor relations between the pilots unions and the airlines, the airlines were increasingly using such reports as a pretext to fire pilots, which led the union to threaten to suspend the program. Many observers felt the negative effects of punishing pilots for errors (cover-ups) were much worse than the gain that might come from firing one or two pilots who made a mistake.[37]

Despite these dangers, many organizations continue to mete out punishment because some behaviors are so damaging to the firm that stopping them is crucial. Moreover, failure to take action might imply acceptance of the offending behavior, and the organization could be held liable for the employee's actions. For example, if a cyberslacking employee downloads and transmits pornography over the company's Internet connection, this practice could be viewed as creating a hostile work environment—opening up the organization to sexual harassment charges. Thus, rather than eliminating punishment altogether, organizations need to strive to punish employees more effectively. A company can take several steps to move in this direction. First, effective discipline programs are *progressive*—that is, they move in incremental steps. A program might start with a simple verbal warning, followed by a written formal notice and then some actual disciplinary action that falls short of termination (such as suspension). Second, punishment should be *immediate* rather than delayed. This characteristic maximizes the perceived contingency between the offending behavior and the punishment, and it minimizes the perception that the offending behavior represents a pretext to punish the person for something else. Third, punishment should be *consistent*, so that the punishment is the same no matter who commits the offense. Fourth, punishment should be *impersonal*—that is, directed at the behavior rather than at the individual as a person. Finally, punishment should be *documented* to construct a "paper trail" of physical evidence that supports the contention that the punishment meted out was progressive, immediate, consistent, and impersonal.

In addition to implementing these five steps, in organizations that employ self-managing teams, it is important to have team members join not only in decisions about who gets rewarded, but also who gets punished.[38] Although group members are often more lenient than hierarchical supervisors, when they allowed to discuss the offense as a group and reach consensus, the group as a whole tends to show much less leniency.[39] Indeed, group-based decisions regarding discipline often resemble the decision that would be made by supervisors working alone. Recognition of this fact is important, because supervisors armed with the support of the work group they represent enjoy a much stronger position when it comes to doling out punishment.

Although the steps described previously might seem like simple and rational procedures that do not need to be spelled out, this perception is not always accurate. The types of offenses that call for punishment often generate strong emotional reactions from managers that short-circuit rationality. Indeed, these disciplinary procedures may seem excruciatingly slow to the offended manager, and they might frustrate his or her need for quick and satisfying retribution. Managers need to be assured that the process is slow but sure. In the end, if the problem employee must be fired, the procedures ensure that the company can prove the action was justified. Otherwise, the company might be sued for "wrongful discharge" and be unable to terminate the offending party.

Social Learning

Social learning theory, as proposed by Albert Bandura, encompasses a theory of observational learning that holds that most people learn behaviors by observing others and then *modeling* the behaviors perceived as being effective. Such observational learning is in marked contrast to the process of learning through direct reinforcement, and it better explains how people learn complex behavioral sequences.

For example, suppose a worker observes a colleague who, after giving bad news to their manager, is punished. Strict reinforcement theory would suggest that, when confronted with the same task, the observing worker will be neither more nor less prone to be the bearer of bad tidings because that person has not personally been reinforced. Social learning theory suggests otherwise. Although the worker may not have directly experienced the fate of a colleague, he or she will nonetheless learn by observation that this manager "shoots the messenger." The employee will probably conclude that the best response in such situations is to keep quiet. Even though the manager might not agree that problems should be covered up, his or her behavior may send precisely this message. Indeed, "fearing the boss more than the competition" has been cited as one of the top ten reasons companies fail.[40]

Besides focusing on learning by observation, social learning theory proposes that people can reinforce or punish their own behaviors; that is, they can engage in *self-reinforcement*. According to Bandura, a self-reinforcing event occurs when (1) tangible rewards are readily available for the taking, (2) people deny themselves free access to those rewards, and (3) they allow themselves to acquire the rewards only after achieving difficult self-set goals.[41] For example, many successful writers, once alone and seated at their workstations, refuse to take a break until they have written a certain number of pages. Obviously, the writers can leave any time they wish. They deny themselves the reward of a rest, however, until they have

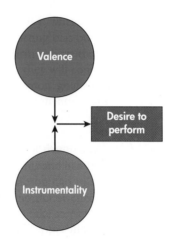

Figure 5.4 **Step 1: The Desire to Perform as a Function of Valence and Instrumentality**

accomplished their self-set goals.[42] Research indicates that this type of self-reinforcement can be used to help people stop smoking, overcome drug addiction, cure obesity, improve study habits, enhance scholastic achievement, and reduce absenteeism.[43]

Valence and instrumentality, the first two parts of our model of motivation, combine to influence the desire to perform (Figure 5.4). People will be motivated to perform at a high level as long as they perceive that receiving high-valence outcomes is contingent upon performing well. Our understanding of the process depicted in Figure 5.4 partly depends on need theories, which explain which outcomes individuals will perceive as having positive valences. In addition, reinforcement theories explain how people learn about contingencies, so they provide insight into the process that makes people want to perform.

Expectancy: Self-Efficacy Theory

Although actually part of Bandura's social learning theory, self-efficacy constitutes an important topic in its own right. **Self-efficacy** refers to the judgments that people make about their ability to execute courses of action required to deal with prospective situations.[44]

Self-Efficacy and Behavior

Individuals high in self-efficacy believe that they can master (or have mastered) some specific task. Self-efficacy determines how much effort people will expend and how long they will persist in the face of obstacles or stressful experiences.[45] When beset with difficulties, people who entertain serious doubts about their capabilities tend to slacken their efforts or give up altogether. In contrast, those who have a strong sense of efficacy tend to exert greater effort to master the challenges, and the positive effects for this characteristic seem to manifest themselves even if one controls for cognitive ability and various other personality traits.[46]

Indeed, if high levels of self-efficacy have a downside, it is the fact that these people will often confidently persist even in the face of consistent feedback indicating that they should change their tactics or lower their self-image.[47] This overconfidence effect also leads people who are high in self-efficacy to underestimate the amount of resources needed to accomplish some difficult goal.[48] However, for the most part, the positive aspects of high self-efficacy seem to outweigh these negative side effects.[49]

Sources of Self-Efficacy

Given that feelings of self-efficacy can greatly influence behavior, it is important to identify the sources of those feelings. Bandura identified four sources of self-efficacy beliefs. First, self-efficacy can reflect a person's *past accomplishments*. Past instances of successful behavior increase personal feelings of self-efficacy, especially when these successes seem attributable to unchanging factors such as personal ability or a manageable level of task difficulty.[50]

The link between self-efficacy theory and social learning theory is made clear in Bandura's second source of self-efficacy beliefs: *observation of others*. Merely watching someone else perform successfully on a task may increase an individual's sense of self-efficacy with respect to the same task. Note, however, that characteristics of the observer and model can influence the effects of observation on feelings of self-efficacy. For instance, the observer must judge the model to be both credible and similar to the observer (in terms of personal characteristics such as ability and experience) if the observation is to influence the individual's efficacy perceptions.

A third source of self-efficacy is *verbal persuasion*. Convincing people that they can master a behavior will, under some circumstances, increase their perceptions of self-efficacy. The characteristics of the source and the target of the communication, however, can affect how the verbal persuasion influences self-efficacy perceptions. Again, people who are perceived as credible and trustworthy are most able to influence others' self-efficacy perceptions in this manner.

Logical verification is another source of self-efficacy perceptions. With logical verification, people can generate perceptions of self-efficacy at a new task by perceiving a systematic relationship between the new task and an already mastered task. For example, if an experienced employee is apprehensive about his or her ability to learn some new software program, the manager should emphasize how many other changes in work procedures this person has successfully managed in the past, and then argue that there is no logical reason why learning this new program will be any different.

Self-efficacy theory is particularly useful for explaining how expectancies are formed and suggesting how they might be changed. Of course, as Figure 5.5 suggests, a person's beliefs will not necessarily translate into motivation unless the person truly desires to excel. Similarly, simply wanting to excel will not bring about high levels of effort unless the person has some belief that such performance is possible.

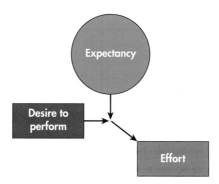

Figure 5.5 **Step 2: Level of Effort as a Function of Desire and Expectancy**

Accuracy of Role Perceptions: Goal-Setting Theory

Role perceptions are people's beliefs about what they are supposed to accomplish on the job and how they should achieve those goals. When these beliefs are accurate, people facing a task know what needs to be done, how long it should take, and who will have the responsibility to carry out the task at hand. Such role accuracy guarantees that the energy devoted to task accomplishment will be directed toward the right activities and outcomes. At the same time, it decreases the amount of energy wasted on unimportant goals and activities. Goal-setting theory can help us understand how to enhance the accuracy of role perceptions.

Important Goal Attributes

Employees are often told, "Do your best." Although this axiom is intended to guide job performance in everyday situations, research has consistently demonstrated that such vague instructions can actually undermine personal performance. In contrast, more than 100 studies support the assertion that performance is enhanced by goals that are both *specific* and *difficult*.[51] Indeed, setting specific goals has improved performance in a wide variety of jobs (Table 5.2). Specific and difficult goals appear to promote greater effort and to enhance persistence, especially when combined with timely feedback and incentives.[52] Specific and difficult goals are especially effective when incorporated into a continuous improvement cycle in which future goals consist of reasonable increments on past goals.[53] They also encourage people to develop effective task strategies and sharpen their mental focus on the task.[54] Their primary virtue, however, is that they direct attention to specific desired results, clarifying priorities and perceptions of both what is important and what level of performance is needed.[55]

However, along with these positive features of difficult goals, it has to be noted that if goals become overly difficult, they can also lead to unethical behaviors.[56] For example, Bernard Ebbers, CEO of WorldCom, stated, "Our goal is not to capture market share or be global, but instead our goal is to be the Number 1 stock on Wall Street." Of course, achieving the latter goal was going to be very difficult if one ignored the first two goals, and Ebbers tried to achieve this by acquiring more and more unrelated businesses.[57] This made it look as though the company was experiencing ever greater revenues in the short term, but without the knowledge of how to achieve market share or expand their markets this could not be sustained over the long term—resulting in one of the largest bankruptcies ever recorded in U.S. history.

Table 5.2 Jobholders Who Have Improved Performance in Goal-Setting Programs

Telephone servicepersons	Loggers
Baggage handlers	Marine recruits
Typists	Union bargaining representatives
Salespersons	Bank managers
Truck loaders	Assembly line workers
College students	Animal trappers
Sewing machine operators	Maintenance technicians
Engineering researchers	Dockworkers
Scientists	Die casters

Source: Adapted from E. A. Locke, "Toward a Theory of Task Motivation and Incentives," *Organizational Behavior and Human Performance* 3 (1968): 145–191.

As another example, Beverly Hall, former National Superintendent of the Year from Atlanta, was arrested in 2013 along with several others when it was learned that the impressive gains she and her colleagues achieved in terms of improving student test scores resulted from a systematic cheating program. Hall's indictment stated she "placed unreasonable goals on educators and protected and rewarded those who achieved targets by cheating." It also alleged that Hall fired principals who raised suspicions about unrealistic test score gains. As one of her co-conspirators noted at the trial, teachers "cheated out of pride, to earn bonuses, to enhance their careers or to keep their jobs," but in all cases "the cheating was in pursuit of unreasonably high goals."[58] Indeed, many have criticized efforts within the field of education to link teacher pay to goals for student achievement measured by standardized test scores and point to this case as indicative of the problems created by this practice.[59]

Although the motivational power of goals is often impressive, one has to be very careful of exactly how goals are expressed, how difficult they will be to achieve, and what exact behaviors they will motivate. This is especially true in team contexts where even if the pressure associated with a goal does not prompt unethical behaviors, it might still trigger suboptimal behaviors. For example, research suggests that groups working toward highly difficult goals often come to consensus too fast, are too conforming in their beliefs, rely too much on formal hierarchical authority when it comes to managing conflict, and focus too much on shared information instead of information unique to each team member. These suboptimal group processes result in so much process loss within the group, that they can often destroy the motivational value associated with the goal.[60]

Goal Commitment and Participation

The extent to which a person feels committed to a goal can also affect performance. As depicted in Figure 5.6, specific and difficult goals tend to lead to increased performance only

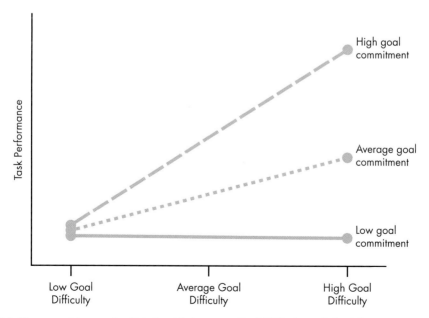

Figure 5.6 Conceptual Interactive Relationship between Goal Difficulty and Goal Commitment

Source: Adapted from H. J. Klein, M. J. Wesson, J. R. Hollenbeck, and B. J. Alge, "Goal Commitment and the Goal Setting Process: Conceptual Clarification and Empirical Synthesis," *Journal of Applied Psychology* 84 (1999): 885–896.

when there is high goal commitment.[61] The requirement that people be committed to goals means that goals must be set carefully because when they are too difficult they are typically met with less commitment. People may view a goal that is set too high as impossible and so reject it altogether.

Fortunately, research has examined several ways to increase commitment to difficult goals. One important factor is the degree to which the goals are public rather than private. In one study, students for whom difficult goals for GPA were made public (posted on bulletin boards) showed higher levels of commitment to those goals relative to students with private goals. Indeed, some organizations are using new technology to promote the positive influence of publically stated goals. For example, Accenture has developed a Facebook-like software program that allows employees to post weekly performance goals. Other employees can check in on the goals and comment on them in terms of whether they are realistic and challenging. Observers can also suggest tips and strategies for helping to accomplish the goals and comment on any behaviors they saw the person do that related to the goals (e.g., "Great job on that sales planning presentation").[62]

Research has also documented a significant positive relationship between need for achievement and goal commitment, suggesting that commitment reflects voluntary dedication to and responsibility for hitting some target.[63] Indeed, the positive relationship between need for achievement and goal commitment is especially strong when the goals are set by workers themselves as opposed to being assigned by an outside party.[64] If the employee is not allowed to set his or her own goals, the next best thing for instilling commitment is to at least let the employee participate in the goal-setting process. Participation promotes commitment, especially in certain cultures such as those characterized by low power distance. We will have more to say about cultural differences in Chapter 15, but for now we will simply note that, in high power distance, people do not expect to participate and hence often show more commitment to assigned goals than those they set for themselves.[65]

Although inspiring commitment to goals is critical, it is also important to recognize that in some cases, goals might need to be revised based upon early feedback. That is, if feedback suggests that a goal that we all thought was difficult in the beginning actually looks to be impossible at some point further down the road, this changes the goal from difficult to impossible, and its original motivational value is lost. At this point, reducing the goal level to some point where it is difficult but still possible might be in order. However, in the face of unforeseen events, simply ignoring the original goal altogether causes problems because this sets a precedent for rewarding people when they meet the goal but not punishing them when they fail to reach the goal. For example, CEO bonuses are traditionally attached to reaching certain financial goals, but in many cases, those executives wind up getting paid anyway even when they fail to meet the goal. For example, Nationwide Mutual Insurance felt it was unfair to blame the CEO for the profit ramifications caused by a rash of tornadoes that struck the United States in 2012 and paid out his bonus despite the fact that he missed all of his goals.[66] This type of "moving the goalposts" is very controversial, however, and is not in the spirit of "paying for performance."

Goals and Strategies

As shown in Table 5.2, goal setting can increase performance on a variety of jobs. Nevertheless, most early research on goal setting consisted of studies that focused attention on relatively simple tasks. More recent research has extended goal-setting theory into more complex task domains. In these situations, however, the links between goals, effort, and performance are less clear. A review of these studies indicates that, while goals have positive effects on all tasks, the magnitude of the effect is stronger for simple tasks than for complex tasks.[67] Figure 5.7 illustrates how the effect of goal difficulty on performance decreases as task complexity increases.

In fact, focusing on narrow goals related to performance might discourage people from experimenting with new strategies and developing new skills, which as we noted earlier, is the key to developing expertise on complex tasks. A performance drop-off often occurs when people switch from well-learned strategies to new and different strategies. For example, if a person has gained a great deal of proficiency with one word-processing program, that individual might express reluctance to upgrade to a new and improved program; while learning the new program, the employee fears that he or she will not work as quickly as was possible with the old program. Indeed, even if the worker is convinced that in the long run he or she will be able to work more rapidly with the new program, the employee might still be unwilling to pay the short-term performance costs of learning the new program.

The term **goal orientation** has been coined to distinguish between people who approach a task with the goal of learning how to improve versus people whose goals focus strictly on performing at a certain level.[68] Individuals with a performance orientation generally want to prove that they are proficient at task, and thus tend to focus on sticking with "tried and true" methods in well-known domains. In contrast, people with learning orientations like to try new and different tasks and often try doing any one task in a variety of different ways. In

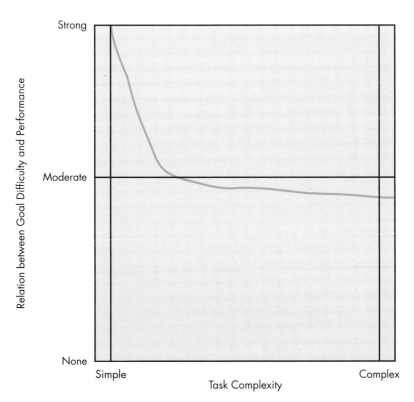

Figure 5.7 Goal Difficulty, Task Complexity, and Performance

Source: Adapted from R. E. Wood, E. A. Locke, and A. J. Mento, "Task Complexity as a Moderator of Goal Effects: A Meta-Analysis," *Journal of Applied Psychology* 72 (1987): 416–425.

general, people with a performance orientation tend to be risk averse, focused on efficiency and try to avoid errors, whereas those high in learning orientation tend to be risk seeking, focused on innovation and try to make discoveries. Although people with a strict performance orientation often perform best on simple, stable, short-term tasks, people with a learning orientation often perform better on complex, dynamic, long-term tasks.[69]

Goal orientation is typically treated as an individual difference variable, in the sense that some people are high on one versus the other, but it can also vary within individuals under certain circumstances. For example, time pressure tends to reduce the level of everyone's learning orientation.[70] In addition, although typically treated as a characteristic of a person, one can also describe groups in these terms and, in general, a group often starts to take on the orientation of its leaders.[71] Thus, the objectives of any managerially inspired goal-setting program must account for the need to perform at a high level as well as the need to create enough slack in the system to allow people to experiment with new and potentially improved task strategies. This seems to be particularly the case for workers who are high in intelligence and hence derive more from potential learning experiences.[72]

Although research on performance strategies has yielded findings that sometimes conflict with the results of other goal-setting studies, it is nevertheless helpful in delineating the specific, role-clarifying effects of goals. In simple tasks, where the *means* to perform a task are clear, specific and difficult goals lead to higher performance because they clarify the *ends* toward which task effort should be directed. In complex tasks, however, the means are not clear. Individuals performing such tasks do not know how to proceed in the best way, so merely clarifying the ends sought is unlikely to enhance performance.

Ability and Experience Revisited

Although this chapter has focused primarily on motivation, task performance is also contingent on the worker's abilities. Chapter 3 discussed abilities at great length, so here we will narrow the focus to how individual differences interact with goal setting and task strategies.

Nonmotivational Determinants of Performance

Two things are worth noting with respect to nonmotivational determinants of performance. First, people lacking the requisite abilities cannot perform a complex task even under the most favorable goal-related circumstances. Second, some subtle relationships exist among goal setting, attention, and cognitive capacity that affect task performance. As you will recall, one way that goal setting affects performance is by directing attention to the kinds of desired results. Kanfer and Ackerman have developed a model that recognizes that different people bring varying amounts of cognitive ability to bear on a task and that this restriction limits how much they can attend to at any one time.[73] Because it diverts attention from the task to the goal, goal setting may be particularly damaging to people who have low ability or who are still learning the task. Such people need to devote all their attention to the task, and goal setting is unlikely to enhance their performance.

Thus, although motivation is critical to performance, we should not forget the lessons learned in Chapter 3 about the importance of ability. For all but the simplest tasks, there is no substitute for ability. In this third step of building our overall motivation model, we can see how motivation and other factors combine to determine performance (Figure 5.8). Specifically, performance will be high when a person puts forth significant effort, directs this effort toward the right outcomes, and has the ability to execute the behaviors necessary for bringing about those outcomes.

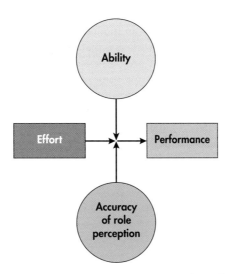

Figure 5.8 **Step 3: Performance as a Function of Effort, Accuracy of Role Perception, and Ability**

Experience and Cyclical Effects

The fourth and final step needed to complete our motivation and performance model deals with the links that make the model dynamic over time. Figure 5.1 includes three arrows that head back left. First, a feedback loop goes from performance to valence. Recall that valence, as a construct, deals with *anticipated* satisfaction, not realized satisfaction. The feedback loop allows for the possibility that an outcome received for performing some task might not bring much real satisfaction to the person when it is actually received. Valence for such an outcome would then decrease relative to its value at an earlier time.

Another link in Figure 5.1 goes from performance to instrumentalities. This loop implies that the outcomes received for performing at some level at one time will affect the person's perceived instrumentalities at later times. If no reward follows high performance, extinction of the performance response could take place, lowering the perceived instrumentality of high performance.

Finally, an arrow goes from performance to expectancy in Figure 5.1. This loop affirms that expectancies and self-efficacy are based at least partially on prior performance. All else being equal, successful performance strengthens self-efficacy and leads to high expectancies. Failing at a task, however, generally leads to lower levels of self-efficacy. Clearly, feedback is central to the motivational process for a number of different reasons.

These three dynamic links in our motivation model suggest that motivation can change over time. For example, Figure 5.1 suggests that even highly motivated people might lose motivation for any of three reasons. First, individuals who start out with high expectancies might discover during job performance that they cannot perform nearly as well as they anticipated. Decreased self-efficacy would lead to reduced expectancy perceptions, and lower motivation would probably result. Second, individuals might discover that performing well on a job does not lead to the desirable outcomes they expected. Motivation could then diminish as projected instrumentalities fail to materialize. Third, experience with the rewards received from performing a job might lead someone to discover faults with the initial valences. That is, the rewards expected to yield satisfaction might not do so.

High-Performance Work Systems

As we noted at the outset of this chapter, in theoretical terms, one of the least controversial statements one can make about paying workers is that it is important to tie pay to job performance. In reality, the implementation of programs to bring about such a relationship often proves quite difficult. To get a feeling for some of the dilemmas involved, consider the following issues that arise when pay-for-performance programs are contemplated.

First, should pay increases be based on outcomes that occur at the individual level (that is, performance of individual workers), the group level (performance of different teams), or the organizational level (performance of the entire business)? If the individual level is used as the standard, the organization might create competition among co-workers and destroy team morale. When pay-for-performance occurs at the group and organizational levels, individuals might find it difficult to see how their own performance relates to group or organizational performance and outcomes.[74] According to expectancy theory terms, these kinds of conditions lower instrumentality.

Second, if the firm decides to pay at the individual level, should it establish the rules for payment in advance (for example, telling workers that they will receive $5 per widget produced)? This plan might sound like a good idea, but prevents the company from accurately forecasting its labor costs; that is, the firm cannot anticipate exactly how many widgets will be produced and therefore how much they are going to have to pay employees. Moreover, because the price and quantity of the product sold or service rendered cannot be known in advance, the organization might not be able to anticipate its revenues. On the other hand, if the firm waits until the end of the year to see how much money is available for merit pay, people will not know in advance exactly how their performance relates to their pay. Moreover, if the organization engages in pay secrecy to protect people's privacy, how can anyone actually know whether the merit system is fair?[75]

Third, how large should incentives be, and how much variability should exist within and between job categories? Research suggests that incentives that are less than 5 percent of the regular salary have little motivational value; thus the company might want to aim for larger incentives.[76] If the overall amount of compensation is fixed, however, larger incentives imply that fewer rewards will be handed out, which can lead to wide variability of pay within the same job category. Such systems tend to engender resentment among workers and hinder collaboration and teamwork.[77]

Fourth, if the company decides to keep incentives at an organizational level, should it base the rewards on cost savings and distribute them yearly, or base them on profits and distribute them on a deferred basis? The calculations and accounting procedures required by cost-savings plans are enormous and complex, but rewards are distributed quickly. Profit-sharing plans are much easier to handle from an accounting perspective but, because the rewards are distributed on a deferred basis, they are less motivating than cost-savings plans.

These questions highlight the complexity inherent in putting into practice the seemingly simple theoretical concept of "paying for performance." Covering all the complexities of these issues is well beyond the scope of this chapter. We will examine, however, the distinguishing features of four kinds of pay-for-performance programs: merit-based plans, incentive plans, cost-savings plans, and profit-sharing plans.

Merit-Pay and Incentive Systems

Individual pay-for-performance plans base financial compensation, at least in part, on the accomplishments of individual workers. Two types of individual programs exist: those based on merit and those based on incentives. Merit-based pay plans are by far the easier to administer and control. These programs assess performance at the end of the fiscal year via subjective ratings of employees made by supervisors. Also at the end of the year, a fixed sum of money is allocated to wage increases. This sum is distributed to individuals in amounts proportional to their performance ratings.

In designing merit-based programs, three major considerations arise. First, what will the average performer receive? Many firms try to ensure that the pay of average performers at least keeps up with inflation. As a result, the midpoint of the rating scale is often tied to the consumer price index (CPI). Typically, this implies an average pay raise in the 2 to 4 percent range, although this will vary depending upon the state of the economy and firm performance.[78]

Second, what will a poor performer receive? Traditionally, companies rarely *lower* an employee's wages; however, raises that fail to cover the CPI are actually wage decreases in terms of buying power. Is it in the firm's best interests to allow the wage increases of poor performers to slip below the inflation level? If so, how much damage does the organization wish to inflict on low performers? How easily replaced are these people if they respond by quitting?

Third, how much will high performers receive? Will high performers at the top of a pay grade receive the same raise as those at the bottom of a higher wage grade? Paying for performance could cause top performers in jobs lower in the hierarchy to surpass (through yearly raises) low performers in upper-level jobs over time. Indeed, to prevent this type of compression, many companies have adopted the practice of *broad banding*. Broad banding simply means reducing the number of hierarchical distinctions between jobs. For example, General Electric has tried to move away from length of service and rank as pay determinants. To do so, it cut the levels of salary grades from twenty-nine to six. As a result, people now have more opportunities to get a raise without a promotion.[79]

The answers to these three questions establish the degree of variability in the reward system and if variability is too low (e.g., the raise is 4 percent for low performers and 6 percent for high performers) this threatens the motivational value of the reward. Why should one put forth heroic efforts for just a 2 percent difference? On the other hand, if the variability is too high (e.g., the raise is 0 percent for low performers and 10 percent for high performers) this could threaten collaboration and teamwork. Why should someone help out the person who got the 10 percent since this came at the cost of others in the unit? If there is a great deal of interdependence inherent in the work, one member of the group might try to sabotage the efforts of another group member to restrict their ability to get higher raises than everyone else. Even short of direct sabotage, a worker who learns some valuable technique that provides a personal competitive advantage over other team members might be reluctant to share this information with them, even though it is in the larger interest of the team and organization to share this valuable information. In terms of managing this dilemma, research suggests that, on average, companies tend to keep the spread between the best and worst performer at around 4 percent.[80]

In contexts where teamwork is important, in addition to supervisors (who have traditionally given the performance ratings that determine merit pay), the process might also include peer ratings. In addition, in the services sector of the economy, high-performance work systems have eliminated the "middle man" (the supervisor). In such companies, merit-pay raises are tied directly to customer service ratings obtained from surveys. For example, at the MGM Grand Hotel in Las Vegas, customer ratings are weighted heavily when making annual merit-pay decisions for workers who engage in a great deal of direct service.[81] In fact, even the U.S. Federal Government has experimented with programs that link a hospital's Medicare and Medicaid reimbursement rates on patient satisfaction surveys.[82]

Some of the problems with merit systems can be reduced if one adopts incentive systems. Incentive systems differ from merit-based systems in three ways. First, incentive programs stipulate the rules by which payment will be made in advance, so that the worker can calculate exactly how much money will be earned if a certain level of performance is achieved. Second, rewards in an incentive program are based on objective measures of performance. Third, incentive systems are usually noncompetitive within the unit, such that all members could receive the incentive if they meet their individual objectives, and one team member's gain does not necessarily imply another team member's loss.

Simple *piecework plans* establish a standard of productivity per time interval, and any productivity beyond that standard is rewarded with a set amount per unit. This type of plan is easy for the worker to understand, and it creates a clear performance to outcome expectancy. However, very few jobs can be totally captured with just one or two objective indicators, and thus most incentive systems often try to employ multiple indicators. For example, WD-40 is a major global manufacturer of lubrication products with operations in the United States, Canada, Latin America, Asia, and Europe. At one time, all of the incentives for the senior executive team were based on global revenues. However, many of the senior executives felt that their lack of ability to control conditions in other countries reduced the motivational value of the incentives. Thus, the company developed a more complicated incentive system where just 20 percent was based on global revenues, and the other 80 percent on local indices. That is, the other 80 percent of the incentive was based on results related to meeting sales targets (50 percent) and meeting profit goals (30 percent) set separately for each country.[83]

Although the incentive formula at WD-40 is still a relatively simple formula to understand, it becomes clear that over time, with highly involved tasks, incentives can become increasingly complex. At some point, if the system gets too complicated, people are unable to figure out what they are going to get paid, and then the system is no longer motivational. For example, in addition to adding more dimensions, incentive systems can also become further complicated by the need to adjust standards over time. If the standard is initially set too low, labor costs can get out of hand. If it is set too high, workers will reject it when they discover that the standard cannot be reached, even with harder work. If the standard is flexible, gradual increases in the standard might be viewed as a manipulative management trick, whereas decreases will cause some workers to try to manipulate the system by lowering output. Furthermore, without built-in safeguards, these programs can lead workers to achieve quantity at the price of quality or ethical violations.[84]

Although incentive systems do not necessarily have to be competitive, in order to control costs, organizations sometimes limit the number of people who can win an incentive. For example, the organization might not be able to provide a Hawaiian vacation to every salesperson, but they might make one available to the highest performer. The minute the incentive becomes competitive like this, it becomes like a merit system in terms of threatening teamwork. For example, Lantech, a small manufacturer of packaging material in Louisville, Kentucky, implemented a bonus-type incentive system built around cost containment, where the manager who cut costs the most won a bonus. The competition within the organization to earn the bonus grew heated, and each person tried to assign costs to others. At one point, the competition became so petty that a manager tried to pass off the cost of his toilet paper to a different division. Pat Lancaster, CEO at Lantech, noted, "I was spending 95 percent of my time on conflict resolution instead of on how to serve our customers." To eliminate these types of problems, Lantech, like many other organizations, eventually scuttled its individual-based plan, replacing it with an organization-level plan.[85]

Profit-Sharing and Cost-Savings Plans

Whereas merit-based plans and incentive plans tie pay to performance at the individual level, profit-sharing and cost-savings plans tie pay to performance at a broader level. Profit-sharing plans distribute organizational profits to employees, and according to recent estimates,

20 percent of U.S. firms have such plans in place. Cash distribution plans provide full payment soon after profits have been determined (annually or quarterly). To reap tax advantages, most plans—indeed, as many as 80 percent—provide deferred payments. In these plans, current profits accumulate in employee accounts, and a cash payment is made only when a worker becomes disabled, leaves the organization, retires, or dies. Of course, not all the company's profits are redistributed. Research suggests that the share of profits distributed may range from a low of 14 percent to a high of 33 percent.[86]

One problem with profit-sharing plans is that employees often find it difficult to see the connection between their activities and their company's profits. This issue is especially apparent when something uncontrollable, such as an overall downturn in the economy, totally eliminates any hope of the organization making a profit in the short term. Similarly, with respect to profit-sharing plans, when multiple businesses are involved, people may struggle to see the link between their efforts and corporate profits. For these reasons, the day-to-day motivational value of these kinds of programs may be questionable. Would a worker who might otherwise quit work an hour early really stop for fear of how it might affect the company's profits?[87] To eliminate this problem, some organizations have adopted cost-savings plans that pay workers bonuses out of the money the company has saved through increased efficiency of its operations. Workers often have more control over the costs of doing business than the company's stock price or profits, so it is easier for them to see the connection between their own work and cost reductions.[88]

We have sampled only a few of the many pay-for-performance programs currently in use, but as you can see, some of these programs are highly complex. You should, however, have some feel for the kinds of issues raised by such programs. Figure 5.9 provides guidance on

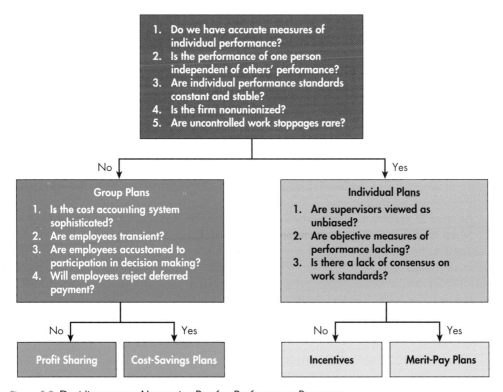

Figure 5.9 Deciding among Alternative Pay-for-Performance Programs

choosing a suitable plan. It explains under what circumstances an individual or a group plan is appropriate and in what situations specific individual or group plans are most effective.

Summary

Our model of motivation and performance is based on *expectancy theory* and incorporates concepts from four other theories of motivation: *need theory, learning theory, self-efficacy theory,* and *goal-setting theory.* The model focuses on explaining three outcomes. The first, desire to perform, is a function of *valences* and *instrumentalities.* A person's desire to perform well will be high when valence rewards are associated with high performance. The second outcome, effort, is a function of desire to perform and *expectancy.* Effort will be forthcoming only when individuals want to perform well and when they believe they can do so. The third outcome, performance, is a function of effort, *accurate role perceptions,* and *ability.* Performance will be high only when individuals with the requisite abilities and knowledge of desired goals and strategies put forth their best effort. The dynamic nature of the motivation process is revealed in the way present levels of performance affect future levels of valence, instrumentality, and expectancy. The complexity of the motivational process can be seen in high-performance work systems and the many issues that must be considered when one attempts to "pay for performance."

Review Questions

1. Recent research suggests that individual needs may be determined more by genetic factors than previously thought. Take each of the need theories described in this chapter and discuss whether this new evidence supports, contradicts, or is irrelevant to that theory.
2. Specific, difficult goals have been suggested to enhance performance, but researchers have also shown that performance will be high only when expectancies are high. You might think that, as goals become increasingly difficult, expectations for accomplishing them would decrease. Can you resolve this apparent contradiction between goal-setting theory and expectancy theory?
3. Analyst Daniel Shore once called motivation researchers "servants of power" because the results of their research were often used to manipulate lower-level workers. Is trying to motivate people necessarily exploitative? Under what conditions might providing external motivation be exploitative? Which theories of motivation do you feel are exploitative? Which ones are not?
4. Imagine two pharmaceutical companies that employ the same job categories but different business strategies. One tries to increase its market share through innovation (developing new and better drugs). The other sticks to established products and tries to increase its market share by lowering costs. Why might the two firms wind up with dramatically different pay-for-performance programs? What types of programs might be most and least suitable to each organization?

Notes

1   L. Scism and J. Hilsenrath, "Workers Stuck in Disability Stunt Economic Recovery," *Wall Street Journal*, April 7, 2013, http://online.wsj.com/article/SB10001424127887323511804578298151374531578.html.

2 M. Saltsman, "Making Work Not Pay," *Wall Street Journal*, April 6, 2013, http://online.wsj.com/article/SB10001424127887323646604578404542118620894.html.

3 L. W. Porter and E. E. Lawler, *Managerial Attitudes and Performance* (Homewood, IL: Irwin, 1968), 107–139.

4 E. Maltby and S. E. Needleman, "Some Small Businesses Opt for the Health Care Penalty," *Wall Street Journal*, April 7, 2013, http://online.wsj.com/article/SB10001424127887323916304578401413507987532.html.

5 J. Marquez, "Wellness: Bad Side Effects," *Workforce Management*, May 5, 2008, 1–3.

6 Ibid.

7 V. H. Vroom, *Work and Motivation* (New York: Wiley, 1964).

8 B. Casselman, "Time Not on the Side of the Jobless," *Wall Street Journal*, March 26, 2012, http://online.wsj.com/article/SB10001424052702303812904577299982932070176.html.

9 B. Casselman, "Unemployment Scars Likely to Last for Years," *Wall Street Journal*, January 9, 2012, http://online.wsj.com/article/SB10001424052970203513604577144483060678656.html.

10 G. F. Dreher and T. H. Cox, "Labor Market Mobility and Cash Compensation: The Moderating Effects of Race and Gender," *Academy of Management Journal* 43 (2000): 890–900.

11 M. Conlin, "Now It Is Getting Personal," *Business Week*, December 18, 2002, 90–92.

12 V. K. G. Lim and Q. S. Sng, "Does Parental Job Insecurity Matter? Money, Anxiety, Money Motives, and Work Motivation," *Journal of Applied Psychology* 91 (2006): 1078–1097.

13 A. M. Grant, "Relational Job Design and the Motivation to Make a Prosocial Difference," *Academy of Management Review* 32 (2007): 393–417.

14 A. M. Grant, "Does Intrinsic Motivation Fuel the Prosocial Fire? Motivational Synergy in Predicting Persistence, Performance, and Productivity," *Journal of Applied Psychology* 93 (2007): 48–58.

15 A. M. Grant, "The Significance of Task Significance," *Journal of Applied Psychology* 93 (2007): 108–124.

16 A. M. Grant, E. M. Campbell, G. Chen, K. Cottone, D. Lapedia, and K. Lee, "Impact and Art of Motivation Maintenance: The Effects of Contact with Beneficiaries on Persistence Behavior," *Organizational Behavior and Human Decision Processes* 103 (2007): 53–67.

17 S. Thau, K. Aquino, and P. M. Poortvliet, "Self-Defeating Behaviors in Organizations: The Relationship between Thwarted Belonging Behaviors and Interpersonal Work Behaviors," *Journal of Applied Psychology* 92 (2007): 840–847.

18 S. E. DeVoe and J. Pfeffer, "Hourly Payment and Volunteering: The Effect of Organizational Practices on Decisions about Time Use," *Academy of Management Journal* 50 (2007): 783–798.

19 A. H. Maslow, "Theory of Human Motivation," *Psychological Reports* 50 (1943): 370–396.

20 M. A. Wahba and L. G. Bridwell, "Maslow Reconsidered: A Review of Research on the Need Hierarchy," *Organizational Behavior and Human Performance* 15 (1976): 121–140.

21 H. A. Murray, *Explorations in Personality* (New York: Oxford University Press, 1938).

22 M. R. Barrick, M. K. Mount, and N. Li, "The Theory of Purposeful Work Behavior: The Role of Personality, Higher-order Goals, and Job Characteristics," *Academy of Management Review* 38 (2010): 132–153.

23 D. C. McClelland, *The Achieving Society* (Princeton, NJ: Van Nostrand Press, 1963).

24 M. Gimein, "Smart Is Not Enough," *Fortune*, January 8, 2001, 124–136.

25 S. Armour, "Higher Pay May Be Layoff Target," *USA Today Online*, June 23, 2003, 1–2.

26 S. E. Markham, K. D. Scott, and G. H. McKee, "Recognizing Good Attendance: A Longitudinal, Quasi-Experimental Field Study," *Personnel Psychology* 55 (2002): 639–660.

27 M. Milian, "A Silent Signal Rewards Customers," *Bloomberg Businessweek*, September 3, 2012, 38.

28 J. S. Lublin, "Can a New Culture Fix Troubled Companies?" *Wall Street Journal*, March 12, 2013, http://online.wsj.com/article/SB10001424127887324096404578356351608725098.html.

29 K. Tyler, "Evaluating Values," *HR Magazine*, April 2011, 57–62.

30 G. Chazan and D. Mattioli, "BP Links Pay to Safety in the Fourth Quarter," *Wall Street Journal*, October 19, 2010, http://online.wsj.com/article/SB10001424052702303496104575560422023190664.html.

31 C. M Barnes, J. Reb, and D. Ang, "More than Just the Mean: Moving to a Dynamic View of Performance-Based Compensation," *Journal of Applied Psychology* 97 (2012): 711–718.

32 G. Colvin, "What It Takes to Be Great," *BusinessWeek*, October 30, 2006, 88–96.

33 K. Grind, *The Lost Bank: The Story of Washington Mutual, the Biggest Bank Failure in American History* (New York: Simon & Schuster, 2012).

34 B. Keoun, "Goldman Sachs May Pay Bonuses Tied to Profit Revenue," *Bloomberg Businessweek*, January 3, 2011, 31–32.

35 L. Kwoh, "When Your Boss Makes You Pay for Being Fat," *Wall Street Journal*, April 5, 2013, http://online.wsj.com/article/SB10001424127887324600704578402784123334550.html.

36 R. L. Solomon, "Punishment," *American Psychologist* 19 (1962): 239–253.

37 A. Pasztor, "U.S. Airways Pilots Halt Voluntary Data-Sharing Program," *Wall Street Journal*, December 15, 2008, C1.

38 H. I. Larkin, L. Pierce, and G. Francesca, "The Psychological Cost of Pay-for-Performance: Implications for the Strategic Compensation of Employees," *Strategic Management Journal* 33 (2012): 1194–1214.

39 R. C. Liden, S. J. Wayne, T. A. Judge, R. S. Sparrowe, M. L. Kraimer, and T. M. Franz, "Management of Poor Performance: A Comparison of Manager, Group Member, and Group Disciplinary Decisions," *Journal of Applied Psychology* 84 (1999): 835–850.

40 R. Charan and J. Useem, "Why Companies Fail," *Fortune*, May 27, 2002, 50–62.

41 A. Bandura, "Self-Reinforcement: Theoretical and Methodological Considerations," *Behaviorism* 4 (1976): 135–155.

42 I. Wallace, "Self-Control Techniques of Famous Novelists," *Journal of Applied Behavioral Analysis* 10 (1977): 515–525.

43 F. H. Kanfer and J. S. Phillips, *Learning Foundations of Behavior Therapy* (New York: John Wiley, 1970).

44 A. Bandura, "Self-Efficacy Mechanism in Human Behavior," *American Psychologist* 37 (1982): 122–147.

45 J. Schaubroeck, S. K. Lam, and J. L. Xie, "Collective Efficacy versus Self-Efficacy in Coping Responses to Stressors and Control: A Cross-Cultural Study," *Journal of Applied Psychology* 85 (2000): 512–525.

46 T. A. Judge, C. L. Jackson, J. C. Shaw, B. A. Scott, and B. L. Rich, "Self-Efficacy and Work Related Performance: The Integral Role of Individual Differences," *Journal of Applied Psychology* 92 (2007): 107–127.

47 J. W. Beck and A. M. Schmidt, "Taken Out of Context? Cross-level Effects of Between-person Self-efficacy and Difficulty on the Within-person Relationship of Self-efficacy with Resource Allocation and Performance," *Organizational Behavior and Human Decision Processes* 119 (2012): 195–208.

48 J. B. Vancouver, K. M. More, and R. J. Yoder, "Self-Efficacy and Resource Allocation: Support for a Nonmonotonic, Discontinuous Model," *Journal of Applied Psychology* 93 (2008): 35–47.

49 A. D. Stajkovic, "Development of a Core Confidence Higher Order Construct," *Journal of Applied Psychology* 91 (2006): 1208–1224.

50 A. P. Tolli and A. M. Schmidt, "The Role of Feedback, Causal Attributions, and Self-Efficacy in Goal Revision," *Journal of Applied Psychology* 93 (2008): 692–701.

51 E. A. Locke, "Toward a Theory of Task Motivation and Incentives," *Organizational Behavior and Human Performance* 3 (1968): 145–191.

52 J. E. Sawyer, W. R. Latham, R. D. Pritchard, and W. R. Bennett, "Analysis of Work Group Productivity in an Applied Setting," *Personnel Psychology* 52 (1999): 927–967.

53 J. M. Phillips, J. R. Hollenbeck, and D. R. Ilgen, "Prevalence and Prediction of Positive Discrepancy Creation: Examining a Discrepancy between Two Self-Regulation Theories," *Journal of Applied Psychology* 81 (1996): 498–511.

54 F. K. Lee, K. M. Sheldon, and D. B. Turban, "Personality and Goal Striving: The Influence of Achievement Goal Patterns, Goal Level, and Mental Focus on Performance and Enjoyment," *Journal of Applied Psychology* 88 (2003): 256–263.

55 A. M. Schmidt and R. P. DeShon, "What to Do? The Effects of Discrepancies, Incentives, and Time on Dynamic Goal Prioritization," *Journal of Applied Psychology* 92 (2007): 928–941.

56 M. E. Schwietzer, L. Ordonez, and B. Douma, "Goal Setting as a Motivator of Unethical Behavior," *Academy of Management Journal* 47 (2004): 422–432.

57 D. Henry and L. Lavelle, "Exploring Options," *BusinessWeek*, February 3, 2003, 78–79.

58 P. Howard, "Former Atlanta Schools Superintendent Reports to Jail in Cheating Scandal," *CNN*, April 3, 2013, http://www.cnn.com/2013/04/02/justice/georgia-cheating-scandal.

59 S. Banchero and K. Maher, "Strike Puts Spotlight on Teacher Evaluation, Pay," *Wall Street Journal*, September 10, 2012, http://online.wsj.com/article/SB10000872396390443921504577643652663814724.html.

60 H. K. Gardner, "Performance Pressure as a Double-edged Sword: Enhancing Team Motivation but Undermining the Use of Team Knowledge," *Administrative Science Quarterly*, 57 (2012): 1–46.

61 H. J. Klein, M. J. Wesson, J. R. Hollenbeck, and B. J. Alge, "Goal Commitment and the Goal Setting Process: Conceptual Clarification and Empirical Synthesis," *Journal of Applied Psychology* 84 (1999): 885–896.

62 J. McGregor, "Performance Review Takes a Page from Facebook," *BusinessWeek*, March 12, 2009, 28–29.

63 H. J. Klein, J. C. Molloy, and C. T. Brinsfield, "Reconceptualizing Workplace Commitment to Redress a Stretched Construct: Revisiting Assumptions and Removing Confounds," *Academy of Management Review* 37 (2012): 130–151.

64 J. R. Hollenbeck, C. R. Williams, and H. J. Klein, "An Empirical Examination of Antecedents of Commitment to Difficult Goals," *Journal of Applied Psychology* 74 (1989): 18–25.

65 C. Sue-Chan and M. Ong, "Goal Assignment and Performance: Assessing the Mediating Roles of Goal Commitment, Self-Efficacy and the Moderating Role of Power Distance," *Organizational Behavior and Human Decision Processes* 89 (2002): 1140–1161.

66 Z. R. Mider and J. Green, "Heads or Tails, Some CEOs Win the Pay Game," *Bloomberg Businessweek*, October 8, 2012, 23–24.

67 R. E. Wood, E. A. Locke, and A. J. Mento, "Task Complexity as a Moderator of Goal Effects: A Meta-Analysis," *Journal of Applied Psychology* 72 (1987): 416–425.

68 S. C. Payne, S. S. Youngblood, and J. M. Beaubien, "A Meta-Analytic Examination of the Goal Orientation Nomological Net," *Journal of Applied Psychology* 92 (2007): 128–150.

69 D. Steele-Johnson, R. S. Beauregard, P. B. Hoover, and A. M. Schmidt, "Goal Orientation and Task Demand Effects on Motivation, Affect, and Performance," *Journal of Applied Psychology* 85 (2000): 724–738.

70 J. W. Beck and A. M. Schmidt, "State-level Goal Orientations as Mediators of the Relationship Between Time Pressure and Performance: A Longitudinal Study," *Journal of Applied Psychology* 98 (2013): 354–363.

71 L. Dragoni and M. Kuenzi, "Better Understanding Work Unit Goal Orientation: Its Emergence and Impact under Different Types of Work Unit Structure," *Journal of Applied Psychology* 97 (2012): 1032–1048.

72 B. S. Bell and S. W. J. Kozlowski, "Goal Orientation and Ability: Interactive Effects on Self-Efficacy, Performance, and Knowledge," *Journal of Applied Psychology* 87 (2002): 497–505.

73 R. Kanfer and P. L. Ackerman, "Motivation and Cognitive Abilities: An Integrative/Aptitude-Treatment Interaction Approach to Skill Acquisition," *Journal of Applied Psychology* 74 (1989): 657–690.

74 L. R. Gomez-Mejia, T. M. Welbourne, and R. M. Wiseman, "The Role of Risk Sharing and Risk Taking under Gainsharing," *Academy of Management Review* 25 (2000): 492–507.

75 B. Hindo, "Mind if I See Your Paycheck?" *Business Week*, June 18, 2007, 40–42.

76 T. R. Zenger and C. R. Marshall, "Determinants of Incentive Intensity in Group-Based Rewards," *Academy of Management Journal* 43 (2000): 149–163.

77 F. Hansen, "Merit-Payoff?" *Workforce Management*, November 3, 2008, 33–39.

78 S. Needleman, "Pay Raises Seen Taking a Hit," *Wall Street Journal*, December 16, 2008, B1.

79 D. Brady, "Secrets of an HR Superstar," *Business Week*, April 9, 2007, 66–68.

80 D. Mattioli, "Raises Creep Back on to Salary Scene," *Wall Street Journal*, May 3, 2010, http://online.wsj.com/article/SB40001424052748704093204575216550390510826.html.

81 C. Huff, "Motivating the World," *Workforce Management*, September 24, 2007, 25–31.

82 S. Pettypiece and S. Armour, "Secret Shoppers in the ER," *Bloomberg Businessweek*, February 4, 2013, 29–30.

83 E. Krell, "All for Incentives, Incentives for All," *HR Magazine*, January 2011, 35–38.

84 C. W. Hamner, "How to Ruin Motivation with Pay," *Compensation Review* 21 (1975): 88–98.
85 P. Nulty, "Incentive Pay Can Be Crippling," *Fortune*, November 13, 1995, 235.
86 S. Hays, "Pros and Cons of Pay for Performance," *Workforce*, February 1999, 69–72.
87 C. Mahoney, "Share the Wealth—and the Headache: Stock Options Are Not All Glory," *Workforce*, June 2000, 119–122.
88 P. K. Zingheim and J. R. Schuster, "Value Is the Goal," *Workforce*, February 2000, 56–61.

Chapter 6

Satisfaction and Stress

Randy Rhodes, the president of Harvest Select, a food processing company in Uniontown, Alabama, thought he was just having a nightmare. He simply could not believe it when he showed up at his plant one day only to find that all of his 160 workers were missing. He had 850,000 pounds of catfish that had to be skinned, gutted, and trimmed for sale, and it would not be a pretty sight (or smell) if he were unable to get that work done. This was not just a bad dream and this experience was not limited to his company. In plants, fields, hotels, and restaurants across the state of Alabama, chickens went unprocessed, tomatoes unpicked, hotel beds unmade, and dishes unwashed as thousands of workers vanished, almost overnight.

The cause of this mass worker exodus was the passage of Alabama House Bill 56, which required police to question people suspected of being in the United States illegally and to forbid people from knowingly hiring illegal immigrants, among other similar provisions. The goal of this legislation was to free up jobs that Governor Robert Bentley said illegal immigrants "had stolen from recession-battered Americans." The unemployment rate in Perry County, where Harvest Select was located, was almost 20 percent. However, few unemployed Alabamians had any interest in the many jobs allegedly made available by the bill, and the new law failed to put even a tiny dent in the unemployment rate while severely hampering operations in a number of Alabama industries. Indeed, the results in Alabama reflected what has been found in large-scale research studies from other regions of the country, where the presence of immigrant labor has had almost no effect on employment levels and wages.[1] For the most part, few Americans compete for the jobs that are taken by immigrant workers due to the undesirable nature of those jobs.

It is not hard to see why many people would be dissatisfied with the jobs at Harvest Select. Employees working at the plant perform manually difficult work slicing up smelly fish for ten hours a day in a cold, wet room for $7.25 an hour with virtually no benefits. Similarly, harvesting tomatoes is another job that attracted very few Alabamians—even those who were unemployed—after the immigrant labor disappeared. Workers head out into the fields at 7 a.m. for a twelve-hour shift that requires them to bend over and gently pry tomatoes out of tangled vines, in temperatures that can exceed 100 °F, for about $60 per day. After a large portion of his tomato crop wound up rotting in his fields, Joe Bearden, who owns a thirty-acre field in Perry County spoke for many employers when he complained that "the governor stepped in and started this bill because he wanted to put people back to work—they're not coming! I've been farming twenty-five years and I can count on one hand the number of Americans that will do this work."

Of course, the comeback to this argument is why anyone should be able to create such terribly dissatisfying jobs in the first place and be entitled to an endless supply of cheap labor.

For example, Alabama's Director of Industrial Relations, Tom Surtees, struck back at some of the local employers. "Don't tell me an Alabamian can't work out in the field picking produce because it's hot," he claimed. "Go into a steel mill, Go into a foundry. Go into numerous other occupations and tell them Alabamians won't do work where it's hot or requires manual labor. The difference being, jobs in Alabama's foundries and steel mills pay better and offer better benefits." Indeed, the stakes of this battle are high in the sense that this is a fight over the basic business model that has been in these industries for decades. As Surtee notes, "Whether an employer in agriculture used migrant workers or whether it's another industry that used illegal immigrants, they had a business model and that business model is going to have to change."[2]

Rhodes and other state employers claim they are stuck with the business model that they have now due to foreign competitors that pay their workers even lower wages. "I'm sorry, but I can't pay those kids $13.00 an hour and then sell my product at a competitive price—it is just not realistic," Rhodes counters. Although it is difficult to predict how this conflict will all play out in the future, it is interesting to note that one of the major adaptations that employers made in the short term was to bring in refugee labor from war-torn countries of Africa and weather-devastated Haiti. Ironically, people admitted to the country as refugees are legally allowed to work the day they arrive and, hence, are not affected by House Bill 56. Scott Beason, a Republican state senator who sponsored the law, is very unhappy with this most recent development, but his hands are tied. He states that "[W]e would prefer that the companies hire native Alabamians," but it is unclear that this is ever going to happen.[3]

Most organizations are not in the "job satisfaction business." For that reason, managers often find it difficult to see the importance of understanding the sources of job dissatisfaction that affect how people react to various jobs. For example, as we see in the Alabama case, the nature of some jobs is so dissatisfying that it is impossible to attract anyone willing to work in those occupations—even people who are unemployed. If an employer cannot line up enough workers to do certain jobs as they are designed, then changes might have to be made or the organization could go out of business. In the cases described above, employers had to go to the extreme of bringing in refugees from another country to do certain jobs, but the long-term sustainability of that solution is questionable.

This is not just the case with low-skill jobs that are physically demanding. Promoting job satisfaction is also critical in jobs where employees work with customers. As Tim Crow, Director of Human Resources at Home Depot, notes, "If people aren't happy, they aren't going to be happy to the customer. That's why morale is so important in our business."[4] Indeed, as we see in this chapter, the link between quality and customer service and worker attitudes is very strong. These attitudes must be considered critical even by managers interested only in profits.

Beyond the service interaction, however, attitudes are also important because they are related to employee retention, and employee retention is also related to customer retention. For example, sales agents at State Farm Insurance stay with the company on average eighteen to twenty years, or two to three times more than the average tenure in the insurance industry. This lengthy tenure allows the average State Farm agent to learn the job and develop long-term relationships with customers that cannot be matched by competitors who might lose half of their sales staff each year. Those long-term relationships can come in handy. For example, during the recent economic downturn, many drivers were letting their auto insurance lapse at many other companies, but this was not the case at State Farm. Because agents at State Farm were close to their customers, they were able to call them and convince them of the importance of not driving uninsured. In some cases, this meant scaling back coverage and, because of the high level of familiarity with their clients, these agents were able to work creatively with them to determine how best to do this. The result in terms of the bottom line is clear: State Farm agents achieve 40 percent higher sales per agent than their competition.[5]

Firms that take advantage of the employee retention–customer retention link remain in the minority, however. Indeed, the massive restructurings and downsizing efforts that have taken place in many organizations in the last few years have left many organizations filled with dissatisfied, stressed, and insecure workers who are ready to abandon their current jobs for new opportunities at a moment's notice.[6] Thus, creating a stable and satisfied workforce serves as another opportunity for one firm to gain a competitive advantage over others in their industry.

Defining Satisfaction and Stress

This chapter focuses on key attitudes and emotions that people experience in the workplace. We begin by defining job satisfaction and job stress. Then, to underline the importance of job satisfaction, we examine the consequences of dissatisfaction and stress, both in human terms and in terms of financial loss. Next, we review the major sources of dissatisfaction and stress in work environments. The chapter ends by discussing methods to manage dissatisfaction and stress in the workplace (see Figure 6.1 for an overview).

Satisfaction

Job satisfaction is "a pleasurable feeling that results from the perception that one's job fulfills or allows for the fulfillment of one's important job values."[7] Our definition of job satisfaction includes three key components: values, importance of values, and perception. Job satisfaction is a function of values, that is, what a person consciously or unconsciously desires to obtain from work. Values are not the same as needs in the sense that needs are best thought of as "objective requirements" of the body that are essential for maintaining life, such as the needs for oxygen and for water. Values, on the other hand, are "subjective requirements" that exist in the person's mind.

The second component of job satisfaction is the *importance* of those values. People differ not only in the values they hold, but also in the weights they give to those values, and these

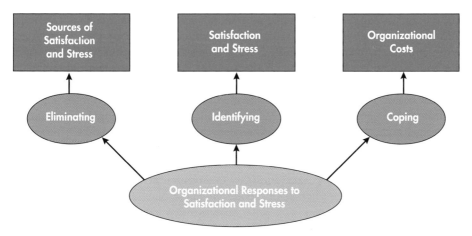

Figure 6.1 **Chapter Overview**

differences critically influence the degree of their job satisfaction. One person might value job security above all else. Another might be most concerned with the opportunity to travel. Yet another person could be primarily interested in doing work that is fun or that helps others. Although the first person might be satisfied by long-term employment, the other two might find little satisfaction in a permanent employment relationship.

The final component of our definition of job satisfaction is *perception*. Satisfaction reflects our perception of the present situation and our values. Recall from Chapter 4 that perceptions might not be completely accurate reflections of objective reality. When they are not perfect, we must look at the individual's perception of the situation—not the actual situation—to understand his or her personal reactions.

Stress

Stress is an unpleasant emotional state that results when someone is uncertain of his or her capacity to resolve a perceived challenge to an important value.[8] As in the case of satisfaction, we might find it easier to understand the nature of stress if we decompose this definition into three key components. The first component, *perceived challenge*, emphasizes that stress arises from the interaction between people and their perceptions of the environment (not necessarily reality). For example, if people are afraid that they might lose their jobs, this can create the preconditions for stress.

The second component of this definition, *importance of values*, is critical for the same reason as was noted in our definition of satisfaction. Unless a challenge threatens some important value, it will not cause stress. For example, the rumored plant closing might not create stress for a worker who is already preparing to retire or a worker who sees many other better employment opportunities on the horizon.

The third component, *uncertainty of resolution*, emphasizes that the person interprets the situation in terms of the perceived probability of successfully coping with the challenge. Obviously, if people believe that they can readily cope with the challenge, they will not experience stress. Perhaps surprisingly, experienced stress is also low if the person sees no possible chance that the problem can be resolved. Under these conditions, a person tends to accept his or her fate with little emotional reaction. Stress is actually highest when the perceived difficulty of the challenge closely matches the person's perceived capacity to meet the demand. Why? As the difficulty level and the ability level approach one another, the outcome becomes increasingly uncertain. This uncertainty about meeting the challenge creates the stress, rather than the fear of a negative outcome.[9] For example, a 2008 poll found that just under 50 percent of workers reported that "economic uncertainty associated with fears that their company might initiate layoffs has caused them to be less productive at work."[10]

The body's physiological reaction to this type of threat once had great survival value. When threatened, the human body produces chemicals that cause blood pressure to rise and divert blood from the skin and digestive organs to the muscles. Blood fats are then released, providing a burst of energy and enhancing blood clotting in case of injury. In fact, even the sweat associated with a stress response serves as a signal to others in close range that the group is being threatened.[11] When the individual faces a prolonged threat, other changes begin that prepare the body for a long battle. For example, the body begins to conserve resources by retaining water and salts. Extra gastric acid is produced to increase the efficiency of digestion in the absence of blood (which has been diverted away from internal organs).[12]

Although these physiological changes probably had adaptive value ages ago, when they readied the person either to physically fight or to flee some threat, the same changes continue to occur today in response to threats, regardless of whether the increased physical capacity they produce is adaptive. For example, workers who hold jobs characterized by many demands over which the employees have little control are three times more likely to suffer from high blood pressure than other workers.[13] The increased physical capacity gained through higher blood pressure will not, however, help these workers cope with the demands they face, and hence they become counter-productive at work.

Moreover, in evolutionary terms, stress episodes typically were events that played out quickly, but this is no longer the case. People might be worried about their situation at work for extended periods, and Hans Selye, a prominent physician and researcher, proposed the **general adaptation syndrome**, which describes the relationship between long-term stress and these physical–physiological symptoms. According to Selye, the body's reaction to chronic stress occurs in three stages (Figure 6.2). In the *alarm stage*, the person identifies the threat. Whether this threat is physical (a threat of bodily injury) or psychological (the threat of losing one's job), the physiological changes described previously ensue. In the *resistance stage*, the person becomes resilient to the pressures created by the original threat. The symptoms that occurred in the alarm stage disappear, even though the stressor remains in place. Resistance seems to rely on increased levels of hormones secreted by the pituitary gland and the adrenal cortex.[14]

If exposure to the threatening stressor continues, the person reaches the *exhaustion stage*. Pituitary gland and adrenal cortex activity slows down, and the person can no longer adapt to the continuing stress. Many of the physiological symptoms that originally appeared in the alarm stage now recur. If stress continues unabated, individuals may suffer **burnout**, which can lead to severe physical damage, including death via coronary failure or heart disease.[15] As a reactive defense mechanism, workers who are burned out also tend to depersonalize the clients or customer they are trying to serve, which further destroys quality of

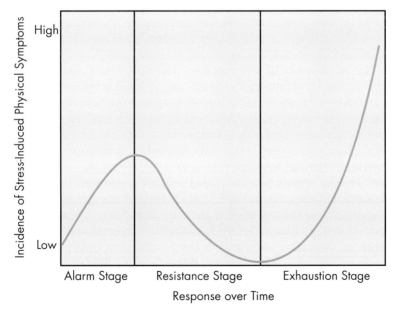

Figure 6.2 The General Adaptation Syndrome

Source: Adapted from the work of Hans Seyle, as reported in E. D. Heaphy and J. E. Dutton, "Positive Social Interactions and the Human Body at Work: Linking Organizations and Physiology," *Academy of Management Review* 33 (2008): 137–162.

service. Thus, burnout has to be prevented and, as we will discuss in more detail later, interventions that help create social support within work groups can often help along these lines.[16]

Organizational Costs of Dissatisfaction and Stress

The previous section focused on the effects of dissatisfaction and stress as measured in terms of human physiology. In this section, we examine the costs of dissatisfaction and stress from an organizational effectiveness perspective. That is, even if we coldly ignore the human costs, important financial reasons exist for monitoring and managing the satisfaction and stress levels of employees.

Performance at the Individual and Organizational Level

Although it was once believed that job satisfaction and job performance were not strongly related, a recent comprehensive analysis of studies that involved 312 organizations and 54,417 employees has revealed a significant, positive correlation between these two variables.[17] A subsequent analysis that examined the timing of effects also makes it clear that, in terms of causal order, attitudes are a cause and not an effect of higher performance.[18]

Employees who are highly engaged with their work put in longer hours and generally see work as its own reward, creating less of a need to set up financial incentives, which as we saw in our last chapter can often backfire.[19] The satisfaction–performance link is especially strong in the service industry where employees have direct, face-to-face contact with customers.[20]

As we noted earlier, in service contexts, there seems to be a direct transfer of attitudes from employees to customers.[21] This relationship was expressed well by a manager at United Airlines who, during a recent period of labor unrest, stated, "[Y]ou can't run a service business when you are at war with your employees."[22] One might wonder whether the relationship between the attitudes of individual workers and their own performance actually translates to higher levels of organizational performance as measured via traditional financial performance indicators, and the evidence is clear that it often does. A recent study by *Fortune* magazine compared the financial performance of the "100 Best Companies to Work For" with a closely matched set of firms that were the same size and in the same industry. In terms of operational performance, the results of this study showed that between 1995 and 2000 the return on assets for the 100 best was 9.3 percent versus 7.3 percent for the control firms. In terms of stock market perceptions, the market-to-book ratio for the 100 best firms was 4.5 versus 2.0 for the controls, suggesting that investors appreciate the competitive value inherent in having a stable and satisfied workforce.[23]

In contrast, some employers have developed negative reputations that can work against their own business interests. For example, "Black Friday," the day after Thanksgiving, is one of the biggest days of the year for U.S. retailers, and is thus, a big day for the nation's largest retailer—Walmart. However, in 2012, 4,000 Walmart employees walked off their jobs to call attention to their dissatisfaction with certain aspects of their jobs, including short, unpredictable hours, as well as low wages and skimpy benefits. This occurred at a time when Walmart was trying to expand into larger cities, but was meeting opposition from local political leaders who believed Walmart was a disruptive and socially dubious citizen. The Black Friday walkout reinforced this belief and one industry insider noted, "A business case could be made that it would be smart for Walmart to figure out a way to improve the situation for their workers."[24]

Health Care Costs

As noted earlier, work-related stress has the potential to greatly affect a person's health and well-being. A fact of current organizational life is that employing organizations bear much of the cost for employee health care. Although wages have risen during the last 30 years, spiraling medical fees and hospital room-and-board charges have increased the cost of patient insurance by three times as much as wage increases over the same period. Indeed, medical insurance and claims costs currently constitute a full 12 percent of payroll for U.S. companies.[25] Analysts have cited legacy costs associated with having to cover employee health expenditures as the single most important factor in explaining the inability of U.S. auto manufacturers to compete with foreign competitors.[26]

These costs were one of the factors that prompted the passage of the new Affordable Care Act, but again, as we saw with Alabama House Bill 56, new legislation often triggers unexpected reactions. For example, one reason that Walmart has tried to restrict the hours of their workers is to keep them at part-time status and thus remove the requirement to pay additional health care costs. Indeed, under the new law, many part-time Walmart employees would make so little money that they would qualify for Medicaid under the new law, which suggests the retailer is seeking to shift the burden of employee health care costs to the federal government. Although this might be a cost-effective, short-term solution, it again reinforces the idea among many state and city governments that Walmart is not a good corporate citizen and that they generate more problems than they solve when they move into your region.[27]

Besides paying for general health insurance, employers are also increasingly finding themselves held liable for specific incidents of stress-related illness. The Occupational Safety and Health Act of 1970 and many state laws hold employing organizations accountable "for all diseases arising out of and in the course of employment."[28] Since research has shown a strong link between stress and mental disorders, this made it possible for an overworked advertising executive who was the victim of a nervous breakdown to successfully sue his employer.[29] Stress and dissatisfaction have also been linked to problem drinking by employees, which can result in direct costs associated with treating these problems, as well as indirect costs associated with increased absenteeism and reduced safety levels associated with problem drinkers at work.[30]

Absenteeism and Turnover

Dissatisfaction and stress not only create direct costs for organizations (that is, health care program expenditures), but also are the source of indirect costs—most notably in the form of absenteeism and turnover. Dissatisfaction is a major reason for absenteeism, an organizational problem that has been estimated to cost $74 billion annually for the overall U.S. economy.[31] Absenteeism in many contexts often spirals out of control because there is a strong element of peer influence on this behavior. Once one sees other co-workers absent from work, the odds of their own absenteeism grows exponentially, and hence supervisors that allow for this behavior in isolated cases often confront a larger systemic problem over time.[32]

Dissatisfaction also triggers organizational turnover which, in turn, has a negative effect on organizational performance.[33] Like absenteeism, there is often a social spiraling effect associated with turnover in the sense that a trickle of turnover can turn into flood under the right conditions.[34] Replacing workers who leave the organization voluntarily is a costly undertaking. For example, according to a recent survey, the cost to replace a single worker ranged from $28,000 (manufacturing) to $40,000 (biotechnology) depending upon the industry.[35] In addition to replacement costs, when workers depart from these jobs, companies lose the knowledge and expertise they might need to be successful. In our last chapter, we noted how it takes extended practice and repetition, sometimes as much as ten years, to truly develop expertise. Thus, turnover among experienced personnel can be especially damaging.

An excellent recent example of this can be seen at the Federal Aviation Authority (FAA), the group that oversees airline safety. The majority of air traffic controllers who currently work for this agency were hired in the mid-1980s after President Ronald Reagan fired over 10,000 controllers who were illegally striking. Now, thirty years later, most of these controllers are nearing the age of retirement, and the FAA is desperately trying to retain these workers for as long as possible, in order to help ease the transition to a younger, less-experienced workforce. The problem, however, is that job dissatisfaction among current controllers is very high, and a mass exodus is taking place. As one departing controller noted, "It is only a matter of time before an accident occurs, and the pervasive feeling among experienced controllers is that I don't want to be there when it happens."[36]

Although safety is the major concern with an organization like the FAA, in the world of business, the worst case is when unhappy, but experienced, employees take jobs with competitors. A company's investment in employee development is then not only lost, but actually winds up as a bonus for a competing firm that gains access to a great deal of knowledge about the competition's operations. This has recently been a problem at Google, where many of its young and talented employees are leaving the organization to try to create their own start-up companies. Many of the ideas for these new start-ups were conceived while these people were working for Google and, all else being equal, Google would rather retain these workers and their ideas than try to compete against them, which is why Google works harder than most organizations to try to keep all its workers happy.[37]

Low Organizational Commitment and Poor Citizenship

Dissatisfaction also contributes to declining organizational commitment. **Organizational commitment** is the degree to which people identify with the organization that employs them. It implies a willingness on the employee's part to put forth a substantial effort on the organization's behalf and his or her intention to stay with the organization for a long time. The subject of organizational commitment has recently attracted a great deal of attention. Many employers fear that the downsizing policies pursued so aggressively by U.S. companies have killed company loyalty. Evidence provided by surveys of U.S. workers bolsters this claim. When asked if employees today are more loyal or less loyal to their companies compared with ten years ago, 63 percent said less loyal and only 22 percent said more loyal.[38] A separate survey indicated that 13 percent of the U.S. workforce was planning to quit their jobs in 2013, which would result in a $2 trillion costs for businesses associated with recruiting, testing, and training new employees.[39]

Unlike U.S. manufacturers, companies like Toyota are committed to no-layoff policies, even in bad economic times, and this leads to a much more loyal workforce. For example, even during the recent economic downturn, when no one was buying cars and Toyota experienced a very public safety-related recall, Toyota avoided layoffs.[40] Even though production was halted, workers came in every day and were either assigned duties to help repair and maintain facilities or were sent to training programs. As Toyota general manager Latondra Newton noted at the time, "We're not just keeping people on the payroll because we're nice. At the end of all of this, our hope is that we'll end up with a more skilled and loyal workforce."[41]

Although formal performance evaluation systems might often prevent someone who is dissatisfied from expressing his or her unhappiness directly (that is, through poor job performance), dissatisfaction can nevertheless have a negative effect on **organizational citizenship behaviors** (OCBs).[42] OCBs are acts that promote the organization's interest, but are not formally a part of any person's documented job requirements. They include behaviors such as volunteering for assignments, going out of one's way to welcome new employees, helping others who need assistance, staying late to finish a task, or voicing one's opinion on critical organizational issues.[43]

OCBs tend to make the organization run more smoothly, but dissatisfied employees rarely engage in them. Instead, employees seem to take a reciprocating approach to these kinds of behaviors; that is, they show a willingness to engage in them only if they feel that the employer goes out of its way as well. For example, one recent study conducted at Fel-Pro, an engine gasket-manufacturing firm in the Midwest, showed that OCBs were high, but only among employees who believed that the company's work–life benefits program helped them and their families.[44] Another study showed that OCBs declined when workers became emotionally exhausted owing to an increase in the number of hours worked, suggesting a quality–quantity trade-off when it comes to stretching workers too far.[45]

Workplace Violence and Sabotage

In the last twenty years, violence in the workplace has developed into a major organizational problem. Workplace homicide is the fastest-growing form of murder in the United States. In terms of being a target of violence, this is especially a problem for women and for supervisors. For example, workplace homicide is the leading cause of death in the workplace for women.[46] Also, although the target of violence can be co-workers, subordinates, or customers, the most likely targets tend to be supervisors.[47] Moreover, homicide is merely the most extreme example of workplace violence—other forms of work-related violence are also proliferating. In any given year, 2 million employees are physically attacked, 6 million are threatened with physical attack, and 16 million suffer from some form of harassment. In terms of being an initiator of violence, this is especially a problem for young and uneducated workers.[48] Most violence that involves organizational insiders is triggered by extreme levels of dissatisfaction and stress on the part of the attacker and, although most people close to the attacker report being aware of their dissatisfaction, almost all were surprised by the violent response.[49]

Organizational sabotage is violence directed at property rather than people. Workers who are dissatisfied might attempt to do damage to company facilities or property. For example, 2,000 workers at Foxconn's Hon Hai Precision factory in China rioted in September 2012 in response to long hours, poor working conditions, and low pay. Employees burned buildings, broke windows, and overturned cars, and the angry mob could be dispersed only by a large contingent of paramilitary police. Three years earlier, the same plant attracted a great deal of world attention when a large number of workers committed suicide by jumping out of buildings. Nets were placed outside the building to catch the would-be jumpers but, over time, anger at the plant has been directed more at the employer—a major manufacturer of Apple iPods and iPads. Hon Hai spokesman, Louis Woo summed up the experience, noting "We cannot argue that manufacturing jobs are exciting for workers. It's kind of boring and requires a lot of hard work, so we may have to change that rather than hoping the workers will change."[50]

Dissatisfied workers can also engage in sabotage by producing faulty products. This can have disastrous effects for both consumers and the company. For example, problems with Firestone tires that were blamed for the deaths of 119 people and 180 legal suits against the company were eventually traced to the actions of disgruntled workers during a period of labor unrest. Failure on the part of workers to follow written procedures—regarding how to treat the "steel" part of steel-belt radial tires—led to tread separation problems that resulted in a large number of accidents. The cost of these safety breakdowns in terms of human life and suffering is incalculable, but the financial repercussions of these failures for Firestone can be well documented. The company was eventually forced to pay out over $40 million in lawsuits and lost over 60 percent of its customer base to competing firms—including the Ford Motor Company, a huge demander of tires that had a long-term, steady relationship with Firestone prior to the incident. The plant where the tires were produced was eventually closed down, putting strikers, strikebreakers, and managers out of their jobs.[51]

Although traditionally organizational sabotage was seen as dealing with vandalism or theft, it is now increasingly being directed at computer information systems. These systems, while protected from external tampering, remain highly vulnerable to manipulation by insiders. For example, Omega Engineering suffered $10 million in losses after one very dissatisfied employee unleashed a software program (a "logic bomb") that deleted critical computer files.[52] Erecting technical barriers to this kind of act, while simultaneously fostering the widespread use of technology within an organization, can be difficult. Often, the only way to prevent such acts is to monitor and eliminate the dissatisfaction that motivates the behavior in the first place.

Sources of Dissatisfaction and Stress

Certain inherent features of organizations can cause dissatisfaction and stress. In this section, we focus on the physical and social environment, the person, the task, and the role.

Physical and Social Environment

A wealth of evidence shows that some physical features of the workplace can stimulate negative emotional reactions in workers, and this of course, was one of the major problems associated with the jobs at Harvest Select in Alabama in the story that opened this chapter. More broadly, studies have shown that *extremes in temperatures* can affect job attitudes as well as performance and decision making. Moreover, research on how people perceive tasks has shown that physical features of the environment, such as *cleanliness, working outdoors*, and *health hazards*, are very important in the way people perceive their tasks.[53] In some cases, all of these negative features come together in one job, and the dissatisfying nature of this work makes it necessary to pay workers a premium just to accept the positions. For example, at the U.S. State Department, the only way the organization could staff the U.S. embassy in Iraq was to offer pay rises in excess of 70 percent, and in some cases even this was not enough.[54]

Of course, one does not have to work outside to suffer from hazards. Recent studies have focused on some very subtle characteristics of the physical environment. Researchers have coined the term *sick-building syndrome* to describe physical structures whose indoor air is contaminated by invisible pollutants. Today, many new buildings are constructed with windows that do not open, which means that workers in these buildings breathe a great deal of recycled air. This air can contain a mixture of carbon monoxide sucked into a building from air intake vents that overhang parking lots, ozone discharged from office printers, chemicals that are emitted by paint, carpet, or new furniture, and even bacteria funneled through heating, ventilation, and cooling systems. This problem has gotten so bad that the U.S. Environmental Protection Agency recently ranked indoor air as one of the top five environmental health risks of our time.[55] Ironically, some of the worst cases of sick-building syndrome are found in hospitals, where in addition to all of these other issues, one can add infection control to the list of problems.[56]

In terms of the social environment, supervisors and co-workers serve as the two primary sources of satisfaction or frustration for the employee. The employee might be satisfied with a supervisor because he or she helps the employee attain some valued outcome, or because they share similar values, attitudes, or philosophy. The greatest degree of satisfaction with supervisors occurs where both kinds of attraction exist, but the negative outcomes associated with abusive supervisors are particularly pronounced.[57] In fact, data from exit interviews show that 75 percent of the reasons cited for leaving a job can be directly tied to the actions or decisions of the direct supervisor.[58]

Lack of support or incivility among co-workers, however, also has measurable effects on employee satisfaction, health, and turnover.[59] Bullying at work has been defined as repeated, health-harming mistreatment by one or more peer perpetrators that takes the form of verbal abuse or offensive conduct that is threatening, humiliating, or intimidating. Just as bullying behavior has come under closer scrutiny in schools, it has also come to the attention of organizations, and a recent survey indicated that 35 percent of workers claim to have been the victim of bullying at work.[60] The negative effect of poor peer-to-peer relations is especially pronounced in organizations that rely on self-managing team-based structures or in situations where people are working in crowded conditions.[61]

In addition to their direct effects on satisfaction, supervisors and co-workers may also be able to buffer their fellow workers from other harmful stressors by providing social support. **Social support** is the active provision of sympathy and caring. Many researchers have suggested that social support from supervisors and co-workers can buffer employees from stress. Figure 6.3 illustrates the notion behind **buffering**. As shown in the figure, the presence of people who are supportive can lower the incidence of stress-related symptoms under conditions of high stress. Evidence for this effect has come largely from research in medical contexts, which shows that recovery and rehabilitation from illness proceed better when the patient is surrounded by caring friends and family. The same seems true for work-related stress—for example, a study of nurses working in stressful units showed that those who received social support were much better able to perform their jobs.[62]

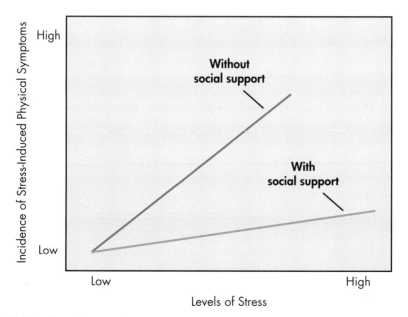

Figure 6.3 How Social Support May Buffer Stress

Personal Dispositions

Because both stress and dissatisfaction ultimately reside within a person, many researchers who have studied these outcomes have focused on individual differences. The term **negative affectivity** describes a dispositional dimension of subjective distress that includes such unpleasant mood states as anger, contempt, disgust, guilt, fear, and nervousness.[63] Negative affectivity is similar to the construct of emotional stability (discussed in Chapter 3) and tends to remain quite stable over time. In fact, recent research has shown that the work attitudes of adults can be predicted from measures of emotional stability and negative affectivity collected when those individuals were children.[64] People who are generally high in negative affectivity tend to focus on both their own negative qualities and those of others. Such people are also more likely to experience significantly higher levels of distress than are individuals who rate low on this dimension. It highlights the fact that some people bring stress and dissatisfaction with them to work, and that these workers may remain relatively dissatisfied regardless of what steps are taken by the organization or the manager.[65]

At the extreme, negative affectivity can turn into clinical depression, which is responsible for the loss of more than 200 million working days in the United States each year. More than 3,000 psychiatric claims are filed annually with the Equal Employment Opportunity Commission (EEOC), making this category the single largest type of claim brought under the Americans with Disabilities Act (ADA).[66] For someone with a diagnosed mental illness such as this, ADA requires employers to make "reasonable accommodations" and that could include more flexible work hours, time off for counseling, or reassigning the employee to a job that is associated with less stress and fewer deadlines.[67]

One constellation of individual-differences variables linked to job satisfaction and performance is labeled "core self-evaluation."[68] An individual's core self-evaluation is defined by his or her standing (low to high) on four different traits: self-esteem, generalized self-efficacy, emotional stability, and internal locus of control (i.e., the belief that one can control one's own destiny through actions and is not a victim of fate). A longitudinal study that started with young people in 1979 and then followed them for a period of twenty-five years found that those who were initially high in core self-evaluation wound up with much higher salaries and job satisfaction relative to people who are low in this characteristic.[69]

One final critical individual-difference variable for predicting stress is the Type A behavior pattern. People with Type A personalities are characterized as being aggressive and competitive, as setting high standards for themselves and others, and as putting themselves under constant time pressure. People with Type B personalities, on the other hand, lack such feelings of urgency. The unrealistic expectations of the impatient, ambitious, and overly aggressive Type A person render him or her particularly susceptible to dissatisfaction and stress. This susceptibility might also account for the fact that the Type A person has twice the risk, as compared with the Type B person, of developing coronary heart disease.[70]

Organizational Tasks

Although we cannot entirely discount the influence of dispositional traits and nonwork experiences, nothing predicts a person's level of workplace satisfaction or stress better than the nature of the work itself.[71] Most stressful jobs tend to be associated with deadline pressures, competitiveness, and physical danger. Innumerable aspects of tasks have been linked to dissatisfaction and stress, but in general, the key factors that determine satisfaction and stress are task complexity, physical strain, and task meaningfulness.

Task Complexity

Although in extreme cases tasks can become overly complex, research generally shows a positive relationship between task complexity and satisfaction. The boredom generated by simple, repetitive jobs that are not mentally challenging has consistently been found to frustrate most workers.[72] This frustration, in turn, manifests itself as dissatisfaction, stress, and ultimately tardiness, absenteeism, and turnover. In some cases, external interventions can alleviate the boredom inherent in these kinds of jobs. For example, research suggests that, for some simple jobs, allowing employees to use personal stereos increases both performance and satisfaction.[73]

Boredom created by lack of task complexity can also hinder performance on certain types of jobs. For example, airport security personnel, air traffic controllers, operators in nuclear power stations, medical technicians, and inspectors on production floors all belong in a class of jobs that require *vigilance*. Such workers must continually monitor equipment and be prepared to respond to critical events. Because such events are rare, however, these jobs are exceedingly boring and hence workers are vulnerable to poor concentration. Ultimately, this inattention can result in performance breakdowns, often with serious consequences.[74]

Work that requires vigilance is especially difficult during nightshift operations, where people struggle to remain alert and awake, especially if they are out of their normal circadian rhythm or the nature of the work is boring (e.g., monitoring a video screen). In fact, recently, a new clinical term—shift work sleep disorder (SWSD)—has been coined to describe the constant fatigue and inability to stay alert that inflicts people who have to work during periods when they should be sleeping. This new disorder also comes with its own treatment, Nuvigil, a drug often called "alertness pills." This new medication is controversial and many doctors question whether a pharmaceutical solution is the best way to stay alert on the job. Robert Basner, the director of Columbia University's Sleep Center notes, "We as a society rely too much on pills and medication, and that is not always the best approach. Caffeine is a very good wake promoting agent and it's a lot cheaper."[75]

In addition, research also suggests that "napping" during the day is also extremely helpful in terms of promoting vigilance and helping shift workers (or workers who simply work late into the night every evening) stay alert. Research suggests that cognitive ability depends on how much sleep one accumulates over a 24-hour period—not just overnight. Rather than fighting a losing battle to stay alert or take potentially addictive pills, it is better to plan ahead and schedule in short sleep interludes into long workdays or shift work.[76] Indeed, as we saw in Chapter 4, for jobs that involve creative problem solving, the brain actually continues to productively work on problems when one is sleeping, thus increasing the probability of generating insights that are unlikely to occur if one is consciously trying to fight off fatigue at the same time one is trying to come up with a new and innovative solution.

Physical Strain

Another important determinant of work satisfaction is the amount of physical strain and exertion involved in the job. As we saw in the Alabama case that opened this chapter, so many people want to avoid work such as cutting fish and picking tomatoes that is hard to find anyone other than refugees willing to take the jobs. This factor is sometimes overlooked in the present age of technology, where much of the physical strain associated with jobs has been removed by automation. Indeed, the very fact that technology continues to advance highlights the degree to which physical strain is universally considered an undesirable work characteristic. Many jobs, particularly those in certain manufacturing industries and in the protective services (police and fire), however, can still be characterized as physically demanding, and it is difficult or impossible to totally eliminate this aspect of the work in those jobs.

Task Meaningfulness

Once one gets beyond the boring and physically demanding nature of work the next most important factor is the degree to which it is meaningful. In our previous chapter on motivation, we discussed how this is a critical aspect of the task when it comes to getting people energized. When people believe that their work has an important impact on other people, they are much more willing to work longer hours.[77] In contrast, when people feel the work does not have meaning, they often react negatively and seek to find alternative employment.[78]

The term **empowerment** has been used to define work that is not only meaningful, but also characterized by autonomy. Empowered workers feel that they can display their competence and make a positive impact on the world—or at least their little corner of it. This belief, in turn, creates a high level of intrinsic motivation that results in high job performance and organizational commitment.[79] For example, at Best Buy headquarters in Minneapolis, the company initiated a program called Results Only Work Environment (ROWE) that eliminated punch clocks and formal scheduling. The program also allowed employees to determine not only their own hours, but also how, when, and where the work was conducted. The program resulted in decreased turnover and costs, and most indicators of productivity actually increased after the change, even though people were spending less physical time at the headquarters itself.[80]

Because empowerment often entails a delegation of authority from supervisors to subordinates, the positive effects of empowering workers tend to be culturally specific. Some countries, such as the United States, are relatively low in power distance (that is, low in terms of accepting status differences between people). In these cultures, empowerment leads to high satisfaction with supervision. On the other hand, in cultures that are high in power distance, such as India, such a program is seen as an abdication of responsibility and leads to dissatisfaction with supervision.[81] We will have much more to say about power distance in Chapter 15, when we deal with international issues.

Organization Roles

The person and the social environment converge in the form of an **organization role**. The person's role in the organization can be defined as the total set of expectations of the person held by both the person and others who make up the social environment. These expectations of behavior include both the formal aspects of the job and the informal expectations of co-workers, supervisors, clients, and customers. They greatly influence how the person responds to the work. Three of the most heavily researched aspects of roles are role ambiguity, role conflict, and role scope.

Role Ambiguity

Role ambiguity consists of the uncertainty or lack of clarity surrounding expectations about a person's role in the organization. It indicates that the worker does not have enough information about what is expected. Role ambiguity can also stem from a lack of information about the rewards for performing well and the punishments for failing. For example, imagine that your college instructor has assigned a term paper but neglected to tell you (1) what topics are pertinent, (2) how long the paper should be, (3) when it is due, (4) how it will be evaluated, and (5) how much it is worth toward the final course grade. Clearly, most people would feel stress under these circumstances, a reaction that can be directly attributed to role ambiguity. High levels of role ambiguity are also associated with lower task performance and the intention to quit one's job.[82]

Role Conflict

Role conflict is the recognition of incompatible or contradictory demands that face the person who occupies a role. It can take many different forms. *Intersender role conflict* occurs when two or more people in the social environment convey mutually exclusive expectations. For example, a middle manager might find that upper management wants to institute severe reprimands for worker absenteeism, whereas the workers expect greater consideration of their needs and personal problems. *Intrasender role conflict* occurs when one person in the social environment holds two competing expectations. For example, a research assistant for a magazine editor might be asked to write a brief but detailed summary of a complex and lengthy article from another source. In attempting to accomplish this task, the assistant might experience considerable distress when trying to decide what to include and what to leave out of the summary. A third form of role conflict is *interrole conflict*. Most people occupy multiple roles, and the expectations for our different roles can sometimes clash. A parent who has a business trip scheduled during a daughter's first piano recital, for example, is likely to feel torn between the demands of the two roles.

Earlier in this chapter, we noted the relatively higher level of financial performance associated with companies that were part of the top 100 best companies to work for as rated by *Fortune* magazine. In terms of how one gets into the top 100, it is instructive to see how many of them directly support their workers in terms of helping them manage role conflict that spills over from life to work. Of the top 100, thirty-three offer on-site day care and twenty-nine offer concierge services.[83] Thirty-one percent of these companies offer fully paid sabbaticals in recognition of the fact that time off for renewal is a major aspiration for many of today's most talented workers.[84]

Role Scope

Role scope refers to the absolute number of expectations that exist for the person occupying a role. Earlier we noted that work that is boring is generally dissatisfying, but the flip side of this problem is the *role overload* situation where there are too many expectations or demands placed on the role occupant. A 2008 survey suggested that role overload is the number one cause of stress at work, with 48 percent of respondents suggesting that this can be attributed to having to do more work with fewer resources.[85] Several aspects of modern workplaces have created problems in the area of role scope.

First, layoffs and reductions in the labor force have often left fewer people to do more work in many large companies. Ironically, as we say in our earlier example at Walmart, at a time when many people cannot get enough hours at work, other people get too many hours. Some of this can be attributed to the incentives that employers face with hourly versus salaried workers. When it comes to hourly workers, their hours are often scarce and unpredictable and scheduled at the last minute. This is often attributed to the fact that hourly work tends to be associated with low fixed costs, and employers want to make sure they do not pay for any unnecessary hours, let alone overtime pay. The idea is to keep a large number of part-time staff on hand to throw at peak demand, but at the same time, prevent any one worker from accumulating the number of hours that would qualify them as "full-time employees" who might qualify for health insurance. On the other hand, salaried workers are associated with high fixed costs and are not subject to overtime pay, and thus, the motivation for employers is to get as many hours as possible from each person, even to the point of getting one person to do the work of two people. As we saw in our last chapter, employers respond to incentives and sometimes these incentives have unintended consequences, like those we see here. These incentives help create a "schizophrenic" labor market where some workers cannot handle the hours that they have to work, whereas others cannot get the hours they want and need.[86]

Second, telecommunications advancements have made it easier for people to take their work home with them. Thus, whereas professional workers in the rest of the developed world have cut back on the number of hours worked per person per year, the United States has gone in the other direction, actually increasing the number of hours worked per year. In addition, in 2012, the average U.S. worker was provided with fourteen days of vacation, but on average used only twelve vacation days.[87] This is half of that taken by Japanese and British workers, one-third of that taken by workers in France and Germany, and one-quarter of that taken by Italians—world leaders in vacation time among industrialized nations.[88] Some are concerned that this is taking a toll on people in terms of stress and health, and have argued that U.S. firms need to strike a better balance between the work and nonwork lives of employees. Indeed, the negative effects of expanding work hours seem to be particularly pronounced for women, who still bear a greater responsibility for housework relative to men, regardless of their employment status.[89]

Eliminating and Coping with Dissatisfaction and Stress

Because the costs associated with employee dissatisfaction and stress can be high, identifying these factors should be a major part of the job description of every manager. Once identified, interventions should target the source of the stress. If it is impossible to eliminate the stressor for some reason, then the manager should at least help employees manage and cope with the stress. In this section, we discuss how to identify, eliminate, and manage dissatisfaction and stress in the workplace.

Identifying Symptoms of Dissatisfaction and Stress

In some cases, employees are afraid to admit that they are stressed and cannot overcome some problem associated with their work. In other cases, workers who are dissatisfied with some facet of their job might not speak out to avoid sounding like chronic complainers. Finally, in yet other cases, the attitudes of some workers could have become so bad that they view reporting dissatisfaction as a waste of time. For this reason, it is critical for managers to monitor the kinds of attitudes via a regular, systematic, and anonymous employee survey program.

Most attempts made to measure worker satisfaction rely on self-reports. A vast amount of data has been gathered on the reliability and validity of many existing scales, and a wealth of data is available on companies that have used these scales in the past, which allows for comparisons across firms. Established scales are excellent starting points when employers seek to assess the satisfaction levels of their employees. An employer would be foolish to "reinvent the wheel" by generating its own versions of measures of these broad constructs. Of course, in some cases, an organization might want to measure its satisfaction among employees (e.g., satisfaction with one health plan versus another health plan). In these situations, the organization might need to create its own scales. This scenario will be the exception rather than the rule, however.

Regardless of which measures are used or how many facets of satisfaction are assessed, a systematic, ongoing program of employee survey research should be a prominent component of any retention strategy for a number of reasons. First, it allows the company to monitor trends over time, thereby enabling the firm to prevent problems in the area of voluntary turnover before they happen. Indeed, one of the most critical trends to watch is the percentage of people who comply by filling out such surveys, because employees who are not willing to be surveyed often have the most negative attitudes.[90]

Second, an ongoing program of survey research provides a means of empirically assessing the effects of changes in policy, such as the introduction of a new performance appraisal system, or personnel, such as the introduction of a new CEO, on worker attitudes. Moreover, when these surveys incorporate standardized scales, they often allow the company to compare itself with others in its industry along the same dimensions. If the firm detects major differences between the organization and the industry as a whole (for example, in satisfaction with pay levels), the company might be able to react and change its policies before it experiences a mass exodus of people moving to the competition.

Finally, with the advent of increased networking capacity in many organizations, the cost of conducting online surveys has never been lower. Computerized versions of many scales perform as well, if not better, when administered over a company's intranet. In addition, the results can be calculated more quickly. Some programs even allow the worker to see where he or she stands relative to co-workers immediately after filling out the survey.[91]

Conducting an organizational opinion survey is not a task that should be taken lightly, because such surveys often raise expectations. For this reason, the organization conducting the survey should be prepared to act on the results if they hope to see any benefit from future surveys. For example, at Sun Healthcare Group, turnover rates among nurses, nurses' aides, and technicians ran at over 150 percent a year. In order to determine the cause of this, the organization conducted an anonymous online survey that revealed unambiguously that employees wanted more opportunities to develop their skills and advance their careers. The organization responded by creating access to training programs that enrolled close to 2,000 workers. Turnover was reduced to 25 percent just three years later, and more and more hiring was based upon employee referrals from nurses who had upgraded their skills and were promoted to higher-level jobs in the system.[92]

Eliminating Dissatisfying and Stressful Conditions

Because the nature of the task influences dissatisfaction and stress so strongly, some of the most effective means of reducing negative reactions to work focus on the task. Job enrichment methods include many techniques designed to add complexity and meaning to a person's work. As the term *enrichment* suggests, this kind of intervention targets jobs that are boring because of their repetitive nature or low scope. Although enrichment cannot always improve all employees' reactions to work, it can prove very useful. This topic will be covered in more depth in Chapter 7 on work design.

Role problems rank immediately behind job problems in terms of creating distress. The role analysis technique is designed to clarify role expectations for a jobholder by improving communication between the person and his or her supervisors, co-workers, subordinates, and perhaps even customers. In role analysis, both the jobholder and the role set members write down their expectations, and then these people gather together to review their lists. Writing down all expectations ensures that ambiguities can be removed and conflicts identified. Where conflicts arise, the group as a whole (perhaps with the assistance of a group facilitator) tries to decide how to resolve these problems. When this kind of analysis is done throughout an organization, instances of overload and underload can be discovered and role requirements might be traded off, allowing for the development of more balanced roles.

Skills training is a means of trying to help the employee change a dissatisfying or stressful condition. For example, at University of Chicago Hospital, many technical employees struggled with interpersonal tasks associated with customers, resulting in conflict with clients and stress at work. Training programs in customer service, critical thinking, and situational judgment were provided, and the technicians were each encouraged to develop their own "Ideal Patient Encounter" associated with their specific job. Complaints from patients dropped precipitously, and the reduction in conflict led to less stress for the technicians, as well as a 33 percent reduction in turnover in those job categories. With this type of training, participants decide on their most important work values. They then learn how to pinpoint goals, identify roadblocks to successful goal accomplishment, and seek the collaboration of co-workers in achieving these goals.[93] In general, skills training gives job incumbents the ability to better predict, understand, and control events occurring on the job, which in turn reduces stress. That is, being able to understand and control these events weakens the effect of perceived stress on job satisfaction.[94]

A person's ability to handle dissatisfying or stressful work experiences is also enhanced when the worker has an opportunity to air any problems and grievances. The formal opportunity to complain to the organization about one's work situation has been referred to as **voice**.[95] Having voice provides employees with an active, constructive outlet for their work frustrations, and leaders who provide voicing opportunities experience less turnover among their direct reports. One step beyond voicing opinions is the chance to take action or make decisions based on one's opinions. *Participation in decision making* (PDM) provides opportunities for workers to have input into important organizational decisions that involve their work and has been found to reduce role conflict and ambiguity. For example, turnover at Crouse Hospital in Upstate New York was reduced from 49 percent to 18 percent after initiating a program that promoted formal, small-group discussion about how to improve patient care at every level of the organization. In addition to the reduction in turnover, cost savings and increased customer service led to an $11 million net gain in 2007 that compared very favorably to the $15 million net loss the hospital recorded prior to the program.[96]

Managing Symptoms of Dissatisfaction and Stress

In some situations, organizations might not be able to sufficiently alter roles, tasks, or individual capacities to reduce dissatisfaction and stress. Here interventions must be aimed at the symptoms of stress. Although not as desirable as eliminating the stressors themselves, eliminating the symptoms is better than no action at all. Some interventions that fall into this category focus exclusively on physiological reactions to stress.

Physical conditioning, particularly in the form of *aerobic exercise*, helps make a person more resistant to the physiological changes, such as high blood pressure, that accompany stress reactions.[97] Many organizations, such as Google, provide on-site gyms in order to promote employee exercise. Another approach to treating stress symptoms is to employ *relaxation techniques*.[98] Under a severe amount of stress (as when preparing a fight-or-flight response), many of the body's muscles tighten. Relaxation programs focus on eliminating tenseness in most of the major muscle groups, including the hand, forearm, back, neck, face, foot, and ankle. Relaxing these muscle groups lowers blood pressure and pulse rate and reduces other physiological stress manifestations, and hence many organizations offer employees training in this skill.[99]

At one time, it was thought that people had no voluntary control over their physiological responses. **Biofeedback** machines, which allow a person to monitor his or her own physiological reactions, have since changed that perception. Indeed, with the appropriate feedback, some people can learn to control brain waves, muscle tension, heart rate, and even body temperature. Biofeedback training teaches people to recognize when these physiological reactions are taking place as well as how to ameliorate these responses when under stress.[100]

A socially supportive environment can reduce stress and buffer employees from stress caused by aversive working conditions.[101] For this reason, many organizations encourage employees to participate in team sports both at work and in their off hours. Ideally, softball and bowling leagues will increase group cohesiveness and support for individual group members through socializing and team effort. Although management certainly cannot ensure that every stressed employee will develop friends, it can make it easier for employees to interact on a casual footing.

Other means of coping with stress that cannot be eliminated at the source focus on allowing the person time away from the stressful environment. Although a person might not feel capable of handling the stress or dealing with the dissatisfying aspects of a particular job indefinitely, it is often possible to do so temporarily. Many employers employ **job rotation**—that is, moving workers from one job to another temporarily—in an effort to give workers a break from stress. Job rotation can do more than simply spread out the stressful aspects of a particular job. It can increase the complexity of the work and provide valuable cross-training in jobs, so that any one person eventually comes to understand many different tasks.

Finally, if the company cannot change the negative aspects of a job, managers should be honest with prospective jobholders about the nature of the work. Many companies hesitate to mention the undesirable aspects of a job when trying to recruit workers for fear that no one will take the job. Fooling someone into taking a job in which he or she would not otherwise be interested, however, is not good for the company or the person. The ultimate result is increased turnover. **Realistic job previews** (RJPs) lower expectations and are likely to attract workers whose values more closely match the actual job situation. RJPs are especially important for applicants who lack work experience or who are going to be working in foreign locations.[102]

Summary

Among the great variety of attitudes and emotions generated in the workplace, the most important are *job satisfaction* and occupational *stress*. Job satisfaction is a pleasurable emotional state resulting from the perception that a job helps the worker attain his or her valued outcomes. Occupational stress, an unpleasant emotional state, arises from the perceived uncertainty that a person can meet the demands of a job. Multiple responses to stress are possible, including physiological responses, behavioral responses, and cognitive reactions. These stress reactions have important consequences for organizations, particularly in terms of the financial costs of healthcare, absenteeism, turnover, and performance failures. Dissatisfaction and stress originate from several sources: the *physical* and *social environment*, the *person*, the *organizational task*, and the *organization role*. A number of different intervention programs can be implemented to eliminate the stress-inducing event, enable the person to avoid or cope with the stressor, or, failing these efforts, at least eliminate the symptoms of stress. These measures include *job enrichment*, *skills training*, *biofeedback*, *job rotation*, and *realistic job previews*.

Review Questions

1. Recall from Chapter 1 some of the many roles that a manager must play. Which of these roles do you think create the most stress? Which are probably the least stressful? From which role do you think most managers derive their greatest satisfaction? Compare your

answers to these three questions and speculate on the relationship between satisfaction and stress for managerial employees.

2. Organizational turnover is generally considered a negative outcome, and many organizations spend a great deal of time, money, and effort trying to reduce it. Can you think of any situations in which an increase in turnover might be just what an organization needs? What are some steps organizations might take to enhance functional types of turnover?

3. Characteristics like negative affectivity and the Type A behavior pattern are associated with aversive emotional states including dissatisfaction and stress. Do you think these tendencies are learned or genetically determined? If they are learned, from a reinforcement theory perspective, what reinforcers might sustain the behaviors associated with them?

4. If off-the-job stress begins to spill over and create on-the-job problems, what do you think are the rights and responsibilities of managers in helping employees overcome these problems? If employees are engaged in unhealthy off-the-job behavior patterns such as smoking, overeating, or alcohol abuse, what are the rights and responsibilities of the employer to change these behaviors? Are such efforts an invasion of privacy? Or do they simply constitute a prudent financial step taken to protect the firm's well-being?

Notes

1 N. Shah, "Do Illegal Immigrants Depress Wages, Job Opportunities?" *Wall Street Journal*, April 12, 2013, http://blogs.wsj.com/economics/2013/04/12/do-illegal-immigrants-depress-wages-job-opportunities/.

2 E. Dwoskin. "Do You Want This Job?" *Bloomberg Businessweek*, November 14, 2011, 70–78.

3 M. Newkirk and G. Doubon, "Legal Immigrants Wanted for Dirty Jobs," *Bloomberg Businessweek*, October 8, 2012, 34–35.

4 J. Marquez, "Rallying the Home Team," *Workforce Management*, July 14, 2008, 24.

5 R. P. McQueen, "Road Risks Rise as More Drivers Drop Insurance," *Wall Street Journal*, December 17, 2008, B1.

6 C. O. Trevor and A. J. Nyberg, "Keeping Your Headcount When All about You Are Losing Theirs," *Academy of Management Journal* 51 (2008): 259–276.

7 E. A. Locke, "The Nature and Causes of Job Dissatisfaction," in M. D. Dunnette, ed., *Handbook of Industrial and Organizational Psychology* (Chicago: Rand McNally, 1976), 901–969.

8 J. E. McGrath, "Stress in Organizations," in M. D. Dunnette, ed., *Handbook of Industrial and Organizational Psychology* (Chicago: Rand McNally, 1977), 1310–1367.

9 J. R. Edwards, "An Examination of Competing Versions of the Person–Environment Fit Approach to Stress," *Academy of Management Journal* 39 (1996): 292–339.

10 J. Smerd and J. Marquez, "Companies Look to Allay Workers' Financial Fears," *Workforce Management*, October 6, 2008, 1–3.

11 S. Reddy, "Why Stress Makes You Sweat," *Wall Street Journal*, February 4, 2013, http://online.wsj.com/article/SB10001424127887323392610457827829052063794.html.

12 D. H. Funkenstein, "The Physiology of Fear and Anger," *Scientific American* 192 (1955): 74–80.

13 S. Shellenbarger, "When Stress Is Good for You," *Wall Street Journal*, January 4, 2012, http://online.wsj.com/article/SB10001424052970204301404577171192704005250.html.

14 E. D. Heaphy and J. E. Dutton, "Positive Social Interactions and the Human Body at Work: Linking Organizations and Physiology," *Academy of Management Review* 33 (2008): 137–162.

15 C. Maslach and M. P. Leiter, "Early Predictors of Job Burnout and Engagement," *Journal of Applied Psychology* 93 (2008): 498–512.

16 P. M. Le Blanc, J. J. Hox, W. B. Schaufeli, T. W. Taris, and M. C. W. Peeters, "Take Care: The Evaluation of a Team-Based Burnout Intervention Program for Oncology Care Providers," *Journal of Applied Psychology* 92 (2007): 213–227.

17 T. A. Judge, C. J. Thoresen, J. E. Bono, and G. K. Patton, "The Job Satisfaction–Job Performance Relationship: A Qualitative and Quantitative Review," *Psychological Bulletin* 127 (2001): 376–407.

18 M. Riketta, "The Causal Relation between Job Attitudes and Performance: A Meta-Analysis of Panel Studies," *Journal of Applied Psychology* 93 (2008): 472–481.

19 J. M. Brett and L. K. Stroh, "Working 61 Plus Hours a Week: Why Do Managers Do It?" *Journal of Applied Psychology* 88 (2003): 67–78.

20 A. M. Susskind, K. M. Kacmer, and C. P. Borchgrevink, "Customer Service Providers' Attitudes Relating to Customer Service and Customer Satisfaction in the Customer–Server Exchange," *Journal of Applied Psychology* 88 (2003): 179–187.

21 A. A. Grandey, "When 'the Show Must Go On': Surface Acting and Deep Acting as Determinants of Emotional Exhaustion and Peer-Related Service Delivery," *Academy of Management Journal* 46 (2003): 86–96.

22 D. Foust, "Why United Is Ready to Unite," *BusinessWeek*, December 3, 2007, 22–24.

23 I. S. Fulmer, B. Gerhart, and K. S. Scott, "Are the 100 Best Better? An Empirical Investigation of the Relationship between Being a 'Great Place to Work' and Firm Performance," *Personnel Psychology* 56 (2003): 965–993.

24 S. Berfield, "Walmart versus Union Backed OUR Walmart," *Bloomberg Businessweek*, December 13, 2012, 55–60.

25 J. Smerd, "Financial Health Incentives on the Rise, but Design Is Key," *Workforce Management*, June 23, 2008, 14.

26 J. Smerd, "Viva Las VEBAs," *Workforce Management*, December 10, 2007, 23.

27 G. Smith, "Walmart's New Health Care Policy Shifts Burden to Medicaid, Obamacare," *Huffington Post*, December 1, 2012, http://www.huffingtonpost.com/2012/12/01/walmart-health-care-policy-medicaid-obamacare_n_2220152.html.

28 U.S. Chamber of Commerce, *Analysis of Workers' Compensation Laws* (Washington, DC: U.S. Chamber of Commerce, 1985): 3.

29 R. Poe, "Does Your Job Make You Sick?" *Across the Board* 9 (1987): 34–43.

30 S. B. Bacharach, P. A. Bamberger, and W. J. Sonnestuhl, "Driven to Drink: Managerial Control, Work-Related Risk Factors, and Employee Problem Drinking," *Academy of Management Journal* 45 (2002): 637–658.

31 M. Conlin, "Shirking Working: The War on Hooky," *BusinessWeek*, November 12, 2007, 70.

32 M. Biron and P. Bamberger, "Aversive Workplace Condition and Absenteeism: Taking Referent Group Norms and Supervisor Support into Account," *Journal of Applied Psychology* 97 (2012): 901–912.

33 T. Y. Park and J. D. Shaw, "Turnover Rates and Organizational Performance: A Meta-analysis," *Journal of Applied Psychology* 98 (2013): 268–309.

34 A. J. Nyborg and R. E. Ployhart, "Context Emergent Turnover (CET) Theory: A Theory of Collective Turnover," *Academy of Management Review* 38 (2013): 109–131.

35 R. Bond, "Turnover Costs," *Workforce Management*, June 23, 2008, 22.

36 J. Marquez, "Taking Flight," *Workforce Management*, June 9, 2008, 1–21.

37 A. Lashinsky, "Where Does Google Go Next?" *Fortune*, May 12, 2008, 33–35.

38 C. L. Cole, "Building Loyalty," *Workforce*, August 2000, 43–48.

39 G. Kranz, "As Career Development Lags, Employees Are Going Places," *Workforce Management*, February 2012, 10.

40 D. Welch, "Toyota Recalls Another 2 Million Cars," *Bloomberg Businessweek*, February 24, 2011, http://www.businessweek.com/autos/autobeat/archives/2011/02/toyota_recalls_another_2_million_cars_apology_needed.html.

41 L. Chappell, "Toyota Plants Idling, but Workers Aren't," *Workforce Management*, September 8, 2008, 22–24.

42 D. W. Organ and M. Konovsky, "Cognitive versus Affective Determinants of Organizational Citizenship Behavior," *Journal of Applied Psychology* 74 (2000): 157–164.

43 J. A. LePine, A. Erez, and D. E. Johnson, "The Nature and Dimensionality of Organizational Citizenship Behavior," *Journal of Applied Psychology* 87 (2002): 52–65.

44 S. J. Lambert, "Added Benefits: The Link between Work–Life Benefits and Organizational Citizenship Behaviors," *Academy of Management Journal* 43 (2000): 801–815.

45 R. Cropanzano, D. E. Rupp, and Z. S. Byrne, "The Relationship of Emotional Exhaustion to Work Attitudes, Job Performance, and Organizational Citizenship Behaviors," *Journal of Applied Psychology* 88 (2003): 160–169.

46 M. Orey, "Attacks by Colleagues Are Creeping Up," *BusinessWeek*, May 7, 2007, 14.

47 M. Inness, M. M. LeBlanc, and J. Barling, "Psychosocial Predictors of Supervisor-, Peer-, Subordinate-, and Service Provider-Targeted Aggression," *Journal of Applied Psychology* 93 (2008): 1401–1411.

48 K. E. Dupre, M. Inness, C. E. Connelly, J. Barling, and C. Hoption, "Workplace Aggression in Teenage Part-Time Employees," *Journal of Applied Psychology* 91 (2006): 987–997.

49 A. M. O'Leary-Kelly, R. W. Griffin, and D. J. Glew, "Organization-Motivated Aggression: A Research Framework," *Academy of Management Review* 21 (1996): 225–253.

50 P. Mozur and T. Orlik, "Hon Hai Riot Shows Squeeze on Chinese Manufacturers," *Wall Street Journal*, September 24, 2012, http://online.wsj.com/article/SB10000872396390444 083304578016163169434552.html.

51 D. Wessel, "The Hidden Cost of Labor Strife," *Wall Street Journal*, January 20, 2002, 1–2.

52 J. Laabs, "Employee Sabotage," *Workforce*, July 2000, 33–42.

53 E. F. Stone and H. G. Gueutal, "An Empirical Derivation of the Dimensions Along Which Characteristics of Jobs Are Perceived," *Academy of Management Journal* 28 (1985): 376–396.

54 M. Scoeff, "Danger and Duty," *Workforce Management*, November 19, 2007, 1–3.

55 M. Conlin, "Is Your Office Killing You? Sick Buildings Are Seething with Molds, Monoxide— and Worse," *BusinessWeek*, June 5, 2000, 114–128.

56 M. Korn, "Managing Mental Health at Work," *Wall Street Journal*, August 28, 2012, http://online.wsj.com/article/SB10000872396390444230504577617381107874516.html.

57 B. J. Tepper, "Consequences of Abusive Supervision," *Academy of Management Journal* 43 (2000): 178–190.

58 J. Laabs, "Will 'To-Die-For' Benefits Really Help Retention?" *Workforce*, July 2000, 62–66.

59 S. Lim, L. M. Cortina, and V. J. Magley, "Personal and Workgroup Incivility: Impact on Work and Health Outcomes," *Journal of Applied Psychology* 93 (2008): 95–107.

60 D. Wescott, "Field Guide to Office Bullies," *Bloomberg Businessweek*, November 26, 2012, 94–95.

61 D. S. Chiaburu and D. A. Harrison, "Do Peers Make the Place? Conceptual Synthesis and Meta-Analysis of Co-Worker Effects on Perceptions, Attitudes, OCBs, and Performance," *Journal of Applied Psychology* 93 (2008): 1082–1103.

62 A. Weintraub, "Nursing: On the Critical List," *BusinessWeek*, June 3, 2002, 81.

63 D. Watson, L. A. Clark, and A. Tellegen, "Development and Validation of Brief Measures of Positive and Negative Affect: The PANAS Scales," *Journal of Personality and Social Psychology* 54 (1988): 1063–1070.

64 T. A. Judge, J. E. Bono, and E. A. Locke, "Personality and Job Satisfaction: The Mediating Role of Job Characteristics," *Journal of Applied Psychology* 85 (2000): 237–249.

65 R. D. Zimmerman, "Understanding the Impact of Personality Traits on Individuals' Turnover Decisions: A Meta-Analysis," *Personnel Psychology* 61 (2008): 309–348.

66 J. Forster, "When Workers Just Can't Cope: New Rulings Clarify What Employers Should and Shouldn't Do," *BusinessWeek*, October 23, 2000, 100–102.

67 Korn, "Managing Mental Health at Work."

68 T. A. Judge, R. Ilies, and Z. Zhang, "Genetic Influences on Core Self-Evaluations, Job Satisfaction, and Work Stress: A Behavioral Genetics Mediated Model," *Organizational Behavior and Human Decision Processes* 117 (2012): 208–220.

69 T. A. Judge and C. Hurst, "How the Rich (and Happy) Get Richer (and Happier): Relationship of Core Self-Evaluations to Trajectories in Attaining Work Success," *Journal of Applied Psychology* 93 (2008): 849–863.

70 K. A. Mathews, "Psychological Perspectives on the Type A Behavior Pattern," *Psychological Bulletin* 91 (1982): 293–323.

71 E. C. Dierdorff and J. K. Ellington, "It's the Nature of the Work: Examining Behavior-Based Sources of Work–Family Conflict across Occupations, *Journal of Applied Psychology* 93 (2008): 883–892.

72 J. E. Edwards, J. A. Scully, and M. D. Brtek, "The Nature and Outcomes of Work: A Replication and Extension of Interdisciplinary Work Design Research," *Journal of Applied Psychology* 85 (2000): 860–868.

73 G. R. Oldham, A. Cummings, L. J. Mischel, J. M. Schmidtke, and J. Zhou, "Listen While You Work? Quasi-Experimental Relations between Personal-Stereo Headset Use and Employee Work Responses," *Journal of Applied Psychology* 80 (1995): 547–564.

74 J. S. Warm, R. Parasuraman, and G. Mathews, "Vigilance Requires Hard Mental Work and Is Stressful," *Human Factors* 50 (2008): 433–441.

75 M. F. Cortez, "Do Sleepy Shift Workers Need a Pick-Me-Up Pill?" *Bloomberg Businessweek*, August 15, 2011, 17–18.

76 D. Wescott, "Do Not Disturb," *Bloomberg Businessweek*, April 23, 2012, 90.

77 A. M. Grant, "Does Intrinsic Motivation Fuel the Prosocial Fire? Motivational Synergy in Predicting Persistence, Performance, and Productivity," *Journal of Applied Psychology* 93 (2007): 48–58.

78 S. Thau, K. Aquino, and P. M. Poortvliet, "Self-Defeating Behaviors in Organizations: The Relationship between Thwarted Belonging Behaviors and Interpersonal Work Behaviors," *Journal of Applied Psychology* 92 (2007): 840–847.

79 G. Chen, B. L. Kirkman, R. Kanfer, D. Allen, and B. Rosen, "A Multilevel Study of Leadership, Empowerment, and Performance in Teams," *Journal of Applied Psychology* 92 (2007): 331–346.

80 E. Frauenheim, "Best Buy and CultureRx," *Workforce Management*, March 26, 2007, 28.

81 C. Rober, T. M. Probst, J. J. Martocchio, F. Drasgow, and J. L. Lawler, "Empowerment and Continuous Improvement in the United States, Mexico, Poland and India: Predicting Fit on the Basis of the Dimensions of Power Distance and Individualism," *Journal of Applied Psychology* 85 (2000): 643–658.

82 S. Gilboa, A. Shirom, Y. Fried, and C. Cooper, "A Meta-Analysis of Work Demand Stressors and Job Performance: Examining Main and Moderator Effects," *Personnel Psychology* 61 (2008): 227–271.

83 J. Schlosser and J. Sung, "The 100 Best Companies to Work For," *Fortune*, January 8, 2000, 148–168.

84 M. Moskowitz and R. Levering, "The 100 Best Companies to Work For," *Fortune*, February 4, 2013, 85–96.

85 W. Wyatt, "Stress Relief," *Workforce Management*, March 3, 2008, 19.

86 S. J. Lambert, "When Flexibility Hurts," *New York Times*, September 19, 2012, http://www.nytimes.com/2012/09/20/opinion/low-paid-women-want-predictable-hours-and-steady-pay.html?_r=0.

87 "The Leisure Gap," *Bloomberg Businessweek*, July 22, 2012, 8–9.

88 D. Brady, "Rethinking the Rat Trap," *BusinessWeek*, August 26, 2002, 142–143.

89 F. Jones, D. B. O'Connor, M. Connor, B. McMillan, and E. Ferguson, "Impact of Daily Mood, Work Hours, and Iso-Strain Variables on Self-Reported Health Behaviors," *Journal of Applied Psychology* 92 (2007): 1731–1740.

90 S. G. Rogelberg, A. Luong, M. E. Sederberg, and D. S. Cristol, "Employee Attitude Surveys: Examining the Attitudes of Non-Compliant Employees," *Journal of Applied Psychology* 85 (2000): 284–293.

91 M. A. Donovan, F. D. Drasgow, and T. M. Probst, "Does Computerizing Paper-and-Pencil Job Attitude Scales Make a Difference? New IRT Analyses Offer Insight," *Journal of Applied Psychology* 85 (2000): 305–313.

92 J. Smerd, "Sun Healthcare Group," *Workforce Management*, March 26, 2007, 32.

93 D. Isen, "Reduce Employee Turnover, Build Customer Loyalty," *Workforce Management*, May 19, 2008, 34.

94 P. E. Spector, "Locus of Control and Well-Being at Work: How Generalizable Are the Findings?" *Academy of Management Journal* 45 (2002): 453–466.

95 E. R. Burris, J. R. Detert, and D. S. Chiaburu, "Quitting before Leaving: The Mediating Effects of Psychological Attachment and Detachment on Voice," *Journal of Applied Psychology* 93 (2008): 912–922.

96 P. J. Kiger, "Crouse Hospital," *Workforce Management*, October 20, 2008, 17.

97 S. Toker and M. Biron, "Job Burnout and Depression: Unraveling Their Temporal Relationship and Considering the Role of Physical Activity," *Journal of Applied Psychology* 97 (2012): 699–710.

98 S. Shellenbarger, "To Cut Office Stress, Try Butterflies and Meditation?" *Wall Street Journal*, October 9, 2012, http://online.wsj.com/article/SB10000872396390443982904578046390545386624.html.

99 H. O. Dickenson, F. Campbell, and F. R. Boyer, "Relaxation Therapies for the Management of Primary Hypertension in Adults: A Cochrane Review," *Journal of Human Hypertension* 22 (2008): 809–820.

100 L. Thompson and M. Thompson, "Effective Stress Management Using Neurofeedback and Biofeedback," *Applied Psychophysiology and Biofeedback* 33 (2008): 243–253.

101 J. R. B. Halbesleben, "Sources of Social Support and Burnout: A Meta-Analytic Test of the Conservation of Energy Hypothesis," *Journal of Applied Psychology* 91 (2006): 1134–1145.

102 K. J. Templer, C. Tay, and N. A. Chandrasaker, "Motivational Cultural Intelligence, Realistic Job Preview, Realistic Living Conditions Preview, and Cross-Cultural Adjustment," *Group and Organization Management* 31 (2006): 154–173.

Part III

Meso Organizational Behavior

Chapter 7

Efficiency, Motivation, and Quality in Work Design

I stand in one spot, about a two- or three-foot area, all night. . . . We do about 32 [welding] jobs per car, per unit. Forty-eight units an hour, eight hours a day. Thirty-two times forty-eight times eight. Figure it out. That's how many times I push that button. . . . You dream, you think of things you've done. I drift back continuously to when I was a kid and what me and my brothers did. . . . [Y]ou're nothing more than a machine. They give better care to that machine than they will to you. They'll have more respect, give more attention to that machine. . . . Somehow you get the feeling that the machine is better than you are.[1]

The other day when I was proofreading [insurance policy] endorsements I noticed some guy had insured his store for $165,000 against vandalism and $5,000 against fire. Now that's bound to be a mistake. They probably got it backwards. . . . I was just about to show it to [my supervisor] when I figured, wait a minute! I'm not supposed to read these forms. I'm just supposed to check one column against another. And they do check. . . . They don't explain this stuff to me. I'm not supposed to understand it. I'm just supposed to check one column against the other. . . . If they're gonna give me a robot's job to do, I'm gonna do it like a robot! Anyway, it just lowers my production record to get up and point out someone else's error.[2]

Few people can build a car by themselves, but companies such as Ford, Toyota, and Volkswagen turn out thousands of cars every year by dividing car building into simple assembly-line jobs. Likewise, insurance policies cannot be underwritten by individuals working alone, but companies such as Allstate, State Farm, and Prudential succeed by breaking down policy preparation into a number of less complicated clerical tasks. As described in Chapter 2, the *division of labor*, in which difficult work is broken into smaller tasks, enables organized groups of people to accomplish tasks that would otherwise be beyond their physical or mental capacities as individuals.

When utilized effectively, the division of labor can lead to the creation of jobs that contribute to satisfaction, success, and significant competitive advantage. Sometimes, however, it leads to the creation of jobs that are monotonous and unchallenging due to oversimplification and the inclusion of too much routine, like the welding and proofreading jobs described above. Why do managers design jobs that are so unappealing? What do they expect to gain by simplifying work? What can be done to counteract the negative effects of oversimplified, routinized tasks—outcomes like detached day-dreaming, social alienation, and careless work? Can oversimplification be avoided completely?

This chapter seeks answers to these questions by examining theories and methods of **work design**, the formal process of dividing an organization's total stock of work into jobs and tasks that its members can perform. Work design stands at the boundary of micro and meso organizational behavior, involving in some instances the creation of jobs to be performed by individuals working alone and in other instances the design of jobs to be performed by the members of groups or teams working together. The chapter begins by describing one approach to work design, the *efficiency perspective*, that originated in the work on scientific management described in Chapter 2. Today this approach is widely used to economize on the costs of routine work activities. Next, the chapter turns to the *motivational perspective*, an approach that arose largely in reaction to problems with the efficiency perspective. This perspective, which is based on ideas about human motivation and satisfaction like those discussed in Chapters 5 and 6, highlights the importance of designing jobs that encourage employee growth and fulfillment. The chapter then describes a third approach, the *quality perspective*, which combines key elements of the efficiency and motivational perspectives. Growing out of the Total Quality Management movement, this perspective focuses primarily on improving innovation and quality through the use of self-managed teams, advanced production technologies, and rigorous process management.

The Efficiency Perspective

To achieve *efficiency*, companies minimize the resources consumed in providing a product or service. Therefore, the **efficiency perspective** on work design is concerned with creating jobs that conserve time, human energy, raw materials, and other productive resources. It is the foundation of the field of **industrial engineering**, which focuses on maximizing the efficiency of the methods, facilities, and materials used to produce commercial products. Methods engineering and work measurement are two areas of industrial engineering that have had especially noticeable effects on the division of labor in modern organizations.

Methods Engineering

Methods engineering is an area of industrial engineering that originated in Frederick Winslow Taylor's work on scientific management (described in Chapter 2). It attempts to improve the methods used to perform work by incorporating two related endeavors—process engineering and human factors engineering.

Process engineering assesses the sequence of tasks required to produce a particular product or service and analyzes the way those tasks fit together into an integrated job. It also examines tasks to see which should be performed by people and which should be carried out by machines, trying to determine how workers can perform their jobs most efficiently.

Process engineers study the product or service to be produced and decide what role, if any, humans should play in its production. They also determine whether some employees should act as managers, directing and controlling the flow of work, and they differentiate the resulting managerial jobs from those of nonmanagerial workers. Process engineers specify the procedures for employees to follow, the equipment they should use, and the physical layout of offices, workstations, and materials-storage facilities.

In contrast to the process engineer's focus on improving work processes, experts in **human factors engineering** (also called **ergonomics**) design machines and work environments so that they better match human capacities and limitations. Table 7.1 summarizes some of the most important areas of study of human factors engineering.

When people make mistakes at work, human factors engineers investigate whether the equipment being used is partially to blame for these mistakes. Are mistakes made when workers use certain kinds of equipment but not others? Can equipment be redesigned so as to

Table 7.1 Human Factors Engineering

Area of study	Examples
Physical aspects of the user–machine interface	Size, shape, color, texture, and method of operation of controls for cars, home appliances, and industrial and commercial equipment.
Cognitive aspects of the user–machine interface	Human understanding of instructions and other information. Style of information exchange between computer and user.
Workplace design and workspace layout	Layout of offices, factories, kitchens, and other places where people work. Design of relationships between furniture and equipment and between different equipment components.
Physical environment	Effects of climate, noise and vibration, illumination, and chemical or biological contaminants on human performance and health.

Source: Adapted from C. T. Morgan, J. S. Cook, A. Chapanis, and M. W. Lund, *Human Engineering Guide to Equipment Design* (New York: McGraw-Hill, 1963).

minimize or even eliminate human error? In most cases, the effects of human fallibility and carelessness can be substantially decreased by minimizing the error-provoking features of jobs and equipment. For example, shape-coded controls like those shown in Figure 7.1 can be used to reduce aircraft accidents caused when pilots activate the wrong control. To help pilots differentiate among control levers without looking at them, two general rules were followed during the design process: (1) the shape of a control should suggest its purpose, and (2) the shape should be distinguishable even when gloves are worn.[3]

Work Measurement: Motion and Time Studies

Besides designing job methods, industrial engineers sometimes examine the motions and time required to complete each job. Although such work can be traced to Taylor's work on scientific management, it is more directly the product of research by Frank and Lillian Gilbreth, who set out to find the "one best way" to do any job. In the course of this pursuit, the Gilbreths developed motion study, a procedure that reduces jobs to their most basic movements. As noted in Chapter 2, each of these basic movements is called a *therblig* (a near reversal of the name *Gilbreth*) and consists of motions such as "search," "grasp," and "assemble." The Gilbreths also developed procedures to specify in advance the time required for each of the movements needed to perform a job. These procedures gave rise to **work measurement**, an area of industrial engineering concerned with measuring the amount of work accomplished and developing standards for performing work of an acceptable quantity and quality. Work measurement includes both micromotion analysis and time-study procedures.

In **micromotion analysis**, industrial engineers analyze the hand and body movements required to do a job. This technique is a direct descendant of the motion-study methods devised by the Gilbreths, whose therbligs continue to be used in current micromotion procedures. Industrial engineers usually conduct micromotion analysis by using a slow-speed film or

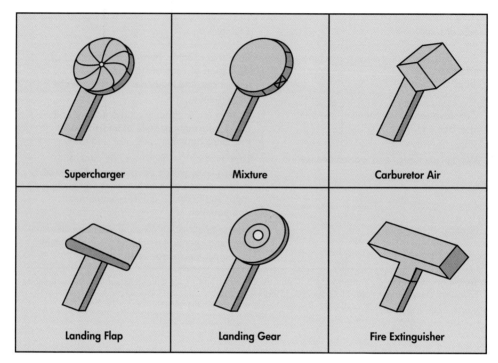

Figure 7.1 Shape-Coding to Reduce Flying Errors

Source: Adapted from C. T. Morgan, J. S. Cook, A. Chapanis, and M. W. Lund, *Human Engineering Guide to Equipment Design* (New York: McGraw-Hill, 1963).

videotape of a person performing his or her job. They then analyze the movements performed in the task and try to improve efficiency by means of principles such as the following:

1. Try to have both hands doing the same thing at the same time or to balance the work of the two hands.
2. Avoid using the hands simply for holding. Use specialized jigs, vises, or clamps instead.
3. Keep all work inside a work area bounded by the worker's reach.
4. Relieve the hands of work wherever possible.
5. Eliminate as many therbligs or as much of a therblig as possible, and combine therbligs when possible.
6. Arrange therbligs in the most convenient order. Each therblig should flow smoothly into the next.
7. Standardize the method of performing the job in the manner that promotes the quickest learning.[4]

As is apparent from these principles, jobs designed by means of micromotion analysis are characterized by economy of motion.

Time-study techniques are used to measure the time actually consumed by job performance. They are also sometimes employed to specify the time that a particular job should take to complete. In **stopwatch time analysis,** an analyst uses a stopwatch (or microchronometer) to time the sequence of motions needed to complete a job. In **standard time analysis,** the analyst matches the results of micromotion analysis with standard time charts to determine the average time that should be required to perform a job. When combined with micromotion analyses, the results of either type of time analysis can be used to create descriptions that identify the therblig motions required to perform a job and the length of time that the job should take to complete.

Evaluating Industrial Engineering and the Efficiency Perspective

Consistent with the efficiency perspective that underlies them, all industrial engineering methods attempt to enhance productivity by simplifying jobs. Often, use of these methods can improve productivity dramatically.[5] There is, however, a danger that simplification will be carried too far, leading to the creation of jobs that are oversimplified and lacking in challenge. Workers performing oversimplified, routine jobs often become bored, resentful, and dissatisfied—attitudes that contribute to problems with workforce absenteeism and turnover. Employees who choose to remain on their jobs may slow down their work pace or resort to sabotage to compensate for the lack of challenge and interest in their work. Performance quantity and quality can suffer as a consequence.

Oversimplification can also have negative health consequences. According to U.S. government sources, far more than 50 percent of all workplace illnesses are attributable to the adverse effects of repetitive stress caused by doing routine jobs again and again. Workers' compensation claims and other expenses related to such injuries cost U.S. employers as much as $20 billion per year, according to estimates made by insurer Aetna Life and Casualty. To deal with this problem, businesses such as the Chrysler Corporation rotate workers among tasks to break up repetition over the course of each working day. Chrysler has also redesigned many jobs and developed special tools to reduce or eliminate repetitive stress.[6] In summary, *the simplification intended to enhance the efficiency of work processes may actually reduce that efficiency, if carried to an extreme.*

The Motivational Perspective

What can be done to counteract the effects of oversimplification, or to make sure that jobs are not oversimplified to begin with? The answer to this question, offered initially by Lillian Gilbreth, is that *jobs should be designed in such a way that performing them creates feelings of fulfillment and satisfaction in their holders.*[7] This idea forms the central tenet of the **motivational perspective** on work design, which suggests that fitting the characteristics of jobs to the needs and interests of the people who perform them provides the opportunity for satisfaction at work.[8] Table 7.2 contrasts this approach with the efficiency perspective discussed in the previous section. Methods of work design that incorporate various elements of the motivational perspective include horizontal job enlargement, vertical job enrichment, comprehensive job enrichment, and sociotechnical enrichment. Some of these approaches are more successful than others in stimulating motivation and feelings of fulfillment and satisfaction, as discussed in the remainder of this section.

Horizontal Job Enlargement

To counteract oversimplification, managers sometimes attempt to boost the complexity of work by increasing the number of task activities entailed in a job. This approach is based on the idea that increasing **job range**, or the number of tasks that a jobholder performs, will reduce the repetitive nature of the job and thus eliminate worker boredom.[9] Increasing job range in this manner is called **horizontal job enlargement**—so named

Table 7.2 Two Perspectives on Work Design

Efficiency perspective	Motivational perspective
Tasks are shaped mainly by technology and organizational needs.	Tasks are shaped at least partly by workers' personal needs.
Tasks are repetitive and narrow.	Tasks are varied and complex.
Tasks require little or no skill and are easy to learn and perform.	Tasks require well-developed skills and are difficult to learn and perform.
The management and performance of work are separated into different jobs.	The management and performance of work are merged in the same jobs.
It is assumed that only one best way to do each job exists.	It is assumed that each job can be performed in several ways.
Tools and methods are developed by staff specialists.	Tools and methods are often developed by the people who use them.
Workers are an extension of their equipment and perform according to its require-ments.	Workers use equipment but are not regulated by it.
The pace of work is often set by a machine.	The pace of work is set by people rather than machines.
Extrinsic rewards (incentive wages) are used to motivate performance.	Intrinsic rewards (task achievements) are used along with extrinsic rewards to motivate performance.
Social interaction is limited or discouraged.	Social interaction is encouraged and, in some cases, required.
Efficiency and productivity are the ultimate goals of work design.	Satisfaction and fulfillment are important goals of work design.

because the job is created out of tasks from the same horizontal "slice" of an organization's hierarchy.

Some horizontal job enlargement programs rely on **job extension**, an approach in which several simplified jobs are combined to form a single new job. For example, an insurance clerk's job that consists solely of proofreading might be extended by adding filing and telephone-answering tasks to it. Similarly, the job of a welder on an automotive assembly line might be extended by adding other assembly operations to it.

Organizations as diverse as Maytag, AT&T, and the civil service have all implemented job extension programs. When a number of simple, readily mastered tasks are combined, however, workers tend to view job extension as giving them more of the same routine, boring work to do. For this reason, although initial efforts seemed promising, most research has suggested that job extension rarely succeeds in reversing oversimplification to the degree necessary to strengthen employee motivation and satisfaction.[10]

In **job rotation**, workers switch jobs in a structured, predefined manner. Rotation of this sort creates horizontal enlargement without combining or otherwise redesigning a firm's jobs. For instance, a supermarket employee might run a checkout lane for a specified period of time and then, after switching jobs with another employee, restock shelves for another set period of time. As workers rotate, they perform a wider variety of tasks than they would if limited to a single job. As with job extension, however, critics have observed that job rotation often achieves little more than having people perform several boring, routine jobs. Thus, although companies such as Ford Motor Company and Western Electric have tried job rotation, it has generally failed to improve worker motivation or satisfaction (although it can help reduce repetitive stress injuries and similar health problems attributable to repetitive work).[11]

Vertical Job Enrichment

The failure of horizontal job enlargement to counteract the undesirable effects of oversimplification has led managers to try a variety of alternative approaches. Many such trials involve attempts to increase **job depth**—that is, the amount of discretion a jobholder has to choose his or her job activities and outcomes. This approach, called **vertical job enrichment**, is based on the work of Frederick Herzberg, an industrial psychologist who studied the sources of employee satisfaction and dissatisfaction at work.[12]

Herzberg, who began his research in the mid-1950s, began by interviewing 200 engineers and accountants in nine companies, asking them to describe incidents at work that made them feel "exceptionally good" or "exceptionally bad" about their jobs. From these interviews, Herzberg concluded that satisfaction (feeling good) and dissatisfaction (feeling bad) should be considered independent concepts, rather than opposite extremes on a single continuum as traditional views had held. This approach suggests that a person might feel more satisfied with his or her job without feeling less dissatisfied, more dissatisfied without feeling less satisfied, and so forth.

As he dug further into his interview data, Herzberg also discovered that certain characteristics of the work situation seemed to influence employee satisfaction, whereas other characteristics appeared to affect employee dissatisfaction. **Motivator factors**, such as achievement or recognition, increased satisfaction. Their absence produced a lack of satisfaction but not active dissatisfaction. In contrast, **hygiene factors**, such as company policy or employees' relationships with their supervisors, were usually associated with dissatisfaction and rarely contributed to a gain in satisfaction.

Armed with this distinction, Herzberg then noticed that only the motivator factors identified in his research seemed able to increase the incentive to work. Hygiene factors, he said, could help maintain motivation but would more often contribute to a decrease in motivation. As indicated in Figure 7.2, many of Herzberg's hygiene factors are the very same work characteristics emphasized by the efficiency perspective on work design. In fact, Herzberg contended that following the principles advocated by Taylor, the Gilbreths, and later specialists in industrial engineering would create oversimplified jobs that could only dissatisfy and demotivate workers. Consequently, he suggested that managers should pay less attention to issues such as working conditions and salary and instead design jobs that incorporated opportunities for growth, achievement, and recognition.

Over the years, many critics have attacked Herzberg's ideas.[13] Among the most serious criticisms are the following:

1. The *critical-incident technique* that Herzberg used, in which he asked people to recall earlier feelings and experiences, is a questionable research method subject to errors in perception or memory and to subconscious biases. Its use leaves the validity of his conclusions open to question.

2. All of Herzberg's interviewees—engineers and accountants—were male members of professional, white-collar occupational groups (few women were engineers or accountants in Herzberg's day). Women, minorities, and members of other occupational groups, such as salespeople or industrial laborers, might have answered Herzberg's questions differently.

3.   Other studies have failed to replicate Herzberg's results. As will be discussed in Chapter 16, which covers research methods, such failure casts doubt on the merits of research findings.
4.   Work design programs based on Herzberg's model almost always fail to stimulate workforce satisfaction of lasting significance.

Because of these questions about its validity, Herzberg's two-factor theory is not a useful guide for managerial actions.[14] Nonetheless, it remains widely known among managers and continues to stimulate interest in questions of motivation, satisfaction, and work design. In addition, it has influenced more recent ideas about work design by highlighting the importance of designing jobs that satisfy *higher-order* desires for growth, achievement, and recognition.

Comprehensive Job Enrichment

Although neither horizontal job enlargement nor vertical job enrichment can counteract oversimplification when implemented separately, **comprehensive job enrichment** programs

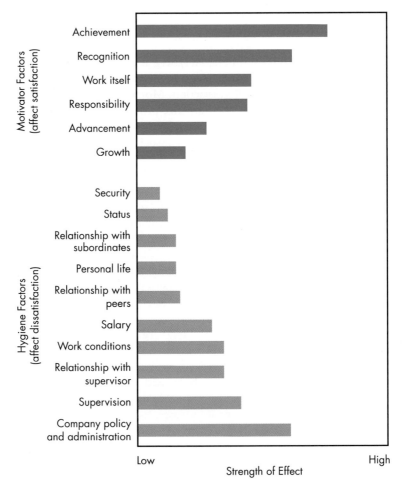

Figure 7.2 Herzberg's Motivator Factors and Hygiene Factors
Source: Adapted from F. Herzberg, B. Mausner, and B. B. Snyderman, *The Motivation to Work* (New York: Wiley, 1959).

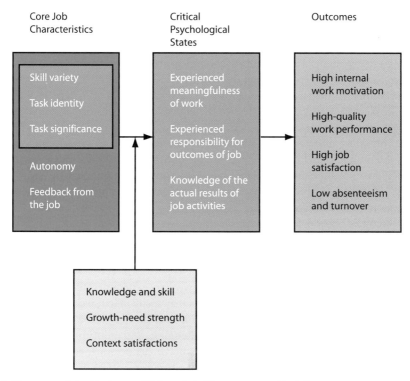

Core Job
Characteristics

Critical
Psychological
States

Outcomes

Figure 7.3 Elements of the Hackman–Oldham Job Characteristics Model

that combine both horizontal and vertical improvements are usually more successful in stimulating motivation and satisfaction. Many such programs are based on the model of work design developed by J. Richard Hackman and Greg Oldham, overviewed in Figure 7.3.[15]

The Hackman–Oldham Model

According to Hackman and Oldham, jobs that are likely to motivate performance and contribute to employee satisfaction exhibit the following five **core job characteristics:**

1. *Skill variety:* the degree to which a jobholder must carry out a variety of activities and use a number of different personal skills in performing the job.
2. *Task identity:* the degree to which performing a job results in the completion of a whole and identifiable piece of work and a visible outcome that can be recognized as the result of personal performance.
3. *Task significance:* the degree to which a job has a significant effect on the lives of other people, whether those people are co-workers in the same firm or other individuals in the surrounding environment.
4. *Autonomy:* the degree to which the jobholder has the freedom, independence, and discretion necessary to schedule work and to decide which procedures to use in carrying out that work.
5. *Feedback:* the degree to which performing the activities required by the job provides the worker with direct and clear information about the effectiveness of his or her performance.

In turn, these five core job characteristics influence the extent to which employees experience three critical psychological states, or personal, internal reactions to their jobs. The first state, *experienced meaningfulness of work*, refers to the degree to which a worker sees his or her job as having an outcome that is useful and valuable to the worker, the company, and the surrounding environment. The second psychological state, *experienced responsibility for work outcomes*, concerns the degree to which the worker feels personally accountable and responsible for the results of their work. The third state, *knowledge of results*, reflects the degree to which the worker maintains an awareness of the effectiveness of his or her work.[16]

Next, each job characteristic influences a particular psychological state. Specifically, skill variety, task identity, and task significance affect the experienced meaningfulness of work. Thus jobholders should feel that their jobs are meaningful if they must use a variety of activities and skills to produce an identifiable piece of work that influences the lives of others. Autonomy, on the other hand, influences the jobholder's experienced responsibility for work outcomes. Consequently, workers who have the discretion to determine their work procedures and outcomes should feel responsible for the results of that work. Finally, feedback determines whether a worker will have knowledge of the results of his or her work. Through information about performance effectiveness that comes from the job itself, the jobholder can maintain an awareness of how effectively he or she is performing.

According to the Hackman–Oldham model, if workers experience all three states simultaneously, four kinds of work and personal outcomes may result. First, workers will tend to view their jobs as interesting, challenging, and important, and they might be motivated to perform them simply because they are so stimulating, challenging, and enjoyable. *High internal work motivation*, or being "turned on" to job performance by its personal consequences, is therefore one possible outcome. Second, experiencing the three critical psychological states and the internal, or intrinsic, motivation they arouse can encourage *high-quality work performance* (and, in some instances, a higher quantity of production as well).[17] Third, workers who experience the three psychological states do so because their work provides them with opportunities for personal learning, growth, and development. As discussed in Chapter 6, these kinds of experiences generally promote *high satisfaction with work*. Fourth, work that stimulates all three psychological states also tends to lead to *lower absenteeism and turnover*.

The Hackman–Oldham model proposes that several moderator variables determine whether the core job characteristics will actually trigger the critical psychological states, leading to the four outcomes just described. The first of these differences is the worker's *knowledge and skill*. To succeed on a job characterized by high levels of the five core job characteristics, a worker must have the knowledge and skill required to perform the job successfully. People who cannot perform a job because they lack the necessary knowledge or skill will merely feel frustrated by their failure, not encouraged. The motivational aims of comprehensive job enrichment will thus be thwarted.

Growth-need strength, or the strength of a worker's need for personal growth, is a second moderator variable that influences the efficacy of the Hackman–Oldham model. Workers who have strong growth needs are attracted to enriched work because it offers the opportunity for growth. In contrast, workers with weak growth needs are likely to feel overburdened by the opportunities offered them. As a consequence, they will try to avoid enriched work and will not derive personal benefit if required to perform it.

Finally, *context satisfactions* can influence the Hackman–Oldham model's applicability. Hackman and Oldham identified several context satisfactions—satisfaction with pay, with job security, with co-workers, and with supervisors. Workers who feel exploited and dissatisfied because they are poorly paid, feel insecure about their jobs, or have abusive co-workers or unfair supervision are likely to view job enrichment as just one more type of exploitation.

Context dissatisfaction can thus negate the expected benefits of comprehensive job enrichment.

Implementation

To put their model to use, Hackman and Oldham developed the **Job Diagnostic Survey** (JDS) a questionnaire that measures workers' perceptions of the five core job characteristics, the three critical psychological states, and certain moderating factors. The deficiencies identified by a JDS analysis of a particular job can be corrected in several ways. To enhance skill variety and task identity, oversimplified jobs can be *combined* to form enlarged modules of work. For example, the production of a toaster could be redesigned so that the entire appliance is constructed by a single employee working alone rather than by a dozen or more people working on an assembly line. *Natural units of work* can be created by clustering similar tasks into logical or inherently meaningful groups. For instance, a data-entry clerk who formerly selected work orders randomly from a stack might be given sole responsibility for the work orders of an entire department or division. This intervention is intended to strengthen both task identity and task significance for the clerk.

To increase task variety, autonomy, and feedback, a firm can give workers the responsibility for *establishing and managing client relationships.* At John Deere & Company, for example, assembly-line workers take stints as traveling salespeople, getting to know their customers' needs and complaints.[18] To increase autonomy, managerial duties can be designed into a particular job through *vertical loading.* Finally, to increase feedback, *feedback channels* can be opened by adding to a job such things as quality-control responsibilities and computerized feedback mechanisms.

Sociotechnical Enrichment

The Hackman–Oldham model focuses on designing individualized units of work, each performed by a single employee. Therefore, it is not appropriate for jobs that must be performed by closely interacting groups of workers. To counteract the negative effects of oversimplified *group work*, managers can instead use a team-based approach.[19] **Sociotechnical enrichment** is one such approach.

Sociotechnical enrichment originated in the early 1950s, when researchers from England's Tavistock Institute set out to correct faults in the processes used to mine coal in Great Britain.[20] Historically, coal had been excavated by teams of miners working closely with each other to pool efforts, coordinate activities, and cope with the physical threats of mining. With the advent of powered coal-digging equipment in the 1930s and 1940s, however, coal mining changed drastically. Teams were split up, and miners often found themselves working alone along the long walls of exposed coal created by the equipment. Mining—normally a hazardous, physically demanding occupation—grew even more unbearable owing to the changes stimulated by the new technology. Miners expressed their dissatisfaction with these circumstances through disobedience, absenteeism, and occasional violence.

The Tavistock researchers soon concluded that the roots of the miners' dissatisfaction lay in the loss of the social interaction that mining teams had provided, which had made the dangerous, demanding job of mining more tolerable. According to the researchers, the technology had been allowed to supersede important social factors. Performance in the mine could be improved only by redressing this balance. Indeed, after small teams were formed to operate and provide support for clusters of powered equipment, production rose substantially.

This finding, along with similar results found at other research sites, led the Tavistock researchers to make the general suggestion that workforce productivity could be hurt when either social or technical factors alone were allowed to shape work processes. They further suggested that work designs that sought to balance social and technological factors—*sociotechnical designs*—would encourage both performance and satisfaction in the workplace.

Stated differently, researchers suggested that employees should work in groups that allow them to talk with each other about their work as they perform their duties. These work groups should include the people whose frequent interaction is required by the production technology being used. For instance, salespeople, register clerks, and stock clerks, who must often interact with each other to serve customers in a department store, should be grouped together to facilitate communication about work. Salespeople and clerks from other departments should not be included in the group, because they do not share job-related interdependencies with the group's members.

In the course of conducting their studies, the Tavistock sociotechnical researchers identified the following work characteristics as critical to worker motivation and satisfaction:

1. The content of each job must be reasonably demanding or challenging and provide some variety, although not necessarily novelty.
2. Performing the job must have perceivable, desirable consequences. Workers should be able to identify the products of their efforts.
3. Workers should be able to see how the lives of other people are affected by the production processes they use and the things they produce.
4. Workers must have decision-making authority in some areas.
5. Workers must be able to learn from the job and go on learning. This requirement implies having appropriate performance standards and adequate feedback.
6. Workers need the opportunity to give and receive help and to have their work recognized by others in the workplace.[21]

This list of characteristics was developed independently of the work of Hackman and Oldham, as the Tavistock group did its research mainly in England and Norway and Hackman and Oldham worked only in the United States. Nonetheless, items (1) through (5) of the Tavistock list are similar to the five core job characteristics of the Hackman–Oldham model. Only item (6) differs from the latter model, and it reflects the emphasis placed by sociotechnical enrichment on the importance of cooperation in groups.

Contemporary sociotechnical designs normally create **semiautonomous groups**. These groups must respond to the management direction needed to ensure adherence to organizational policies, but they are otherwise responsible for managing group activities. Within each such group,

> [i]ndividuals must move about within the group spontaneously and without being ordered to do so, because it is necessary to the efficient functioning of the [group]. . . . If we observe the group in action, we will see movements of individuals between different jobs. When an especially heavy load materializes at one work station and another is clear for the moment, we will see the person at the latter spontaneously move to help out at the former. . . . It is a natural and continuous give and take within a group of people, the object being to attain an established production target. . . . The group members are not merely carrying out a certain number of tasks. They are also working together, on a continuing basis, to coordinate different tasks, bearing responsibility, and taking whatever measures are necessary to cope with the work of the entire unit.[22]

As they work together in this manner, the members of a semiautonomous group are able to do the following:

1. Rotate in and out of tasks to enhance skill variety.
2. Work together on a group product that is a whole, identifiable piece of work.
3. Influence the lives of other members of the group and the lives of those who consume the group's output.
4. Decide as a group who will belong to the group and what tasks the group members will perform.
5. Obtain feedback from group members about task performance.
6. Count on the help and support of other group members if it is needed.

When it proceeds in this manner, the work of semiautonomous groups is rich in the psychological requirements identified by sociotechnical researchers as enhancing workforce motivation and satisfaction.[23]

Implementation

Figure 7.4 contrasts a traditional assembly line with semiautonomous groups. As shown in the figure, the decision to adopt sociotechnical design principles has important implications for shop-floor operations. In both panels of the figure, workers are assembling automotive engines. In the upper panel, each worker performs a simplified job that consists of taking a part from a storage bin and attaching it to a partially completed engine as it moves along a conveyor. In the lower panel, workers are clustered into semiautonomous groups, each of which removes a bare engine block from a conveyor loop, assembles a complete engine from parts in surrounding storage bins, and returns the finished engine to the conveyor loop for transportation to other assembly operations. As suggested by this example, sociotechnical work designs typically eliminate traditional assembly-line operations.

Evaluating the Motivational Perspective

Consistent with the motivational perspective that underlies them, all enlargement and enrichment techniques are aimed at designing jobs that satisfy the needs and interests of their holders. As noted earlier, methods that consist solely of horizontal job enlargement or vertical job enrichment have largely failed to achieve this goal. Methods of work design that incorporate *both* horizontal enlargement and vertical enrichment, however, have proven more effective in stimulating workforce motivation and satisfaction in a wide variety of situations.[24]

Some doubts have been raised about various elements of the Hackman–Oldham model. For example, studies have sometimes failed to verify the existence of the five distinct job characteristics identified in the model.[25] It is also unclear whether JDS questionnaire items measure objective, stable job characteristics or subjective, changing worker opinions.[26] Some researchers have even questioned whether job characteristics like those identified by Hackman and Oldham truly influence motivation and satisfaction. They suggest that employees' feelings about themselves and their work might instead be affected more profoundly by the opinions of other people in the surrounding social context.[27] This idea will be considered further in Chapter 14, when we discuss *social information processing* and organizational culture. Finally, some disagreement exists as to whether the moderators identified by Hackman and Oldham actually influence the model's applicability.[28]

Traditional Assembly Line

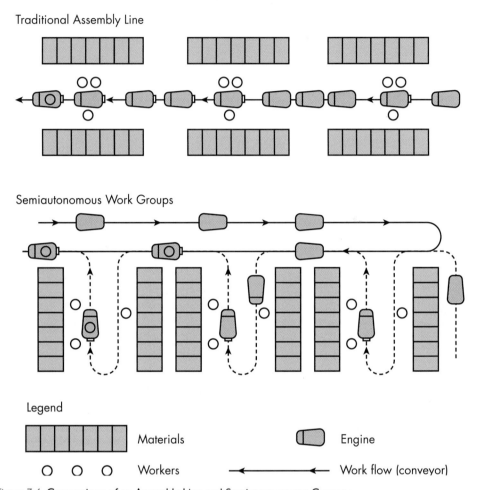

Semiautonomous Work Groups

Legend

▯▯▯▯▯▯ Materials	⬠ Engine
○ ○ ○ Workers	◄─────◄── Work flow (conveyor)

Figure 7.4 Comparison of an Assembly Line and Semiautonomous Groups

Source: Adapted from N. J. Kemp, T. Wall, C. W. Clegg, and J. L. Cordery, "Autonomous Work Groups in a Greenfield Site: A Comparative Study," *Journal of Occupational Psychology* 56 (2011): 271–288.

Nonetheless, the Hackman–Oldham model has served as the basis of successful work design programs implemented at many well-respected companies, including Texas Instruments, AT&T, Motorola, and Xerox. Such programs are not without their drawbacks. In particular, they are usually incompatible with assembly-line production processes. To enrich jobs using the Hackman–Oldham approach, a firm must almost always abandon the sort of simplified, repetitive tasks that serve as the foundation of assembly lines. Consequently, companies with substantial investments in modernized assembly lines are often reluctant to try Hackman–Oldham enrichment. In addition, 5 to 15 percent of the workforce typically lacks the skills, growth needs, or context satisfactions needed to realize the benefits of such work; those workers are likely to be "overstretched" by enriched work. Therefore, a cluster of unenriched jobs must be maintained if the firm wants to avoid displacing a significant number of its employees.

The sociotechnical enrichment approach was first implemented in Europe, where it influenced the design of jobs in firms such as Norsk Hydro, Volvo, Saab-Scania, and the Orrefors

Glass Works. Since then, U.S. companies including Xerox, Cummins Engine, IBM, Polaroid, and General Electric have also experimented with sociotechnical work design, and investigation has shown that this approach yields virtually the same outcomes stimulated by the Hackman–Oldham method.[29] Sociotechnical work designs do not always improve productivity or reduce absenteeism and turnover, but they do strengthen motivation, satisfaction, and similar workplace attitudes.[30] In addition, as is true for programs based on the Hackman–Oldham model, experience suggests that a small but significant number of workers are likely to resist sociotechnical enrichment. Consequently, either a few jobs must be left unchanged or managers must be prepared to deal with the overstretching problem.

The Quality Perspective

Within the last three decades, a third perspective on work design has emerged as researchers and managers have sought new ways to improve the quality of goods and services produced in North America. Founders of the **quality perspective** include W. Edwards Deming, Philip B. Crosby, and Joseph M. Juran, three U.S. quality experts who inspired widespread adoption of an approach known as *Total Quality Management* (TQM).[31] TQM is guided by an overarching emphasis on making *continuous* improvements in quality throughout the process of planning objectives, organizing work, designing products, undertaking production, and monitoring results.[32]

Reflecting this emphasis, advocates of the quality perspective recommend the use of self-management, teamwork, and technology to stimulate innovation and flexibility, so that companies can produce high-quality products and respond effectively to changing customer demands.[33] As part of this perspective, quality circles, self-managed teams, automation and robotics, and process management have been introduced throughout North America and have significantly affected the way work is designed and performed.

Quality Circles

Quality circles (QCs) are small groups of employees, ranging in size from roughly three to thirty members, who meet on company time to identify and resolve job-related problems. Although usually thought of as a Japanese management technique, QCs were actually invented in the United States and exported to Japan by Deming and Juran during the Allied occupation that followed World War II.[34] In North America, companies such as Westinghouse, Procter & Gamble, and Ford have implemented QCs to achieve the following goals:

1. Reduce assembly errors and enhance product quality.
2. Inspire more effective teamwork and cooperation in everyday work groups.
3. Promote a greater sense of job involvement and commitment.
4. Increase employee motivation.
5. Create greater decision-making capacity.
6. Substitute problem prevention for problem solving.
7. Improve communication in and between work groups.
8. Develop harmonious relations between management and employees.
9. Promote leadership development among nonmanagerial employees.[35]

Ordinarily, QC membership is voluntary and remains stable over time. The amount of time spent in QC activities can range from one hour per month to a few hours every week. Topics of discussion can include quality control, cost reduction, improvement of production techniques, production planning, and even long-term product design.[36] Over the course of many meetings, the activities of a typical QC proceed through a series of steps:

1. Members of the QC raise issues about their work and workplace in a group discussion coordinated by their supervisor or a specially trained facilitator. Often, the facilitator is an internal change agent with expertise in micro organization development.
2. QC members examine these concerns and look for ways to collapse or integrate them into specific projects. For instance, concerns about production speed and raw-material quality might be grouped together in a production methods project. Concerns about workplace safety and worker health could be combined into a work environment project.
3. Members perform initial analyses of their QC's projects using various group decision-making techniques and tools, including data gathering, graphs, checklists, or charts.
4. QC members reach consensus decisions about the feasibility and importance of different projects, deciding which ones to abandon and which ones to pursue.
5. Representatives from the QC make a presentation or recommendation to management that summarizes the work of their group.
6. Management reviews the recommendation and makes a decision. Often, the decision is that QC members will have the opportunity to implement and assess their own recommendations.[37]

Many companies that suffer the negative consequences of job oversimplification are unable or unwilling to modify production equipment or methods to the extent required by the Hackman–Oldham and sociotechnical models. In some of these firms, managers have attempted to use QCs to counteract the negative effects of overzealous job specialization and simplification. QCs fight oversimplification by giving employees the opportunity to participate in the management of their jobs, and they do not require the modification of existing work technologies. For example, employees who work on an assembly line for thirty-nine hours each week might meet as a QC group during the fortieth hour to evaluate the assembly line's performance and prepare for the following week's work. They might also meet in an extended session on a monthly basis to discuss more complicated issues and resolve more difficult problems.

Such monthly sessions offer an opportunity for QC members to engage in more managerial activity, group autonomy, and information exchange than allowed by the regular QC meetings. To the extent that QC meetings focus workers' attention on the outputs of the entire assembly line, they may also reinforce task identity and task significance.

Self-Managing Teams

Self-managing teams take the general orientation of QCs a step further, by grouping employees together into *permanent* teams and empowering each team with the authority to manage itself.[38] Such teams resemble the semiautonomous groups investigated in Tavistock's sociotechnical research, except that self-managing teams have greater autonomy.[39] This difference is attributable to the recent emergence of computer networks, which provide self-managing groups with the ability to interact with one another and exchange information about company goals, job assignments, and ongoing production progress without the assistance of an intervening hierarchy of managers.[40]

Among the management responsibilities allotted to each self-managing team is the duty of continually assessing the work of the team and redesigning the jobs of the team's members. To enable teams to fulfill this responsibility, team members receive training in how to design jobs and assess performance quality and efficiency. Techniques taught to team members include many of the industrial engineering procedures described earlier in this chapter.

For example, the members of self-managing teams might analyze each of the team's jobs by performing stopwatch time studies, micromotion analyses, ergonomic equipment assessments, or similar investigations, all in an effort to improve each job's efficiency. Inefficient jobs are either eliminated or redesigned by the team. The newly designed jobs are then retested, assessed, and, if successful, adopted throughout the plant.

Automation and Robotics

Automation is a third approach available to managers who seek to improve quality. Like other TQM approaches, it also has implications for the design of jobs. For many years, automation in the form of assembly-line manufacturing created some of the most oversimplified and demotivating jobs in industry. Today, however, with the invention of automated technologies that can totally replace people in production processes, automation is sometimes used instead to eliminate repetitive, physically demanding, mistake-prone work.[41] Such jobs frequently utilize **industrial robots**, or machines that can be programmed to repeat the same sequence of movements over and over again with extreme precision. Robots have been introduced throughout the automotive industry, taking over various painting and parts installation jobs. Robots have also moved from the factory floor to the operating room, performing such functions as precision hip replacement and cancerous tumor radiation.[42]

Robots are not without their flaws. At General Motors, for example, employees regularly tell stories of one robot busily smashing the windshields installed by another robot, or a group of robots painting each other instead of the cars passing by them on the assembly line. Proper programming is obviously a critical aspect of introducing robots into the workplace,[43] and careful planning, implementation, and adjustment are essential. In addition, experience has shown that building a robot capable of performing anything more than the simplest of jobs is often cost-prohibitive. Consequently, the U.S. population of robots is far less than the hundreds of thousands once predicted. Nonetheless, robots provide an effective way to cope with many repetitive jobs that people do not want to do or cannot perform well.[44]

Computer-integrated manufacturing in the form of *flexible manufacturing cells* is another type of automated technology introduced in the name of TQM, albeit one that focuses on adaptability rather than robotic repetitiveness. Products made in such cells include gearboxes, cylinder heads, brake components, and similar machined-metal components used in the automotive, aviation, and construction-equipment industries. Companies throughout Europe, Japan, and North America are also experimenting with using flexible manufacturing cells to manufacture items out of sheet metal.[45]

Each flexible manufacturing cell consists of a collection of automated production machines that cut, shape, drill, and fasten metal components together. These machines are connected to each other by convertible conveyor grids that allow for quick rerouting to accommodate changes from one product to another. It is possible, for instance, to produce a small batch of automotive door locks and then switch over to fabricate and finish a separate batch of crankshafts for automotive air-conditioner compressors. The conversion simply involves turning some machines on and others off and then activating those conveyors that interconnect the machines that are in use—and operations of this sort are normally computer controlled. When employed in this manner, the same collection of machines can manufacture a wide variety of products without substantial human involvement and without major alteration of the cell.[46]

Workers in a flexible manufacturing cell need never touch the product being manufactured, nor must they perform simple, repetitive production tasks. Instead, their jobs focus on the surveillance and decision making required to initialize different cell configurations and oversee equipment operations. Often, a cell's workforce forms a self-managing team to accommodate the sizable amount of mutual adjustment that must occur to manage occasional crises and keep production flowing smoothly. Under such circumstances, employees in a flexible manufacturing cell have enriched jobs that allow them to exercise expertise in teamwork, problem solving, and self-management.[47]

Process Management

Process management is an approach intended to map, improve, and standardize organizational processes in order to reduce variance in the outcomes of those processes and increase organizational efficiency as a consequence.[48] In the 1980s, the approach consisted of the TQM programs that gave rise to the quality perspective. In the decades since that time it has developed further into programs ranging from ISO 9000 certification to Six Sigma management and lean manufacturing implementation. In the United States, extraordinary achievements are recognized each year by receipt of the Malcolm Baldrige National Quality Award, administered by the National Institute of Standards and Technology.

All programs within the area of process management share several common features. First, all focus on the standardization of work practices, to ensure quality and uniformity in the outcomes of those practices. Second, all encourage employees to apply a consistent set of problem-solving procedures (and most involve significant training in those procedures). Third, all involve rigorous measurement of outcomes in order to assess variance and trigger corrective action.[49] As is apparent from this description, process management thus encourages significant employee involvement in managerial processes, and at the same time it contributes to the standardization of work processes and employee behaviors.

Evaluating the Quality Perspective

In many respects, the quality perspective represents a hybrid of the efficiency and motivational perspectives on work design. For instance, QCs allow employees to enjoy at least modest satisfaction under conditions in which work processes are shaped mainly by concerns about productive efficiency. Self-managed teams enable their members to satisfy needs for social- and growth-oriented outcomes partly by requiring them to work together to apply many of the work design methods conforming to the efficiency perspective. Automation—perhaps the peak of mechanical efficiency—releases employees from jobs devoid of satisfying elements. Process management increases employee involvement in workplace decision making but focuses attention on efficient resource utilization.

What effects does this "middle ground" approach have on performance and satisfaction in the workplace? Evidence identifying the effects of QCs as a form of job enrichment is sketchy. The information that is available suggests that QCs have little effect on productivity but can enhance feelings of satisfaction and involvement significantly.[50] The magnitude of such effects is usually smaller than the results produced by job enrichment programs based on the Hackman–Oldham model or the Tavistock sociotechnical model. This discrepancy is understandable, however, because workers who participate in QCs must still perform unenriched jobs during most of their time spent at work.

Evidence concerning the job enrichment effects of self-managing groups is even more meager. Extrapolation from research on semiautonomous groups and QCs suggests that self-management should improve team members' satisfaction and perhaps performance, and anecdotal accounts seem to support this contention.[51] Researchers have also noted that the quality standards developed and then observed in TQM teams can severely limit autonomy, which in turn reduces potential motivational gains, but workers who are able to alternate between adhering to existing standards and working to create new ones report significant satisfaction with their jobs.[52]

Research on the work design effects of automation is similarly lacking. At its core, automation represents a return to the efficiency perspective of industrial engineering. Some jobs resist enrichment, and it is more effective to turn them over to machines than to attempt to convert them into interesting, enjoyable work for people. Among both the old jobs that remain and the new ones that are created by adoption of innovation, the danger exists that human satisfaction may be ignored during the job design process. Nevertheless, research suggests that employees in flexible manufacturing cells do show signs of increased motivation, satisfaction, and improved performance if the tasks they perform provide greater autonomy than was available before the introduction of automation.[53]

Finally, a study of the effects of process management on workforce outcomes has shown that statistical process management practices can increase the motivation and satisfaction of workers who are involved in those practices as data interpreters and decision makers.[54] Although these results are promising, additional research is required to determine their generalizability and to expand consideration to the variety of other outcomes also expected to be affected by improvements in work design.[55]

To summarize, the relevant evidence seems to support the conclusion that work design implementations stimulated by the quality perspective can have positive effects on workforce motivation, satisfaction, and productivity. This evidence is not conclusive, and additional information is needed before the perspective's true benefits can be determined.[56]

Summary

Contemporary work design began with Frederick Taylor, Frank and Lillian Gilbreth, and other experts whose work on *industrial engineering* served as the foundations of the *efficiency perspective* on work design. Within this perspective, *methods engineering* attempts to improve the methods used to perform work, and *work measurement* examines the motions and time required to complete each job. A second approach to work design was first developed when Frederick Herzberg differentiated between *motivator* and *hygiene factors*. Other specialists later extended this perspective by introducing early models of *horizontal job enlargement* and *vertical job enrichment*. The *motivational perspective* emerged as work progressed on *comprehensive job enrichment programs* and on *sociotechnical job enrichment*. A third approach, the *quality perspective*, then emerged as experience with *Total Quality Management* programs indicated that *quality circles, self-managing teams, automation*, and *process management* could be used as alternatives to traditional job assignments during the process of work design. Incorporated in this third perspective were elements of both the efficiency and the motivational perspectives that preceded its development.

Review Questions

1. Explain how following Taylor's principles of scientific management can simplify the jobs in an organization. What are some positive effects of this simplification? What negative effects might occur?

2. What do the fields of process engineering and human factors engineering have in common? How do they differ from one another? Are they more likely to enhance satisfaction or efficiency? Why?

3. How does the quality perspective differ from the efficiency and motivational perspectives? What similarities does it share with each of the other two? How do concerns about quality affect the design of jobs?
4. The quality perspective includes quality circles, self-managed teams, automation, and process management. Which of these approaches would you *not* select to enrich jobs in a newly built assembly line? Why not? Which would you use to design jobs that resist all attempts at enrichment?

Notes

1 S. Terkel, *Working* (New York: Avon, 1972), 221–223.
2 B. Garson, *All the Livelong Day: The Meaning and Demeaning of Routine Work* (New York: Penguin Books, 1977), 171.
3 C. T. Morgan, J. S. Cook, A. Chapanis, and M. W. Lund, *Human Engineering Guide to Equipment Design* (New York: McGraw-Hill, 1963).
4 M. E. Mundel, *Motion and Time Study: Improving Productivity*, 7th ed. (Englewood Cliffs, NJ: Prentice Hall, 1993).
5 M. A. Campion, "Ability Requirement Implications of Job Design: An Interdisciplinary Perspective," *Personnel Psychology* 42 (1989): 1–24; M. A. Campion and C. L. McClelland, "Interdisciplinary Examination of the Costs and Benefits of Enlarged Jobs: A Job Design Quasi Experiment," *Journal of Applied Psychology* 76 (1991): 186–198; J. R. Edwards, J. A. Scully, and M. D. Brtek, "The Measurement of Work: Hierarchical Representation of the Multimethod Job Design Questionnaire," *Personnel Psychology* 52 (1999): 305–334; J. R. Edwards, J. A. Scully, and M. D. Brtek, "The Nature and Outcomes of Work: A Replication and Extension of Interdisciplinary Work-Design Research," *Journal of Applied Psychology* 85 (2000): 860–868; M. Elnekave and I. Gilad, "Rapid Video-Based System for Advanced Work Measurement," *International Journal of Production Research* 44 (2006): 271–290.
6 M. Galen, M. Mallory, S. Siwolop, and S. Garland, "Repetitive Stress: The Pain Has Just Begun," *BusinessWeek*, July 13, 1992, 142–146; "Repetitive Motion Disorders Lead Increase in Job Illnesses," *New York Times*, November 16, 1990, D7; "Chrysler Agrees to Curtail Repetitive Tasks for Workers," *Lansing State Journal*, November 3, 1989, 4B; see also M. van Tulder, A. Malmivaara, and B. Koes, "Repetitive Strain Injury," *The Lancet* 369 (2007): 1815–1822.
7 L. M. Gilbreth, *The Psychology of Management* (New York: Macmillan, 1921), 19.
8 G. R. Salancik and J. Pfeffer, "An Examination of Need-Satisfaction Models of Job Attitudes," *Administrative Science Quarterly* 22 (1977): 427–456; S. Wood, M. Van Veldhoven, M. Croon, and L. M. de Menezes, "Enriched Job Design, High Involvement Management and Organizational Performance: The Mediating Roles of Job Satisfaction and Well-being," *Human Relations* 65 (2012): 419–445.
9 The classic piece on this approach to counteracting oversimplification is C. R. Walker and R. H. Guest, *The Man on the Assembly Line* (Cambridge, MA: Harvard University Press, 1952).
10 J. D. Kilbridge, "Reduced Costs through Job Enlargement: A Case," *Journal of Business* 33 (1960): 357–362; J. F. Biggane and A. Stewart, "Job Enlargement: A Case Study," in L. E. Davis and J. C. Taylor, eds., *Design of Jobs* (New York: Penguin, 1972), 264–276; G. E. Susman, "Job Enlargement: Effects of Culture on Worker Responses," *Industrial Relations* 12 (1973): 1–15; S. K. Parker, "Enhancing Role Breadth Self-Efficacy: The Roles of Job Enrichment and Other Organizational Interventions," *Journal of Applied Psychology* 83 (1998): 835–852.
11 F. M. Kuijer, B. Visser, and H. C. G. Kemper, "Job Rotation as a Factor in Reducing Physical Workload at a Refuse Collecting Department," *Ergonomics* 42 (1999): 1167–1178; C. Gaudart, "Conditions for Maintaining Aging Operators at Work: A Case Study Conducted at an Automobile Manufacturing Plant," *Applied Ergonomics* 31 (2000): 453–462; A. Mikkelsen and O. Saksvik, "Impact of a Participatory Organizational Intervention on Job Characteristics and Job Stress," *International Journal of Health Services* 29 (1999): 871–893; R. W. Griffin, *Task Design: An Integrative Approach* (Glenview, IL: Scott, Foresman, 1982), 25; J. Keir, K. Sanei, and M. W. Holmes, "Task Rotation Effects on Upper Extremity and Back Muscle Activity," *Applied Ergonomics*, 42 (2011): 814–819.

12 F. Herzberg, B. Mausner, and B. B. Snyderman, *The Motivation to Work* (New York: Wiley, 1959).

13 For example, see R. J. House and L. A. Wigdor, "Herzberg's Dual-Factor Theory of Job Satisfaction and Motivation: A Review of the Empirical Evidence and a Criticism," *Personnel Psychology* 20 (1967): 369–389; M. D. Dunnette, J. Campbell, and M. D. Hakel, "Factors Contributing to Job Dissatisfaction in Six Occupational Groups," *Organizational Behavior and Human Performance* 2 (1967): 146–164; J. Schneider and E. A. Locke, "A Critique of Herzberg's Classification System and a Suggested Revision," *Organizational Behavior and Human Performance* 6 (1971): 441–458; D. Schwab and L. L. Cummings, "Theories of Performance and Satisfaction: A Review," *Industrial Relations* 9 (1970): 408–430; R. J. Caston and R. Braito, "A Specification Issue in Job Satisfaction Research," *Sociological Perspectives* 28 (1985): 175–197.

14 Griffin, *Task Design*; also see J. R. Hackman, "On the Coming Demise of Job Enrichment," in E. L. Cass and F. G. Zimmer, eds., *Man and Work in Society* (New York: Van Nostrand, 1975), 45–63.

15 J. R. Hackman and G. R. Oldham, *Work Redesign* (Reading, MA: Addison-Wesley, 1980); J. R. Hackman and G. R. Oldham, "Motivation through the Design of Work: Test of a Theory," *Organizational Behavior and Human Performance* 16 (1976): 250–279; K. H. Roberts and W. H. Glick, "The Job Characteristics Approach to Task Design: A Critical Review," *Journal of Applied Psychology* 86 (1981): 193–217; R. J. Aldag, S. H. Barr, and A. Brief, "Measurement of Perceived Task Characteristics," *Psychological Bulletin* 99 (1981): 415–431; Y. Fried and G. R. Ferris, "The Validity of the Job Characteristics Model: A Review and Meta-Analysis," *Personnel Psychology* 40 (1987): 287–322; B. T. Loher, R. A. Noe, N. L. Moeller, and M. Fitzgerald, "A Meta-Analysis of the Relation of Job Characteristics to Job Satisfaction," *Journal of Applied Psychology* 70 (1985): 280–289; F. Morgeson and S. E. Humphrey, "The Work Design Questionnaire (WDQ): Developing and Validating a Comprehensive Measure for Assessing Job Design and the Nature of Work," *Journal of Applied Psychology* 91 (2006): 1321–1339; S. E. Humphrey, J. D. Nahrgang, and F. Morgeson, "Integrating Motivational, Social, and Contextual Work Design Features: A Meta-Analytic Summary and Theoretical Extension of the Work Design Literature," *Journal of Applied Psychology* 92 (2007): 1332–1356.

16 Hackman and Oldham, "Motivation through the Design of Work," 256–257.

17 R. A. Katzell, Bienstock, P., and H. Faerstein, *A Guide to Worker Productivity Experiments in the United States 1971–1975* (New York: New York University Press, 1977), 14; E. A. Locke, D. B. Feren, V. M. McCaleb, K. N. Shaw, and A. T. Denny, "The Relative Effectiveness of Four Methods of Motivating Employee Performance," in K. D. Duncan, M. M. Gruneberg, and D. Wallis, eds., *Changes in Working Life* (London: Wiley, 1980), 363–388; R. E. Kopelman, "Job Redesign and Productivity: A Review of the Evidence," *National Productivity Review* 4 (1985): 237–255. See also D. Morrison, J. Cordery, A. Giradi, and R. Payne, "Job Design, Opportunities for Skill Utilization, and Intrinsic Job Satisfaction," *European Journal of Work and Organizational Psychology* 14 (2005): 59–79.

18 K. Kelly, "The New Soul of John Deere," *BusinessWeek*, January 31, 1994, 64–66.

19 F. Morgeson, G. J. Medsker, and M. A. Campion, "Job and Team Design," *Handbook of Human Factors and Ergonomics* 15 (2012): 428–457.

20 E. L. Trist and K. W. Bamforth, "Some Social and Psychological Consequences of the Longwall Method of Coal-Getting," *Human Relations* 4 (1951): 3–38; E. Mumford, "The Story of Sociotechnical Design: Reflections on its Successes, Failures, and Potential," *Information Systems Journal* 16 (2006): 317–342.

21 Adapted from F. E. Emery and E. Thorsrud, *Democracy at Work: The Report of the Norwegian Industrial Democracy Program* (Leiden, Netherlands: H. E. Stenfert Kroese, 1976), 14.

22 D. Jenkins, trans., *Job Reform in Sweden: Conclusions from 500 Shop Floor Projects* (Stockholm: Swedish Employers' Confederation, 1975), 63–64.

23 N. J. Kemp, T. Wall, C. W. Clegg, and J. L. Cordery, "Autonomous Work Groups in a Greenfield Site: A Comparative Study," *Journal of Occupational Psychology*, 56 (2011): 271–288.

24 Apparently, the motivational effects of Hackman–Oldham enrichment grow stronger over time, as a study by Griffin indicated that productivity increased over the course of four years. However, the same study suggested that initial improvements in satisfaction triggered by Hackman–Oldham enrichment may disappear over the same period of time. See R. W. Griffin, "Effects of Work Redesign on Employee Perceptions, Attitudes, and Behaviors: A Long-Term Investigation," *Academy of Management Journal* 34 (1991): 425–435.

25 Studies that have confirmed the existence of five distinct characteristics include R. Katz, "Job Longevity as a Situational Factor in Job Satisfaction," *Administrative Science Quarterly* 23 (1978): 204–223; R. Lee and A. R. Klein, "Structure of the Job Diagnostic Survey for Public Service Organizations," *Journal of Applied Psychology* 67 (1982): 515–519. Studies that have failed to reveal confirmatory evidence include R. B. Dunham, "The Measurement and Dimensionality of Job Characteristics," *Journal of Applied Psychology* 61 (1976): 404–409; J. Gaines and J. M. Jermier, "Functional Exhaustion in a High Stress Organization," *Academy of Management Journal* 26 (1983): 567–586; J. L. Pierce and R. B. Dunham, "The Measurement of Perceived Job Characteristics: The Job Diagnostic Survey vs. the Job Characteristics Inventory," *Academy of Management Journal* 21 (1978): 123–128; and D. M. Rousseau, "Technological Differences in Job Characteristics, Job Satisfaction, and Motivation: A Synthesis of Job Design Research and Sociotechnical Systems Theory," *Organizational Behavior and Human Performance* 19 (1977): 18–42.

26 Objectivity is suggested by studies such as R. W. Griffin, "A Longitudinal Investigation of Task Characteristics Relationships," *Academy of Management Journal* 42 (1981): 99–113; E. F. Stone and L. W. Porter, "Job Characteristics and Job Attitudes: A Multivariate Study," *Journal of Applied Psychology* 60 (1975): 57–64; and C. T. Kulik, G. R. Oldham, and H. Langner, "Measurement of Job Characteristics: Comparison of the Original and the Revised Job Diagnostic Survey," *Journal of Applied Psychology* 73 (1988): 462–466. Other studies that seem to support the subjectivity side of the argument include A. Brief and R. J. Aldag, "The Job Characteristic Inventory: An Examination," *Academy of Management Journal* 21 (1978): 659–670; H. Birnbaum, J. L. Farh, and G. Y. Y. Wong, "The Job Characteristics Model in Hong Kong," *Journal of Applied Psychology* 71 (1986): 598–605.

27 G. R. Salancik and J. Pfeffer, "A Social Information Processing Approach to Job Attitudes and Task Design," *Administrative Science Quarterly* 23 (1978): 224–253; C. S. Wong, C. Hui, and K. S. Law, "A Longitudinal Study of the Job Perception–Job Satisfaction Relationship: A Test of the Three Alternative Specifications," *Journal of Occupational and Organizational Psychology* 71 (1998): 127–146.

28 A. Brief and R. J. Aldag, "Employee Reactions to Job Characteristics: A Constructive Replication," *Journal of Applied Psychology* 60 (1975): 182–186; H. Sims and A. D. Szilagyi, "Job Characteristic Relationships: Individual and Structural Moderators," *Organizational Behavior and Human Performance* 17 (1976): 211–230.

29 R. E. Walton, "From Control to Commitment in the Workplace," *Harvard Business Review* 63 (1985): 76–84; J. C. Taylor and D. F. Felten, *Performance by Design: Sociotechnical Systems in North America* (Englewood Cliffs, NJ: Prentice Hall, 1993).

30 A. H. van de Zwaan and J. De Vries, "A Critical Assessment of the Modern Sociotechnical Approach within Production and Operations Management," *International Journal of Production Research* 38 (2000): 1755–1767; C. W. Clegg, "Sociotechnical Principles for System Design," *Applied Ergonomics* 31 (2000): 463–477; J. L. Cordery, W. S. Mueller, and L. M. Smith, "Attitudinal and Behavioral Effects of Autonomous Group Working: A Longitudinal Field Study," *Academy of Management Journal* 34 (1991): 464–476; C. A. Pearson, "Autonomous Work Groups: An Evaluation at an Industrial Site," *Human Relations* 45 (1992): 905–936; see also F. Morgeson and S. E. Humphrey, "Job and Team Design: Toward a More Integrative Conceptualization of Work Design," *Research in Personnel and Human Resources Management* 27 (2008): 39–91.

31 T. A. Lowe and J. M. Mazzoo, "Three Preachers, One Religion," *Quality* 25 (1986): 32–37. See also W. E. Deming, *Out of the Crisis* (Cambridge, MA: MIT Center for Advanced Engineering Study, 1986); B. Crosby, *Quality Is Free* (New York: McGraw-Hill, 1979); and J. M. Juran, *Juran on Leadership for Quality* (New York: Free Press, 1989).

32 R. J. Schonberger, "Is Strategy Strategic? Impact of Total Quality Management on Strategy," *Academy of Management Executive* 6 (1992): 80–87; J. W. Dean, Jr., and J. R. Evans, *Total Quality: Management, Organization, and Strategy* (St. Paul, MN: West, 1994); J. D. Westphal, R. Gulati, and S. M. Shortell, "Customization or Conformity? An Institutional and Network Perspective on the Content and Consequences of TQM Adoption," *Administrative Science Quarterly* 42 (1997): 366–394.

33 R. Blackburn and B. Rosen, "Total Quality and Human Resources Management: Lessons Learned from Baldrige Award-Winning Companies," *Academy of Management Executive* 7 (1993): 49–66.

34 W. L. Mohr and H. Mohr, *Quality Circles: Changing Images of People at Work* (Reading, MA: Addison-Wesley, 1983), 13.

35 D. L. Dewar, *The Quality Circle Handbook* (Red Bluff, CA: Quality Circle Institute, 1980), 17–104.

36 G. R. Ferris and J. A. Wagner III, "Quality Circles in the United States: A Conceptual Reevaluation," *Journal of Applied Behavioral Science* 21 (1985): 155–167.

37 B. R. Lee, "Organization Development and Group Perceptions: A Study of Quality Circles," Ph.D. dissertation, University of Minnesota, 1982; M. Robson, *Quality Circles: A Practical Guide*, 2nd ed. (Hants, UK: Gower, 1988), 47–62.

38 E. Molleman, "Modalities of Self-Managing Teams: The 'Must,' 'May,' 'Can,' and 'Will' of Local Decision Making," *International Journal of Operations and Productivity Management* 20 (2000): 889–910; C. C. Manz and H. Sims, "Leading Workers to Lead Themselves," *Administrative Science Quarterly* 32 (1987): 106–128.

39 A. H. van de Zwaan and E. Molleman, "Self-Organizing Groups: Conditions and Constraints in a Sociotechnical Perspective," *International Journal of Manpower* 19 (1998): 301–329; J. R. Barker, "Tightening the Iron Cage: Concertive Control in Self-Managed Organizations," *Administrative Science Quarterly* 38 (1993): 408–437.

40 M. Hammer and J. Champy, *Reengineering the Corporation: A Manifesto for Business Revolution* (New York: Harper Business, 1993).

41 J. M. Hoc, "From Human–Machine Interaction to Human–Machine Cooperation," *Ergonomics* 43 (2000): 833–843; R. Parasuraman, T. B. Sheridan, and C. D. Wickens, "A Model for Types and Levels of Human Interaction with Automation," *IEEE Transactions on Systems, Man, and Cybernetics, Part A: Systems and Humans* 30 (2000): 286–297.

42 S. Baker, "A Surgeon Whose Hands Never Shake," *BusinessWeek*, October 4, 1993, 111–114.

43 D. Sharon, J. Harstein, and G. Yantian, *Robotics and Automated Manufacturing* (London: Pitman, 1987).

44 T. Kilborn, "Brave New World Seen for Robots Appears Stalled by Quirks and Costs," *New York Times*, July 1, 1990, C7.

45 O. Port, "Brave New Factory," *BusinessWeek*, July 23, 2001, 75–76; R. B. Kurtz, *Toward a New Era in U.S. Manufacturing* (Washington, DC: National Academy Press, 1986), 3.

46 A. Aston and M. Arndt, "The Flexible Factory," *BusinessWeek*, May 5, 2003, 90–91; R. Jaikumar, "Postindustrial Manufacturing," *Harvard Business Review* 44 (1986): 69–76.

47 P. Senker, *Towards the Automatic Factory: The Need for Training* (New York: Springer-Verlag, 1986), 27–43; G. Liu, R. Shah, and R. G. Schroeder, "Linking Work Design to Mass Customization: A Sociotechnical Systems Perspective," *Decision Sciences* 37 (2006): 519–545.

48 M. Benner and M. Tushman, "Exploitation, Exploration, and Process Management," *Academy of Management Review* 28 (2003): 238–254.

49 T. Vogus and T. Welborne, "Structuring for High Reliability: HR Practices and Mindful Processes in Reliability-Seeking Organizations," *Journal of Organizational Behavior* 24 (2003): 877–903; L. L. Gilson, J. E. Mathieu, C. E. Shalley, and T. M. Ruddy, "Creativity and Standardization: Complementary or Conflicting Drivers of Team Effectiveness?" *Academy of Management Journal* 48 (2005): 521–531; R. Schroeder, K. Linderman, C. Liedtke, and A. S. Choo, "Six Sigma: Definition and Underlying Theory," *Journal of Operations Management* 26 (2008): 536–554.

50 R. Steel and R. F. Lloyd, "Cognitive, Affective, and Behavioral Outcomes of Participation in Quality Circles: Conceptual and Empirical Findings," *Journal of Applied Behavioral Science* 24 (1988): 1–17; H. H. Greenbaum, I. T. Kaplan, and W. Metlay, "Evaluation of Problem Solving Groups: The Case of Quality Circle Programs," *Group and Organization Studies* 13 (1988): 133–147; K. Buch and R. Spangler, "The Effects of Quality Circles on Performance and Promotions," *Human Relations* 43 (1990): 573–582; R. Steel, K. R. Jennings, and J. T. Lindsey, "Quality Circle Problem Solving and Common Cents: Evaluation Study Findings from a United States Federal Mint," *Journal of Applied Behavioral Science* 26 (1990): 365–381.

51 J. D. Orsburn, L. Moran, E. Musselwhite, and J. H. Zenger, *Self-Directed Work Teams: The New American Challenge* (Homewood, IL: Irwin, 1990); M. J. Zbaracki, "The Rhetoric and Reality of Total Quality Management," *Administrative Science Quarterly* 43 (1998): 602–636.

52 J. R. Hackman and R. Wageman, "Total Quality Management: Empirical, Conceptual, and Practical Issues," *Administrative Science Quarterly* 40 (1995): 309–342; B. Victor, A. Boynton, and T. Stephens-Jahng, "The Effective Design of Work under Total Quality Management," *Organization Science* 11 (2000): 102–117.

53 S. Adler, "Workers and Flexible Manufacturing Systems: Three Installations Compared," *Journal of Organizational Behavior* 12 (1991): 447–460; but see J. W. Dean, Jr., and S. A. Snell, "Integrated Manufacturing and Job Design: Moderating Effects of Organizational Inertia," *Academy of Management Journal* 34 (1991): 776–804.

54 M. Rungtusanatham, "Beyond Quality: The Motivational Effects of Statistical Process Control," *Journal of Operations Management* 19 (2001): 653–673.

55 S. J. Cullinane, J. Bosak, C. Flood, and E. Demerouti, "Job Design under Lean Manufacturing and its Impact on Employee Outcomes," *Organizational Psychology Review* 23 (2012): 47–89.

56 J. W. Dean, Jr., and D. E. Bowen, "Management Theory and Total Quality: Improving Research and Practice through Theory Development," *Academy of Management Review* 19 (1994): 392–419; D. A. Waldman, "The Contributions of Total Quality Management to a Theory of Work Performance," *Academy of Management Review* 19 (1994): 510–536; R. Reed, D. J. Lemak, and J. C. Montgomery, "Beyond Process: TQM Content and Firm Performance," *Academy of Management Review* 21 (1996): 173–202.

Chapter 8

Interdependence and Role Relationships

Although most CEOs cite the communitarian ideal that "we are all in this together" when speaking publically to their employees, when it comes to the rewards for everyone's efforts, there are big differences in outcomes for different people in any organization. In 2013, the average CEO of an American company earned 354 times more than the average employee in the same firm.[1] And this is just the average. Some CEOs can make many more times the average wages of the employees they lead. For example, Ronald Johnson's compensation was 1,795 times more than the average wages of JCPenneys associates at the underperforming department store chain.[2] Disparities such as these have fueled a debate about whether CEO compensation is fair because, as labor organizer Brandon Rees has noted, "[such disparities create] the perception that the CEO is creating all the value for an organization."[3]

Certainly, the CEO is a major player when it comes to affecting the organization's outcomes because the decisions made by the top executive at a major corporation can have a disproportionate impact on the organization's bottom line. In addition, most CEOs have also amassed a long history of unique work experience and they often work over eighty hours a week. Hence the inputs provided by the CEO might justify higher outcomes relative to the average employee, especially if their efforts are instrumental in helping the organization succeed.

However, in many cases, CEOs are rewarded handsomely even when their organizations fail. Kevin Crutchfield, the CEO of energy company Alpha Natural Resources, was paid a $6 million dollar bonus in 2011 despite the fact that Alpha was the second worst performer among all firms listed on the New York Stock Exchange. In addition, the ratios of CEO pay to average employee pay in U.S. companies are far out of line with those of companies in Europe, nor are these ratios representative of what was found in U.S. companies historically. For example, in 1992, the ratio of CEO pay to average employee pay was only 42.

Empirical research suggests that when the ratio of CEO to average employee pay exceeds 20 to 1, it begins to have negative effects on average employee productivity, attributable to resentment and perceptions of unfairness. Some companies, such a Whole Foods Market Inc., try to make sure this ratio never exceeds this precise 20:1 ratio, and Whole Foods has tracked this ratio carefully from the day the company was founded. Ratio tracking was not a common practice in organizations until 2010, when the "internal pay equity provision" of the Dodd-Frank Wall Street Reform and Consumer Protection Act mandated that publically held companies report this value. The Dodd-Frank reforms were passed, in 2010, in the wake of the financial crisis, when the U.S. government had to bail out many failed institutions. The internal pay equity provision of Dodd-Frank was intended to expose these kinds of income disparities to potential investors.[4]

Clearly, investors, the government, CEOs, and average employees in an organization are all interdependent upon one another for financial success. Still, as you can see, the nature of this interdependence—and the way that rewards for success are shared—is an open debate. In the last chapter, we discussed jobs and how jobs can be designed to enhance the fit between tasks and individual people. Jobs and the individuals who hold these jobs do not exist in a vacuum, however. Rather, in organizations, jobs and individuals are linked to each other, and much of the competitive success of an organization can be traced to how well the relationships between jobs and individuals are managed. Thus, managers need to know about various factors that affect people as they *work together*, and that is the focus of this chapter.

We begin this chapter by identifying several different patterns of *interdependence* that develop among people and connect them as they work with one another. Next, we note that people occupy specific *roles* in the networks of interdependence they share with others, and we examine the process of *communication*, which is the glue that holds role occupants together. At no time is this communication more important than when people are first introduced into their organizational roles; thus we will pay particular attention to *socialization* processes through which individuals learn about the roles they are expected to fill. Finally, we conclude the chapter by examining *equity theory* as a framework for judging and enhancing the quality of relationships between individuals and organizations in terms of fairness. If people feel that they are being treated fairly in their organizational relationships, the quality of relationships will be high, and over time this can lead to trust and a long-term focus on well-coordinated efforts. However, if this trust is violated and people feel that they are being treated unfairly, this can destroy teamwork.[5]

Patterns of Interdependence and Organizational Roles

People in organizations share a rich variety of connections. Their work might require them to associate with one another as a regular part of job performance. They might band together to share resources, such as access to valuable equipment or financial resources, even when their work does not require direct contact between individuals. Such connections make interpersonal relationships a very important aspect of organizational life. Among both individuals and groups, these relationships take the form of patterns or networks of interdependence.

Types of Interdependence

In the workplace, interdependence typically takes one of the four forms diagrammed in Figure 8.1: pooled, sequential, reciprocal, or comprehensive interdependence.

Pooled interdependence occurs when people draw resources from a shared source but have little else in common. Resources pooled together in this manner might include money, equipment, raw materials, information, or expertise. As the simplest form of interdependence, pooled interdependence requires little or no interpersonal interaction. In a company such as Metropolitan Life Insurance, for example, individual data-entry specialists draw off a common pool of work that must be entered into the firm's computers. Each person works alone to perform the task of entering information, however. That is, the task itself requires little interaction with other employees.

Sequential interdependence consists of a chain of one-way interactions in which people depend on those individuals who precede them in the chain. People earlier in the chain, however, remain independent of those who follow them. Thus, sequentially interdependent relationships are said to be *asymmetric*, meaning that some people depend on others who do not, in turn, depend on them. For example, employees at Steelcase who work on an assembly

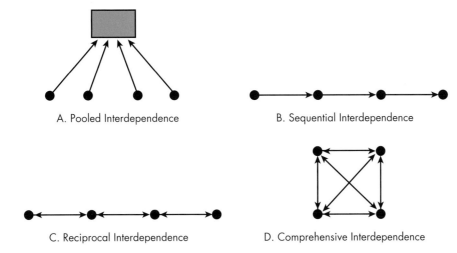

A. Pooled Interdependence

B. Sequential Interdependence

C. Reciprocal Interdependence

D. Comprehensive Interdependence

Figure 8.1 **Types of Interdependence**

line manufacturing office furniture are connected by sequential interdependence. Workers earlier in the line produce partial assemblies, which workers later in the line complete.

By its very nature, sequential interdependence prevents people at the end of the chain from performing their jobs unless people at the head of the chain have already carried out their tasks. On the other hand, people at the head of the chain can complete their tasks no matter what people at the other end do. Research shows that sequential systems like this are very sensitive to differences either between people in their performance (two workers who operate at different speeds) or between the same person at different times (a worker who operates faster in the morning than in the afternoon). Performance variability can "starve" workers down the line if the work moves too slow or "block" the line if it moves faster than the next person can handle it. Thus, people who are dependent tend to experience more stress and feel less powerful in these asymmetric relationships than those who are independent.[6]

In **reciprocal interdependence**, a network of two-way relationships ties a collection of people together. A good example of this kind of interdependence is the relationship between a sales force and a clerical staff. Sales representatives rely on clerks to complete invoices and process credit card receipts, and clerks depend on salespeople to generate sales. Reciprocal interdependence also occurs among the members of a hospital staff. Doctors depend on nurses to check patients periodically, administer medications, and report alarming symptoms. Nurses, in turn, depend on doctors to prescribe medications and to specify the nature of symptoms associated with potential complications.

Reciprocal interdependence always involves some sort of direct interaction, such as face-to-face communication, telephone conversations, or written instructions. As a result, people who are reciprocally interdependent are more tightly interconnected than are individuals who are interconnected by either pooled or sequential interdependence. Reciprocal interdependence incorporates symmetric, two-way interactions in which each person depends on the person who depends on him or her. The symmetric nature of this relationship makes people feel more equal to one another with respect to power and promotes helping behavior going in both directions.[7]

Comprehensive interdependence develops in a tight network of reciprocal interdependence. It is the most complex form of interdependence because everyone involved is reciprocally interdependent with the others. As in reciprocal interdependence, people who depend on one another interact directly. In comprehensive interdependence, however, these interactions tend to be more frequent, more intense, and of greater duration than in any other type of interdependence.

In the brand-management groups that oversee the development of new products at firms such as Colgate-Palmolive and Procter & Gamble, for example, product designers, market researchers, production engineers, and sales representatives are all linked by a completely connected network of two-way relationships. The product designers interact with the market researchers, product engineers, and sales representatives. The market researchers also interact with the product engineers and the sales staff, who in turn interact with each other. In groups that experience comprehensive interdependence, systems that allow for direct peer monitoring and input into performance appraisals are critical for long-term success and viability.[8]

Implications of Interdependence

The type of interdependence that connects people together in interpersonal relationships has several important managerial implications. First, a greater potential for conflict arises as the complexity of the interdependence grows in moving from pooled to comprehensive interdependence. Sharing a greater number of interconnections and being more tightly connected increase the likelihood that differences in opinions, goals, or outcomes will be noticed and disputed, and this can be particularly an issue in self-managing groups that cannot simply turn to a leader to resolve all their discrepancies.[9] In groups like this, small conflicts can often escalate and spiral up over time, often leading to major conflicts in the future.[10] Indeed, all the evidence seems to suggest that trust builds up very slowly over time, but breaks down very quickly.[11]

Second, the loss of individuals due to turnover becomes more important as the intensity of the interdependence increases. One person's departure requires that few relationships be rebuilt under conditions of pooled or sequential interdependence. In situations characterized by reciprocal or comprehensive interdependence, however, many more relationships must be redeveloped if a new individual is introduced into the system. In some cases of extreme interdependence, the loss of even a single person can make everyone else perform below par, and it can take a very long time to get the group back up to the level of trust that they had experienced formerly.[12]

Third, comprehensive interdependence can stimulate greater flexibility and enable groups of people to adapt more quickly to changing environments than groups unified by less complex forms of interdependence. As discussed more fully in Chapter 9, this flexibility requires that greater attention be paid to maintaining continued interdependence, and it can contribute to *process loss* and reduced productivity if managed unwisely.

Fourth, the type of interdependence has implications for the design of motivational systems. Group-level goals and group-level feedback are associated with high performance in organizations utilizing sequential, reciprocal, or comprehensive interdependence, but individual-level goals and performance feedback work best for people connected via pooled interdependence.[13]

Role Taking and Role Making

As interdependent people associate with one another and gain experience with interpersonal relations, they come to expect other individuals to behave in specific ways. These expectations might be based partially on the formal job descriptions that each person has but typically go well beyond the written description of the job. Expectations such as these, and the behaviors they presuppose, form the **roles** that individuals occupy in interpersonal relations.[14] Chapter 6 introduced the concept of work-related roles, which were described there as a source of dissatisfaction and stress. This chapter will elaborate on the concept of a role, using it as a framework for understanding how interpersonal relationships develop and sometimes break down.

As indicated in Table 8.1, the behavioral expectations that make up such roles can include formal *established task elements* that are generally determined by a company's management as well as many other informal *emergent task elements* that evolve over time as interpersonal relations develop and mature.[15]

Established task elements are the parts of a role that arise because the role occupant is expected to perform a particular *job*. A job is a formal position, often accompanied by a written statement of the tasks it entails. Such written statements, called *job descriptions*, are generally prepared by managers or specialists with expertise in job analysis and description. When such descriptions exist, a fair amount of agreement usually exists at the outset regarding what constitutes the established task elements of a role.

Because job descriptions are prepared before the fact by people who do not actually perform the job, they are often incomplete. Moreover, most do not account for job incumbents' personal characteristics or the complex and dynamic environments in which jobs must be performed. Thus, as a person begins to do a job, it often becomes clear that tasks omitted from the written job description must be performed to successfully fulfill the role. These added-on tasks are referred to as **emergent task elements**. Rather than being written down, these emergent elements tend to be assumed and taken for granted. For example, although managing the moods of employees might not be a written element in a manager's job description, some managers realize that they need to do this in order to keep things running smoothly, and employees soon begin to expect this behavior on the part of managers. Thus, what started out as discretionary, soon becomes expected.[16] Over time, people develop systems of implicit expectations and coordination with one another that are enacted without a great deal of explicit communication.[17] In well-developed groups like these, each person specializes in keeping track of specific types of information and knowledge, and these **transactional memory systems** make the group much more efficient in terms of processing information. Each group member does not have to remember every important fact, but instead only needs to know "who knows what" and how to tap into that person's expertise.[18]

Table 8.1 **Elements of Work Roles**

Established task elements	Emergent task elements
1. Created by managers or specialists, independently of the role incumbent	1. Created by everyone who has a stake in how the role is performed, including the role incumbent
2. Characterized by elements that are objective, that are formally documented, and about which there is considerable consensus	2. Characterized by elements that are subjective, not formally documented, and open to negotiation
3. Static and relatively constant	3. Constantly changing and developing

Source: Adapted from D. R. Ilgen and J. R. Hollenbeck, "The Structure of Work: Job Design and Roles," in M. Dunnette, ed., *Handbook of Industrial Organizational Psychology* (Houston, TX: Consulting Psychologist Press, 1993), 165–207.

Established and emergent task elements can be combined in different ways. At one extreme is the *bureaucratic prototype*, in which the role occupant performs few duties other than the ones written in a job description. When people move into these highly prescribed roles, they engage in role taking. Many low-level jobs in automated, assembly-line factories are of this type. At the other extreme is the *loose-cannon prototype*, in which emergent elements greatly outnumber few established elements. When people move into this kind of loosely defined role, they engage in role making—a term that highlights the degree to which the role occupant "builds or constructs" his or her own role. Organizations are structured in terms of roles rather than in terms of the unique acts of specific individuals. Consequently, they can remain stable despite persistent turnover of personnel. For this reason, roles are of crucial importance to organizations and a central concern for those charged with managing organizational behavior.

Norms and Role Episodes

As indicated in Figure 8.2, the expectations that make up roles and give shape to interpersonal relations are called **norms**. Norms develop over time through repeated interaction; in many instances, group members might not even be aware that they exist.[19] For example, in a class, norms direct students to sit down and wait for the instructor to begin the day's activities. Norms might also direct students to participate in class discussions and exercises. Without such norms, each class meeting would require the instructor to reestablish the basic rules of behavior and set an agenda for the day. You would, therefore, have much less time available to pursue the learning activities on the schedule.

In organizations, norms exist for both the job's formal requirements, or its established task elements, and the job's generally agreed-upon informal rules, or emergent task elements. Either type may evolve from a variety of sources. Sometimes *precedents* that are established in early exchanges simply persist over time and become norms. For example, students take certain seats on the first day of class and, even though the instructor might not establish a formal seating arrangement, the students might tend to return to the same seats for each session. Norms might also be *carryovers* from other situations. In such instances, people might generalize from what they have done in the past in other, similar situations. For instance, a person might stand when making a presentation at a meeting because he or she was required to stand in prior meetings. Sometimes norms reflect *explicit statements from others*. A part-time summer worker, for instance, might be told by more experienced workers to "slow down and save some work for tomorrow."

Finally, some *critical historical event* might influence norms. Suppose, for example, that a lower-level worker leaks important company secrets to a competitor. In response to this

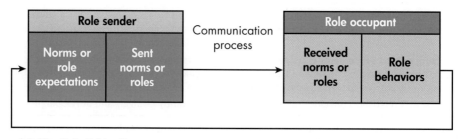

Figure 8.2 The Role-Taking Process

Source: Adapted from D. Katz and R. L. Kahn, *The Social Psychology of Organizations* (New York: Wiley, 1978), 112.

incident, a norm could evolve that requires all sensitive information to be typed by managers, not delegated to lower-level staff members. This new norm might even be written into a job description, thus taking what was once an informal, emergent element and converting it to a formal, established element. If this occurs over and over again, the organization can become full of written rules and procedures, which makes it very rigid and bureaucratic. Thus, something that starts out as an adaptive process (formalizing norms), if left unchecked, can become a maladaptive process (excessive formalization). Because of this, it is critical to distinguish pivotal norms from peripheral norms.

Adherence to the first type of norms, **pivotal norms**, is an absolute requirement if interpersonal relations are to persist and work is to be performed without major interruption. Failure to adopt such norms threatens the survival of existing interpersonal relations and continued interdependence. For example, in 2009, Starbucks garnered a great deal of negative publicity when one of its franchises fired three workers who were part of a group trying to unionize the company's workers. This is a potential violation of one of the major components of the Fair Labor Standards Act and, for that reason, against the law. This is a pivotal norm, and management does not have the discretion to fire workers who are trying to organize a union. However, beyond this, as a company, Starbucks also tried to maintain an image that suggested to both future employees and customers that it was socially aware and sensitive to worker rights. Organizations do not necessarily have to be socially aware or sensitive to worker rights, therefore, this would be considered a **peripheral norm**. Peripheral norms are not formally required, but they can strongly influence the character of interpersonal relations if they are violated. For example, according to one public relations expert in the industry, many customers "picked up the narrative that Starbucks is posing to be somebody they are not," and this hurt sales in some regions.[20]

Another type of peripheral norm might be the practice of sharing detailed financial information with all employees. This kind of "open-book management" is not required, but many organizations routinely practice it anyway because it has been shown to promote employee trust and willingness to cooperate.[21] In the wake of recent corporate scandals, some CEOs have moved in this direction voluntarily.[22] In other cases, union leaders and shareholders have pressed for it more directly.[23] In still other cases, the government has threatened to demand it, suggesting that there might be a need for laws that would convert open-book management from a peripheral norm to a pivotal norm.[24]

Whether interdependent individuals adopt pivotal and peripheral norms, such norms have important consequences for their behaviors and performance as members of groups and organizations. As Table 8.2 indicates, *individual adjustment*, or the acceptance or rejection

Table 8.2 Norms and Individual Adjustment

		Pivotal norms	
		Accept	Reject
Peripheral norms	Accept	Conformity	Subversive rebellion
	Reject	Creative individualism	Open revolution

Source: Adapted from E. H. Schein, *Organization Psychology* (Upper Saddle River, NJ: Pearson Education, Inc.), 100.

of these norms, leads to four basic behavior patterns: conformity, subversive rebellion, open revolution, and creative individualism.

When role occupants choose to accept both pivotal and peripheral norms, the resulting **conformity** is marked by a tendency to try to fit in with others in a loyal but uncreative way. People who conform to all norms become caretakers of the past. So long as tasks remain unchanged and the work situation is stable, conformity can facilitate productivity and performance. Conversely, it can endanger the organization's long-term survival if tasks or the surrounding situation change significantly. In groups where conformity is very high, individual differences are largely eliminated and one can predict behavior better by examining the norms rather than the individual person's own thoughts and tendencies. For example, most groups have strong norms for how important attendance is and, when a person moves from a group with norms that have zero tolerance for absenteeism to a group where the standards are less strict, that person's rate of absenteeism tends to go up.[25]

When individuals accept peripheral norms but reject pivotal ones, the result is **subversive rebellion**. That is, people conceal their rejection of norms that are critical to the survival of existing interpersonal relations by acting in accordance with less important ones. This outward show of conformity could make it possible for rebellious members to continue occupying important roles. If their number is large, however, their failure to adhere to important pivotal norms could jeopardize the survival of ongoing interpersonal relations.

Open revolution might break out if role occupants reject both pivotal and peripheral norms. If only a few individuals revolt, they might be pressured to conform or asked to leave. Interpersonal relations dominated by open revolution, however, might simply fall apart; for example, the norms in many Chinese factories had historically presumed that workers would work long hours for low pay. However, the 2012 riot at Hon Hai's Foxconn factory in Shanxi province proved to be a watershed event. Though it started as a minor argument between two young workers, it quickly escalated into a pitched battle that involved over 2,000 employees and 5,000 paramilitary forces. The two workers, who everyone agrees started the riot, were from different regions and had just got off a stressful shift at the factory, which makes iPod and iPads. The work was boring and low paid. When frustrations boiled over, a small argument turned into a shoving and pushing match. Witnesses claim that security workers at the plant overreacted to the incident and began brutally beating the two young people.[26]

At that point, hundreds of workers rushed the security personnel and a melee erupted. Soon additional security personnel were called to the scene, followed by increasing numbers of restive workers. A major revolt was under way. When it was over, forty people were hospitalized and the facility had to be shut down for days after fires and looting left gutted sections of the sprawling industrial campus, which housed close to 80,000 workers.[27] Soon after the Foxconn riot, questions were raised about the changing nature of the Chinese workforce and how these changes are challenging the norms and the business model that underlies all of Chinese manufacturing. Specifically, the riot put a spotlight on the tension between Chinese factories that base their business model on low-cost strategies that create low-scope jobs and unpleasant working conditions, and a new generation of Chinese workers who seem less willing to tolerate those conditions. For example, one worker who was involved in the riot spoke for many when she stated that "some people are just not satisfied that Foxconn pays us so little and asks us to work long hours."[28]

In **creative individualism**, individuals accept pivotal norms but reject peripheral ones. This behavior ensures continued productivity and survival. It also opens the door to the individual creativity needed to develop new ways of doing things. Creative individualism is, therefore, especially desirable when dealing with change in tasks or work situations. It ensures that individuals have the freedom to invent new responses to changing conditions. This type of creativity is often sought because norms do not always remain effective over time.

Norms develop through a series of role episodes. A **role set** comprises a collection of people who interact with a role occupant and serve as the source of the norms that influence that person's behaviors (see Figure 8.2). A typical role set includes such people as an employee's supervisor, peers, and subordinates, other members of the employee's functional unit, and members of adjacent functional units that share tasks, clients, or customers. Members of the role set communicate norms to the role occupant via *role-sending messages.*

Some role-sending messages are informational, telling the role occupant what is going on. Others attempt to influence the role occupant (for example, by letting him or her know what punishments will follow if the individual disregards norms). Some of these messages might be directed toward accomplishing organizational objectives. Others could be unrelated to, or even contrary to, official requirements.

As long as the role occupant complies with these expectations, role senders will attend to their own jobs. If the role occupant begins to deviate from expectations, however, the role senders, their expectations, and their means of enforcing compliance will become quite visible. For example, although the recipes of famous chefs are not covered directly by intellectual property laws, there are strong norms in the restaurant industry associated with "stealing" other people's recipes. For example, in France, a chef who is found to have stolen recipes will be called out in public by his peers. If it happens once, he or she will become the victim of derision, practical jokes, or isolation. If it happens more than once, the group itself will collude to make it difficult for the person to find work anywhere in the region.[29]

Although the members of the organization communicate the dos and don'ts associated with a role through the *sent role*, the *received role* actually has the most immediate influence on the behavior of the role occupant. As discussed later in this chapter, factors that influence the process of communication can distort a message or cause it to be misunderstood. Even when messages are communicated effectively, role occupants often fail to meet senders' role expectations. Several types of role conflict (as discussed in Chapter 6) can prevent a role receiver from meeting the expectations of a sender.

First, *intersender role conflict* may place competing, mutually exclusive demands on the role occupant. A person who meets one sender's expectations might violate the expectations of another. In addition, *interrole conflict*, caused by occupying two roles at once (for example, being a manager and a parent), can create stress both at home and at work.[30] Thus, women who have primary care responsibilities for children or grandparents often experience *role overload* due to competing demands. Professional positions that come with salaries and benefits create a number of fixed costs and employers are motivated to recoup these costs by working people in these types of jobs very long hours. In contrast, when workers are being paid by the hour, employers are motivated to avoid overtime pay and, perhaps, even health benefits by keeping everyone's hours below forty or thirty hours a week. People who want to work more but cannot get enough hours may experience *role underload*.[31] Although this might make some sense for the bottom line, research suggests that organizations that help employees achieve some degree of work–life balance often generate a more loyal and dedicated workforce.[32]

Finally, the role occupant might experience *person–role conflict* and have some ideas about how the role should be performed that conflict with the role sender's demands. For example, in 2012, when Eric Snowden, who worked at the U.S. National Security Agency, learned that the government was illegally tapping the cell phones of millions of Americans, he had to choose between keeping this secret as part of his role at the agency or blowing the whistle on the government as part of his role as a concerned citizen.[33] People who are experiencing person–role conflict and respond by whistleblowing in the way that Snowden did are often accused of being traitors or disloyal, however, this kind of active dissent has historically proven to be an important check on institutions that may become too powerful.[34] Thus, role making and taking is a process characterized not by unilateral demands and forced acceptance but instead by flexibility and sometimes give-and-take negotiation that breaks down into conflict. Indeed, the amount of flexibility in terms of how tightly or loosely roles are regulated is emerging as one of the most important aspects of cultural differences between countries.[35]

Communication Processes in Interdependent Relationships

In Figure 8.2, a straight line was drawn between the sent role and the received role to denote the communication of a message between members of the role set and the role occupant. A more detailed representation of the process of communication breaks it into three general stages: (1) encoding information into a message, (2) transmitting the message via a medium, and (3) decoding information from the received message.[36] Because problems can develop at any one of these stages, it is important to understand what happens at each stage, and how this might translate into barriers to effective communication.

Communication Messages and Media

Encoding is the process by which a communicator's abstract idea is translated into the symbols of language and thus into a message that can be transmitted to someone else. The idea is subjective and known only to the communicator. Because it employs a common system of symbols, the message can be understood by other people who know the communicator's language.

The *medium*, or the carrier of the message, exists outside the communicator and can be perceived by everyone. We can characterize media by the human senses on which they rely: oral speech, which uses hearing; written documentation, which uses vision or touch (Braille); and nonverbal communication, which might use at least four of the five basic senses.

Nowhere is technology having a greater effect on the workplace than in the area of communication media. Facsimile (fax), electronic mail (e-mail), chat rooms, text messaging, social networking sites, cellular phones, and the capacity to tweet have created an ever increasing menu of options in terms of finding the best medium for each message. Thus, learning how to match the medium with the message has never been more challenging.

Oral communication relies predominantly on the sense of hearing; its symbols are based on sounds and consist of spoken language. Face-to-face conversations, meetings, and telephone calls are the most commonly used forms of communication in organizations. As you will recall from Chapter 1, as much as 75 percent of a manager's time is devoted to meetings and telephone calls.[37] Oral communications offer the advantage of speed. One can encode information quickly, and the feedback cycle is rapid. If receivers are unclear about the message, they can immediately ask for clarification. Presenting a proposal orally, for example, provides much more opportunity for answering questions than does preparing a written report. Oral messages are generally efficient in handling the day-to-day problems that arise in groups and organizations. In addition, strong narratives and story-telling skills are necessary to help convey emotionally laden information or information related to the organization's core values, especially if these are changing.[38]

Lack of communication skills on the part of either party in the communication process can reduce the virtues of oral communication, however. In some cases, the cost of these breakdowns can be so severe that the organization might go to great lengths to promote effective oral communication. For example, medical doctors have often been criticized as being ineffective communicators and 40 percent of malpractice suits cite a breakdown in physician–patient communication as a factor in the patient's negative outcome. This problem was considered so important to administrators of the Medicare program that they began to survey patients regarding their doctor's communication skills so that they could reward and punish ineffective communicators as part of the Hospital Consumers Assessment of Healthcare Providers and Systems (HCAHPS) program introduced in 2012. Many hospitals are responding to this with training programs in which physicians are taught to face patients directly and to let them speak for at least two minutes without being interrupted. Physicians are also trained to show compassion and empathy when providing information and then to quiz patients after the information has been provided to insure that they understood the message. Protocols such as these have been found to increase patient adherence to treatments by 20 percent.[39]

Sometimes *written communication* is preferred over oral communication. Although written messages are more slowly encoded, they allow the communicator to use more precise language. A sentence in a labor contract, for example, can be rewritten many times to ensure that everyone involved knows exactly what it means. The aim is to minimize the possibility of any future confusion or argument over interpretation. Written materials also provide a permanent copy of the communication that can be stored and retrieved for later purposes. For example, a supervisor might write a formal memo to an employee, noting that she has been late for work ten of the last eleven days and warning that failure to arrive on time will result in her dismissal. If the behavior continues, the supervisor has documentary evidence that the employee received fair warning.

Indeed, one of the problems caused by newer communication media, such as text messages, e-mail, and tweets, is that people get confused regarding the strengths and weaknesses of the media. For example, most people treat e-mail as if it is a form of oral communication, ignoring grammar, writing style, and form, in return for quick and informal communication. Many e-mails are "zipped off" in a hurry, without a great deal of planning and forethought as to their content and expression. However, e-mail is in fact a written form of communication that leaves a paper trail, providing written documentation of ideas that one might later regret. Thus, when Merrill Lynch stock analyst Henry Blodgett told his clients in a formal letter to "accumulate" a certain stock and a day later told a friend in an e-mail that the same stock was "a piece of crap," he set the stage for a $100 million conflict-of-interest lawsuit.[40] Indeed, recovered e-mails are more often than not the "smoking gun" evidence that forms the basis for many of the legal actions brought against unethical organizations, including suits where the charge is destruction of e-mail evidence.[41]

In addition to oral and written communication, owing to our long evolutionary history, humans have developed nonverbal ways to communicate. Nonverbal messages are often underestimated in terms of their power. For example, you can gauge how interested two people are in a conversation by their timing of responses to one another's messages. When two people are intently interested in the conversation, they often anticipate one another's thoughts and respond quickly, often completing each other's sentences. Slow rhythms in conversation, on the other hand, signal a lack of interest or understanding. Similarly, like our evolutionary ancestors, humans often mimic each other in conversations where there is a high interest level, adopting the hand and head motions of those whom they admire. Failure to mimic implies a lack of attention, agreement, or respect and is a sign that one is not getting through to the intended audience.[42]

To complete the communication process, the message sent must be subjected to decoding, a process in which the message is translated in the mind of the receiver. When all works well, the resulting idea or mental image corresponds closely to the sender's idea or mental image. Unfortunately, myriad things can go wrong and render communication ineffective. The term **noise** refers to the factors that can distort a message. Noise can occur at any stage of the process and is particularly problematic when two people are from different cultures.[43]

Barriers to Effective Communication

A variety of organizational, interpersonal, and individual factors can hinder communication within groups or organizations. For instance, the nature of the physical space occupied by jobholders inevitably affects patterns of communication. If an organization wants to promote the development of interpersonal relations, it must place people in close physical proximity. People who work closely together have more opportunities to interact and are more likely to form lasting relationships than are people who are physically distant from one another. This is even true if people who are physically distant can communicate frequently via electronic media like e-mail. For this reason, many organizations invest in richer electronic communication media such as video conferencing or Skype that allow people to "see" one another. Although helpful in terms of developing cohesiveness and trust, rich media do not seem to be a total replacement for face-to-face interpersonal communication, which is important in this regard.[44]

Whether the purpose of the communication is to inform or persuade, the *credibility* of the source will largely determine whether the role occupant internalizes the message. Credibility refers to the degree to which the information provided by the source is believable, and it is a function of three factors:

1.   Expertise, or the communicator's knowledge of the topic at hand.
2.   Trustworthiness, or the degree to which the recipient believes the communicator has no hidden motives.
3.   Consistency between the communicator's words and actions.

Credibility is low whenever the source of the communication is uninformed, is untrustworthy, or acts in a way that contradicts his or her words. For example, after the war with Iraq, the failure of the United States to uncover weapons of mass destruction (WMDs) led many to question the administration's credibility because Iraq's alleged possession of WMDs was one of the primary justifications for the war. This perception was particularly acute when it became clear that some of the evidence that the president mentioned in a nationally televised speech to the nation was based on forged documents.[45] Although few believed that the president knew that the evidence was forged nor that he had deliberately misled the public, the fact that he was uninformed because of failure within the intelligence community still harmed his credibility.

A *power imbalance* between a role sender and a role occupant can also impede communication. For example, *upward communication* flows from people low in the organizational hierarchy to people above them. Because people at upper levels of the hierarchy have a great deal of power to reward and punish employees at lower levels, the latter are sometimes inhibited in their upward communication. Insecure lower-level workers might tend to forget about losses and exaggerate gains when reporting information upward, leaving managers at upper levels with a distorted sense of reality. Similarly, lower-level employees who are unsure about how to perform their jobs or critical aspects of the organization's mission might be reluctant to ask questions, fearing to appear less than knowledgeable. Some organizations, such as DuPont, will actually conduct anonymous polls of the lower-level employees to gauge what they do and do not seem to know about the company, in order to get an unbiased assessment of how well they are communicating to all levels.[46] Upper-level managers who fail to do this might also get a distorted view of the competencies and knowledge of those who serve under them.

Some leaders unwittingly contribute to this problem, by "shooting the messenger" or surrounding themselves with "yes people." In this context, the manager receives only positive feedback on his or her personal performance or the performance of the organization, setting the manager up for future failure. The pervasiveness of this problem has led many top leaders to turn to executive coaches, who provide an external and often painful assessment of the manager's weaknesses in the realm of interpersonal relations. As one such executive coach has noted, "CEOs get hired for their skills but fired for their personalities."[47] The research evidence suggests that this kind of coaching can have modest effects in terms of improving the manager's receptivity to negative feedback, which in turn enhances his or her performance.[48]

Finally, distortion can occur because of jargon. **Jargon** is an informal language shared by long-tenured, central members of units. Within a small closed group, it can be extremely useful. It maximizes information exchange with a minimum of time and symbols by taking advantage of the shared training and experience of its users. On the other hand, because jargon is likely to confuse anyone lacking the same training and experience, it can create a barrier to communication with new members or between different groups. Often technical specialists use jargon unconsciously and might find it difficult to express themselves in any other terms. This habit can become a permanent disability, greatly reducing people's career opportunities outside their own small groups.

Socialization to New Roles

Although effective communication is always important within organizations, perhaps at no time is it more critical than when a person assumes a new role. **Socialization** is the procedure through which people acquire the social knowledge and skills necessary to correctly assume new roles in a group or an organization.[49] This process of "learning the ropes" entails much more than simply learning the technical requirements associated with one's job. It also deals with learning about the group or organization, its values, its culture, its past history, its potential, and the role occupant's position in the overall scheme. Although most people think of socialization only in terms of someone joining a group or organization for the first time, in fact socialization is an ongoing process. It occurs whenever an individual moves into a new role within the group or organization. A role can be considered "new" for an individual as long as it differs from the previous role on any one of three dimensions: functional, hierarchical, or inclusionary.

The *functional* dimension reflects differences in the tasks performed by members of a group or an organization. Figure 8.3A shows the typical functional groupings of a conventional business organization: marketing, production, accounting, human resources, research and development, and finance. Similarly, Figure 8.3B depicts the functional groupings common to many universities: the schools of business, engineering, medicine, social sciences, law, and arts and letters. The roles performed in each group are quite distinct, because the jobholders are trying to accomplish different aspects of the organization's overall mission.

The *hierarchical* dimension concerns the distribution of rank and authority in a group or an organization. As you will recall from Chapter 1, a hierarchy establishes who is officially responsible for the actions of whom. In traditional organizations, this dimension takes the shape of a pyramid, in which fewer people occupy the highest ranks. The roles performed by people higher in the pyramid differ from the roles assumed by individuals lower in the pyramid

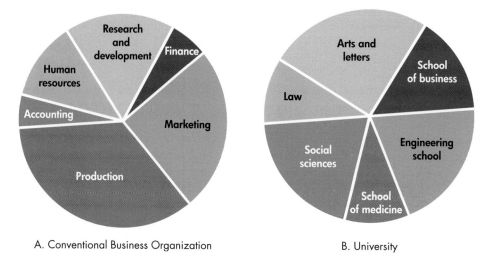

A. Conventional Business Organization   B. University

Figure 8.3 The Functional Dimensions of Organizations

largely in that the former have greater authority and power. In a highly centralized organization, this triangle is often rather steep. Figure 8.4A depicts one such pyramid, representing the hierarchical structure of a hypothetical military organization. In a more decentralized organization, fewer levels of authority exist and the hierarchical pyramid looks flatter. As indicated in Figure 8.4B, city police departments usually have fewer levels of hierarchy than an army. Most employees are arresting officers, the highest rank is captain, and only two genuine levels of hierarchy separate the top and the bottom.

The *inclusionary* dimension reflects the degree to which an employee of an organization finds himself or herself at the center or on the periphery of things. As shown in Figure 8.5, a person might move from being an outsider, beyond the organization's periphery, to being an informal leader, at the center of the organization. A job applicant, or outsider, joins the organization and becomes a newcomer, just inside the periphery. For this employee to move further along the radial dimension shown in Figure 8.5, others must accept the newcomer as a full member of the organization. This move can be accomplished only by proving that the individual shares the same assumptions as others about what is important and what is not. Usually, newcomers must first be tested—formally or informally—as to their abilities, motives, and values before they are granted inclusionary rights and privileges.

Women, minorities, and people from different cultures often find it particularly difficult to advance along this dimension in traditional organizations, and organizations can often speed their development by creating "social networks" that make it easy for them to find similar others throughout the organization. This opens up communication channels and opportunities for interaction and mentorship that might not have otherwise been possible.[50] The provision of specialized socialization programs targeted to these types of subgroups can also be instrumental in speeding up the adjustment process.[51]

Socialization occurs whenever an individual crosses boundaries in any of the three dimensions—for instance, transferring between functional departments or being promoted to a position of higher authority. When moving across functional boundaries, the key concern is the person–job fit, and the major attributes considered during this transition are the person's knowledge, skills, and abilities. For the hierarchical and inclusionary boundaries, the person's values and personality traits seem to become more relevant concerns.[52]

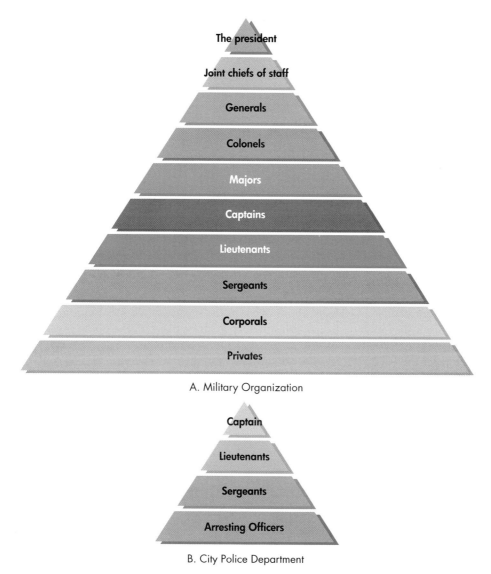

Figure 8.4 The Hierarchical Dimension of Organizations

Socialization is likely to be particularly intense when a person crosses all three boundaries at once. When a person joins a new organization, he or she crosses the inclusionary boundary, moving from nonmember to member status, and crosses functional and hierarchical boundaries by joining a particular functional unit, such as the advertising department, at a specific hierarchical level, such as account executive. It is at this time that the organization has the most instructing and persuading to accomplish. It is also the time when a person might have the least accurate expectations and, therefore, is most susceptible to being taught and influenced.[53] If handled well, this instruction can lead to increased role clarity, self-efficacy and social acceptance, which in turn promotes commitment to the role, job performance, and retention.[54]

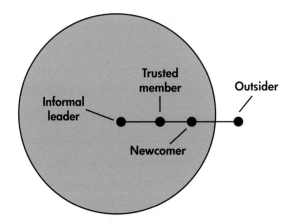

Figure 8.5 The Inclusionary Dimension of Organizations
Source: Adapted from D. Katz and R. L. Kahn, *The Social Psychology of Organizations* (New York: Wiley, 1978), 112.

Socialization Goals and Tactics

Although instructing individuals about their roles is part of all socialization programs, different firms may seek to accomplish different goals in this process. Some organizations might pursue a **role custodianship** response. Here, recipients of socialization take a care-taker's stance toward their roles. They do not question the status quo but instead conform to it. A popular expression in the U.S. Marine Corps, paraphrased from Tennyson's poem "Charge of the Light Brigade," is "Ours is not to question why; ours is but to do or die." When an organization hopes instead that recipients of socialization will change either the way their roles are performed or the ends sought through role performance, it might have **role innovation** as a goal.

Firms can use any of several tactics in socializing new members, each of which has different effects. As shown in Figure 8.6, we can classify these strategies along four critical dimensions to help understand their likely consequences: (1) collective–individual, (2) sequential–random, (3) serial–disjunctive, and (4) divestiture–investiture. The first alternative in each pair brings about a custodianship response from the new member. The second alternative of each pair leads the recipient toward role innovation.

In *collective socialization*, recipients are put in groups and go through socialization experiences together. This method is characteristic of military boot camps, fraternities, sororities, and management-training courses. In collective processes, the recruits accomplish much of the socialization themselves. For example, Marine Corps recruits might abuse one another verbally or even physically in a way that the formal institution never could.

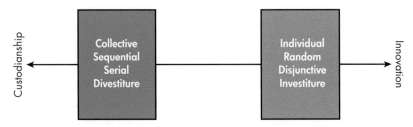

Figure 8.6 The Custodianship–Innovation Continuum and Its Socialization Techniques

In *individual socialization*, the second alternative in this pair, new members are taken one at a time and put through unique experiences. This treatment is characteristic of apprenticeship programs or on-the-job learning. It yields much more variable results than collective socialization does, and its success depends heavily on the qualities of the individual recruit.

In the second dimension of socialization, the alternative of *sequential socialization* takes new members through a set sequence of discrete and identifiable steps leading to the target role. A physician's training, for example, includes several observable steps: the undergraduate pre-med program, medical school, an internship, and a residency. A person must complete all of these steps before taking specialist board examinations. Usually, in sequential processes, each stage builds on the prior stage. The algebra teacher socializing the student to the world of math, for example, notes that geometry will be easy if the person understands algebra. The geometry teacher, in turn, explains that trigonometry will be painless if the student appreciates geometry. This type of presentation helps recruits stay focused on the current stage. It minimizes the discouragement that comes with the knowledge that they have a long journey to reach the ultimate goal.

At the other end of the second dimension are *random socialization* processes, in which learning experiences have no apparent logic or structure. Steps of the socialization process are unknown, ambiguous, or continually changing. Training for a general manager, for example, tends to be much less rigorously specified than that for a medical professional. Some managers rise from lower ranks, some come from other organizations, and some come straight from business school programs.

Socialization strategies also differ along a third dimension that concerns the amount of help and guidance provided to new members as they learn their new roles. In *serial socialization*, experienced members of the organization teach individuals about the roles they will assume. The more experienced employees serve as role models or mentors for the new members. Observing and discussing issues with these role models is the primary means by which newcomers gather information.[55] In police departments, for example, rookies are assigned as partners to older, veteran officers. Some observers have suggested that this practice creates a remarkable degree of intergenerational stability in the behaviors of police officers. This method of socialization also allows recruits to see into the future—that is, to get a glimpse of their future role. This knowledge can be good or bad, depending on the person doing the socialization. For this reason, organizations need to take great care in assigning mentors to new members. Supervisors are another potential source for delivering serial socialization to new workers, and research suggests that newcomers experience a much better perception of person–organization fit when supervisors take the time to develop a personal relationship with each new hire.[56]

In *disjunctive socialization*, new members must learn by themselves how to handle a new role. For example, the first partner in a tradition-bound law firm who is not a native English speaker might find few people (if any) who have faced her unique problems. She could be completely on her own in coping with the challenges of her new position. Disjunctive socialization is sometimes created when organizations "clean house"—that is, sweep out the older members of the organization and replace them with new personnel. Such a shakeup causes almost all employees of the firm to relearn their roles. Typically the organization hopes that the result will bring more creativity in problem solving, as this kind of move eliminates individuals who might have taught others the established way of doing things.

The fourth dimension of socialization deals with the degree to which a socialization process confirms or denies the value of an individual's personal identity. *Divestiture socialization* ignores or denies the value of the individual's personal characteristics. The organization wants to tear new members down to nothing and then rebuild them as completely new and different individuals. Some organizations require either explicitly or implicitly that recruits sever old relationships, undergo intense harassment from experienced members, and engage in the "dirty work" of the trade (work that is associated with low pay and low status) for long periods. In contrast, *investiture socialization* affirms the value to the organization of the recruit's particular personal characteristics. The organization says, in effect, "We like you just the way you are" and encourages the new employee to view the organization as a place for self-expression. It implies that, rather than changing the new member, the organization hopes that the recruit will change the organization. Under these conditions, the organization might try to make the recruit's transition process as smooth and painless as possible.[57]

Designing Socialization Programs

The strategy employed in designing a socialization program depends on the goals of that program. If the intention is to foster a custodianship response, a group or an organization is best served by a strategy that is collective, sequential, and serial and that involves divestiture. In this way, every socialization recipient will start with the same "clean slate" and receive the same experiences in the same order.

For example, the French Foreign Legion is an organization with a 175-year history of competitive excellence in an industry where success is measured in terms of life and death rather than dollars and cents. Much of its achievement can be attributed to its socialization practices, which clearly aim to instill a custodianship response in new members. The socialization task confronting the Foreign Legion is formidable. Recruits come from more than a hundred different countries and must be assembled into a cohesive unit in which members are willing to risk their lives for strangers. Far from being the "cream of the crop," most applicants are fugitive criminals, ex-convicts, dishonorably discharged members of regular armies, ex-mercenaries, and other men running from their past for some reason.[58]

For this applicant pool, one major attraction of the Foreign Legion is the fact that it is probably the only employer in the world that does not request any formal proof of identification before hiring. Indeed, the first step of the socialization program is to assign new names and nationalities to all recruits. Along with their former identities, most recruits must also say goodbye to their native tongue, because multilingualism is not appreciated. This organization has one official language: French. New recruits are then whisked off to train in exotic locales—the jungles of French Guiana or the deserts of Chad—far from their homes, families, and friends. Their training includes many of the task-specific fighting skills that one would imagine, but the standards for proficiency are much higher than those of NATO armies. Many individuals cannot stand up to the hardships of this training and drop out, leaving only a small core of the most committed members.[59]

While few businesses may want to emulate all of the socialization tactics practiced by the Foreign Legion, its example does offer some lessons for organizations whose socialization goals are to instill change in recruits. Changing recruits into conforming organizational members requires sacrificing old identities and behavior patterns and assuming new identities and behavior patterns. This change is instilled by disconnecting new members from their pasts and challenging them to realize a new future.

If the goal is to not change the individual, but rather to help the individual change the organization, the opposite tactics should be employed. That is, to promote innovation, a group or organization is better served by a strategy that provides a unique and individualized program for each recipient and places value on each recipient's particular personality, characteristics, and style.[60] In this alternative type of socialization program, individuals need to proactively seek feedback and build relationships, and this is enhanced when they are high on the traits of extroversion and openness to experience.[61] Research indicates that two different types of networks need to be established in building these relationships: first, a small and dense set of relationships with people who work directly with the newcomer; and, second, a broader, more superficial network with people from different departments and levels of the organization. The first network is critical for learning one's current job and role, and the latter is instrumental for planning for one's future roles in the organization.[62]

Regardless of its goals and strategies, and the degree to which it allows individuals to proactively socialize themselves, a good socialization program will teach new role occupants about the history, values, people, language, and culture of the group or organization in which membership is sought. If conducted properly, it will enhance the understanding of the person's role and increase his or her commitment to the organization's goals.[63]

Quality of Interpersonal Role Relationships

Given the importance of role relationships within organizations, it is critical to have a framework whereby the quality of these relationships can be judged and enhanced. *Equity theory* is a theory of social exchange that focuses on the "give and take" of various relationships, such as supervisors and subordinates. It describes the process by which people determine whether they have received fair treatment in their relationships.

Equity and Social Comparisons

As shown in Figure 8.7, equity theory holds that people make judgments about relational fairness by forming a ratio of their perceived investments (or inputs, I) and perceived rewards (or outcomes, O). They then compare this ratio to a similar ratio reflecting the perceived costs and benefits of some other reference person. Equity theory does not require that outcomes or inputs be equal for equity to exist. Individuals who receive fewer desirable outcomes than someone else might still feel fairly treated if they see themselves contributing fewer inputs than the other person. Thus, a new entry-level employee might not feel that it is unfair if the CEO is paid more, because there is a corresponding perception that the CEO brings more to the relationship. At some point, however, as we noted in the vignette that opened this chapter, this ratio may be perceived as getting out of alignment.[64]

Table 8.3 lists other possible inputs and outcomes that might be incorporated in equity comparisons in work organizations. When factors other than these seem to determine outcomes, this might be perceived as unfair. For example, a person's gender should not influence their pay, however, even when one holds the occupation constant, men often out-earn women. In fact, even in female-dominated occupations such as nursing, men are paid 16 percent more than women performing the same job. The fact that men earn higher wages and get promoted faster than women in female-dominated industries such as nursing has been referred to as the "glass elevator"—the flipside of the "glass ceiling," which refers to women's documented struggle to get promoted in male-dominated fields.[65]

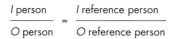

Figure 8.7 **Algebraic Expression of How People Make Equity Comparisons**

Table 8.3 Inputs and Outcomes in Equity Theory

Inputs	Outcomes
Education	Pay
Intelligence	Satisfying supervision
Experience	Seniority benefits
Training	Fringe benefits
Skill	Status symbols
Social status	Job perquisites
Job effort	Working conditions
Personal appearance	
Health	
Possession of tools	

Distributive, Procedural, and Interactive Justice

Equity theory provides a simple framework for understanding how people decide whether they are being treated fairly in their relationships. Even with this simple framework, however, it can prove difficult to achieve widespread perceptions of justice in organizations for several reasons. First, equity judgments are based on individual *perceptions* of inputs and outcomes, and perceptions of the same inputs or outcomes may differ markedly from one person to the next. There can also be cultural differences in how different groups weigh their own inputs and outputs. For example, one study found that people from individualistic cultures like the United States were much more likely to overestimate their own personal inputs (in order to "stand out") relative to people from collectivist cultures like Japan, where people tend to underestimate their own personal inputs (in order to "blend in"). This can make it very difficult to see eye to eye on what is fair, thus leading to many more impasses and fewer negotiated settlements that are accepted by each side.[66]

Second, it is difficult to predict who will be chosen as the reference person. For example, in our earlier example involving CEO pay, we saw that most CEOs use other CEOs as their reference person, and thus they do not perceive their pay requests as unfair. In fact, most compensation committees actually compute a ratio that compares the CEO to the second highest paid employee.[67] This often results in high executive pay cascading down the organization since it is in the best interest of each level of management to pad the salaries of those directly below them.[68] In contrast to either CEOs or executive compensation committees, the average taxpayer uses himself or herself as a reference person when considering CEO salaries and, therefore, the average taxpayer finds CEO pay to be outrageously unfair, especially when the company being led by that CEO is performing poorly.[69]

Outside the CEO suite, where pay disclosure is legally mandated, many organizations try to prevent social comparisons among employees by keeping pay details secret. However, in team-based structures, there is a push for transparency that is tightly focused on equity among insiders in order to promote teamwork. This emphasis on "internal equity" often comes into conflict with the need to recruit new hires externally, however. For example, one high tech firm that went to an open salary model found that external recruits used this as a starting point to leverage higher salaries. This new higher salary then "trickled down" to all of the insiders creating a major hike in labor costs. The company eventually took all the salary data offline, trying to make it more difficult for employees to leverage this information toward their own ends.[70]

Third, in addition to outcomes and inputs, people are keenly sensitive to the procedures through which allocation decisions are made and the manner in which these decisions are communicated. We can distinguish between three kinds of justice perceptions. **Distributional justice** refers to the judgments that people make with respect to the input/outcome ratios they experience relative to the ratios experienced by others with whom they identify (that is, *reference persons*). The degree to which perceptions of distributional justice translate into the type of anger and resentment that might harm or sever the relationship, however, depends at least partially on perceptions of procedural and interactional justice. In some instances, managers can maintain a perception of fairness and trust even in the face of some pretty negative outcomes, if they carefully manage these "nondistributional" aspects of justice.[71]

Whereas distributive justice focuses on "ends," procedural justice and interactional justice focus on "means." If the methods and procedures used to arrive at and implement decisions that affect the employee negatively are seen as fair, the reaction is likely to be much more positive than otherwise.[72] Table 8.4 details the factors that determine whether **procedural justice** will be applied. Even if someone experiences a decision that may harm him or her in an outcome sense (for example, by being passed over for a promotion), the organization can minimize the amount of anger and resentment felt by the employee by focusing on the procedures used to make the decision and showing that they were consistent, unbiased, accurate, correctable, representative, and ethical. For example, most people will react negatively to being laid off by their employer, but research shows that if the employer can show that the rules followed when making the decisions met these criteria, people will react much less negatively.[73] In other contexts where difficult decisions have to be made, allowing people to participate in the decision-making process may also increase perceptions of procedural justice.[74]

Promoting perceptions of procedural justice among employees is important for a number of other reasons. Workers who feel that organizational procedures are just are much more likely to engage in *organizational citizenship behaviors* (OCBs) relative to other workers.[75]

Table 8.4 Six Determinants of Procedural Justice

1. Consistency	The procedures are applied consistently across time and other people.
2. Bias suppression	The procedures are applied by a person who has no vested interest in the outcome or prior prejudices regarding the individual.
3. Information accuracy	The procedure is based on information that is perceived to be true.
4. Correctability	The procedure has built-in safeguards that allow for appealing mistakes or bad decisions.
5. Representativeness	The procedure is informed by the concerns of all groups or stakeholders (co-workers, customers, owners) affected by the decision, including the individual who is being harmed.
6. Ethicality	The procedure is consistent with prevailing moral standards as they pertain to issues such as invasion of privacy or deception.

Indeed, this can have a trickle-down effect in that, if managers experience procedural justice, they will often engage in citizenship behaviors toward their subordinates who, in turn, will reciprocate with more OCBs directed toward management—creating a positive, self-reinforcing cycle.[76] This can help establish a climate of procedural justice throughout the work unit, which has been shown to promote group performance and reduce absenteeism.[77] This is especially the case in organizations that are structured in a mechanistic fashion and rely a great deal on formalized rules and procedures to promote coordination.[78]

Whereas procedural justice deals with the manner in which a decision was reached, **interactional justice** focuses on the interpersonal nature of the implementation of the outcomes. Table 8.5 lists the four key determinants of interactional justice. When the decision is explained well and implemented in a fashion that is socially sensitive, considerate, and empathetic, this approach might help diffuse some of the resentment produced by a decision that, in an outcome sense, might be seen as unfair to a particular employee.[79] For example, a manager confronted with the task of laying off a worker would do well to use Table 8.5 as a checklist. Indeed, as one experienced manager notes, when it comes to layoff decisions, "the primary thing we try to do is let them leave with their self-esteem."[80] As is the case with procedural justice, interactional justice tends to trickle down in an organization, such that supervisors who are treated with this kind of fairness respond with this kind of fairness down the line— and vice versa.[81]

Over time, if a relationship is characterized as being high on all three dimensions of justice, then trust will develop. In a trusting relationship, each member of the exchange has faith in the other, knowing that he or she will be judged fairly and that the other will act in accordance with his or her needs.[82] Developing trust is critical because it ensures that the two people need not constantly direct their attention and effort at negotiating the short-term inputs and outputs of their relationship. It is especially crucial in today's decentralized, networked organizations that rely on teams, because trust replaces formal, hierarchical authority as a control mechanism, and hence trust is strongly related to organizational performance in these kinds of contexts.[83]

Instead, in a trusting relationship, people take a long-term focus, where the expectation of fair treatment in the long run precludes the necessity of frequent "equity checks." People in trusting relationships spend less time and attention on maintaining the relationship, which means that they can direct their effort and attention toward working together productively to meet their interdependence needs. Thus a much stronger relationship between motivation and performance exists in groups characterized by trust.[84] A trusting culture arises where the level of trust is high across all relationships within a group. Groups with this kind of culture show high levels of group cohesion and spontaneous helping behavior relative to low-trust groups.[85] Figure 8.8 depicts the relationships between the three types of justice, trust, and work outcomes.

Table 8.5 Four Determinants of Interactional Justice

1. Explanation	Emphasizes aspects of procedural fairness that justify the decision
2. Social sensitivity	Treats the person with dignity and respect
3. Consideration	Listens to the person's concerns
4. Empathy	Identifies with the person's feelings

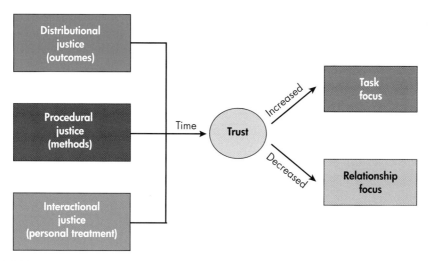

Figure 8.8 The Relationship between Justice, Trust, and Work Outcomes

Responses to Inequity

Perceptions of inequity create unpleasant emotions. When people feel that they are receiving a greater share of outcomes than they deserve, they might feel guilty. Having a sense of guilt can often be an important positive characteristic for leaders or team members, because it prompts them to go out of their way to reduce inequities that they perceive in the workplace. In contrast, perceiving oneself as coming up short in the equity comparison results in anger—a much stronger emotion than guilt. Such anger could make a person want to retaliate against the partner in the relationship, especially if the person is low in agreeableness or negative affectivity.[86] Indeed, the tension associated with inequity could motivate the person to take any of several actions in response.

First, the individual might *alter his or her personal inputs.* For example, in decision-making teams, if one team member perceives that his or her opinion is not being given any weight by the leader, he or she might cease contributing to the group's discussion or withhold critical information needed to make a good decision.[87] This person might even recruit other team members to his or her cause and alter the power relationship between the leader and the group as a whole.[88] Of course, the classic response associated with withholding inputs among workers covered by a collective bargaining agreement is to go on strike. For example, in 2012, when the City of Chicago threatened to remove some of the job security protections that went along with tenure in the public school system, the Chicago Teachers Union responded by having 26,000 teachers walk off the job.[89] In contexts where there is no collective bargaining agreement, anger resulting from unfair treatment might encourage people to form a union, as was the case at WalMart that same year.[90]

A second possible response to inequity is to try to *alter personal outcomes.* For example, individuals who feel that they are relatively underpaid might demand raises or sue their employer for higher pay. For example, an increasingly common type of lawsuit involves workers who claim violations of standard wage and hour laws when they fail to get paid for overtime work. Professional and managerial workers are exempt from this law, but it is not always clear who exactly is a manager or a professional and who is not, and employers paid out over $1 billion as a result of such suits in 2006 alone.[91] If this kind of legal response is not possible, some employees might even resort to illegal methods to get even with their employer, and perceptions of injustice have been directly linked to measures of employee theft.[92] Finally, some employees conclude that, if you can't take it with you, you can always break it, and sabotage is an especially likely response to perceived injustice when the individual feels powerless to effect change in any other more legitimate form.[93]

A third way of responding to inequity is to use *cognitive distortion*—that is, to rationalize the results of one's comparisons. For example, people can distort their perceptions of outcomes. In one study, people who were underpaid for a particular task justified this underpayment by stating that their task was more enjoyable than the task performed by people who were overpaid—even though the tasks were identical. This type of over-justification effect has been documented in a number of contexts.[94] One example of this can be seen in the behavior of interns, who often provide a great deal of service to organizations despite being unpaid. The interns might justify this to themselves by noting that they are gaining valuable job experience that offsets the lack of pay. However, if the work actually being done by an intern would otherwise go to a "real employee," then this is an unfair labor practice according to the law, and several ex-interns have successfully sued companies who found it cost effective to simply slap the term "intern" on a real job.[95]

A fourth way to restore equity is to take some action that will *change the behavior of the reference person*. Workers who, according to their peers, perform too well on piece-rate systems often earn the derogatory title of "rate buster." Research has shown that, if such name calling fails to constrain personal productivity, more direct tactics may be invoked. In one study, researchers coined the term "binging" to refer to a practice in which workers periodically punched suspected rate busters in the arm until they reduced their level of effort. Finally, if all else fails, equity can be secured by *leaving an inequitable situation*. Turnover and absenteeism are common means of dealing with perceptions of unfairness in the workplace, and more often than not, the employees that leave are those with the best talent and, therefore, the best alternative employment opportunities.[96] Although organizations concerned about retention frequently focus on pay and benefits, exit interviews of employees who leave companies often reveal that the driving factor was either a poor relationship between the individual and his or her supervisor or lack of supporting relationships among co-workers.[97]

Managing Inequitable Situations

In a perfect world, managers could ensure that every employee felt equitably treated at all times. Given the wide variety of inputs and outputs that employees might consider relevant and the many reference people who might be called on in comparisons, however, there will inevitably be situations in which the manager is confronted with an employee who is angry and feels that he or she has been treated unfairly. In these circumstances, the manager's first step should be to try to change the actual source of the inequity. For example, the manager might seek to increase the outcomes the aggrieved individual receives (for example, through a pay raise) or decrease the inputs that the aggrieved individual must contribute (for example, by reduced responsibilities).

For example, at McDonald's restaurant chain, the difference in revenue between one of their top managers and their average manager is roughly $200,000 a year. Unfortunately, these top managers also have the best alternative employment opportunities, and thus their turnover rate is quite high, bordering on 50 percent. In order to prevent these managers from terminating their relationship with the company, the human resource department created a new retirement program in 2008 that boosted savings for this group. McDonald's basically agreed to double any 401(k) savings for these managers. That is, if a manager put $5,000 into a 401(k) plan, McDonald's would double that with a $10,000 donation. This program helped build loyalty and resulted in a reduction of turnover of over 33 percent.[98]

If true change cannot be initiated, the manager's second step might be to change the aggrieved person's perceptions of the situation, by persuading the worker to focus on outcomes of which he or she might be unaware (for example, the added chances of being promoted given those responsibilities) or inputs the worker takes for granted (for example, not being asked to travel or work weekends). The manager can also try to switch the reference person being utilized by the aggrieved individual to someone in an even worse position (for example, by noting how many people with similar jobs have been laid off).

As a last resort, if a manager cannot change either the conditions or the perceptions of the angry individual, he or she might be left with only excuses and apologies. With an excuse, the manager basically admits that the person was treated unfairly, but implies that the problem was beyond the manager's control. With an apology, the manager admits both harm and responsibility, but shows remorse and denies that the inequity is truly representative of the past and future of the relationship. A successful apology is usually accompanied by some form of compensation that, at least symbolically, restores equity in the relationship. In today's increasingly litigious society, these kinds of apologies are increasingly rare since they might be seen as an admission of guilt by parties who may be interested in suing their employer. This is unfortunate because a good sincere apology is often a cheap, fast, and effective way to eliminate the problems caused with a specific perceived injustice, and it has been shown to actually result in reduced lawsuits.[99]

For example, Joette Schmidt, vice president of America West Airlines, went on the *Today* show and was confronted with a passenger, Sheryl Cole, who was thrown off a recent America West flight for making a joke about security. Instead of trying to defend the company, Schmidt looked directly into the camera and stated, "I'm here primarily to apologize to Ms. Cole. We overreacted." Cole, who had spent her first few minutes on camera harshly criticizing the airline, was visibly caught off guard, and immediately softened her stance, responding, "I appreciate the apology, and I am sympathetic to America West right now, knowing that they are going through a tough time."[100] This shows the power of simple apologies to restore equity in relationships that have been damaged. The three main goals that one has to accomplish to restore a damaged relationship are to reduce negative affect, restore a positive exchange, and then gradually rebuild trust, all of which can be triggered by a good sincere apology.[101]

If nothing else, a good apology shows that the two sides of the relationship see things the same way, and legitimizes the world view of the offended party. Poor apologies accomplish very little, and as seen in the case of famed cyclist Lance Armstrong, can actually make things worse. Many viewers felt that Armstrong's apologies on the *Oprah Winfrey Show* regarding his past lies about illegal blood doping during competitions denied responsibility and diminished the harm caused by his behavior on other people involved in the case. Public opinion polls following the airing of the show documented that people disliked Armstrong more after the apology than before it.[102] Clearly, this was a case where the attempt to manage an inequitable situation failed miserably—but, at least Armstrong felt a need to apologize. As we saw in our opening vignette, many CEOs of poorly performing companies that still reap huge salaries do not even see a need to apologize.

Summary

This chapter discussed the three key ingredients of all interpersonal relations: interdependence, roles, and communication. Different types of interdependence form among people who are joined together in interpersonal relations. *Pooled interdependence* is the simplest of these forms; increasingly more complex forms are *sequential, reciprocal,* and *comprehensive interdependence. Roles* form among interdependent individuals to guide their behaviors as they interact with one another. They capture the expectations that members of a *role set* have for the person occupying a given work role. Roles can be differentiated along *functional, hierarchical,* and *inclusionary* dimensions. *Socialization* is the process through which individuals learn about their roles. Depending on the goal of socialization, different communicators, using different tactics, might be required to strengthen *custodianship* or *innovation* expectations. Just as socialized roles form the building blocks of interpersonal relations, *communication* is the cement that holds these blocks together. It involves the encoding, transmission, and decoding of information sent from one person to another via a communication medium. Equity theory is a theoretical framework that helps explain how people judge the fairness of their relationships. This theory provides a great deal of practical guidance in terms of managing perceptions of *distributional, procedural,* and *interactional justice.*

Review Questions

1. Of the four types of interdependence discussed in this chapter, which type is most adversely affected by turnover among organizational members? Which type of interdependence is most adversely affected by turnover in group leadership? How might the nature of the turnover process affect the kind of interdependence built into groups?
2. Socialization refers to the effect that the group or organization has on the individual. This effect tends to be greatest when the individual is moving through more than one dimension simultaneously (for example, functional and hierarchical). In contrast, when is the individual most likely to have the greatest effect on the organization? (Are there honeymoon periods? Do lame ducks have any influence?) How might your answer depend on the tactics of socialization initially employed to bring the individual into the group or organization?
3. What role do ceremonies play in the socialization process of someone crossing an important organizational boundary? In terms of the three kinds of boundaries that a person can traverse, where are ceremonies most frequently encountered, and why? What role do ceremonies play in the motivation of group members who are not crossing a boundary but are merely observers at the affair?
4. In communication, it has been said that "the medium is the message." What factors should be considered when choosing a medium for one's communication? Some of the greatest leaders of all time actually wrote very little. What might explain why people who are perceived as strong leaders avoid leaving a paper trail? When might writing be used to enhance leadership?
5. According to equity theory, how do people judge whether they have been treated fairly? What effects can these judgments have on workplace performance? How can these effects be managed?

Notes

1   M. Trottman, "Corporate Pay: One CEO = 354 Workers," *Wall Street Journal*, April 16, 2013, http://blogs.wsj.com/corporate-intelligence/2013/04/16/corporate-pay-one-ceo-354-workers/.
2   E. B. Smith and P. Kuntz, "Some CEOs Are More Equal than Others," *Bloomberg Businessweek*, May 2, 2013, 71–75.

3 Z. R. Mider and J. Green, "Heads or Tails, Some CEOs Win the Pay Game," *Bloomberg Businessweek*, October 8, 2012, 23–24.

4 L. Kwoh, "Firms Resist Pay Equity Rules," *Wall Street Journal*, June 26, 2012, http://online. wsj.com/news/articles/SB10001424052702304458604577490842584787190.

5 H. Y. Li, J. B. Bingham, and E. E. Umphress, "Fairness from the Top: Perceived Procedural Justice and Collaborative Problem Solving in New Product Development," *Organization Science* 18 (2007): 200–216.

6 R. Gulati, "Dependence Asymmetry and Joint Dependence in Inter-Organizational Relationships: Effects of Embeddedness on a Manufacturer's Performance in Procurement Relationships," *Administrative Science Quarterly* 52 (2007): 32–69.

7 S. B. de Jong, G. S. D. Van der Vegt, and E. Molleman, "The Relationships among Asymmetry in Task Dependence, Perceived Helping Behavior, and Trust," *Journal of Applied Psychology* 92 (2007): 1625–1637.

8 M. L. Loughry and H. L. Tosi, "Performance Implications of Peer Monitoring," *Organization Science* 19 (2008): 876–890.

9 C. W. Langfred, "The Downside of Self-Management: A Longitudinal Study of the Effects of Conflict on Trust, Autonomy, and Task Interdependence in Self-Managing Teams," *Academy of Management Journal* 50 (2007): 885–900.

10 D. L. Ferrin, M. C. Bligh, and J. C. Kohles, "It Takes Two to Tango: An Interdependence Analysis of the Spiraling of Perceived Trustworthiness and Cooperation in Interpersonal and Intergroup Relations," *Organizational Behavior and Human Decision Processes* 107 (2008): 161–178.

11 M. D. Johnson, J. R. Hollenbeck, S. E. Humphry, D. R. Ilgen, D. Jundt, and C. J. Meyer, "Cutthroat Cooperation: Asymmetrical Adaptation to Changes in Team Reward Structures," *Academy of Management Journal* 49 (2006): 103–119.

12 D. Z. Levin, E. A. Whitener, and R. Cross, "Perceived Trustworthiness of Knowledge Sources: The Moderating Impact of Relationship Length," *Journal of Applied Psychology* 91 (2006): 1163–1171.

13 R. Wageman, "Interdependence and Group Effectiveness," *Administrative Science Quarterly* 40 (1995): 145–179.

14 E. C. Dierdorff and F. P. Morgeson, "Consensus in Work Role Requirements: The Influence of Discrete Occupational Context on Role Expectations," *Journal of Applied Psychology* 92 (2007): 1228–1241.

15 D. R. Ilgen and J. R. Hollenbeck, "The Structure of Work: Job Design and Roles," in M. Dunnette, ed., *Handbook of Industrial Organizational Psychology* (Houston, TX: Consulting Psychologist Press, 1993), 165–207.

16 G. Toegl, M. Kilduff, and N. Anand, "Emotion Helping by Managers: An Emergent Understanding of Discrepant Role Expectations and Outcomes," *Academy of Management Journal* 56 (2013): 334–357.

17 R. Rico, M. Sanchez-Manzanares, F. Gil, and C. Gibson, "Team Implicit Coordination Processes: A Team Knowledge-Based Approach," *Academy of Management Journal* 33 (2008): 163–184.

18 Z. X. Zhang, P. S. Hempel, Y. L. Han, and D. Tjosvold, "Transactive Memory System Links Work Team Characteristics and Performance," *Journal of Applied Psychology* 92 (2007): 1722–1730.

19 J. L. Levine, E. T. Higgens, and H. Choi, "Development of Strategic Norms in Groups," *Organizational Behavior and Human Decision Processes* 82 (2000): 88–101.

20 M. Goldstein, "Starbucks' Karma Problem," *BusinessWeek*, January 12, 2009, 26–27.

21 B. Johnson, "25 Ideas for a Changing World," *BusinessWeek*, August 26, 2002, 70–72.

22 J. Useem, "From Heroes to Goats and Back Again: How Corporate Leaders Lost Our Trust," *Fortune*, November 18, 2002, 40–48.

23 A. Borrus, "Executive Pay: Labor Strikes Back," *BusinessWeek*, May 26, 2003, 46.

24 J. Cummings, J. Schlesinger, and M. Schoeder, "Bush Crackdown on Business Fraud Is Sure Signal that New Era Is Here," *Wall Street Journal*, July 10, 2002, 1–5.

25 P. Bamberger and M. Biron, "Group Norms and Excessive Absenteeism: The Role of Peer Referent Others," *Organizational Behavior and Human Decision Processes* 103 (2007): 179–196.

26 D. Barboza and K. Bradsher," Foxconn Factory in China Is Closed after Worker Riot," *New York Times*, September 23, 2012, http://www.nytimes.com/2012/09/25/technology/foxconn-plant-in-china-closed-after-worker-riot.html.

27 P. Mozur and T. Orlink, "Hon Hai Riot Undermines Squeeze on Chinese Manufacturers," *Wall Street Journal*, September 24, 2012, http://online.wsj.com/news/articles/SB1000087 23963904440833045780161631694 34552.

28 P. Mozur, "New Labor Attitudes Fed into China Riot," *The Wall Street Journal Online*, September 26, 2012, http://online.wsj.com/article/SB10000872396390444454920457802 0342979518814.html.

29 E. Fauchart and E. von Hipple, "Norms-Based Intellectual Property Systems: The Case of French Chefs," *Organization Science* 19 (2008): 187–201.

30 E. C. Dierdorff and J. K. Ellington, "It's the Nature of the Work: Examining Behavior-Based Sources of Work–Family Conflict," *Journal of Applied Psychology* 93 (2008): 883–892.

31 S. J. Lambert, "When Flexibility Hurts," *New York Times*, September 19, 2012, http://www.nytimes.com/2012/09/20/opinion/low-paid-women-want-predictable-hours-and-steady-pay.html.

32 J. H. Wayne, W. J. Casper, R. A. Mathews, and T. D. Allen, "Family Supportive Perceptions and Organizational Commitment: The Mediating Role of Work-Family Conflict and Enrichment and Partner Attitudes," *Journal of Applied Psychology* 98 (2013): 606–622.

33 D. Nissenbaum, "Grand Jury Probes Firm that Cleared Snowden," *Wall Street Journal*, August 3, 2013, http://online.wsj.com/news/articles/SB1000142412788732399700457864263 900358822.

34 D. Barrett, "Snowden Says Obama's Failed Promises Motivated Leaks," *Wall Street Journal*, June 17, 2013, http://blogs.wsj.com/washwire/2013/06/17/snowden-says-obamas-failed-promises-motivated-leaks/.

35 M. J. Gelfand, L. H. Nishi, and J. L. Raver, "On the Nature and Importance of Cultural Tightness-Looseness," *Journal of Applied Psychology* 91 (2008): 1225–1244.

36 C. Shannon and W. Weaver, *The Mathematical Theory of Communication* (Urbana: University of Illinois Press, 1948), 17.

37 H. Mintzberg, *The Nature of Managerial Work* (New York: Harper & Row, 1973), 22.

38 J. P. Kotter, "Combating Complacency," *BusinessWeek*, September 15, 2008, 54–55.

39 L. Landro, "The Talking Cure for Health Care," *The Wall Street Journal Online*, April 8, 2013, http://online.wsj.com/news/articles/SB10001424127887323362880457834622396 0774296.

40 R. C. Varchaver, "The Perils of Email," *Fortune*, February 17, 2003, 96–102.

41 C. Gasparino, "How a String of E-Mail Came to Haunt CSFB, Star Banker," *Wall Street Journal*, February 28, 2003, 1–6.

42 A. Pentland, "The Power of Nonverbal Communication," *Wall Street Journal*, October 20, 2008, C1.

43 C. M. Solomon, "Communicating in a Global Environment," *Workforce*, November 1999, 50–55.

44 K. W. Rockmann and G. B. Northcraft, "To Be or Not to Be Trusted: The Influence of Media Richness on Defection and Deception," *Organizational Behavior and Human Decision Processes* 107 (2008): 106–122.

45 P. Wilson, "White House Acknowledges Iraq Uranium Claim Wrong," *USA Today*, July 8, 2003, 1.

46 R. Charan, "What DuPont Did Right," *BusinessWeek*, January 19, 2009, 36–37.

47 M. Conlin, "CEO Coaches," *BusinessWeek*, November 11, 2002, 98–104.

48 J. W. Smither, "Can Working with an Executive Coach Improve Multisource Feedback Ratings over Time? A Quasi-Experimental Field Study," *Personnel Psychology* 56 (2003): 23–44.

49 J. Van Maanen and E. H. Schein, "Toward a Theory of Organizational Socialization," in B. Staw and L. L. Cummings, eds., *Research in Organizational Behavior* (Greenwich, CT: JAI Press, 1979), 209–264.

50 D. Brady and J. McGregor, "What Works in Women's Networks," *BusinessWeek*, June 18, 2007, 58–60.

51 J. Y. Fan and J. P. Wanous, "Organizational and Cultural Entry: A New Type of Orientation Program for Multiple Boundary Crossings," *Journal of Applied Psychology* 93 (2008): 1390–1400.

52 A. L. Kristof-Brown, "Perceived Applicant Fit: Distinguishing between Recruiters' Perceptions of Person–Job and Person–Organization Fit," *Personnel Psychology* 53 (2000): 643–671.

53 C. E. Lance, R. J. Vandenberg, and R. M. Self, "Latent Growth Models of Individual Change: The Case of Newcomer Adjustment," *Organizational Behavior and Human Decision Processes* 83 (2000): 107–140.

54 T. N. Bauer, T. Bodner, B. Erdogan, D. M. Truxillo, and J. S. Tucker, "Newcomer Adjustment during Organizational Socialization: A Meta-Analytic Review of Antecedents, Outcomes, and Consequences," *Journal of Applied Psychology* 92 (2007): 707–721.

55 C. Ostroff and S. W. J. Kozlowski, "Organizational Socialization as a Learning Process: The Role of Information Acquisition," *Personnel Psychology* 45 (1992): 849–874.

56 D. M. Sluss and B. S. Thompson, "Socializing the Newcomer: The Mediating Role of Leader-Member Exchange," *Organizational Behavior and Human Decision Processes*, 125 (2012): 114–125.

57 D. M. Cable, F. Gino, and B. R. Staats, "Breaking Them In or Eliciting Their Best? Reframing Socialization around Newcomers' Authentic Self-Expression," *Administrative Science Quarterly* 58 (2013): 1–36.

58 H. Molesky, "Defeat and Its Consequences," *Wall Street Journal*, January 12, 2005, B1–B2.

59 S. Romero, "Training Legionnaires to Fight (and Eat Rodents)," *New York Times*, December 1, 2008, A1.

60 B. E. Ashforth and A. M. Saks, "Socialization Tactics: Longitudinal Effects on Newcomer Adjustment," *Academy of Management Journal* 39 (1996): 149–178.

61 C. R. Wanberg and J. D. Kammeyer-Mueller, "Predictors and Outcomes of Proactivity in the Socialization Process," *Journal of Applied Psychology* 85 (2000): 373–385.

62 E. W. Morrison, "Newcomers' Relationships: The Role of Social Network Ties during Socialization," *Academy of Management Journal* 45 (2002): 1149–1160.

63 H. J. Klein and N. A. Weaver, "The Effectiveness of an Organizational-Level Orientation Program in the Socialization of New Hires," *Personnel Psychology* 53 (2000): 47–66.

64 T. Kalwarski, "Extravagant Executive Pay Shows No Signs of Moderation," *BusinessWeek*, September 1, 2008.

65 B. Casselman, "Male Nurses Make More Money," *Wall Street Journal*, February 25, 2013, http://blogs.wsj.com/economics/2013/02/25/male-nurses-make-more-money/.

66 M. J. Gelfand, "Culture and Egocentric Perceptions of Fairness in Conflict and Negotiation," *Journal of Applied Psychology* 87 (2002): 833–845.

67 J. Marquez, "Shareholders Set to Increase Their Attack on Executive Pay," *Workforce Management*, March 3, 2008, 6.

68 J. B. Wade, C. A. O'Reilly, and T. G. Pollock, "Overpaid CEOs and Underpaid Managers: Fairness and Executive Compensation," *Organization Science* 17 (2006): 527–544.

69 S. Berfield, "Mad as Hell on Main Street," *BusinessWeek*, October 6, 2008, 26–28.

70 R. E. Silverman, "Psst . . . This Is What Your Co-Worker Is Being Paid," *Wall Street Journal*, January 29, 2013, http://online.wsj.com/news/articles/SB100014241278873236449045 78272034121941000.

71 M. A. Korsgaard, S. E. Brodt, and E. M. Whitener, "Trust in the Face of Conflict: The Role of Managerial Trustworthy Behavior and Organizational Context," *Journal of Applied Psychology* 87 (2002): 312–319.

72 J. Brockner, A. Y. Fishman, J. Reb, B. Goldman, S. Spiegel, and C. Garden, "Procedural Fairness, Outcome Favorability, and Judgments of an Authority's Responsibility," *Journal of Applied Psychology* 92 (2007): 1657–1671.

73 C. O. Trevor and A. J. Nyberg, "Keeping Your Headcount When All about You Are Losing Theirs: Downsizing, Voluntary Turnover Rates, and the Moderating Role of HR Practices," *Academy of Management Journal* 51 (2008): 259–276.

74 Q. M. Robinson, N. A. Moye, and E. A. Locke, "Identifying a Missing Link between Participation and Satisfaction: The Mediating Role of Procedural Justice Perceptions," *Journal of Applied Psychology* 84 (1999): 585–593.

75 S. J. Wayne, L. M. Shore, W. H. Bommer, and L. E. Tetrick, "The Role of Fair Treatment and Rewards in Perceptions of Organizational Support and Leader–Member Exchange," *Journal of Applied Psychology* 87 (2002): 590–598.

76 B. J. Tepper and E. C. Taylor, "Relationships among Supervisors' and Subordinates' Procedural Justice Perceptions and Organizational Citizenship Behaviors," *Journal of Applied Psychology* 46 (2003): 97–105.

77 J. A. Colquitt, R. A. Noe, and C. L. Jackson, "Justice in Teams: Antecedents and Consequences of Procedural Justice Climate," *Personnel Psychology* 55 (2002): 83–109.

78 M. Ambrose and M. Schminke, "Organization Structure as a Moderator of the Relationship between Procedural Justice, Interactional Justice, Perceived Organizational Support, and Supervisory Trust," *Journal of Applied Psychology* 88 (2003): 295–305.

79 M. C. Kernan and P. J. Hanges, "Survivor Reactions to Reorganization: Antecedents and Consequences of Procedural, Interpersonal, and Informational Justice," *Journal of Applied Psychology* 87 (2002): 916–928.

80 K. K. Spors, "If You Fire People, Don't Be a Jerk about It," *Wall Street Journal*, December 22, 2008, C1.

81 Q. M. Roberson and I. O Williamson, "Trickle Down Perceptions of Supervisor Perceptions of Interactional Justice: A Moderated Mediation Model," *Journal of Applied Psychology* 98 (2013): 678–689.

82 R. C. Mayer and J. H. Davis, "The Effect of the Performance Appraisal System on Trust for Management: A Quasi-Experiment," *Journal of Applied Psychology* 85 (2000): 123–136.

83 S. D. Salamon and S. L. Robinson, "Trust that Binds: The Impact of Collective Felt Trust on Organizational Performance," *Journal of Applied Psychology* 93 (2008): 593–601.

84 K. T. Dirks, "The Effects of Interpersonal Trust on Work Group Performance," *Journal of Applied Psychology* 84 (1999): 445–455.

85 S. E. Naumann and N. Bennett, "A Case for Procedural Justice Climate: Development and Test of a Multilevel Model," *Academy of Management Journal* 43 (2000): 81–89.

86 D. P. Skarlicki, R. Folger, and P. Tesluk, "Personality as a Moderator in the Relationship between Fairness and Retaliation," *Academy of Management Journal* 42 (1999): 100–108.

87 S. Tangirala and R. Ramanujam, "Employee Silence on Critical Work Issues: The Cross Level Effects of Procedural Justice Climate," *Personnel Psychology* 61 (2008): 37–68.

88 J. S. Christian, M. S. Christian, A. S. Garza, and A. P. J. Ellis, "Examining Retaliatory Responses to Justice Violations and Recovery Attempts in Teams," *Journal of Applied Psychology* 97 (2012): 1218–1232.

89 S. Banchero and K. Maher, "Strike Puts Spotlight on Teacher Evaluation and Pay," *Wall Street Journal*, September 10, 2012.

90 S. Berfield, "WalMart Versus WalMart," *Bloomberg Businessweek*, December 17, 2012, 55–60.

91 M. Orey, "Wage Wars," *BusinessWeek*, October 1, 2007, 51–60.

92 S. E. Needleman, "Businesses Say Theft by Their Workers Is Up," *Wall Street Journal*, December 11, 2008, C1.

93 M. L. Ambrose, M. A. Seabright, and M. Schminke, "Sabotage in the Workplace: The Role of Organizational Justice," *Organizational Behavior and Human Performance* 89 (2002): 947–965.

94 M. R. Forehand, "Extending Overjustification: The Effect of Perceived Reward-Giver Intention on Responses to Rewards," *Journal of Applied Psychology* 85 (2000): 919–931.

95 J. Sanborn, "Hard Labor: Inside the Backlash Against Unpaid Internships," *Bloomberg Businessweek*, May 21, 2012, 17.

96 M. S. Breslin, "Retention Strategies Need to Be Reengineered," *Workforce Management*, August, 2013, 10.

97 S. M. Lilienthal, "What Do Departing Workers Really Think of Your Company?" *Workforce*, October 2000, 71–85.

98 L. Young, "Supersizing the 401(k)," *BusinessWeek*, January 12, 2009, 38–40.

99 M. Orey, "The Vanishing Trial," *BusinessWeek*, April 30, 2007, 38–39.

100 M. France, "The Mea Culpa Defense," *BusinessWeek*, August 26, 2002, 76–78.

101 K. T. Dirks, Roy J. Lewickik, and A. Zaheer, "Repairing Relationships within and between Organizations: Building a Conceptual Foundation," *Academy of Management Review* 34 (2009): 68–84.

102 B. Schrotenboer, "For Lance Armstrong, Sorry Seems to Be the Hardest Word," *USA Today*, May 28, 2013, http://www.usatoday.com/story/sports/2013/05/27/for-armstrong-forgiveness-is-not-saying-sorry/2364137/.

Chapter 9

Group Dynamics and Team Effectiveness

Procter & Gamble (P&G) has always been known as an innovative company where the business strategy is based on the idea that consumers will pay a premium price for cutting-edge products. Most P&G brands cost close to 20 percent more than their competitors, and this added revenue helps fuel a research-and-development (R&D) budget that exceeded $2 billion in 2012—*twice* the industry average. Historically, P&G did not just tweak existing products in small ways but invented entirely new product categories such as Crest fluoride toothpaste, Tide laundry detergent, Pampers disposable diapers, Pringles stackable potato chips, and Folger's freeze-dried coffee.

More often than not, these major innovations came about when members of cross-functional research teams leveraged technologies already used in P&G products to come up with entirely new products and product categories. For example, Crest Whitestrips combined bleaching technology based on detergent products, glue technology from the paper business, and film-bonding technology from the food wrap business. The cross-functional research teams employed by P&G worked in a centralized unit that was largely isolated from the day-to-day operational concerns that drove the short-terms interests of the three major divisions of the company (beauty care, household care, and health and well-being).[1]

All that changed, however, when new CEO A. G. Lafley took over the company and decided to decentralize R&D teams, placing them under the separate divisions. The new research teams at P&G tended to be less cross-functional, with team members drawn from within each division. In addition, profit pressures that were present at the division level, but not in place when R&D was a separate unit, demanded a more short-term focus for product development. Rather than major revolutionary breakthroughs, these teams tended to engage in more incremental innovation based on making minor adjustments to existing products. For example, the sleep-aid ZzzQuil was really just the cold remedy NyQuil with two of its three major ingredients removed. As one industry analyst noted, ZzzQuil "is a distraction that won't move the growth needle much at a company as big as P&G."[2]

Worse yet, other innovations such as Tide Pods—perfectly measured packets of detergent—actually reduced revenue by preventing consumers from using too much detergent with every load, a widespread tendency. A separate industry analyst went so far as to claim that this innovation "is killing the laundry detergent category." In general, in the time period between 2003 and 2009, sales from new launches at P&G shrank by 50 percent—a figure that is hardly sustainable given its business strategy. Many consumers, unimpressed by the novelty of the new products, simply switched to cheaper substitutes made by rivals such as Unilever.[3]

P&G's chief technology officer, Bruce Brown, admitted in 2012 that the company's ability to create new blockbusters had "dried up a bit," and in an effort to help generate bolder innovation, he recentralized R&D teams under a new and separate "new business creation and innovation division." These teams were throwbacks to the old cross-functional research teams that had helped to build P&G. They were given a long-term horizon and tasked to come up with more revolutionary ideas for inventing new products rather than tinkering or reformulating existing products.[4]

History will judge whether these changes at P&G can help the company get "back to the future." For our purposes, it illustrates some of the critical issues associated with creating and managing teams. A single person working alone cannot accomplish very much, and the relative success of the human species on this planet is traceable to the ability of people to work together and coordinate their efforts. Contemporary organizations are recognizing the power of work teams and are increasingly structuring themselves around flexible project teams that are temporally bound—individual jobs that exist in isolation on the organization chart—rather than fixed.

Clearly, team building is a very popular trend in contemporary organizations both large and small.[5] However, as team building gains greater favor in organizations (some might call it a fad), managers need to keep in mind that teams are often the solution to one set of problems and the source of a second set of problems. Indeed, many organizations currently list the inability to find people with good teamwork skills as one of their most difficult challenges.[6] Thus, this chapter discusses the management of group and team performance. We begin by examining how groups are formally constituted in organizations and by exploring the processes within groups that give rise to a sense of group identity and purpose. After laying this groundwork, we identify several critical factors that can influence the decision to have individuals work alone or work in groups. Next, we identify the special type of group called a *team*, discussing how to "set the stage" and then "manage the process" so as to derive the benefits of teamwork while avoiding some of the potential pitfalls associated with teams. The ability to understand and execute a role within a team seems to be a skill that has value across many different organizations and career stages.[7] Developing this skill is the goal of this chapter.

Formation and Development of Groups

A *group* is a collection of two or more people who interact with one another in a way such that each person influences, and is influenced by, the others.[8] The members of a group draw important psychological distinctions between themselves and people who are not group members. For example, in our opening story, the cross-functional teams that were built by P&G early in its history identified with the R&D division. However, teams eventually became embedded within the operational divisions and identified with those units instead. Since group membership says a great deal about who the group really is, in many groups, membership is often granted very selectively and, in some cases, the higher the selectivity, the stronger the psychological identification with the group. Generally, group members share ten characteristics:

1.   They define themselves as members.
2.   They are defined by others as members.
3.   They identify with one another.
4.   They engage in frequent interaction.
5.   They participate in a system of interlocking roles.
6.   They share common norms.
7.   They pursue shared, interdependent goals.

8.   They feel that membership in the group is rewarding.
9.   They have a collective perception of unity.
10. They stick together in any confrontation with other groups.[9]

These distinctions provide the group with boundaries and a sense of permanence. They lend it a distinct identity and separate it from other people and other groups.

Teams are a special type of group that, in addition to these properties, also possess some degree of skill differentiation, authority differentiation, and temporal stability.[10] Teams that are high in skill differentiation have members whose unique skill sets make it impossible to substitute one member for another. For example, the players on a professional baseball team typically specialize in one position, and thus arbitrarily moving players into different positions would dramatically alter the team's ability to compete. Authority differentiation means that some members of the group have more power than others in terms of decision making. When a team is high in authority differentiation, one formal leader may make all the decisions, whereas in a team that is low in authority differentiation, each member has one vote when it comes to making a decision. Finally, high temporal stability means that the team has a long past and is expected to have a long future, whereas a team short in temporal stability only plans on being together for a very limited period of time. Groups that are low on all three of these characteristics are more loosely coupled relative to teams. These three differences between teams and groups make a big difference when it comes to determining effectiveness.

Some tasks are so large, require so many different skills, and may last for such a long time period or get repeated so often that no single individual or loosely structured group can accomplish the task. Complex surgical procedures, for example, require at least a surgeon, an anesthesiologist, and a surgical nurse. In this instance, it makes no sense to question whether these three individuals could perform more operations working alone versus working together. The skill set required of each person is so complex that no person could perform an operation by himself or herself.

Team-based structures offer two primary advantages over traditional hierarchical structures. First, they enable organizations to bring products to market faster than would be possible in systems in which experts work sequentially—for instance, designers handing over drawings to engineers, who then hand over specifications to manufacturers, who then deliver a product to marketers. If the designers envision a project that will be too difficult to produce or too challenging to market, this problem is spotted early by teams, when it is easier to rectify. This kind of quick self-correction is most likely to occur when customers are recruited to play a role in the team. For example, Xerox routinely places customers on project development teams, and the unique and important perspective brought by these team members has been directly attributed to many innovations, including the first "two-engine" copier, which allows people to make copies even when one of the machine's engines is down and being serviced. Sales for the new two-engine copiers have been very high and were jump-started by the fact that virtually every customer who worked on the development team eventually bought some of the machines for their own companies.[11]

Second, team-based structures eliminate the need for having multiple levels of middle management, giving workers autonomy over decisions that were previously the province of managers. Autonomy has a powerful, positive effect on workforce motivation, as indicated in Chapter 5, and trimming the number of managers reduces administrative overheads.[12] Indeed, when autonomous team-based structures are combined with the motivational force of employee ownership, firms can gain a great deal of competitive advantage over their traditionally structured rivals. For example, W. L. Gore, maker of Gore-Tex waterproof fabric, has no fixed hierarchy, no fixed job titles, and no formal job descriptions. Instead, this employee-owned company is organized around flexible teams that move from project to project depending on the swings in demand for various products. This flexibility means the firm can produce more fabric than its competitors with fewer people, and the saved labor costs are then reinvested in the company, increasing its value for the employee owners.[13]

A group is effective when it satisfies three important criteria:

1. *Production output.* The product of the group's work must meet or exceed standards of quantity and quality defined by the organization. *Group productivity* is a measure of this product, and the speed with which fast-forming groups can accomplish their objectives is ever more critical.[14]
2. *Member satisfaction.* Membership in the group must provide people with short-term satisfaction and facilitate their long-term growth and development. If it does not, members will leave and the group will cease to exist. Furthermore, because how people feel about the group tends to be contagious, dissatisfaction with the group can spread quickly if it is not managed appropriately.[15]
3. *Capacity for continued cooperation and adaptation.* The interpersonal processes that the group uses to complete a task should maintain or enhance members' capacity to work together and adapt over time. Groups that are not able to learn from their experiences and adapt and cooperate flexibly over time cannot remain viable.[16]

Thus, an effective group is able to satisfy immediate demands for performance and member satisfaction, while making provisions for long-term survival, learning, and adaptation. These three criteria are all slightly different from each other, and in some cases a manager needs to be careful not to promote one goal in the short term (productivity) and unwittingly harm another one in the long term (long-term continuity). Over the long term, the three tend to come together, however, and teams develop a form of "implicit coordination" in which a high level of collaboration effectiveness can be achieved with a minimum amount of communication, misunderstanding, and conflict.[17] For example, a recent study of basketball teams in the National Basketball Association (NBA) showed that the longer a group stayed together, the better they performed because team members were better able to learn and exploit subtle differences in each player's strengths and weaknesses. This kind of "tacit knowledge" did not develop in teams that were constantly changing their rosters, and this put them at a severe competitive disadvantage.[18]

Group Formation

In most organizations, groups are formed based on similarities either in what people do or in what they make.[19] To illustrate these two contrasting approaches to **group formation**, imagine a company that makes wooden desks, bookshelves, and chairs. To produce each product, four basic activities are required:

1. A receiver must unpack and stock the raw materials required for the product.
2. A fabricator must shape and assemble the raw materials into a partially completed product.
3. A finisher must complete the assembly operation by painting and packaging the product.
4. A shipper must dispatch the finished products to the organization's customers.

Also imagine that the company's manufacturing workforce consists of twelve employees, who are organized into three assembly lines consisting of four employees each. One employee on each line performs each of the four basic work activities. The company must decide whether to group the twelve employees by the tasks they perform, called **functional grouping**, or by the flow of work from initiation to completion, called **work flow grouping**. In the story that opened this chapter, when P&G placed all its research personnel into one specialized R&D unit, this set up the creation of functional groups. In contrast, when research personnel at P&G were distributed to the three operational divisions, this set up the creation of groups based on workflow.

Each alternative structure offers significant advantages and disadvantages. Consider first what functional grouping, or grouping by the means of production, can offer the firm. Figure 9.1 shows how the four tasks from each assembly line can be grouped together so that the four resulting work groups consist of people with the same sets of abilities, knowledge, and skills.

Functional work groups help integrate and coordinate employees who perform similar tasks. Employees in such groups can exchange information about task procedures, sharpening their knowledge and skills. They can also help one another out when necessary. This sort of cooperation can greatly enhance productivity. In addition, functional grouping can allow the organization to take advantage of other cost savings. Suppose that the receivers for all three assembly lines in Figure 9.1 need only five hours per day to complete their work; they remain idle for the remaining three hours. If receiving is handled in a single work group, the firm can economize by employing two receivers instead of three. The third receiver can be moved elsewhere in the company to perform a more productive job, and the company can derive substantial benefit from improved efficiency in the use of human resources.

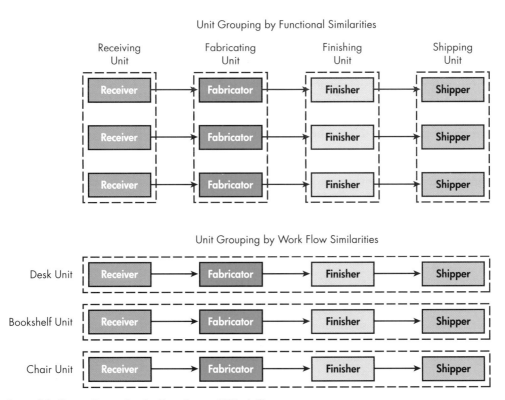

Figure 9.1 Group Formation by Function and Work Flow

On the negative side, functional grouping separates people performing different tasks along the same flow of work. This differentiation can encourage slowdowns that block the flow, thereby reducing productivity. For instance, suppose the finisher on the desk assembly line has nothing to do and wants the desk fabricator to speed up so as to provide more work. Because of functional grouping, the two people are members of different groups, and no simple way exists for them to communicate with each other directly. Instead, the desk finisher must rely on hierarchical communication linkages between the fabricating and finishing groups. The finisher must tell the supervisor of the finishing group about the problem. The finishing supervisor must notify the superintendent overseeing all manufacturing operations. The manufacturing superintendent must talk with the supervisor of the fabricating group. Finally, the fabricating supervisor must tell the desk fabricator to work more quickly. Meanwhile, productivity suffers because of the absence of direct communication along the flow of work created by these "functional silos."

Now consider what happens if work groups are created on the basis of work flow. In the furniture company example, a different flow of work is associated with each of its three product lines (desks, bookshelves, and chairs). The lower panel of Figure 9.1 illustrates the results of choosing this approach. The primary strengths of work flow grouping relate to the fact that this approach integrates all activities required to manufacture a product or provide a service. Each separate work flow is completely enclosed within a single group. If employees who fill different functions along the assembly line need to coordinate with each other to maintain the flow of work, they can do so without difficulty.

Owing to its encouragement of integration, work flow grouping also enhances organizational adaptability. Operations on any of the furniture company's three assembly lines can be halted or stopped without affecting the rest of the company. Suppose, for example, that the desk assembly line in the company is shut down because of poor sales. To simulate this situation, cover the upper assembly line in the bottom panel of Figure 9.1 with a piece of paper. You can see that neither of the remaining two groups will be affected in any major way. Under functional grouping, however, the firm would not enjoy the same degree of flexibility. If you cover the upper assembly line in the top panel of Figure 9.1, you will note that all four of the groups created by functional grouping would be affected by the interruption in desk production.

A recent example of this can be seen when Vikram Pandit took over as the new CEO at Citigroup. In order to speed up decision making and flexibility, Pandit broke down functional silos at Citigroup and created semiautonomous teams for different regions of the country. His regional managers became "mini-CEOs" who did not have to get all their ideas for new products or personnel practices approved by central headquarters. As Pandit noted, "taking this approach makes sense because change is occurring so rapidly in today's world that the old command-and-control mentality doesn't work."[20] Teams structured in this way tend to learn and innovate more about customers and products, whereas teams structured along functional lines tend to learn more and innovate around technology and work processes.[21]

Despite its strengths, however, work flow grouping does not permit the scale economies associated with functional grouping. In work flow grouping, people who perform the same function cannot help or substitute for one another. In addition, they will inevitably duplicate one another's work, adding to the firm's overall costs. For example, at Citigroup, two different autonomous managers could both conduct a salary survey separately, when for efficiency reasons one survey might have met the needs of both. Moreover, it becomes very difficult for people who perform the same task to trade information about issues such as more efficient work procedures and ways to improve task skills.

Just as functional grouping does not allow the adaptability of work flow grouping, work flow grouping does not produce the economic efficiency of functional grouping. The alternative structures also place different demands on managers, in the sense that managing a unit grouped around work flow is often a more complex job where the manager has a high degree of autonomy; whereas the manager of a unit grouped around functional similarity has a simpler task but one where the manager is more interdependent on other managers. For this reason, managers of groups organized around work flow often need to be higher in cognitive ability than managers of groups organized around functional similarities.[22] Thus, although many different types of groups are possible, each type inevitably has its own set of strengths and weaknesses.

Group Development

In most organizations, choices between functional and work flow grouping are made by managers who must decide whether efficiency or adaptability should be given a higher priority. Group formation is, therefore, a process of determining the formal, established characteristics of groups. A second process, *group development*, allows informal aspects of groups to emerge. As groups develop, members modify formally prescribed group tasks, clarify personal roles, and negotiate group norms. Research indicates that these developmental processes tend to advance through the four stages shown in Figure 9.2: initiation, differentiation, integration, and maturity.[23]

The first stage of group development, **initiation**, is characterized by uncertainty and anxiety. Potential members focus on getting to know each other's personal views and abilities. In the beginning, they often discuss neutral topics that have little bearing on the group's purpose, such as the weather and local news. As they gain familiarity with one another and begin to feel more comfortable, members begin discussing general work issues and each person's likely relationship to the formally prescribed task of the group. Attention now concentrates on determining which behaviors should be considered appropriate and what sorts of contributions people should be expected to make to the group. As ideas are exchanged and discussed, people who have the option might decide whether to join or leave the group.

When a group enters the second stage of development, **differentiation**, conflicts can erupt as members try to reach agreement on the purpose, goals, and objectives of the group. Strong

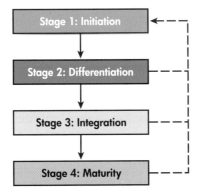

Figure 9.2 Stages in Group Development

Source: Adapted from B. W. Tuckman, "Developmental Sequence in Small Groups," *Psychological Bulletin* 63 (1965): 384–399.

differences of opinion might emerge as members try to achieve consensus on exactly how they will accomplish the group's formally prescribed task. Sorting out who will do what when, where, why, and how and what reward members will receive for their performance often proves to be extremely difficult. Sometimes disagreements about members' roles in the group become violent enough to threaten the group's very existence. If successful, however, differentiation creates a structure of roles and norms that allows the group to accomplish missions that its members could not accomplish by working alone.

Having weathered the differentiation stage, group members must resolve conflicts over other crucial issues in the third stage of group development, **integration**. Integration focuses on reestablishing the central purpose of the group in light of the structure of roles developed during differentiation. Members might define the task of the group in informal terms that modify the group's formal purpose and reflect their own experiences and opinions. Reaching a consensus about the group's purpose helps develop a sense of group identity among members and promotes cohesiveness within the group. It also provides the foundation for the development of additional rules, norms, and procedures to help coordinate interactions among members and facilitate the pursuit of group goals. Many groups tend to hit this stage near the halfway point of a project, and this has been referred to as a point of **punctuated equilibrium**. The halfway point is significant because it is easy for the group members to estimate their final progress by simply multiplying what they have accomplished at the point by two. In most cases, this projection creates anxiety, causes an abrupt change in the group's motivation and willingness to compromise with others, and thus helps accelerate the group's move to stage four.[24]

In the final stage of group development, **maturity**, members fulfill their roles and work toward attaining group goals. Many of the agreements reached about goals, roles, and norms may take on formal significance, being adopted by management and documented in writing. Formalizing these agreements helps to ensure that people joining the group at this stage will understand the group's purpose and way of functioning. Even at this late stage, a group might be confronted with new tasks or new requirements for performance. Changes in the group's environment or in its members could make it necessary to return to an earlier stage and reenter the development process. For example, a new member might challenge the past norms and try to change them in a manner that may help the group adapt to new developments in the task environment. Being open to this kind of "minority influence" is important for maintaining a group's long-term viability over time. Without this kind of influence, the group may grow stale and gradually lose its effectiveness and ability to innovate.[25] Thus group development is a dynamic, continuous process in which informal understandings support or sometimes displace the formal characteristics of the group and its task.

Not every group passes through all four stages of development in a predictable, stepwise manner, and there is a great deal of variability in how fast this process proceeds for different groups, which of course has implications for competitive advantage. For example, to speed up this process, IBM created an "innovation portal," which was essentially a glorified chat room, where any employee with a new idea could recruit new team members and line up other resources for launching some new product. Armed with this technology, an IBM project leader can build a global team in less than an hour and develop a prototype in thirty days, which compares to an average of six months prior to the introduction of the portal. After just one year in operation, the portal had attracted contributions from over 90,000 would-be innovators and was attributed to helping to develop ten new products, all of which eventually turned a profit.[26]

In addition to the provision of technology, several other steps can be taken to help speed the developmental process of teams so that they reach the maturity stage as fast as possible.

First, most teams go through discernible cycles or performance episodes that are marked by goal-setting, planning, task execution, and feedback/reflection cycles. In many cases, there are time-cycle trade-offs such that the more cycles a group goes through the faster it develops. Thus a group that does four small projects over the course of a year develops faster than a group that does one twelve-month project.[27]

Second, distributing power equally in the group so that one person does not dominate decision making also seems to speed development. Having to reach a consensus or win a group vote creates a context conducive to information sharing and debate that can be stifled by autocratic leadership.[28] For this and other reasons, organizations that rely heavily on teams tend to perform better when they use peer evaluations as a major part of the performance appraisal process.[29] Some firms even go beyond the workgroup itself and solicit input via crowdsourcing methods where everyone who might have encountered an employee can weigh in on their performance. In companies that rely on this method, as many as twenty to twenty-five peers might weigh in on someone's performance. This is especially helpful where people work on many different project teams and hence no one person or team really gets to see exactly in how many ways an employee might be contributing across the organization.[30]

Third, group-based rewards where everyone receives the same bonus for successful group accomplishment also seem to engage people more actively in teamwork, giving everyone an equal stake in the team's outcome.[31] In teams where some individuals in the group receive more rewards than others, this can promote dysfunctional competition within the group and harm cooperation and helping behavior.[32] Finally, stress seems to trigger individualistic orientations and decision making and, to the extent that new teams can be shielded from a great deal of stress, this can also help promote faster development to maturity.[33]

Group versus Individual Productivity

Are people necessarily more productive when they work in groups than when they work alone? Based on the growing prevalence of groups and teams in organizations, it appears that many people believe the answer to this question is "yes." However, a large body of research indicates that groups of individuals working together are sometimes less productive than the same number of people working alone.[34] First, although teams often bring more information to bear on problem solving, much of this knowledge often fails to manifest itself in the team's deliberations.[35] Second, although groups are often able to come up with more creative ideas relative to individuals, this is usually only the case when the members have worked together for an extended time period. Groups of strangers rarely produce creative or innovative ideas.[36] Instead, it seems that, although there are some trade-offs, members of groups need to have a great deal of familiarity both with the task and with the team to achieve high levels of success.[37]

Finally, it often takes longer to make decisions in a group—especially if one must arrive at consensus. For example, many have blamed Sony's inability to match Apple in terms of speed of introducing new products with Sony's culture and the stress they place on developing consensus at all levels prior to the introduction of a new product or process. In fact, when Ty Roberts was recruited away from Apple to Sony, he struggled to introduce change even though that was what he was explicitly recruited to do. He noted that "Sony is not like Apple. You can't just tell people to do something. It's all about building consensus here, and is often a slow and difficult process where one person or department can bring decision-making to a halt."[38]

Process Loss

Adding more people to a group increases the human resources that the group can put to productive use. Thus, as depicted in Figure 9.3, the *theoretical* productivity of a group should rise in direct proportion to the size of the group. In reality, after an initial rise, a group's *actual productivity* falls as its size continues to increase. The difference between what a group actually produces and what it might theoretically produce constitutes **process loss**.[39] Process loss results from the existence of obstacles to group productivity, the most influential of which are production blocking, group-maintenance activities, and social loafing.

Production blocking occurs when people get in each other's way as they try to perform a group task—for example, when one member of a moving van crew carries a chair through a doorway and another member waits to carry a box of clothing through the same doorway. A recent instance of this can be seen in the case of the *M.S. Costa Concordia*, a large cruise ship that struck a rock formation off the coast of Italy. Even though the ship sank very slowly and only 150 yards from shore, thirty-two lives were lost due to the lack of coordination among crew members.[40] The *Costa Concordia* was carrying over 3,000 passengers and had the largest crew in the industry. However, for most of this misadventure, the crew simply got in the way of each other and of panicking passengers who struggled just to get through doorways, let alone to man lifeboats in an orderly fashion.[41]

There are many sources of process loss, and all of these get worse as group size increases. For example, although it might seem minor, if the group fails to start a meeting until all members show up, then the member who arrives last and late has essentially blocked everyone else at the meeting from using that time productively.

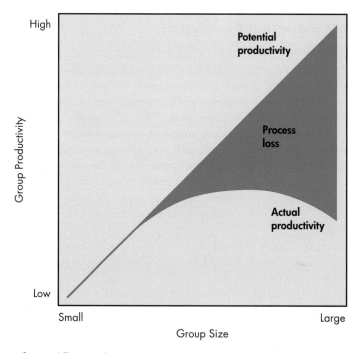

Figure 9.3 **Group Size and Process Loss**
Source: Adapted from I. D. Steiner, *Group Processes and Productivity* (New York: Academic Press, 1972).

Once the group is finally assembled, another form of production blocking is caused by the fact that only one person can effectively talk at once. In this context, it might be difficult for some members to get their ideas discussed. This is especially a problem if some members of the group like to talk a great deal and wind up stealing time from everyone else in the group that has to listen. Some companies use "stand up meetings" where no one is allowed to sit down as a means of keeping meetings moving. Stand up meetings tend to be 33 percent shorter than sit-down meetings and no less productive. The company Hashrocket, a software development firm located in Jacksonville, Florida, takes this idea one step forward and makes anyone who wants to talk at the meeting hold a ten-pound medicine ball while they speak—a sure way to prevent long-winded oration.[42]

Of course, with modern technology, one does not have to be in the same room to waste another person's time and pointless e-mail exchanges can also block production. One insidious form of production blocking that occurs with e-mail is the "Reply All" option, where one person can send a message to dozens or even hundreds of people who could not care less, but nevertheless have to spend time reading and deleting the message. In some cases, carelessly clicking "Reply All," instead of selecting "Reply," can wind up splattering private or proprietary information across the Internet. Some firms have gone so far as to technologically eliminate the "Reply All" option on their e-mail interfaces to prevent this kind of production blocking.[43]

In addition, for a group to function effectively over time, its members must fulfill the requirements of several **group-maintenance roles**. Each of these roles helps to ensure the group's continued existence by building and preserving strong interpersonal relations among its members. These roles include the following:

- *encouragers*, who enhance feelings of warmth and solidarity within the group by praising, agreeing with, and accepting the ideas of others
- *harmonizers*, who attempt to minimize the negative effects of conflicts among the group's members by resolving disagreements fairly, quickly, and openly and by relieving interpersonal tension
- *standard setters*, who raise questions about group goals and goal attainment and set achievement standards against which group members can evaluate their performance.[44]

Group-maintenance activities support and facilitate a group's continued functioning, but they can also interfere with productive activity. For instance, members of a management team who disagree about a proposal must spend time not only on improving the proposal but also on harmonizing among themselves, diverting valuable time and effort and reducing the group's productivity. Like production blocking problems, group-maintenance problems become worse as group size increases. Members of large groups tend to perceive much less social support in the group relative to members of small teams.[45] In addition, large team size also results in a greater difficulty to establish trust among members because of the inability to monitor and enforce norms.[46]

Process loss can also result from **social loafing**, the choice by some members of a group to take advantage of others by doing less work, working slower, or in other ways decreasing their own contributions to group productivity.[47] According to economists, social loafing—also called *free riding*—makes sense from a loafer's perspective if the rewards that his or her group receives for productivity are shared more or less equally among all group members. A loafer can gain the same rewards bestowed on everyone else without having to expend personal effort. Unless someone else in the group takes up the slack, even one person's loafing can lower the entire group's productivity. In the worst-case scenario, the other team members who witness the social loafer might feel that they are being taken advantage of, and then begin to reduce their level of effort as well. If this happens, the group as a whole begins to look more and more like its worst member, and unless this is managed it creates a huge amount of process loss.[48] Social loafing can be prevented in a number of different ways, but two central practices are to make sure that each person's contribution to the group is both identifiable (so they feel accountable) and unique (so they feel indispensable).[49]

As with the other forms of process loss we have seen, social loafing becomes more pronounced in larger groups where one sees diffusion of responsibility, wherein everyone expects someone else to take the initiative for doing something that no one winds up doing. Thus, it is fair to conclude that, on average, people working in smaller groups are more productive than people in larger groups.[50] As suggested by Figure 9.4, this relationship can be traced to several factors. First, small groups simply have fewer members who might get in each other's way. Clearly, production blocking caused by *physical constraints* is less likely to occur in small groups than in large ones. Second, group size influences productivity by affecting the amount of *social distraction* that people experience when they work in a group. The smaller the group, the less likely that group members will distract one another and interrupt behavioral sequences that are important to the task. Third, smaller groups have lower *coordination requirements* because the fewer members a group has, the fewer the inter-dependencies that must be formed and maintained. Fourth, group size is related to the incidence of *behavioral masking*. The behaviors of a group member can be masked or hidden by the simple presence of other members. The smaller the group, the easier it is to observe each member's behavior, and this visibility in turn affects the frequency of social loafing, a problem discussed earlier. Finally, group size influences the *diffusion of responsibility*—the sense that

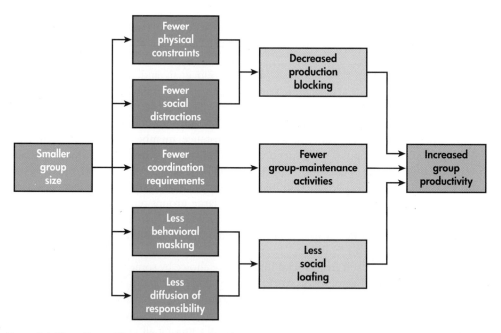

Figure 9.4 How Group Size Affects Group Productivity

Source: Adapted from R. Z. Gooding and J. A. Wagner III, "A Meta-Analytic Review of the Relationship between Size and Performance: The Productivity and Efficiency of Organizations and their Subunits," *Administrative Science Quarterly* 30 (1985): 462–481.

responsibility is shared broadly rather than shouldered personally. In a small group, each person is more apt to feel personally responsible for group performance and effectiveness.[51]

Given the widespread and pervasive negative effects of large team size, one would think that managers would try to avoid creating large groups, but research suggests just the opposite. Managers systematically tend to overvalue the practice of adding members to teams and underestimate the problems caused by increased group size—a concept so common that it has been given its own label—the *team-scaling fallacy*.[52] Rather than building ever larger teams, a better response is to create a "multiteam system," where instead of creating one large twenty-person team, a manager might, instead, create four five-person teams where there is functional specialization between teams. This achieves many of the advantages a manager might seek to gain from trying to increase group size (better representation or ability to handle large problems) but avoids many of the liabilities associated with large teams. Multiteam systems represent a "team-of-teams" approach where there is interdependence between teams, but this is enacted through a small set of boundary spanners rather than having each and every member trying to coordinate with each and every other member.[53]

The rules that apply to teams within multiteam systems often differ from prescriptions that would be made for traditional stand-alone autonomous teams. For example, autonomous teams should be empowered to make their own decisions and, for that reason, tend to benefit from decentralized control.[54] Because of the interdependence between teams that work as part of multiteam systems, they tend to demand slightly more centralized control relative to smaller stand-alone self-managing autonomous teams.[55] On the other hand, they tend to be less centralized relative to traditional subunits within a tight, formal bureaucratic structure. Thus, multiteam systems create the potential to gain many of the benefits associated with small team size and, at the same time, allow organizations to tackle large-scope problems.[56]

Group Synergy

Whereas process loss focuses on the reduction of productivity attributed to putting people into groups, the concept of **group synergy** deals with the opposite phenomenon—productivity of a group that exceeds expectation based on the potential individual contributions. Figure 9.5 shows the relationship between group productivity and group size under conditions of group synergy.

Although process loss is the more common outcome, group synergy is possible, and much of the remainder of this chapter is devoted to identifying those conditions where synergy happens more frequently. Indeed, for each of the three factors that can cause process loss, a corresponding factor exists that could account for group synergy. For example, whereas in production blocking individuals get in one another's way, **social facilitation** may allow the presence of others to increase an individual's performance.

The mere presence of others can be facilitating for a number of reasons. Perhaps most important, in a group context, one person who is unskilled or inexperienced can model his or her behavior on the behavior of others in the group who are more skilled and experienced. For example, research shows that teams that are composed of new and old members are particularly powerful because of the ability of older members to transfer their knowledge and experience quickly to new members who would otherwise take years to learn many aspects of the work on their own. In return, new members can help their older counterparts with introducing new ideas and technologies to the work.[57] A real-world example of this can be seen at Randstad, a New York-based employment agency that systematically pairs workers in their twenties with workers in their fifties and sixties. These two-member teams work together with their desks facing one another, hence creating a very intense shared experience for each person.[58]

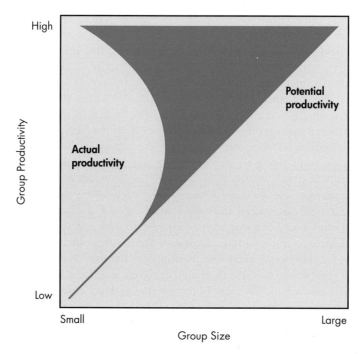

Figure 9.5 Group Size and Synergy
Source: Adapted from I. D. Steiner, *Group Processes and Productivity* (New York: Academic Press, 1972).

Similarly, although it takes time to build and maintain interpersonal relationships in the group, under many conditions the presence of close interpersonal relationships promotes helping behaviors, where one member of the team takes over some of the workload of another member who might be overwhelmed at that moment in time. Although not part of anyone's formal job description, this type of helping behavior is essential when there are unpredictable and uneven workloads.[59] The key, however, is to make sure that the right people are receiving the help they need because sometimes, left on their own, people have a tendency to help those who are most able to help them in return and not those who actually need the most help.[60]

Finally, although some people respond to working in groups by social loafing, the within-group competition aspect of group tasks motivates other people to work harder than they would have if left on their own. Research shows that some amount of within-group competition can increase the speed of individual members, and that this effect is particularly pronounced on the group's worst member (the potential social loafer).[61] Indeed, some tasks might be so boring or monotonous that the only way to inspire workers is by creating a competition out of the situation. Although this type of within-group competition must be monitored so that it does not interfere with larger group goals, the fact that it can work in certain situations shows that forming groups can increase or decrease the efforts of individuals.

Keys to Team Effectiveness: Setting the Stage

As noted earlier, in the initial stage of group formation, a decision must be made with respect to whether the group will employ functional grouping or work flow grouping (reexamine Figure 9.1). This decision is important because it is a primary determinant of how much task interdependence the group experiences. Task interdependence refers to the degree to which team members interact cooperatively and work interactively to complete tasks. The level of task interdependence is related to performance on both cognitive and behavioral tasks as well as commitment to the team.[62]

Task Structure

In addition, task interdependence also has implications for how teams react to losing a member, in the sense that turnover is more disruptive when task interdependence is high.[63] When task interdependence is high, two other aspects of structuring the team can promote coordination and performance. First, structures that rotate members through different roles via cross-training help create shared mental models among team members, which, in turn, promote coordination and mutual support.[64] Indeed, this kind of "within-person" functional diversity (where one person has varied experiences) seems to be even more important than "cross-unit" functional diversity (where different people each bring a unique experience) in terms of promoting effective team performance.[65] Members of cross-functional teams often struggle to communicate effectively due to their different backgrounds.[66] Thus, any form of shared experience can help overcome this problem.[67] Beyond cross-training, in self-managed teams, rotating the leadership position is also instrumental in promoting cooperation and participation among members, because all team members get a "big picture" appreciation of how all the parts sum to the whole.[68]

In addition to directly affecting group performance and commitment to the group, interdependence influences the relationship between member attributes and group performance. For example, a highly useful typology for classifying group tasks breaks them down into additive, disjunctive, and conjunctive tasks.[69] In an **additive task**, each group member contributes to group performance in proportion to his or her ability, so that the sum of the individual team members' abilities equals the team performance. Shoveling snow is an example of an additive task—the amount of snow shoveled by a group of people is the sum of the amounts that each group member could shovel alone. Additive tasks are low in interdependence.

A **disjunctive task** is structured such that one person could perform it effectively alone as long as he or she had the requisite resources (information, cognitive ability, and so on). Solving an algebra problem is an example of a disjunctive task, in the sense that the solution to such a problem depends on the most capable group member—once one person has solved the problem, the team's task is complete (this type of task is sometimes referred to as a "Eureka" task). Disjunctive tasks are moderately high in task interdependence, because the people who do not solve the task are dependent on the one person who can solve the task; the person who solves the task, however, is not really dependent on the others.

In a **conjunctive task**, in contrast, the group's level of performance depends on the resources that the least able group member brings to the task. For example, the speed with which a team of mountain climbers can reach the top of a cliff is a close function of how fast the slowest, weakest member can climb. A common expression in team contexts is that "a chain is only as strong as its weakest link"; this saying indicates how teams are often characterized as performing conjunctive tasks. The unique skills that each person brings to the task and their lack of interchangeability mean that, if one team member fails to perform his or her role, then the entire team will fail because no one else is equipped to carry out those duties.[70]

Communication Structure

Once a decision on task structure is made and roles have been designed, the next question becomes who within the team can talk to whom. This issue deals with **communication**

structure. If the members of a group cannot exchange information about their work, the group cannot function effectively. A viable communication structure is, therefore, crucial to group productivity. For managers, it is important to know about the different kinds of group communication structures and to be able to implement those that encourage the greatest productivity.

In research on group communication and productivity, five structures have received considerable attention: the wheel, Y, chain, circle, and completely connected communication network (Figure 9.6). The first three of these networks are the most centralized, in that a central member can control information flows in the group. In contrast, in the decentralized circle and completely connected networks, all members are equally able to send and receive messages.

The five communication networks differ in several ways:

- the *speed* at which information can be transmitted
- the *accuracy* with which information is transmitted
- the degree of *saturation*, which is high when information is distributed evenly in a group and low when some members have significantly more information than others
- the *satisfaction* of members with communication processes and the group in general.

As shown in Figure 9.6, communication speed and accuracy in a group are affected both by the nature of the group's communication network and by the relative complexity of the

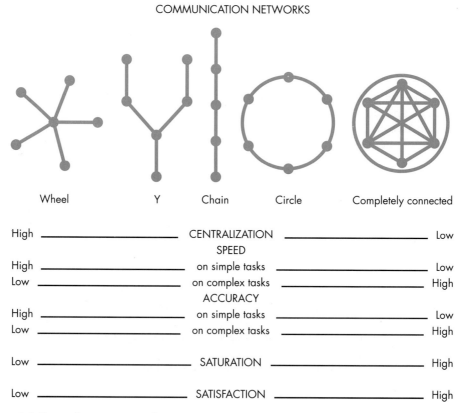

COMMUNICATION NETWORKS

| Wheel | Y | Chain | Circle | Completely connected |

High		CENTRALIZATION		Low
		SPEED		
High		on simple tasks		Low
Low		on complex tasks		High
		ACCURACY		
High		on simple tasks		Low
Low		on complex tasks		High
Low		SATURATION		High
Low		SATISFACTION		High

Figure 9.6 Group Communication Structures and Group Effectiveness

Source: Adapted from information presented in M. E. Shaw, *Group Dynamics: The Psychology of Small Group Behavior* (New York: McGraw-Hill, 1976), 262–314.

group's task. Group tasks can range from *simple* tasks, which involve physical demands but little mental effort or need for communication among co-workers, to *complex* tasks, which require greater mental effort, less physical exertion, and significant communication.[71]

When a task is simple and communication networks are centralized, both speed and accuracy are higher. Centralization facilitates the minimal communication required to succeed at simple tasks. When tasks are simple and communication networks are decentralized, however, speed and accuracy are lower because extra people are involved in communication. In contrast, when tasks are relatively complex, centralized communication networks lower both speed and accuracy because people serving as network hubs succumb to **information overload**. Overload and its effects are less likely to occur in decentralized networks, as more people process information and share responsibilities for communication. Both network saturation and member satisfaction are generally higher in decentralized networks. Everyone is informed and fully involved in the communication process and the task. (The exception to this rule involves centralized networks, where the one person located at the hub of the network is usually very satisfied.)

To summarize, centralization increases the productivity of groups in performing simple tasks that require little or no communication but generally reduces member satisfaction. In contrast, decentralization increases not only the productivity of groups in performing complex tasks that require much communication, but also member satisfaction and perceptions of group potency.[72] The decentralized network, therefore, provides an efficient *and* effective way of organizing communication when the group must tackle complex tasks. Indeed, changes in communication media have allowed organizations to increasingly employ decentralized communication networks where anyone who has access to video-conferencing technology or easily available technology such as Skype can communicate face-to-face.[73] Some companies, such as Accenture, have gone as far as eliminating the company's headquarters so that the company's consultants can spend more time at the client's site.[74] IBM also employs a great deal of virtual work arrangements, but finds that if its team members do not meet face-to-face at least once a week, team performance and satisfaction suffer.[75]

Group Composition

As we noted earlier, it is important to keep teams small in size. Nevertheless, the question of "who is on the team" is just as important as how many. Having the appropriate level of expertise in the right positions ensures that the team can accomplish its tasks and subgoals. Clearly, having individuals with the right skills, abilities, knowledge, or dispositions is critical for all jobs—whether they are part of a team or not—but it is especially critical for teams because of the interdependence that exists among team members. Under such circumstances, the effective execution of one person's role becomes a critical resource needed by others so that they can, in turn, execute their own roles. This consideration is also critical with conjunctive tasks because the team will be only as good as its weakest member.

In addition to considering each team member's standing on critical abilities, traits, and characteristics, in team contexts one must decide whether to construct the team so that the members are diverse (different) or homogeneous (the same) on these characteristics. In discussing issues related to diversity, we focus on four different types of diversity and how they combine to create faultlines or shared mental models.

Functional Diversity

Functional diversity means that each member of the team differs in terms of educational background or area of task expertise. This is the defining characteristic of cross-sectional teams, and a large body of evidence indicates that, on complex tasks, heterogeneity on this characteristic is highly valuable—especially if people with different skills can communicate effectively and manage the debate that is likely to ensue from their different backgrounds and experiences.[76] The group also benefits when team members are aware of the different skills represented by each member, and they respect the training that the others have received.[77] It is important that members have a mindset that accurately captures the need for the unique skills that each member brings to the task and do not assume that their own job is the most important.[78] Finally, strong transformational leadership that focuses cross-functional teams on the larger team goals and can help mediate disagreements between its members is also essential in terms of promoting success and viability.[79]

Personality Diversity

Turning to personality traits, the degree to which one wants people to be diverse or homogeneous on personality characteristics depends upon the nature of the trait. With certain traits, such as conscientiousness, all members should have the same level of this characteristic. If some members rate very high on it, but others rate very low, this discrepancy might create the type of social loafing situation that starts fights and destroys group cohesiveness. Moreover, because they feel as though the other members are taking advantage of them, highly conscientious team members might withhold effort; ultimately, they might be indistinguishable from low-conscientiousness members. Another virtue of highly conscientious team members deals with propensity to seek and offer help or support to other members. People who are high in conscientiousness are often the first to provide assistance to others when it is needed, and they are the least likely to ask for help from others when it is not needed.[80] In addition to conscientiousness, it is also helpful when groups are composed of individuals who tend to be all high in emotional stability because in contexts where members might disagree about means or ends, high levels of emotional stability on the part of all the team members can prevent conflict from spiraling out of control.[81]

With other traits, such as extroversion, it is best to build in heterogeneity. If all members are high on extroversion, a power struggle arises as everyone tries to dominate the group. Alternatively, if everyone in the group is low on this trait, no leadership emerges and the group will flounder. Consequently, heterogeneity is preferred so that the group includes some people who are comfortable leading and others who are comfortable following. Similarly, some degree of variance in agreeableness is also valuable, because one disagreeable member can prevent the team from making decisions too quickly. Indeed, some leaders will assign the role of "devil's advocate" to some team members to simulate the benefits that come about from having at least one person who is disagreeable. Heterogeneity in characteristics such as personality, values, and interests is often referred to as "deep-level psychological diversity" and, although this sometimes creates short-term problems in the group formation differentiation stage, it has generally been found to have long-term value in terms of team viability and performance.[82]

Gender Diversity

Owing to the increased demographic diversity of the labor pool, beyond the effects of functional and personality diversity, one also has to consider diversity in demographic characteristics. Demographic diversity can promote team effectiveness because people from different backgrounds can tap into different social networks to gather information and new ideas.[83] In some cases, just having one single member from a different demographic group within an otherwise homogeneous group can have a substantial impact. For example, research on gender diversity in teams seems to imply that it only takes the introduction of one female member to an all-male group to significantly reduce the level of excessive risk taking in that group.[84] The positive impact of a single person who differs from others in the group is especially likely if that person's unique role is appreciated (and hence they are distinctive), as opposed to when their unique status is not valued (and hence they are just conspicuous).[85] For the most part, however, being a token female member in an all-male group on a task that has been traditionally male dominated is stressful, especially when the group is large.[86]

Cultural Diversity

Given the increased frequency of international joint ventures, it is also important to consider the role of demographic and cultural diversity in groups. Although this kind of diversity has great potential to lead to new ideas and insights, group composition issues can often thwart this potential. In terms of cultural diversity, a more complex pattern emerges relative to what is seen with diversity along functional, personality, or gender lines. To understand how cultural heterogeneity plays out, one needs to recognize that the eventual culture adopted by the team, referred to as a *hybrid culture*, represents a mixture of the cultures brought by individual team members. If all members of the team come from the same culture except one (for example, three American members and one Chinese), the hybrid culture naturally closely resembles the culture most of the members share, and the lone member from a different culture adapts. This type of convergence can lead to high performance. Similarly, when all of the members come from different cultures (for example, one American, one German, one Chinese, and one South African), no culture dominates, and the members must jointly construct a hybrid culture that is unique and idiosyncratic to that team. Although these teams might struggle initially, they eventually arrive at a hybrid culture. Indeed, teams can perform quite well under these conditions.

A problem seems to arise, however, when one subset of group members shares a dominant culture and the others do not share this culture (for example, two Americans, one German, and one South African). In this instance, a struggle ensues, and the team often fails to arrive at a hybrid culture. In teams with this type of "moderate" homogeneity, the dominant group (in this example, the two Americans) is not strong enough to assert the primacy of its particular culture, but still strong enough to resist adopting a new, unique, and idiosyncratic culture. Under these conditions, teams often perform poorly. Research suggests that culture is an all-or-nothing proposition: Highly homogeneous or heterogeneous teams can be effective, but teams with moderate levels of heterogeneity tend to struggle.[87]

Faultlines: Diversity Convergence

The formation of distinct subgroups within the overall team is always a potential threat to viability of any team.[88] The effects of diversity seem to be particularly pronounced when multiple dimensions of diversity converge and create a strong set of subgroups within the larger group that threaten to break apart and go their own way. For example, imagine a four-person group composed of two men and two women, two marketing experts and two engineers, and two people from the United States and two people from France. One way this diversity could configure itself is such that the two males were also both engineers and both from the United States, and the two women were both marketing experts from France. In this configuration, the group has a strong faultline because all three dimensions of diversity converge, and it is easy to predict how this group might break apart into two subgroups. In contrast, the same level of diversity could be configured in a group where one of the men was an engineer, but one of the women was an engineer also. Similarly one of the marketing experts was a man and one was a woman. Finally one of the men was from France and one was from the United States. In this second configuration, there is no strong faultline, and it is harder to see how the group is likely to fall apart.[89]

Strong faultlines have been found to negatively impact group performance and viability.[90] Training group members to value diversity can often offset these negative effects. However, it is still better if one can cross-categorize people and avoid strong faultlines. One way to achieve this is through reward structures that place people who differ on other dimensions into "subteams" that have a common goal and all obtain the same reward for meeting that goal. This type of cooperative goal creates a new dimension of diversity where two people who differ on one dimension (gender) are the same when it comes to rewards.[91]

Shared Mental Models

Regardless of whether the team members differ on skills, traits, or culture, the critical consideration is their ability to arrive at a shared mental model about each other and the task at hand. Teams with shared mental models enjoy a great deal of coordination with a minimum of communication, but sharing mental models yields benefits beyond coordination. First, high levels of mutual understanding create the conditions necessary for learning from experience, in the sense that most people in the team are likely to learn the same lessons from past successes and failures.[92] The mutual understanding that arises via shared mental models also helps the team diagnose problems with a member who, for one reason or another, is not meeting the expectations of the team. This type of mutual understanding among team members provides a system of checks and balances that is especially critical given the interdependence and specialization that characterize teams.[93]

Keys to Team Effectiveness: Managing the Process

Once the group is structured and composed, the next step in promoting group performance is to make sure the group engages in effective group processes. This implies that all members put forth their best effort so that the group can become cohesive over time. It also means that the group develops approaches for managing group conflict, which is often inevitable when people have different opinions or goals.

Motivation in Groups

Member motivation is an important factor that affects group productivity and must be managed to minimize process loss and maximize synergy. A major aspect of motivation in team contexts is getting people to sacrifice their own self-interests for the overall good of the collective. As is true for research on individuals, studies of group performance have substantiated that setting specific, difficult group goals has a strong positive effect on group productivity, especially in contexts where goals are paired with feedback and incentives.[94] Goal accomplishment, in turn, tends to increase the group's collective self-efficacy, which makes it even more resilient to setbacks and able to overcome future challenges.[95]

Even if not tied directly to goals, the nature of rewards that groups receive has a big impact on the nature of the group's dynamics. Two fundamentally different types of group rewards exist: cooperative and competitive. **Cooperative group rewards** are distributed *equally* among the members of a group. That is, the group is rewarded *as a group* for its successful performance, and each member receives exactly the same reward. This compensation technique does not recognize individual differences in effort or performance but, rather, rewards employees' efforts to coordinate their work activities and to share information with one another.[96] As a result, the cooperative reward system ignores the possibility that some members will make greater contributions to group task performance than others. As discussed in Chapter 8, the inequity caused by this type of reward distribution can demotivate group members who are high performers.

Under the **competitive group rewards** system, group members are rewarded for successful performance *as individuals in a group*. They receive *equitable* rewards that vary based on their individual performance. This system, which relies on the idea that high group performance requires all members to perform at their highest capacity, rewards individuals who accomplish more than their peers. It provides a strong incentive to individual effort, thereby enhancing individual productivity. Unfortunately, it can also pit group members against one another in a struggle for greater personal rewards. In such a case, the cooperation and coordination needed to perform group tasks might never develop, and group performance might suffer.

Which of these two approaches is likely to ensure the highest group productivity? The answer depends on the degree of task interdependence. Higher levels of task interdependence require group members to work closely together. For this reason, cooperative rewards, which encourage cooperation and coordination, promote group productivity when paired with high task interdependence.[97] In contrast, lower task interdependence—either complete independence or pooled interdependence—enables the members of a group to work independently. In this case, competitive rewards motivate high personal performance and lead to increased group productivity, as depicted in Figure 9.7.[98]

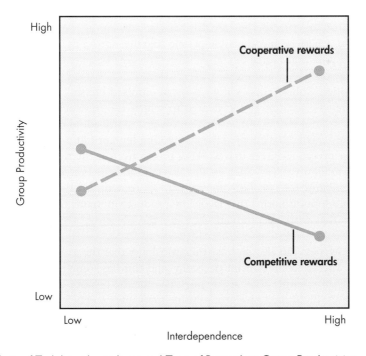

Figure 9.7 Effects of Task Interdependence and Type of Reward on Group Productivity

Source: Adapted from R. Wageman, "Interdependence and Group Effectiveness," *Administrative Science Quarterly* 40 (1995): 145–180.

Group Cohesiveness

A group's **cohesiveness** reflects the degree to which a group sticks together. In a cohesive group, members feel attracted to one another and to the group as a whole. A variety of factors encourage group cohesiveness:

1. *Shared personal attitudes, values, or interests.* People who share the same attitudes, values, or interests are likely to be attracted to one another.
2. *Agreement on group goals.* Shared group goals encourage members to work together. When members participate in determining their purpose and goals, they get to know and influence one another.
3. *Frequency of interaction.* Frequent interaction and the physical closeness afforded by it encourage members to develop the mutual understanding and intimacy that characterize cohesiveness.
4. *Group size.* Smaller groups are more likely to be cohesive than larger groups, because physical proximity makes it easier for their members to interact.
5. *Group rewards.* Cooperative group rewards that encourage interaction can stimulate cohesiveness, especially when members must perform interdependent tasks.
6. *Favorable evaluation.* Recognition given to a group for effective performance can reinforce feelings of pride in group membership and group performance.
7. *External threats.* Threats to a group's well-being that originate from outside the group can strengthen its cohesiveness by providing a common enemy that motivates a unified response. That is, conflict between groups can promote cohesion within groups.
8. *Isolation.* Being cut off from other groups can reinforce members' sense of sharing a common fate, again motivating a unified response.

The last two of these factors, external threats and isolation, can be particularly strong factors that bind otherwise incompatible people together into a tight cohesive unit. Group cohesiveness is a potential source of competitive advantage because cohesive groups need to spend less energy on group-maintenance activities and can, instead, focus all their effort on alternative activities. Cohesiveness is not always an unmixed blessing, however.

First, cohesiveness does affect the degree to which the members of a group *agree* on productivity norms, but it does not ensure that the group will adopt *high* productivity norms. If a highly cohesive group has adopted norms favoring high productivity, its productivity will be high, because everyone agrees that working productively is the right thing to do (see the upper-right cell in Figure 9.8).[99] Such groups also tend to be persistent and are more likely to struggle through barriers to goal accomplishment.[100] In contrast, the productivity of highly cohesive groups adopting norms that favor low productivity tends to be quite low, because everyone agrees that working productively is *not* the objective (see the lower-right cell in Figure 9.8).

Second, cohesiveness can also increase the probability that the group will come to premature consensus when making difficult decisions, and this has sometimes been referred to as *groupthink*.[101] That is, rather than argue and hash out the positive and negative features of various alternatives, highly cohesive groups sometimes agree too quickly on the first idea that is offered up. This is especially the case if the group is isolated from outside sources of influence and the leader is the person who came up with the first idea. Dissenting opinions are either directly squelched or not shared with the team by members who self-censor their own misgivings. This flawed and incomplete process often leads to disastrous outcomes that outsiders, in the light of hindsight bias, severely criticize.

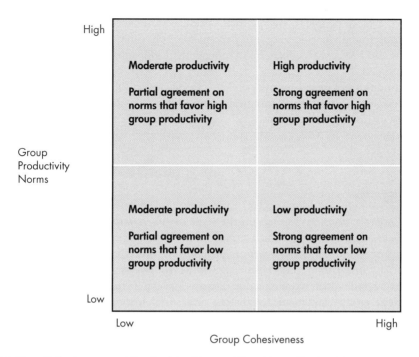

Figure 9.8 How Cohesiveness and Productivity Norms Affect Group Productivity

Source: Adapted from L. Berkowitz, "Group Standards, Cohesiveness, and Productivity," *Human Relations* 7 (1954): 509–519.

Group Conflict

Groups that lack cohesiveness often experience a great deal of within-team conflict. Just as cohesiveness is not always an unmixed blessing when it comes to group performance, so too conflict is not always undesirable. Groups can experience two types of conflict: cognitive and mixed-motive. In **cognitive conflict**, all group members agree on the goals sought, but differ in their views on how those goals can be best met. With this type of conflict, members can still cooperate and do not necessarily compete. This type of conflict focuses on task procedures rather than on the people involved. Cognitive conflict within groups can lead to effective debate, and it often generates well-thought-out, highly effective decisions.[102] As we noted earlier, some groups try to actually create this type of conflict structurally by creating the role of "devil's advocate," that is, a team member whose primary job is to question and critique the team's ideas. Although this kind of "contrived dissent" is better than nothing when it comes to preventing premature consensus, it is not nearly as potent as genuine dissent that comes from team members who truly believe the group is heading down the wrong track.[103] In general, any steps that teams take to make it safer for people to express dissent without fear of being labeled "disloyal" promotes more effective decision-making processes.[104]

Alternatively, groups can experience **mixed-motive conflict**. In these situations, group members might not agree on the goals being sought, and this type of conflict can prove difficult to overcome. Because mixed-motive conflict often hinges on differences in values, and given the centrality of values to people, this kind of conflict can quickly become personal and emotional, and hence needs to be carefully managed.[105] Unlike in cognitive conflict, where the best ideas for approaching the problem might win out in a group discussion, such discussions rarely persuade people to change their values. Left unchecked, this kind of conflict will lead the group to reduce its level of interdependence over time, and in many ways the group breaks apart and reverts to a collection of independent individuals looking out for their own personal interests.[106]

Under conditions of mixed-motive conflict, a formal leader might have to make a unilateral decision or create some type of political compromise or voting procedure to overcome the inability to reach group consensus. We have more to say about this type of conflict and ways to manage it in Chapter 10 (on leadership) and Chapter 11 (power, politics, and conflict).

Summary

Groups in organizations are formed on the basis of *functional grouping*, which favors efficiency, or *work flow grouping*, which enhances flexibility. Informal characteristics emerge during the process of *group development* as groups pass through the four stages of *initiation*, *differentiation*, *integration*, and *maturity*. Owing to *process loss*, groups are usually less productive than individuals working alone. Process loss can be traced to the effects of production blocking, group-maintenance activities, and social loafing. Owing to *group synergy*, groups can sometimes be more productive than individuals working alone; this gain can be traced to social facilitation, the need for affiliation, and within-group competition. *Teams* are a special type of group characterized by high levels of interdependence, work flow grouping, and differentiated knowledge, skills, and abilities possessed by team members. Because teams are not always more effective than individuals working alone, managers need to pay particular attention to the group's *task and communication structure, size and composition, goals and incentives,* and *cohesiveness and conflict.*

Review Questions

1. What are the three criteria of group effectiveness? Why is group effectiveness assessed in terms of all three criteria instead of being measured solely by group productivity?
2. What influence do group goals have on member motivation? What effects do group rewards have on motivation? What implications do your answers have for managers who must motivate individuals to perform productively in groups?
3. Explain why centralized communication structures enhance the productivity of groups performing simple tasks but depress the performance of groups performing complex jobs. What sort of structure would you recommend for a group of accountants who are auditing the books of a large manufacturing firm? Why?
4. Why is work flow grouping more flexible than functional grouping? If your company sold pencils, pens, and notebook paper, which type of grouping would provide the greatest benefit? Why?

Notes

1   J. Bussey, "The Innovator's Enigma," *Wall Street Journal*, October 4, 2012, http://online. wsj.com/news/articles/SB10000872396390443493304578036753351798378.
2   R. Plant, "Incremental Innovation or Breakthroughs? Consider P&G's Tide Pod," *Wall Street Journal*, September 16, 2013, http://blogs.wsj.com/experts/2013/09/16/incremental-innovation-or-breakthroughs-consider-pgs-tide-pod/.

3 P. Ziobro and S. Ng, "Is Innovation Killing the Soap Business?" *Wall Street Journal*, April 3, 2013, http://online.wsj.com/news/articles/SB10001424127887323916304578400521297972496.

4 L. Coleman-Lochner and C. Hymowitz, "At P&G, the Innovation Well Runs Dry," *Bloomberg Businessweek*, September 12, 2010, http://www.businessweek.com/articles/2012-09-06/at-procter-and-gamble-the-innovation-well-runs-dry.

5 P. Strozniak, "Small Company Executives Tell How Team Development Improves Productivity and Profits," *Industry Week*, September 18, 2000, 21–23.

6 G. Fosler, "Forecasting Talent Shortages," *Business Week*, November 19, 2007, 8.

7 T. V. Mumford, C. H. Van Iddekinge, F. P. Morgeson, and M. A. Campion, "The Team Role Test: Development and Validation of Team Role Knowledge Situational Judgment Test," *Journal of Applied Psychology* 93 (2008): 250–267.

8 M. E. Shaw, *Group Dynamics: The Psychology of Small Group Behavior* (New York: McGraw-Hill, 1981), 8.

9 D. Cartwright and A. Zander, *Group Dynamics: Research and Theory* (New York: Harper & Row, 1968), 46–48.

10 J. R. Hollenbeck, B. Beersma, and M. E. Schouten, "Beyond Team Types: A Dimensional Scaling Conceptualization for Team Description," *Academy of Management Review* 37 (2012): 82–106.

11 N. Byrnes, "Xerox' New Design Team: Customers," *BusinessWeek*, May 7, 2007, 72.

12 J. B. Carson, P. E. Tesluk, and J. A. Marrone, "Shared Leadership in Teams: An Investigation of Antecedent Conditions and Performance," *Academy of Management Review* 50 (2007): 1217–1234.

13 L. Harrison, "We're All the Boss," *Time*, April 17, 2002, 41–43.

14 A. Majchrzak, S. L. Jarvenpaa, and A. B. Hollingshead, "Coordinating Expertise among Emergent Groups Responding to Disasters," *Organization Science* 18 (2007): 147–161.

15 R. Ilies, D. T. Wagner, and F. P. Morgeson, "Explaining Affective Linkages in Teams: Individual Differences in Susceptibility to Contagion and Individualism–Collectivism," *Journal of Applied Psychology* 92 (2007): 1140–1148.

16 J. M. Wilson, P. S. Goodman, and M. A. Cronin, "Group Learning," *Academy of Management Review* 32 (2007): 1041–1059.

17 R. Rico, M. Sanchez-Manzanares, F. Gil, and C. Gibson, "Team Implicit Coordination: A Team Knowledge-Based Approach," *Academy of Management Review* 33 (2008): 163–184.

18 S. L. Berman, J. Down, and C. W. Hill, "Tacit Knowledge as a Source of Competitive Advantage in the National Basketball Association," *Academy of Management Journal* 45 (2002): 13–31.

19 H. Mintzberg, *The Structuring of Organizations* (Englewood Cliffs, NJ: Prentice Hall, 1979), 108–129.

20 J. Marquez, "Banking on a New Structure," *Workforce Management*, May 19, 2008, 1–3.

21 H. Bresman and M. Zellmer-Bruhn, "The Structural Context of Team Learning: Effects of Organizational Structure and Team Structure on Internal and External Learning," *Organization Science* 24 (2013): 1120–1139.

22 J. R. Hollenbeck, H. Moon, A. P. Ellis, B. J. West, D. R. Ilgen, L. Sheppard, C. O. Porter, and J. A. Wagner, "Structural Contingency Theory and Individual Differences: Examination of External and Internal Person–Environment Fit," *Journal of Applied Psychology* 87 (2002): 509–606.

23 B. W. Tuckman, "Developmental Sequence in Small Groups," *Psychological Bulletin* 63 (1965): 384–399.

24 A. Chang, P. Bordia, and J. Duck, "Punctuated Equilibrium and Linear Progression: Toward a New Understanding of Group Development," *Academy of Management Journal* 46 (2003): 106–117.

25 A. M. Grant and S. V. Patil, "Challenging the Norm of Self-Interest: Minority Influence and Transitions to Helping Norms in Work Units," *Academy of Management Review* 37 (2102): 547–568.

26 P. Engardio, "Managing a Global Workforce," *BusinessWeek*, August 20, 2007, 48–52.

27 J. E. Mathieu and W. Schulze, "The Influence of Team Knowledge and Formal Plans on Episodic Team Process–Performance Relationships," *Academy of Management Journal* 49 (2006): 605–619.

28 K. J. Klein, J. C. Zeigert, and Y. Xiao, "Dynamic Delegation: Hierarchical, Shared and Deindividualized Leadership in Extreme Action Teams," *Administrative Science Quarterly* 51 (2006): 590–621.

29 G. L. Stewart, S. H. Courtright, and M. R. Barrick, "Peer-Based Control in Self-Managing Teams: Linking Rational and Normative Influence with Individual and Group Performance," *Journal of Applied Psychology* 97 (2012): 435–447.

30 R. E. Silverman and L. Kwoh, "Peer Performance Reviews Take Off," *Wall Street Journal*, July 31, 2012, http://online.wsj.com/news/articles/SB100008723963904441303045775611700013717112.

31 Z. X. Zhang, P. S. Hempel, Y. L. Han, and D. Tjosvold, "Transactive Memory System Links Work Team Characteristics and Performance," *Journal of Applied Psychology* 92 (2007): 1722–1730.

32 B. Beersma, J. R. Hollenbeck, D. E. Conlon, S. E. Humphrey, H. Moon, and D. R. Ilgen, "Cutthroat Cooperation: The Effects of Team Role Decisions on Adaptation to Alternative Reward Structures," *Organizational Behavior and Human Decision Processes* 108 (2009): 131–142.

33 A. P. J. Ellis, "System Breakdown: The Role of Mental Models and Transactive Memory in the Relationship between Acute Stress and Team Performance," *Academy of Management Journal* 49 (2006): 576–589.

34 G. W. Hill, "Group versus Individual Performance: Are N + 1 Heads Better than One?" *Psychological Bulletin* 9 (1982): 517–539.

35 F. C. Brodbeck, R. Kerschreiter, A. Mojzisch, and S. Schulz-Hardt, "Group Decision Making under Conditions of Distributed Knowledge: The Information Asymmetries Model," *Academy of Management Review* 32 (2007): 459–479.

36 A. Taylor and H. R. Greve, "Superman or the Fantastic Four? Knowledge Combination and Experience in Innovative Teams," *Academy of Management Journal* 49 (2006): 723–740.

37 J. A. Espinosa, S. A. Slaughter, R. E. Kraut, and J. D. Herbsleb, "Familiarity, Complexity, and Team Performance in Geographically Distributed Software Development," *Organization Science* 18 (2007): 613–630.

38 C. Edwards, K. Hall, and R. Grover, "Sony Chases Apple's Magic," *BusinessWeek*, December 10, 2008, 48–51.

39 I. D. Steiner, *Group Processes and Productivity* (New York: Academic Press, 1972). We use the term *process loss* somewhat broader than Steiner, applying it to all decrements in group productivity.

40 S. Meichry and G. Castonguay, "Costa Chief Blames 'Human Error' for Crash," *Wall Street Journal*, January 16, 2012, http://online.wsj.com/article/SB10001424052970204555904577164310019563418.html.

41 S. Meichtry and N. Zevi, "Shipwrecked Liner's Command Faces More Scrutiny," *Wall Street Journal*, January 16, 2012, http://online.wsj.com/article/SB10001424052970204468004577162540796139040.html.

42 R. E. Silverman, "No More Angling for the Best Seat; More Meetings Are Stand-up Jobs," *Wall Street Journal*, February 2, 2012, http://online.wsj.com/news/articles/SB10001424052970204652904577193460472598378.

43 M. Rosenwald, "Re:Re;Re; Confidential," *Bloomberg Businessweek*, November 26, 2012, 100.

44 K. Benne and P. Sheats, "Functional Roles of Group Members," *Journal of Social Issues* 2 (1948): 42–47.

45 J. S. Mueller, "Why Individuals in Larger Groups Perform Worse," *Organizational Behavior and Human Decision Processes* 117 (2012): 111–124.

46 D. Bennett, "The Dunbar Number, from the Guru of Social Networks," *Bloomberg Businessweek*, January 10, 2013, http://www.businessweek.com/articles/2013-01-10/the-dunbar-number-from-the-guru-of-social-networks.

47 A. Shepperd, "Productivity Loss in Performance Groups: A Motivation Analysis," *Psychological Bulletin* 113 (1993): 67–81.

48 C. L. Jackson and J. A. LePine, "Peer Responses to a Team's Weakest Link: A Test and Extension of LePine and Van Dyne's Model," *Journal of Applied Psychology* 88 (2003): 459–475.

49 K. H. Price, D. A. Harrison, and J. H. Gavin, "Withholding Inputs in Team Contexts: Member Composition, Interaction Processes, Evaluation Structure, and Social Loafing," *Journal of Applied Psychology* 91 (2006): 1375–1384.

50 R. Z. Gooding and J. A. Wagner III, "A Meta-Analytic Review of the Relationship between Size and Performance: The Productivity and Efficiency of Organizations and their Subunits," *Administrative Science Quarterly* 30 (1985): 462–481.

51 J. George, "Extrinsic and Intrinsic Origins of Perceived Social Loafing in Organizations," *Academy of Management Journal* 43 (2000): 81–92.

52 B. R. Staats, K. L. Milkman, and C. R. Fox, "The Team Scaling Fallacy: Underestimating the Declining Efficiency of Larger Teams," *Organizational Behavior and Human Decision Processes* 118 (2012): 132–142.

53 R. B. Davison, J. R. Hollenbeck, D. R. Ilgen, C. M. Barnes, and D. Sleesman, "Coordinated Action in Multiteam Systems," *Journal of Applied Psychology* 97 (2012): 808–824.

54 N. M. Loinkova, M. J Pearsall, and H. P. Sims, "Examining the Differential Longitudinal Performance of Directive versus Empowering Leadership in Teams," *Academy of Management Journal* 56 (2013): 573–596.

55 K. Lanaj, J. R. Hollenbeck, D. R. Ilgen, C. M. Barnes, and S. Harmon, "The Double-Edged Sword of Decentralized Planning in Multiteam Systems," *Academy of Management Journal* 56 (2013): 735–757.

56 S. Grobart, "Hooray for Hierarchy," *Bloomberg Businessweek*, January 14, 2013, 74.

57 K. Lewis, M. Belliveau, B. Herndon, and J. Keller, "Group Cognition, Membership Change, and Performance: Investigating the Benefits and Detriments of Collective Knowledge," *Organizational Behavior and Human Decision Processes* 103 (2007): 1 59–178.

58 S. Berfield, "Bridging the Generation Gap," *Business Week*, September 17, 2007, 60–61.

59 C. M. Barnes, J. R. Hollenbeck, D. T. Wagner, D. S. DeRue, J. D. Nahrgang, and K. M. Schwind, "Harmful Help: The Costs of Backing-Up Behavior in Teams," *Journal of Applied Psychology* 93 (2008): 529–539.

60 G. S. Van der Vegt, J. S. Bunderson, and A. Oosterhof, "Expertness Diversity and Interpersonal Helping in Teams: Why Those Who Need the Most Help End Up Getting the Least," *Academy of Management Journal* 49 (2006): 877–893.

61 B. Beersma, J. R. Hollenbeck, S. E. Humphrey, H. Moon, D. E. Conlon, and D. R. Ilgen, "Cooperation, Competition, and Team Performance: Towards a Contingency Approach," *Academy of Management Journal* 46 (2003): 572–590.

62 J. W. Bishop and K. D. Scott, "An Examination of Organizational and Team Commitment in a Self-Directed Team Environment," *Journal of Applied Psychology* 85 (2000): 439–450.

63 D. S. DeRue, J. R. Hollenbeck, M. D. Johnson, D. R. Ilgen, and D. K. Jundt, "How Different Team Downsizing Approaches Influence Team-Level Adaptation and Performance," *Academy of Management Journal* 51 (2008): 182–196.

64 M. Marks, M. J. Sabella, C. S. Burke, and S. J. Zaccaro, "The Impact of Cross-Training on Team Effectiveness," *Journal of Applied Psychology* 87 (2002): 3–13.

65 J. S. Bunderson and K. M. Sutcliffe, "Comparing Alternative Conceptualizations of Functional Diversity in Management Teams: Process and Performance Effects," *Academy of Management Journal* 45 (2002): 875–893.

66 E. E. Jones and J. R. Kelly, "The Psychological Costs of Knowledge Specialization in Groups: Unique Expertise Leaves You Out of the Loop," *Organizational Behavior and Human Decision Processes* 121 (2103): 174–182.

67 A. Majchizaik, P. H. B. More, and S. Jaraj, "Transcending Knowledge Differences in Cross-Functional Teams," *Organization Science* 23 (2012): 951–970.

68 A. Erez, J. A. LePine, and H. Elms, "Effects of Rotated Leadership and Peer Evaluations on the Functioning and Effectiveness of Self-Managed Teams: A Quasi-Experiment," *Personnel Psychology* 55 (2000): 929–948.

69 I. D. Steiner, *Group Processes and Productivity* (New York: Academic Press, 1972).

70 J. A. LePine, J. R. Hollenbeck, D. R. Ilgen, and J. Hedlund, "Effects of Individual Differences on the Performance of Hierarchical Decision-Making Teams: Much More than 'g'," *Journal of Applied Psychology* 82 (1997): 803–811.

71 J. A. Wagner III and R. Z. Gooding, "Shared Influence and Organizational Behavior: A Meta-Analysis of Situational Factors Expected to Moderate Participation–Outcome Relationships," *Academy of Management Journal* 30 (1987): 524–541.

72 W. Lester, B. M. Meglino, and M. A. Korsgaard, "The Antecedents and Consequences of Group Potency: A Longitudinal Investigation of Newly Formed Groups," *Academy of Management Journal* 45 (2002): 352–368.

73 J. Getty, "Pants Required: Attending Meetings When Working from Home," *Wall Street Journal*, May 16, 2012, http://blogs.wsj.com/atwork/2012/05/16/pants-required-attending-meetings-when-working-from-home/.

74 J. Marquez, "Connecting a Virtual Workforce," *Workforce Management*, September 22, 2008, 18–25.

75 M. Conlin, "Out of Sight, Yes; Out of Mind, No," *Business Week*, February 18, 2008.

76 T. Simons, L. H. Pelled, and K. A. Smith, "Making Use of Difference: Diversity, Debate, and Decision Comprehensiveness in Top Management Teams," *Academy of Management Journal* 42 (1999): 662–673.

77 R. L. Moreland and L. Myaskovsky, "Exploring the Performance Benefits of Group Training: Transactive Memory or Improved Communication," *Organizational Behavior and Human Decision Processes* 82 (2000): 117–133.

78 D. van Knippenberg, W. P. von Ginkel, and A. C. Homan, "Diversity Mindsets and the Performance of Diverse Teams," *Organizational Behavior and Human Decision Processes* 121 (2013): 183–193.

79 S. J. Shin and J. Zhou, "When Is Educational Specialization Heterogeneity Related to Creativity in Research and Development Teams? Transformational Leadership as a Moderator," *Journal of Applied Psychology* 92 (2007): 1709–1721.

80 C. O. Porter, J. R. Hollenbeck, D. R. Ilgen, A. P. Ellis, B. J. West, and H. Moon, "Backing Up Behaviors in Teams: The Role of Personality and Legitimacy of Need," *Journal of Applied Psychology* 88 (2003): 391–403.

81 B. H. Bradley, A. C. Klotz, B. E. Postelwaite, and K. G. Brown, "Ready to Rumble: How Team Personality Composition and Task Conflict Interact to Improve Performance," *Journal of Applied Psychology* 98 (2013): 385–392.

82 S. E. Humphrey, J. R. Hollenbeck, C. J. Meyer, and D. R. Ilgen, "Trait Configurations in Self-Managed Teams: A Conceptual Examination of the Use of Seeding for Maximizing and Minimizing Trait Variance in Teams," *Journal of Applied Psychology* 92 (2007): 885–892.

83 A. Joshi, "The Influence of Organizational Demography on the External Networking Behavior of Teams," *Academy of Management Review* 31 (2006): 583–595.

84 J. A. LePine, J. R. Hollenbeck, D. R. Ilgen, and A. Ellis, "Gender Composition, Situational Strength, and Team Decision-Making Accuracy: A Criterion Decomposition Approach," *Organizational Behavior and Human Decision Processes* 88 (2002): 445–475.

85 J. A. Chatman, A. D. Boisnier, S. E. Spataro, C. Anderson, and J. L. Berdahl, "Being Distinctive versus Being Conspicuous: The Effects of Numeric Status and Sex-Stereotyped Tasks on Individual Performance in Groups," *Organizational Behavior and Human Decision Processes* 107 (2008):141–160.

86 J. Wegge, C. Roth, B. Neubach, K. H. Schmidt, and R. Kanfer, "Age and Gender Diversity as Determinants of Performance and Health in a Public Organization: The Role of Task Complexity and Group Size," *Journal of Applied Psychology* 93 (2008): 1301–1313.

87 P. C. Earley and E. Mosakowski, "Creating Hybrid Cultures: An Empirical Test of Transnational Team Functioning," *Academy of Management Journal* 43 (2000): 26–49.

88 A. M. Carton and J. N. Cummings, "A Theory of Subgroups in Work Teams," *Academy of Management Review* 37 (2012): 441–470.

89 D. Lau and J. K. Murnighan, "Demographic Diversity and Faultlines: The Compositional Dynamics of Organizational Groups," *Academy of Management Review* 23 (1998): 325–340.

90 A. C. Homan, D. van Knippenberg, G. A. van Kleef, and C. K. W. De Dreu, "Bridging Faultlines by Valuing Diversity: Diversity Beliefs, Information Elaboration, and Performance in Diverse Work Groups," *Journal of Applied Psychology* 92 (2007): 1189–1199.

91 A. C. Homan, J. R. Hollenbeck, S. E. Humphrey, D. van Knippenberg, D. R. Ilgen, and G. van Kleef, "Facing Differences with an Open Mind: Openness to Experience, Salience of Intra-Group Differences, and Performance of Diverse Work Groups," *Academy of Management Journal* 33 (2008): 1110–1123.

92 A. Gurtner, F. Tachan, N. K. Semmer, and C. Nagele, "Getting Groups to Develop Good Strategies: Effects of Reflexivity Interventions on Team Processes, Team Performance, and Shared Mental Models," *Organizational Behavior and Human Decision Processes* 102 (2007): 127–142.

93 W. P. van Ginkel and D. van Knippenberg, "Group Information Elaboration and Group Decision Making: The Role of Shared Task Representations," *Organizational Behavior and Human Decision Processes* 104 (2008): 82–97.

94 J. E. Sawyer, W. R. Latham, R. D. Pritchard, and W. R. Bennett, "Analysis of Work Group Productivity in an Applied Setting: Application of a Time Series Panel Design," *Personnel Psychology* 52 (2000): 927–968.

95 K. Tasa, S. Taggar, and G. H. Seijts, "The Development of Collective Efficacy in Teams: A Multilevel and Longitudinal Perspective," *Journal of Applied Psychology* 92 (2007): 17–27.

96 C. K. W. De Dreu, "Cooperative Outcome Interdependence, Task Reflexivity, and Team Effectiveness: A Motivated Information Processing Perspective," *Journal of Applied Psychology* 92 (2007): 628–638.

97 S. J. Wang and Y. J. He, "Compensating Nondedicated Cross-Functional Teams," *Organization Science* 19 (2007): 753–765.

98 R. Wageman, "Interdependence and Group Effectiveness," *Administrative Science Quarterly* 40 (1995): 145–180.

99 L. Berkowitz, "Group Standards, Cohesiveness, and Productivity," *Human Relations* 7 (1954): 509–519.

100 P. E. Tesluk and J. E. Mathieu, "Overcoming Roadblocks to Effectiveness: Incorporating Management of Performance Barriers into Models of Work Group Effectiveness," *Journal of Applied Psychology* 84 (1990): 200–217.

101 M. E. Turner and A. R. Pratkanis, "Twenty-Five Years of Groupthink Theory and Research: Lessons from the Evaluation of a Theory," *Organizational Behavior and Human Decision Processes* 73 (1998): 105–115.

102 S. Alper, D. Tjosvold, and K. S. Law, "Conflict Management, Efficacy and Performance in Organizational Teams," *Personnel Psychology* 52 (2000): 625–642.

103 S. Schultz-Hardt, M. Jochims, and D. Frey, "Productive Conflict in Group Decision Making: Genuine and Contrived Dissent as Strategies to Counteract Biased Information Seeking," *Organizational Behavior and Human Decision Processes* 88 (2002): 563–586.

104 B. H. Bradley, B. E. Postelwaite, A. C. Klotz, and M. R. Handami, "Reaping the Benefits of Task Conflict in Teams: The Critical Role of Team Psychological Safety Climate," *Journal of Applied Psychology* 97 (2012): 151–158.

105 K. J. Behfar, R. S. Peterson, E. A. Mannix, and W. M. K. Trochim, "The Critical Role of Conflict Resolution in Teams: A Close Look at the Links between Conflict Type, Conflict Management Strategies, and Team Outcomes," *Journal of Applied Psychology* 93 (2008): 170–188.

106 C. W. Langfred, "The Downside of Self-Management: A Longitudinal Study of the Effects of Conflict on Trust, Autonomy, and Task Interdependence in Self-Managing Teams," *Academy of Management Journal* 50 (2007): 885–900.

Chapter 10

Leadership of Groups and Organizations

When Marissa Mayer was selected to be CEO of Yahoo! in 2012, she became only the twentieth female CEO of a Fortune 500 company and, at age 37, the youngest. Although the engineering-dominated tech industry has long been a bastion for men, Yahoo!'s choice to go with this specific woman as its new leader made perfect sense for a number of reasons. First, in recent years, women have become the leading users of technology. Women, for example, perform more Web searches than men. Women, too, spend more time on social-networking sites and they shop online more than men. Women are more likely than men to carry a smartphone or tablet. Consumers drive technology now. The days when businesses provided the most revenue are over, a fact that many companies, such as Research In Motion (RIM), the maker of the BlackBerry, learned the hard way.[1]

Although the stereotype for a software engineer probably would not be exemplified by a strikingly beautiful woman who has been featured in a *Vogue* photo shoot, Marissa Mayer's programming skills are beyond reproach.[2] She was one of the founding members of Google (Employee #20). She ran Google's original search engine design team, contributed significantly to the development of products such as Gmail and Google Maps, and was often trotted out as the company's spokesperson because of her media savvy. Her tech background did not go unnoticed by investors, one of whom observed specifically that "any company that has information and data as its core ought to have a techie running it."[3]

This rare combination of technical skills and social skills made Mayer a very popular choice to turn around the poorly performing Yahoo! brand. In terms of product markets, Yahoo! was experiencing declining revenues and market share. In fact, the company's share of online advertising revenue dropped from 16 percent in 2009 to 9 percent in 2012. In terms of labor markets, employee morale was at an all-time low, resulting in high rates of turnover among its most-talented engineers. In terms of leadership, the company was a disaster, having gone through seven different CEOs in the last five years alone—the last of which was fired when it became public knowledge that he lied on his resume.[4]

Mayer moved quickly to make changes at Yahoo! that she felt were needed in order to restore the company. One of her first and most controversial decisions was to end Yahoo!'s long-time policy allowing flextime at work. Because she was expecting her first child when her selection was announced (also making her the only pregnant CEO of a Fortune 500 firm), this move surprised many observers, and disappointed many feminists, however, there were two specific issues that led to Mayer's somewhat controversial policy change.[5]

First, internal evidence from VPN logs showed that Yahoo!'s work-at-home staff did not seem to be working very hard when measured in terms of hours actually logged. The perception that some Yahoo! employees were abusing the privilege was widespread and created conflict with employees who were on-site or workers who were not abusing the privilege. Second, Mayer believed that Yahoo! needed to come up with creative solutions to compete with Google and Facebook, which had siphoned off users and advertisers from Yahoo! over the years. Mayer stressed that "people are more productive when they are alone, but they are more collaborative and innovative when they're together."[6] Thus, the decision was a strategic choice regarding how to best compete in that industry—no more, no less. It was also a powerful signal that people had better drop any stereotypes that might hold for this specific female leader.

As noted in the previous chapter, few important tasks or goals can be accomplished by one person working alone. Indeed, this fact largely explains why so many groups and organizations exist in our society. Nevertheless, few groups or organizations can accomplish much without the help of a single individual acting as a leader. Leadership is the force that energizes and directs groups. Many have suggested that the pool of available leaders is smaller today than it has ever been, and leadership development has been rated the number one human capital challenge facing organizations today.[7]

Given the centrality of leadership to the behavior of people in groups and to organizational achievement, it is important that we understand how leaders emerge and what qualities make them effective. This chapter focuses on this topic, showing how leadership is a complex function involving a leader, followers, and situations. All too often, people who want to learn about leadership focus too much on the leader and not enough on the followers and the situation. As we can see from the example that opened this chapter, however, the criteria by which leaders are selected are constantly changing, and someone who might have been successful in the past might not be able to survive in the new era, where one needs to meet the needs of a more diverse set of stakeholders. Thus, the leadership at RIM and Yahoo! were both slow to react to changes in the tech industry, but at least Yahoo! took dramatic steps with its new leader, Marissa Mayer, to respond to change.

Because of its centrality to organizational effectiveness, you should not be surprised to learn that a large number of theories have been proposed about leadership. Trying to explain them all might leave you more confused about the topic than when you started. Conversely, ignoring important approaches so as to simplify our discussion might give you a false impression about the real subtlety and complexity of the leadership process. If leadership were a simple process, everyone would be a great leader—which is hardly the case. In fact, a recent survey indicated that 83 percent of those questioned felt there was a leadership vacuum in their organization.[8] Given this state of affairs, superior leadership processes serve as another area where one firm can gain competitive advantage over another.

To facilitate the process of learning about the many different theories of leadership, this chapter begins by presenting a single conceptual framework, *the integrated leadership model*, which encompasses the other theories. This arrangement reflects our emphasis on the three elements that go into leadership: *the leader, the followers,* and *the situation*; and the three factors that characterize the leader, that is, his or her *traits, behaviors,* and *decision-making styles.* Our general approach to leadership asserts that no one trait, behavior, or decision-making style is always going to result in leadership success but, instead, certain followers or situations require one set of traits, behaviors, and styles, whereas other followers or situations might demand an alternative set of traits, behaviors, and styles. With this framework in place, we then examine individual theories, fitting them into a single overall scheme. This model is comprehensive in reflecting the many ingredients that contribute to effective leadership—but concise in classifying these ingredients and showing how they can be applied in different organizational situations.

The Integrated Leadership Model

Most people have a difficult time expressing exactly what the word *leadership* means. Indeed, even experts offer conflicting definitions of this term. Nevertheless, when asked to name strong leaders throughout history, people respond in a remarkably consistent way. Table 10.1 lists a number of people who are almost always cited as strong leaders. This list should give you an idea of how difficult it is to develop a definition of leadership that is specific enough to be useful, yet broad enough to include people who differ so greatly from one another. What traits do the people in the table share in common?

One characteristic shared by the people listed in Table 10.1 is their *ability to influence others.* The use of influence certainly should be paramount in any definition of leadership. Influence is not the only piece of the leadership puzzle, however. For example, would you consider an armed robber who enters a subway train and induces passengers to hand over their personal belongings to be a leader? Most people would recognize this person's influence, but would not consider this act one of leadership. Instead, a leader's influence must to some degree be *sanctioned by followers.* In some situations, a person might be compelled to lead; in other cases, a leader might be merely tolerated for a short time. Whatever the circumstances, the idea that followers voluntarily surrender control over their own behavior to someone else forms an integral part of any definition of leadership.

Finally, a complete definition of leadership must describe the context in which leadership occurs and the symbolism captured in the leader. Leadership occurs in *goal-oriented* group contexts. Leaders who set difficult goals for their followers experience higher levels of performance, especially if the leader is trusted and sets goals that are difficult but not impossible.[9] This statement does not mean that moving the group toward its goal is a leader's only function. Leaders also serve an important *symbolic* function for both group members and outsiders. Thus, during the recent economic downturn, there was a rash of CEO firings that sent a symbolic message to everyone within those organizations about how the future needed to be different from the past. Indeed, research shows that CEO firings double in recessions relative to other economic periods, despite the fact that no real evidence suggests that this improves matters in large organizations—other than being symbolic.

Still, this type of symbolism is important, because every employee cannot possibly understand all that goes on in the organization and one cannot fire the entire organization when things are going poorly. As noted in Chapter 4, when the complexity of a stimulus exceeds a person's cognitive capacity the individual attempts to simplify the stimulus, and the leader provides the means for much of this simplification. The leader offers a logically compelling and emotionally satisfying focal point for people who are trying to understand the causes and consequences of organized activity. Focusing on the leader reduces organizational

Table 10.1 Conventional Examples of Strong Leaders

Adolf Hitler	Martin Luther King, Jr.
Mahatma Gandhi	Napoleon Bonaparte
Mao Zedong	Moses
Franklin D. Roosevelt	Abraham Lincoln
Winston Churchill	Golda Meir
John F. Kennedy	Nelson Mandela

complexities to simple terms that people can more readily understand and communicate.[10] This simplifying aspect of leadership can often be dysfunctional and, therefore, we need to resist such unsophisticated descriptions of the leadership process.

The negative implications of equating the leader with the organization as a whole becomes particularly salient when larger-than-life leaders engage in negative behaviors that threaten the whole firm. For example, in 2012, Paula Deen Enterprises, which consists of a restaurant chain, television shows, publications, cooking paraphernalia, and the like, all based on the outsized personality of the celebrity chef Paula Deen, came crashing down when it became clear that she hid the fact that she had diabetes and that she used the n-word while organizing a Southern Plantation-style wedding at her house. All of a sudden, the quirky southern cook—who made her name being a foil to sensible diet regimens by serving hamburgers on donuts—seemed much less charming and quaint. All of the business units that comprised Paula Deen Enterprises suffered when everything associated with her became poison to advertisers and consumers.[11] Thus, the symbolic function associated with leadership means that leaders have a big impact on organizational outcomes—both good and bad—and many people can succeed or suffer based solely on the action of a single person.

With these points in mind, we define **leadership** as the use of noncoercive and symbolic influence to direct and coordinate the activities of the members of an organized group toward the accomplishment of group objectives.[12] In defining leadership, it is important to distinguish between leaders and managers. Recall from Mintzberg's overview of managerial roles (see Chapter 2) that the role of leader is just one of ten roles commonly occupied by managers. Leadership, according to Mintzberg, deals explicitly with guiding and motivating employees. From this point of view, leadership is merely one of many managerial tasks.[13]

Edward Hollander has suggested that the leadership process is best understood as the occurrence of mutually satisfying interactions among leaders and followers within a particular situational context. As Figure 10.1 indicates, the *locus of leadership* appears where these three forces—*leaders, followers,* and *situations*—come together. In Hollander's view, we can understand leadership only by gaining an appreciation of the important characteristics of these three forces and the ways in which they interact.

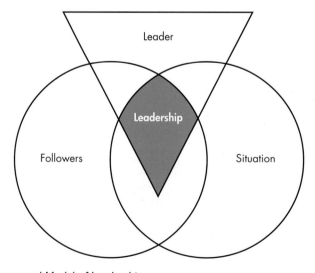

Figure 10.1 **The Integrated Model of Leadership**

To better appreciate the influence of followers on leadership, return to Table 10.1 and ask yourself the following questions. Could a person with Adolf Hitler's totalitarian character-istics have risen to power in the United States following the Vietnam War, where opposing almost any government act was virtually a national pastime? Could Martin Luther King, Jr.'s peaceful, patient approach to civil rights have worked for Central European Muslims in their opposition to the Serbians, who seemed to seek nothing less than their extermination? Can anyone establish a position of leadership with a group of intellectuals who reject the very idea that they need to be led? These questions underline the complex nature of leadership and the contribution of the situation in making a leader successful.

Universal Approaches to Leadership

Not all theories about leadership emphasize the three-dimensional character of the leadership process as proposed by Hollander. The earliest probes into the nature of leadership focused almost exclusively on leader characteristics (rather than on followers or situations). These *universal theories* emphasized the traits and abilities, typical behaviors, and decision-making styles that made leaders different from nonleaders.

Leader Traits

The earliest approaches to leadership held that leaders were born, not made. In 1869, Sir Francis Galton argued that the traits of great leaders were inherited. Studies of the physical characteristics of leaders have yielded weak but consistent relationships between a person's *energy level* and the ability to rise to positions of leadership. Large-scale research projects involving hundreds of leaders and thousands of followers suggest that the perceived amount of time and energy that the leader devotes to the job is a major determinant of follower ratings of leader effectiveness. Certainly, anecdotal reports support the notion that many leaders simply work harder than average individuals, and many CEOs report working eighty hours a week.[14]

As we saw in our opening story with respect to Marissa Mayer's programming abilities, specific *technical skills* and *task knowledge* are also related to success in leadership, although this is especially the case at lower levels in the organization. Knowing how to get the job done and, perhaps, being the most knowledgeable person with respect to the task, both help leadership emergence in the beginning. Over time, however, as one climbs higher in the organizational hierarchy, this becomes less and less a virtue as one often has to manage talented people whose skills within their own technical specialties exceed those of the leader. This is the major reason why many leaders "plateau" at middle levels of an organization, when the skills that got them to that place are no longer relevant for breaking through to the next level.[15]

At the highest levels of an organization, the complexity of running a major business means that one needs to have a "question to statement ratio" that is heavily skewed toward questions to prevent being blindsided. For example, historians have noted that John F. Kennedy was an effective leader during turbulent times because he was a skilled interrogator. He was both comfortable expressing what he did not know and a master in terms of tapping into other people's knowledge and quickly assimilating their expertise.[16] This can also be seen in the case of billionaire Warren Buffett, who routinely would bring in investors who were "short-selling" his business units (i.e., questioning their future prospects) to his annual meetings. Buffett would interrogate these individuals to see what was driving their negative assessments and used this information to form more nuanced and less-biased judgments of what was happening in his own companies.[17] It is easy for those at the top of the organization to get out of touch with their large and diverse operations, especially if those who report to them tend to "forget about the losses and exaggerate the wins" for their own benefit.

In terms of personality traits, the evidence suggests that there are weak but consistent relationships between four of the five characteristics identified by the five-factor model (see Chapter 3). Many leaders tend to be extroverted, for example, because it helps them feel comfortable talking and taking charge in group contexts that would be difficult for an introvert. This is especially the case if the extroverted leader is matched with relatively introverted employees.[18] People also seem to prefer leaders who are calm and emotionally stable. Indeed, even things as small as using foul language can make some followers think the leader is out of control. For example, Carol Bartz, one of seven Yahoo! CEOs in five years—and the CEO who preceded Marissa Mayer—was fired because of her constant use of profane language that unnerved many workers and customers.[19]

Openness to experience is also a valuable trait in leaders because it helps them learn the right lessons from experience.[20] In general, some young leaders struggle with leadership at large organizations due to their lack of experience. For example, Facebook's founder Mark Zuckerberg, was, at twenty-seven, the youngest CEO of a major company in 2012, and many business and finance observers traced the difficulties associated with Facebook's original IPO (initial public offering) to his inexperience.[21] However, Zuckerberg, who is very high in openness to experience, proved to be a quick learner and without this trait even the most experienced leaders eventually fail. Finally, conscientiousness is also related to leadership for two specific reasons. First, highly conscientious people are competitive and strive to achieve, and so this helps them to "get ahead" in organizations. But recall that in our definition of leadership, we noted that this kind of influence has to be sanctioned by followers. Hence, the fact that conscientious individuals also have a strong sense of duty and trustworthiness means this also helps them "get along."[22]

In general, although many of these individual characteristics are related to leadership, the effects of these traits tend to depend on characteristics of the situation or the followers.[23] Keeping these exceptions in mind, however, the weak magnitude and contingent nature of the relationships between leadership and the personal traits of leaders ultimately prompted researchers to explore other approaches to understanding this important concept.

Leader Decision-Making Styles

Whereas the research discussed previously dealt with leader traits, other early research in the area of leadership focused more specifically on how leaders make decisions and how these styles affect subordinates' rates of productivity and general satisfaction. Research in this tradition has examined three decision-making styles: (1) laissez-faire, (2) authoritarian, and (3) democratic. The **laissez-faire leader** leaves the group alone to do whatever it wants, and most consider this to be an abdication of leadership. Research clearly shows that laissez-faire leadership fails to yield positive results for the group in terms of performance or satisfaction.[24] In an interesting account of her tenure at Enron, whistleblower Sherron Watkins noted that CEO Ken Lay's laissez-faire style leadership at the failed organization left him clueless and was a major reason for all of the unethical activity that took place there under his stewardship. Watkins noted that when it comes to leadership "clueless is far worse than toxic because at least with toxic you can begin to predict behaviors. With clueless, what you would expect from a boss can vary widely from their actual behavior. Crooks are much easier to deal with than fools."[25]

The **authoritarian leader** is almost the opposite of the laissez-faire leader, and makes virtually all decisions by him- or herself. Members of groups led by authoritarian leaders can be highly productive, but only when members are closely supervised.[26] Also, the evidence seems to suggest that authoritarian leadership tends to trickle down in an organization, in the sense that middle-level managers who have authoritarian bosses tend to act more authoritarian themselves.[27] For example, Apple's Steve Jobs was famous for being an authoritarian leader who only trusted his own vision and rarely listened to others. He was often rude and dismissive to his direct reports, and much of this "trickled down" the organization all the way to the production floor.[28]

In contrast, the **democratic leader** works with the group to help members come to their own decisions. Results of studies on leader decision styles suggest that most groups prefer a democratic leader to those employing the alternative styles, and like the authoritarian leadership style, this approach also tends to trickle down to lower levels of the organization.[29] As with leader traits, however, research has revealed only modest correlations between this leader style and group performance. Subsequent research has indicated that democratic leadership is not always the single best approach for *all* followers and all situations. For example, research on cross-cultural differences suggests that, while workers from some countries, such as Denmark, perform very well under democratic leadership, workers from other countries, such as Russia, perform very poorly under participative leaders.[30]

Leader Behaviors

A third school of early leadership research focused on the behaviors exhibited by leaders. Based on interviews with supervisors and clerical workers at the Prudential Insurance Company, researchers concluded that two general classes of supervisory behavior exist: **employee-oriented behavior**, which aims to meet the social and emotional needs of group members, and **job-oriented behavior**, which focuses on careful supervision of employees' work methods and task accomplishment. Early studies indicated that work attitudes were better and productivity was higher in the groups led by supervisors who displayed employee-oriented behaviors.[31]

Another set of early studies that relied on questionnaires rather than interviews reached similar conclusions about leader behavior. After analyzing workers' responses to a questionnaire through a sophisticated statistical procedure called *factor analysis*, researchers concluded that most supervisory behaviors could be assigned to one of two dimensions: **consideration** or **initiating structure**.[32] Table 10.2 shows some items from the Leader Behavior Description Questionnaire (LBDQ) that evolved from these original studies. The consideration dimension closely resembles the employee-centered orientation, in that both dimensions address the individual and social needs of workers. For example, Craig Jelinek, the CEO of Costco, leads an organization that is as devoted to meeting the needs of its workers as it is to meeting the needs of its customers. Workers at Costco receive generous health benefits and are paid $21 an hour—compared to $12 an hour for employees at one of its competitors—Sam's Club, a division of Wal-Mart. Costco business strategy is to offer low prices like Wal-Mart, but make up for its higher employee expenses by charging a higher annual membership fee. The theory at Costco is that in return for this higher fee, customers experience more satisfied and engaged service providers. This, in turn, promotes customer loyalty, operationalized in terms of their willingness to continue to pay the higher membership fee, year in and year out. This theory has been borne out by experience, and Costco boasts the highest return rates for customers and the lowest rate of turnover among employees of any other large retailer in the industry. Jelinek notes that "This is not Harvard grad school stuff. We sell quality stuff at the

Table 10.2 Items Similar to Those in the Leader Behavior Description Questionnaire

Consideration items:

1. Is easy to get along with
2. Puts ideas generated by the group into operation
3. Treats everyone the same
4. Lets followers know of upcoming changes
5. Explains actions to all group members

Initiating-structure items:

1. Tells group members what is expected
2. Promotes the use of standardized procedures
3. Makes decisions about work methods
4. Clarifies role relationship among group members
5. Sets specific goals and monitors performance closely

Source: Adapted from R. M. Stodgill and A. E. Coons, *Leader Behavior: Its Description and Measurement* (Columbus: Ohio State University, Bureau of Business Research, 1957), 75.

best possible price. If you treat consumers with respect and treat employees with respect, good things are going to happen to you."[33]

Moving from consideration to initiating structure, it is clear that this dimension resembles the job-centered orientation in that both are concerned with the clarification of work processes and expectations. Rather than being mutually exclusive (that is, if a person is high on one dimension, he or she must be low on the other), these two dimensions are somewhat independent (that is, a person can be high on one dimension, and high, medium, or low on the other). If anything, a small positive correlation exists between the two dimensions, in that leaders who are considerate also seem to rate slightly higher on initiating structure.

Based on this early research, Blake and Mouton developed the notion of the managerial grid, proposing that a leader needs to rate highly in terms of both concern for people and concern for production to be truly effective.[34] This approach was suggested to be "the one best way" to lead (that is, regardless of followers or situations). Blake and Mouton subsequently developed an elaborate training program to move managers in that direction. Managers find the program appealing because it points to two specific sets of behaviors—consideration and initiating structure—in which they can engage to enhance the attitudes and performance of their group. Despite its appeal, however, the managerial grid approach lacks support from rigorous scientific studies. In fact, some investigators have even labeled the whole idea a myth.[35] In terms of outcomes, an approach that is high on initiating structure tends to reduce mistakes but not help group creativity, whereas an approach that is high in consideration seems to have the opposite set of effects.[36] Indeed, creativity seems to be consistently associated with high levels of consideration, and abusive supervisors tend to squelch innovation at all levels of the organization.[37]

Transformational Leadership

Perhaps because of the weaknesses associated with universal approaches that emphasize traits, behaviors, or decision-making styles, subsequent universal approaches were developed that incorporated all three aspects of leadership simultaneously. Among these are theories of **transformational leadership**, which emphasize the ability of the leader to communicate new visions of an organization to followers.[38] Transformational leaders can be characterized by their traits, behaviors, and decision-making styles. In terms of traits, transformational leaders are often called *charismatic leaders* because of the centrality of this trait to their effectiveness, as well as their tendency to rely on moralistic emotional appeals rather than calculative, instrumental, or financial appeals, which tend to be employed more by transactional leaders.[39] In some cases, it does not even matter whether the emotion displayed by the leader is positive (enthusiasm) or negative (agitation) but, rather, the intensity of the emotion is critical for communicating importance and urgency.[40] In terms of behaviors, transformational leaders raise followers' awareness of the importance of group goals, and increase the degree to which employees identify with such goals.[41] Transformational leaders often induce individuals to sacrifice their own goals for the goals of the group or sacrifice the goals of their own specific group for some larger, more meaningful organizational purpose.[42] They "raise the stakes" of organizational performance by convincing subordinates of the importance of the leader's values and vision, as well as the dangers of deviating from this vision.[43]

This vision and emphasis on change distinguishes transformational leaders from more ordinary leaders.[44] Transformational leaders accomplish this by creating a strong identification between the leader and the follower, as well as increasing the strength of the bond among the followers themselves, thus enhancing group cohesiveness and collective self-efficacy.[45] Indeed, the social and value-oriented nature of charismatic leadership is best revealed by research that shows that perceptions of charisma spread much faster among people who are in the same social network (friends), as opposed to the same physical location or task network.[46]

Still, many transformational leaders also engage in behaviors that most would characterize as transactional, and the two styles are often complementary and not mutually exclusive.[47] Indeed, as we have seen in previous studies of leadership, there seem to be contingencies associated with the success of this leadership style that make it more effective in some situations or with some followers relative to others. For example, research indicates that, with respect to followers, charismatic leadership is more effective with followers who are collectivistic rather than individualistic.[48] In terms of situations, it also seems to be more effective when there is direct contact between the leader and the followers, as opposed to when the relationship is indirect.[49] Charismatic leadership also seems to be more effective when the task is not necessarily intrinsically satisfying or important on its own merits.[50]

Finally, charismatic leadership also seems to be less important in contexts where people perceive high levels of procedural justice, suggesting that trust in procedures can serve as a substitute for the role of a charismatic leader.[51]

We discuss the concept of substitutes for leadership in more detail in a later section of this chapter. For now, we merely assert that, as these findings suggest, the evidence argues against the notion that there is any "one best way" of leading, regardless of followers and situations. The primary problem of all the approaches we have discussed is that they specify one best way to lead (for example, be extroverted or initiate structure, or use a democratic leadership style) regardless of the characteristics of followers and situations. This led to weak results in terms of predicting or explaining leader emergence and effectiveness, and started many people wondering just how critical leadership really was to large organizations. As we see in the next section, some began to argue that leadership might be irrelevant.

Leader Irrelevance

Advocates of leader irrelevance, a situation-based approach to understanding leadership, emphasize that situations are much more important determinants of events than leader characteristics, for several reasons.[52] First, factors outside the leader's control tend to affect outcomes more than anything a leader might do. Especially when one is dealing with large organizations in complex, dynamic and hostile environments, the efforts of a single individual might simply be overmatched by the circumstances. For example, the $5 million Ibrahim Prize for Achievement in African Leadership was to be given out each year to recognize democratically elected leaders in Africa who served their constituents with honor. Unfortunately, dire conditions on the continent have made it such that the award has been withheld three out of the last four years. Apparently no one was able to rise to the occasion under these circumstances, and the chairman of the committee overseeing the award noted that "If we are going to have a prize for exceptional leadership, we have to stick to that and not compromise."[53]

Second, even leaders at relatively high levels tend to have unilateral control over only a few resources. In very large organizations, even a highly charismatic person's impact is diluted, especially given the short tenure of many top leaders.[54] Moreover, the discretionary use of any set of resources is constrained by the leader's accountability to other people both inside and outside the organization. Even the CEO of a major corporation must answer to shareholders, consumers, government regulators, and other people in the company. For example, when Toyota announced that it was searching for a new CEO, no one really expected a major departure from business as usual at the company. As one industry analyst noted, "No matter who takes over at Toyota, it may not make a huge difference. Unlike a more personality-driven company where a new executive may take the company in a new direction, Toyota has taken a more cautious approach to its management style. Toyota values making decisions slowly and building consensus among all employees before moving forward."[55]

Finally, the selection process through which all leaders must go filters people such that those in leadership positions tend to act in similar ways. For example, when the leadership succession team at soup producer Campbell's went searching for a new CEO, they limited themselves to long-time insiders who embodied many of the characteristics of the previous set of CEOs. Afraid to make a mistake, the selection committee took a very cautious, "stay-the-course," approach that wound up selecting Denise Morrison, an eighteen-year veteran at the company. This choice was met with disappointment by some industry analysts who noted that the company was losing market share to General Mills, which owns the Progresso brand, and was seemingly unable to gain any ground internationally. Only two out of twenty analysts who study this industry thought this was a good choice given the firm's declining performance, and one noted that, "You could say, 'Let's get some new blood in here,' but she is another Campbell's disciple reluctant to take a fresh look at the business and shake things up."[56] Indeed, research suggests that organizations only tend to go against the historical grain of their leadership profile when confronted with massive failures.[57]

The failure to find robust direct relationships between leader traits, behaviors, and decision-making styles promoted this kind of anti-leadership sentiment. In fact, it can be quite useful to remember that leaders are often victims of their environments rather than masters of their domain. Even so, research on leadership continued, and more contemporary approaches maintained that leadership did provide some value. These approaches suggested, however, that the value of leadership was a highly contingent phenomenon that could not be captured by "one best way" approaches that dominated the early research in this area. The theories discussed next all acknowledge these types of leader–follower–situation interactions.

Characteristics of Followers and Situations

All of the theories described above focused primarily on the leader, in terms of traits, behaviors, and decision-making style. The inability of these theories to adequately explain variance in leadership performance has led many to consider factors beyond the leader alone and to a shift in focus on followers and on situations confronting leaders. In this section, we analyze several of the theories that expand the conversation about leadership.

Vertical Dyad Linkage

An approach to leadership that emphasizes the characteristics of followers is the *vertical dyad linkage* (VDL) theory of leadership. A **vertical dyad** consists of two persons who are linked hierarchically, such as a supervisor and a subordinate. Most studies that involve measurements of leader consideration or initiating structure average subordinates' ratings of leaders. VDL proponents, however, argue that there is no such thing as an "average" leadership score. Instead, they insist, each supervisor–subordinate relationship is unique. A supervisor might be considerate toward one person but not another. Similarly, the leader may initiate structure for some workers but not others.

The importance of distinguishing dyadic from average scores has received broad research support. For example, Figure 10.2 compares the strength of the relationship between (1) leader consideration and follower satisfaction; and (2) leader initiating structure and follower role clarity as measured by both dyadic scores and average scores.[58] As shown in the figure, the relationships based on dyadic scores were much stronger than the relationships based on average scores. This finding suggests that leaders do behave differently with different subordinates and that these differences spill over into worker reactions.[59]

The VDL approach also suggests that leaders tend to classify subordinates as either in-group members or out-group members. According to this theory, *in-group members* are willing and able to do more than the tasks outlined in a formal job description.[60] Once they have been identified, the leader gives these individuals more latitude, authority, and consideration, and they respond by providing even higher levels of citizenship behavior over and above the normal call of duty.[61] The impact of being an in-group member is especially powerful when one's leader has a strong in-group relationship with his or her own leader.[62]

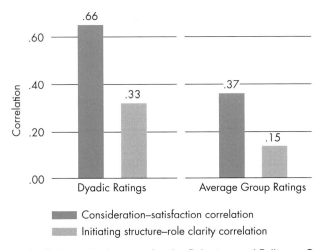

Figure 10.2 **Measuring the Relationship between Leader Behaviors and Follower Outcomes by Dyadic Ratings and Average Group Ratings**

Source: Adapted from G. Graen, "Role-Making Processes within Complex Organizations," in *Handbook of Industrial and Organizational Psychology*, ed. M. D. Dunnette (Chicago: Rand McNally, 1976), 1210–1259.

Out-group members, on the other hand, either cannot or will not expand their roles beyond formal requirements. Leaders assign these individuals more routine tasks, give them less consideration, and communicate less often with them. Because their status is more tenuous relative to in-group members, out-group members tend to become very risk averse and unwilling to take chances for fear of making mistakes.[63] This is especially the case in contexts where an out-group member is working for a leader who has relatively low power and access to resources owing to a precarious relationship with his or her own leader.[64]

Whether distinguishing among subordinates in this manner improves a leader's effectiveness depends on the leader's reasons for placing some people in the in-group and others in the out-group. Research shows that performance is not always the reason for separating members into in-groups and out-groups; indeed, if these kinds of distinctions are based on non-performance-related demographic information (such as race or gender), then this classification can interfere with leader effectiveness.[65] Highly competent and committed workers might differ demographically from their supervisors but could excel if given in-group status and support. Indeed, when leaders differentially weigh the opinions of their followers based on their competence, highly effective results often follow.[66]

Life-Cycle Model

Whereas the previous approach focused on leader traits and behaviors, the next approach features the leader's decision-making style, emphasizing how it combines with characteristics of followers to determine leadership effectiveness. According to the *life-cycle model* developed by Paul Hersey and Kenneth Blanchard, the effectiveness of a leader's decision-making style depends largely on followers' level of maturity.[67] This model proposes two basic dimensions on which decision-making style may vary: task orientation and relationship orientation.

The life-cycle model suggests that these two dimensions combine to form four distinct types of decision styles: telling, selling, participating, and delegating. The *telling style* is characterized by high task orientation and low relationship orientation—the leader simply tells the follower what to do. The *selling style* is characterized by both high task and high relationship orientations such that the leader tries to convince subordinates that the decision is appropriate. The *participating style* is marked by a high relationship orientation but a low task orientation. The leader who uses this style of decision making includes subordinates in discussions so that decisions are made by consensus. Finally, in the *delegating style*, which is low on both task and relationship orientations, the leader actually turns things over to followers and lets them make their own decisions.

According to Hersey and Blanchard, the type of decision-making style that a leader should adopt depends on the level of maturity of the followers (Figure 10.3). The model suggests that, for followers at very low levels of maturity, telling is the most effective leadership decision style. As followers move from very low to moderately low levels of maturity, a selling style becomes more effective. That is, the leader in this case should act as an opinion leader.[68] When followers show a moderately high level of maturity, participating is the most effective style. At the very highest levels of follower maturity, the delegating style leaves followers essentially on their own.

For example, when he served as the basketball coach for the U.S. Olympic team in 2012, Mike Krzyzewski noted that he had to take a completely different approach with his all-star team of professional talent compared to his approach for running his college program at Duke University. Krzyzewski noted that, "In college, you have youngsters who need to adapt to me and our culture and our program. I'm their guide. When you have players like Kobe Bryant, LeBron James, and Carmelo Anthony, you cannot come in and just tell them what to

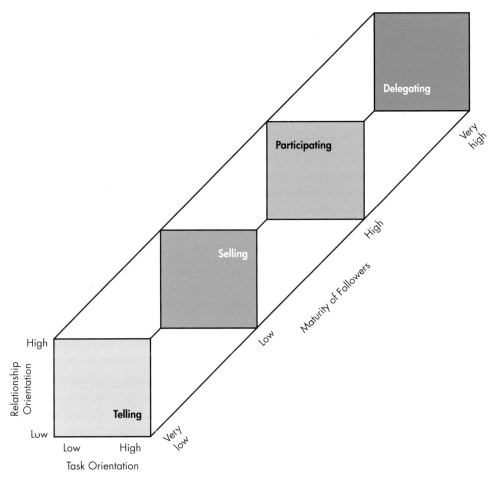

Figure 10.3 The Life-Cycle Model of Leadership in Four Dimensions

Source: Adapted from P. Hersey and K. Blanchard, *Management of Organizational Behavior* (Englewood Cliffs, NJ: Prentice Hall, 1991).

do. I had to give them a chance to take ownership of the team by doing things that they found to be good."[69]

Although empirical research has not supported the life-cycle model completely, the notion that performance will be higher in matched situations is supported at one level of maturity— the lowest. That is, with workers at low levels of maturity, the telling style is slightly more effective in eliciting good performance than the other styles. Also, in terms of stages of group development, a more directive telling style seems to be more appropriate for early stages of the group development process, whereas more participative or delegating styles seem to work better as the group matures over time.[70]

Three of this model's four dimensions are easily seen. Relationship orientation can be low (bottom half of the rectangular box model) or high (top half). Task orientation can also be low (left half of the model) or high (right half). Follower maturity ranges from very low (front of the model) to very high (back). The fourth dimension, leader effectiveness, is represented by the highlighted cell at each follower-maturity level. For example, at the high-maturity level, the highlighting of the cell for the participating leader style—which is high on relationship orientation and low on task orientation—indicates that at this level this style should be the most effective.

Substitutes for Leadership

Whereas the VDL approach to leadership places a great deal of weight on leader behaviors and the characteristics of followers, the **substitutes for leadership** theory emphasized leader behaviors and the situation. Although not as extreme as the anti-leadership approaches, this theory argues that traditional leader behaviors, such as initiating structure and consideration, are sometimes made irrelevant by certain characteristics of situations.[71] That is, characteristics of situations can act to *substitute* for leader behavior. Figure 10.4 illustrates the effect of a substitute. Here consideration leads to follower satisfaction when boring tasks must be performed. When tasks are intrinsically satisfying, however, the satisfying nature of the task substitutes for leader behavior; leader consideration has no effect in this case, because satisfaction is already high.

One review of the scientific literature on this topic suggests that the most powerful substitutes for leadership relate to both characteristics of the task and the organization as a whole. In general, leadership tends to be neutralized in situations where tasks are intrinsically satisfying and good objective feedback about task performance is provided. For example, in many small technical companies, the programmers are so intrinsically motivated by the challenging

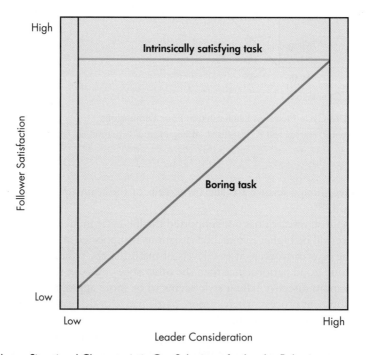

Figure 10.4 How a Situational Characteristic Can Substitute for Leader Behavior

Source: Adapted from P. M. Podsakoff, S. B. MacKenzie, and W. H. Bommer, "Meta-Analysis of the Relationships between Kerr and Jermier's Substitutes for Leadership and Employee Job Attitudes, Role Perceptions, and Performance," *Journal of Applied Psychology* 81 (1996): 380–399.

nature of the work and immediate feedback about whether or not their programs run effect-ively that this substitutes for strong leadership that might be necessary under the opposite conditions.[72]

Strong and cohesive work groups can also substitute for leadership in the sense that the team as a whole will perform many of the functions that might be served by a formal leader.[73] Again, in the area of technology, a great deal of programming is performed by teams that may (1) select their own members, (2) train their own members, and (3) evaluate their own members in terms of rewards or retention. Of these three activities, the third is often the most difficult to accomplish without a formal leader. As one team member at Gore-Tex notes with respect to their own self-managing teams, "Some poorly performing workers can some-times go unchecked for too long."[74] This becomes even more problematic if the group becomes more cohesive over time and some members start to cover the tracks of their low performing friends.

Finally, leadership can also be neutralized in organizations that are highly formalized, that is, organizations that develop a large number of written rules and procedures for most jobs. Well-established written rules and procedures take the place of initiating structure, however, there is still room in such organizations for leaders who display consideration. In contrast, cohesive work groups tend to substitute for leadership consideration but still leave room for supervisors who can initiate structure.[75]

Comprehensive Theories of Leadership

Whereas all four of the interactive approaches discussed earlier deal with two of the three forces identified in the transactional model of leadership (leader–follower–situation), the comprehensive leadership theories discussed in this section account for all three simultan-eously. The three comprehensive theories that we examine next differ only in that each tends to focus on a particular leader characteristic—either a personal characteristic, a behavioral orientation, or a decision-making style.

Fiedler's Contingency Theory

Think for a moment of someone you dislike when you have to work together. In fact, consid-ering all of your co-workers in the past, who do you remember as being the worst? Now rate this person on the qualities listed in the scale shown in Table 10.3. If you described your *least-preferred co-worker* (LPC) in relatively harsh terms, then contingency theory would suggest that you are most likely to take a *task orientation* toward leadership. Task-oriented

Table 10.3 Items Similar to Those on the Least-Preferred Co-Worker Scale

Agreeable	8	7	6	5	4	3	2	1	Disagreeable
Closed-minded	1	2	3	4	5	6	7	8	Open-minded
Courteous	8	7	6	5	4	3	2	1	Rude
Agitated	1	2	3	4	5	6	7	8	Calm
Dull	1	2	3	4	5	6	7	8	Fascinating

Source: Adapted from F. E. Fiedler, "Engineering the Job to Fit the Manager," *Harvard Business Review* 43 (1965): 115–122.

leaders emphasize completing tasks successfully, even at the expense of interpersonal relations. A task-oriented leader finds it difficult to overlook the negative traits of a poorly performing subordinate. On the other hand, if you described your LPC in relatively positive terms, you are likely to take a *relationship orientation* toward leadership. Relationship-oriented leaders, according to this theory, are permissive, considerate leaders who can maintain good interpersonal relationships even with workers who are not contributing to group accomplishment.

The leader's orientation toward either tasks or relationships is the central piece of this complex and controversial theory of leadership that was proposed by Fred Fiedler.[76] Fiedler's model is called a *contingency theory of leadership* because it holds that the effectiveness of a leader's orientation depends on both the followers *and* the situation. A leadership situation can be placed along a continuum of favorability, depending on three factors. First, **leader–follower relations** are considered good if followers trust and respect the leader. Good relations are obviously more favorable for leader effectiveness than poor relations. Second, **task structure** is high when a group has clear goals and a clear means for achieving these goals. High task structure is more favorable for the leader than low task structure. Third, **position power** is the ability to reward or punish subordinates for their behavior. For example, middle-level managers who might be constrained in their ability to reward and punish most of the people they have to influence, have less position power than a CEO.[77]

Fiedler's analysis of a number of studies that used the LPC scale suggested that task-oriented leaders are most effective in situations that are either extremely favorable or extremely unfavorable. Relationship-oriented leaders, on the other hand, achieve their greatest success in situations of moderate favorability. Although this was one of the first comprehensive theories of leadership, and is hence important historically, the theory has been criticized on numerous grounds as being "too data driven." According to his critics, Fiedler started with a set of results that he tried to explain, rather than with a logical, deductive theory. In addition, the LPC measure itself has aroused controversy. Critics have questioned what the scale actually measures and how well it measures this variable.[78]

Vroom–Yetton Decision Tree Model

Fiedler's comprehensive model focused on personality characteristics of the leader. In contrast, the *decision tree model of leadership* developed by Victor Vroom and his colleagues emphasizes the fact that leaders achieve success through effective decision making.[79] Vroom's model recognizes four general styles of leadership decision making: *authoritarian, consultative, delegation,* and *group based.* These alternatives are then broken down into seven specific decision styles: three that are appropriate to both individual and group decisions, two that are appropriate only to decisions involving individual followers, and two that are appropriate only to decisions that involve an entire group of followers (see Table 10.4).

Like all comprehensive theories of leadership, the decision tree model proposes that the most effective leadership style depends on characteristics of both the situation and the followers. Specifically, the model asks eight questions—three about the situation and five about the followers—to determine which of the seven leadership styles outlined in Table 10.4 is best. The decision tree presented in Figure 10.5 makes the question-and-answer process easy. Responding to questions A through H leads to one of eighteen answers, each of which identifies one or more decision-making styles that are appropriate to the problem confronted. To choose among two or more styles, the leader must decide whether to maximize the speed of decision making or the personal development of subordinates.

Table 10.4 The Seven Decision Styles in the Vroom–Yetton Decision Tree Model of Leadership

For all problems:

AI You solve the problem or make the decision yourself, using information available to you at the time.

AII You obtain any necessary information from subordinates and then decide on the solution to the problem yourself. You may or may not tell subordinates what the problem is in getting the information from them. The role played by your subordinates in making the decision is clearly one of providing specific information that you request, rather than one of generating or evaluating solutions.

CI You share the problem with the relevant subordinates individually, getting their ideas and suggestions without bringing them together as a group. Then *you* make the decision. This decision may or may not reflect your subordinates' influence.

For individual problems:	*For group problems:*
GI You share the problem with one of your subordinates, and together you analyze the problem and arrive at a mutually satisfactory solution in an atmosphere of free and open exchange of information and ideas. You both contribute to the resolution of the problem, with the relative contribution of each being dependent on knowledge rather than formal authority.	DI You delegate the problem to one of your subordinates, providing any relevant information that you possess, but giving your subordinate responsibility for solving the problem independently. Any solution that the person reaches will receive your support.
CII You share the problem with your subordinates in a group meeting. In this meeting you obtain their ideas and suggestions. Then *you* make the decision, which may or may not reflect your subordinates' influence.	GII You share the problem with your subordinates as a group. Together you generate and evaluate alternatives and attempt to reach agreement (consensus) on a solution. Your role is much like that of chairperson, coordinating the discussion, keeping it focused on the problem, and making sure that the critical issues are discussed. You do not try to influence the group to adopt "your" solution and are willing to accept and implement any solution that has support of the entire group.

Note: A stands for authoritarian, C for consultative, D for delegative, and G for group based.

Source: Adapted from V. H. Vroom, "Leadership," in *Handbook of Industrial and Organizational Psychology*, ed. M. D. Dunnette (Chicago: Rand McNally, 1976).

Autocratic approaches favor speed, whereas consultative or group approaches favor employee growth.

For example, suppose you are a corporate vice president who has just been given the responsibility for starting up a new plant in a developing country, and you must choose a plant manager. Should it be one of your five current and highly experienced plant managers? Should it be someone from outside the firm who has had experience working overseas? Should it be a citizen of the target country? As vice president, you might move through the decision tree as follows:

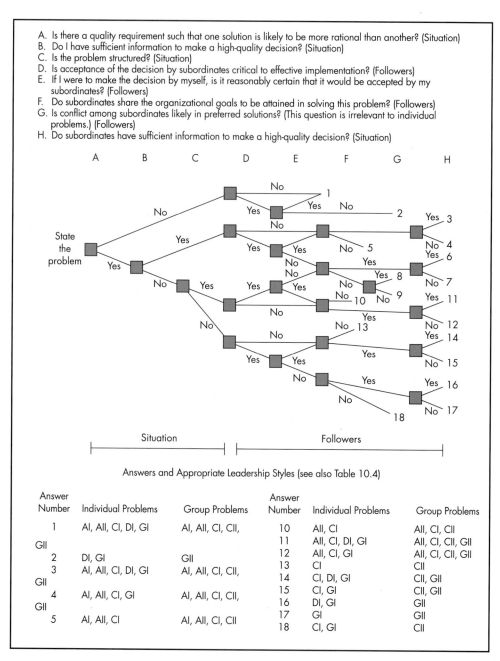

A. Is there a quality requirement such that one solution is likely to be more rational than another? (Situation)
B. Do I have sufficient information to make a high-quality decision? (Situation)
C. Is the problem structured? (Situation)
D. Is acceptance of the decision by subordinates critical to effective implementation? (Followers)
E. If I were to make the decision by myself, is it reasonably certain that it would be accepted by my subordinates? (Followers)
F. Do subordinates share the organizational goals to be attained in solving this problem? (Followers)
G. Is conflict among subordinates likely in preferred solutions? (This question is irrelevant to individual problems.) (Followers)
H. Do subordinates have sufficient information to make a high-quality decision? (Situation)

Answers and Appropriate Leadership Styles (see also Table 10.4)

Answer Number	Individual Problems	Group Problems	Answer Number	Individual Problems	Group Problems
1	AI, AII, CI, DI, GI	AI, AII, CI, CII, GII	10	AII, CI	AII, CI, CII
2	DI, GI	GII	11	AII, CI, DI, GI	AII, CI, CII, GII
3	AI, AII, CI, DI, GI	AI, AII, CI, CII, GII	12	AII, CI, GI	AII, CI, CII, GII
4	AI, AII, CI, GI	AI, AII, CI, CII, GII	13	CI	CII
5	AI, AII, CI	AI, AII, CI, CII	14	CI, DI, GI	CII, GII
			15	CI, GI	CII, GII
			16	DI, GI	GII
			17	GI	GII
			18	CI, GI	CII

Figure 10.5 The Vroom–Yetton Decision Tree Model of Leadership

Source: Adapted from V. H. Vroom, "Leadership," in *Handbook of Industrial and Organizational Psychology*, ed. M. D. Dunnette (Chicago: Rand McNally, 1976).

Question A: Yes. Some managers might be better suited than others.

Question B: No. You, the vice president, might not know all the interests or past experience that would be relevant to the assignment.

Question C: No. This problem is a new one for the company, and thus no clear guidelines dictate what steps to take.

Question D: Yes. Your current managers could all find good jobs with other firms in their own country if they refused the overseas job.

Question E: No. The decision will have too large an effect on subordinates' lives.

Question F: Yes. They have been with the company a long time and are committed to the organization.

Question H: No. Only you, the vice president, know about many details of the assignment.

The "no" response to question H leads to answer number 17. This answer, applied to a group problem, eliminates both autocratic and consultative styles and recommends the GII group-based decision-making style.

Early studies of the model's usefulness asked managers to think about past decisions that were effective or ineffective and had them trace their decision processes back to see whether they had followed the model's prescriptions. When the managers' decision-making processes were consistent with the model, 68 percent of decisions were effective, compared to only 22 percent when decisions violated the model. Research also indicates that most managers' natural decision-making processes seem to violate the model's prescriptions. In particular, managers tend to overuse the consultative CII style and underutilize the group-based GII style. The difference between these two styles is subtle but critical; the leader retains ultimate decision-making responsibility in the first but not the second. Giving up this ultimate responsibility is difficult for many leaders, because they know they could ultimately be blamed for the employees' mistakes.[80]

Path–Goal Theory

The most comprehensive theory of leadership to date and the theory that best exemplifies all aspects of the transactional model is the *path–goal theory of leadership*.[81] At the heart of the path–goal theory is the notion that the leader's primary purpose is to motivate followers by clarifying goals and identifying the best paths to achieve those goals. Because motivation is essential to the leader role, this approach is based on the expectancy theory of motivation (described in Chapter 5) and emphasizes the three motivational variables that leaders can influence through their behaviors or decision-making styles: (1) valences, (2) instrumentalities, and (3) expectancies.

The job of the leader, according to the path–goal theory, is to manipulate these three factors in desirable ways. Correspondingly, the theory's proponents recommend that leaders fulfill three major roles. First, leaders need to *manipulate follower valences* by recognizing or arousing needs for outcomes that the leader can control. Second, leaders must *manipulate follower instrumentalities* by ensuring that high performance results in satisfying outcomes for followers via contingent rewards and punishments.[82] Third, leaders need to *manipulate follower expectancies* by reducing frustrating barriers to performance. This can often be accomplished by leveraging the leader's larger social network for the benefit of the subordinates, whose networks are more constrained.[83]

The path–goal theory proposes that four behavioral styles can enable leaders to manipulate the three motivational variables: (1) directive, (2) supportive, (3) participative, and (4)

Table 10.5 The Path–Goal Theory's Four Behavioral Styles

Directive leadership	The leader is authoritarian. Subordinates know exactly what is expected of them, and the leader gives specific directions. Subordinates do not participate in decision making.
Supportive leadership	The leader is friendly and approachable and shows a genuine concern for subordinates.
Participative leadership	The leader asks for and uses suggestions from subordinates but still makes the decisions.
Achievement-oriented leadership	The leader sets challenging goals for subordinates and shows confidence that they will attain these goals.

Source: Adapted from R. T. Keller, "A Test of the Path–Goal Theory of Leadership with Need for Clarity as a Moderator in Research and Development Organizations," *Journal of Applied Psychology* 74 (1989): 208–212.

achievement-oriented leadership. As described in Table 10.5, these styles are composed both of behaviors, such as initiating structure, and of decision-making styles, such as the authoritarian approach. In each case, the leader's effectiveness depends on follower and situation characteristics. Much like the substitutes for leadership approach, the path–goal theory recognizes that situational characteristics can make leader behavior unnecessary or impossible.

Researchers have tested small parts of the path–goal model. Some of their findings are as follows:

- *Leader* participative behavior results in satisfaction in *situations* where the task is nonroutine, but only for *followers* who are nonauthoritarian.[84]
- *Leader* supportive behavior results in *follower* satisfaction, but only in *situations* where the task is highly structured.
- *Leader* achievement-oriented behavior results in improved performance, but only when *followers* are committed to goals.[85]

Perhaps because the theory is so complex, no one has yet undertaken a comprehensive study of the path–goal theory that tests every variable. The theoretical framework provided by the path–goal theory, however, is an excellent one for generating, testing, and understanding the complexities of the leadership process. Moreover, its tie to the expectancy theory of motivation makes it particularly suitable for leadership as conceptualized by Mintzberg— that is, the leader as a group motivator. So, for example, if someone wants to motivate technical workers to assume leadership roles, that person needs to (1) make sure leadership roles are valued (and not given short-shrift compared to technical competence); (2) help people see the link between assuming leadership roles and rewards; and (3) help people develop the skills they need so that their expectations for success in leadership roles is enhanced. Indeed, these are the three exact steps currently taking place in companies such as GE and IBM that are well known for their leadership development programs. Many technical companies currently faced with leadership succession problems are trying to develop similar programs.[86] The overall goal of these programs is to produce dual-threat leaders like Marissa Mayer, who have both the technical skills and social influence skills to lead in a complex and dynamic environment.[87]

The Integrated Leadership Model Revisited

This chapter began with a discussion of an integrated model of leadership and expressed a view of leadership as a complex interaction involving characteristics of the leader, the followers, and the situation. These ideas provided a framework for our discussion of several theories of leadership that vary in breadth and emphasis. Figure 10.6 depicts the dynamic relationships among the elements of these several theories as they fit together in an *integrated model of leadership*. At the core of this model is the notion that the purpose of leaders is to meet the performance and satisfaction needs of individual group members. Through their abilities and personality characteristics, their behaviors, and their decision-making styles, leaders must affect their followers' valences, instrumentalities, and expectancies.

The first key to applying this model to your own leadership situation is to engage in self-assessment to learn your standing on various traits (for example, extroversion or LPC), behavioral tendencies (on dimensions such as consideration and initiating structure), and decision-making style (autocratic, consultative, participative, delegative). High levels of self-awareness are critical for leadership effectiveness and can often be raised through 360-degree feedback interventions like those discussed in Chapter 4.[88]

Leaders must recognize that these phenomena are affected by a variety of follower characteristics. A trait, behavior, or decision style that works well with one group of followers is unlikely to work well with another group. Thus, the second key to applying this model to your own leadership situation is to make a critical assessment of those people who are following you, in terms of their maturity, competence, and cohesiveness, to determine the degree of match between their characteristics and yours.

Finally, the situation that leaders find themselves in will also affect the relationship between the leaders' traits, behaviors, and decision styles on the one hand, and group effectiveness on the other. Thus, the third key to applying this model is that leaders need to study the

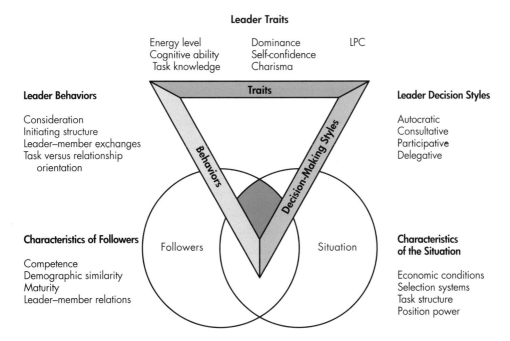

Figure 10.6 **The Fully Articulated Integrated Model of Leadership**

situation they are in (for example, in terms of task structure or the leader's power to change certain conditions like the overall economy) to determine what kinds of leadership will be most effective with this specific configuration of followers and situation. Effective leadership requires careful analysis of, and reaction to, the three forces—leader, followers, and situation—highlighted in the integrated framework you have learned about in this chapter. Although this might seem complex, as we saw in the story that opened this chapter dealing with Yahoo! and Marissa Mayer, the criteria for what makes for an excellent leader are constantly changing. A leader cannot simply assume that what worked well for one group of followers in one situation is likely to work for all followers in all situations.

Summary

Leadership differs from management in that leading is merely one task of managerial work. The emergence and continued success of a *leader* is a complex function of personal characteristics, characteristics of the *followers*, and characteristics of the *situation*. Important personal characteristics of a leader seem to include high extroversion and conscientiousness, as well as task knowledge. Important dimensions of leader behavior include *consideration* of employee needs (sometimes referred to as a *relationship orientation* or concern for people), *initiating structure* (sometimes referred to as a *task orientation* or concern for production), and leader–member exchange behaviors that separate subordinates into in-groups and out-groups. Leaders also differ in terms of their decision-making styles. *Authoritarian* leaders make all decisions for their followers. Leaders who take a *laissez-faire* approach leave followers to do as they please. Leaders may also take a *democratic* approach, working actively with followers to ensure that all group members have a chance to contribute to a task. According to the *integrated model of leadership*, the effectiveness of these different behaviors and decision-making styles is contingent on characteristics of the followers and of the situation. Followers differ along several important dimensions. They might be highly knowledgeable, mature, professional, and committed to the organization and its mission, or they might be quite the opposite. Different leadership styles will be required to work effectively with followers with different characteristics or in different situations.

Review Questions

1. Theories of leadership differ in terms of how adaptable they suggest the leader can be. Of the theories discussed in this chapter, choose two that suggest the leader is inflexible and two that suggest the leader is readily adaptable. Which of these two conflicting perspectives seems more likely to be true? Are leaders born or are they made?
2. Most of the early research on leadership involved leaders who were almost exclusively white and male. Demographic research suggests that increasingly fewer of the new entrants in the labor force will be white males. Which theories of leadership might need to be seriously reexamined because of this change? Which do you feel will generalize well to the new workforce?
3. This chapter discussed the LPC scale. Although no such instrument exists, what if there were a least-preferred leader scale? Who would be your least-preferred leader? Why? Can you think of followers other than yourself, or situations other than the one you face, for which this person might be an excellent leader?
4. Although we can think of a few exceptions, in general people who achieve preeminence as leaders in business organizations do not achieve success as political leaders. What are some characteristics of leaders, followers, or situations that make this kind of transition difficult

Notes

1 A. Efrati and J. Letzing, "Google's Mayer Takes Over as Yahoo Chief," *Wall Street Journal*, July 17, 2012, http://online.wsj.com/news/articles/SB100014240527023037549045775 31230541447956.

2 Jacob Weisberg, "Yahoo's Marissa Mayer: Hail to the Chief," *Vogue*, August 16, 2013, http://www.vogue.com/magazine/article/hail-to-the-chief-yahoos-marissa-mayer/#1.

3 B. Stone, "Reading the Mind of Marissa Mayer," *Bloomberg Businessweek*, July 23, 2012, 30–31.

4 R. Foroohar, "She's Feeling Luck: Why Mother-to-Be Marissa Mayer Is a Smart Pick to Reinvent a Laboring Yahoo," *Bloomberg Businessweek*, July 30, 2012, 17.

5 E. Klein, "Mom-to-Be in the Corner Office," *Bloomberg Businessweek*, July 30, 2012, 8.

6 R. Bell, "Turning Their Backs on Telecommuting," *Workforce Management*, April 2013, 46.

7 F. Hanson, "Building Better Leaders . . . Faster," *Workforce Management*, June 9, 2008, 25–28.

8 S. Caudron, "Where Have All the Leaders Gone?" *Workforce*, December 2002, 29–31.

9 C. D. Crossley, C. D. Cooper, and T. S. Wernsing, "Making Things Happen Through Challenging Goals: Leader Proactivity, Trust, and Business-Unit Performance," *Journal of Applied Psychology* 98 (2013): 540–549.

10 J. R. Meindl and S. B. Ehrlich, "The Romance of Leadership and the Evaluation of Organizational Performance," *Academy of Management Journal* 30 (1987): 91–109.

11 A. Woolner and F. Gillette, "Southern Comfort," *Bloomberg Businessweek*, July 3, 2013, 21–23.

12 A. Jago, "Leadership: Perspectives in Theory and Research," *Management Sciences* 28 (1982): 315–336.

13 H. Mintzberg, *The Nature of Managerial Work* (New York: Harper & Row, 1973).

14 J. M. Brett and L. K. Stroh, "Working 61 Hours a Week: Why Managers Do It," *Journal of Applied Psychology* 88 (2003): 67–78.

15 J. Bos, "Top Trends in Training and Leadership Development," *Workforce Management*, November 19, 2007, 35–38.

16 J. Reingold, "Meet Your New Leader," *CNNMoney.com*, November 14, 2008, 1.

17 J. Zweig, "Lesson from Buffett: Doubt Yourself," *Wall Street Journal*, May 5, 2013, http://blogs.wsj.com/moneybeat/2013/05/05/a-lesson-from-buffett-doubt-yourself/.

18 A. M. Grant, F. Gino, and D. A. Hoffman, "Reversing the Extraverted Leadership Advantage: The Role of Employee Proactivity," *Academy of Management Journal* 54 (2011): 528–550.

19 J. S. Lublin, "A Curse upon Your Career," *Wall Street Journal*, May 24, 2012, http://online.wsj.com/news/articles/SB10001424052702304840904577422683764866606.

20 D. S. DeRue, J. D. Nahrgang, J. R. Hollenbeck, and K. Workman, "A Quasi-Experimental Study of After-Event Reviews and Leadership Development," *Journal of Applied Psychology* 97 (2102): 997–1015.

21 S. E. Ante and J. S. Lublin, "Young CEO's: Are They Up to the Job?" *Wall Street Journal*, February 7, 2012, http://online.wsj.com/article/SB10001424052970203315804577207131063501 196.html.

22 S. V. Marinova, H. Moon, and D. Kamdar, "Getting Ahead or Getting Along? The Two-Facet Conceptualization of Conscientiousness and Leadership Emergence, *Organization Science* 24 (2013): 1257–1276.

23 T. A. Judge, J. E. Bono, R. Ilies, and M. W. Gerhart, "Personality and Leadership: A Qualitative and Quantitative Review," *Journal of Applied Psychology* 87 (2002): 765–780.

24 T. R. Hinken and C. A. Schriesheim, "An Examination of Non-Leadership," *Journal of Applied Psychology* 93 (2008): 1234–1248.

25 S. Truglia, "How to Live with the S.O.B.," *BusinessWeek*, September 1, 2008, 51.

26 K. Lewin, R. Lippitt, and R. K. White, "Patterns of Aggressive Behavior in Experimentally Created Social Climates," *Journal of Social Psychology* 10 (1939): 271–301.

27 S. Aryee, Z. X. Chen, L. Y. Sun, and Y. A. Debrah, "Antecedents and Outcomes of Abusive Supervision," *Journal of Applied Psychology* 92 (2007): 191–201.

28 R. B. Williams, "Why Steve Jobs Was Not a Leader," *Psychology Today*, April 7, 2012, http://www.psychologytoday.com/blog/wired-success/201204/why-steve-jobs-was-not-leader.

29 M. J. Gelfand, L. M. Leslie, K. Keller, and C. de Dreu, "Conflict Cultures in Organizations: How Leaders Shape Conflict Cultures and the Organization-Level Consequences," *Journal of Applied Psychology* 97 (2012): 1131–1147.

30 D. B. Welsh, F. Luthans, and S. M. Summer, "Managing Russian Factory Workers: The Impact of U.S.-Based Behavioral and Participative Techniques," *Academy of Management Journal* 36 (1993): 58–79.

31 N. C. Morse and E. Reimer, "The Experimental Change of a Major Organizational Variable," *Journal of Abnormal and Social Psychology* 52 (1956): 120–129.

32 R. M. Stodgill and A. E. Coons, *Leader Behavior: Its Description and Measurement* (Columbus: Ohio State University, Bureau of Business Research, 1957), 75.

33 B. Stone, "How Cheap Is Craig Jelinek?" *Bloomberg Businessweek*, June 6, 2013, 55–58.

34 R. Blake and J. S. Mouton, *The Managerial Grid III: The Key to Leadership Excellence* (Houston, TX: Gulf, 1985); R. Blake and A. A. McCanse, *Leadership Dilemmas—Grid Solutions* (Houston, TX: Gulf, 1991), 21–31.

35 L. L. Larson, J. G. Hunt, and R. Osburn, "The Great Hi–Hi Leader Myth: A Lesson from Occam's Razor," *Academy of Management Journal* 19 (1976): 628–641.

36 M. J. Neubert, K. M. Kacmer, D. S. Carlson, L. B. Chonko, and J. A. Roberts, "Regulatory Focus as a Mediator of the Influence of Initiating Structure and Servant Leadership on Employee Behavior," *Journal of Applied Psychology* 93 (2008): 1220–1233.

37 D. Liu, H. Liao, and R. Loi, "The Dark Side of Leadership: A Three-level Investigation of the Cascading Effect of Abusive Supervision on Employee Creativity," *Academy of Management Journal* 55 (2012): 1187–1212.

38 J. M. Burns, *Leadership* (New York: Harper & Row, 1979), 2.

39 A. Erez, V. F. Misangyi, D. E. Johnson, M. A. LePine, and K. C. Halverson, "Stirring the Hearts of Followers: Charismatic Leadership as the Transferal of Positive Emotions," *Journal of Applied Psychology* 93 (2008): 602–616.

40 M. Venus, D. Staam, and D. van Knippenberg, "Leader Emotion as a Catalyst of Effective Leader Communication of Visions, Value-Laden Messages, and Goals," *Organizational Behavior and Human Decision Processes* 122 (2013): 53–68.

41 F. O. Walumbwa, B. J. Avolio, and W. C. Zhu, "How Transformational Leadership Weaves Its Influence on Individual Job Performance: The Role of Identification and Efficacy Beliefs," *Personnel Psychology* 61 (2008): 793–825.

42 M. A. Hogg, D. van Knippenberg, and D. E. Rast, "Intergroup Leadership in Organizations: Leading across Group and Organization Boundaries," *Academy of Management Review* 37 (2012): 232–255.

43 M. E. Brown and L. K. Trevino, "Socialized Charismatic Leadership, Values Congruence, and Deviance in Work Groups," *Journal of Applied Psychology* 91 (2006): 954–962.

44 D. M. Herold, D. B. Felder, S. Caldwell, and Y. Liu, "The Effects of Transformational and Change Leadership on Employees' Commitment to Change: A Longitudinal Study," *Journal of Applied Psychology* 93 (2008): 346–357.

45 G. Chen and P. D. Bliese, "The Role of Different Levels of Leadership in Predicting Self- and Collective Efficacy: Evidence for Discontinuity," *Journal of Applied Psychology* 87 (2002):549–556.

46 J. C. Pastor, J. R. Meindl, and M. C. Mayo, "A Network Effects Model of Charisma Attributions," *Academy of Management Journal* 45 (2002): 410–420.

47 B. M. Bass, B. J. Avolio, D. I. Jung, and Y. Berson, "Predicting Unit Performance by Assessing Transformational and Transactive Leadership," *Journal of Applied Psychology* 88 (2003): 207–218.

48 J. Schaubroeck, S. S. K. Lim, and S. A. Cha, "Embracing Transformational Leadership: Team Values and the Impact of Leader Behavior on Team Performance," *Journal of Applied Psychology* 92 (2007): 1020–1030.

49 T. Dvir, D. Eden, B. J. Avolio, and B. Shamir, "Impact of Transformational Leadership on Follower Development and Performance: A Field Experiment," *Academy of Management Journal* 45 (2002): 735–744.

50 R. T. Keller, "Transformational Leadership, Initiating Structure, and Substitutes for Leadership: A Longitudinal Study of Research and Development Team Performance," *Journal of Applied Psychology* 91 (2006): 202–210.

51 D. De Cremer and D. van Knippenberg, "How Do Leaders Promote Cooperation?" *Journal of Applied Psychology* 87 (2002): 858–866.

52 J. Pfeffer, "The Ambiguity of Leadership," *Academy of Management Review* 2 (1977): 104–112.

53 P. McGroaty, "No Award for African Leadership," *Wall Street Journal*, October 15, 2012, http://online.wsj.com/news/articles/SB10000872396390443675404578058190334025104.

54 Y. Ling, M. H. Lubatkin, Z. Simsek, and J. F. Viega, "The Impact of Transformational CEOs on the Performance of Small- to Medium-Sized Firms: Does Organizational Context Matter?" *Journal of Applied Psychology* 93 (2008): 923–934.

55 N. Shirouzu and J. Murphy, "Toyota to Change Leader amid Sales Slump," *Wall Street Journal*, December 24, 2008, A1.

56 D. Brady and M. Boyle, "Recipe for a CEO," *Bloomberg Businessweek*, June 27, 2011, 62–66.

57 J. Smerd, "Heirs Not Apparent," *Workforce Management*, December 1, 2007, 1–3.

58 G. Graen, "Role-Making Processes within Complex Organizations," in M. D. Dunnette, ed., *Handbook of Industrial and Organizational Psychology* (Chicago: Rand McNally, 1976), 1210–1259.

59 C. A. Schriesheim, S. L. Castro, and F. J. Yammarino, "Investigating Contingencies: An Examination of the Impact of Span of Supervision and Upward Controllingness on Leader–Member Exchange Using Traditional and Multivariate Within- and Between-Entities Analysis," *Journal of Applied Psychology* 85 (2000): 659–677.

60 D. A. Hoffman, F. P. Morgeson, and S. J. Gerras, "Climate as a Moderator of the Relationship between Leader–Member Exchange and Content-Specific Citizenship: Safety Climate as an Exemplar," *Journal of Applied Psychology* 88 (2003): 170–178.

61 R. Ilies, J. D. Nahrgang, and F. D. R. Morgeson, "Leader–Member Exchange and Citizenship Behaviors: A Meta-Analysis," *Journal of Applied Psychology* 92 (2007): 269–277.

62 S. Tangirala, S. G. Green, and R. Ramanujam, "In the Shadow of the Boss's Boss: Effects of Supervisors' Upward Exchange Relationships on Employees," *Journal of Applied Psychology* 92 (2007): 309–320.

63 Z. G. Chen, W. Lam, and J. A. Zhong, "Leader–Member Exchange and Member Performance: A New Look at Negative Feedback-Seeking Behavior and Team-Level Empowerment Climate," *Journal of Applied Psychology* 92 (2007): 202–212.

64 B. Erdogen and J. Enders, "Support from the Top: Supervisors' Perceived Organizational Support as a Moderator of Leader–Member Exchange to Satisfaction and Performance Relationships," *Journal of Applied Psychology* 92 (2007): 321–330.

65 A. S. Rosette, "Race Influences How Leaders Are Assessed," *Wall Street Journal*, January 3, 2012, http://online.wsj.com/news/articles/SB10001424052970203899504577128973024950032.

66 R. C. Liden, S. J. Wayne, and D. Stilwell, "A Longitudinal Study on the Early Development of Leader–Member Exchanges," *Journal of Applied Psychology* 78 (1993): 662–674.

67 P. Hersey and K. Blanchard, *Management of Organizational Behavior* (Englewood Cliffs, NJ: Prentice Hall, 1991).

68 S. K. Lam and J. Schaubroeck, "A Field Experiment Testing Frontline Opinion Leaders as Change Agents," *Journal of Applied Psychology* 85 (2000): 987–995.

69 M. Krzyzewski, "Hard Choices," *Bloomberg Businessweek*, July 16, 2012, 72.

70 N. M. Lorinkova, M. J. Pearsall, and H. P. Sims, "Examining the Differential Longitudinal Performance of Directive Versus Empowering Leadership in Teams," *Academy of Management Journal* 56 (2013): 573–596.

71 P. M. Podsakoff, S. B. MacKenzie, and W. H. Bommer, "Meta-Analysis of the Relationships between Kerr and Jermier's Substitutes for Leadership and Employee Job Attitudes, Role Perceptions, and Performance," *Journal of Applied Psychology* 81 (1996): 380–399.

72 R. E. Silverman, "Some Tech Firms Ask: Who Needs Managers?" *Wall Street Journal*, August 6, 2013, http://online.wsj.com/news/articles/SB10001424127887323420604578652051466314748.

73 N. Li, D. S. Chiaburu, B. L. Kirkman, and Z. T. Xie, "Spotlight on the Followers: An Examination of Moderators of Relationships Between Transformational Leadership and Subordinates Citizenship and Taking Charge," *Personnel Psychology* 66 (2013): 225–260.

74 R. E. Silverman "Who's the Boss? There Isn't One," *Wall Street Journal*, June 19, 2012, http://online.wsj.com/news/articles/SB10001424052702303379204577474953586383604.

75 F. E. Fiedler, "Engineering the Job to Fit the Manager," *Harvard Business Review* 43 (1965): 115–122.

76 C. A. Schriesheim, B. D. Bannister, and W. H. Money, "Psychometric Properties of the LPC Scale: An Extension of Rice's Review," *Academy of Management Review* 4 (1979): 287–290.

77 M. Korn, "What It's Like Being a Middle Manager Today," *Wall Street Journal*, August 5, 2013.

78 V. H. Vroom, "Leadership," in M. D. Dunnette, ed., *Handbook of Industrial and Organizational Psychology* (Chicago: Rand McNally, 1976), 912.

79 V. H. Vroom and A. G. Jago, "The Role of the Situation in Leadership," *American Psychologist* 62 (2007): 17–24.

80 R. J. House, "A Path–Goal Theory of Leadership Effectiveness," *Administrative Science Quarterly* 16 (1971): 321–338.

81 P. M. Podsakoff, W. H. Bommer, and N. P. Podsakoff, "Relationships between Leader Reward and Punishment Behavior and Subordinate Attitudes, Perceptions, and Behaviors: A Meta-Analytic Review of Existing and New Research," *Organizational Behavior and Human Decision Processes* 99 (2006): 113–142.

82 P. Balkundi and D. A. Harrison, "Ties, Leaders, and Time in Teams: Strong Inference about Network Structure's Effects on Team Viability and Performance," *Academy of Management Journal* 40 (2006): 49–68.

83 R. T. Keller, "A Test of the Path–Goal Theory of Leadership with Need for Clarity as a Moderator in Research and Development Organizations," *Journal of Applied Psychology* 74 (1989): 208–212.

84 J. E. Stinson and T. W. Johnson, "A Path–Goal Theory of Leadership: A Partial Test and Suggested Refinements," *Academy of Management Journal* 18 (1975): 242–252.

85 M. Erez and I. Zidon, "Effect of Goal Acceptance on the Relationship between Goal Difficulty and Performance," *Journal of Applied Psychology* 69 (1984): 69–78.

86 P. Burrows, "The Least Popular Job in Silicon Valley," *Bloomberg Businessweek*, October 3, 2011, 39–40.

87 R. M. Fuller and B. Hanson, "Do Techies Make Good Leaders?" *Wall Street Journal*, August 22, 2012, http://online.wsj.com/news/articles/SB10001424052748704548604575097531072898668.

88 A. D. Walker, J. W. Smither, and D. A. Waldman, "A Longitudinal Examination of Concomitant Changes in Team Leadership and Customer Satisfaction," *Personnel Psychology* 61 (2008): 547–577.

Part IV

Macro Organizational Behavior

Chapter 11

Power, Politics, and Conflict

Walmart is ubiquitous in the U.S. retail economy and is making inroads into other markets throughout the world. The company is a prominent employer in each of the towns and cities in which it does business. For both of these reasons, Walmart's employment practices are increasingly the subject of public debate. Entering this debate are more than 4,000 current employees comprising the Organization United for Respect at Walmart, or *OUR Walmart*, who have staged protests outside Walmart's stores to voice their concerns about company policies and seek public support for their efforts. High on OUR Walmart's list of demands are full-time jobs with predictable schedules instead of part-time jobs with hours that can change every few weeks, wages and benefits generous enough to support workers' families, and a company culture of respect for employees and the company alike.[1]

In banding together and reaching out to the surrounding community, the members of OUR Walmart have entered into the political realm, seeking to advance their agenda by using coalition politics and public support to increase their power relative to that of the company. Far from being the exception, political tactics in the pursuit of shared interests are commonplace in contemporary organizations. Power, politics, and conflict in organizations can increase productivity and efficiency—or reduce them substantially. Political processes can even determine organizational existence and strategic direction. Restructuring, often stimulated as much by internal power struggles as by external market conditions, is prompting managers to search out new strategic directions for their firms. In the process, political considerations are altering the careers of thousands of employees—both managers and nonmanagers. At the same time that these events are creating opportunities for some, they are costing many others their jobs.[2]

Understanding power, politics, and conflict is therefore critical to managerial success—and survival—in today's business organizations. To provide this understanding, Chapter 11 begins with a discussion of the nature, sources, and consequence of power. Next, it turns to the closely related topic of organizational politics, the process through which people acquire and use power to get their way. Finally, it examines conflict, describing the origins, results, and resolution of political confrontation in organizations.

Power in Organizations

When asked to define *power*, many people recall master politicians such as Great Britain's wartime Prime Minister Winston Churchill or former U.S. President Bill Clinton describing power as the ability to influence the behaviors of others and persuade them to do things they would not otherwise do.[3] For other people, images of the less powerful come to mind, leading them to define power as the ability to avoid others' attempts to influence their behavior. In truth, both of these views are correct. That is, **power** is the ability both to influence the conduct of others and to resist unwanted influence in return.[4]

According to David McClelland, people are driven to gain and use power by a need for power—which he calls *nPow*—that is learned during childhood and adolescence.[5] This need for power can have several different effects on the way people think and behave. Generally speaking, people with high nPow are competitive, aggressive, prestige-conscious, action oriented, and prone to join groups. They are likely to be effective managers if, in addition to pursuing power, they also do the following:

- use power to accomplish organizational goals instead of using it to satisfy personal interests
- coach subordinates and use participatory management techniques rather than autocratic, authoritarian methods
- remain aware of the importance of managing interpersonal relations but avoid developing close relationships with subordinates.[6]

McClelland's research has suggested that seeking power and using it to influence others are not activities to be shunned or avoided in and of themselves. In fact, the process of management *requires* that power be used.

Interpersonal Sources of Power

If management requires the use of power, then what is the source of a manager's power? In their pioneering research, John French and Bertram Raven sought to answer this question by identifying the major bases, or sources, of power in organizations.[7] As indicated in Table 11.1, they discovered five types of power: reward, coercive, legitimate, referent, and expert power.

Reward power is based on the ability to allocate desirable outcomes—either the receipt of positive things or the elimination of negative things. Praise, promotions, raises, desirable job assignments, and time off from work are outcomes that managers often control. If they can make decisions about the distribution of such rewards, managers can use them to acquire and maintain reward power. Similarly, eliminating unwanted outcomes, such as unpleasant working conditions or mandatory overtime, can be used to reward employees. For instance, police officers who receive clerical support to help complete crime reports generally look at this reduction of paperwork as rewarding.

Table 11.1 **Five Types of Power and Their Sources**

Type of power	Source of power
Reward	Control over rewarding outcomes
Coercive	Control over punishing outcomes
Legitimate	Occupation of legitimate position of authority
Referent	Attractiveness, charisma
Expert	Expertise, knowledge, talent

Source: Adapted from J. R. French, Jr., and B. Raven, "The Bases of Social Power," in D. Cartwright, ed., *Studies in Social Power* (Ann Arbor: Institute for Social Research, University of Michigan, 1959), 150–165.

Whereas reward power controls the allocation of desirable outcomes, **coercive power** is based on the distribution of undesirable outcomes—either the receipt of something negative or the removal of something positive. People who control punishing outcomes can get others to conform to their wishes by threatening to penalize them in some way. That is, coercive power exploits fear. To influence subordinates' behaviors, managers might resort to punishments such as public scoldings, assignment of undesirable tasks, loss of pay, or, taken to the extreme, layoffs, demotions, or dismissals.

Legitimate power is based on norms, values, and beliefs that teach that particular people have the legitimate right to govern or influence others. From childhood, people learn to accept the commands of authority figures—first parents, then teachers, and finally bosses. This well-learned lesson gives people with authority the power to influence other people's attitudes and behaviors. In most organizations, authority is distributed in the form of a hierarchy (Chapter 2). People who hold positions of hierarchical authority are accorded legitimate power by virtue of the fact that they are office holders. For example, the vice president of marketing at a firm such as Philip Morris issues orders and expects people in subordinate positions to obey them because of the clout that being a vice president affords.

Have you ever admired a teacher, a student leader, or someone else whose personality, way of interacting with other people, values, goals, and other characteristics were exceptionally attractive? If so, you probably wanted to develop and maintain a close, continuing relationship with that person. This desire can provide this individual with **referent power**. Someone you hold in such esteem is likely to influence you through his or her attitudes and behaviors. In time you might come to identify with the admired person to such an extent that you begin to think and act alike. Referent power is also called *charismatic power*.

Famous religious leaders and political figures often develop and use referent power. Mahatma Gandhi, John F. Kennedy, Martin Luther King, Jr., and Nelson Mandela, for example, have all used personal charisma to profoundly influence the thoughts and behaviors of others. Of course, referent power can also be put to more prosaic use. Consider advertising's use of famous athletes and actors to help sell products. Athletic shoe manufacturers such as Nike, Reebok, and Adidas, for example, employ sports celebrities as spokespeople in an effort to influence consumers to buy their products. Similarly, movie producers try to ensure the success of their films by including well-known stars in the cast.

Expert power derives from the possession of expertise, knowledge, and talent. People who are seen as experts in a particular area can influence others in two ways. First, they can provide other people with knowledge that enables or causes those individuals to change their attitudes or behavior. For example, media critics provide reviews that shape people's attitudes about new books, movies, music, and television shows. Second, experts can demand conformity to their wishes as the price for sharing their knowledge. For instance, doctors, lawyers, and accountants provide advice that influences their clients' choices. Auto mechanics, plumbers, and electricians also exert a great deal of influence over customers who are not themselves talented craftspeople.

Conformity Responses to Interpersonal Power

How do employees respond when managers use the different kinds of power identified by French and Raven? According to Herbert Kelman, three distinctly different types of reactions are likely to occur as people respond to attempts to influence their behavior. As indicated in Table 11.2, they are compliance, identification, and internalization.[8]

Table 11.2 Three Responses to Interpersonal Power

Level	Description
Compliance	Conformity based on desire to gain rewards or avoid punishment. Continues as long as rewards are received or punishment is withheld.
Identification	Conformity based on attractiveness of the influencer. Continues as long as a relationship with the influencer can be maintained.
Internalization	Conformity based on the intrinsically satisfying nature of adopted attitudes or behaviors. Continues as long as satisfaction continues.

Source: Adapted from H. C. Kelman, "Compliance, Identification, and Internalization: Three Processes of Attitude Change," *Journal of Conflict Resolution* 2 (1958): 51–60.

Compliance ensues when people conform to the wishes or directives of others so as to acquire favorable outcomes for themselves in return. They adopt new attitudes and behaviors not because these choices are agreeable or personally fulfilling but, rather, because they lead to specific rewards and approval or head off specific punishments and disapproval. People are likely to continue to display such behaviors only as long as the favorable outcomes remain contingent on conformity.

Of the various types of power identified by French and Raven, reward and coercive power are the most likely to stimulate compliance, because both are based on linking employee performance with the receipt of positive or negative outcomes. Employees who work harder because a supervisor with reward power has promised them incentive payments are displaying compliance behavior. Similarly, employees who work harder to avoid punishments administered by a supervisor with coercive power are likely to continue doing so only while the threat of punishment remains salient.

Identification occurs when people accept the direction or influence of others because they identify with the power holders and seek to maintain relationships with them—not because they value or even agree with what they have been asked to do. French and Raven's concept of referent power is based on the same sort of personal attractiveness as is identification. Consequently, referent power and identification are likely to be closely associated with each other. Charismatic leaders are able to continue influencing other people's behaviors for as long as identification continues.

Finally, through *internalization*, people may adopt others' attitudes and behaviors because this course of action satisfies their personal needs or because they find those attitudes and behaviors to be congruent with their own personal values. In either case, they accept the power holders' influence wholeheartedly. Both legitimate and expert power can stimulate internalization, as these forms of power rely on personal credibility—the extent to which a person is perceived as truly possessing authority or expertise. This credibility can be used to convince people of the intrinsic importance of the attitudes and behaviors they are being asked to adopt.

Internalization leads people to find newly adopted attitudes and behaviors personally rewarding and self-reinforcing. A supervisor who can use her expertise to convince colleagues to use consultative leadership (see Chapter 10) can expect the other managers to continue consulting with their subordinates long after she has withdrawn from the situation. Likewise, a manager whose legitimate power lends credibility to the orders he issues can expect his subordinates to follow those orders even in the absence of rewards, punishments, or charismatic attraction.

A Model of Interpersonal Power: Assessment

French and Raven describe the different kinds of interpersonal power used in organizations, and Kelman identifies how people respond to this use. Although valuable as a tool for understanding power and its consequences, the model integrating these ideas, shown in Figure 11.1, is not entirely without fault. Questions arise as to whether the five bases of power are completely independent, as proposed by French and Raven, or whether they are so closely interrelated as to be virtually indistinguishable from one another. The idea that reward, coercive, and legitimate power often derive from company policies and procedures, for instance, has led some researchers to subsume these three types of power in a single category labeled **organizational power**. Similarly, because expert and referent power are both based on personal expertise or charisma, they have sometimes been lumped together into the category of **personal power**.

In fact, French and Raven's five bases of power might be even more closely interrelated than this categorization would suggest. In their study of two paper mills, Charles Greene and Philip Podsakoff found that changing just one source of managerial power affected employees' perceptions of three other types of power.[9] Initially, both paper mills used an incentive payment plan in which supervisors' monthly performance appraisals determined the employees' pay. At one mill, the incentive plan was changed to an hourly wage system in which seniority determined an employee's rate of pay. The existing incentive plan was left in place at the other mill. Following this change, the researchers found that employees at the first mill perceived their supervisors as having significantly less reward power—as we might expect. Surprisingly, however, they also saw significant changes in their supervisors' punishment, legitimate, and referent power. As shown in Figure 11.2, they attributed significantly more punishment power, a little less referent power, and substantially less legitimate power to their supervisors.

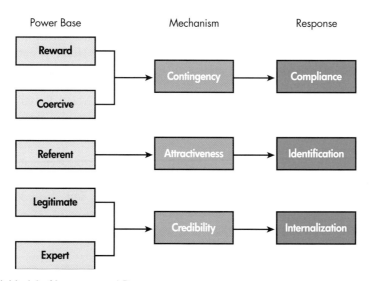

Figure 11.1 A Model of Interpersonal Power

Source: Adapted from H. C. Kelman, "Compliance, Identification, and Internalization: Three Processes of Attitude Change," *Journal of Conflict Resolution* 2 (1958): 51–60; M. Sussmann and R. P. Vecchio, "A Social Influence Interpretation of Worker Motivation," *Academy of Management Review* 7 (1982): 177–186.

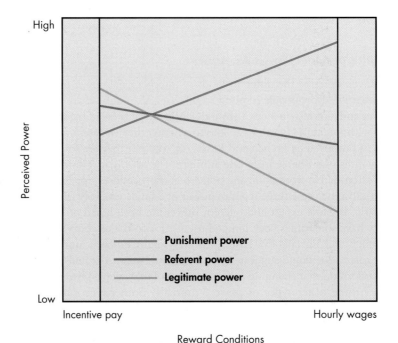

Figure 11.2 **Effects of a Change in Method of Payment on Perceived Bases of Power**
Source: Adapted from C. N. Greene and P. M. Podsakoff, "Effects of Withdrawal of a Performance-Contingent Reward on Supervisory Influence and Power," *Academy of Management Journal* 24 (1981): 527–542.

In contrast, employees in the second mill, where the incentive plan remained unchanged, reported no significant changes in their perceptions of their supervisors' reward, punishment, legitimate, and referent power. Because all other conditions were held constant in both mills, employees' changed perceptions in the first mill could not be attributed to other unknown factors. Instead, their perceptions of reward, coercive, legitimate, and referent power proved to be closely interrelated. This finding suggests that four of the five types of power identified by French and Raven appear virtually indistinguishable to interested observers.[10]

Despite this limitation, the model created by joining French and Raven's classification scheme with Kelman's theory is useful in analyzing social influence and *interpersonal* power in organizations. Managers can use this model to help predict how subordinates will conform to directives based on a particular type of power. For example, is the use of expertise likely to result in long-term changes in subordinates' behavior? Since the model shown in Figure 11.1 indicates that internalization is stimulated by the use of expert power, long-term behavioral changes are quite probable. Alternatively, subordinates might find the model useful as a means of understanding—and perhaps influencing—the behaviors of their superiors. For instance, an employee interested in influencing his boss to permanently change her style of management would be well advised to try using personal expertise.

Structural Sources of Power

In addition to the interpersonal sources discussed so far, power also derives from the *structure* of patterned work activities and flows of information found in every organization. Chapter 12

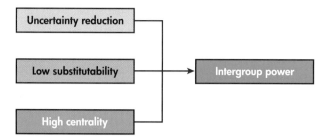

Figure 11.3 The Critical Contingencies Model of Power

Source: Adapted from D. J. Hickson, C. R. Hinings, C. A. Lee, R. H. Schenck, and J. M. Pennings, "A Strategic Contingencies Theory of Intraorganizational Power," *Administrative Science Quarterly* 16 (1971): 216–229.

will examine the topic of organizational structure in detail. The discussion here will, therefore, be limited to those characteristics of organizations that shape power relations—uncertainty reduction, substitutability, and centrality. As depicted in Figure 11.3, these three variables combine to form the critical contingencies model of power.[11]

Uncertainty Reduction

Critical contingencies are the things that an organization and its various parts need in order to accomplish organizational goals and continue surviving. The raw materials needed by a company to manufacture goods are critical contingencies. So, too, are the employees who make these goods, the customers who buy them, and the banks that provide loans to buy inventory and equipment. Information can also be a critical contingency.

Consider the financial data used by banks to decide whether to grant loans, or the mailing lists employed by catalog merchandisers to locate prospective customers. Uncertainty about the continued availability of such critical contingencies can threaten the organization's well-being. If a purchasing manager cannot be certain that she can buy raw materials at reasonable prices, then her organization's ability to start or continue productive work is compromised. Similarly, when a marketing department reports shifting consumer tastes, the firm's ability to sell what it has produced is threatened. Thus, as explained by Gerald Salancik and Jeffrey Pfeffer, the critical contingencies model of power is based on the principle that "those [individuals or groups] most able to cope with [their] organization's critical problems and uncertainties acquire power"[12] by trading *uncertainty reduction* for whatever they want in return.

One way to reduce uncertainty is by gaining *resource control*—that is, by acquiring and maintaining access to those resources that might otherwise be difficult to obtain.[13] A human resources management department might be able to reduce an important source of uncertainty in an organization that has experienced problems in attracting qualified employees if it can hire and retain a productive workforce. Similarly, a purchasing department that can negotiate discounts on raw materials can help reduce uncertainty related to whether the firm can afford to continue to produce its line of goods. Each of these departments, by delivering crucial resources and thereby reducing success-threatening uncertainty, can gain power.[14]

Information control offers another way to reduce uncertainty in organizations. Providing information about critical contingencies is particularly useful when such information can be used to predict or prevent threats to organizational operations.[15] Suppose, for example, that a telecommunication company's legal department learns of impending legislation that will restrict the company's ability to buy additional television stations unless it divests itself of the stations it already owns. By alerting management and recommending ways to form subsidiary companies to allow continued growth, the firm's legal department can eliminate much uncertainty for the firm.

A third way to reduce uncertainty is to acquire *decision-making control*—that is, to have input into the initial decisions about what sorts of resources will be critical contingencies. At any time, events might conspire to give certain groups power over others. This power, in turn, allows its possessors to determine the rules of the game or to decide such basic issues as what the company will produce, to whom it will market the product, and what kinds of materials, skills, and procedures will be needed. In the process, those already in power can make the contingencies they manage even more important to organizational well-being. In this manner, power can be used to acquire power of even greater magnitude—"the rich get richer."[16]

Substitutability

Whether individuals or groups gain power as a result of their success in reducing uncertainty depends partly on their **substitutability**. If others can serve as substitutes and reduce the same sort of uncertainty, then individuals or departments that need help in coping with uncertainty can turn to a variety of sources for aid. Hence no single source is likely to acquire much power under such a scenario. For example, a legal department's ability to interpret laws and regulations is unlikely to yield power for the department if legal specialists working in other departments can fulfill the same function. When substitutes are readily available, other departments can ignore the pressures of any particular group, so each group's ability to amass power is undermined.

If others can get help in coping with uncertainty only from the target group or person, however, this group or person is clearly in a position to barter uncertainty reduction for desired outcomes. For example, a research and development (R&D) group that serves as a company's sole source of new product ideas can threaten to reduce the flow of innovation if the firm does not provide the desired resources. The less substitutability present in a situation, the more likely that a particular group or person will be able to amass power.[17]

Centrality

The ability of a group or person to acquire power is also influenced by its **centrality**, or its position within the flow of work in the organization.[18] The ability to reduce uncertainty is unlikely to affect a group's power if no one outside the group knows that it has this ability and no one inside the group recognizes the importance of the ability. Simply because few other people know of its existence, a clerical staff located on the periphery of a company is unlikely to amass much power, even if its typing and filing activities bring it in direct contact with critically important information. When uncertainty emerges that the staff could help resolve, it is likely to be ignored because no one is aware of the knowledge and abilities possessed by the staff members.

The Critical Contingencies Model: Assessment

Despite a few criticisms, research strongly supports the critical contingencies model's suggestion that power is a function of uncertainty reduction, substitutability, and centrality.[19] An analysis of British manufacturing firms in business during the first half of the twentieth century confirms this idea.[20] The analysis revealed that accounting departments dominated organizational decision making in the Great Depression era preceding World War II because they kept costs down at a time when money was scarce. After the war ended, power shifted to purchasing departments as money became more readily available and strong consumer demand made access to plentiful supplies of raw materials more important. During the 1950s, demand dropped so precipitously that marketing became the most important problem facing British firms. As a result (and as predicted by the model), marketing and sales departments that succeeded in increasing company sales gained power over important decision-making processes.

In another study, researchers examined twenty-nine departments of the University of Illinois, looking at the departments' national reputations, teaching loads, and financial receipts from outside contracts and grants.[21] Their results indicated that each department's ability to influence university decision making was directly related to its reputation, teaching load, and grant contributions.

In addition, the amount of contract and grant money brought in from outside sources had an especially strong effect on departmental power. Contracts and grants provide operating funds critical to the survival of a public institution such as the University of Illinois. Thus, as predicted by the critical contingencies model, the power of each department in the university was directly related to its ability to contribute to the management of critical contingencies.

An even more intriguing piece of evidence supporting the critical contingencies model was discovered by Michel Crozier, a French sociologist who studied a government-owned tobacco company located just outside Paris.[22] As described by Crozier, maintenance mechanics in the tobacco company sought control over their working lives by refusing to share knowledge needed to repair crucial production equipment. The mechanics memorized repair manuals and then threw them away so that no one else could refer to them. In addition, they refused to let production employees or supervisors watch as they repaired the company's machines. They also trained their replacements in a closely guarded apprenticeship process, thereby ensuring that outsiders could not learn what they knew. Some mechanics even altered equipment so completely that the original manufacturer could not figure out how it worked. In this manner, the tobacco company's maintenance mechanics retained absolute control over the information and skill required to repair production equipment. In essence, the maintenance personnel ran the production facility as a result of the information they alone possessed about its equipment.

Crozier's account of the tobacco factory mechanics illustrates the usefulness of the critical contingencies model in explaining why people who have hierarchical authority and formal power sometimes lack the influence needed to manage workplace activities. If subordinates have the knowledge, skills, or abilities required to manage critical contingencies, thereby reducing troublesome uncertainties, they might gain enough power to disobey their hierarchical superiors. In turn, as long as superiors must depend on subordinates to manage such contingencies, it will be the subordinates—not the superiors—who determine which orders will be followed and which will be ignored.[23]

In sum, the critical contingencies model appears to describe the structural bases of power quite accurately. Its utility for contemporary managers lies in the observation that the roots of power lie in the ability to solve crucial organizational problems. Managers must understand and exploit this simple premise because such knowledge can help them acquire and keep the power needed to do their jobs.

Politics and Political Processes

Politics can be defined as activities in which individuals or groups engage so as to acquire and use power to advance their own interests. In essence, politics is power in action.[24] Although political behavior can be disruptive, it is not necessarily bad. The unsanctioned, unanticipated changes wrought by politics can, in fact, enhance organizational well-being by ridding companies of familiar but dysfunctional ways of doing things.[25] Nonetheless, because politics has a negative connotation, political behavior is seldom discussed openly in organizations. In fact, managers and employees might even deny that politics influences organizational activities. Research indicates, however, that politicking *does* occur and that it has measurable effects on organizational behavior.[26]

Personality and Politics

Why do people engage in politics? As with power in general, certain personal characteristics predispose people to exhibit political behaviors. For example, some people have a need for power (nPow), as identified by McClelland and discussed previously. Just as nPow drives people to seek out influence over others, it also motivates them to use this power for political gain.

Other researchers have suggested that people who exhibit the personality characteristic of **Machiavellianism**—the tendency to seek to control other people through opportunistic, manipulative behaviors—may also be inclined toward politics. In addition, studies have indicated that self-conscious people might be less likely than others to become involved in office politics because they fear being singled out as a focus of public attention and being evaluated negatively for engaging in politics. This fear keeps them from seeking power and using it for personal gain.[27]

Conditions That Stimulate Politics

In addition to personality characteristics such as nPow and Machiavellianism, certain conditions encourage political activity in organizations (see Figure 11.4). One such condition is *uncertainty* that can be traced to ambiguity and change (see Table 11.3). Uncertainty can hide or disguise people's behaviors, enabling them to engage in political activities that would otherwise be detected and prohibited. It can also trigger political behavior because it gives people a reason to be political—they might resort to politics in efforts to find ways to reduce uncertainty and provide them with added power and other personal benefits.

Besides uncertainty, other conditions that encourage political behavior include *organizational size, hierarchical level, membership heterogeneity,* and *decision importance.* Politicking is more prevalent in larger organizations than in smaller ones.[28] The presence of a greater number of people is more likely to hide the behaviors of any one person, enabling him or her to engage in political behaviors with less fear of discovery. Politics is also more common

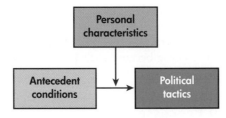

Figure 11.4 A Model of the Emergence of Politics

Source: Adapted from G. R. Ferris, G. S. Russ, and P. M. Fandt, "Politics in Organization," in R. A. Glacalone and P. Rosenfield, eds., *Impression Management in the Organization* (Hillsdale, NJ: Erlbaum, 1989), 143–170.

Table 11.3 Types of Uncertainty That Encourage Politics

Interruptions in the availability of critical resources or of information about these resources.

Ambiguity (no clear meaning) or equivocality (more than one possible meaning) in the information that is available.

Poorly defined goals, objectives, work roles, or performance measures.

Unclear rules for such things as who should make decisions, how decisions should be reached, or when decision making should occur.

Change of any type—for example, reorganization, budgetary reallocations, or procedural modifications.

Dependence on other individuals or groups, especially when that dependence is accompanied by competitiveness or hostility.

Source: Adapted from D. R. Beman and T. W. Sharkey, "The Use and Abuse of Corporate Politics," Business Horizons 30 (1987): 26–30; A. Raia, "Power, Politics, and the Human Resource Professional," Human Resource Planning 8 (1985): 198–209; J. P. Kotter, "Power, Dependence, and Effective Management," Harvard Business Review 55 (1977): 125–136.

among middle and upper managers, because the power required to engage in politics is usually concentrated among managers at these levels. In heterogeneous organizations, members share few interests and values and therefore see things very differently. Under such circumstances, political processes are likely to emerge as members compete to decide whose interests will be satisfied and whose will not. Finally, important decisions stimulate more politics than unimportant decisions do simply because less important issues attract less interest and attention.

Political Tactics

When personal characteristics and surrounding conditions favor them, a variety of political tactics might surface. Each tactic is intended to increase the power of one person or group relative to others. When power increases, so does the likelihood that the person or group will be able to seek out and acquire self-interested gains.[29]

Acquiring Interpersonal Power: Forming Affiliations

Forming **coalitions** or political affiliations with each other represents an important way for people to increase their power and pursue political gain beyond their individual grasp.[30] By banding together, people can share their collective control over rewards or punishments. They can also combine their expertise, legitimacy, and charisma. For instance, collective bargaining enables union members to obtain wages and conditions far superior to those that they could demand as individuals. Conversely, companies form trade associations so as to exchange information about collective bargaining and union agreements.

As part of the process of forming political affiliations, favors might be used to create a sense of indebtedness. People who pursue this tactic can increase the dependence of others by building up a bank of favors that are owed them. In the U.S. Congress, for instance, representatives from industrial regions will vote for bills providing farm subsidies with the understanding that farm-state representatives will reciprocate by supporting bills that secure industrial assistance grants.

Besides exchanging favors, people engaging in politics sometimes use cooptation to preserve their interests in the face of adversity. In **cooptation**, former rivals become transformed into allies, often by involving them in planning and decision-making processes.[31] Colleges and universities often use this tactic during periods of campus unrest, inviting student protesters to join university representatives on administrative committees. Making opponents part of the team often silences their objections, but carries the risk of making major changes in plans and decisions.

Finally, ingratiation and impression management can be used to build and maintain political relationships. *Ingratiation* is the use of praise and compliments to gain the favor or acceptance of others. Similarly, *impression management* involves behaving in ways intended to build a positive image. Both can increase personal attractiveness, thereby raising the likelihood that others will seek a close relationship.[32]

Acquiring Structural Power: Controlling Critical Resources

As suggested by the critical contingencies model of power, controlling the supply of a critical resource gives people power over those whose success or survival depends on having that resource. A warehouse manager, for example, can decide which orders will be filled immediately and which will be delayed. As a political tool, power of this sort can be used to ensure that personal interests are satisfied. Similarly, controlling access to information sources provides power over those who need that information to reduce uncertainty. Political players often attempt to control access to the people who are sources of important information or expertise. Managers, for instance, might shield the staff specialists who advise them from others in their firm. Engineers who are working on new product development are often sequestered from other employees; cost accountants might be separated from other members of a company's accounting department. Such employees are an important resource because they possess critical information that is unavailable elsewhere.

To succeed as a political tactic, controlling access to important resources, information, or people requires eliminating substitutes for these critical resources and discrediting alternative definitions of what is critical. The presence of substitutes counteracts attempts to gain power by controlling critical resources because it neutralizes political efforts. In addition, successful control of critical resources requires that people have at least the centrality needed to identify which resources are critical and which are not.

Negative Politics

If all else fails, a person may sometimes gain the political upper hand by attacking or blaming others, or making them *scapegoats* for failures.[33] Another tactic is to denigrate or belittle others' accomplishments. Either approach involves a direct attack on the interpersonal sources of power that others might possess in an attempt to weaken their political positions, thereby creating doubt about their ability to control rewards and punishments or reducing their credibility, legitimacy, or attractiveness. Negative politicking can also justify the creation of substitute sources of critical resources or information or reduction of the degree of centrality enjoyed by a person or group. After all, who would want an incompetent individual or group in charge of something that is critically important to organizational survival?

Managing Destructive Politics

You can easily imagine some of the consequences when people band together, hoard resources, or belittle each other for no other reason than to get their own way. Morale can suffer; battle lines between contending individuals or groups might impede important interactions; energy that should go into productive activities might, instead, be spent on planning attacks and counterattacks if politicking is left uncontrolled. For this reason, controlling political behavior is a major part of every manager's job.[34]

Set an Example

One way to manage destructive politics is to set an example. Managers who do not tolerate deceit and dirty tricks and who refuse to engage in negative politics themselves make it clear that such political tactics are inappropriate. Subordinates are thus discouraged from engaging in destructive political activities. In contrast, managers who engage in negative politics— blaming their mistakes on others, keeping critical information from others—convey the message that politics is acceptable. Little wonder, then, that subordinates in such situations are themselves prone to politicking.

Communicate Openly

Sharing all relevant information with co-workers and colleagues can thwart the effects of destructive politics. Managers who communicate openly with their peers, superiors, and subordinates eliminate the political advantage of withholding information or blocking access to important people. Information that everyone already knows cannot be hoarded or hidden. In addition, open communication ensures that everyone understands and accepts resource allocations. Such understanding eliminates the attractiveness of political maneuvers intended to bias distribution procedures. Shrinking the potential benefits of destructive politicking lessens the incidence of political behaviors.

Reduce Uncertainty

A third way to minimize destructive political behavior is to reduce uncertainty. Clarifying goals, tasks, and responsibilities makes it easier to assess people's behaviors and brings politics out into the open. Expanding decision-making processes by consulting with subordinates or involving them in participatory decision-making processes helps make the resulting decisions understandable and discourages undercover politicking.

Manage Informal Coalitions and Cliques

Managing informal coalitions and cliques can also help reduce destructive politics. Influencing the norms and beliefs that steer group behaviors can ensure that employees continue to serve organizational interests. When cliques resist less severe techniques, job reassignment becomes a viable option. Group politicking is thereby abolished by eliminating the group.

Confront Political Game Players

A fifth approach to managing politics is to confront political game players about their activities. When people engage in politics despite initial attempts to discourage them from this course of action, a private meeting between superior and subordinate might be enough to curb the subordinate's political pursuits. If not, disciplinary measures might become necessary. Punishments such as a public reprimand or a period of layoff without pay ensure that the costs of politicking outweigh its benefits. If this approach does not work, managers who must cope with damaging politics might have no choice except to dismiss political game players.

Anticipate the Emergence of Damaging Politics

In any effort intended to control political behavior, awareness and anticipation are critical. If managers are aware that circumstances are conducive to politicking, they can try to prevent the emergence of politics. Detection of any of the personal characteristics or favorable conditions discussed earlier should be interpreted as a signal indicating the need for management intervention *before* destructive politics crop up.

Conflict in Organizations

Conflict—a process of opposition and confrontation that can occur in organizations between either individuals or groups—occurs when parties exercise power in the pursuit of valued goals or objectives and obstruct the progress of other parties.[35] Key to this definition is the idea that conflict involves the use of power in confrontation, or disputes over clashing interests. Also important is the notion that conflict is a process—something that takes time to unfold, rather than an event that occurs in an instant and then disappears. Finally, to the extent that obstructing progress threatens effectiveness and performance, the definition implies that conflict is a problem that managers must be able to control.

Is Conflict Necessarily Bad?

Conflict might seem inherently undesirable. In fact, many of the models of organization and management discussed in Chapter 2 support this view. Classic theorists often likened organizations to machines and portrayed conflict as symptomatic of breakdown of these machines. Managers in the days of Henri Fayol and Frederick Taylor concerned themselves with discovering ways either to avoid conflict or to suppress it as quickly and forcefully as possible.

In contrast, contemporary theorists argue that conflict is not necessarily bad.[36] To be sure, they say, *dysfunctional* conflict—confrontation that hinders progress toward desired goals—does occur. For example, protracted labor strikes leave both managers and employees with bad feelings, cost companies lost revenues and customers, and cost employees lost wages and benefits. Current research, however, suggests that conflict is often *functional*, having positive effects such as the following:

- Conflict can lessen social tensions, helping to stabilize and integrate relationships. If resolved in a way that allows for the discussion and dissipation of disagreements, it can serve as a safety valve that vents pressures built up over time.
- Conflict lets opposing parties express rival claims and provides the opportunity to readjust the allocation of valued resources. Resource pools can thus be consumed more effectively owing to conflict-induced changes.
- Conflict helps maintain the level of stimulation or activation required to function innovatively. In so doing, it can serve as a source of motivation to seek adaptive change.
- Conflict supplies feedback about the state of interdependencies and power distributions in an organization's structure. The distribution of power required to coordinate work activities then becomes more clearly apparent and readily understood.
- Conflict can help provide a sense of identity and purpose by clarifying differences and boundaries between individuals or groups. Such outcomes are discussed in greater detail later in this chapter.[37]

At the very least, conflict can serve as a red flag signaling the need for change. Believing that conflict can have positive effects, contemporary managers try to manage or resolve disagreements rather than avoid or suppress them.

Conditions That Stimulate Conflict

For conflict to occur, three key conditions must exist: interdependence, political indeterminism, and divergence. *Interdependence* is found where individuals, groups, or organizations depend on each other for assistance, information, feedback, or other coordinative relations.[38] As indicated in Chapter 8, four types of interdependence—pooled, sequential, reciprocal, and comprehensive—can link parties together. Any such linkages can serve as sources of conflict. For example, two groups that share a pool of funds might fight over who will receive money to buy new office equipment. Similarly, employees organized along a sequential assembly process might disagree about the pace of work. In the absence of interdependence, however, parties have nothing to fight about and, in fact, might not even know of each other's existence.

The emergence of conflict also requires *political indeterminism*, which means that the political pecking order among individuals or groups is unclear and subject to question. If power relations are unambiguous and stable, and if they are accepted as valid by all parties, appeals to authority will replace conflict, and differences will be resolved in favor of the most powerful. Only a party whose power is uncertain will gamble on winning through conflict rather than by appealing to power and authority. For this reason, individuals and groups in a newly reorganized company are much more likely to engage in conflict than are parties in an organization with a stable hierarchy of authority.

Finally, for conflict to emerge, there must be *divergence*, or differences or disagreements deemed worth fighting over.[39] For example, differences in the functions they perform can lead individuals or groups to have *varying goals*. Table 11.4 describes some differences in the goal orientations of marketing and manufacturing groups. In this example, each group's

Table 11.4 Differences in Goal Orientations: Marketing and Manufacturing

Goal focus	Marketing approach	Manufacturing approach
Product variety	Customers demand variety	Variety causes short, often uneconomical production runs
Capacity limits	Manufacturing capacity limits productivity	Inaccurate sales forecasts limit productivity
Product quality	Reasonable quality should be achievable at a cost that is affordable to customers	Offering options that are difficult to manufacture undermines quality
New products	New products are the firm's lifeblood	Unnecessary design changes are costly
Cost control	High cost undermines the firm's competitive position	Broad variety, fast delivery, high quality, and rapid responsiveness are not possible at low cost

Source: Adapted from B. S. Shapiro, "Can Marketing and Manufacturing Coexist?" *Harvard Business Review* 55 (September–October 1977): 104–114.

approach reflects its particular orientation—marketing's focus on customer service, manufacturing's concern with efficient production runs. In such situations, conflicts can occur over whose goals to pursue and whose to ignore.

Individuals and groups might also have different *time orientations*. For example, tasks such as making a sale to a regular customer require only short-term planning and can be initiated or altered quite easily. In contrast, tasks such as traditional assembly-line manufacturing operations necessitate a longer time frame because such activities require extensive preplanning and cannot be changed easily once they have begun. Certain tasks, such as the strategic planning activities that plot an organization's future, might even require time frames of several decades. When parties in a firm have different time orientations, conflicts can develop regarding which orientation should regulate task planning and performance.

Often, *resource allocations* among individuals or groups are unequal. Such differences usually stem from the fact that parties must compete with each other to get a share of their organization's resources. When the production department gets new tablet devices to help schedule weekly activities, the sales department might find itself forced to do without the software it wants for market research. In such instances, someone wins and someone loses, laying the groundwork for additional rounds of conflict.

Another source of conflict can be the practices used to *evaluate* and *reward* groups and their members. Consider, for example, that manufacturing groups are often rewarded for their efficiency, which is achieved by minimizing the quantity of raw materials consumed in production activities. Sales groups, on the other hand, tend to be rewarded for their flexibility, which sometimes sacrifices efficiency. Conflict often arises in such situations as each group tries to meet its own performance criteria or tries to force others to adopt the same criteria.

In addition, *status discrepancies* invite conflict over stature and position. Although the status of a person or group is generally determined by its position in the organization's hierarchy of authority—with parties higher in the hierarchy having higher status—sometimes other criteria influence status.[40] For instance, a group might argue that its status should depend on the knowledge possessed by its members or that status should be conferred on the basis of such factors as loyalty, seniority, or visibility.

Conflict can emerge in *jurisdictional disputes* when it is unclear who has responsibility for something. For example, if the personnel and employing departments both interview a prospective employee, the two groups might dispute which has the ultimate right to offer employment and which must take the blame if mistakes are made.

Finally, individuals and groups can differ in the *values, assumptions,* and *general perceptions* that guide their performance. Values held by the members of a production group, which stress easy assembly, for instance, might differ from the values held by the R&D staff, whose members favor complex product designs. These values can clash, leading to conflict, whenever researchers must fight for demanding product specifications that production personnel dismiss as unnecessarily complicated.

Effects of Conflict

Conflict affects relationships among people and groups in many ways. Especially when conflict occurs between groups, several important effects can be predicted to occur within the opposing groups.[41]

First, as noted in Chapter 9, external threats such as intergroup conflict bring about *increased group cohesiveness*. As a result, groups engaged in conflict become more attractive and important to their own members. Ongoing conflict also stimulates an *emphasis on task performance*. All efforts within each conflicting group are directed toward meeting the challenge posed by other groups, and concerns about individual members' satisfaction diminish in importance. A sense of urgency surrounds task performance; defeating the enemy becomes uppermost, and much less loafing occurs.

In addition, when a group faces conflict, otherwise reluctant members will often submit to *autocratic leadership* to manage the crisis, because they perceive participatory decision making as slow and weak. Strong, authoritarian leaders often emerge as a result of this shift. A group in such circumstances is also likely to place much more emphasis on standard procedures and centralized control. As a result, it becomes characterized by *structural rigidity*. By adhering to established rules and creating and strictly enforcing new ones, the group seeks to eliminate any conflicts that might develop among its members and to ensure that it can succeed repeatedly at its task.

Other changes can occur in the relations between conflicting groups. Hostility often surfaces in the form of hardened *"we–they" attitudes*. Each group sees itself as virtuous and the other groups as enemies. Intense dislike often accompanies these negative attitudes. As attitudes within each group become more negative, group members might develop *distorted perceptions* of opposing groups. The resulting negative stereotyping can create even greater differences between groups and further strengthen the cohesiveness within each group.

Eventually, negative attitudes and perceptions of group members can lead to a *decrease in communication* among conflicting groups. The isolation that results merely adds to the conflict, making resolution even more difficult to achieve. At the same time, conflicting groups often engage in *increased surveillance* intended to provide information about the attitudes, weaknesses, and likely behaviors of other groups.

Negotiation and Restructuring

A variety of conflict-management techniques have been developed to help resolve conflicts and deal with the kinds of negative effects just described. In general, these techniques are of two types: bargaining and negotiation procedures that focus on managing *divergence* among the interests of conflicting parties, and restructuring techniques that focus on managing *interdependence* between conflicting individuals and groups.

Managing Diverging Interests

Bargaining and negotiation are two closely associated processes that are often employed to work out the differences in interests and concerns that generate conflict. **Bargaining** between conflicting parties consists of offers, counteroffers, and concessions exchanged in a search for some mutually acceptable resolution. **Negotiation**, in turn, is the process in which the parties decide what each will give and take in this exchange.[42]

In the business world, relations between management and labor are often the focus of bargaining and negotiation. Both processes also occur elsewhere in organizations, however, as people and groups try to satisfy their own desires and control the extent to which they must sacrifice so as to satisfy others. In tight economies, for example, groups of secretaries who are dependent on the same supply budget might have to bargain with each other to see who will get new office equipment and who will have to make do with existing equipment. A company's sales force might try to negotiate favorable delivery dates for its best clients by offering manufacturing personnel leeway in meeting deadlines for other customers' orders.

In deciding which conflicting interests will be satisfied, parties engaged in bargaining and negotiation can choose the degree to which they will assert themselves and look after their own interests. They can also decide whether they will cooperate with their adversary and put its interests ahead of their own. Five general approaches to managing divergent interests exist that are characterized by different mixes of assertiveness and cooperativeness:[43]

1   *Competition* (assertive, uncooperative) means overpowering other parties in the conflict and promoting one's own concerns at the other parties' expense. One way to accomplish this aim is by resorting to authority to satisfy one's own concerns. Thus the head of a group of account executives might appeal to the director of advertising to protect the group's turf from intrusions by other account execs.

2.   *Accommodation* (unassertive, cooperative) allows other parties to satisfy their own concerns at the expense of one's own interests. Differences are smoothed over to maintain superficial harmony. A purchasing department that fails to meet budgetary guidelines because it deliberately overspends on raw materials in an effort to satisfy the demands of production groups is trying to use accommodation to cope with conflict.

3.   *Avoidance* (unassertive, uncooperative) requires staying neutral at all costs or refusing to take an active role in conflict resolution procedures. The finance department that "sticks its head in the sand," hoping that dissension about budgetary allocations will simply blow over, is exhibiting avoidance.

4.   *Collaboration* (assertive, cooperative) attempts to satisfy everyone by working through differences and seeking solutions in which everyone gains. A marketing department and a manufacturing department that meet on a regular basis to plan mutually acceptable production schedules are collaborating.

5.   *Compromise* (midrange assertive, cooperative) seeks partial satisfaction of everyone through exchange and sacrifice, settling for acceptable rather than optimal resolution. Contract bargaining between union representatives and management typically involves significant compromise by both sides.

As indicated in Table 11.5, the appropriateness of each of these approaches depends on the situation and, in many cases, on the time pressure for a negotiated settlement. Beyond these general alternatives, experts on organizational development have devised an assortment of more specific techniques for conflict management that are based on structured sessions of bargaining and negotiation. Several of these techniques will be described in detail in Chapter 14, which deals with culture, change, and organization development.

Managing Structural Interdependence

In addition to divergence in interests, conflict requires interdependence. It can, therefore, be managed or resolved by restructuring the connections that tie conflicting parties together.[44] One way to accomplish this goal is to *develop superordinate goals*, identifying and pursuing a set of performance targets that conflicting parties can achieve only by working together. Sharing a common goal requires the parties to look beyond their differences and learn to cooperate with each other. In the automobile industry, for instance, unions and management, fearing plant closures, have forgone adversarial relations to strengthen the competitiveness of automotive firms. In many companies, teamwork has replaced conflict in the pursuit of the superordinate goal of producing high-quality products for today's world markets.

Expanding the supply of critical resources is another way to restructure. This strategy removes a major source of conflict between individuals and groups that draw from the same supply. Pools of critical resources are not easily enlarged—which is what makes them critical,

Table 11.5 Application of Different Styles of Managing Divergence

Style	Application
Competing	When quick, decisive action is required. On important issues where unpopular solutions must be implemented. On issues vital to organizational welfare when your group is certain that its position is correct. Against groups that take advantage of noncompetitive behavior.
Accommodating	When your group is wrong and wants to show reasonableness. When issues are more important to groups other than yours. To bank favors for later issues. To minimize losses when your group is outmatched and losing. When harmony and stability are especially important.
Avoiding	When a conflict is trivial or unimportant. When there is no chance that your group will satisfy its own needs. When the costs of potential disruption outweigh the benefits of resolution. To let groups cool down and gain perspective. When others can resolve the conflict more effectively.
Collaborating	To find an integrative solution when conflicting concerns are too important to be compromised. When the most important objective is to learn. To combine the ideas of people with different perspectives. To gain commitment through the development of consensus. To work through conflicting feelings between groups.
Compromising	When group concerns are important but not worth the disruption associated with more assertive styles. When equally powerful groups are committed to pursuing mutually exclusive concerns. To achieve temporary settlements. To arrive at expedient resolutions under time pressure. As a backup when neither competing nor problem-solving styles are successful.

Source: Adapted from K. W. Thomas, "Conflict and Conflict Management," in *Handbook of Industrial and Organizational Psychology*, ed. M. D. Dunnette (Chicago: Rand McNally, 1976), 889–935.

of course. When this method is successful, it decreases the amount of interdependence between parties, which then compete less for available resources. For example, one way to eliminate interoffice conflicts over the availability of shared computers is to buy a network of personal computers for every department. Some organizations purchase large quantities of used computers at reduced prices instead of a few new ones at full retail price.

A third way to manage conflict by restructuring interdependence is to *clarify existing relationships* and make the political position of each party readily apparent. If it is feasible, this political clarification affects interdependence by strengthening everyone's understanding of how and why they are connected. It also reduces the political indeterminism that must exist for conflict to occur.

A fourth approach is to *modify existing structural relationships*. This strategy includes a number of mechanisms that either uncouple conflicting parties or modify the structural linkage between them.[45] Two such mechanisms—the **decoupling mechanisms** of slack resources and self-contained tasks—manage conflict by eliminating the interdependence that must exist for conflict to occur.

Slack resources help decouple otherwise interconnected individuals and groups by creating buffers that lessen the ability of one party to affect the activities of another. Suppose one person assembles telephone handsets, and another person connects finished handsets to telephone bodies to form fully assembled units. The two employees are sequentially interdependent, because the second person's ability to perform the work is contingent on the first person's ability to complete the task. The second employee cannot work if the first employee stops producing. If a buffer inventory is created—a supply of finished handsets—on which the second worker can draw when the first worker is not producing anything, we have (at least temporarily) decoupled the two individuals.

In contrast, the creation of *self-contained tasks* involves combining the work of two or more interdependent parties and then assigning this work to several independent parties. If the original parties are groups, then the self-contained groups are usually staffed by employees drawn from each of the interdependent groups. For example, engineering and drafting groups might have problems coordinating engineering specifications and the drawings produced by the drafting group. These two groups might be re-formed into several independent engineering–drafting groups. After this restructuring, the original two groups no longer exist. Key interdependencies that lie outside the original groups are contained within redesigned groups and can be managed without crossing group boundaries or involving outside managers.

Sometimes concerns about minimizing inventory costs rule out the use of slack resources. Among U.S. manufacturers, for instance, the cost of carrying excessive inventory is a major concern and has stimulated increasing interest in just-in-time (JIT) procedures. Using JIT, inventory is acquired only as needed, eliminating the cost of having unused items lying around. In addition, work often cannot be divided into self-contained tasks. For example, the task of producing the parts required to make a car and assembling them into a final product is so immense that many individuals and groups (in fact, many companies) must be involved. In such cases, existing structural relationships might be modified instead by means of various **unit-linking mechanisms**.

Network information systems are one such mechanism. These systems consist of mainframe computers with remote terminals or network servers connected to personal computers that can be used to input and exchange information about organizational performance. If you have taken courses in computer science, you have probably worked with a computer network similar to the *intranets* now used in businesses. Managers use such systems to communicate among themselves and to store information for later review. The networks facilitate the transfer of large amounts of information up and down an organization's hierarchy of authority. In addition, they support lateral exchanges among interdependent individuals and groups. In the process, they facilitate communication that might otherwise develop into misunderstandings and lead to conflict. The fact that many organizations have recently added the corporate position of chief information officer (CIO) reflects the growing use of network information systems to manage interdependent, potentially conflictful relationships.[46]

A second type of unit-linking mechanism consists of several *lateral linkage devices* that managers can use to strengthen communication between interdependent parties. In one of these, an employee might be assigned a *liaison position* in which he or she is responsible for seeing that communications flow directly and freely between interdependent groups. The liaison position represents an alternative to hierarchical communication channels. It reduces both the time needed to communicate between groups and the amount of information distortion likely to occur. The person occupying a liaison position has no authority to issue direct orders but, rather, serves as a neutral third party and relies on negotiation, bargaining, and persuasion. This person is called on to mediate between groups if conflict actually emerges, resolving differences and moving the groups toward voluntary intergroup coordination.[47]

The liaison position is the least costly of the lateral linkage devices. Because one person handles the task of coordination, minimal resources are diverted from the primary task of production. In addition, because the position has no formal authority, it is the least disruptive of normal hierarchical relationships. Sometimes, however, a liaison position is not strong enough to manage interdependence relations. Managers then have the option of turning to another type of lateral linkage device, *representative groups*, to coordinate activities among interdependent parties. Representative groups consist of people who represent the interdependent individuals or groups, and who meet to coordinate the interdependent activities.

Two kinds of representative groups exist. One, called a *task force*, is formed to complete a specific task or project and then disbanded. Representatives get together, talk out the differences among the parties they represent, and resolve conflicts before they become manifest. For this reason, companies such as Colgate-Palmolive and Procter & Gamble form product task groups by drawing together members from advertising, marketing, manufacturing, and product research departments. Each product task group identifies consumer needs, designs new products that respond to these needs, and manages their market introduction. Once a new product is successfully launched, the product task group responsible for its introduction is dissolved, and its members return to their former jobs.

The other type of representative group is a more or less permanent structure. Like the members of the task force, the members of this group, called a *standing committee*, represent interdependent parties, but they meet on a regular basis to discuss and resolve ongoing problems. The standing committee is not assigned a specific task, nor is it expected to disband at any particular time. An example of a standing committee is a factory's Monday morning production meeting. At that meeting, representatives from production control, purchasing, quality assurance, shipping, and various assembly groups overview the week's production schedule and try to anticipate problems.

Like task forces, standing committees use face-to-face communication to manage interdependence problems and resolve conflict-related differences. Despite their usefulness in this regard, both of these linkage devices are more costly than the liaison position. Through process loss, their group meetings inevitably consume otherwise productive resources. In addition, because representative groups (especially task forces) are sometimes designed to operate outside customary hierarchical channels, they can prove quite disruptive to normal management procedures.

When neither liaison positions nor representative groups solve intergroup conflict problems, the company might use a third type of lateral linkage device, called an *integrating manager*. Like the liaison position, the integrating manager mediates between interdependent parties. Unlike the liaison position, however, this individual has the formal authority to issue orders and expect obedience. He or she can tell interdependent parties what to do to resolve conflict. Project managers at companies such as Rockwell International and Lockheed fill the role of integrating manager. They oversee the progress of a project by ensuring that the various planning, designing, assembling, and testing groups work together successfully.

Normally, when coordinating the efforts of groups, an integrating manager issues orders only to group supervisors. Giving orders to the people who report to these supervisors might confuse employees, as employees might feel that they were being asked to report to two supervisors. Because an integrating manager disrupts normal hierarchical relationships by short-circuiting the relationships between the group supervisors and their usual superior, this device is used much less often than either the liaison position or representative groups.

Occasionally, even integrating managers cannot provide the guidance needed to manage conflict through structural means. In these rare instances, a fourth type of lateral linkage device, called the *matrix organization structure*, is sometimes employed. Matrix structures are the most complicated of the mechanisms used to coordinate group activities and resolve intergroup conflicts, and they are extremely costly to sustain.[48] The matrix organization structure will be discussed in greater detail in Chapter 12, which covers organization structure, because it is both a conflict resolution device and a specific type of structure. For now, we conclude by suggesting that matrix structures are appropriate only when all other intergroup mechanisms have proved ineffective.

Summary

Power is the ability to influence others and to resist their influence in return. Compliance, identification, and internalization are outcomes that can result from the use of five types of interpersonal power—*reward, coercive, legitimate, referent,* and *expert* power. Power also grows out of uncertainty surrounding the continued availability of *critical contingencies*. It is therefore based on the ability to *reduce this uncertainty* and is enhanced by low *substitutability* and high *centrality.*

Politics is a process through which a person acquires power and uses it to advance the individual's self-interests. It is stimulated by a combination of personal characteristics and antecedent conditions and can involve a variety of tactics, ranging from controlling supplies of critical resources to attacking or blaming others. Several techniques are employed to manage politicking, including setting an example and confronting political game players.

Conflict is a process of opposition and confrontation that requires the presence of interdependence, political indeterminism, and divergence. It can be managed through *bargaining* and *negotiation*, or it can be resolved by restructuring interdependence relations through the use of various *decoupling* or *unit-linking mechanisms.*

Review Questions

1. Is power being exercised when a manager orders a subordinate to do something the subordinate would do even without being ordered? When a subordinate successfully refuses to follow orders? When a manager's orders are followed despite the subordinate's reluctance?

2. How does uncertainty encourage politics? What can managers do to control this antecedent condition?

3. Why does intergroup conflict require interdependence? How does political indeterminism influence whether this sort of conflict will occur? Based on your answers to these two questions, how can managers resolve intergroup conflicts without attempting to reduce divergence?

4. How does an integrating manager differ from a liaison position? Which of the two is more likely to prove successful in resolving a longstanding conflict? Given your answer, why isn't this "stronger" approach the only option used in organizations?

Notes

1   S. Berfeld, "Walmart vs. Walmart: Can a Group of Loyal—and Loud—Employees Force the World's Biggest Retailer to Change How It Treats Its Workers?" *Bloomberg Businessweek,* December 12, 2012, 54–58; R. Dudley, "Wal-Mart Union Protests Fail to Deter Bargain-Seekers," *Bloomberg,* November 23, 2012, http://www.bloomberg.com/news/2012-11-23/

wal-mart-union-protests-fail-to-deter-bargain-seekers.html; J. Eidelson, "The Great Walmart Walkout," *The Nation*, December 19, 2012, http://www.thenation.com/article/171868/great-walmart-walkout.

2 J. A. Byrne, W. Zeller, and S. Ticer, "Caught in the Middle: Six Managers Speak Out on Corporate Life," *BusinessWeek*, September 12, 1988, 80–88.

3 R. A. Dahl, "The Concept of Power," *Behavioral Science* 2 (1957): 201–215; A. Kaplan, "Power in Perspective," in R. L. Kahn and E. Boulding, eds., *Power and Conflict in Organizations* (London: Tavistock, 1964), 11–32; and R. M. Emerson, "Power Dependence Relations," *American Sociological Review* 27 (1962): 31–41.

4 V. V. McMurray, "Some Unanswered Questions on Organizational Conflict," *Organization and Administrative Sciences* 6 (1975): 35–53.

5 D. C. McClelland, *Power: The Inner Experience* (New York: Irvington, 1975), 3–29; D. C. McClelland and D. H. Burnham, "Power Is the Great Motivator," *Harvard Business Review* 54 (1976): 100–110; A. Delbecq, R. J. House, M. S. de Luque, and N. R. Quigley, "Implicit Motives, Leadership, and Follower Outcomes: An Empirical Test of CEOs," *Journal of Leadership and Organizational Studies* 19 (2012): 397–406. For an updated discussion of the psychology of power, see J. Pfeffer and C. T. Fong, "Building Organization Theory from First Principles: The Self-Enhancement Motive and Understanding Power and Influence," *Organization Science* 16 (2005): 372–388.

6 McClelland and Burnham, "Power Is the Great Motivator."

7 J. R. French, Jr., and B. Raven, "The Bases of Social Power," in D. Cartwright, ed., *Studies in Social Power* (Ann Arbor: Institute for Social Research, University of Michigan, 1959), 150–165; G. Yukl, "Use Power Effectively," in E. A. Locke, ed., *Blackwell Handbook of Principles of Organizational Behavior* (Malden, MA: Blackwell, 2004), 242–247; for a recent extension, see N. B. Kurland and L. H. Pelled, "Passing the Word: Toward a Model of Gossip and Power in the Workplace," *Academy of Management Review* 25 (2000): 428–438.

8 H. C. Kelman, "Compliance, Identification, and Internalization: Three Processes of Attitude Change," *Journal of Conflict Resolution* 2 (1958): 51–60.

9 C. N. Greene and M. Podsakoff, "Effects of Withdrawal of a Performance-Contingent Reward on Supervisory Influence and Power," *Academy of Management Journal* 24 (1981): 527–542.

10 Another criticism of this model relates to problems with the measures and methods used to study the French and Raven classification scheme. For further information about these problems and their effects on power research, see G. A. Yukl, *Leadership in Organizations* (Englewood Cliffs, NJ: Prentice Hall, 1981), 38–43; M. Podsakoff and C. A. Schreisheim, "Field Studies of French and Raven's Bases of Power: Critique, Reanalysis, and Suggestions for Future Research," *Psychological Bulletin* 97 (1985): 387–411.

11 D. J. Hickson, C. R. Hinings, C. A. Lee, R. H. Schneck, and J. M. Pennings, "A Strategic Contingencies Theory of Intraorganizational Power," *Administrative Science Quarterly* 16 (1971): 216–229; J. Pfeffer and G. R. Salancik, *The External Control of Organizations: A Resource Dependence Perspective* (New York: Harper & Row, 1978), 231; J. Pfeffer, *Power in Organizations* (Marshfield, MA: Pitman, 1981), 109–122.

12 G. R. Salancik and J. Pfeffer, "Who Gets Power and How They Hold On to It: A Strategic-Contingency Model of Power," *Organizational Dynamics* 5 (1977): 3–4.

13 R. M. Kanter, "Power Failures in Management Circuits," *Harvard Business Review* 57 (1979): 65–75.

14 R. H. Miles, *Macro Organizational Behavior* (Santa Monica, CA: Goodyear, 1980), 171–172.

15 G. A. Crawford, "Information as a Strategic Contingency: Applying the Strategic Contingencies Theory of Intraorganizational Power to Academic Libraries," *College and Research Libraries* 58 (1997): 145–155; Miles, *Macro Organizational Behavior*, 171.

16 G. R. Salancik and J. Pfeffer, "The Bases and Uses of Power in Organizational Decision Making," *Administrative Science Quarterly* 19 (1974): 470.

17 Hickson et al., "A Strategic Contingencies Theory," 40.

18 D. Krackhardt, "Assessing the Political Landscape: Structure, Cognition, and Power in Organizations," *Administrative Science Quarterly* 35 (1990): 342–369; D. J. Brass and M. E. Burkhardt, "Potential Power and Power Use: An Investigation of Structure and Behavior," *Academy of Management Journal* 36 (1993): 441–470; H. Ibarra, "Network Centrality, Power, and Innovation Involvement: Determinants of Technical and Administrative Roles," *Academy of Management Journal* 36 (1993): 471–501; H. Ibarra and S. B. Andrews, "Power, Social Influence, and Sense Making: Effects of Network Centrality and Proximity on Employee

Perceptions," *Administrative Science Quarterly* 38 (1993): 277–303; W. Tsai, "Knowledge Transfer in Intraorganizational Networks: Effects of Network Position and Absorptive Capacity on Business Unit Innovation and Performance," *Academy of Management Journal* 44 (2001): 996–1004.

19 W. G. Astley and E. J. Zajac, "Intraorganizational Power and Organizational Design: Reconciling Rational and Coalitional Models of Organization," *Organization Science* 2 (1991): 399–411.

20 H. A. Landsberger, "A Horizontal Dimension in Bureaucracy," *Administrative Science Quarterly* 6 (1961): 299–332.

21 Salancik and Pfeffer, "The Bases and Uses of Power"; see also J. Pfeffer and G. R. Salancik, "Organizational Decision Making as a Political Process: The Case of a University Budget," *Administrative Science Quarterly* 19 (1974): 135–151.

22 M. Crozier, *The Bureaucratic Phenomenon* (Chicago: University of Chicago Press, 1964), 153–154.

23 D. Mechanic, "Sources of Power of Lower Participants in Complex Organizations," *Administrative Science Quarterly* 7 (1962): 349–364; L. W. Porter, R. W. Allen, and H. L. Angle, "The Politics of Upward Influence in Organizations," in B. M. Staw and L. L. Cummings, eds., *Research in Organizational Behavior* 3 (Greenwich, CT: JAI Press, 1981), 109–150; R. S. Blackburn, "Lower Participant Power: Toward a Conceptual Integration," *Academy of Management Review* 6 (1981): 127–131; S. M. Farmer and J. M. Maslyn, "Why Are Styles of Upward Influence Neglected? Making the Case for a Configurational Approach to Influences," *Journal of Management* 25 (1999): 653–682.

24 R. W. Allen, D. L. Madison, L. W. Porter, A. Renwick, and B. T. Mayes, "Organizational Politics: Tactics and Characteristics of Its Actors," *California Management Review* 22 (1979): 77–83; B. T. Mayes and R. W. Allen, "Toward a Definition of Organizational Politics," *Academy of Management Review* 2 (1977): 672–678; V. Murray and J. Gandz, "Games Executives Play: Politics at Work," *Business Horizons* 23 (1980): 11–23; Pfeffer, *Power in Organizations*, 6.

25 Miles, *Macro Organizational Behavior*, 155.

26 W. A. Hochwater, L. Perrewe, G. R. Ferris, and R. Guercio, "Commitment as an Antidote to the Tension and Turnover Consequences of Organizational Politics," *Journal of Vocational Behavior* 55 (1999): 277–297; L. A. Witt, M. C. Andrews, and K. M. Kacmar, "The Role of Participation in Decision-Making in the Organizational Politics–Job Satisfaction Relationship," *Human Relations* 53 (2000): 341–358; M. Valle and L. Perrewe, "Do Politics Perceptions Relate to Political Behaviors? Tests of an Implicit Assumption and Expanded Model," *Human Relations* 53 (2000): 359–386; S. Zivnuska, K. M. Kacmar, L. A. Witt, D. S. Carlson, and V. K. Bratton, "Interactive Effects of Impression Management and Organizational Politics on Job Performance," *Journal of Organizational Behavior* 25 (2004): 627–640; D. C. Treadway, G. Ferris, W. Hochwater, L. Perrewe, L. A. Witt, and J. M. Goodman, "The Role of Age in the Perceptions of Politics–Job Performance Relationship: A Three-Study Constructive Replication," *Journal of Applied Psychology* 90 (2005): 872–881; G. R. Ferris, D. C. Treadway, L. Perrewe, R. L. Brouer, C. Douglas, and S. Lux, "Political Skill in Organizations," *Journal of Management* 33 (2007): 290–320.

27 D. C. McClelland, "The Two Faces of Power," *Journal of International Affairs* 24 (1970): 32–41; R. Christie and F. L. Geis, *Studies in Machiavellianism* (New York: Academic Press, 1970), 1–9; G. R. Ferris, G. S. Russ, and M. Fandt, "Politics in Organizations," in R. A. Giacalone and Rosenfeld, eds., *Impression Management in the Organization* (Hillsdale, NJ: Erlbaum, 1989), 143–170.

28 T. J. Chen, H. Chen, and Y. H. Ku, "Resource Dependency and Parent-Subsidiary Capability Transfers," *Journal of World Business*, 47 (2012): 259–266.

29 Pfeffer, *Power in Organizations*; R. L. Daft and R. M. Steers, *Organizations: A Micro/Macro Approach* (Glenview, IL: Scott, Foresman, 1986), 488–489; Allen et al., "Organizational Politics," 77–83.

30 W. B. Stevenson, J. B. Pearce, and L. W. Porter, "The Concept of Coalition in Organization Theory and Research," *Academy of Management Review* 10 (1985): 256–268.

31 M. Gargiulo, "Two-Step Leverage: Managing Constraints in Organizational Politics," *Administrative Science Quarterly* 38 (1993): 1–19.

32 E. E. Jones, *Ingratiation* (New York: Appleton-Century-Crofts, 1964); C. B. Wortman and J. A. W. Linsenmeier, "Interpersonal Attraction and Techniques of Ingratiation in Organizational

Settings," in B. M. Staw and G. R. Salancik, eds., *New Directions in Organizational Behavior* (Chicago: St. Clair Press, 1977), 133–178; G. Harrell-Cook, G. R. Ferris, and J. H. Dulebohn, "Political Behaviors as Moderators of the Perceptions of Organizational Politics–Work Outcomes Relationships," *Journal of Organizational Behavior* 20 (1999): 1093–1105; K. M. Kacmar and D. S. Carlson, "Effectiveness of Impression Management Tactics across Human Resource Situations," *Journal of Applied Social Psychology* 29 (1999): 1293–1315; W. H. Turnley and M. C. Bolino, "Achieving Desired Images while Avoiding Undesired Images: Exploring the Role of Self-Monitoring in Impression Management," *Journal of Applied Psychology* 86 (2001): 351–360; J. D. Westphal and I. Stern, "Flattery Will Get You Everywhere (Especially if You Are a Male Caucasian): How Ingratiation, Boardroom Behavior, and Demographic Minority Status Affect Additional Board Appointments of U.S. Companies," *Academy of Management Journal* 50 (2007): 267–288.

33 W. Boeker, "Power and Managerial Dismissal: Scapegoating at the Top," *Administrative Science Quarterly* 37 (1992): 400–421.

34 The political management techniques described in this section are based partly on discussions in R. Vecchio, *Organizational Behavior*, 2nd ed. (Chicago: Dryden Press, 1991), 281–282; and G. Moorhead and R. W. Griffin, *Organizational Behavior*, 3rd ed. (Boston: Houghton Mifflin, 1992), 306–307.

35 Miles, *Macro Organizational Behavior*, 122.

36 R. E. Quinn, *Beyond Rational Management: Mastering the Paradoxes and Competing Demands of High Performance* (San Francisco: Jossey-Bass, 1988), 2; A. C. Amason, "Distinguishing the Effects of Functional and Dysfunctional Conflict on Strategic Decision Making: Resolving a Paradox for Top Management Teams," *Academy of Management Journal* 39 (1996): 123–148; D. Tjosvold, C. Hui, D. Z. Ding, and J. Hu, "Conflict Values and Team Relationships: Conflict's Contribution to Team Effectiveness and Citizenship in China," *Journal of Organizational Behavior* 24 (2002): 69–88; but for a contrasting position see C. K. W. De Dreu, "The Virtue and Vice of Workplace Conflict: Food for (Pessimistic) Thought," *Journal of Organizational Behavior* 29 (2007): 5–18.

37 L. Coser, *The Functions of Social Conflict* (New York: Free Press, 1956), 154; Miles, *Macro Organizational Behavior*, 123; J. Wall and R. R. Callister, "Conflict and Its Management," *Journal of Management* 21 (1995): 515–558.

38 Miles, *Macro Organizational Behavior*, 131.

39 Ibid., 132–138; J. M. Ivancevich and M. T. Matteson, *Organizational Behavior and Management*, 3rd ed. (Homewood, IL: Irwin, 1993), 340–344.

40 D. Ulrich and J. B. Barney, "Perspectives on Organizations: Resource Dependence, Efficiency, and Population," *Academy of Management Review* 9 (1984): 471–481.

41 M. Sherif and C. W. Sherif, *Groups in Harmony and Tension* (New York: Harper, 1953), 229–295; A. D. Szilagyi, Jr., and M. J. Wallace, Jr., *Organizational Behavior and Performance*, 4th ed. (Glenview, IL: Scott, Foresman, 1987), 301; J. L. Gibson, J. M. Ivancevich, and J. H. Donnelly, Jr., *Organizations: Behavior, Structure, Process*, 7th ed. (Homewood, IL: Irwin, 1991), 308–309; Ivancevich and Matteson, *Organizational Behavior and Management*, 344–347; J. Hinds and D. E. Bailey, "Out of Sight, Out of Sync: Understanding Conflict in Distributed Teams," *Organization Science* 14 (2003): 615–632; J. Hinds and M. Mortensen, "Understanding Conflict in Geographically Distributed Teams: The Moderating Effects of Shared Identity, Shared Context, and Spontaneous Communication," *Organization Science* 16 (2005): 290–307; C. W. Langfred, "The Downside of Self-Management: A Longitudinal Study of the Effects of Conflict on Trust, Autonomy, and Task Interdependence in Self-Managed Teams," *Academy of Management Journal* 50 (2007): 885–900.

42 J. Z. Rubin and B. R. Brown, *The Social Psychology of Bargaining and Negotiation* (New York: Academic Press, 1975), 3; R. J. Lewicki and J. R. Litterer, *Negotiation* (Homewood, IL: Irwin, 1985); W. L. Adair and J. M. Brett, "The Negotiation Dance: Time, Culture, and Behavioral Sequences in Negotiation," *Organization Science* 16 (2005): 33–51.

43 K. W. Thomas, "Conflict and Conflict Management," in M. D. Dunnette, ed., *Handbook of Industrial and Organizational Psychology* (Chicago: Rand McNally, 1976), 889–935; also see K. W. Thomas, "Toward Multidimensional Values in Teaching: The Example of Conflict Behaviors," *Academy of Management Review* 2 (1977): 472–489; K. W. Thomas, "Conflict and Conflict Management: Reflections and Update," *Journal of Organizational Behavior* 13 (1992): 265–274; S. Altmae, K. Turk, and O. S. Toomet, "Thomas-Kilmann's Conflict

Management Modes and their Relationship to Fiedler's Leadership Styles," *Baltic Journal of Management* 8 (2012): 42–63.

44 M. Sherif, "Superordinate Goals in the Reduction of Intergroup Conflict," *American Journal of Sociology* 63 (1958): 349–356; J. R. Galbraith, "Organization Design: An Information Processing View," *Interfaces* 4 (1974): 28–36; and Pfeffer, *Power in Organizations.*

45 J. R. Galbraith, *Designing Complex Organizations* (Reading, MA: Addison Wesley, 1973), 14–18

46 J. R. Galbraith, *Competing with Flexible Lateral Organizations* (Reading, MA: Addison-Wesley, 1994); T. Smart, "Jack Welch's Cyber-Czar," *BusinessWeek*, August 5, 1996, 82–83; A. L. Sprout, "The Internet inside Your Company," *Fortune*, November 27, 1995, 161–168.

47 D. E. Conlon, P. J. Carnevale, and W. H. Ross, "The Influence of Third Party Power and Suggestions on Negotiation: The Surface Value of Compromise," *Journal of Applied Social Psychology* 24 (1994): 1084–1113.

48 L. R. Burns and D. R. Wholey, "Adoption and Abandonment of Matrix Management Programs: Effects of Organizational Characteristics and Interorganizational Networks," *Academy of Management Journal* 36 (1993): 106–138.

Chapter 12

Structuring the Organization

Omega Solutions LLC, located in Troy, Michigan, contracts with other companies to provide human resources services that range from payroll and tax management to benefits administration. Formerly a small firm conducting business in a regional market, Omega could rely on the entrepreneurial spirit of its employees and the leadership of its owners to attract customers, assess their needs, and provide appropriate services. Now, however, Omega has grown to become a national competitor, requiring the company to increase the size of its workforce while developing formal departments and lines of authority to coordinate the work of the larger staff. What was once handled by word-of-mouth among co-workers now requires a management hierarchy and formalized procedures.[1]

In contrast, in nearby Detroit, General Motors (GM), one of the world's leading auto manufacturers, has intentionally reduced its size by eliminating its Oldsmobile, Pontiac, and Saturn brands and many of the employees and factories that produced them. The goal of these changes is to streamline U.S. operations and redirect GM's competitive focus toward developing markets around the world. Former ways of managing the company's work and workforce, which typically relied on centralized decision making and a tall hierarchy of managers, have given way to increasingly decentralized processes and a flatter management hierarchy. GM sees itself as needing to become more flexible and less reliant on rules and regulations. To become an adaptable, global competitor, GM is reinventing the way it is structured.[2]

For both Omega and GM, changes in the scope of company operations have led to changes in **organization structure**, the relatively stable network of interconnections or interdependencies among the different people and tasks that make up an organization.[3] Like the steel framework of a building or the skeletal system of the human body, an organization's structure differentiates among its parts even as it helps to keep those parts interconnected. In so doing, it creates and reinforces relationships of interdependence among the people and groups within it. Balancing this structural *integration* and *differentiation* is an important challenge facing today's managers. The ability to create a workable balance between the two can determine whether a company succeeds in organizing work activities in a way that allows something meaningful to be accomplished.[4]

An organization's structure enables the people within it to work together, thereby accomplishing things beyond the abilities of unorganized individuals. To help their employees achieve this feat in the most effective manner, managers of companies like Omega or GM must know how to structure their organization in a way that will enhance employee performance, control the costs of doing business, and keep the organization abreast of changes in the surrounding environment. They must, therefore, understand the basic design and specific features of the various types of structures they might choose to implement in their company, and they must be aware of the likely advantages and disadvantages of each structural type.

To cultivate this understanding and awareness, this chapter introduces the basic elements of an organization's structure—how coordination is established among interdependent people and jobs, how teams and groups are formed through departmentation and joined together in a hierarchy, and how information and decision making are distributed within this hierarchy so as to stimulate continued coordination and maintain effective interdependence. Using these basic elements, the chapter then describes a variety of structural types that an organization might adopt, and it examines some of the strengths and weaknesses of each. After studying this chapter, you should be able to recognize a wide range of structural features and organization structures, and you should understand the most important advantages and disadvantages of each of these different structural types.

Structural Coordination

Achieving structural integration is an important challenge facing all managers, requiring them to make decisions about how to coordinate relationships among the interdependent people and groups they manage. *Coordination* is a process through which otherwise disorganized actions become integrated so as to produce a desired result. For example, if appropriately coordinated, different parts of the human body work together to produce complex behaviors. The arms follow a trajectory plotted by the eyes so as to catch a ball. The hands hold a car's steering wheel at the same time that the foot depresses the accelerator pedal. It would be very difficult—if not impossible—to catch a ball without first seeing it and judging its path. It would be dangerous to accelerate or even move the car without being able to coordinate the control of its direction.

In a similar manner, through coordination the members of an organization are able to work together to accomplish outcomes that would otherwise be beyond the abilities of any one person working alone. The primary means by which organizational activities are integrated—the **basic coordination mechanisms** of mutual adjustment, direct supervision, and standardization—enable the organization to perform complex activities by bringing together the efforts of many individuals.[5]

Basic Coordination Mechanisms

Mutual adjustment is coordination accomplished through person-to-person communication processes in which co-workers share job-related information.[6] The simplest of the three basic coordination mechanisms, it consists of the exchange among co-workers of knowledge about how a job should be done and who should do it. It might occur through face-to-face communication, or it could take place with the aid of electronic mediation (e.g., a cell phone or a polycom system). A group of factory maintenance mechanics examining service manuals and discussing how to fix a broken conveyor belt is coordinating job efforts by means of mutual adjustment. Similarly, sales managers getting together via Skype to discuss their company's market position are using mutual adjustment to coordinate among themselves. In both of these examples, information is exchanged among people who can exercise at least partial control over the tasks they are discussing. Unless the co-workers doing the communicating possess this control, they cannot successfully coordinate their activities with mutual adjustment.

Direct supervision, a second type of coordination mechanism, occurs when one person takes responsibility for the work of a group of others.[7] As part of this responsibility, a direct supervisor acquires the authority to decide which tasks must be performed, who will perform them, and how they will be linked to produce the desired result. A direct supervisor can then issue orders to subordinates, verify that these orders have been followed, and redirect subordinates as needed to fulfill additional work requirements. The owner of a grocery store is functioning as a direct supervisor when, having instructed an employee to restock the shelves, she finds that the clerk has completed the job and directs him next to change the signs advertising the week's specials. In this example, as in every instance of direct supervision, an individual with the authority to issue direct orders is able to coordinate activities by telling subordinates what to do.

Standardization, a third type of coordination mechanism, is itself a collection of four different mechanisms that coordinate work by providing employees with standards and procedures that help them determine how to perform their tasks, thereby alleviating their need to communicate with one another or consult their supervisor to find out what to do. Coordination via standardization requires that standards be set and procedures designed—in the process of *formalization*, or the development of formal, written specifications—before the work is actually undertaken.[8] So long as formalized, "drawing-board" plans are followed and the work situation remains essentially unchanged, interdependent relationships can be reproduced again and again, and coordination can be sustained.

One form of standardization, *behavioral standardization*, involves specification of the behaviors or work processes that employees must perform in order to accomplish their jobs. Some of these behaviors link each job with other jobs in the organization, such as the requirement that the holder of an assembly-line job place finished items on a conveyor that transports them to other employees for further work. In this way, the need for other types of coordination among jobs is reduced. Behavioral standardization originates in the process of *formalization by job*, also called *job analysis*, in which the sequence of steps required to perform each job is identified and documented in writing. The written documentation is referred to as a *job description*. In Burger King's corporate kitchen, for example, job analysts develop procedures manuals containing job descriptions that specify how long company employees should cook each type of food served, what condiments should be used to flavor the food, and how workers should package the food for purchase.

Output standardization, a second type of standardization, involves the formal designation of output targets or performance goals. So long as everyone coordinated by output standardization accomplishes his or her goals, the work that is handed off from one employee to the next remains consistent and no one needs to engage in further coordination. The process of establishing written targets and goals is sometimes called *formalization by work flow*, because it produces standards that coordinate interdependence by directing and stabilizing the flow of work in a firm—as exemplified by the set of standards for display-screen brightness, keyboard responsiveness, and exterior appearance prepared for workers who assemble notebook computers.

Unlike employees working under behavioral standardization, people coordinated by output standardization are free to decide for themselves *how* to attain their goals. For instance, posted monthly sales goals indicate levels of performance that insurance sales representatives are expected to achieve, but do not specify particular behaviors required to achieve them. Consequently, output standardization allows a degree of autonomy not permitted by behavioral standardization. As indicated in Chapters 5 through 7, this difference is important because autonomy can have positive effects on employee motivation, satisfaction, and success at work.

A third type of standardization, *skill standardization*, relies on the specification of skills, knowledge, and abilities needed to perform tasks competently. Skilled employees seldom need to communicate with one another to figure out what to do, and they can usually predict with reasonable accuracy what other similarly skilled employees will do. Consequently, on jobs staffed by such employees, there might be much less need to coordinate in other ways among people and jobs.

Skill standardization can be implemented in either of two ways: by hiring professionals from outside the organization or by training employees already working within the firm. As part of their education, *professionals* learn a generalized code of conduct that shapes their behavior on the job, enriching or in some cases replacing the local rules and regulations of the employing firm. As a result, professionals can be brought into a firm to perform work for which useful written specifications do not exist or cannot be prepared.[9] In contrast, in *training*, the knowledge and skills needed to perform the work of an organization are acquired within the organization itself. Such training, as provided by the employing organization, is purposely organization specific and often job specific.

Because skill standardization is aimed at regulating characteristics of people rather than jobs, it is used most often in situations where neither behaviors nor output standards can be easily specified. Few experts agree, for example, on the precise behaviors in which high school teachers should engage while teaching. In addition, general consensus exists that the output indicators for the job of teaching, such as course grades and standardized test scores, have questionable validity as measures of teaching success: grades can be artificially inflated and test scores can be influenced by pretest coaching. For this reason, instead of specifying expected behaviors or outputs, school districts often mandate that their teachers be certified by a state agency. Achieving such certification typically requires that teachers not only hold certain educational degrees, but also provide evidence of having acquired specific knowledge and skills. As a result, all teachers hired by a school district that requires state certification should possess a more or less standardized set of job qualifications or skills and be similarly able to perform their jobs.

Finally, *norm standardization* is present when the members of a group or organization share a set of beliefs about the acceptability of particular types of behavior, leading them to behave in ways that are generally approved. At Honda, for example, corporate norms promote the importance of producing high-quality automobiles. Workers on Honda's U.S. lines who adopt these norms as their own do not need to be directed by a supervisor to produce high-quality products. Instead, the norms of the larger company influence them to behave in ways that enhance product quality. Accepting shared norms and behaving accordingly reduce the need to coordinate activities in other ways because they increase the likelihood that people will behave appropriately and consistently over time.

As described in Chapter 8, organizations use *socialization* to teach important behavioral norms to employees, particularly newcomers. To the extent that these norms regulate activities required to coordinate the flow of work, coordination by norm standardization can be enacted without formalized written rules and procedures. This approach lies at the heart of the system of coordination used in many companies in Japan and South Korea. Asian companies use practices such as reciting company mottos before beginning work each day or singing company songs during social outings after work to constantly remind employees of the firms' norms and to ensure compliance with these norms. In less obvious forms, norm standardization is cropping up with increasing frequency in North American organizations. For instance, at Hewlett-Packard employees learn the history of their company. Along the way, they hear stories about the company's founders and early management that illustrate which behaviors are presently considered appropriate at Hewlett-Packard and which are not. In addition to being entertaining, these stories promote important company norms.

Choosing among the Mechanisms

Managers charged with managing an organization's structure continually confront the need to make choices among the basic coordination mechanisms summarized in Table 12.1. In most situations, two or more of these mechanisms are used concurrently to integrate work activities in and among the groups in an organization. In such instances, one serves as the primary mechanism used to solve most coordination problems. The others, if present, serve as secondary mechanisms that supplement the primary mechanism, backing it up in case it fails to provide enough integration.

Managers must decide which mechanism will serve as the primary means of coordination and which (if any) will act as secondary mechanisms. In general, two factors influence such choices: (1) the number of people whose efforts must be coordinated to ensure the successful performance of interdependent tasks and (2) the relative stability of the situation in which the tasks must be performed.[10] In small groups, containing twelve or fewer people, coordination is often accomplished by everyone doing what comes naturally. Employees communicate face-to-face or electronically using mutual adjustment to fit their individual task behaviors into the group's overall network of interdependence. No other coordination mechanism is needed, and none is used. Family farms and neighborhood restaurants are often organized around this type of coordination.

Suppose, however, that a group includes more than twelve people—as many as twenty, thirty, or even forty—who use mutual adjustment alone to coordinate their activities. As depicted in Figure 12.1, the number of needed communication links rises geometrically as the number of individuals rises arithmetically; that is, although two people need only one link, three people need three links, six people need fifteen links, and so on. Clearly, the members of larger groups must spend so much time communicating with one another that very little time is left for task completion. This sort of *process loss* (discussed in Chapter 9) diminishes group productivity in such instances.

For this reason, direct supervision is typically employed instead of mutual adjustment in larger groups as the primary means of coordinating group activities. In communicating information to subordinates, the direct supervisor acts as a proxy for the group as a whole. To use an analogy,

Table 12.1 Basic Coordination Mechanisms

Mechanism	Definition
Mutual adjustment	Face-to-face communication in which co-workers exchange information about work procedures
Direct supervision	Direction and coordination of the work of a group by one person who issues direct orders to the group's members
Standardization	Planning and implementation of standards and procedures that regulate work performance
Behavior standardization	Specification of sequences of task behaviors or work processes
Output standardization	Establishment of goals or desired end results of task performance
Skill standardization	Specification of the abilities, knowledge, and skills required by a particular task
Norm standardization	Encouragement of attitudes and beliefs that lead to desired behaviors

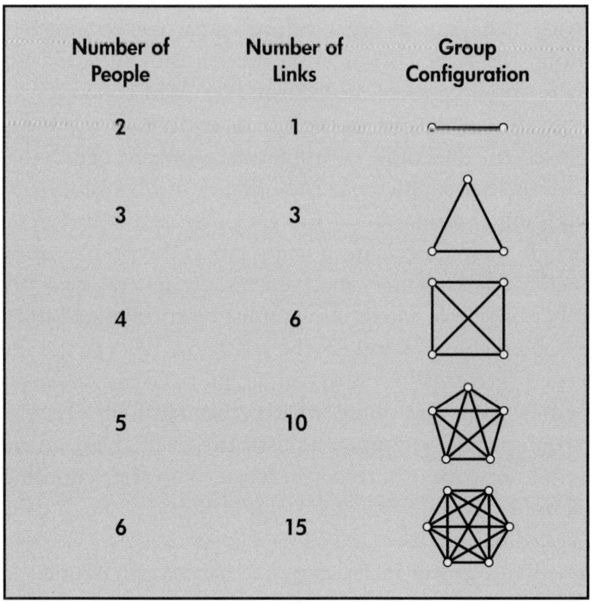

Number of People	Number of Links	Group Configuration
2	1	
3	3	
4	6	
5	10	
6	15	

Figure 12.1 Group Size and Mutual Adjustment Links

the direct supervisor functions like a switching mechanism that routes telephone messages from callers to receivers. The supervisor originates direct orders and collects performance feedback, while channeling information from one interdependent group member to another.

In such situations, mutual adjustment serves as a supplementary coordination mechanism: when the direct supervisor is unavailable or does not know how to solve a particular problem, employees communicate among themselves to try to figure out what to do and how to do it. Besides clarifying how direct supervision functions as a basic coordination mechanism, the telephone-switching analogy helps to explain the failure of direct supervision to coordinate the activities of members in even larger groups (for example, groups containing fifty or more individuals). Just as a switching mechanism can become overloaded by an avalanche of telephone calls, in successively larger groups the direct supervisor becomes increasingly burdened by the need to obtain information and channel it to the appropriate people. Ultimately, he or she will succumb to information overload, failing to keep up with subordinates' demands for information and coordination.

At this point, standardization is likely to replace direct supervision as the primary means of coordination. Coordination by standardization can prevent information overload by greatly reducing or eliminating the amount of communication needed for effective coordination. In this type of system, workers perform specified task behaviors, produce specified task outputs, use specified task skills, or conform to specified workplace norms. Thanks to the guidance provided by such standardization, members of very large groups can complete complex, interdependent networks of task activities with little or no need for further coordination.

Where standardization serves as the primary means of coordination, direct supervision and mutual adjustment remain available for use as secondary coordination mechanisms. On an assembly line, for instance, direct supervision might be used to ensure that workers adhere to formal behavioral standards. Mutual adjustment might also be employed on the assembly line to cope with machine breakdowns, power outages, or other temporary situations in which standard operating procedures are ineffective and direct supervision proves insufficient.

Standardization requires stability. If the conditions envisioned during the planning of a particular standardization program change, the program's utility could be lost. For example, behavioral specifications that detail computerized check-in procedures are likely to offer few benefits to hotel registration personnel who face a long line of guests and a dead computer screen. Mutual adjustment often reemerges in such instances, assuming the role of the primary basic coordination device. The process loss associated with mutual adjustment in these situations is simply tolerated as a necessary cost of staying in business.

The three means of coordination form a continuum, as depicted in Figure 12.2.[11] As coordination needs progress from left to right along the continuum, mechanisms to the left are not completely abandoned. All the way to the right end of the continuum, standardization, direct supervision, and secondary mutual adjustment remain available to supplement the mutual adjustment that serves as the primary means of coordination.

A critical trade-off exists between the *costs* of using a particular mechanism and the *flexibility* it permits. Mutual adjustment requires neither extensive planning nor the hierarchical differentiation of an organization's membership into supervisors and subordinates. Therefore, it affords a high degree of flexibility. However, each new use of mutual adjustment generates new coordination costs, and these costs tend to add up over time and become quite significant. They can take the form of time, effort, and similar resources that are consumed by communication activities and thus must be diverted away from task-related endeavors. In sum, what might appear to be a nearly cost-free approach to coordination can actually become very costly.

In contrast, the initial costs of standardization are quite high. The process of developing standards and procedures often requires the services of highly paid specialists, and otherwise productive resources must be diverted toward the design and implementation of standardization programs. Yet, once designed and implemented, such programs no longer consume resources of major significance. The large initial costs of standardization can therefore be amortized—spread over long periods of time and across long production runs. The result is an extremely low cost per incidence of coordination, which is less expensive than mutual adjustment over the long run. As mentioned earlier, however, standardization requires that the work situation remain essentially unchanged, because dynamic conditions would render existing standards obsolete. Thus it lacks the flexibility of mutual adjustment.

The flexibility of direct supervision lies between the extremes associated with mutual adjustment and standardization. Because direct supervision presupposes a hierarchy of authority, it lacks the spontaneity and fluidity of mutual adjustment. Yet, because it requires much less planning than standardization, direct supervision is more flexible. Not surprisingly, its coordination costs also fall between those of mutual adjustment and standardization. Although direct supervision requires fewer costly communication links than mutual adjustment, new coordination costs are generated for every supervisory action taken owing to the process loss that still occurs.

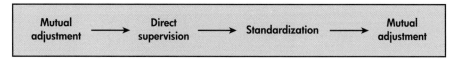

Figure 12.2 Continuum of Coordination Mechanisms

Departmentation

In addition to deciding how to coordinate interdependent activities, managers shaping an organization's structure must determine how to cluster the groups or teams produced via group formation. As indicated in Chapter 9, managers can form groups of co-workers on the basis of *functional* similarities, resulting in efficient but relatively inflexible groups of functional specialists. Alternatively, they can create groups based on *work flow* similarities, producing flexible but relatively inefficient teams that blur functional distinctions. Managers apply much the same logic to the job of linking the resulting groups together into a larger organization. The result consists of two types of **departmentation**.[12]

To illustrate these two alternatives, think of an organization that consists of four functional areas—marketing, research, manufacturing, and accounting—and three product lines—automobiles, trucks, and small gasoline engines. Figure 12.3 depicts this firm. In the figure, each box represents one of the four functions. Each of the horizontal work flows, represented by a series of arrows, stands for one of the three product lines. Dashed lines illustrate the alternative forms of departmentation.

The upper diagram in Figure 12.3 shows one type of departmentation, called *functional departmentation*. It is the equivalent of functional grouping but, rather than forming groups of individuals, the focus here is on forming groups that are themselves composed of groups. In the diagram, all marketing groups are combined into a single marketing department, all research groups are combined into a single research department, and so forth.

As with functional grouping, the *departments* that result from functional departmentation are economically efficient. In each department, members can trade information about their

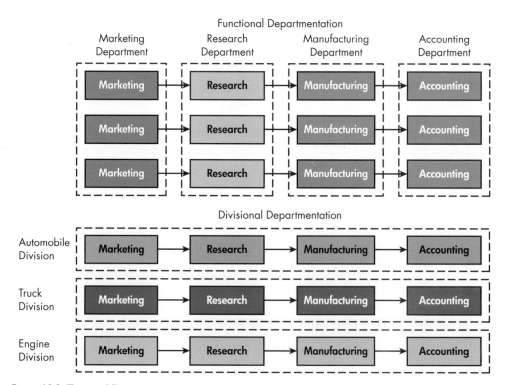

Figure 12.3 Types of Departmentation

functional specialty and improve their skills. Managers can also reduce overstaffing or duplication of effort by reassigning redundant employees elsewhere in the firm. Changes to any of the product lines crossing a particular department, however, require reorganization of the entire department. In other words, departments lack the flexibility to deal easily with change. In contrast, the second type of departmentation shown in the lower diagram of Figure 12.3, called *divisional departmentation*, is equivalent to using work flow grouping to cluster groups together into larger units. Instead of being grouped into marketing, manufacturing, research, and accounting departments, the organization's activities are grouped into product divisions—an automobile division, a truck division, and a gasoline engine division.

Alternatively, when an organization's clients differ more dramatically than its products, the organization's work might be grouped based on differences in the clients served. For instance, the company might include a military contracts division, a wholesale distribution division, and an aftermarket parts division. Following a third approach, an organization with operations spread throughout the world might be grouped geographically into North American, Asian, and European divisions.

Any of these alternatives offers the organization division-by-division flexibility. Each division can tailor its response to the unique demands of its own market. For example, Toyota's Lexus might decide to redesign its luxury market automobiles to be more conservative without worrying about the effects of this move on other Toyota products and markets. Some of the economic efficiency of functional departmentation is sacrificed, however, because effort is duplicated across the organization's various product lines. Lexus's product design studios duplicate those of Toyota, but the two studios cannot be consolidated without losing divisional flexibility. As with group formation, managers making divisional departmentation decisions face a trade-off between economy and flexibility.

By clustering related groups, departmentation of either type accentuates similarities that facilitate the management of intergroup relations. Specifically, in an organization structured around functional departmentation, groups in the same department share the same specialized knowledge, language, and ways of looking at the company's business. For instance, the members of a marketing department all share the same general marketing know-how. They discuss topics such as market segmentation and market share, and they generally agree that the best way to ensure their company's success is by appealing to customer needs. A manager charged with coordinating different groups in the marketing department can base his or her actions on this common knowledge, language, and viewpoint despite having to deal with several different groups of employees. Thus the manager can manage them using the same basic management approach.

Similarly, in an organization structured around divisional departmentation, groups in the same division share interests in the same basic line of business. Thus all employees in the truck division of a company such as General Motors or Ford are concerned about doing well in the truck industry. This commonality allows the manager of a division to treat groups performing different functions—marketing, manufacturing, research, and so forth—in much the same way, without having to tailor management practices to the functional specialty of each particular group.

Nonetheless, whether functional or divisional departmentation is used, the process of clustering related groups together also creates gaps or discontinuities between the resulting departments or divisions. In many instances, the kinds of conflict described in Chapter 11 can arise where these gaps occur. As indicated in that chapter, unit-linking mechanisms—ranging from intranets to matrix structuring—can be deployed to manage and resolve such conflicts.

Hierarchy and Centralization

A **hierarchy** reflects the differentiation of rank that occurs as group formation processes and departmentation procedures work together to create clusters of groups and layers of managers having responsibility for the activities of particular clusters. In Figure 12.4A, each of the small squares represents an assembly-line employee who works on one of the company's four lines, located in two separate buildings. Work groups, one per assembly line, are formed by grouping each line's workers together into a single group. In return, these groups are clustered into two larger groups, paralleling the two buildings that house assembly operations. Finally, these two "groups of groups" are themselves clustered together into a single assembly department. Figure 12.4B depicts the same pattern of clustering, but diagrams it in the familiar "organization chart" form that accentuates the presence of a hierarchy.

Once formed, a hierarchy can be used to control intergroup relations. A manager having hierarchical authority over a particular collection of groups can act as a direct supervisor and use this authority to issue orders that, when followed, will help coordinate activities among those groups. For instance, the manager having hierarchical authority over all manufacturing groups of the company depicted in the upper diagram in Figure 12.3 can use that authority to smooth the flow of information among groups of manufacturing employees formed through functional departmentation. Alternatively, the manager of the automobile division shown in the lower diagram in Figure 12.3 can facilitate work flows among employees in the divisions created through divisional departmentation. In turn, interdependencies that span different departments or divisions can be coordinated by managers higher in the organization's hierarchy. For example, problems between the manufacturing department and the marketing, research, or accounting departments shown in the upper diagram can be handled by the executive responsible for overseeing the various department managers. Hierarchical authority, then, can be used to coordinate relations among groups by extending the scope of direct supervision.

The use of hierarchy to coordinate intergroup relations differs from one organization to the next in terms of which level of managers—top, middle, or supervisory—has the ultimate authority to make decisions and issue orders. Left to their own devices, many top managers

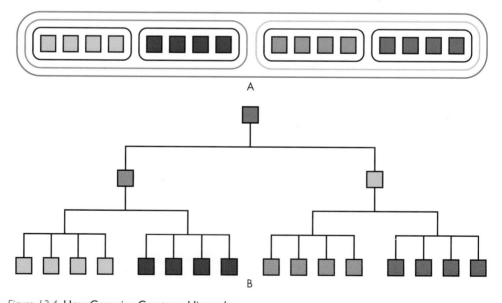

Figure 12.4 **How Grouping Creates a Hierarchy**

in North America would favor **centralization**, or the concentration of authority and decision making at the top of a firm.[13] Centralization affords top managers a high degree of certainty. Because they alone make the decisions in centralized firms, they can be sure not only that decisions are made, but also that those decisions are made in accordance with their own wishes. In addition, centralization can minimize the time needed to make decisions because few people are involved in the decision-making process.

However, **decentralization** has become increasingly common in modern organizations. In decentralized organizations, authority and decision making are dispersed downward and outward in the hierarchy of managers and employees. Several factors push otherwise reluctant top managers toward its implementation. First, some decisions require top managers to weigh a great deal of information. Managers might become overloaded by the task of processing this vast amount of information and therefore find it useful to involve more people in the decision-making process. Second, decentralization might be stimulated by a need for flexibility. If local conditions require that different parts of an organization respond differently, managers of those organizational groups must be empowered to make their own decisions. Third, decentralization might prove useful in dealing with employee motivation problems if those problems can be solved by granting employees control over workplace practices and conditions. In any of these cases, the failure to decentralize can seriously undermine attempts to coordinate intergroup relations.

Types of Organization Structure

The choice to emphasize standardization as a primary means of coordination leads to the creation of a bureaucratic organization structure. As noted in Chapter 2, Weber's bureaucracy is a form of organization in which rules, regulations, and standards are written down and used to govern member behaviors. In contrast, the choice to place primary emphasis on either of the other means of coordination also entails the choice to bypass bureaucracy or reduce its presence in a firm. Between complete bureaucracy and no bureaucracy lies a continuum of structures, each incorporating specific configurations of departmentation and centralization. These different structures are described next.

Prebureaucratic Structures

As their name suggests, **prebureaucratic structures** lack the standardization that is the defining characteristic of bureaucracies. They can be used successfully only in organizations so small in size and so simple in purpose that mutual adjustment or direct supervision provides the coordination needed to maintain interdependence.

In the most basic type of prebureaucratic structure, the **simple undifferentiated structure**, coordination is accomplished solely by mutual adjustment. That is, co-workers interact with one another to determine how to coordinate work among themselves. Because communicating with other people is natural for most of us, mutual adjustment is easy to initiate and relatively simple to sustain. For this reason, simple undifferentiated structures can often be established and perpetuated fairly easily.

As Figure 12.5 suggests, a simple undifferentiated structure lacks a hierarchy of authority. Such a structure is nothing more than an organization of people who decide what to do by communicating with each other as they work. No single individual has the authority to issue orders, and few, if any, written procedures guide performance. A group of friends who decide to open a small restaurant, gift shop, or similar sort of business might, at the outset, adopt this type of structure for the business.

Figure 12.5 **The Simple Undifferentiated Structure**

The primary strengths of simple undifferentiated structures are their simplicity and extreme flexibility. Especially when they are organized around face-to-face communication, they can develop spontaneously and be reconfigured almost instantly. For example, just as adding another member to a small classroom discussion group is likely to cause only a momentary lapse in the group's activities, adding another worker to a family-run convenience store will have little long-term effect on coordination among the store's workers.

A major weakness of simple undifferentiated structures is their limitation to small organizations. Suppose you are a member in an advertising firm employing twenty-five or thirty people. It would be difficult or impossible to rely on mutual adjustment alone to ensure that the firm's accounts were properly handled, because process loss would inevitably undermine the usefulness of face-to-face coordination among such a large number of individuals. So many interpersonal links would be required that valuable time and effort would be lost in the struggle to maintain some degree of organization.

A related weakness is the failure of simple undifferentiated structures to provide the coordination needed to accomplish complex tasks. For example, it is unlikely that a simple undifferentiated structure of twelve or fewer people could succeed at mass-producing automobiles. Complicated work requires a more complicated organization structure.

In the second type of prebureaucratic structure, the **simple differentiated structure**, direct supervision replaces mutual adjustment as the primary means of coordination. Organizations with simple differentiated structures are a common part of everyday life—a local grocery store or neighborhood gas station, for example. As shown in Figure 12.6, this type of structure is organized as a small, centralized hierarchy. One person (usually the firm's owner or the owner's management representative) retains the hierarchical authority needed to coordinate work activities by means of direct supervision. Mutual adjustment is used to deal with coordination problems that direct supervision cannot resolve. For example, while the owner of a small insurance agency is at the post office retrieving the morning mail, clerks in the agency may talk among themselves to decide who will answer the telephone and who will process paperwork until the owner returns.

The simple differentiated structure can coordinate the activities of larger numbers of people than can the simple undifferentiated structure. By shifting to direct supervision, it eliminates some of the process loss associated with reliance on mutual adjustment alone. In addition, because its decision-making powers are centralized in the hands of a single person, an organization with a simple differentiated structure can respond rapidly to changing conditions. At the same time, this structure affords a good deal of flexibility because it avoids standardization.

The simple differentiated structure's weaknesses include its inability to coordinate the activities of more than about fifty people and its failure to provide the integration needed to accomplish complex tasks. A group of people is just as unlikely to organize itself to produce cars by using a combination of direct supervision and mutual adjustment as it is to organize itself to carry out such a task by using mutual adjustment alone. A single direct supervisor would soon be overwhelmed by the vast amount of information required to know what cars to produce, which parts to order, how to assemble them properly, and so forth.

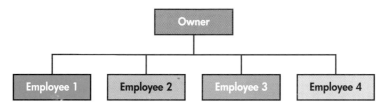

Figure 12.6 **The Simple Differentiated Structure**

Bureaucratic Structures

Both kinds of prebureaucratic structures are likely to be overwhelmed by the coordination requirements of complicated tasks. Some combination of standardization of behaviors, outputs, skills, or norms is required to deal with such tasks, because standardization of any type greatly reduces the amount of information that must be exchanged and the number of decisions that must be made as work is being performed. In the **bureaucratic structures** that arise as standardization emerges as the primary means of coordination, direct supervision and mutual adjustment are retained as secondary mechanisms that take effect when standardization fails to meet all coordination needs. This combination of coordination mechanisms allows organizations with bureaucratic structures to integrate the variety of jobs needed to perform complicated, demanding work.

The **functional structure** is the most basic form of bureaucratic structure, and can be adopted by organizations that are larger than the fifty or so members whose activities can be coordinated via a simple differentiated structure, yet not so large that they do business in several different locations or serve widely differing groups of clientele. Locally owned banks, department stores, or manufacturing plants typically have functional structures.

Such structures are characterized by three key attributes. First, because they are bureaucratic structures, functional structures are based on coordination by standardization. Most often they will rely on behavioral standardization, although output standardization is also used in functional structuring. Second, these structures are organized according to functional departmentation. That is, groups within them are clustered into departments according to the functions their members perform, such as marketing, manufacturing, or accounting. Third, functional structures are usually centralized. Most, if not all, important decisions are made by one person or a few people at the tops of firms with functional structures—especially decisions related to the formation of organizational goals and objectives.

As Figure 12.7 suggests, one easy way to determine whether a particular firm has a functional structure is to examine the titles held by its vice presidents. If the firm has a bureaucratic structure and all of its vice presidents have titles that indicate what their subordinates do (for example, vice president of manufacturing, vice president of marketing, vice president of research and development), the firm has a functional structure. If one or more vice presidents have other sorts of titles (for instance, vice president of the consumer finance division or vice president of European operations), the firm has another type of structure (described later).

The primary strength of the functional structure is its economic efficiency. Standardization minimizes the long-term costs of coordination. In addition, centralization makes it possible for workers to focus their attention on their work rather than taking time out to make decisions. Functional structures, however, have a critical weakness: they lack significant flexibility. The standardization that provides so much efficiency not only takes lengthy formalization (planning and documentation) to implement, but also requires that the same standards

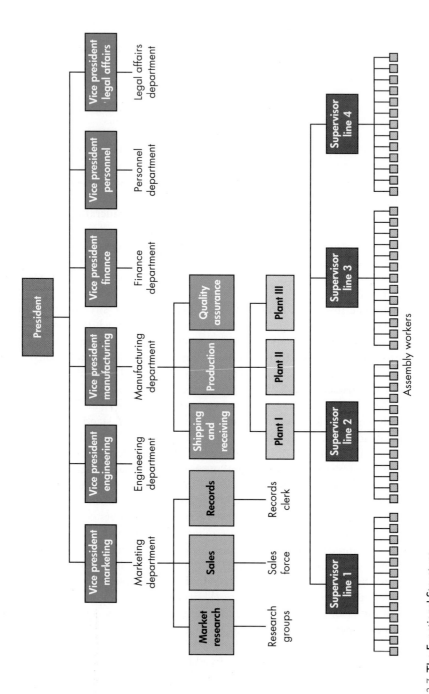

Figure 12.7 The Functional Structure

be followed repeatedly. This inflexibility reduces the functional structure's ability to cope with instability or change. Functional departmentation adds to this rigidity, because changes to any work flow in a company organized by functional departmentation necessarily affect the other work flows in the organization.

A functional structure can coordinate the work of an organization effectively if the firm limits itself to one type of product, manufactures this product in a single geographic location, and sells to no more than a few different types of clients. Of course, many organizations produce multiple types of products, do business in several locations, or seek to serve a wide variety of clients. Such diversity of products, locations, or clients injects variety into the information that a firm needs to make managerial decisions. This variety overloads the centralized decision-making processes on which the functional structure is based. In such situations, other structures can prove more useful.

The **divisional structure** is a second type of bureaucratic structure. As such, it is characterized by standardization of any of several types, most often standardization of behaviors, outputs, or skills. Unlike functional structures, however, divisional structures are moderately decentralized. Decision making is pushed downward by one or two hierarchical layers, so a company's vice presidents and sometimes their immediate subordinates share in the process of digesting information and making key decisions. Divisional departmentation is another feature that distinguishes divisional structures from functional structures. Groups in divisional structures are clustered together according to similarities in products, geographic locations, or clients. For this reason, divisional structures are sometimes called product structures, geographic structures, or market structures.

Figure 12.8 depicts three divisional structures, based on product similarities, geographic similarities, and client similarities. Each differs from the functional structure diagrammed in Figure 12.7, since in each of the structures in Figure 12.8 the vice presidential titles of *line* divisions include product, geographic, or client names. Note, however, that vice presidents of *staff* divisions in these divisional structures have titles that sound like functions—for example, vice president of legal affairs or vice president of corporate finance.

The divisional structure's departmentation scheme and moderate decentralization imbue it with a degree of flexibility not found in the functional structure.[14] Each division can react to issues concerning its own product, geographic region, or client group without disturbing the operation of other divisions. It remains securely connected to the rest of the organization, however, and is not allowed to drift away from the overall organization's goals and objectives. For example, the vice president of consumer electronics, shown in the upper panel of Figure 12.8, can make decisions affecting the production and sales of clock radios and steam irons without consulting with the company's president or other vice presidents, but he or she cannot decide to redirect the division into another line of products.

The limited degree of independence afforded the divisions in a divisional structure allows one to stop doing business without seriously interrupting the operations of the others. For example, the division of Boeing that fulfills military contracts could discontinue doing business without affecting work in the firm's civilian aircraft division. Remember, however, that each division in such a structure is itself organized like a functional structure, as indicated in Figure 12.8. As a result, a particular division cannot change products, locations, or clients without incurring serious interruptions in its own internal operations. Thus a decision at Boeing to service NASA contracts in its military division would require substantial reorganization of that division.

The flexibility that is the main strength of divisional structures comes at the price of increased costs arising from duplication of effort across divisions. For example, every division is likely to have a separate sales force, even though that structure means that salespeople from

A. Product Structure

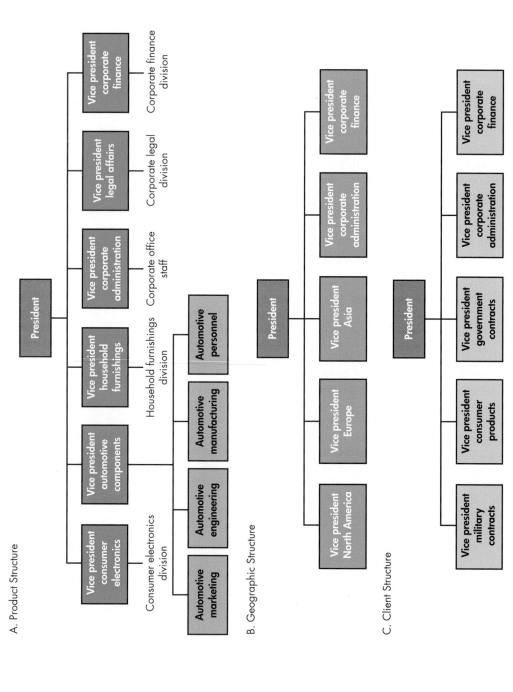

B. Geographic Structure

C. Client Structure

Figure 12.8 Divisional Structures

several different divisions might visit the same customer. The primary weakness of divisional structures is the fact that they are, at best, only moderately efficient.

Matrix structures, like divisional structures, are bureaucratic structures adopted by organizations that must integrate work activities related to a variety of products, locations, or customers. However, firms that have implemented matrix structures, such as Monsanto, Prudential Insurance, and Chase Manhattan Bank, need even more flexibility than is possible with divisional structures.[15] They try to achieve this flexibility by reintegrating functional specialists across different product, location, or customer lines. Because matrix structures use functional and divisional departmentation simultaneously to cluster together structural groups, they are also called *simultaneous structures.*

Figure 12.9 illustrates the matrix structure of a firm that has three divisions, each of which manufactures and sells a distinct product line. Each box or unit in the matrix represents a distinct group composed of a small hierarchy of supervisors and one or more structural groups having both functional and divisional responsibilities. For example, Unit 1 is a consumer electronics marketing group, composed of units that market televisions, radios, cellular telephones, and other electronic merchandise. Unit 2 is an automotive components engineering group, consisting of engineering units that design automobile engines, suspensions, steering assemblies, and other such items. Unit 3 is a household products manufacturing group, made up of facilities that produce furniture polishes, floor waxes, window cleaners, and other household supplies. Note that staff groups in a matrix structure are often excluded from the matrix itself. The three staff departments shown in the diagram—personnel, finance, and legal affairs—provide advice to top management but are not parts of the matrix.

Mutual adjustment is the primary means of coordination within the upper layers of a matrix structure, and decision making is decentralized among matrix managers. Both of these characteristics enable top managers to reconfigure relationships among the cells in the matrix, promoting extreme flexibility. Because of their dual responsibilities, each matrix cell has two bosses: a functional boss and a divisional boss. This arrangement violates Fayol's principle of unity of command (Chapter 2). Thus mutual adjustment must also be used in the upper layer of each cell to cope with conflicting orders from above.

Beneath the upper layer of each cell, standardization is used to integrate work activities. Both direct supervision and lower-level mutual adjustment serve as supplementary mechanisms that coordinate cell-level activities. For instance, once managers at the top of the matrix structure shown in Figure 12.9 have decided to manufacture a new kind of floor wax, formalization is used to develop new standards. Standardization is then used to coordinate activities in the units in the household products manufacturing cell that carry out the production of this new product. Direct supervisors help employees learn the new standards and work to correct deficiencies in the standards as they become apparent. In addition, employees engage in mutual adjustment to cope with problems that their supervisor cannot resolve.

As is apparent, a matrix structure basically consists of a simple differentiated structure designed into the upper layers of a bureaucracy—including the president and vice presidents, plus the individuals who manage each of the cells shown in Figure 12.9. This simple structure injects mutual adjustment into an otherwise bureaucratic organization so as to encourage communication, coordination, and flexibility among the managers who oversee organizational operations.

The primary strength of matrix structures derives from their extreme flexibility. They can adjust to changes that would overwhelm other bureaucratic structures. Nonetheless, matrix structures are relatively rare, because they are extremely costly to operate. In part, this costliness stems from the proliferation of managers in matrix firms, as a matrix requires two complete sets of vice presidents. Matrix structures also incorporate the same sort of

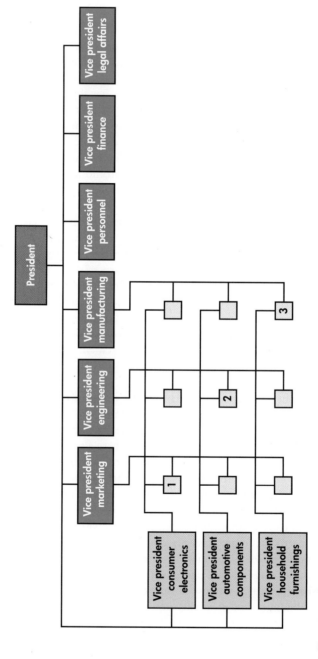

Figure 12.9 The Matrix Structure

duplication of effort—multiple sales forces, for instance—that make divisional structures so expensive to operate. Moreover, because employees near the top must deal with two bosses and often conflicting orders, working in a matrix can be extremely stressful. This stress can lead to absenteeism, turnover, and ultimately lower productivity and higher human resource costs.[16]

More important, matrix structures are economically inefficient because they rely on mutual adjustment as their primary coordination mechanism, despite extremely costly levels of process loss. Matrix structuring, therefore, represents the decision to tolerate costly coordination so as to secure high flexibility. Firms that choose matrix structures and function effectively thereafter are generally those that face high degrees of change that would destroy them if they could not easily adapt to their dynamic environment. In effect, they choose the lesser of two evils—the inefficiency of a matrix rather than dissolution. Firms that attempt matrix organization, but later abandon it, tend not to face the degree of change required to justify the costs of the matrix approach.

A fourth form of bureaucratic structure, the **multiunit structure**, achieves high flexibility in extremely large organizations by decoupling the divisions of an organization rather than by further integrating divisional elements along functional lines, as in a matrix structure. A multiunit structure emerges when the divisions of a divisional structure are permitted to separate themselves from the rest of the organization and develop into autonomous, self-managed business units.[17] Each business unit is allowed to fend for itself, with little or no interference from the *holding unit* that oversees the complete firm. Companies including General Electric, Ford, Xerox, and Alco Standard have variations of this form of structure.[18]

Figure 12.10 shows a multiunit structure. All multiunit structures are organized around divisional departmentation, but each "division" is actually a self-sufficient business concern. Compared with other kinds of bureaucratic structures, multiunit structures are extremely decentralized. Unit managers several levels below the holding unit's CEO have the authority to define their unit's purpose and formulate its mission. At the same time, routine activities within each business unit are coordinated as much as possible by standardization, often involving the standardization of skills or norms to control the costs of process loss.

A major strength of the multiunit structure is its ability to provide the coordination required to manage extremely large or complex organizations, albeit in parts, without incurring the high costs of the matrix structure. Unfortunately, multiunit structures suffer from some degree of inefficiency inasmuch as their divisional departmentation means substantial duplication of effort. Another drawback is that multiunit structures are not useful when strong links are needed between the various parts of the organization. For example, it is difficult to imagine organizing a hospital as a multiunit structure. Too many transfers of patients and treatment information are required among the units of a hospital to allow many of them to operate autonomously.

Postbureaucratic Structures

Within the past thirty years, many organizations have found it necessary to be more flexible than allowed by even the most flexible form of bureaucracy. Some have grown extremely large—employing hundreds of thousands of individuals, producing a tremendous variety of goods or services, and doing business in every corner of the world. Others have found themselves competing in industries characterized by massive change occurring on a continual basis. As a result, attention has turned to forming information-rich organization structures, grounded in computerized communication networks and coordinated by technology-aided mutual adjustment, that can successfully deal with extreme complexity and identify change

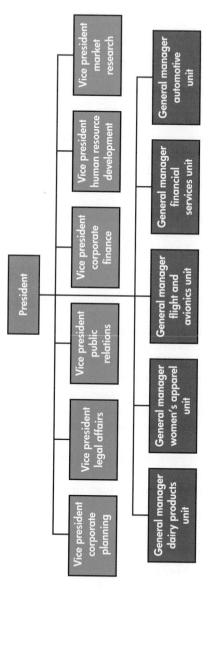

Figure 12.10 The Multiunit Structure

before it threatens organizational viability. In the process, managers have begun to experiment with two new kinds of **postbureaucratic structures**: modular and virtual structures.

A **modular structure**, also called a *network structure*, consists of a collection of autonomous modules or cells interconnected by a computerized intranet.[19] In such structures, self-managing teams, grouped according to process, assume supervisory duties and use mutual adjustment to coordinate internal work activities. An intranet ties teams together horizontally, allowing for mutual adjustment among teams needed to manage interdependent efforts, and provides the vertical information flows required to ensure firmwide collaboration. Computer-mediated networks thus supplant hierarchy and centralization as the primary means of coordinating interdependence among groups.

The modular structure can be quite flexible, as different configurations of modules can be strung together to accomplish the various tasks that might confront a firm. For example, the collection of research, production, and marketing modules assembled in a biotechnology firm to develop and distribute an influenza vaccine can be disbanded and recombined with others to perform research on cell development and market the firm's new anticancer discovery.

Modular flexibility comes at the price of significant process loss, however, owing to the redirection of otherwise productive resources toward self-management activities. This loss is less than that experienced in matrix structures and is viewed as essential to organizational success and survival.

In the **virtual structure**, several organizations attain the performance capacities of a single, much larger firm while retaining extreme flexibility and significant efficiency.[20] The label *virtual structure* is patterned after the term *virtual memory*, which refers to a way of making a computer act as though it has more memory capacity than it actually possesses. Analogously, virtual structuring provides a way to make an organization act as though it has more productive capacity than it actually controls. A structure of this type develops when a company forms a network of alliances with other companies to quickly exploit a business opportunity. Thus a virtual structure is not a single organization, but rather a temporary collection of several organizations.

Levi Strauss, Atlas Industrial Door, and Dell Computer are some of the better-known companies currently implementing aspects of the virtual structuring approach.[21] In virtual structures, each firm focuses on doing the thing it does best—its core competency in design, manufacturing, marketing, or any other necessary function—and together the firms form a "best of everything" organization. During the period of its temporary existence, a virtual structure resembles a loosely coupled functional structure where each "department" is an otherwise autonomous company. Connecting the various companies together is an intranet of computerized information-processing systems that takes the place of hierarchy in coordinating interdependence relationships among companies. Such coordination is accomplished mainly by mutual adjustment through e-mail, teleconferencing, and similar electronic linkages.

The temporary nature of the virtual structure is the source of its flexibility, because companies can be added or eliminated as the situation warrants. In the face of this flexibility, the virtual structure's efficiency comes from each company's singular focus on doing what it does best. Thus it would seem that the virtual structure overcomes the efficiency-versus-flexibility trade-offs evident among the other structures just discussed. It does have some drawbacks, however. Considerable efficiency might be sacrificed by virtual structuring, owing to the cost of coordinating efforts spread among several otherwise independent firms. These costs inhibit the use of virtual structures in all but the most turbulent situations.[22]

Summary

An organization's *structure* is a network of interdependencies among the people and tasks that make up the organization. It is created and sustained by the *basic coordination mechanisms* of *mutual adjustment, direct supervision,* and *standardization,* all of which coordinate interdependent relationships among people and groups. Structure emerges as the groups in an organization become clustered together during *functional* or *divisional departmentation.* The resulting departments or divisions are also coordinated by means of *hierarchy* and *centralization.*

Standardization, when used as the primary means of coordination, is the hallmark of *bureaucracy.* Depending on the mix of coordination mechanisms, departmentation, and centralization chosen by the managers of a firm, various types of *prebureaucratic, bureaucratic,* or *postbureaucratic* structures may be produced. These include the *simple undifferentiated structure,* the *simple differentiated structure,* the *functional structure,* the *divisional structure,* the *matrix structure,* the *multiunit structure,* the *modular structure,* and the *virtual structure.* Each structural type offers its own strengths and weaknesses, most of which involve trade-offs between efficiency and flexibility.

Review Questions

1. Given that an organization's structure integrates and differentiates activities in the organization, tell which of the following structural characteristics provide integration and which produce differentiation: basic coordination mechanisms, departmentation, hierarchy, and centralization.
2. Explain why standardization requires stability. Why is mutual adjustment so much more flexible? How does direct supervision fit between the two extremes? Which mechanism(s) would you use to coordinate a television-assembly group of fifty employees? Six custom jewelry makers? A dozen door-to-door magazine salespeople? Why?
3. Explain how professionalization, training, and socialization can be used to create standardization. Based on what you have learned in other chapters, name some additional purposes that these three processes serve in organizations.
4. What kinds of departmentation can be used to cluster groups together? How do departmentation and hierarchy work together to resolve coordination problems among departments or divisions?

Notes

1   G. Anglebrandt, "When Success Needs Structure," *Crain's Detroit Business,* May 20, 2013, 11–12.
2   D. Welch, "Ed Whitcre's Battle to Save GM from Itself," *Bloomberg Businessweek,* May 9, 2010, 48–55; D. Welch, "Akerson Grabs the Wheel," *Bloomberg Businessweek,* August 30, 2010, 64–67; D. Welch, "Dan Akerson is Not a Car Guy," *Bloomberg Businessweek,* August 29, 2011, 56–60.
3   J. G. March and H. A. Simon, *Organizations* (New York: Wiley, 1958), 4; J. D. Thompson, *Organizations in Action* (New York: McGraw-Hill, 1967), 51; W. R. Scott, *Organizations: Rational, Natural, and Open Systems,* 3rd ed. (Englewood Cliffs, NJ: Prentice Hall, 1992), 15.
4   P. R. Lawrence and J. W. Lorsch, "Differentiation and Integration in Complex Organizations," *Administrative Science Quarterly* 12 (1967): 1–47; P. R. Lawrence and J. W. Lorsch, *Organization and Environment* (Homewood, IL: Irwin, 1967), 7; R. L. Daft, *Essentials of Organization Theory and Design* (Cincinnati, OH: South-Western, 2007).
5   Lawrence and Lorsch, "Differentiation and Integration," 2–3; March and Simon, *Organizations,* 160; J. R. Galbraith, *Designing Complex Organizations* (Reading, MA: Addison-Wesley, 1973), 4.

6 Thompson, *Organizations in Action*, 62.

7 H. Mintzberg, *Structuring of Organizations* (Englewood Cliffs, NJ: Prentice Hall, 1979), 3–4.

8 Ibid., 5.

9 R. H. Hall, "Professionalism and Bureaucratization," *American Sociological Review* 33 (1968): 92–104; J. Hage and M. Aiken, "Relationship of Centralization to Other Structural Properties," *Administrative Science Quarterly* 12 (1967): 72–91.

10 Mintzberg, *Structuring of Organizations*, 7–9; H. Mintzberg, "The Structuring of Organizations," in J. B. Quinn, H. Mintzberg, and R. M. James, eds., *The Strategy Process: Concepts, Contexts, and Cases* (Englewood Cliffs, NJ: Prentice Hall, 1988), 276–304.

11 Mintzberg, *Structuring of Organizations*, 7.

12 P. N. Khandwalla, *The Design of Organizations* (New York: Harcourt Brace Jovanovich, 1977), 489–497; A. Walker and J. Lorsch, "Organizational Choice: Product versus Function," *Harvard Business Review* 46 (1968): 129–138.

13 D. S. Pugh, D. J. Hickson, C. R. Hinings, and C. Turner, "Dimensions of Organization Structure," *Administrative Science Quarterly* 13 (1968): 65–91; J. Hage and M. Aiken, "Relationship of Centralization to Other Structural Properties"; P. M. Blau, "Decentralization in Bureaucracies," in M. N. Zald, ed., *Power in Organizations* (Nashville, TN: Vanderbilt University Press, 1970), 42–81; N. M. Carter and J. B. Cullen, "A Comparison of Centralization/Decentralization of Decision Making Concepts and Measures," *Journal of Management* 10 (1984): 259–268; R. Mansfield, "Bureaucracy and Centralization: An Examination of Organizational Structure," *Administrative Science Quarterly* 18 (1973): 477–478; N. S. Argyres and B. S. Silverman, "R&D, Organization Structure, and the Development of Corporate Technological Knowledge," *Strategic Management Journal* 25 (2004): 929–958; W. G. Ouchi, "Power to the Principles: Decentralization in Three Large School Districts," *Organization Science* 17 (2006): 298–307.

14 R. E. Hoskisson, C. W. L. Hill, and H. Kim, "The Multidivisional Structure: Organizational Fossil or Source of Value?" *Journal of Management* 19 (1993): 269–298; J. R. Galbraith, "The Evolution of Enterprise Organization Designs," *Journal of Organization Design* 1 (2012): 1–13.

15 R. C. Ford and W. A. Randolph, "Cross Functional Structures: A Review and Integration of Matrix Organization and Project Management," *Journal of Management* 18 (1992): 267–294; T. Sy and S. Cote, "Emotional Intelligence: A Key Ability to Succeed in the Matrix Organization," *Journal of Management Development* 23 (2004): 437–455.

16 L. R. Burns, "Matrix Management in Hospitals: Testing Theories of Matrix Structure and Development," *Administrative Science Quarterly* 34 (1989): 349–368; L. R. Burns and D. R. Wholey, "Adoption and Abandonment of Matrix Management Programs: Effects of Organizational Characteristics and Interorganizational Programs," *Academy of Management Journal* 36 (1993): 106–138.

17 J. A. Wagner III, "Organizations," in A. E. Kasdin, ed., *Encyclopedia of Psychology* (New York: Oxford Press, 2000), 14–20.

18 M. Hammer and J. Champy, *Reengineering the Corporation: A Manifesto for Business Revolution* (New York: Harper Business, 1993); S. Lubove, "How to Grow Big yet Stay Small," *Forbes*, December 7, 1992, 64–67; M. Rothschild, "Coming Soon: Internal Markets," *Forbes ASAP*, June 7, 1993, 19–21.

19 M. A. Schilling and H. K. Steensma, "The Use of Modular Organizational Forms: An Industry-Level Analysis," *Academy of Management Journal* 44 (2001): 1149–1168; G. DeSanctis, J. T. Glass, and I. M. Ensing, "Organizational Designs for R&D," *Academy of Management Executive* 16 (2002): 55–66; R. E. Miles and C. C. Snow, "The New Network Firm: A Spherical Structure Built on a Human Investment Philosophy," *Organizational Dynamics* 23 (1995): 5–18; R. E. Miles, C. C. Snow, J. A. Matthews, and H. C. Coleman, Jr., "Organizing in the Knowledge Age: Anticipating the Cellular Form," *Academy of Management Executive* 11 (1997): 7–24; A. Oberg and P. Walgenbach, "Hierarchical Structures of Communication in a Network Structure," *Scandinavian Journal of Management* 24 (2008): 183–198; J. A. Mathews, "Design of Industrial and Supra-Firm Architectures: Growth and Sustainability," *Journal of Organization Design* 1 (2012): 42–63.

20 G. DeSanctis and P. Monge, "Communication Processes for Virtual Organizations," *Organization Science* 10 (1999): 693–703; G. G. Dess, A. M. A. Rasheed, K. J. McLaughlin, and R. L. Priem, "The New Corporate Architecture," *Academy of Management Executive* 9 (1995): 7–20; R. E. Miles and C. C. Snow, "Organizations: New Concepts for New Forms,"

California Management Review 28 (1986): 62–73; M. K. Ahuja and K. M. Carley, "Network Structure in Virtual Organizations," *Organization Science* 10 (1999): 741–757; L. H. Lin and I. Y. Lu, "Adoption of Virtual Organization by Taiwanese Electronics Firms: An Empirical Study of Organization Structure Innovation," *Journal of Organizational Change Management* 18 (2005): 184–200.

21 W. H. Davidow and M. S. Malone, *The Virtual Corporation: Structuring and Revitalizing the Corporation for the 21st Century* (New York: Harper Collins, 1992); J. A. Byrne, R. Brandt, and O. Port, "The Virtual Corporation: The Company of the Future Will Be the Ultimate in Adaptability," *BusinessWeek*, February 8, 1993, 99–102; J. A. Byrne, "The Futurists Who Fathered the Ideas," *BusinessWeek*, February 8, 1993, 103; M. Malone and W. Davidow, "Virtual Corporation," *Forbes ASAP*, December 7, 1992, 102–107; J. W. Verity, "A Company that's 100% Virtual," *BusinessWeek*, November 21, 1994, 85; D. Greising, "The Virtual Olympics," *BusinessWeek*, April 29, 1996, 64–66; I. Ivan, C. Ciurea, and M. Doinea, "Collaborative Virtual Organizations in Knowledge-based Economy," *Informatica Economica* 16 (2012): 143–154.

22 D. Tapscott, D. Ticoll, and A. Lowy, "Internet Nirvana," *E-Company*, December 2000, 99–108.

Chapter 13

Technology, Environment, and Organization Design

There was a time in the 1990s when BlackBerry cell phones were the must-have business accessory. In fact, the phones were so essential to processes of business communication—voice communication, composing and reading e-mail, scheduling and tracking appointments, storing and retrieving contact information, and the like—that users coined the term "Crackberry" to highlight the addictive relationship that often developed between themselves and their BlackBerries. The company that made them, Research in Motion (RIM), had a stranglehold on the business communication market up until in 2007, when Apple introduced the touchscreen iPhone and a deluge of specialized business apps. Soon after, Google launched its Android operating system and "Droid" smartphones from such manufacturers as Samsung, HTC, and Motorola. By 2012, Apple had surpassed RIM to become the top seller of company-issued cellular devices, and Android phones were quickly closing the gap. By its own admission, RIM was no longer the dominant provider of cell phones for the business market. In an effort to regain lost ground, in 2013 RIM changed its name to BlackBerry and introduced a new product, the BlackBerry Z10, intended to appeal to touchscreen users and restore the company's competitive position. Meanwhile, Microsoft introduced Windows Phone 8, its latest touchscreen operating system designed to run on phones manufactured by Nokia and others. Whether BlackBerry can survive, let alone regain its former position of dominance, is considered highly questionable by industry experts.[1]

How can a company like BlackBerry lose sight of its surrounding environment and fail to realize that change is necessary? More importantly, what can an organization do to minimize the likelihood that it will fail to see changes in its environment? Both are questions of organization design—the process of managing organization structure and fitting an organization's structure to pertinent business conditions—that have important implications for the competitiveness and continued survival of all business organizations. Whether they are maintaining existing structures or implementing new ones, managers must know about the different types of structures as well as the key strengths and weaknesses of each structural type. In addition, they must be able to diagnose and react to the various factors that influence the effectiveness of each type of structure, and they must recognize how a particular structure matches up with their company's specific business situation.

This chapter presents an adaptive model of organization design that provides guidance to managers engaged in structuring modern organizations. It begins by discussing the concept of organizational effectiveness, which is the ultimate goal of structural management. It then examines some of the most influential contingency factors that govern the effectiveness of alternative structures. In the process, the chapter identifies which of the various structures described in Chapter 12 work best under each of several kinds of business conditions.

An Adaptive Model of Organization Design

Is there a single *best* type of organizational structure? The fact that many different kinds of structures exist suggests that no one type will be suitable for all organizations. Instead, each form of organization structure possesses unique strengths and weaknesses that make it appropriate for some situations but not for others. Structuring an organization involves making well-considered choices among the various alternatives available.

Organization design is the process of making these choices. In this process, managers diagnose the situation confronting their organization and then select and implement the structure that seems most appropriate. The process of organization design is consciously adaptive and is guided by the principle, illustrated in Figure 13.1, that the degree to which a particular type of *structure* will contribute to the *effectiveness* of an organization depends on *contingency factors* that impinge on the organization and shape its business.[2]

Organizational Effectiveness

Organizational effectiveness, which is the desired outcome of organization design, is a measure of an organization's success in achieving its goals and objectives. Relevant goals and objectives might include targets pertaining to profitability, growth, market share, product quality, efficiency, stability, or similar outcomes.[3] An organization that fails to accomplish its goals is ineffective because it is not fulfilling its purpose.

An effective organization must also satisfy the demands of the various **constituency groups** that provide it with the resources necessary for its survival. As suggested by Figure 13.2, if a company satisfies customers' demands for desirable goods or services, it will probably continue to enjoy its customers' patronage. If it satisfies its suppliers' demands for payment in a timely manner, the suppliers will probably continue to provide it with needed materials. If it satisfies its employees' demands for fair pay and satisfying work, it will probably be able to retain its workers and recruit new employees. If it satisfies its stockholders' demands for profitability, it will probably enjoy continued access to equity funding.[4] If a firm fails to satisfy any one of these demands, however, its effectiveness will be weakened, because the consequent loss of needed resources, such as customers or employees, will threaten its continued survival.

Effectiveness differs from **organizational productivity** in that productivity measures do not take into account whether a firm is producing the *right* goods or services.[5] A modern company producing more glass milk bottles than ever before is productive but is not effective because most milk companies now sell their products in paper or plastic containers.

Effectiveness also differs from efficiency. **Organizational efficiency** means minimizing the raw materials and energy consumed by the production of goods and services. This parameter is often stated as the ratio of inputs consumed per units of outputs produced—for instance, the number of labor hours expended in manufacturing a bicycle.[6] Efficiency means *doing the job right*, whereas effectiveness means *doing the right job*. That is, effectiveness is a measure of

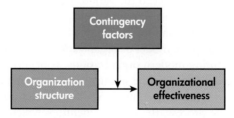

Figure 13.1 The Contingency Model of Organization Design

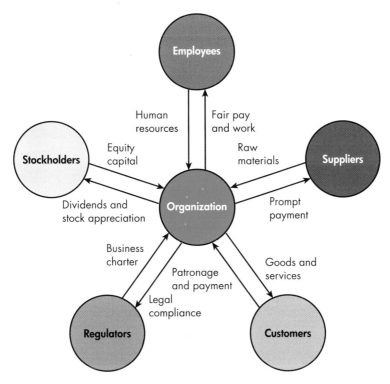

Figure 13.2 **Types of Constituency Groups and Their Demands**

whether a company is producing what it should produce in light of the goals, objectives, and constituency demands that influence its performance and justify its existence.

Structural Alternatives

The structure of an organization strongly influences its effectiveness. For each firm, one type of structure—whether simple undifferentiated, simple differentiated, functional, divisional, multiunit, matrix, modular, or virtual—will have the greatest positive effect on its ability to meet its goals and satisfy its constituencies. To clarify the fundamental differences among the various types of structures, we sometimes classify alternatives along a dimension ranging from *mechanistic* to *organic.*[1]

At one extreme on this continuum, purely **mechanistic structures** are machinelike. They permit workers to complete routine, narrowly defined tasks—designed according to the dictates of the efficiency perspective discussed in Chapter 7—in an efficient manner, but they lack flexibility. Extremely mechanistic structures are centralized, having *tall hierarchies* of vertical authority and communication relationships such as the one depicted in the upper panel of Figure 13.3. They are also characterized by large amounts of standardization, as indicated in Table 13.1.

At the other extreme on the same continuum, purely **organic structures** are analogous to living organisms in that they are flexible and able to adapt to changing conditions. In such structures, the motivational and quality perspectives on job design described in Chapter 7 have greater influence on the way tasks are developed and performed, which in turn allows

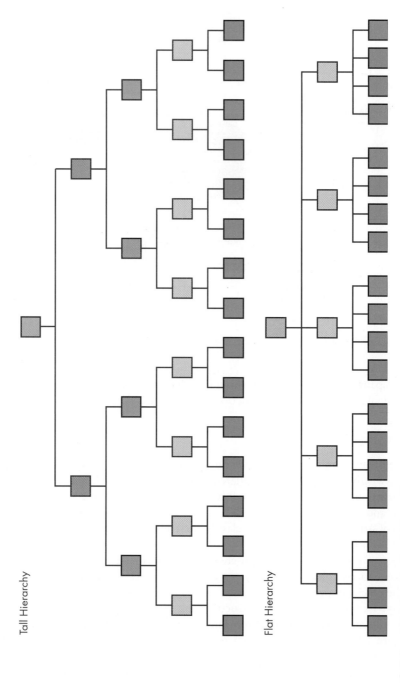

Tall Hierarchy

Flat Hierarchy

Figure 13.3 Tall and Flat Organizational Hierarchies

Table 13.1 Comparison of Mechanistic and Organic Structures

Characteristics of mechanistic structures	*Characteristics of organic structures*
Tasks are highly specialized. It is often not clear to members how their tasks contribute to accomplishment of organizational objectives.	Tasks are broad and interdependent. Relation of task performance to attainment of organizational objectives is emphasized.
Tasks remain rigidly defined unless they are formally altered by top management.	Tasks are continually modified and redefined by means of mutual adjustment among task holders.
Specific roles (rights, duties, technical methods) are defined for each member.	Generalized roles (acceptance of the responsibility for overall task accomplishment) are defined for each member.
Control and authority relationships are structured in a vertical hierarchy.	Control and authority relationships are structured in a network characterized by both vertical and horizontal connections.
Communication is primarily vertical, between superiors and subordinates.	Communication is both vertical and horizontal, depending on where the needed information resides.
Communication mainly takes the form of instructions and decisions issued by superiors, performance feedback, and requests for decisions sent from subordinates.	Communication takes the form of information and advice.
Loyalty to the organization and obedience to superiors are mandatory.	Commitment to organizational goals is more highly valued than is loyalty or obedience.

Source: Adapted from T. Burns and G. M. Stalker, *The Management of Innovation* (London: Tavistock, 1961), 120–122.

employees more control over their work and affords the organization increased adaptability. Owing to their flexibility, however, organic structures lack the single-minded focus required to perform routine work in the most efficient manner.

The different parts of extremely organic structures are connected by decentralized networks in *flat hierarchies*, like the one shown in the lower panel of Figure 13.3. The emphasis placed on horizontal relationships means that fewer vertical layers are required to process information and manage activities. In addition, organizations with organic structures typically rely more heavily on mutual adjustment and less critically on standardization. Computerized information networks take on greater importance as modes of coordination and communication among interdependent tasks.

Not all organizations represent such extreme cases. In reality, a particular type of structure might be mechanistic in some respects and organic in others. The more mechanistic the structure, the more efficient but less flexible it will be. The more organic the structure, the more flexible but less efficient it will be. These differences in efficiency and flexibility can be traced to the mechanisms used to coordinate work activities. As indicated in Chapter 12, standardization incorporates low long-term coordination costs and thus serves as the basis for mechanistic efficiency. Mutual adjustment, on the other hand, is quite flexible and therefore provides the source of organic flexibility.

Differences in the efficiency and flexibility of mechanistic and organic structures are also attributable to differences in centralization. On the one hand, the greater centralization of mechanistic structures encourages efficient specialization, with centralized decision makers gaining ever growing expertise in decision making. On the other hand, the greater decentralization of organic structures facilitates adaptive responsiveness, as decentralized decision makers located throughout an organization can lead its parts in several different adaptive directions at once. IBM's efforts to decentralize company operations illustrate this point quite well. As formerly organized, IBM was so centralized that decisions about the design, manufacture, and sales of personal computers were made by the same headquarters managers who also made decisions about larger mainframe computers and midsize minicomputers. With IBM's current organization, managers of IBM's personal computer lines can decide to introduce new products or enter new markets without consulting with, or affecting the operations of, other parts of the firm.

Structural Contingencies

In light of the contrasting strengths and weaknesses of the various types of structures, it is critically important that managers identify key **structural contingency factors** that can help determine whether a particular type of structure will function successfully in their organization.

These factors constitute the situation—both within the organization and in the surrounding environment—that managers must perceive and diagnose correctly to determine how to conduct their business most effectively. The remainder of this chapter considers some of the most important of these contingency factors and describes how each influences structural choice.

Life-Cycle Contingencies: Age and Stage of Development

Company age and stage of development are **life-cycle contingencies** associated with organizational growth. As organizations age and mature, they often grow out of one type of structure and into another.[8] This process can be envisioned as a series of developmental stages, as described in Table 13.2.

At the *inception* stage, one person or a small group of people create an organization and identify the firm's initial purpose. As commitment to this purpose develops, initial planning and implementation bring the firm to life. If the organization proves initially successful, it may experience rapid growth. As routines emerge, workers might invent general rules to preserve customary ways of doing things. Little, if any, formal coordination occurs, however. Mutual adjustment or direct supervision usually suffices as the primary means of unit coordination. Consequently, the organization takes on one of the prebureaucratic forms of structure—either simple undifferentiated or simple differentiated—with the choice depending on the effects of other contingency considerations discussed later in this chapter.

During the second developmental stage, *formalization*, work becomes divided into different functional areas, the organization develops systematic evaluation and reward procedures, and its direction is determined through formal planning and goal setting. As the organization continues to grow, professional managers first supplement and then replace the firm's owners, becoming the day-to-day bosses who run the company. In addition, decision making becomes increasingly centralized. Management emphasizes efficiency and stability, and work becomes routine as tasks are designed in accordance with the efficiency perspective on job

Table 13.2 Stages in Organizational Maturation

Stage	Primary characteristics	Structural type
Inception	Determination of firm's purpose Growth of commitment Initial planning and implementation Reliance on mutual adjustment	Prebureaucratic
Formalization	Rapid growth and change Development of routine activities Division of work into functions Systematic evaluation and rewards Formal planning and goal setting Emphasis on efficiency and stability	Bureaucratic (functional)
Elaboration	Search for new opportunities Diversification, decentralization Maturation and continued growth	Bureaucratic (divisional)
Transformation	Large size, either real or virtual Flattened organization hierarchy Massive change and complexity Emphasis on flexibility	Postbureaucratic

design. In the process, standardization emerges as the means by which coordination is achieved. As a consequence, the organization's structure becomes bureaucratic and, typically, functional.

To adapt to changing conditions and to pursue continued growth, a firm that has progressed to the third stage, *elaboration*, seeks out new product, location, or client opportunities. As the company's business diversifies, its centralized management loses the ability to coordinate work activities, and a need develops for decentralization and divisional departmentation. If the firm continues to mature even further, continued growth and diversification might require yet more structural elaboration. Although the company's structure remains bureaucratic, management must consider reliance on mutual adjustment, no matter how costly, to cope with the firm's greater complexity or need for greater flexibility. The motivation and quality perspectives influence job design at this point, as standardization fades in importance and employees gain greater control over their work. Whether the specific type of structure possessed by the firm will be divisional, matrix, or multiunit depends on the effects of other contingency factors.

Finally, an organization that has advanced to the fourth developmental stage, known as *transformation*, finds itself confronted by extremes of both change and complexity in its business situation. To compete, the company enters into the process of *mass customization*, wherein it relies on skilled teams and advanced technologies to tailor mass-produced goods or services to the unique demands of different clientele.[9] The quality perspective on job design is fully apparent at this stage of development. Autonomous teams use both mutual adjustment and decentralization to manage themselves and to coordinate with one another by sharing information on computerized networks. The pyramidal hierarchy developed during the stages of formalization and elaboration becomes transformed into a flattened, horizontal structure characterized by process flows and peer relationships. These flows and relationships might be wholly contained within the organization itself, or they might extend outward and into other firms. The organization adopts a postbureaucratic structure, either modular or virtual, depending on the influence of additional contingency effects discussed later.

The four-stage developmental model just described suggests that as older organizations grow more complex, similarly, their structures and the jobs within them become more complicated. Note, however, that not every organization progresses through every developmental stage. For instance, a family-owned convenience store might never grow beyond the stage of inception. Such notable companies as Apple Computer and Coca-Cola have yet to grow beyond elaboration. In addition, some companies leap over one or more stages as they develop—for example, starting out with formalization or elaboration, or moving directly from initiation to transformation. Not every company starts small, nor do all firms invest in bureaucracy. Nonetheless, the fact remains that increasing age is accompanied by a tendency to progress from prebureaucratic structures developed during the stage of inception, to bureaucratic structures developed during formalization and elaboration, and then to postbureaucratic structures developed during transformation. As an organization advances through this sequence of stages and structures, its management faces a progression of new contingency factors at each stage. This progression is the focus of the remainder of this chapter.

Inception Contingencies

Organizations at the developmental stage of inception are typically new, small, and fairly simple in form. Consequently, they are most likely to have prebureaucratic structures. It follows that the organization design choice confronting managers concerns which prebureaucratic structure to adopt—simple undifferentiated or simple differentiated. Both alternatives are relatively organic, despite the ownership-related direct supervision found in simple differentiated structures. Because they share this general similarity, considerations regarding trade-offs between mechanistic efficiency and organic flexibility have little relevance. Instead, the choice between the two prebureaucratic structures is influenced by the contingency factor of organization size.

Organization size can be defined in several ways:

- the number of members in an organization
- the organization's volume of sales, clients, or profits
- its physical capacity (e.g., the number of beds in a hospital or the number of rooms in a hotel)
- the total financial assets it controls.[10]

For our purposes, size is considered to be the number of members or employees within the organization—that is, the number of people whose activities must be integrated and coordinated.

Defined in this manner, the size of an organization affects its structure mainly by determining which of the three coordination mechanisms—mutual adjustment, direct supervision, or standardization—is most appropriate as the primary means of coordination. As indicated in Chapter 12, in extremely small organizations containing twelve or fewer people, mutual adjustment alone can provide adequate coordination without incurring overwhelming process loss. If more than about a dozen people try to coordinate by means of mutual adjustment alone, however, so much process loss occurs that performance declines substantially. Thus the activities of larger numbers of people—thirty, forty, or fifty—are better coordinated by direct supervision, because such supervision reduces the number of coordination linkages that must be maintained. In even larger organizations, direct supervision succumbs to information overload. Standardization must, therefore, be implemented instead to reduce information-processing demands and sustain coordinated efforts.

This relationship between organization size and coordination mechanism has especially strong contingency effects on choices between the two prebureaucratic structural alternatives. Simple undifferentiated structures, coordinated solely by means of mutual adjustment, can be used to effectively integrate the people and tasks that make up very small organizations. Simple differentiated structures, with their reliance on direct supervision, become the necessary choice for organizations that grow in size beyond a dozen or so individuals. For managers of small organizations who must choose among alternative prebureaucratic structures, organization size influences structural choice and effectiveness through its effects on coordination.

Formalization and Elaboration Contingencies

As an organization grows beyond fifty people or so, simple undifferentiated structures and simple differentiated structures become overwhelmed by coordination requirements. As the primary means of coordination, mutual adjustment becomes extremely expensive, and direct supervision is bogged down by rapidly multiplying information-processing needs. As a consequence, standardization assumes the role of primary coordination mechanism. For this reason, organizations that have progressed beyond the stage of inception and outgrown pre-bureaucratic structures must consider the adoption of more bureaucratic forms of structure.

Relative to prebureaucratic structures, bureaucratic structures are more mechanistic and, therefore, more standardized and often more centralized. However, the four types of bureaucratic structures also differ from one another along these same dimensions. Functional structures are the most mechanistic, owing to their standardization and high level of centralization. Divisional structures are substantially less mechanistic, owing to their reduced centralization, but still quite mechanistic relative to the remaining structural alternatives. Matrix structures are even less mechanistic and, therefore, more organic, owing to their greater decentralization and reliance on mutual adjustment among managers of matrix cells. Finally, multiunit structures are the least mechanistic of the four bureaucratic structures, reflecting the extreme decoupling that occurs among their parts and the high levels of decentralization that result.

Consequently, for managers trying to decide which bureaucratic structure to implement, the trade-off between mechanistic efficiency and organic flexibility plays a major role in shaping structural choices. Related to this trade-off, the most influential contingency factors at the formalization and elaboration stages of development consist of the organization's core technology and the environment that surrounds the firm.[11]

Core Technology

An organization's **technology** includes the knowledge, procedures, and equipment used to transform unprocessed resources into finished goods or services.[12] **Core technology** is a more specific term that encompasses the dominant technology used in performing work in the operational center of the organization. Core technologies are found in the assembly lines at GM, Ford, and Chrysler, in the fast-food kitchens at Wendy's, in the employment and job-training offices in state and federal agencies, and in the reactor buildings where electricity is generated at nuclear power plants. This section introduces two contingency models that delineate basic differences in core technology: the Woodward manufacturing model and the Thompson service model. Both propose that core technology influences the effectiveness of an organization by placing particular coordination requirements on its structure.

Woodward's Manufacturing Technologies

Joan Woodward, a British researcher who began studying organizations in the early 1950s, was an early proponent of the view that an organization's technology can have tremendous effects on its structural effectiveness.[13] She initially studied 100 British manufacturing firms, examining their organizational structures and their relative efficiency and success in the marketplace. While analyzing her data, Woodward discovered that not all companies with the same type of structure were equally effective. Theorizing that these differences in effectiveness might be traced to differences in core technologies, Woodward devised a classification scheme to describe three basic types of manufacturing technology: small-batch production, mass production, and continuous-process production.

Small-batch production (also called *unit production*) is a technology for the manufacture of one-of-a-kind items or small quantities of goods designed to meet unique customer specifications. Such items range from specialized electronic instruments, weather satellites, and space shuttles to hand-tailored clothing. To make this kind of product, craftspeople work alone or in small, close-knit groups. Because customer specifications change from one order to the next, the organization finds it almost impossible to predict what will be required on the next job. Thus the work in firms using small-batch technologies varies in unpredictable ways.

This unpredictability causes small-batch technologies to influence organizational structures and effectiveness. It impedes planning and, therefore, makes it difficult to coordinate by means of standardization. Not surprisingly, it is impossible to plan legitimate standards for use in a future that cannot be foreseen. Instead, employees must decide for themselves how to perform their jobs. When employees work alone, they are guided by their own expertise and by customer specifications. When employees work in groups, they coordinate with one another by means of mutual adjustment.

Woodward found that mutual adjustment played a pivotal role in coordinating small-batch production. In her research, she showed that, among organizations using this type of technology, firms with organic structures were significantly more likely to be successful than companies with mechanistic structures. Of the four types of bureaucratic structures likely to be adopted during the developmental stages of formalization and elaboration, according to Woodward's findings, multiunit structuring would appear more likely to provide the greatest autonomy and support for technological flexibility. The matrix structure, itself a massive lateral linkage mechanism, is another suitable alternative.

The other lateral linkage mechanisms described in Chapter 11—liaison positions, representative groups, and integrating managers—can also be positioned in functional and divisional structures to increase mutual adjustment and introduce greater flexibility. In this way, otherwise mechanistic structures can be made at least modestly organic. Thus it follows that functional or divisional structures with extensive lateral linkages can prove effective when paired with small-batch technology. As with all other technology-based decisions, which one of this reduced set of structural alternatives is best suited to the needs of a particular organization becomes clearer after consideration of the environmental contingencies discussed later in this section.

In Woodward's second type of technology, *mass production* (also referred to as *large-batch production*), the same product is produced repeatedly, either in large batches or in long production runs. For instance, rather than producing a few copies of this book each time an order was received, the publisher initially printed thousands of copies in a single run and warehoused them to fill incoming orders. Other examples of mass production range from word-processing pools, in which business records are transcribed in large batches, to manufacturing operations in which thousands of Ford Explorers are made on an assembly line that remains virtually unchanged for several years.

As these examples suggest, work in mass-production technologies is intentionally repetitive and remains so for extended periods of time. Employees perform the same jobs over and over, knowing that the work they do tomorrow will be the same as the work done today. The existence of this stability and routine facilitates planning and formalization. As a result, a company is likely to use standardization to reduce the long-term costs of coordination. Woodward's research revealed that mass-production firms with mechanistic structures were far more likely to be effective than those with organic structures. Therefore, mechanistic structures—functional or divisional—are more apt to enhance effectiveness than are more organic alternatives.

In the third type of technology identified in Woodward's research, *continuous-process production*, automated equipment makes the same product in the same way for an indefinite period of time. For instance, at Marathon Petroleum, one refinery unit makes nothing but gasoline, another unit refines motor oil, and a third unit produces only diesel fuel. The equipment used in this type of technology is designed to produce one product and cannot readily be switched over to manufacture a different product. There is no starting and stopping once the equipment has been installed. Machines in continuous-process facilities perform the same tasks without interruption.

Of the three types of technology described by Woodward, continuous-process production involves the most routine work. Few changes, if any, occur in production processes, even over the course of many years. For this reason, it seems logical to assume that organizations using continuous-process production would be most effective if structured along mechanistic lines.

Interestingly, however, closer examination reveals that very few of the people involved in continuous-process production perform routine, repetitive jobs. Rather, machines perform these jobs. The people act as "exception managers," monitoring production equipment by watching dials and gauges, checking machinery, inspecting finished goods, and handling the problems that arise when this equipment fails to function properly. Although some of these problems occur repeatedly and can be planned for in advance, a significant number are emergencies that have never happened before and cannot be anticipated with acceptable accuracy.

Because some of the most critical work performed by people in continuous-process production technologies is highly unpredictable, standardization is not feasible. Mutual adjustment, sometimes in conjunction with direct supervision, is therefore the dominant mode of coordination. Technicians who oversee production equipment manage unusual events by conferring with each other and devising solutions to emergencies as they arise. It is not surprising that Woodward found that firms using continuous-process production technologies were most effective when structured organically. In these circumstances, laterally linked functional or divisional structures, or matrix or multiunit structures, are the most likely to encourage effectiveness.

In the years since Woodward conducted her studies, advances in computers, robotics, and automation have led to the identification of another type of manufacturing technology, known as *flexible-cell production*. As described in Chapter 7, this type of technology is characterized by a group, or cell, of computer-controlled production machines, which are connected by a flexible network of conveyors that can be rapidly reconfigured to adapt the cell for different production tasks. This technology is typically used to produce a wide variety of machined metal parts, such as pistons for car engines or parts for the lock on the front door of your home. Conceivably, however, it could be used to manufacture virtually any kind of product.[14]

As in continuous-process production, automated equipment performs the work in flexible cells. The only people involved are technicians who monitor the equipment and handle problems. Whereas continuous-process production facilities can make only a single product, however, flexible cells can make many different things. In this respect, flexible-cell production resembles small-batch production. It is an efficient method of producing one-of-a-kind items or small quantities of similar items built to satisfy unique customer specifications.

Inasmuch as Woodward found mutual adjustment to be the most effective coordination mechanism for both continuous-process and small-batch production technologies, an organic structure would seem most suitable for a firm using flexible-cell production. Indeed, a study of 110 manufacturing firms in New Jersey revealed a significant positive relationship between organic structuring and the effectiveness of organizations with flexible cells.[15] This information updates Woodward's research, suggesting that companies employing flexible-cell technologies are likely to be more effective if they adopt laterally linked functional or divisional structures, or matrix or multiunit structures, to coordinate work activities.

Thompson's Service Technologies

Because Woodward focused her research solely on manufacturing firms, her contingency model is applicable only to technologies used to produce tangible goods. Today, however, firms that provide services such as real estate sales, appliance repair, or investment planning make up an increasingly critical element of the U.S. economy as well as the economies of other countries around the world. Another contingency model, developed by James D. Thompson, is quite useful because it examines the technologies often employed in these service organizations. These technologies, which are diagrammed in Figure 13.4, include mediating technology, long-linked technology, and intensive technology.[16] In the figure, circles represent employees, and arrows represent flows of work.

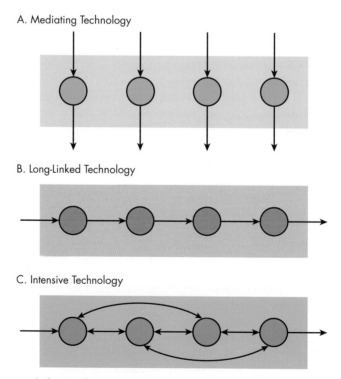

Figure 13.4 Thompson's Service Technologies

A *mediating technology* provides services that link clients together. For example, banks connect depositors who have money to invest with borrowers who need loans; insurance companies enable their clients to pool risks, permitting one person's losses to be covered by joint investments; and telephone companies provide the equipment and technical assistance that people need to talk with one another from separate locations.

When mediating technology is used to provide a service, employees usually serve each client individually. Consequently, as depicted in Figure 13.4A, bank tellers and workers in other mediating technologies normally perform their jobs without assistance from others in their organization. Assuming adequate training, a single bank teller can handle a deposit or withdrawal without seeking help from other tellers. At the same time, however, the teller and other workers might share equipment such as the central computer that keeps track of all bank transactions.

Although individual employees work independently in a mediating technology, many perform the same job. Coordination in such firms is needed to ensure that workers provide consistently high-quality service and offer the same basic service to each client. Thus managers in service firms develop lists of the different types of clients that their organization is likely to serve and devise standard operating procedures to be followed while serving each type of client. For example, a bank teller will follow one procedure while serving a client who is making a savings account deposit, a second procedure when assisting a client who is making a loan payment, and a third procedure when helping a client open a new checking account. This standardization of behaviors means that firms using mediating technologies are most likely to be effective when structured mechanistically. Either functional or divisional structures would be suitable for such firms.

Thompson's second type of technology, *long-linked technology*, is analogous to Woodward's mass-production technology. Both refer to sequential chains of simplified tasks. A service sector example of this type of technology is the state employment agency that requires all clients to follow the same lockstep procedures. Each client moves along an "assembly line," starting with registration and progressing through assessment, counseling, training, and placement activities. Figure 13.4B diagrams the sequential movement from one station to the next that characterizes long-linked technology.

Like firms that use mass-production technology, organizations that use long-linked technology coordinate by means of standardization. According to Thompson, mechanistic structuring is likely to enhance the effectiveness of a firm using long-linked technology. This finding suggests that long-linked technology is most effectively paired with functional or divisional structures.

Intensive technology, the third type of technology in Thompson's model, consists of work processes whose configuration may change as employees receive feedback from their clients. The specific array of services to be rendered to a particular patient in a hospital, for example, depends on the patient's symptoms. A patient who enters the hospital's emergency room complaining of chest pains might be rushed to an operating room and then to a cardiac-care unit. A patient with a broken arm might be shuttled from the emergency room to the radiology lab for an X-ray and then returned to the emergency room for splinting. A patient with less clear-cut symptoms might be checked into a hospital room for further observation and testing (see Figure 13.4C).

To accommodate the needs of each client, a firm using intensive technology must be able to reorganize itself again and again. Above all, it must have flexibility. Moreover, because the needs of future clients cannot be forecast accurately, the behaviors required of the workers in such a firm are too unpredictable to be successfully formalized. Both flexibility and unpredictability require the use of mutual adjustment as a coordinating mechanism. Thus, firms using intensive technology will be best served by laterally linked functional or divisional structures, or matrix or multiunit structures.

Technological Contingencies: Integration

Both the Woodward and Thompson technology models help identify which general form of organization structure is most likely to enhance the effectiveness of a firm whose primary operations incorporate a specific type of core technology. As indicated in Table 13.3, standardization and mechanistic structuring generally enhance the effectiveness of firms using core technologies that are suited to more routine work—mass-production, mediating, and long-linked technologies. Mutual adjustment and organic structuring, in contrast, promote effectiveness in firms that use core technologies suited to unpredictable, often rapidly changing requirements—small-batch, continuous-process, flexible-cell, and intensive technologies.[17]

The External Environment

An organization's **environment** encompasses everything outside the organization. Suppliers, customers, and competitors are part of an organization's environment, as are the governmental bodies that regulate its business, the financial institutions and investors that provide it with funding, and the labor market that contributes its employees. In addition, general factors such as the economic, geographic, and political conditions that impinge on the firm are part of its environment. Central to this definition is the idea that the term *environment* refers to things external to the firm.[18] The internal "environment" of a firm, more appropriately called the company's culture, is distinctly different and will be discussed in Chapter 14.

Table 13.3 Technological Contingencies

Industry type	Technology	Structural category	Structural types	Example
Manufacturing	Small batch	Organic	Laterally linked functional or divisional, matrix	Scientific instrument fabricator
	Mass production	Mechanistic	Functional, divisional	Television manufacturer
	Continuous process	Organic	Laterally linked functional or divisional, matrix	Petroleum refinery
	Flexible cell	Organic	Laterally linked functional or divisional, matrix	Auto parts supplier
Service	Mediating	Mechanistic	Functional, divisional	Bank
	Long linked	Mechanistic	Functional, divisional	Cafeteria
	Intensive	Organic	Laterally linked functional or divisional, matrix	Hospital

As a structural contingency factor affecting organizations in the stages of formalization and elaboration, the environment influences structural effectiveness by placing certain coordination and information-processing restrictions on the firm. Five specific environmental characteristics influence structural effectiveness: change, complexity, uncertainty, receptivity, and diversity.

Environmental change concerns the extent to which conditions in an organization's environment change unpredictably. At one extreme, an environment is considered stable if it does not change at all or if it changes only in a cyclical, predictable way. An example of a stable environment is the one that surrounds many of the small firms in Amish communities throughout the Midwestern United States. Amish religious beliefs require the rejection of many modern conveniences, such as automobiles, televisions, and gasoline-powered farm equipment. As a consequence, Amish blacksmiths, farmers, and livestock breeders have conducted business in much the same way for generations. Another stable environment surrounds firms that sell Christmas trees. The retail market for cut evergreen trees is predictably strong in November and December but weak at other times of the year.

At the other extreme, an environment is considered dynamic when it changes over time in an unpredictable manner. Because the type of dress deemed stylish changes so frequently in many parts of the world, the environment surrounding companies in the fashion industry is quite dynamic. Similarly, the environment surrounding companies in the consumer electronics industry has changed dramatically in recent years. Breakthrough products such as high-definition televisions and smartphones have created entirely new industries and markets.

Environmental change affects the structure of an organization by influencing the predictability of the firm's work and, therefore, the method of coordination used to integrate work activities.[19] Stability allows managers to complete the planning needed to formalize organizational activities. Firms operating in stable environments can use standardization as their primary coordination mechanism and will typically elect to do so to reduce long-term coordination costs. Mechanistic structures—functional or divisional—are the most likely to prove effective in such instances.

In contrast, it is difficult to establish formal rules and procedures in dynamic environments. In fact, it is useless for managers to try to plan for a future they cannot foresee. Members of an organization facing a dynamic environment must adapt to changing conditions instead of relying on inflexible, standardized operating procedures. Dynamism in the environment leaves management with little choice but to rely on mutual adjustment as a primary coordination mechanism. The organic structuring of laterally linked functional or divisional structures, or matrix or multiunit structures, is therefore appropriate.

Environmental complexity is the degree to which an organization's environment is complicated and therefore difficult to understand. A simple environment is composed of relatively few component parts—for example, suppliers, competitors, or types of customers—so little can affect organizational performance. A locally owned gas station does business in a relatively simple environment. It orders most of its supplies from a single petroleum distributor, does business almost exclusively with customers who want to buy gasoline or oil for their cars, and can limit its attention to the competitive activities of a fairly small number of nearby stations. On the other hand, a complex environment incorporates a large number of separable parts. The environments of aviation firms such as Boeing and Airbus Industries are extremely complex, including an enormous number of suppliers and many types of customers.

Complexity influences structural effectiveness by affecting the amount of knowledge and information that people must process to understand the environment and cope with its demands.[20] To demonstrate this effect, consider an inexpensive digital watch. If you disassembled this watch, you would probably have little trouble putting it back together again, because it has very few parts—a computer chip programmed to keep time, a digital liquid-crystal face, a battery, and a case. With only a few minutes of practice or simple instructions, you could quickly learn to assemble this watch. Now suppose the pieces of a Rolex watch were spread out before you. Could you reassemble the watch? Probably not, because it includes an overwhelming number of springs, screws, gears, and other parts. Learning to assemble a Rolex properly would require extensive training and much practice.

Similarly, the organization facing a simple environment—one with few "parts"—can understand environmental events and meet the challenges they pose by using a minimal amount of knowledge and processing little new information. A local restaurant that is losing business can determine the reason for its plight simply by telephoning a few prospective customers and asking them for their comments. In contrast, organizations in complex environments—environments with many "parts"—must draw on a considerable store of knowledge and process an overwhelming amount of information to understand environmental events.

Environmental complexity affects organizational structures by influencing the suitability of centralized decision making. As indicated in Chapter 12, centralization is characterized by decision making that is limited to a selected group of top managers. It therefore limits the number of people available to digest information and determine its meaning. Because simple environments require little information processing, organizations operating in such environments can be centralized and function quite effectively.

Because environmental complexity requires the ability to process and understand large amounts of information, however, centralized organizations in complex environments can suffer the effects of information overload. One possible way to cope with information overload is to invest in computerized management information systems. The usual net effect of such investment is actually to *increase* the amount of environmental information available, thereby contributing to *additional* information overload. A more successful way to handle the problem of information overload due to environmental complexity is to involve more individuals in information-processing activities. Thus organizations that are attempting to cope with complex environments often decentralize decision making. That way, they include more people—more brains—in the process of digesting and interpreting information.

In addition to pointing out distinctive environmental differences, the two environmental dimensions of change and complexity combine in the manner shown in Figure 13.5 to define yet another important environmental characteristic: **environmental uncertainty**. Uncertainty reflects a lack of information about environmental factors, activities, and events.[21] It undermines an organization's ability to manage current circumstances and plan for the future. To cope with uncertainty, organizations try to find better ways of acquiring information about the environment. This effort often involves the creation of boundary-spanning positions that can strengthen the information linkage between an organization and its environment.[22]

A *boundary spanner* is a member or unit of an organization that interacts with people or firms in the organization's environment.[23] Salespeople who have contact with customers, purchasing departments that deal with suppliers of raw materials, and top managers who in their figurehead roles represent the company to outsiders are all boundary spanners. When they take on boundary-spanning roles, employees or organizational units perform several functions:

- They monitor the environment for information that is relevant to the organization.
- They serve as gatekeepers, simplifying incoming information and ensuring that it is routed to the appropriate people in the firm.

- They warn the organization of environmental threats and initiate activities that protect it from those dangers.
- They represent the organization to other individuals or to other firms in its environment, providing them with information about the organization.
- They negotiate with other organizations to acquire raw materials and sell finished goods or services.
- They coordinate any other activities that require the cooperation of two or more firms.[24]

When carried out successfully, these activities enable boundary spanners to provide their organization with information about its environment that can help make change and complexity more understandable.

Environmental receptivity, which ranges from munificent to hostile, is the degree to which an organization's environment supports the organization's progress toward fulfilling its purpose. In a munificent environment, a firm can acquire the raw materials, employees, technology, and capital resources needed to perform productively.[25] Such an environment enables the firm to find a receptive market for its products. The firm's competitors, if any, do not threaten its existence. Regulatory bodies do not try to impede its progress. For example, the environment surrounding McDonald's fast-food chain at the time of its founding was munificent. Few other fast-food franchises existed, labor was plentiful in the post-Korean War era, and a convenience-minded middle class was emerging throughout North America.

In a hostile environment, the opposite situation prevails. An organization may have great difficulty acquiring or might be unable to acquire needed resources, employees, knowledge,

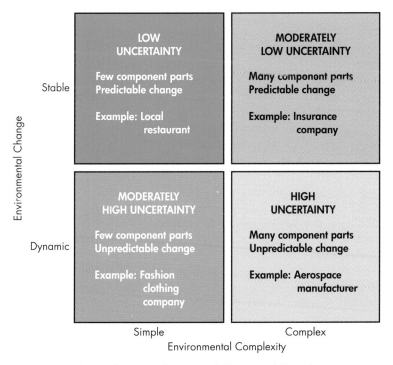

Figure 13.5 Environmental Uncertainty as a Function of Change and Complexity

Source: Adapted from R. B. Duncan, "Characteristics of Organizational Environments and Perceived Environmental Uncertainty," Administrative Science Quarterly 17 (1972): 313–327.

or money. Customer disinterest, intense competition, or severe regulation may also threaten the firm's future. For instance, Altria and other members of the tobacco industry have been forced to cope with extreme hostility in North America owing to widespread concerns about the health hazards of smoking. During the 1990s, U.S. defense contractors faced similar hostility as the Cold War ended and the demand for defense weaponry diminished.[26]

Environmental hostility, though normally temporary, represents a crisis that must be handled quickly and decisively if the firm is to survive. An organization facing such hostility either finds a way to deal with it—for example, by substituting one raw material for another, marketing a new product, or lobbying against threatening regulations—or ceases to exist. For example, tobacco companies have contributed to the campaign funds of politicians known to be against the passage of antismoking laws, and defense contractors have merged with other companies to convert to peacetime manufacturing.

To deal with the crisis of a hostile environment, firms that are normally decentralized in response to environmental complexity may centralize decision making for a limited period of time.[27] This temporary centralization facilitates crisis management. Because it reduces the number of people who must be consulted to make a decision, the organization can respond to threatening conditions more quickly. It is important to emphasize that centralization established in response to a hostile environment should remain in effect only as long as the hostility persists. When the threat ends, a firm dealing with a complex environment will perform effectively again only if it reinstates decentralized decision making.

Environmental diversity refers to the number of distinct environmental sectors or domains served by an organization. A firm in a uniform environment serves a single type of customer, provides a single kind of product, and conducts its business in a single geographic location. That is, it serves only a single domain. A campus nightclub that caters to the entertainment needs of local college students, for example, operates in a uniform environment. So does a building-materials firm whose sole product is concrete, which it sells only to local contractors. In contrast, an organization in a diverse environment produces an assortment of products, serves various types of customers, or has offices or other facilities in several geographic locations. It does business in several different domains. Dell, for instance, sells computers to businesses, universities, and the general public. General Electric produces durable consumer goods, financial services, jet engines, and locomotives. Volkswagen markets cars in North America, South America, Europe, and Asia.

Environmental diversity affects an organization by influencing the amount of diversity that must be built into its structure.[28] In organizations with uniform environments, managers can use functional departmentation to group units together. Because firms in uniform environments face only a single domain, they must focus on only information about a single kind of environment and react to only a single set of environmental events. Functional departmentation, which facilitates this sort of unified information processing and response, is therefore sufficient in such situations. The absence of environmental diversity permits the firms to operate effectively without significant internal diversification.

In organizations with diverse environments, however, management must use divisional departmentation to gather work associated with each product, customer, or location into its own self-contained division. Companies in diverse environments face a number of distinct domains and must acquire information about each to satisfy its particular demands. Divisional departmentation allows such firms to keep track of each domain separately and to respond to the demands of one domain independently of other domains. Without this type of structure, work on one product might impede work on other products, services rendered to one type of customer might detract from services provided to other types of customers, or operations at one location might affect operations at other locations.

Environmental uniformity, then, favors functional departmentation and suggests the need for a functional structure. In contrast, environmental diversity requires divisional departmentation and either a divisional, matrix, or multiunit structure, depending on other contingency factors.

Environmental Contingencies: Integration

As just indicated, organizational environments have five distinct characteristics: change, complexity, uncertainty, receptivity, and diversity. Diagnosing the nature of a firm's environment during the process of organization design requires that managers perform five environmental analyses more or less simultaneously. The decision tree shown in Figure 13.6 can help guide this process. Each question in the figure deals with one of the environmental characteristics just examined. Note that it is not necessary to ask a separate question about uncertainty, because this property is a combination of change and complexity and, therefore, is assessed implicitly by the answers to questions 1 and 2.

1. *Is the environment stable or dynamic?* The answer to this question identifies the amount of change in the environment and helps determine whether standardization or mutual adjustment is likely to be more effective as a coordination mechanism for the firm. Stable environments either do not change or change in a predictable, cyclical manner, thereby permitting the use of standardization. Dynamic environments change in unpredictable ways and require mutual adjustment.

2. *Is the environment simple or complex?* This answer relies on an assessment of environmental complexity and will indicate whether centralization or decentralization is more appropriate for the firm. Simple environments are more readily understood and accommodate centralization. Complex environments require a great deal of information processing and therefore exert pressure toward decentralization.

3. *Is the environment munificent or hostile?* This question is relevant only if an organization has a complex environment and decentralized decision making. How it is answered gauges environmental receptivity and indicates whether temporary centralization is necessary. Munificent environments are resource-rich and allow for continued decentralization, whereas hostile environments are resource-poor and stimulate crises that mandate temporary centralization.

4. *Is the environment uniform or diverse?* To respond to this question, a manager must evaluate environmental diversity so as to determine which form of departmentation to use. Environmental uniformity supports the structural uniformity of functional departmentation. Environmental diversity requires the structural diversity of divisional departmentation.

Transformation Contingencies

Transition beyond bureaucratic structuring occurs because the standardization intended to stimulate efficient performance can, in some instances, actually reduce efficiency and productivity. This reduction can happen for several reasons. For instance, the very existence of bureaucratic rules and procedures can encourage the practice of following them to the letter. Some employees might interpret rules that were intended to describe minimally acceptable levels of performance as describing the maximum level of performance for which they should aim. As a result, their performance might suffer.

In addition, rigid adherence to rules and regulations can discourage workers from taking the initiative and being creative, and the organization can subsequently lose its ability to anticipate

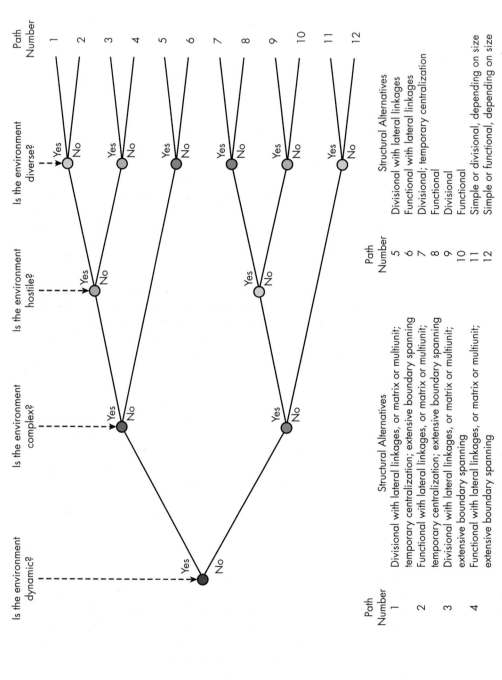

Figure 13.6 Decision Tree: Environmental Contingency Dimensions

or adapt to changing conditions. During the late twentieth century, rules that required lengthy approval reviews for even minor design changes limited the ability of many U.S. firms then in the consumer electronics industry to improve existing products or introduce new ones. As a result, once dominant U.S. companies such as General Electric and Sunbeam are no longer major participants in markets for everything from hair-curling irons to stereo receivers. Forgone flexibility can cost organizations precious markets—and sometimes even their survival.

Standardization can also undermine efficiency by narrowing the scope of workplace activities to the point where employees feel bored and unchallenged. Oversimplification caused by too much standardization can contribute to serious problems of workforce motivation and, as a consequence, poor performance.[29] Groups of workers may develop informal social structures in which low productivity is the norm. Employees might even turn to dangerous horseplay or costly sabotage to break up the monotony or to "get even" with a company they perceive as insensitive and uncaring. Sometimes the job redesign and enrichment procedures described in Chapter 7 can provide sufficient relief in such circumstances. In other cases, nothing short of organizational restructuring will succeed in countering the effects of over-specialization.

In sum, the standardization that characterizes all bureaucratic structures can have important drawbacks. To the degree that these drawbacks impede efficiency, bureaucracy fails to achieve its intended purpose and can threaten the organization's success and continued well-being. Firms facing this danger have grown beyond the developmental stages of formalization and elaboration, and now find themselves entering into the stage of transformation.

Managers of organizations in the stage of transformation confront the challenge of dealing with business conditions that require the resources of a large organization but the flexibility of a small one. Global competition, technological volatility, and trends toward mass customization of products and services often contribute to this challenge.[30] Owing to the drawbacks just described, bureaucratic structures often depress organizational performance under such circumstances. For this reason, entry into the stage of transformation is accompanied by the task of converting bureaucratic structures into either of two postbureaucratic alternatives: the modular structure or the virtual structure.

Both of these postbureaucratic structures are organic, meaning that they are based on decentralized decision making and mutual adjustment conducted with the assistance of computerized networks rather than on centralization and hierarchy with direct supervision or standardization. As a consequence, both are quite flexible. Choices between the two involve trade-offs between completing the entire process of design, production, and distribution within the confines of a single organization, in the case of the modular structure, and relying on a network of several organizations connected by temporary alliances, in the case of the virtual structure. At this advanced stage of growth and development, choices pertaining to organization design are influenced by two contingency factors: environmental turbulence and transaction costs.

Environmental Turbulence

The term **environmental turbulence** describes the speed and scope of change that occurs in the environment surrounding an organization. High turbulence is characterized by simultaneous and extremely high levels of environmental change, complexity (i.e., uncertainty), and diversity, as well as rapid technological advances including the use of team-managed technologies. Such conditions, sometimes labeled *hypercompetitive*, require flexibility beyond the limits of bureaucracy, necessitating progression to postbureaucratic structures.[31] At the other extreme, low turbulence exists when levels of environmental change, complexity, diversity, and technological considerations are not simultaneous or less extreme in effect. The flexibility required by such conditions can be supplied in traditional bureaucratic structures by adding lateral linkages or opting for matrix or multiunit structuring, as suggested by the technological and environmental contingency models discussed earlier.

By determining the degree of flexibility and adaptability an organization must have to perform effectively, the level of environmental turbulence can also act as a contingency factor that influences choices between the two postbureaucratic alternatives. Compared with bureaucratic structures, modular structures are far more flexible.[32] For instance, General Electric's decision to allow its units to function as independent entities has enabled each of the company's businesses—consumer finance, jet engines and avionics, military contracting, and so on—to adapt itself to its own competitive situation without affecting the operations of other units.

Relying on temporary associations, as in virtual structures, allows for even greater flexibility. Such associations, in the form of short-term contracts or longer-term joint-venture relationships, are easier to modify and eliminate than are the interconnections among parts of a single firm.[33] Whereas high levels of environmental turbulence push for the adoption of modular structures, extremely high levels encourage the use of virtual structures.

Transaction Costs

Decisions about "doing it yourself" in a modular structure versus "contracting it out" in a virtual structure also boil down to a comparison of the costs of sustaining a single organization and maintaining a unified structure, on the one hand, with the costs of writing acceptable contracts and, on the other, ensuring contractual compliance. As suggested by economist Oliver Williamson, such **transaction costs** represent a second contingency factor that influences whether managers opt for the permanence of a single organization or the transience of temporary relationships.[34]

Transaction costs associated with preserving a single company or maintaining contractual relationships are affected by two important considerations. First, people are limited in the amount of information they can process, and greater complexity in a particular business situation creates a need for information processing that can prove overwhelming. This situation makes contracting out work difficult because it increases feelings of uncertainty on the part of contractors. In turn, uncertainty increases the reluctance of prospective contractors to consign costly resources or commit to long-term relationships. Consider, for instance, the situation in which you are looking for an apartment to rent. Are you likely to sign a lease for an apartment if you have never seen it, if monthly payments have yet to be specified, or if the lease period may change without notice? Or are you more likely to sign a lease when you know exactly which apartment you will live in, what your monthly payments will be, and how long the lease will last? For most people, the uncertainty of the first alternative makes it the less attractive of the two options.

In contrast, creating a single organization can help in coping with human limitations in the face of complexity because it affords a sense of social stability and permanence. Containing business transactions within a single organization also allows the use of basic coordination mechanisms and makes it easier to involve many more people in decision making. All of these factors help reduce the uncertainty of work relationships. People who opt for co-ops or condominiums instead of apartments are, to some extent, buying into a permanent organization. This type of organization provides them with the greater stability of permanent ownership and unites them with other owners who share similar interests in housing quality and affordability. Items that might otherwise require a contract among co-owners can be handled through periodic meetings in which the owners discuss problems and negotiate acceptable solutions.

Second, contracting becomes more difficult and the transaction costs of contractual relationships are increased by the threat that one or more contractors will use deception and seek to profit at the expense of the others. The threat of opportunism becomes especially troublesome when few prospective contractors are available, because the low substitutability affords them power, which in turn enables them to demand special treatment (see Chapter 11). Opportunism also emerges as an issue when uncertainty hides the true intentions of contractors, blocking efforts to verify their honesty. In the absence of such verification, contractors are well advised to prepare for the worst and expect deceit. Costly surveillance should be conducted to detect opportunism before it can prove destructive.

Thus, considerations of bounded rationality and complexity drive up the transaction costs of contracting. In such situations—where uncertainty about the future undermines temporary relationships—the modular structure is favored. Likewise, concerns about opportunism increase the transaction costs of contracting and favor the modular structure. In contrast, the virtual structure is preferable when prospective contractors can negotiate good-faith contracts that are fair to all parties, honest in intention, and verifiable in every regard.[35]

Final Considerations

For large organizations that have progressed through the developmental stages of formalization and elaboration, transition to a modular structure is a matter of forming teams and giving them autonomy by decentralizing operations and reducing middle management. Transition to the virtual structure is more dramatic, requiring massive downsizing and the formation of contractual relationships. GM's North American operations are headed in this direction as its management has sold off many of the company's parts-manufacturing facilities and now purchases completed subassemblies such as automotive interiors, drivetrains, and bodies from outside contractors.

For small organizations that have jumped directly from inception or early formalization to transition, adoption of a modular structure means rapid growth through merger or internal expansion. In contrast, movement into a virtual structure requires the identification of prospective contractors and development of contractual relationships.

If successful, transitions that occur during the stage of transformation result in postbureaucratic structures that enable companies to act as both large and small entities simultaneously. Through mutual adjustment and decentralization, firms are able to realize extensive flexibility. Through large size, whether real or virtual, firms are able to control the scope of resources needed to accomplish complex tasks in an efficient manner. Key to the success of such organizations are the information-processing networks that tie their members together. In the absence of modern computer equipment and the intranets or internets it supports, postbureaucratic structures could not exist.

Summary

Organization design is the process of structuring an organization to enhance its *organizational effectiveness* in the light of the *contingency factors* with which it must deal. As they develop, organizations grow through the stages of *inception, formalization, elaboration*, and *transformation*. During inception, structural effectiveness is influenced by the contingency factors of *organization size* and *ownership norms*. Managers choose between the prebureaucratic alternatives of the simple undifferentiated and simple differentiated structures. During the stages of formalization and elaboration, structural effectiveness becomes a function of the contingency factors of *core technology* and *external environment*. Managers then choose between the bureaucratic alternatives of functional, divisional, matrix, and multiunit structures. During the stage of transformation, structural effectiveness is shaped by the contingency factors of *environmental turbulence* and *transaction costs*. In this stage, managers choose between the postbureaucratic alternatives of modular and virtual structures.

Review Questions

1. Name a specific business organization in your community and identify three of its most important constituency groups. What interests do each of the constituency groups expect the organization to fulfill? How does the organization's structure affect its ability to satisfy these interests? Is the company effective?

2. Why do organizations in the inception stage usually have prebureaucratic structures? What effects does organization size have on organization design at this stage?

3. Explain why environmental change impedes an organization's ability to coordinate by means of standardization. What sort of coordination is used instead? Why does environmental complexity push an organization toward decentralization?

4. How does the developmental stage of transformation differ from the stages of formalization and elaboration? Why does this difference push the organization toward the adoption of a postbureaucratic structure? How do environmental turbulence and transaction costs affect the process of organization design at this developmental stage?

Notes

1 P. Burrows and H. Miller, "Research in Motion: The Living Dead?" *Bloomberg Businessweek*, January 30, 2012, 36–37; S. Armour, "The First Five Years of Mass Obsession," *Bloomberg Businessweek*, June 25, 2012, 34–36; K. Tofel, "BlackBerry 10 is RIM's Last, Best Comeback Attempt," *Bloomberg Businessweek*, January 29, 2013, http://www.businessweek.com/articles/2013-01-29/blackberry-10-is-rim-s-last-best-comeback-attempt; C. Ngak, "Research in Motion Launches BlackBerry 10, Changes Corporate Name," *Bloomberg Businessweek*, January 30, 2013, http://www.cbsnews.com/news/research-in-motion-launches-blackberry-10-changes-corporate-name/; J. Brustein, "BlackBerry Gives Up on Its Tablet, while Consumers Give Up on Its Phones," June 28, 2013, http://www.businessweek.com/articles/2013-06-28/blackberry-gives-up-on-its-tablet-while-consumers-give-up-on-its-phones.

2 R. L. Priem and J. Rosenstein, "Is Organization Theory Obvious to Practitioners? A Test of One Established Theory," *Organization Science* 11 (2000): 509–524; J. Birkinshaw, R. Nobel, and J. Ridderstråle, "Knowledge as a Contingency Variable: Do the Characteristics of Knowledge Predict Organization Structure?" *Organization Science* 13 (2002): 274–289.

3 J. L. Price, "The Study of Organizational Effectiveness," *Sociological Quarterly* 13 (1972): 3–15; S. Strasser, J. D. Eveland, G. Cummings, O. L. Deniston, and J. H. Romani, "Conceptualizing the Goal and System Models of Organizational Effectiveness: Implications for Comparative Evaluative Research," *Journal of Management Studies* 18 (1981): 321–340; Y. K. Shetty, "New Look at Corporate Goals," *California Management Review* 22 (1979): 71–79.

4 Constituency models of effectiveness and other examples of constituencies and their interests are discussed by P. S. Goodman, J. M. Pennings, and Associates, *New Perspectives on Organizational Effectiveness* (San Francisco: Jossey-Bass, 1977); J. A. Wagner III and B. Schneider, "Legal Regulation and the Constraint of Constituent Satisfaction," *Journal of Management Studies* 24 (1987): 189–200; and R. F. Zammuto, "A Comparison of Multiple Constituency Models of Organizational Effectiveness," *Academy of Management Review* 9 (1984): 606–616. Related stakeholder models are discussed by R. E. Freeman, *Strategic Management: A Stakeholder Approach* (Boston: Pitman, 1984); C. W. L. Hill and T. M. Jones, "Stakeholder-Agency Theory," *Journal of Management Studies* 29 (1992): 131–154; T. Donaldson and L. E. Preston, "A Stakeholder Theory of the Corporation: Concepts, Evidence, and Implications," *Academy of Management Review* 20 (1995): 65–91; and T. A. Kochan and S. A. Rubinstein, "A Stakeholder Theory of the Firm: The Saturn Partnership," *Organization*

Science 11 (2000): 367–386; K. N. Jun and E. Shiau, "How Are We Doing? A Multiple Constituency Approach to Civic Association Effectiveness," *Nonprofit and Voluntary Sector Quarterly*, 41 (2012): 632–655.

5 R. Z. Gooding and J. A. Wagner III, "A Meta-Analytic Review of the Relationship between Size and Performance: The Productivity and Efficiency of Organizations and Their Subunits," *Administrative Science Quarterly* 30 (1985): 462–481; H. A. Haveman, "Organizational Size and Change: Diversification in the Savings and Loan Industry after Deregulation," *Administrative Science Quarterly* 38 (1993): 20–50; P. Dass, "Relationship of Firm Size, Initial Diversification, and Internationalization with Strategic Change," *Journal of Business Research* 48 (2000): 135–146.

6 Gooding and Wagner, "A Meta-Analytic Review."

7 T. Burns and G. M. Stalker, *The Management of Innovation* (London: Tavistock, 1961), 119–122; J. A. Courtright, G. T. Fairhurst, and L. E. Rogers, "Interaction Patterns in Organic and Mechanistic Systems," *Academy of Management Journal* 32 (1989): 773–802; V. L. Barker and M. A. Mone, "The Mechanistic Structure Shift and Strategic Reorientation in Declining Firms Attempting Turnarounds," *Human Relations* 51 (1998): 1227–1258.

8 L. Greiner, "Evolution and Revolution as Organizations Grow," *Harvard Business Review* 50 (1972): 37–46; J. R. Kimberly, R. H. Miles, and Associates, *The Organizational Life Cycle* (San Francisco: Jossey-Bass, 1980); R. F. Quinn and K. Cameron, "Organizational Life Cycles and Shifting Criteria of Effectiveness: Some Preliminary Evidence," *Management Science* 29 (1983): 29–34; G. Westerman, F. W. McFarlan, and M. Iansiti, "Organization Design and Effectiveness over the Innovation Life Cycle," *Organization Science* 17 (2006): 230–238; R. Phelps, R. Adams, and J. Bessant, "Life Cycles of Growing Organizations: A Review with Implications for Knowledge and Learning," *International Journal of Management Reviews* 9 (2007): 1–30.

9 S. M. Davis, *Future Perfect* (Reading, MA: Addison-Wesley, 1987); B. J. Pine II, *Mass Customization: The New Frontier in Business Competition* (Boston: Harvard University Press, 1993).

10 J. R. Kimberly, "Organizational Size and the Structuralist Perspective: A Review, Critique, and Proposal," *Administrative Science Quarterly* 21 (1976): 571–597; P. Y. Martin, "Size in Residential Service Organizations," *Sociological Quarterly* 20 (1979): 569–579; Gooding and Wagner, "A Meta-Analytic Review," 463.

11 C. C. Miller, W. H. Glick, Y. Wang, and G. P. Huber, "Understanding Technology–Structure Relationships: Theory Development and Meta-Analytic Theory Testing," *Academy of Management Journal* 34 (1991): 370–399; D. Miller, "Environmental Fit versus Internal Fit," *Organization Science* 3 (1992): 159–178; J. J. Ebben and A. C. Johnson, "Efficiency, Flexibility, or Both? Evidence Linking Strategy to Performance in Small Firms," *Strategic Management Journal* 26 (2005): 1249–1259.

12 C. Perrow, "A Framework for the Comparative Analysis of Organizations," *American Sociological Review* 32 (1967): 194–208; D. Rousseau, "Assessment of Technology in Organizations: Closed versus Open System Approaches," *Academy of Management Review* 4 (1979): 531–542; M. J. Hatch, *Organization Theory: Modern, Symbolic, and Postmodern Perspectives* (Oxford, UK: Oxford University Press, 2013), 127–157.

13 J. Woodward, *Management and Technology* (London: Her Majesty's Stationery Office, 1958). See also Woodward's *Industrial Organization: Theory and Practice* (London: Oxford University Press, 1975).

14 G. Moslemipour, T. S. Lee, and D. Rilling, "A Review of Intelligent Approaches for Designing Dynamic and Robust Layouts in Flexible Manufacturing Systems," *International Journal of Advanced Manufacturing Technology* 60 (2012): 11–27.

15 F. M. Hull and P. D. Collins, "High Technology Batch Production Systems: Woodward's Missing Type," *Academy of Management Journal* 30 (1987): 786–797; R. Parthasarthy and S. P. Sethi, "The Impact of Flexible Automation on Business Strategy and Organizational Structure," *Academy of Management Review* 17 (1992): 86–111.

16 J. D. Thompson, *Organizations in Action* (New York: McGraw-Hill, 1967), 15–18.

17 Perrow, "A Framework for the Comparative Analysis of Organizations"; R. G. Hunt, "Technology and Organization," *Academy of Management Journal* 13 (1970): 235–252; W. H. Starbuck, "Organizational Growth and Development," Chapter 11 in *Handbook of Organizations*, ed. J. G. March (New York: Rand McNally, 1965); Courtright, Fairhurst, and Rogers, "Interaction Patterns in Organic and Mechanistic Systems."

18 A. C. Bluedorn, R. A. Johnson, D. K. Cartwright, and B. R. Barringer, "The Interface and Convergence of the Strategic Management and Organizational Environment Domains," *Journal of Management* 20 (1994): 201–262; A. J. Verdu-Jover, F. J. Llorens-Montes, and V. J. Garcia-Morales, "Environment-Flexibility Coalignment and Performance: An Analysis in Large versus Small Firms," *Journal of Small Business Management* 44 (2006): 334–349.

19 Burns and Stalker, *The Management of Innovation*; C. R. Hinings, D. J. Hickson, J. M. Pennings, and R. E. Schneck, "Structural Conditions of Intraorganizational Power," *Administrative Science Quarterly* 19 (1974): 22–44; R. B. Duncan, "Multiple Decision-Making Structures in Adapting to Environmental Uncertainty: The Impact of Organizational Effectiveness," *Human Relations* 26 (1973): 273–291.

20 R. B. Duncan, "Characteristics of Organizational Environments and Perceived Environmental Uncertainty," *Administrative Science Quarterly* 17 (1972): 313–327; J. R. Galbraith, *Designing Complex Organizations* (Reading, MA: Addison-Wesley, 1973), 4–6.

21 Galbraith, *Designing Complex Organizations*, 4.

22 O. O. Sawyerr, "Environmental Uncertainty and Environmental Scanning Activities of Nigerian Manufacturing Executives: A Comparative Analysis," *Strategic Management Journal* 14 (1993): 287–299.

23 J. S. Adams, "The Structure and Dynamics of Behavior in Organization Boundary Roles," in M. D. Dunnette, ed., *Handbook of Industrial and Organizational Psychology* (Chicago: Rand McNally, 1976), 1175–1199.

24 H. Aldrich and D. Herker, "Boundary Spanning Roles and Organization Structure," *Academy of Management Review* 2 (1977): 217–239; R. H. Miles, *Macro Organizational Behavior* (Santa Monica, CA: Goodyear, 1979), 320–339; R. L. Daft and R. M. Steers, *Organizations: A Micro/Macro Approach* (Glenview, IL: Scott, Foresman, 1986), 299.

25 G. J. Castrogiovanni, "Environmental Munificence: A Theoretical Assessment," *Academy of Management Review* 16 (1991): 542–565.

26 D. Greising, L. Himelstein, J. Carey, and L. Bongiorno, "Does Tobacco Pay Its Way?" *Business Week*, February 19, 1996, 89–90; J. Carey, L. Bongiorno, and M. France, "The Fire This Time," *Business Week*, August 12, 1996, 66–68; C. Farrell, M. J. Mandel, T. Peterson, A. Borrus, R. W. King, and J. E. Ellis, "The Cold War's Grim Aftermath," *Business Week*, February 24, 1992, 78–80.

27 H. Mintzberg, *Structuring of Organizations* (Englewood Cliffs, NJ: Prentice Hall, 1979), 281; M. Yasi-Ardekani, "Effects of Environmental Scarcity on the Relationship of Context to Organizational Structure," *Academy of Management Journal* 32 (1989): 131–156.

28 Thompson, *Organizations in Action*, 25–38.

29 G. R. Carroll, "The Specialist Strategy," *California Management Review* 26 (1984): 126–137.

30 R. L. Daft and A. Y. Lewin, "Where Are the Theories for the 'New' Organization Forms? An Editorial Essay," *Organization Science* 4 (1993): i–vi; S. K. Fixson, Y. Ro, and J. K. Liker, "Modularisation and Outsourcing: Who Drives Whom? A Study of Generational Sequences in the US Automotive Cockpit Industry," *International Journal of Automotive Technology and Management* 5 (2005): 166–183; N. Siggelkow and J. W. Rivkin, "Speed and Search: Designing Organizations for Turbulence and Design," *Organization Science* 16 (2005): 101–122; T. Buganza and R. Verganti, "Life-Cycle Flexibility: How to Measure and Improve Capability in Turbulent Environments," *Journal of Product Innovation Management* 23 (2006): 393–407.

31 F. E. Emery and E. Trist, "The Causal Texture of Organizational Environments," *Human Relations* 18 (1965): 21–32; R. D'Aveni, *Hypercompetition: Managing the Dynamics of Strategic Maneuvering* (New York: Free Press, 1994); H. W. Volberda, "Toward the Flexible Form: How to Remain Vital in Hypercompetitive Environments," *Organization Science* 7 (1996): 359–374.

32 M. A. Schilling and H. K. Steensma, "The Use of Modular Organization Forms: An Industry-Level Analysis," *Academy of Management Journal* 44 (2001): 1149–1168; D. C. Galunic and K. M. Eisenhardt, "Architectural Innovation and Modular Corporate Forms," *Academy of Management Journal* 44 (2001): 1229–1250; G. Hoetker, "Do Modular Products Lead to Modular Organizations?" *Strategic Management Journal* 27 (2006): 501–518.

33 J. Pfeffer and G. R. Salancik, *The External Control of Organizations: A Resource Dependence Perspective* (New York: Harper & Row, 1978); N. Modig, "A Continuum of Organizations Formed to Carry Out Projects: Temporary and Stationary Organization Forms," *International*

Journal of Project Management 25 (2007): 807–814; E. J. de Waard and E. H. Kramer, "Tailored Task Forces: Temporary Organizations and Modularity," *International Journal of Project Management* 26 (2008): 537–546.

34 O. Williamson, *Markets and Hierarchies: Analysis and Antitrust Implications* (New York: Free Press, 1975). See also J. R. Commons, *Institutional Economics* (Madison: University of Wisconsin Press, 1934); R. H. Coase, "The Nature of the Firm," *Economica N.S.* 4 (1937): 386–405; and A. A. Alchian and H. Demsetz, "Production, Information Costs, and Economic Organization," *American Economic Review* 62 (1972): 777–795.

35 For related discussions, see P. S. Ring and A. H. Van de Ven, "Structuring Cooperative Relationships between Organizations," *Strategic Management Journal* 13 (1992): 483–498; J. T. Mahoney, "The Choice of Organizational Form: Vertical Financial Ownership versus Other Methods of Vertical Integration," *Strategic Management Journal* 13 (1992): 559–584.

Chapter 14

Culture, Change, and Organization Development

Early in 2013, the magazine publishing industry was abuzz with the news that Meredith Corporation, publisher of *Better Homes and Gardens, Parents, Family Circle*, and *Ladies' Home Journal*, was in talks to acquire Time, Inc.'s lifestyle and style and entertainment holdings, which included *People* and *InStyle* magazines. Weeks later, it became obvious that the hoped-for merger would not occur. Publicly, the failure was blamed on a variety of business considerations, including Meredith's limited interest in *Time, Fortune, Money*, and *Sports Illustrated* and Time, Inc.'s concerns about ownership of London-based Time-Warner subsidiary IPC Media. Privately, representatives from the two companies also noted that the cultures of the two corporations simply did not allow a single company to emerge. On one hand, Time Inc. was North America's largest publisher of general interest magazines and Time-Warner's offices were located in New York City, contributing to the big-city/big-company culture that existed within the firm. On the other hand, Meredith's magazines were aimed at limited audiences sometimes considered unfashionable and its headquarters were located in Des Moines, Iowa, lending a more Midwestern, conservative feel to the company. Whereas a Meredith business meeting might include a lunch of kale salad and rosemary-infused lemonade served in a company conference room, Time, Inc. executives were more likely to meet at Michael's for dry-aged steaks and later at the Lamb's Club for after-work cocktails. The two companies, and the two groups of employees, could not find common cultural ground, and this failure was, in the end, a very important reason why the merger did not take place.[1]

Managing the organization as an organization is a complex, demanding task. As discussed in Chapters 11 through 13, the management of macro organizational behavior requires that managers deal with issues of power, conflict, structure, and organization design. In addition, as will be discussed in this chapter, managers must assess and actively shape the culture of norms, values, and ways of thinking that influence behavior throughout the firm. As they deal with all of these issues, managers must also solve problems originating in change processes and the outcomes these processes bring into being. For this reason, Chapter 14 discusses the topics of organizational culture, change, and development. It first focuses on organizational culture, indicating how a firm's culture consists of surface elements that people use to make sense of their organization as well as deeper norms and values that stabilize cultural understandings over time. Next, the chapter discusses issues associated with change in organizations, focusing particular attention on changing organization cultures, and introduces organization development as a process of change planning and management. It concludes by describing specific organization development interventions that managers can use to initiate change aimed at resolving many of the problems identified throughout this book.

Organization Culture

Every *formal* organization of prescribed jobs and structural relationships includes an *informal* organization characterized by unofficial rules, procedures, and interconnections.[2] This informal organization arises as employees make spontaneous, unauthorized changes in the way things are done. In discussing emergent role characteristics (Chapter 8) and group development (Chapter 9), we have already discussed to some extent how day-to-day adjustments occur in organizations. As these informal adjustments shape and change the formal way of doing things, a culture of attitudes and understandings emerges that is shared among co-workers. This culture is a "pattern of basic assumptions—invented, discovered, or developed [by a firm's members] to cope with problems of external adaptation and internal integration—that has worked well enough to be considered valid and, therefore, to be taught to new members as the correct way to perceive, think, and feel in relation to those problems."[3] An organization's **culture** is therefore an informal, shared way of perceiving life and membership in the organization that binds members together and influences what they think about themselves and their work.

In the process of helping to create a mutual understanding of organizational life, organizational culture fulfills four basic functions. First, it *gives members an organizational identity*. That is, sharing norms, values, and perceptions provides people with a sense of togetherness that promotes a feeling of common purpose. Second, it *facilitates collective commitment*. The common purpose that grows out of a shared culture tends to elicit feelings of attachment among all those who accept the culture as their own. Third, it *promotes organizational stability*. By nurturing a shared sense of identity and commitment, culture encourages lasting integration and cooperation among the members of an organization. Fourth, it shapes behavior by *helping members make sense of their surroundings*. An organization's culture serves as a source of shared meanings that explain why things occur in the way that they do.[4] By fulfilling these four basic functions, the culture of an organization serves as a sort of social glue that helps reinforce persistent, coordinated behaviors at work. In so doing, an organization's culture can enhance its performance and serve as a valuable source of competitive advantage.[5]

Elements of Organization Culture

Deep within the culture of every organization is a collection of fundamental norms and values that shape members' behaviors and help them understand the surrounding organization. In companies such as 3M, cultural norms and values emphasize the importance of discovering new materials or technologies and developing them into new products. In other companies, such as Apple and Whirlpool, cultural norms and values focus on attaining high product quality.[6] Such fundamental norms and values serve as the ultimate source of the shared perceptions, thoughts, and feelings constituting the culture of an organization.[7]

These fundamental norms and values are expressed and passed from one person to another through *surface elements* of the culture, such as those overviewed in Table 14.1, that help employees interpret everyday organizational events.[8] One type of surface element, **ceremonies**, exemplifies and reinforces important cultural norms and values. Ceremonies include special events in which the members of a company celebrate the myths, heroes, and symbols of their culture.[9] In sales-focused organizations such as Mary Kay or Amway, annual ceremonies are held to recognize and reward outstanding sales representatives. Holding these ceremonies is intended to inspire sales representatives who have been less

Table 14.1 Surface Elements of Organization Cultures

Element	Description
Ceremonies	Special events in which organization members celebrate the myths, heroes, and symbols of their firm
Rites	Ceremonial activities meant to communicate specific ideas or accomplish particular purposes
Rituals	Actions that are repeated regularly to reinforce cultural norms and values
Stories	Accounts of past events that illustrate and transmit deeper cultural norms and values
Myths	Fictional stories that help explain activities or events that might otherwise be puzzling
Heroes	Successful people who embody the values and character of the organization and its culture
Symbols	Objects, actions, or events that have special meanings and enable organization members to exchange complex ideas and emotional messages
Language	A collection of verbal symbols that often reflect the organization's particular culture

effective to adopt the norms and values of their successful colleagues. Whether they personify the "Mary Kay approach" or the "Amway philosophy," the people who are recognized and rewarded in these ceremonies greatly enhance the attractiveness of their companies' cultural underpinnings.

Often, organizational ceremonies incorporate various **rites**, or ceremonial activities meant to send particular messages or accomplish specific purposes.[10] For instance, *rites of passage* are used to initiate new members into the organization and can convey important aspects of the culture to them. In some businesses, new recruits are required to spend considerable time talking with veteran employees and learning about cultural norms and values by listening to stories about their experiences at work. In other companies, the rite of passage consists of a brief talk about company rules and regulations delivered by a human resources staff member to newcomers during their first day at work. Little more than a formal welcoming, it does not really help newcomers learn about the culture of the firm.

When employees are transferred, demoted, or fired because of low productivity, incompatible values, or other personal failings, *rites of degradation* may draw the attention of others to the limits of acceptable behavior. Today, rites of degradation are typically deemphasized, involving little more than quiet reassignment. In the past, they were occasionally much more dramatic. In the early days of NCR—when it was still National Cash Register—executives who had incurred the founder's wrath sometimes learned that they had lost their jobs by discovering their desks burning on the lawn in front of corporate headquarters.

Rites of enhancement also emphasize the limits of appropriate behavior, but in a positive way. These activities, which recognize increasing status or position in a firm, can range from simple promotion announcements to intricate recognition ceremonies, such as the Mary Kay and Amway ceremonies just described.

In *rites of integration*, members of an organization become aware of the common feelings that bond them together. Official titles and hierarchical differences might be intentionally ignored in rites of this sort so that members can get to know one another as people rather than as managers, staff specialists, clerks, or laborers. At many companies, TGIF—Thank God It's Friday—parties are held every week to give employees the opportunity to chat informally over pizza and drinks. Company picnics, golf outings, softball games, and holiday parties can also serve as rites of integration.

A rite that is repeated on a regular basis becomes a **ritual**, a ceremonial event that continually reinforces key norms and values. The morning coffee break, for example, is a ritual that can strengthen important workplace relationships. So, too, is the annual stockholder meeting held by management to convey cultural norms and values to company shareholders. Just as routine coffee breaks enable co-workers to gossip among themselves and reaffirm important interpersonal relationships, annual stockholder meetings give the company the opportunity to strengthen connections between itself and people who would otherwise have little more than a limited financial interest in its continued well-being.

Stories are accounts of past events with which all employees are familiar and that serve as reminders of cultural values.[11] As organization members tell stories and think about the messages conveyed by the stories, the concrete examples described in this manner facilitate their later recall of the concepts presented. Stories also provide information about historical events in the development of a company that can improve employees' understanding of the present. In one organization, for example,

> employees tell a story about how the company avoided a mass layoff when almost every other company in the industry . . . felt forced to lay off employees in large numbers. The company . . . managed to avoid a layoff of 10 percent of their employees by having everyone in the company take a 10 percent cut in salary and come to work only nine out of ten days. This company experience is thus called the 'nine-day fortnight.'[12]

As a story, it vividly captures a cultural value—namely, that looking after employees' well-being is the right thing to do. Present-day employees continue to tell the story because it reminds them that their company will avoid layoffs as much as possible during economic downturns.

A **myth** is a special type of story that provides a fictional but plausible explanation for an event or thing that might otherwise seem puzzling or mysterious. Ancient civilizations often created myths about gods and other supernatural forces to explain natural occurrences, such as the rising and setting of the sun, the phases of the moon, and the formation of thunderstorms. Similarly, the members of a modern-day organization might develop fictionalized accounts of the company's founders, origins, or historical development to provide a framework for explaining current activities in their firm.

In many instances, organizational myths contain at least a grain of truth that, ultimately, makes them sound completely true. For example, myths retold throughout General Motors (GM) about the management prowess of Alfred P. Sloan, one of the company's earliest chief executives, are based in part on a study of GM's structure and procedures that Sloan performed from 1919 to 1920.

Heroes are people who embody the values of an organization and its culture:

> Richard A. Drew, a banjo-playing college dropout working in 3M's research lab during the 1920s, [helped] some colleagues solve a problem they had with masking tape. Soon

thereafter, DuPont came out with cellophane. Drew decided he could do DuPont one better and coated the cellophane with a colorless adhesive to bind things together—and Scotch tape was born. In the 3M tradition, Drew carried the ball himself by managing the development and initial production of his invention. Moving up through the ranks, he went on to become technical director of the company and showed other employees just how they could succeed in similar fashion at 3M.[13]

Heroes such as 3M's Drew serve as role models, illustrating personal performance that is not only desirable but attainable. Like stories, heroes provide concrete examples that make the guiding norms and values of a company readily apparent.

Symbols are objects, actions, or events to which people have assigned special meanings. Company logos, flags, and trade names are all familiar symbols. For example, Mercedes' three-point star logo is synonymous with quality in most people's minds, and even the youngest children know that the McDonald's arches mark the locations of fast-food restaurants. Symbols represent a conscious or unconscious association with some wider, usually more abstract, concept or meaning.[14] In organizations, they might include official titles, such as chief operating officer. Private dining rooms, official automobiles, or airplanes also might be given symbolic status. Sometimes even the size of an employee's office or its placement or furnishings have special symbolic value.[15]

Symbols mean more than might seem immediately apparent. For instance, despite the fact that a reserved parking space consists of just a few square feet of asphalt, it might symbolize its holder's superior hierarchical status or clout. It is this ability to convey a complex message in an efficient, economical manner that makes symbols so useful and important:

> When two people shake hands, the action symbolizes their coming together. The handshake may also be rich in other kinds of symbolic significance. Between freemasons it reaffirms a bond of brotherhood and loyalty to the order to which they belong. Between politicians it is often used to symbolize an intention to cooperate and work together. The handshake is more than just a shaking of hands. It symbolizes a particular kind of relationship between those involved.[16]

Clearly, symbols are absolutely necessary to communication. They convey emotional messages that cannot easily be put into words. Without symbols, many of the fundamental norms and values of an organization's culture could not be shared among organizational members.

Language is another means of sharing cultural ideas and understandings. In many organizations, the language used by members reflects the organization's particular culture.[17] Silicon Valley companies were well known for referring to the use of loaned funding in terms of "burn rate." *Bandwidth*, a term once used by Internet firms to indicate bit rate, has now become part of the language of the larger U.S. national culture.[18]

Managing Organization Culture

Organizational culture grows out of informal, unofficial ways of doing things. In turn, it influences the attitudes that employees hold and the behaviors in which they engage at work, thereby shaping the way that employees perceive and react to formally defined jobs and structural arrangements.[19] These relationships arise because cultural norms and values provide **social information** that helps employees determine the meaning of their work and the organization around them.[20] For example, in a company that follows a policy of promotion from within—wherein managers are chosen from among eligible subordinates rather than being hired from outside the firm—employees tend to view their jobs as critical to personal success. By encouraging employees to perceive success as something to be valued and pursued, cultural norms stressing the importance of hard work also encourage the development of a need for achievement (see Chapter 5) and motivate high productivity. In sum, as indicated in Figure 14.1, cultural norms and values convey social information that can influence the way people choose to behave on the job. They do so by affecting the way employees perceive themselves, their work, and the organization.

Can organizational culture be managed? It might seem that the answer to this question should be "no" for the following reasons:

1. Cultures are so spontaneous, elusive, and hidden that they cannot be accurately diagnosed or intentionally changed.
2. Considerable experience and deep personal insight are required to truly understand an organization's culture, making management infeasible in most instances.
3. Several subcultures might exist within a single organizational culture, complicating the task of managing organizational culture to the point where it becomes impossible.
4. Cultures provide organization members with continuity and stability. As a consequence, members are likely to resist even modest efforts at cultural management or change because they fear discontinuity and instability.[21]

Many experts disagree with these arguments, however, and suggest that organizational cultures can be managed by using either of two general approaches.

In the first approach, **symbolic management**, managers attempt to influence deep cultural norms and values by shaping the surface cultural elements, such as symbols, stories, and ceremonies that people use to express and transmit cultural understandings.[22] Managers can accomplish this shaping in several ways. For example, they can issue public statements about their vision for the future of the company. They can recount stories about themselves and the company. They can use and enrich the shared company language. In this way, managers not

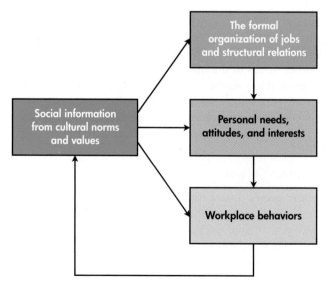

Figure 14.1 Cultural Elements as Social Information

only communicate the company's central norms and key values, but also devise new ways of expressing them.

Managers who practice symbolic management realize that every managerial behavior broadcasts a message to employees about the organization's norms and values. They consciously choose to do specific things that will symbolize and strengthen a desirable culture. The fact that symbolic management involves the manipulation of symbols is apt to lead some managers to underestimate its importance. Telling stories, performing ceremonies, and anointing heroes might seem unnecessary to managers who do not understand the import- ance of managing culture. In reality, playing down the importance of symbolic management can have disastrous consequences. Managers at companies such as Walt Disney agree that managing symbols—and the culture they support—is critical to organizational success.[23]

The second approach to managing organizational culture is to use **organization develop- ment** (OD) interventions.[24] OD interventions, such as those described in the following section, can contribute to cultural management by helping the members of an organization progress through the following steps:

1. *Identifying current norms and values.* OD interventions typically require people to list the norms and values that influence their attitudes and behaviors at work. This kind of list gives members insight into the organization culture.
2. *Plotting new directions.* OD interventions often make it possible for the members of an organization to evaluate present personal, group, and organization goals and to consider whether these goals represent the objectives they truly want to achieve. Such evaluations often point out the need to plot new directions.
3. *Identifying new norms and values.* OD interventions that stimulate thinking about new directions also provide organization members with an opportunity to develop new norms and values that will promote a move toward the desirable new goals.
4. *Identifying culture gaps.* To the extent that current (step 1) and desired (step 3) norms and values are articulated, the OD process enables organization members to identify culture gaps—that is, the differences between the current and desired situations.
5. *Closing culture gaps.* OD interventions give people the opportunity to reach agreements stating that new norms and values should replace old ones and that every employee should take responsibility for managing and reinforcing change.[25]

When people engage in behaviors that are consistent with the new norms and values developed in an OD intervention, they reduce culture gaps and, in effect, change the organization's culture.

Change and Organization Development

Besides stimulating and solidifying cultural change, **organization development** entails the more general process of planning, implementing, and stabilizing the results of any type of organizational change. In addition, the OD field of research specializes in developing and assessing specific **interventions**, or change techniques.[26] As both a management process and a field of research, OD is characterized by five important features:

1. *OD emphasizes planned change.* The OD field evolved out of the need for a systematic, planned approach to managing change in organizations. OD's emphasis on planning distinguishes it from other processes of change in organizations that are more spontan- eous or less methodical.

2. *OD has a pronounced social–psychological orientation.* OD interventions can stimulate change at many different levels—interpersonal, group, intergroup, or organizational. The field of OD is, therefore, neither purely psychological (focused solely on individuals) nor purely sociological (focused solely on organizations) but, rather, incorporates a mixture of both orientations.
3. *OD focuses primary attention on comprehensive change.* Although every OD intervention focuses on a specific organizational target, the effects on the total system are seen as equally important. No OD intervention is designed and implemented without considering its broader implications.
4. *OD is characterized by a long-range time orientation.* Change is an ongoing process that can sometimes take months—or even years—to produce the desired results. Although managers often face pressures to produce quick, short-term gains, the OD process is not intended to yield stopgap solutions.
5. *OD is guided by a change agent.* OD interventions are designed, implemented, and assessed with the help of a *change agent,* an individual who may be a specialist within the organization or a consultant brought in from outside the firm, and who serves as both a catalyst for change and a source of information about the OD process.[27]

Together, these five features suggest the following definition: *Organization development is a planned approach to interpersonal, group, intergroup, and organizational change that is comprehensive, long-term, and under the guidance of a change agent.*

Resistance to Change

Change means to alter, vary, or modify existing ways of thinking or behaving. In organizations, change is both an important impetus and a primary product of OD efforts, reshaping the ways in which people and groups work together. Change in organizations is pervasive, meaning that it is a normal and necessary part of being organized.[28]

Whenever managers attempt to set any change in motion, however, they must expect resistance, because people tend to reject what they perceive as a threat to the established way of doing things. The more drastic the change, the more intense the resulting resistance is likely to be.

Setting change in motion requires identifying and overcoming sources of resistance, on the one hand, and encouraging and strengthening sources of support, on the other hand. **Force field analysis** is a diagnostic method that diagrams the array of forces acting for and against a particular change in a graphic analysis. This tool is useful for managers and change agents who are attempting to visualize the situation surrounding a prospective change.

Figure 14.2 depicts a typical force field analysis. The figure includes two lines: one representing an organization's present situation and the other representing the organization after the desired change has been implemented. Forces identified as supporting change are shown as arrows pushing in the direction of the desired change, and forces resisting change are drawn as arrows pushing in the opposite direction. The length of each arrow indicates the perceived strength of the force relative to the other forces in the force field. The specific situation represented in the figure occurred a decade ago, when GM established production facilities in Lansing, Michigan, intended to produce a new line of luxury cars aimed at retaking market share recently lost to European and Asian nameplates such as Lexus, Infiniti, and BMW. Forces resisting this change included the following:

- differing perceptions among GM's managers about the need for new products and production facilities (as opposed to continuing to sell minor modifications of existing lines)
- differing perceptions of the importance of new products
- employee concerns at GM's other plants about the social disruption likely to occur as old work groups disbanded to staff the new production facilities
- bureaucratic inertia stemming from the rules and procedures used to coordinate existing ways of doing things
- employee fears about not being able to cope with the demands of new production technologies.

Opposing these forces were others supporting change:

- U.S. consumer interests in greater sportiness in luxury automobiles
- a drive among auto manufacturers to introduce team based production technologies and greater factory automation in order to increase quality and control costs
- a general sense of unease in the U.S. auto industry.

In the end, forces supporting change won out, with GM launching new Cadillac models that proved to be quite successful in the marketplace. There is, however, no universal, fail-safe way to overcome the resistant factors identified in a force field analysis. Of the many options available, six are used most often:

1. *Education and communication.* Information about the need and rationale for a prospective change can be disseminated through one-on-one discussions, group meetings, and written memos or reports. An educational approach is most appropriate where change is being undermined by a lack of information or where available information is

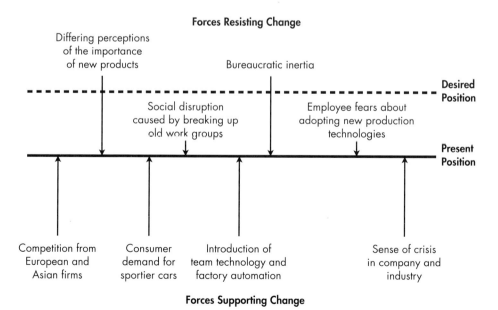

Figure 14.2 Force Field Analysis

inaccurate. Its strength is that, once persuaded through education, people will often help with the implementation of change. Its primary weakness is that education can be quite time-consuming if many people must be involved.

2. *Participation and involvement.* Individuals who will be affected by an intervention should be involved in its design and implementation. Thus employees should meet in special committees or task forces to participate in the decision making. Participation works well when the information required to manage change is dispersed among many people and when employees who have considerable power are likely to resist change if they are not directly involved in the initiation. This approach facilitates information exchange among people and breeds commitment among the people involved, but it can slow down the process if participants design an inappropriate change or stray from the task at hand.

3. *Facilitation and support.* Needed emotional support and training in topics related to organizational behavior should be provided through instructional meetings and counseling sessions for employees affected by a change. This method is most useful when people are resisting change because of problems with personal adjustment. Although no other method works as well with adjustment problems, facilitation efforts can consume significant amounts of time and money and still fail.

4. *Bargaining and negotiation.* Bargaining with resistant employees can provide them with incentives to change their minds. This technique is sometimes used when an individual or group with the power to block a change is likely to lose out if the change takes place. Negotiation can be a relatively easy way to avoid such resistance but can prove costly if it alerts other individuals and groups that they might be able to negotiate additional gains for themselves.

5. *Hidden persuasion.* Covert efforts can sometimes be implemented on a selective basis to persuade people to support desired changes. This approach is employed when other tactics will not work or are too costly. It can be a quick and inexpensive way to dissolve resistance, but can lead to future problems if people feel that they are treated unfairly. Covert persuasion might seem overly manipulative in retrospect, even if it leads to suitable results.

6. *Explicit and implicit coercion.* Power and threats of negative consequences may be employed to change the minds of resistant individuals. Coercion tends to be favored when speed is essential and individuals initiating change possess considerable power. It can overcome virtually any kind of resistance. Its weakness is that it can risk leaving people angry.[29]

Action Research

Organization development is a structured, multistep process. The **action research model** is a detailed variation of this process that promotes adherence to the scientific method (see Chapter 16) and places particular emphasis on post-change evaluation.[30] As indicated in Figure 14.3, it consists of seven stages, with the latter four forming a recurrent cycle.

In the initial stage of action research, *problem identification*, someone in an organization perceives problems that might be solved with the assistance of an OD change agent. Specific problem statements can usually be formulated at this stage. Sometimes, however, problem identification cannot progress beyond an uneasy feeling that something is wrong. Consultation with a change agent might then be required to crystallize the problems.

In the second stage, *consultation*, the manager and change agent clarify the perceived problems and consider ways of dealing with them. During this discussion, they assess the degree of fit between the organization's needs and the change agent's expertise. If the agent fits the situation, action research progresses to the next stage. If not, then another change agent is sought and consultation begins anew.

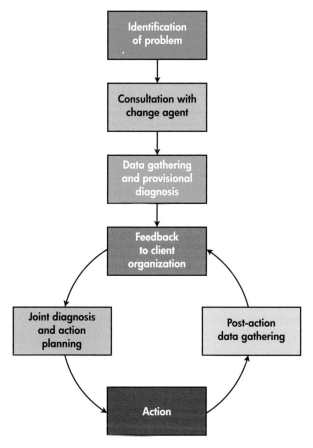

Figure 14.3 The Action Research Model

Source: Adapted from W. French, "Organization Development: Objectives, Assumptions, and Strategies," *California Management Review* 12 (1969): 23–30.

In the third stage, *data gathering and provisional diagnosis*, the change agent initiates the diagnostic process by gathering data about the organization and its perceived problems. The agent observes, interviews, and questions employees and analyzes performance records. A member of the organization may assist during this process, facilitating the agent's entry into the firm and providing access to otherwise hidden or unavailable data. The change agent concludes this stage by examining the data and performing a provisional analysis and diagnosis of the situation.

Next, during the stage of *feedback to the client organization*, the change agent submits data and provisional diagnosis to the client organization's top management group. Informing top management at an early point that the OD process is under way is crucial for securing the managerial support that any OD effort must have to succeed. During the feedback presentation, the change agent must be careful to preserve the anonymity of people serving as sources of information. Identifying them could jeopardize their openness and willingness to cooperate later, especially if they possess information that might prove unflattering to management or portray the organization in negative terms.

During the fifth stage of action research, *joint diagnosis and action planning*, the change agent and the top management group discuss the meaning of the data, their implications for organizational functioning, and needs for additional data gathering and diagnosis. At this point, other people throughout the organization might also become involved in the diagnostic process. Sometimes, employees meet in feedback groups and react to the results of top management's diagnostic activities. At other times, work groups elect representatives, who then meet to exchange views and report back to their co-workers. If the firm is unionized, union representatives are usually consulted as well. Throughout the action research process, the change agent must be careful not to impose any interventions on the client organization. Instead, members of the organization should deliberate jointly with the change agent and work together to develop wholly new interventions and plan specific action steps.

Next, the company puts the plan into motion and executes its action steps. In addition to the jointly designed intervention, the *action* stage might involve such activities as additional data gathering, further analysis of the problem situation, and supplementary action planning. Because action research is a cyclical process, data are also gathered after actions have been taken during the stage of *post-action data gathering and evaluation*. Here the purpose of the activity is to monitor and assess the effectiveness of an intervention. In their evaluation, groups in the client organization review the data and decide whether they need to rediagnose the situation, perform more analyses of the situation, and develop new interventions. During this process, the change agent serves as an expert on research methods as applied to the process of development and evaluation. In filling this role, the agent might perform data analyses, summarize the results of these analyses, guide subsequent rediagnoses, and position the organization for further intervention.

Organization Development Interventions

Many different OD interventionsvperhaps hundreds—can be selected on the basis of data gathered through action research and used to facilitate the stages of joint diagnosis and action planning, action, and post-action data gathering and evaluation just described. This section overviews eight of these interventions. As indicated in Table 14.2, they differ from one another in terms of target and depth.

The **target** of an OD intervention is the intervention's focus. Interpersonal, group, inter-group, and organizational relations can all serve as targets of OD interventions. Associated

Table 14.2 Organization Development Interventions

| Target | Focal problem | Depth | |
		Shallow	Deep
Interpersonal relations	Problem fitting in with others	Role negotiation technique	Sensitivity training
Group relations and leadership	Problem with working as a group	Process consultation	Team development
Intergroup relationships	Problem with relationships between groups	Third-party peacemaking	Intergroup team building
Organization-wide relationships	Problem with functioning effectively	Survey feedback	Open system planning

with these targets are various kinds of problems, as shown in Table 14.2 and indicated in earlier chapters of this book.

An intervention's **depth** reflects the degree or intensity of change that the intervention is designed to stimulate.[31] A *shallow* intervention is intended mainly to provide people with information or to facilitate communication and minor change. In contrast, a *deep* intervention is intended to effect massive psychological and behavioral change. An intervention of this type challenges basic beliefs, values, and norms in an attempt to bring about fundamental changes in the way people think, feel, and behave.

Interpersonal Interventions

Interpersonal interventions focus on solving problems with interpersonal relations, such as those described in Chapter 8. Depending on the particular intervention, the organization might attempt to redefine personal roles, clarify social expectations, or strengthen sensitivity to others' needs and interests.

Role Negotiation Technique

The **role negotiation technique** (RNT), an interpersonal intervention of moderately shallow depth, is intended to help people form and maintain effective working relationships.[32] As indicated in Chapter 8, people at work fill specialized *roles* in which they are expected to engage in specific sorts of behavior. Often, however, they lack a clear idea of what their roles entail, or they are overburdened by role demands. RNT (as diagrammed in Figure 14.4) is intended to reduce role ambiguity and conflict by clarifying interpersonal expectations and responsibilities.

To initiate an RNT intervention, the occupant of a problematic role contacts a change agent about his or her problem and receives instruction from the agent on the RNT procedure. The role occupant then works alone to analyze the rationale for the role as well as its place in the organizational network of interpersonal relations. This individual tries to learn how to use his or her role in meeting personal, group, and organizational goals.

Next, the role occupant discusses the results of the analysis in a meeting attended by everyone whose work is directly affected by his or her role. During this discussion, the change agent lists on a blackboard or flipchart the specific duties and behaviors of the role as identified by the role occupant. The rest of the group suggests corrections to this list. Behaviors are added or deleted until the role occupant is satisfied that the role he or she performs is defined accurately and completely.

In the next phase of the RNT process, the change agent directs attention to the role occupant's expectations of others. To begin this step, the role occupant lists his or her expectations of those roles that are connected with his or her own. The group then discusses and modifies these expectations until everyone agrees on them. Afterward, all participants have the opportunity to modify their expectations about the person's role, in response to his or her expectations of them. Thus, as its name indicates, RNT involves a process of negotiation. The person who is the focus of the intervention can ask others to do things for him or her, and others can ask the role occupant to do something for them in return.

In the final step of the RNT, the role occupant writes a summary or profile of his or her role as it has been defined through the RNT process. This profile specifies which behaviors are required and which are discretionary. Thus it constitutes a clearly defined listing of the role-related activities that the role occupant will perform. The meeting then continues, focusing on the roles of the other RNT participants, until all relevant interpersonal relationships have been clarified.

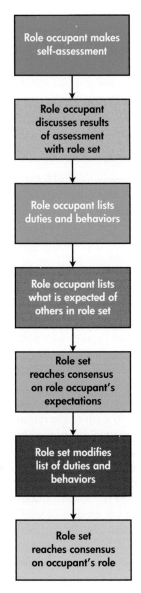

Figure 14.4 Steps in the Role Negotiation Technique

Sensitivity Training

As a deep interpersonal intervention, **sensitivity training** focuses on developing greater sensitivity to oneself, to others, and to one's relations with others.[33] Designed to promote emotional growth and development, it typically takes place in a closed session away from work. It might involve a collection of people who do not know each other, a group of people who are well acquainted, or a combination of both. A sensitivity training session may last for a period as brief as half a day or go on for several days. It is begun by a change agent, who announces that he or she will serve solely as a nondirective resource. The change agent then lapses into silence, leaving the participants with neither a leader nor an agenda to guide inter-personal activities. Putting people in such an ambiguous situation forces them to structure relations among themselves and, in the process, question long-held assumptions about them-selves, about each other, and about how to conduct interpersonal relationships.[34]

Sensitivity training participants take part in an intense exchange of ideas, opinions, beliefs, and personal philosophies as they struggle with the process of structuring interpersonal relations. Here is a description of one four-day session:

> The first evening discussion began with a rather neutral opening process, which very soon led to strongly emotional expression of concern. . . . By the second day the participants had begun to express their feelings toward each other quite directly and frankly, something they had rarely done in their daily work. As the discussion progressed it became easier for them to accept criticism without becoming angry or wanting to strike back. As they began to express long-suppressed hostilities and anxieties, the "unfreezing" of old attitudes, old values, and old approaches began. From the second day onward the discussion was spontan-eous and uninhibited. From early morning to long past midnight, the process of self-examination and confrontation continued. They raised questions they had never felt free to ask before. Politeness and superficiality yielded to openness and emotional expression and then to more objective analysis of themselves and their relationships at work. They faced up to many conflicts and spoke of their differences. There were tense moments, as suspicion, distrust, and personal antagonisms were aired, but most issues were worked out without acrimony.[35]

By completing this process, people learn more about their own personal feelings, inclinations, and prejudices and about what other people think of them.

A word of warning: Sensitivity training is a deep intervention that can initiate profound psychological change. Participants typically engage in intensely critical assessments of themselves and others that can be both difficult and painful. Therefore, the change agent overseeing sensitivity training *must* be a trained professional who can help participants deal with criticism in a constructive manner. In the absence of expert help, participants could risk serious psychological harm.[36]

Group Interventions

Group interventions are designed to solve problems with group or team performance and leadership, such as those identified in Chapters 7 through 10. In general, these interventions focus on helping the members of a group learn how to work together to fulfill the group's task and maintenance requirements.

Process Consultation

Process consultation is a relatively shallow, group-level OD intervention. In a process consulta-tion intervention, a change agent meets with a work group and helps its members examine group processes such as communication, leadership and followership, problem solving, and cooperation. The specific approach taken during this exploration, which varies from one situ-ation to another, might include group meetings in which the following activities take place:

1. The change agent asks stimulus questions that direct attention to relationships among group members. Ensuing discussions between group members might focus on ways to

improve these relationships as well as ways that such relationships can influence group productivity and effectiveness.

2. A process analysis session is held, during which the change agent watches the group as it works. This session is followed by additional feedback sessions in which the change agent discusses his or her observations about how the group maintains itself and how it performs its task. Supplementary feedback sessions might also allow the change agent to clarify the events of earlier sessions for individual group members.

3. The change agent makes suggestions that may pertain to group membership, communication, interaction patterns, and the allocation of work duties, responsibilities, and authority.[37]

Whatever the change agent's approach in a given situation, his or her primary focus in process consultation is on making a group more effective by getting its members to pay more attention to important *process* issues—that is, to focus on *how* things are done in the group rather than *what* is being done (the issues that normally dominate a group's attention). The ultimate goal of process consultation is to help the group improve its problem-solving skills by enhancing the ability of members to identify and correct faulty group processes.[38]

Team Development

Team development is a deep, group-level extension of interpersonal sensitivity training. In a team development intervention, a group of people who work together on a daily basis meet over an extended period of time to assess and modify group processes.[39] Throughout these meetings, participants focus their efforts on achieving a balance of basic components of teamwork, such as the following:

*   an understanding of and commitment to common goals
*   involvement of as many group members as possible, to take advantage of the complete range of skills and abilities available to the group
*   analysis and review of group processes on a regular basis, to ensure that sufficient maintenance activities are performed
*   trust and openness in communication and relationships
*   a strong sense of belonging on the part of all members.[40]

To begin team development, the group first engages in a lengthy diagnostic meeting, in which a change agent helps members identify group problems and map out possible solutions. The change agent asks members to observe interpersonal and group processes and to be prepared to comment on what they see. In this way, group members work on two basic issues: looking for solutions to problems of everyday functioning that have arisen in the group, and observing the way group members interact with each other during the meeting.

Based on the results of these efforts, team development then proceeds in two specific directions. First, the change agent and group implement the interventions chosen during diagnosis to solve the problems identified by the group. Second, the change agent initiates group sensitivity training to uncover additional problems that might otherwise resist detection:

> As the group fails to get [the change agent] to occupy the traditional roles of teacher, seminar leader, or therapist, it will redouble its efforts until in desperation it will disown him and seek other leaders. When they too fail, they too will be disowned, often brutally. The group will then use its own brutality to try to get the [change agent] to change his task by eliciting his sympathy and care for those it has handled so roughly. If this

maneuver fails, and it never completely fails, the group will tend to throw up other lead-ers to express its concern for its members and project its brutality onto the consultant. As rival leaders emerge it is the job of the consultant, so far as he is able, to identify what the group is trying to do and explain it. His leadership is in task performance, and the task is to understand what the group is doing "now" and to explain why it is doing it.[41]

Group sensitivity training is really an interpersonal sensitivity training intervention conducted with an intact workgroup. It enables co-workers to critique and adjust the inter-personal relations problems that inevitably arise during the workday. For this reason, the same cautions mentioned for interpersonal sensitivity training are also relevant to group sens-itivity training. Only a change agent trained to manage the rigors and consequences of a deep intervention should take a leadership role in this type of exercise.

Intergroup Interventions

Intergroup interventions focus on solving many of the intergroup problems identified in Chapter 11. In general, these problems concern conflict and associated breakdowns in inter-group coordination. Thus OD interventions developed to manage intergroup relations involve various open communication techniques and conflict resolution methods.

Third-Party Peacemaking

Third-party peacemaking is a relatively shallow intervention in which a change agent seeks to resolve intergroup misunderstandings by encouraging communication between or among groups. The change agent, who is not a member of any of the groups and is referred to as a third party, guides a meeting between the groups.[42] To be productive, the meeting must be characterized by the following attributes:

1. *Motivation*. All groups must be motivated to resolve their differences.
2. *Power*. A stable balance of power must be established between the groups.
3. *Timing*. Confrontations must be synchronized so that no one group can gain an inform-ation advantage over another.
4. *Emotional release*. People must have enough time to work through the negative thoughts and feelings that have built up between the groups. In addition, they need to recognize and express their positive feelings.
5. *Openness*. Conditions must favor openness in communication and mutual understanding.
6. *Stress*. There should be enough stress— enough pressure—on group members to motivate them to give serious attention to the problem, but not so much that the problem appears intractable.[43]

The change agent facilitates communication between the groups both directly and indir-ectly. He or she may interview group members before an intergroup meeting, help construct a meeting agenda, monitor the pace of communication between groups during the meeting or actually referee the interaction. Acting in a more subtle, indirect way, the change agent might schedule the meeting at a neutral site or establish time limits for intergroup interaction. The whole process can be as short as an afternoon, though it is more likely to last as long as several months of weekly sessions. Through these sessions, group members begin to learn things about one another and their relationships that can help them focus on common interests and begin to overcome conflictive tendencies.

Intergroup Team Building

Intergroup team building is a deep intervention that has three primary aims:

1. to improve communication and interaction between work-related groups
2. to decrease counter-productive competition between the groups
3. to replace group-centered perspectives with an orientation that recognizes the necessity for various groups to work together.[44]

As indicated in Figure 14.5, during the first step of intergroup team building, two groups (or their leaders) meet with an OD change agent and discuss whether relationships between

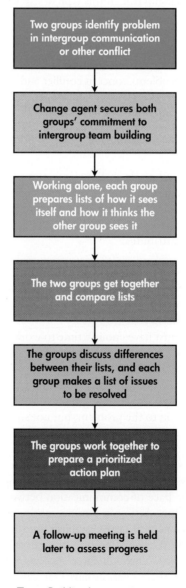

Figure 14.5 Steps in an Intergroup Team-Building Intervention

the groups can be improved. In the second step, if both groups agree that this goal is feasible, the change agent asks both groups to commit themselves to searching for ways to improve their relationship.

The groups then move to the third step of intergroup team building. The two groups meet in separate rooms, and each makes two lists. One list includes the group's perceptions, thoughts, and attitudes toward the other group. The other list describes their thoughts about what the other group is likely to say about them.

In the fourth step, the two groups reconvene and compare their lists. Each group can compare its view of the other group with the way the other group expects to be seen. Discrepancies uncovered during this comparison are discussed during the fifth step, when the groups meet separately. Each reacts to what it has learned about itself and the other group and then lists important issues that need to be resolved between the two groups.

During the sixth step, the two groups meet again and compare the lists of issues, setting priorities. They then work together on an action plan to resolve the issues based on their priority. They assign individual responsibilities and target dates for completion. The final step is a follow-up meeting held later to assess progress made to date. At that time, additional actions are planned as required to ensure that intergroup cooperation will continue over the long run.

Organizational Interventions

Organizational interventions are intended to deal with structural and cultural problems, such as those identified in Chapters 12 and 13 as well as those mentioned earlier in this chapter. Some of these interventions are directed at improving communication and coordination within the organization. Others focus on diagnosing and strengthening relations between the organization and its external environment.

Survey Feedback

The main purpose of **survey feedback** is to stimulate information sharing throughout the entire organization; planning and implementing change are of secondary importance.[45] Thus this technique is a relatively shallow, organization-level intervention.

The survey feedback procedure normally proceeds in four stages. First, under the guidance of a trained change agent, top management engages in preliminary planning, deciding such questions as who should be surveyed and what questions should be asked. Other organization members may also participate in this stage if their expertise or opinions are needed. Second, the change agent and his or her staff administer the survey questionnaire to all organization members. Depending on the kinds of questions to be asked and issues to be probed, the survey questionnaire might include any of the diagnostic questions provided in this book. Third, the change agent categorizes and summarizes the data. After presenting this information to management, he or she holds group meetings to let everyone who responded to the questionnaire know the results. Fourth, the groups that received the feedback information hold meetings to discuss the survey. The group leaders (perhaps a supervisor or an assistant vice president) help groups interpret the data—that is, diagnose the results and identify specific problems, make plans for constructive changes, and prepare to report on the data and proposed changes with groups at the next lower hierarchical level. The change agent usually acts as a process consultant during these discussions to ensure that all group members have an opportunity to contribute their opinions.

Survey feedback differs dramatically from the traditional questionnaire method of gathering information. In survey feedback, not only are data collected from everyone, from the highest to the lowest level of the hierarchy, but everyone in the organization also participates in analyzing the data and in planning appropriate actions. These key characteristics of survey feedback reflect OD's basic values, which stress the criticality of participation as a means of encouraging commitment to the organization's goals and stimulating personal growth and development.

Open System Planning

Open system planning is a fairly deep, organization-level intervention that is distinguished by its focus on the organization as a system open to its surrounding environment. The primary purpose of open system planning is to help the members of an organization devise ways to accomplish their firm's mission in light of the demands and constraints that originate with constituency groups in the organization's environment. As indicated in Chapter 13, these groups might include raw material suppliers, potential employees, customers, government regulators, and competitors.

As shown in Figure 14.6, the intervention involves five steps:

1. *Identification of the core mission or purpose.* The members of the organization meet and, through open discussion, define the firm's basic goals, purpose, and reason for existence.
2. *Identification of important constituency groups.* Participants identify the environmental constituencies that can affect the firm's ability to accomplish its goals and purpose.
3. *"Is" and "ought" planning.* Participants describe current relationships between the organization and its constituencies. They consider each constituency separately, focusing on the importance and duration of the relationship. Other factors probed include the frequency with which the parties come in contact with one another and the organization's ability to sense and react to changes in the constituency group. Participants then determine how satisfactory the relationship *is* to both organization and constituency. If this assessment uncovers deficiencies, participants specify what the relationship *ought* to be if it is to satisfy both sides.
4. *Current responses to constituency groups.* Participants assess the organization's current response to each constituency group by answering these questions: What does this constituency want from us? What are we currently doing to respond to this demand? Is our current response moving us closer to where we want to be in relation to our company's goals and purpose?
5. *Action planning.* If the current situation is not what it ought to be, and if the organization's current response to its constituency groups is inadequate, participants face the final task of deciding how to redirect the firm's behavior. In planning corrective action, they usually consider these questions: What actions should be taken, and who should take them? What resource allocations are necessary? What timetable should be set? When should each action start and finish? Who will prepare a progress report, and when will it be due? How will actions be evaluated to verify that progress is proceeding in the desired direction?[46]

Unlike most other OD interventions, open system planning directs primary attention to factors *outside* the organization that can influence organizational performance. It is especially useful in providing a structured, yet participatory, way to establish a firm's purpose and set the goals required to accomplish this purpose. Open system planning can also help identify critical environmental contingencies during the process of organization design. This exercise encourages the development of a better fit between an organization's structure and its environment.

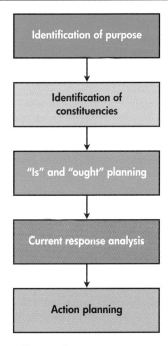

Figure 14.6 Steps in an Open System Planning Invention

Evaluating Change and Development

No matter what type of organization development intervention is used, the concluding stage of the OD process always consists of an evaluation of the technique's effectiveness. Based on the results of this evaluation, efforts may be devoted to ensuring that newly developed attitudes, values, and behaviors become permanent fixtures in the organization. Alternatively, OD may begin anew, and additional interventions might be initiated to stimulate further change. Table 14.3 contains a checklist of questions that can prove helpful in deciding which criteria to use and how to measure them when evaluating the effectiveness of OD.

Table 14.3 **Criteria for Evaluating Change Efforts**

Criterion	Suggested questions
Overall results:	
Desired outcomes	1. What were the intended outcomes of the intervention? How do they compare with the outcomes actually realized?
Guiding assumptions	2. How explicit were the assumptions that guided the intervention? Did experience prove them to be both valid and appropriate? Did everyone understand and agree with the intervention's purpose as a result?
Theory foundation	3. How consistent with current theories of organization behavior and OD are these assumptions? Was everything currently known with regard to the intervention's focus and purpose incorporated in the intervention?

Table 14.3 **Continued**

Criterion	Suggested questions
Phase of intervention:	
Identification	4. What was the reason for starting the intervention? Who was initially involved? Was the intervention undertaken because of a broadly felt need or a narrow set of special interests?
Consultation	5. What activities were performed at the start of the intervention process? Who was involved in them? Was the intervention implemented prematurely, without adequate diagnosis? Did unnecessary resistance arise as a result?
Data gathering	6. What specific data collection and provisional diagnostic activities took place? Were they carried out fully and effectively?
Feedback and planning	7. What aspects of the organization were diagnosed to determine the target and depth of the intervention that was implemented? How was the intervention planned, and who planned it? How were resources used in this effort? How explicit and detailed were the plans that resulted?
Action	8. What was actually done? When was it done? Who did it? How do the answers to these questions compare with the action plan as initially developed?
Post-action	9. Was post-action evaluation included from the outset as part of the intervention? Were deficiencies identified during evaluation corrected through a careful, planned modification of the intervention or its action plan?
External factors:	
Workforce traits	10. Were the results of the intervention affected, either positively or negatively, by workforce characteristics (such as age, gender, education, or unemployment level)?
Economy	11. What was the state of the economy and the firm's market at the time of the intervention? Did economic factors affect the success of the intervention?
Environment	12. How much did the organization's environment change over the course of the intervention? Are the intended results of the intervention still desirable given the organization's current environment?
Internal factors:	
Size	13. How large is the organization? Did its size permit access to the resources required for the intervention to succeed?
Technology	14. What is the organization's primary product, and what sort of technology is used to make it? Do the results of the intervention mesh or conflict with the requirements of this technology?
Structure	15. How mechanistic or organic is the organization's structure? Do the results of the intervention mesh or conflict with this structure?
Culture	16. What are the organization's prevailing norms and values concerning change? Concerning involvement in OD interventions?

Source: Adapted from N. Tichy and J. N. Nisberg, "When Does Work Restructuring Work? Organizational Innovations at Volvo and GM," *Organizational Dynamics* 5 (Summer 1976): 13–36; W. L. French, "A Checklist for Organizing and Implementing an OD Effort," in W. L. French, C. H. Bell, Jr., and R. A. Zawacki, eds., *Organization Development: Theory, Practice, and Research,* rev. ed. (Plano, TX: Business Publications, 1983), 451–459.

As suggested by the checklist, resources are expended to acquire the outcomes generated by the OD process. Consequently, OD's effectiveness must be judged partly in terms of its outcomes. In addition, measuring its effectiveness requires remembering why the process was undertaken initially and assessing what took place during each stage of the OD process. This procedure guarantees that an OD effort labeled "effective" not only accomplished its intended purpose, but did so in a manner that left everyone more informed about the process of change and ways to manage it. Finally, the effects of external and internal factors, whether positive or negative, on the OD process must be examined and cataloged for subsequent reference. With this knowledge, the factors that support change can be revisited when needed again in the future, and the ones that are resistant can be anticipated and neutralized.

Summary

The *culture* of an organization consists of deep-seated norms and values as well as surface expressions of these norms and values. The latter include *ceremonies, rites, rituals, stories, myths, heroes, symbols,* and *language.* Culture is a cohesive force that influences the way that the firm's members perceive the formal organization, their behaviors, and themselves. *Symbolic management* and *organization development* (OD) interventions can be used to manage the culture of an organization.

Organization development is both a field of research and a collection of *interventions* intended to stimulate planned change in organizations. Associated with OD is a concern about managing resistance to change and strengthening forces that favor change. *Force field analysis* is a technique that can be used to aid in the pursuit of these complementary goals. The *action research model* describes how *change agents* often manage the OD process.

OD interventions differ in terms of the types of organizational behavior that are their *targets* and the *depth* of change stimulated. The *role negotiation technique* and *sensitivity training* are interventions of increasing depth that target interpersonal problems. *Process consultation* and *team development* are group interventions of increasing depth. *Third-party peacemaking* and *intergroup team building* are increasingly deep intergroup interventions. *Survey feedback* and *open system planning* are organization-level interventions of increasing depth. To be considered completely successful, OD efforts should conclude with an evaluation of program effectiveness.

Review Questions

1. As a manager, you face the task of reversing cultural norms that currently favor low performance. How can you accomplish this task? What role do the surface elements of culture play in your plan?
2. How do cultural norms and values act as social information? What effects does this information have on organizational behavior? Why should managers take social information into account when designing jobs and structuring the organization?
3. Which of the OD interventions described in this chapter would you choose for each of the following situations: a person who understands his or her role in a group but cannot seem to get along with co-workers; a group of people who get along with one another but are less productive than expected; an organization suffering from poor internal communication; an organization unsure about its place in the broader business environment?
4. Why is it always important to evaluate the results of an OD intervention? What kinds of information should you collect and consider during an evaluation?

Notes

1 F. Gillette, "The Publishing Company that Beat the Internet," *Bloomberg Businessweek*, June 9, 2013, 62–65; C. Haughney, "How will Magazine Titans Merge? Carefully," *New York Times*, February 25, 2013, 65; A. Chozick, "Time Warner Ends Talks with Meredith and Will Spin Off Time Inc. into Separate Company," *New York Times*, March 6, 2013, 44.

2 A. S. Tannenbaum, *Social Psychology of the Work Organization* (London: Tavistock Publications, 2013).

3 E. H. Schein, *Organizational Culture and Leadership* (San Francisco: Jossey-Bass, 1985), 9.

4 L. Smircich, "Concepts of Culture and Organizational Analysis," *Administrative Science Quarterly* 28 (1983): 339–358; S. G. Harris, "Organizational Culture and Individual Sensemaking: A Schema-Based Perspective," *Organization Science* 5 (1994): 309–321; E. H. Schein, "Organizational Culture," *American Psychologist* 45 (1990): 109–119; A. D. Brown and K. Starkey, "The Effect of Organizational Culture on Communication and Information," *Journal of Management Studies* 31 (1994): 807–828.

5 J. B. Sørensen, "The Strength of Corporate Culture and the Reliability of Firm Performance," *Administrative Science Quarterly* 47 (2002): 70–91; A. Zuckerman, "Strong Corporate Cultures and Firm Performance: Are There Tradeoffs?" *Academy of Management Executive* 16 (2002): 158–160; P. Pyoria, "Informal Organizational Culture: The Foundation of Knowledge Workers' Performance," *Journal of Knowledge Management* 11 (2007): 16–30: M. Alveson, *Understanding Organizational Culture*, 2nd ed. (Thousand Oaks, CA: Sage, 2013).

6 T. E. Deal and A. A. Kennedy, *Corporate Cultures: The Rites and Rituals of Corporate Life* (Reading, MA: Addison-Wesley, 1982), 15.

7 H. M. Trice and J. M. Beyer, *The Cultures of Work Organizations* (Englewood Cliffs, NJ: Prentice Hall, 1993), 1–2; E. H. Schein, *Organizational Culture and Leadership*, 2nd ed. (San Francisco: Jossey-Bass, 1992), 3–27.

8 M. J. Hatch, "The Dynamics of Organizational Culture," *Academy of Management Review* 18 (1993): 657–693; L. K. Gundry and D. M. Rousseau, "Critical Incidents in Communicating Culture to Newcomers: The Meaning Is the Message," *Human Relations* 47 (1994): 1063–1088.

9 Deal and Kennedy, *Corporate Cultures*, 63.

10 J. M. Beyer and H. M. Trice, "How an Organization's Rites Reveal its Culture," *Organizational Dynamics* 15 (1987): 3–21; Trice and Beyer, *The Cultures of Work Organizations*, 107–127.

11 J. Martin, "Stories and Scripts in Organizational Settings," in A. Hastorf and A. Isen, eds., *Cognitive Social Psychology* (New York: Elsevier-North Holland, 1982), 225–305; C. D. Hansen and W. M. Kahnweiler, "Storytelling: An Instrument for Understanding the Dynamics of Corporate Relationships," *Human Relations* 46 (1993): 1391–1409; D. M. Boje, "The Storytelling Organization: A Study of Story Performance in an Office-Supply Firm," *Administrative Science Quarterly* 36 (1991): 106–126; D. M. Boje, "Stories of the Storytelling Organization: A Postmodern Analysis of Disney as 'Tamara-Land'," *Academy of Management Journal* 38 (1995): 997–1035; L. Naslund and F. Pemer, "The Appropriated Language: Dominant Stories as a Source of Organizational Inertia," *Human Relations* 65 (2012): 89–110.

12 A. L. Wilkins, "Organizational Stories as Symbols Which Control the Organization," in L. R. Pondy, P. J. Frost, G. Morgan, and T. C. Dandridge, eds., *Organizational Symbolism* (Greenwich, CT: JAI Press, 1983), 81–92.

13 Deal and Kennedy, *Corporate Cultures*, 40–41.

14 D. A. Gioia, "Symbols, Scripts, and Sensemaking," in H. P. Sims, ed., *The Thinking Organization* (San Francisco: Jossey-Bass, 1986), 48–112.

15 J. Pfeffer, *Power in Organizations* (Marshfield, MA: Pitman, 1981), 50.

16 G. Morgan, P. J. Frost, and L. R. Pondy, "Organizational Symbolism," in L. R. Pondy, P. J. Frost, G. Morgan, and T. C. Dandridge, eds., *Organizational Symbolism* (Greenwich, CT: JAI Press, 1983), 3–38.

17 Trice and Beyer, *The Cultures of Work Organizations*, 90.

18 R. Brandt, "The Billion-Dollar Whiz Kid," *BusinessWeek*, April 13, 1987, 68–76; K. I. Rebello and E. I. Schwartz, "Microsoft: Bill Gates' Baby Is on Top of the World. Can It Stay There?" *BusinessWeek*, February 24, 1992, 60–64.

19 C. A. O'Reilly III, J. Chatman, and D. F. Caldwell, "People and Organizational Culture: A Profile Comparison Approach to Assessing Person–Organization Fit," *Academy of Management*

Journal 34 (1991): 487–516; J. E. Sheridan, "Organizational Culture and Employee Retention," *Academy of Management Journal* 35 (1992): 1036–1056.

20 G. R. Salancik and J. Pfeffer, "A Social Information Processing Approach to Job Attitudes and Task Design," *Administrative Science Quarterly* 23 (1978): 224–253; R. E. Rice and C. Aydin, "Attitudes toward New Organizational Technology: Network Proximity as a Mechanism for Social Information Processing," *Administrative Science Quarterly* 36 (1991): 219–244; H. Ibarra and S. B. Andrews, "Power, Social Influence, and Sense Making: Effects of Network Centrality and Proximity on Employee Perceptions," *Administrative Science Quarterly* 38 (1993): 277–303; C. J. Bean and E. M. Eisenberg, "Employee Sensemaking in the Transition to Nomadic Work," *Journal of Organizational Change Management* 19 (2006): 210–222; D. Ravasi and M. Schultz, "Responding to Organizational Identity Threats: Exploring the Role of Organizational Culture," *Academy of Management Journal* 49 (2006): 433–458.

21 J. B. Miner, *Organizational Behavior: Performance and Productivity* (New York: Random House, 1988), 571; H. M. Trice and J. M. Beyer, "Using Six Organizational Rites to Change Culture," in R. H. Kilmann, M. J. Saxon, and R. Serpa, eds., *Gaining Control of the Corporate Culture* (San Francisco: Jossey-Bass, 1985), 370–399.

22 J. Pfeffer, "Management as Symbolic Action: The Creation and Maintenance of Organizational Paradigms," in L. L. Cummings and B. M. Staw, eds., *Research in Organizational Behavior*, vol. 3 (Greenwich, CT: JAI Press, 1981) 1–52; R. F. Dennehy, "The Executive as Storyteller," *Management Review*, March 1999, 40–43.

23 B. Dumaine, "Creating a New Company Culture," *Fortune*, January 15, 1990, 127–131; S. Fox and Y. Amichai-Hamburger, "The Power of Emotional Appeals in Promoting Organizational Change Programs," *Academy of Management Executive* 15 (2001): 84–93; C. Kane-Urrabazo, "Management's Role in Shaping Organizational Culture," *Journal of Nursing Management* 14 (2006): 188–194.

24 J. J. van Muijen, "Organization Culture," in P. J. D. Drenth, H. Thierry, and C. J. deWolff, eds., *Handbook of Work and Organizational Psychology*, 2nd ed. (East Sussex, UK: Psychology Press, Ltd., 2013), 113–131.

25 Miner, *Organizational Behavior*, 574–575; R. H. Kilmann, *Beyond the Quick Fix* (San Francisco: Jossey-Bass, 1984), 105–123.

26 G. L. Lippitt, P. Longseth, and J. Mossop, *Implementing Organizational Change* (San Francisco: Jossey-Bass, 1985), 3; E. Fagenson and W. W. Burke, "The Current Activities and Skills of Organization Development Practitioners," *Academy of Management Proceedings*, August 13–16, 1989, 251; L. E. Greiner and T. G. Cummings, "Wanted: OD More Live than Dead!" *Journal of Applied Behavioral Science* 40 (2004): 374–391; J. Wirtenberg, "Assessing the Field of Organization Development," *Journal of Applied Behavioral Science* 40 (2004): 465–479.

27 A. C. Filley, R. J. House, and S. Kerr, *Managerial Process and Organizational Behavior*, 2nd ed. (Glenview, IL: Scott, Foresman, 1976), 488–490; W. L. French and C. H. Bell, Jr., *Organization Development: Behavioral Science Interventions for Organizational Improvement*, 4th ed. (Englewood Cliffs, NJ: Prentice Hall, 1990), 21–22.

28 H. Tsoukas and R. Chia, "On Organizational Becoming: Rethinking Organizational Change," *Organization Science* 13 (2002): 567–582; N. Beck, J. Bruderl, and M. Woywode, "Momentum or Deceleration? Theoretical and Methodological Reflections on the Analysis of Organizational Change," *Academy of Management Journal* 51 (2008): 413–435.

29 J. P. Kotter and L. A. Schlesinger, "Choosing Strategies for Change," *Harvard Business Review* 57 (1979): 102–121; J. M. Ivancevich and M. T. Matteson, *Organizational Behavior and Management*, 2nd ed. (Homewood, IL: Irwin, 1990), 621–622; J. A. Wagner III, "Use Participation to Share Information and Distribute Knowledge," in E. A. Locke, ed., *The Blackwell Handbook of Principles of Organizational Behavior* (Oxford, UK: Blackwell, 2000), 304–315; J. E. Dutton, S. J. Ashford, R. M. O'Neill, and K. A. Lawrence, "Moves that Matter: Issue Selling and Organizational Change," *Academy of Management Journal* 44 (2001): 716–736.

30 W. French, "Organization Development: Objectives, Assumptions, and Strategies," *California Management Review* 12 (1969): 23–30; J. M. Bartunek, "Scholarly Dialogues and Participatory Action Research," *Human Relations* 46 (1993): 1221–1233; F. Heller, "Another Look at Action Research," *Human Relations* 46 (1993): 1235–1242; J. R. B. Halbesieben, H. K. Osburn, and M. D. Mumford, "Action Research as a Burnout Intervention," *Journal of Applied Behavioral Science* 42 (2006): 244–266; J. Trullen and J. M. Bartunek, "What a

Design Approach Offers to Organization Development," *Journal of Applied Behavioral Science* 43 (2007): 23–40; L. S. Luscher and M. W. Lewis, "Organizational Change and Managerial Sensemaking: Working through Paradox," *Academy of Management Journal* 51 (2008): 221–240.

31 R. Harrison, "Choosing the Depth of Organizational Intervention," *Journal of Applied Behavioral Science* 6 (1970): 181–202.

32 I. Dayal and J. M. Thomas, "Operation KPE: Developing a New Organization," *Journal of Applied Behavioral Science* 4 (1968): 473–506; V. D. Miller, J. R. Johnson, Z. Hart, and D. L. Peterson, "A Test of Antecedents and Outcomes of Employee Role Negotiation Ability," *Journal of Applied Communication Research* 27 (1999): 24–48; J. Watkins and R. A. Luke, "Role Negotiation: Sorting Out the Nuts and Bolts of Day-to-Day Staff Supervision," *Federal Probation* 55 (1991): 18–23; A. Aritzeta, S. Swailes, and B. Senior, "Belbin's Team Role Model: Development, Validity, and Applications for Team Building," *Journal of Management Studies* 44 (2007): 96–118.

33 J. P. Campbell and M. D. Dunnette, "Effectiveness of T-Group Experiences in Managerial Training and Development," *Psychological Bulletin* 65 (1968): 73–104; P. Sachdev, "Cultural Sensitivity Training through Experiential Learning: A Participatory Demonstration Field Education Project," *International Social Work* 40 (1997): 7–36.

34 E. Aronson, "Communication in Sensitivity Training Groups," in W. L. French, C. H. Bell, Jr., and R. A. Zawacki, eds., *Organization Development: Theory, Practice, and Research* (Plano, TX: Business Publications, 1983), 249–253.

35 G. David, "Building Cooperation and Trust," in A. J. Marrow, D. G. Bowers, and S. E. Seashore, eds., *Management by Participation* (New York: Harper & Row, 1967), 99–100.

36 C. A. Bramlette and J. H. Tucker, "Encounter Groups: Positive Change or Deterioration," *Human Relations* 34 (1981): 303–314; S. Satoh, N. Morita, I. Matsuzaki, E. Seno, S. Obata, M. Yashikawa, T. Okada, A. Nishimura, T. Konishi, and A. Yamagimi, "Brief Reactive Psychosis Induced by Sensitivity Training: Similarities between Sensitivity Training and Brainwashing Situations," *Psychiatry and Clinical Neurosciences* 50 (1996): 261–265.

37 E. H. Schein, *Process Consultation* (Reading, MA: Addison-Wesley, 1968), 102–103; C. F. Paul and A. C. Gross, "Increasing Productivity and Morale in a Municipality: Effects of Organization Development," *Journal of Applied Behavioral Science* 17 (1981): 59–78.

38 Schein, *Process Consultation*, 135; J. C. Quick and E. H. Schein, "The Next Frontier: Edgar Schein on Organizational Therapy," *Academy of Management Executive* 14 (2000): 32–44; E. H. Schein, "The Concept of 'Client' from a Process Consultation Perspective: A Guide," *Journal of Organizational Change Management* 10 (1997): 22–24; C. C. Hebard, "A Story of Real Change," *Training and Development* 52 (1998): 47–64; R. Weir, L. Stewart, G. Browne, J. Roberts, A. Gafni, S. Easton, and L. Seymour, "The Efficacy and Effectiveness of Process Consultation in Improving Staff Morale and Absenteeism," *Medical Care* 35 (1997): 334–353; M. A. Diamond, "Telling Them What They Know," *Journal of Applied Behavioral Science* 44 (2008): 348–364.

39 R. T. Golembiewski, *Approaches to Planned Change, Part I: Orienting Perspectives and Micro-Level Interventions* (New York: Marcel Dekker, 1979), 301; H. Prager, "Cooking Up Effective Team Building," *Training and Development* 53 (1999): 14–15; D. J. Svyantek, S. A. Goodman, L.t L. Benz, and J. A. Gard, "The Relationship between Organizational Characteristics and Team Building Success," *Journal of Business and Psychology* 14 (1999): 265–283.

40 G. L. Lippitt, *Organization Renewal* (New York: Appleton-Century-Crofts, 1969), 107–113.

41 A. K. Rice, *Learning for Leadership* (London: Tavistock, 1965), 65–66.

42 P. S. Nugent, "Managing Conflict: Third-Party Interventions for Managers," *Academy of Management Executive* 16 (2002): 139–154.

43 R. E. Walton, *Interpersonal Peacemaking: Confrontation and Third Party Consultation* (Reading, MA: Addison-Wesley, 1969), 94–115.

44 R. R. Blake, H. A. Shepard, and J. S. Mouton, *Managing Intergroup Conflict in Industry* (Houston, TX: Gulf, 1965), 36–100; R. Beckhard, *Organization Development: Strategies and Models* (Reading, MA: Addison-Wesley, 1969), 33–35.

45 F. C. Mann, "Studying and Creating Change," in W. G. Bennis, K. D. Benne, and R. Chin, eds., *The Planning of Change* (New York: Holt, Rinehart and Winston, 1961), 605–613; V. M. C. van Geen, "The Measure and Discussion Intervention: A Procedure for Client Empowerment and Quality Control in Residential Care Homes," *Gerontologist* 37 (1997):

817–822; M. A. Peter, "Making the Hidden Obvious: Management Education through Survey Feedback," *Journal of Nursing Administration* 24 (1994): 13–19; S. Silver, "Implementing and Sustaining Empowerment," *Journal of Management Inquiry* 15 (2006): 47–58.

46 W. G. Dyer, *Strategies for Managing Change* (Reading, MA: Addison-Wesley, 1984), 149–150; B. H. Kleiner, "Open Systems Planning: Its Theory and Practice," *Behavioral Science* 31 (1986): 189–204.

Part V

Conclusion

Chapter 15

International Organizational Behavior

In today's global economy, it is increasingly difficult to find a company whose business activities do not cross national borders. For instance, Jeep, identified in a recent poll as the quintessential American brand, is now marketing a Grand Cherokee SUV built on a chassis shared with Italian auto manufacturer Fiat. Among a ranking of cars and trucks deemed "most American" on the basis of domestic parts content and assembly, Japanese manufacturer Toyota's Camry ranks number two and Honda's Odyssey is number four. American soft drink manufacturer PepsiCo is a major player in snack food markets in Ukraine, Turkmenistan, and Kyrgyzstan. European aircraft manufacturer Airbus assembles its A320 jetliner in a plant located in Brookley, Alabama. More than half of British consumer products giant Unilever's sales are in emerging markets, including Indonesia, Brazil, and India. In these examples and many others, to refer to a company as "American," "Japanese," or "English" does not yield an accurate picture of the firm's multinational reach.[1]

With multinationalization and globalization come differences in nationality and culture within organizations that can have significant effects on micro, meso, and macro organizational behavior. These differences can complicate the jobs of contemporary managers because they require that management practices developed in one cultural region be modified for use in others. Managers in these circumstances *must* take international differences into consideration if they expect to gain competitive advantage from cultural diversity and succeed in global markets.

This chapter focuses on some of the most important international differences that have been identified in organizational research, examining the effects they can have on the management of organizational behavior. It begins with the introduction of a five-dimensional model that is useful in highlighting differences among national cultures. Next, it discusses effects that the differences mapped by the five dimensions can have on organizations and their members. The chapter concludes by considering the managerial implications of such international differences, focusing on a basic framework for fitting the management practices described in this book—which are primarily North American in origin and cultural focus—to the job of managing people and organizations throughout the world.

International Dimensions

How do cultures differ from one region of the world to another? In what ways are the **national cultures** of different countries comparable? What effects do cultural differences have on people's attitudes and behaviors in organizations? In a groundbreaking study, Dutch researcher Geert Hofstede set out to answer these questions by surveying employees in IBM offices located in forty countries throughout the world. As he examined the data from 116,000 questionnaires, Hofstede discovered that most differences among national cultures could be captured by a model composed of four cross-cultural dimensions: *uncertainty avoidance, masculinity–femininity, individualism–collectivism*, and *power distance*.[2] In later research, Canadian researcher Michael Harris Bond found a fifth dimension, *long-term/short-term orientation*, which Hofstede later added to his model.[3]

Uncertainty Avoidance

The degree to which people are comfortable with ambiguous situations and with the inability to predict future events with assurance is called **uncertainty avoidance**. At one extreme of this dimension, people with weak uncertainty avoidance feel comfortable even though they are unsure about current activities or future events. Their attitudes are expressed in the following statements:

- Life is inherently uncertain and is most easily dealt with if taken one day at a time.
- It is appropriate to take risks in life.
- Deviation from the norm is not threatening; tolerance of differences is essential.
- Conflict and competition can be managed and used constructively.
- There should be as few rules as possible, and rules that cannot be kept should be changed or eliminated.[4]

At the other extreme, people characterized by strong uncertainty avoidance are most comfortable when they feel a sense of certainty about the present and future. Their attitudes about uncertainty and associated issues can be stated as follows:

- The uncertainty inherent in life is threatening and must be fought continually.
- Having a stable, secure life is important.
- Deviant people and ideas are dangerous and should not be tolerated.
- Conflict and competition can unleash aggression and must be avoided.
- Written rules and regulations are needed; if people do not adhere to them, the problem is human frailty, not defects in the rules and regulations themselves.[5]

In national cultures characterized by high uncertainty avoidance, behavior is motivated at least partly by people's fear of the unknown and by attempts to cope with this fear. Often, people in such cultures try to reduce or avoid uncertainty by establishing extensive formal rules. For instance, having detailed laws about marriage and divorce diminishes uncertainty about the structure and longevity of family relationships. If uncertainty proves unavoidable, people with a cultural aversion to uncertainty might hire "experts" who seem to have the ability to apply knowledge, insight, or skill to the task of transforming something uncertain into something understandable. These experts need not actually accomplish anything, so long as they are perceived as understanding what others do not.

People with an uncertainty aversion might also engage in rituals intended to help them cope with the anxiety aroused by uncertainty. For example, they might develop extensive plans and forecasts designed to encourage speculation about the future and to make it seem more understandable and predictable. Plans and forecasts dispel anxiety, even if they prove largely invalid. For this reason, although people living in highly changeable climates often joke about the inaccuracy of local weather forecasts, many still tune into televised weather forecasts every night to plan what to wear and do the next day.

Masculinity–Femininity

Hofstede used the term *masculinity* to refer to the degree to which a culture is founded on values that emphasize independence, aggressiveness, dominance, and physical strength. According to Hofstede, people in a national culture characterized by extreme masculinity hold beliefs such as the following:

- Sex roles in society should be clearly differentiated; men are intended to lead and women to follow.
- Independent performance and visible accomplishments are what count in life.
- People live to work.
- Ambition and assertiveness provide the motivation behind behavior.
- People admire the successful achiever.[6]

Femininity, according to Hofstede, describes a society's tendency to favor such values as interdependence, compassion, empathy, and emotional openness. People in a national culture oriented toward extreme femininity hold such beliefs as the following:

- Sex roles in society should be fluid and flexible; sexual equality is desirable.
- The quality of life is more important than personal performance and visible accomplishments.
- People work to live.
- Helping others provides the motivation behind behavior.
- People sympathize with the unfortunate victim.[7]

Together, the extremes of masculinity and femininity delineate the dimension of **masculinity–femininity** in Hofstede's analysis of cross-cultural differences. One important effect of the differences mapped by this dimension is the way a nation's work is divided into jobs and distributed among its populace. In masculine national cultures, women are forced to work at lower-level jobs. Managerial work is seen as the province of men, who are portrayed as having the ambition and independence of thought required to succeed at decision making and problem solving. Women also receive less pay and recognition for their work than do their male counterparts. Only in "feminine" occupations such as teacher or nurse or in supporting roles such as secretary or clerk are women allowed to manage themselves. Even then, female supervisors must often imitate their male bosses to gain acceptance as managers.

In contrast, equality between the sexes is the norm in feminine national cultures. Neither men nor women are considered to be better managers, and no particular occupation is seen as masculine or feminine. Both sexes are equally recognized for their work, and neither is required to mimic the behavior of the other for the sake of acceptance in the workplace.

Individualism–Collectivism

According to Hofstede, **individualism–collectivism** is a dimension that traces cultural tendencies to emphasize either satisfying personal needs or looking after the needs of the group. From the viewpoint of individualism, pursuing personal interests is seen as being more important, and succeeding in the pursuit of these interests is critical to both personal and societal well-being. If each person takes care of personal interests, then everyone will be satisfied. Consistent with this perspective, the members of individualistic national cultures espouse the following attitudes:

- "I" is more important than "we." People are identified by their personal traits.
- Success is a personal achievement. People function most productively when working alone.
- People should be free to seek autonomy, pleasure, and security through their own personal efforts.
- Every member of society should take care of his or her personal well-being and the well-being of immediate family members.[8]

In contrast, the collectivist perspective emphasizes that group welfare is more important than personal interests. People who hold this view believe that only by belonging to a group and looking after its interests can they secure their own well-being and that of the broader society. For this reason, the members of collectivistic national cultures tend to ignore personal needs for the sake of their groups, ensuring group welfare even if personal hardships must be endured. They agree on the following points:

- "We" is more important than "I." People are identified by the characteristics of the groups to which they belong.
- Success is a group achievement. People contribute to group performance, but groups alone function productively.
- People can achieve order and security and fulfill their duty to society only through group membership.
- Every member of society should belong to a group that will secure members' well-being in exchange for loyalty and attention to group interests.[9]

In national cultures oriented toward the individualistic end of the dimension, membership in a group is something that can be initiated and terminated whenever convenient. A person does not necessarily have a strong feeling of commitment to any of the groups to which he or she belongs. In more collectivistic national cultures, however, changes in membership status can be traumatic. Joining and leaving a group can be likened to finding and then losing one's sense of identity. The collectivist feels a very strong, enduring sense of commitment to the group.[10]

Power Distance

Power distance is a dimension that reflects the degree to which the members of a society accept differences in power and status among themselves. In national cultures that tolerate only a small degree of power distance, norms and values specify that differences in people's ability to influence others should be minimal; instead, political equality should be encouraged. People in these cultures show a strong preference for participatory decision making and tend to distrust autocratic, hierarchical types of governance. They hold the following beliefs:

- Superiors should consider subordinates as "people just like me," and subordinates should regard superiors in the same way.
- Superiors should be readily accessible to subordinates.
- Using power is neither inherently good nor inherently evil; whether power is good or evil depends on the purposes for, and consequences of, its use.
- Everyone in a society has equal rights, and these rights should be universally enforced.[11]

In contrast, national cultures characterized by a large degree of power distance support norms and values stipulating that power should be distributed hierarchically, instead of being shared more or less equally. People in these cultures favor using authority and direct supervision to coordinate people and jobs. They hold the following beliefs:

- Superiors and subordinates should consider each other to be different kinds of people.
- Superiors should be inaccessible to subordinates.
- Power is a basic fact of society; notions of good and evil are irrelevant.
- Power holders are entitled to special rights and privileges.[12]

Power distance influences attitudes and behaviors by affecting the way that a society is held together. When the members of a national culture favor only a small degree of power distance, citizens have a strong, direct voice in determining national policy. Conversely, authoritarian, autocratic government is the hallmark when societal norms and values favor larger power distance.

Short-Term/Long-Term Orientation

The dimension of **short-term/long-term orientation** reflects the extent to which the members of a national culture are oriented toward the recent past and the present versus being oriented toward the future. In national cultures characterized by a short-term orientation, individuals believe the following:

- It is important to respect traditions and to remember past accomplishments.
- To forget history is to risk repeating past mistakes.
- Failing activities should be halted immediately.
- Resources should be consumed now without worrying about the future.

Thus the short-term orientation supports immediate consumption and opposes the deferral of pleasure and satisfaction. People tend to avoid unpleasant tasks, even if they are necessary to ensure a pleasurable future.

In contrast, in national cultures with a long-term orientation, people agree on the following points:

- It is important to look ahead and to envision the future.
- History is likely to repeat itself only if looking to the past obscures visions of the future.
- Perseverance in the face of adversity can overcome failure.
- Resources should be saved to ensure a prosperous future.[13]

A longer-term orientation favors the opposite strategy—that is, doing what is necessary now, whether pleasant or unpleasant, for the sake of future well-being. Short-term/long-term orientation thus influences people's willingness to endure hardship in the present and defer pleasurable experiences into the future.

Effects on Organizational Behavior

Hofstede and Bond's five-dimensional model does not lack critics. For instance, a study that used Hofstede's original four dimensions to assess the societal values of American, Japanese, and Taiwanese managers in Taiwan revealed problems with measurement validity and reliability (see Chapter 16 for a discussion of these kinds of problems).[14] In addition, other researchers have proposed competing frameworks, such as the cultural dimensions model introduced by Shalom Schwartz and associates, and the GLOBE taxonomy developed by Robert House and colleagues.[15] Nonetheless, the Hofstede–Bond model is considered by many to be the most comprehensive cross-cultural framework currently available, and it can stimulate useful insights into ways in which organizational behavior varies from one national culture to another. For this reason, it serves as the conceptual foundation of the rest of this chapter.

Cultural Trends: Four Scenarios

Table 15.1 summarizes the average scores on the five dimensions for each of forty-four countries. In the table, larger numbers signify greater amounts of uncertainty avoidance, masculinity, individualism, power distance, or longer-term orientation. The cultural distinctions quantified in this table reflect a variety of differences in the way people think and behave in different national cultures. To explore some of these differences, try using the five dimensions of the model to explain the following four scenarios:

1. *Feelings about progress.* Being modern and future-oriented is highly valued in China. From the modernist perspective, something that has existed for many years might seem old-fashioned or obsolete. In Russia, however, tradition, the status quo, and the past are more highly revered. To a traditionalist, familiar things are perceived as trustworthy, proven, and worthwhile. Which dimension explains this difference?

2. *Tendencies toward confrontation or consensus.* In Greece, it is important to smooth over differences to preserve agreement. Emphasis is placed on building consensus among co-workers and avoiding personal confrontation. In Denmark, conflict and confrontation are accepted or even encouraged. Conflict is perceived to be a signal of the need for change. How can this difference be explained?

3. *Locus of control.* The national culture of Australia instills a sense of personal responsibility for the outcomes of individual behaviors. Rewarding people for personal performance is considered a logical consequence of the value that Australians place on personal accountability. In Pakistan, however, people focus on external social causes to explain similar outcomes. Giving people rewards for personal performance seems unwarranted because of cultural beliefs that behaviors are strongly influenced by outside forces. How can you explain this difference?

4. *Status and social position.* In India, status is accorded on the basis of family, class, ethnicity, and even accent. High-status people can impose their will on lower-status people, even when both are equally knowledgeable and competent. In New Zealand, status is earned through personal achievement, and shared governance by majority rule or participatory decision making is valued more highly than personal fiat. Expertise outranks social position in determining who will be involved in decision-making procedures. What lies beneath this difference?[16]

Were you able to explain the first scenario? Differing attitudes toward progress are produced by cross-cultural differences in short-term/long-term orientation. Cultures like that of Russia, which incorporate short-term orientations (10 on short-term/long-term orientation, as

Table 15.1 A Comparison of Cultural Characteristics

National culture	Uncertainty avoidance	Masculinity– femininity	Individualism– collectivism	Power distance	Short-term/long-term orientation
Argentina	86	56	46	49	—
Australia	51	61	90	36	—
Austria	70	79	55	11	—
Belgium	94	54	75	65	—
Brazil	76	49	38	69	—
Canada	48	52	80	39	—
Chile	86	28	23	63	—
China	60	50	20	80	118
Colombia	80	64	13	67	—
Denmark	23	16	74	18	—
Finland	59	26	63	33	—
France	86	43	71	68	30
Germany	65	66	67	35	31
Great Britain (United Kingdom)	35	66	89	35	—
Greece	112	57	35	60	—
Hong Kong	29	57	25	68	96
India	40	56	48	77	—
Indonesia	48	46	14	78	25
Iran	59	43	41	58	—
Ireland	35	68	70	28	—
Israel	81	47	54	13	—
Italy	75	70	76	50	—
Japan	92	95	46	54	80
Mexico	82	69	30	81	—
Netherlands	53	14	80	38	44
New Zealand	49	58	79	22	—
Norway	50	8	69	31	—
Pakistan	70	50	14	55	—
Peru	87	42	16	64	—
Philippines	44	64	32	94	—
Portugal	104	31	27	63	—
Russia	90	40	50	95	10
Singapore	8	48	20	74	—
South Africa	49	63	65	49	—
Spain	86	42	51	57	—
Sweden	29	5	71	31	—
Switzerland	58	70	68	34	—
Taiwan	69	45	17	58	—
Thailand	64	34	20	64	—
Turkey	85	45	37	66	—
United States	46	62	91	40	29
Venezuela	76	73	12	81	—
West Africa	54	46	20	77	16
Yugoslavia	88	21	27	76	—

Source: Adapted from G. Hofstede, "Motivation, Leadership, and Organization: Do American Theories Apply Abroad?" *Organizational Dynamics* 9 (1980): 42–63; and G. Hofstede, "Cultural Constraints in Management Theories," *Academy of Management Executive* 7 (1993): 81–94.

indicated in Table 15.1), honor tradition and feel threatened by new ways of doing things. Cultures like that of China, which include long-term orientations (118 on short-term/long-term orientation), more readily embrace modern ways.

The second scenario focuses on conflict avoidance, a cultural tendency that is closely associated with uncertainty avoidance. Conflict creates uncertainty, and cultures that cannot deal with uncertainty, like the Greek culture (112 on uncertainty avoidance), prefer to avoid the competition and aggression that conflict unleashes. In contrast, cultures that can tolerate uncertainty, like the Danish culture (23 on uncertainty avoidance), can cope with conflict as well.

The third scenario concerns locus of control and arises out of cross-cultural differences based on individualism and collectivism. On the one hand, the sense of personal responsibility stimulated by believing that the locus of control for personal behavior lies inside the individual is consistent with the norms and values of an individualistic national culture like that of Australia (90 on individualism–collectivism). On the other hand, the focus on social causes as the source of behaviors that is prompted by an external locus of control is compatible with the cultural collectivism of countries like Pakistan (14 on individualism–collectivism).

The fourth scenario shows how cultural differences in power distance can affect the way status and social position are accorded and perceived. Cultures like that of India in which status and position are seen as birthrights—the special-privilege approach—also tend to be oriented toward large power distance (77 in Table 15.1). In contrast, cultures in countries like New Zealand in which status and position are awarded according to personal abilities—the equal opportunity approach—are more inclined toward smaller power distance (22 in the table).

Organizational Effects

The four scenarios illustrate how the Hofstede–Bond five-dimensional model can diagnose differences in national culture and help identify some of the cultural roots of everyday customs and behaviors. To understand how these cultural differences can influence organizational behavior, consider first the national culture of the United States and its effects on American theories and practices. As shown in Table 15.1, the U.S. national culture is extremely individualistic (91) and oriented toward larger degrees of power distance (40) than many of the other cultures included in Hofstede's study. If attention is limited to these two cultural characteristics—to simplify the discussion—a few brief examples will suffice to show how U.S. national culture shapes and affects organizational behavior in American firms.

As indicated in Chapter 5, work behaviors in U.S. companies are influenced most strongly by the receipt of rewards expected to satisfy personal needs, especially when those rewards are distributed in proportion to personal performance. Thus American firms often use piece-rate wages or commission payments tied to personal performance to encourage productivity, and these tactics typically succeed in the United States as motivational devices. As suggested by the Hofstede–Bond model, this tendency is consistent with the strong individualism of U.S. national culture and of individualistic proclivities to perceive (1) work as something that people accomplish alone and (2) rewards as allocated fairly when received according to personal—not group—achievements.

In addition, as described in Chapter 10, American models of leadership suggest that leading is largely a process of directing the behaviors and strengthening the motivation of individual employees. Individualism requires that leaders in U.S. firms use direct supervision to coordinate the work of their subordinates, so that success at personal jobs, in turn, leads to fulfillment of group and organizational goals. The leader is the "glue" that keeps groups of co-workers from falling apart. Large power distance justifies the leader's use of the power necessary to accomplish this feat.

Finally, American organizations often reflect the tenet that large firms should be structured as hierarchies in which rules and procedures govern employee behaviors, in the manner indicated in Chapter 12. The type of direct supervision undertaken as part of the task of being a leader is implemented when rules and procedures fail to provide the necessary guidance. This kind of hierarchical structuring requires workers to agree with the belief that differences in power are a normal part of everyday life. It is made possible by the fact that U.S. national culture favors norms supportive of a relatively large degree of power distance.

Cross-Cultural Differences

To further understand how the differences highlighted in the Hofstede–Bond model can influence behavior in organizations, consider the various areas of organizational behavior as practiced in organizations throughout the world.

Decision Making

On an Israeli **kibbutz** (kibbutzim, pl.)—a self-contained community, often located along Israel's national border and organized around deeply held religious principles—decision making is shared among the adult membership, being vested in the kibbutz's general assembly rather than in the hands of a small management group. The general assembly, which is the principal governing body of the kibbutz, meets once per week in most kibbutzim. Topics considered in assembly meetings may include the purchase, cleaning, and repair of kibbutznik clothing, as all clothing is collectively owned, or the practices used to raise and educate kibbutz children, as children are raised in communal quarters. Participation in assembly meetings is nearly universal, because all members who are kibbutz-born and age nineteen or older or who have completed a one-year naturalization program can vote on the issues.

The secretariat, an administrative board consisting of elected officials, is empowered only to implement policies approved by the kibbutz assembly. No official is permitted to act outside assembly mandates. Each is elected by the assembly, serves a fixed term of office, and cannot hold the same office for more than one consecutive term. As a result, the ability of any office holder to amass the power needed to make decisions autonomously is strictly limited.[17]

In a similar vein, traditional Japanese organizations are known for their use of *ringisei*, a consensus-based process of decision making in which managers circulate proposals among subordinates to gain their approval before implementing decisions. Such a scheme increases commitment, reduces resistance to change, and can minimize the time required to implement the results of decision-making processes. However, the decision-making process itself can consume a considerable amount of time.[18]

In contrast to the Israeli and Japanese approaches, Korean businesses seldom use groups to make decisions. Instead, members of the families that own Korea's *chaebol* conglomerates make all corporate decisions themselves and require subordinates to implement them without question. Although Korean firms sometimes employ an approach that outwardly resembles Japanese consensus decision making, it is actually a process of communicating management decisions already made, because employees are not allowed to suggest significant changes.[19]

In sum, Israeli kibbutz and Japanese and Korean organizations differ in terms of the extent to which members can influence decisions and decision-making processes. This difference is explained by the contrasting levels of power distance evident in the national cultures of Israel

(13), Japan (54), and Korea (Korean power distance was not measured in the Hofstede and Bond studies, but is similar in level to that of Hong Kong [68] and Singapore [74]). Lower power distance, which minimizes hierarchical differences, encourages decentralized decision making among an organization's membership. Higher power distance, which encourages hierarchical differentiation, also favors the retention of decision making at the top of the organization.

Motivation

Japanese motives and motivation are influenced by the relatively strong collectivism that characterizes Japan's national culture (46 in Table 15.1). For the current managers of large Japanese corporations, managing motivation is primarily a matter of stimulating in each employee a sense of loyalty, obligation, and dependence on superiors and co-workers. The resulting feelings reinforce the collectivism that holds Japanese organizations together. In particular, the practice in larger Japanese firms of offering lifetime employment (to age fifty-six) to their permanent employees greatly encourages workers to display loyalty to the company. Japanese employees find it difficult to behave disloyally toward a firm that is willing to commit itself to them up to their retirement.[20]

Collectivistic loyalty is also encouraged in large Japanese firms by the *nenko* system of wage payment. Under the *nenko* system, the employee's pay consists of a basic wage plus merit supplements and job-level allowances. The basic wage, which constitutes about 55 percent of total pay, includes the employee's starting wage plus yearly increases. Those increases are determined by (in order of importance) seniority or length of service with the company, age, and supervisory ratings on such qualities as seriousness, attendance, performance, and cooperativeness.[21]

Merit supplements account for an additional 15 percent of the employee's pay and are based on supervisory assessments of specific job behaviors. In principle, they are meant to reward exemplary performance. In fact, merit supplements are heavily influenced by seniority because they are calculated as a percentage of the basic wage. Moreover, junior employees' performance is typically rated below senior employees' work regardless of any real differences between the two.[22] Clearly, Japanese merit supplements reward loyalty and longevity with the company.

Job-level allowances, which account for about 30 percent of each Japanese worker's total pay, reflect the importance of each worker's job in relation to the other jobs in the organization. Such allowances might sound similar to the pay increments that result in the United States from job-evaluation procedures. In Japan, however, each employee's position in the hierarchy of jobs—which affects his or her job-level allowance—is more directly influenced by seniority than by skill.[23]

Thus seniority is the single most important factor in determining a Japanese worker's compensation. It affects the basic wage, merit supplements, and job-level allowances. The large Japanese firm resembles an idealized family in the sense that its employees spend their lives in a stable social setting and receive positions of increasing social importance as they grow older.[24] Along with the *nenko* method of financial compensation, this family-like system provides its members with social rewards for emphasizing loyalty to the company over all other concerns. Employees' decisions to attend work and to perform productively grow out of their sense of loyalty and obligation to the collectivistic firm.

Work Design

Jobs in Scandinavian automotive manufacturers tend to be organized less around the assembly-line processes commonly found in the United States, Japan, and elsewhere, and more according to the principles of reflective production. Embodied in these principles are the following ideas:

1. Assembly work must be viewed in a wide context on the shop floor. It includes not only the assembly itself, but also the preceding phases (that is, controlling the materials, structuring the materials and tools) and the subsequent phases (that is, final inspection and, if necessary, adjustment and further inspection). The vertical division of labor is also affected in that assembly workers assume responsibility for certain administrative tasks. This new concept of assembly work calls for workers' own reflections.
2. In reflective production, the assembly work itself becomes intellectualized and therefore meaningful. Work teams are able to rebalance their own work.
3. Established empirical knowledge of grouping and restructuring work tasks is a basic precondition for the realization of efficient and humane production systems.[25]

Thus, from the perspective of reflective production, employees are encouraged to develop an understanding of the entire manufacturing process and contribute to its design. Signified are values of work as an intellectual and humane activity; these values are consistent with the extremely high femininity demonstrated by Swedish (5 in Table 15.1) and Norwegian (8 in Table 15.1) national cultures.

Leadership

Consistent with cultural proclivities favoring low power distance (31 in Table 15.1), managers in Sweden often do not supervise employees directly, nor do they always issue direct orders to coordinate work activities. Instead, they function as boundary spanners who facilitate the flow of work between groups, while allowing employees to handle intragroup coordination responsibilities themselves. Managers also resolve conflicts within groups and help members communicate with one another in the course of participatory decision making. Thus managers act more as facilitators or social catalysts than as direct supervisors.

As shown in Figure 15.1, groups and committees fulfill leadership functions in many Swedish firms.[26] The **works council**, for example, is composed of worker representatives who are elected by their peers and management representatives who are appointed by top

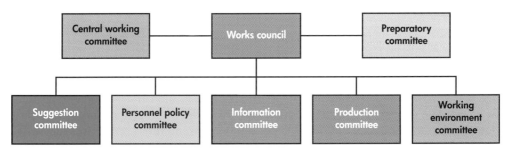

Figure 15.1 The Structure of Advisory Committees in a Scandinavian Firm

management. An organization usually has only one works council, which assumes responsibility for developing the overall organizational policies and procedures. Works councils have little or no direct decision-making power, but they provide a forum in which worker representatives can express their opinions and thereby be instrumental in shaping the mission and strategic direction of the firm. They are usually supported by several general advisory committees located lower in the organization hierarchy, which also provide leadership. These advisory groups might include suggestion committees, personnel policy committees, or information committees. Their purpose is to contribute advice on general problems or issues lying outside the domains of the special-interest committees (described next).

Special-interest committees, which are also composed of worker and manager representatives, provide the works council with advice on specific issues, such as job design, plant sanitation, personnel practices, and environmental safety. These committees cooperate with middle management to produce yearly reports that assist works councils with the task of formulating company policies. Such reports might include an analysis of water and air pollution produced by the company, a set of guidelines for curbing absenteeism, or a proposal on ways to reduce the amount of costly inventory kept on hand. As a whole, then, leadership in Swedish organizations often comes from groups in which employees and management work together to influence company policies and procedures.

Organization Structure

The structures of family businesses in China reflect the ideology of patrimonialism, which brings together elements of paternalism, hierarchy, mutual obligation, responsibility, and familialism that grow out of the Chinese national culture's high collectivism (20) and power distance (80). Chinese family businesses are typically small in size and take on simple structures that limit them to only a single business function, such as production, sales, or logistics. All employees are expected to help execute this function, resulting in a negligible division of labor. Formalized rules and systems of roles are largely lacking or completely absent. Correspondingly, interpersonal relationships and feelings take priority over concerns with organizational efficiency and effectiveness in determining whether structural arrangements are considered appropriate. Informal groups and personal loyalty replace standardized coordination and formal structuring in such organizations.[27]

Showing the effects of a similar pattern (albeit lesser absolute amounts) of collectivism (46) and power distance (54), the structures of most large Japanese corporations resemble the hierarchical, pyramidal structures of many U.S. companies. In fact, Japanese organization charts often show the same hierarchy of vertical relationships that characterize a U.S. firm's organization chart. In Japanese firms, however, these vertical relationships are often patterned after the parent–child (*oyabun–kobun*) relationships of traditional Japanese families. In the organizational version of this relationship, a subordinate is encouraged to feel loyal and obligated to his or her superior as well as dependent on the superior. This feeling of dependence, in turn, encourages—in fact, requires—acquiescence to the superior's demands.[28]

Another significant feature of Japanese organizational structures relates to communication patterns. In traditionally structured organizations elsewhere in the world, the vertical lines of command that appear in organization charts are meant to serve as the primary formal channels of communication. To communicate with a colleague in another department or division, an employee is expected to pass a message up the hierarchy to a superior, who then sends it downward to the final recipient. In Japanese corporations, however, certain formally designated *horizontal* relationships are accorded the same degree of importance as the vertical relationships depicted in the organization chart. These horizontal relationships, which allow communication to flow across the hierarchy rather than having to go up and down, connect managers who entered the company at the same time. They are encouraged by the group socialization that managers receive on first entering the company—other members of the manager's group become lifetime contacts throughout the company. In addition, such relationships are encouraged by the practice of rotating Japanese managers among the different functional areas of the firm—marketing, accounting, production, finance, and so forth. As a result, each manager becomes more of a generalist than a specialist and can cultivate a collection of horizontal linkages that unites him or her with management peers across functional boundaries.[29]

Together, the kinds of dependence relations and communication patterns formed in Japanese organizations create a **latticework structure** of vertical and horizontal relationships among the company's managers. Continuing relations among management peers from different functional areas, such as marketing and manufacturing, help stimulate harmony and coordination between functional groups. Nonetheless, in large Japanese firms, decision-making authority remains highly centralized. This combination of central control and strong relationships among peers is unique to the latticework structure of large Japanese corporations.

Organizational Change

In general, national cultures that are highly supportive of organizational change tend to have low power distance, high individualism, and low uncertainty avoidance.[30] Consequently, one would expect cultural resistance to organizational change to be quite high in Russia (with measures of 95, 50, and 90 for power distance, individualism–collectivism, and uncertainty avoidance, respectively)—a supposition that has been borne out by recent experience.[31]

Interestingly, however, in Korea, Japan, and Taiwan (three other countries with cultural profiles similar to that of Russia), innovation and change are relatively common. This apparent paradox can be explained by the pronounced long-term orientation in such cultures (80 for Japan), which strongly emphasizes persistence and adaptive growth in the face of challenge and adversity.[32]

Managing International Differences

Diagnosing and understanding the primary features of national cultures—as in the previous examples—are critical to success in the management of international organizational behavior, because this exercise represents the first step toward determining whether familiar management practices must be reconfigured before being used abroad. A glance back at Table 15.1 indicates that the national cultures of the United States and Canada, for example, are approximately equal in terms of power distance, uncertainty avoidance, masculinity, and individualism. Owing to this similarity, U.S. managers can expect to succeed in Canada, and Canadian managers can anticipate working effectively in the United States, without making major adjustments to customary management practices.

According to Hofstede's findings, however, the level of uncertainty avoidance in Denmark (23) is about half that in the United States (46) and Canada (48). As a result, North American managers will likely find it necessary to change their normal way of doing things if they must work in Denmark. More generally, managers working in national cultures characterized by weaker uncertainty avoidance must learn to cope with higher levels of anxiety and stress, while reducing their reliance on planning, rulemaking, and other familiar ways of absorbing uncertainty. On the other side of the coin, managers working in cultures with stronger uncertainty avoidance must learn not only to accept, but also to participate in, the development of seemingly unnecessary rules and apparently meaningless planning to help other organization members cope with stressful uncertainty. Rituals that at first glance might seem useless or even irrational might, in fact, serve the very important function of diminishing an otherwise intolerable level of uncertainty.

Next, consider the dimension of masculinity–femininity. Female managers working in cultures characterized by more cultural masculinity than in their own culture face the prospect of receiving less respect at work than they feel they deserve. To cope with gender discrimination of this sort, a female manager might want to seek out male mentors in senior management to secure her place in the organization. Conversely, male managers in national cultures marked by more cultural femininity than their own must control their aggressive tendencies and learn to treat members of both sexes with equal dignity and respect. Acting as mentors, female managers can demonstrate that women are as adept at their jobs as men.

The next dimension to be examined is individualism–collectivism. Managers who must work in national cultures that are more individualistic than their own must first learn to cope with the sense of rootlessness that comes from the absence of close-knit group relationships. They must learn not to be embarrassed by personal compliments, despite their belief that success stems from group effort. At work, they must develop an understanding of the importance of rewarding individuals equitably and adjust to the idea that organizational membership is impermanent. Conversely, managers attempting to work in cultures that are more collectivistic than their own must adjust to demands for self-sacrifice in support of group well-being. They must also learn to accept equal sharing in lieu of equity and exchange at work. Consequently, they must refrain from paying individual employees compliments and, instead, praise group performance. In addition, managers adjusting to collectivistic national cultures must understand that belonging to an organization in such cultures means more than just forming a temporary association; it is an important basis of each employee's personal identity.

Managers who work in cultures that favor less power distance may initially feel discomfort stemming from the unfamiliar decentralization of authority and a perceived loss of control. They must learn to be less autocratic and more participatory in their work with others. On the other hand, managers facing cultural tendencies toward more power distance must accept the role that centralization and tall hierarchies play in maintaining what is deemed to be an acceptable level of control. They must adopt a more authoritarian, autocratic style of management. Indeed, they might find that subordinates, if asked to participate in decision making, will refuse on the grounds that decision making is management's rightful job.

Finally, short-term/long-term orientation may have its greatest effect during the planning activities that represent an integral part of management. For managers who are most familiar with a short-term orientation, working in a culture characterized by a long-term orientation will require them to pay less attention to past successes or failures and more attention to future possibilities as they set organizational objectives and define group and individual goals. In contrast, managers from cultures with long-term orientations must accept that colleagues with short-term orientations will spend considerable energy looking backward in time to decide how to approach the future. Traditional approaches will likely be favored over innovation and creativity, and much attention might be paid to avoiding the mistakes of history. Although the cross-cultural differences just described are readily evident among contemporary national cultures, some have suggested that management practices throughout the world are growing more alike.[33] Consistent with this idea, practices developed in one culture are occasionally borrowed for use in another. For instance, in the United States, teams of co-workers are being formed where employees once worked as individuals, in interventions patterned after Scandinavian work design programs. Quality circles resembling the Japanese groups have become so prevalent that they are now considered part of the U.S. approach to job design. In addition, U.S. business organization structures are becoming flatter and more participatory as downsizing reduces the size of management staffs and as reengineering breaks down barriers separating tasks and task groups. All of these changes are occurring as U.S. companies strive to become more flexible and market-oriented.

Such trends seem to support the **convergence hypothesis**, which suggests that national cultures, organizations, and management practices throughout the world are becoming more homogeneous.[34] In a review of studies that examined this hypothesis, John Child found both evidence for convergence and evidence for divergence (that is, continued cross-cultural differences). Interestingly, studies that supported convergence typically focused on organizational variables, such as structure and technology, whereas studies that revealed divergence usually dealt with employee attitudes, beliefs, and behaviors.[35] Child concluded that organizations themselves might be becoming more alike throughout the world, but that people in these organizations are maintaining their cultural distinctiveness. Management in a multicultural world currently requires an understanding of cultural differences and will continue to do so for quite some time.

In closing, the five dimensions introduced in this chapter form a model that highlights important differences among national cultures. As you use this model in the future, remember that each dimension simplifies the kinds of variations that exist among the world's national cultures. Such simplification is the necessary consequence of the goal of researchers like Hofstede and Bond, who seek to create theories and models that can be readily understood and used in many situations.[36] Realize also that this simplification encourages stereotyping—that is, the perception that all members of a particular culture are alike in some specific way. Always keep in mind the fact that beneath societal similarities like those discussed in this chapter lie subtle differences among people, who also vary along the lines identified in the Hofstede–Bond model. For example, although both the U.S. and the Canadian national cultures are highly individualistic, a significant number of people in North America are collectivists.[37] For this reason, you should exercise caution when employing the five-dimensional model, lest you overlook relatively less conspicuous, but nonetheless influential, cultural complexities and dissimilarities.

Summary

Whether comparisons are made within a single *national culture* or across different national cultures, no two organizations are exactly alike. Likewise, no two people in the world hold exactly the same beliefs and values. Thus the discussions in this chapter necessarily involved generalization. Not every Japanese organization has a fully developed *latticework structure*, and not every kibbutz is completely collectivistic. Nevertheless, firms in a particular national culture tend to be more like each other than they are like organizations in other national cultures. Moreover, people in the same national culture tend to think and act more similarly than do people from different cultures.

Cross-cultural differences exist and can have significant effects on organizational behavior. The most important of these cross-cultural differences are captured by five dimensions: *uncertainty avoidance, masculinity–femininity, individualism–collectivism, power distance*, and *short-term/long-term orientation*. Differences in individualism–collectivism and power distance seem to explain many of the differences that can be detected among management practices throughout the world. Considered together, these five dimensions are helpful in understanding why people in a particular national culture behave as they do and can prove useful to managers as they strive to adapt familiar management practices for use in unfamiliar cultures.

Review Questions

1. Compared with the national culture of Sweden, what level of uncertainty avoidance characterizes the national culture of the United States? In which country would you expect to find greater evidence of ritualistic behavior? Why? How would your answers to these questions change if you were asked to compare the United States and Greece?
2. Hofstede's findings indicated that U.S. national culture at the time of his research was more masculine than many of the other national cultures he examined. In your opinion, is U.S. culture still as masculine as Hofstede's research suggests? Why or why not?
3. According to Hofstede's research, the three most individualistic national cultures are found in the United States, Australia, and the United Kingdom. Can you think of a reason why these three countries share this cultural characteristic? Does your answer also explain the relatively strong individualism of the Canadian national culture?
4. Would you expect the structures of organizations in Denmark to be taller or flatter than those of organizations in the United States? Why? How are organization structures in Mexico likely to compare with those in Denmark and the United States?

Notes

1 C. Woodyard, "Patriotic Brand," *Lansing State Journal*, July 3, 2013, 6B; S. Davis, "Three Lansing-Made Cars on Top 10 List," *Lansing State Journal*, June 26, 2013, 1A–2A; D. Stanford, "PepsiCo Prepares for a Snack War in Russia," *Bloomberg Businessweek*, March 4, 2013, 21–22; M. Boyle, "Unilever: Taking on the World, One Stall at a Time," *Bloomberg Businessweek*, January 7, 2013, 18–20; E. Dwoskin, "Alabama Opens Its Wallet to Woo Airbus," *Bloomberg Businessweek*, April 22, 2013, 25–26.
2 G. Hofstede, "Motivation, Leadership, and Organization: Do American Theories Apply Abroad?" *Organizational Dynamics* 9 (1980): 42–63; G. Hofstede, *Culture's Consequences: International Differences in Work-Related Values* (Beverly Hills, CA: Sage, 1984); G. Hofstede, *Culture's Consequences: International Differences in Work-Related Values*, 2nd ed. (Thousand Oaks, CA: Sage, 2001); G. Hofstede and G. J. Hofstede, *"Cultures and Organizations: Software of the Mind*, 2nd ed. (Thousand Oaks, CA: Sage, 2005); M. Minkov, *Cross-Cultural Analysis: The Science and Art of Comparing the World's Modern Societies and Their Cultures* (Thousand Oaks, CA: Sage, 2013).
3 G. Hofstede, "Cultural Constraints in Management Theories," *Academy of Management Executive* 7 (1993): 81–94.
4 Hofstede, "Motivation, Leadership, and Organization," 47.
5 Ibid.
6 Ibid., 49.
7 Ibid.; G. Hofstede, *Masculinity and Femininity: The Taboo Dimension of National Cultures* (Thousand Oaks, CA: Sage, 1998).
8 Ibid., 48.
9 Ibid.
10 H. C. Triandis, *Individualism and Collectivism* (Boulder, CO: Westview Press, 1995); M. Erez and P. C. Earley, *Culture, Self-Identity, and Work* (New York: Oxford University Press, 1993); J. A. Wagner, "Utilitarian and Ontological Variation in Individualism-Collectivism," *Research in Organizational Behavior* 24 (2002): 301–345.
11 Hofstede, "Motivation, Leadership, and Organization," 46.
12 Ibid.
13 Hofstede, "Cultural Constraints," 90.
14 R. Yeh, "Values of American, Japanese, and Taiwanese Managers in Taiwan: A Test of Hofstede's Framework," *Academy of Management Proceedings* (1988): 106–110.
15 S. H. Schwartz and W. Bilsky, "Toward a Universal Psychological Structure of Human Values," *Journal of Personality and Social Psychology* 53 (1987): 550–562; R. J. House, P. J. Hanges, M. Javidan, P. W. Dorfman, and V. Gupta, *Culture, Leadership, and Organizations: The GLOBE Study of 62 Societies* (Thousand Oaks, CA: Sage, 2004); G. Hofstede, "What did GLOBE Really Measure? Researchers' Minds versus Respondents' Minds," *Journal of International Business* 37

(2006): 882–896; J. S. Chhokar, F. C. Brodbeck, and R. J. House, *Culture and Leadership Across the World: The GLOBE Book of In-Depth Studies of 25 Societies* (New York: Lawrence Erlbaum Associates, 2012).

16 For additional examples, see L. Sayles, "A 'Primer' on Cultural Dimensions," *Issues and Observations of the Center for Creative Leadership* 9 (1989): 8–9.

17 Y. Criden and S. Gelb, *The Kibbutz Experience* (New York: Herzl Press, 1974), 37–57; J. Blasi, *The Communal Experience of the Kibbutz* (New Brunswick, NJ: Transaction Books, 1986), 112; L. Goldstein, "Kibbutz Tzuba: Meeting the Social and Economic Challenges of a Changing Israeli Society," *Journal of the International Academy for Case Studies* 13 (2007): 57–69; M. Palgi and S. Reinharz, *One Hundred Years of Kibbutz Life: A Century of Crisis and Reinvention* (New Brunswick, NJ: Transaction Publishers, 2011).

18 C. Isac, "Characteristics of Japanese Decision Making by Consensus," *Annals of the University of Petrosani, Economics* 3 (2003): 123–126; S. P. Sethi, N. Namiki, and C. L. Swanson, *The False Promise of the Japanese Miracle: Illusions and Realities of the Japanese Management System* (Boston: Pitman, 1984), 34–41.

19 C. Chang and N. Chang, *The Korean Management System: Cultural, Political, Economic Foundations* (Westport, CT: Quorum, 1994); R. Kienzle and M. Shadur, "Developments in Business Networks in East Asia," *Management Decision* 35 (1997): 23–32; J. H. Lee and A. S. Gaur, "Managing Multi-Business Firms: A Comparison between Korean Chaebols and Diversified U.S. Firms," *Journal of World Business* (forthcoming 2013), http://papers.ssrn.com/sol3/papers.cfm?abstract_id=2160424.

20 R. E. Cole, *Japanese Blue Collar* (Berkeley: University of California Press, 1971), 72–100; R. Dore, *British Factory—Japanese Factory* (Berkeley, CA: University of California Press, 1973), 74–113; E. Fingleton, "Jobs for Life," *Fortune*, March 20, 1995, 119–125; J. Hamaaki, M. Hori, S. Maeda, and K. Murata, "Changes in the Japanese Employment System in the Two Lost Decades," *Industrial and Labor Relations Review* 65 (2012): 102–135. Note that lifetime employment occurs only in large firms and applies to no more than one-third of Japan's labor force; for further information, see T. K. Oh, "Japanese Management: A Critical Review," *Academy of Management Review* 1 (1976): 14–25.

21 Cole, *Japanese Blue Collar*, 75.

22 Dore, *British Factory—Japanese Factory*, 112.

23 Cole, *Japanese Blue Collar*, 79; Dore, *British Factory—Japanese Factory*, 390.

24 R. Clark, *The Japanese Company* (New Haven, CT: Yale University Press, 1979), 38.

25 K. Ellegard, D. Jonsson, T. Enstrom, M. Johansson, L. Medbo, and B. Johansson, "Reflective Production in the Final Assembly of Motor Vehicles: An Emerging Swedish Challenge," *International Journal of Operations and Production Management* 12 (1992): 117–133; A. M. Francesco and B. A. Gold, *International Organizational Behavior* (Upper Saddle River, NJ: Prentice Hall, 1998).

26 D. E. Zand, "Collateral Organization: A New Change Strategy," *Journal of Applied Behavioral Science* 10 (1974): 63–89; H. Lindestadt and G. Rosander, *The Scan Vast Report* (Stockholm: Swedish Employers' Confederation [SAF], 1977), 3–12; F. E. Emery and E. Thorsrud, *Democracy at Work* (Leiden, Netherlands: Kroese, 1976), 27–32; J. F. Bolweg, *Job Design and Industrial Democracy: The Case of Norway* (Leiden, Netherlands: Martinus Nijhoff, 1976), 98–109.

27 M. Chen, *Asian Management Systems: Chinese, Japanese, and Korean Styles of Business* (New York: Routledge, 1995).

28 Dore, *British Factory—Japanese Factory*; Peter F. Drucker, *Management* (New York: Harper & Row, 1974); N. Hatvany and C. V. Pucik, "Japanese Management Practices and Productivity," *Organizational Dynamics* 9 (1981): 5–21; A. D. Bhappu, "The Japanese Family: An Institutional Logic for Japanese Corporate Networks and Japanese Management," *Academy of Management Review* 25 (2000): 409–415.

29 Cole, *Japanese Blue Collar*; R. J. Samuels, "Looking Behind Japan Inc.," *Technology Review* 83 (1981): 43–46.

30 A. Harzing and G. Hofstede, "Planned Change in Organizations: The Influence of National Culture," in P. Bamberger and M. Erez, eds., *Research in the Sociology of Organizations: Cross-Cultural Analysis of Organizations* (Greenwich, CT: JAI Press, 1996).

31 S. Michailova, "Contrasts in Culture: Russian and Western Perspectives on Organizational Change," *Academy of Management Executive* 14 (2000): 99–112.

32 Harzing and Hofstede, "Planned Change in Organizations."

33 C. Kerr, J. T. Dunlop, F. H. Harbison, and C. A. Meyers, *Industrialism and Industrial Man* (Cambridge, MA: Harvard University Press, 1960), 282–288; J. K. Galbraith, *The New Industrial State* (Boston: Houghton Mifflin, 1967), 11–21; F. Harbison, "Management in Japan," in F. Harbison and C. A. Meyers, eds., *Management in the Industrial World: An International Analysis* (New York: McGraw-Hill, 1959), 249–264.

34 P. J. Dowling and R. S. Schuler, *International Dimensions of Human Resource Management* (Boston: PWS-Kent, 1990), 163–164.

35 J. Child, "Culture, Contingency, and Capitalism in the Cross-National Study of Organizations," in L. L. Cummings and B. M. Staw, eds., *Research in Organizational Behavior* (Greenwich, CT: JAI Press, 1981), 303–356; D. Faulkner, R. Pitkethly, and J. Child, "International Mergers and Acquisitions in the UK 1985–94: A Comparison of National HRM Practices," *International Journal of Human Resource Management* 13 (2002): 106–122.

36 W. Thorngate, "'In General' vs. 'It Depends': Some Comments on the Gergen–Schlenker Debate," *Personality and Social Psychology Bulletin* 2 (1976): 404–410; K. E. Weick, *The Social Psychology of Organizing*, 2nd ed. (Reading, MA: Addison-Wesley, 1979).

37 J. A. Wagner III and M. K. Moch, "Individualism–Collectivism: Concept and Measure," *Group and Organization Studies* 11 (1986): 280–304; J. A. Wagner III, "Studies of Individualism– Collectivism: Effects on Cooperation in Groups," *Academy of Management Journal* 38 (1995): 152–172.

Chapter 16

Evidence-Based Management: Critical Thinking and Continuous Learning

"When I was growing up," observes Chris Argyris, a leading academic management scholar for the past four decades, "managers used to say they hired a hand, and they really meant it. But today they say they hire minds. In a world where minds are hired, learning becomes essential."[1] Certain features of organizations, such as their hierarchical structure, management style, and the like, however, make it difficult for people to learn—and to learn what works and what does not. Learning often comes from an error detection and correction process and, in many organizations, admitting to a mistake can get a person in trouble. Suggesting that one's supervisor has made an error can result in even more trouble.

For example, recent evidence from the U.S. Institute for Medicine has documented that 25 percent of patients who check into a hospital in the United States are actually harmed by the experience, and that 98,000 patients die every year from routine medical errors. U.S. surgeons operate on the wrong body part as often as forty times a week, and if medical errors were treated as a disease, it would be the sixth leading cause of death in the United States.[2] This is the equivalent of four or more jumbo jets crashing every year, and whereas the aviation industry—not to mention government regulators—would certainly conduct a painstaking investigation as well as ground affected planes, in the medical community, routine errors often go unreported. In fact, rather than trying to learn from routine errors, in many hospitals problems are swept under the rug. Patients are asked to sign "gag orders" that prevent them from saying anything negative about their doctors, and lawyers for hospitals make never speaking about an error publicly a condition of any lawsuit settlement.

As you can see, some kinds of organizations are powerfully motivated to deny that any error has taken place. So are individuals and, ironically, the smarter one is, the better he or she is at "spinning" the evidence in order to deny the error or blame it on someone else. Although spinning the evidence has short-term personal value in terms of promoting one's career, the organization might lose an opportunity to prevent that same error from happening again. This is especially true when the organization is powerfully motivated in another way, to learn from mistakes and put policies in place to ensure that the mistake event will not happen again—and when such organizations cultivate and reward employees for their willingness to point out errors in the first place.

Learning Organizations

Firms that systematically try to avoid this trap are called *learning organizations*. Four primary features of learning organizations set them apart from their competitors. First, such firms critically analyze experiences of their employees and other stakeholders to maximize their capacity to learn from past successes and failures.[3] This practice has been referred to as *evidence-based management*. For example, at MemorialCare, a six-hospital nonprofit organization based in California, managers track the performance of doctors on several measures, including complications and readmissions (patients who have to return to the hospital for the same problem). Even though doctors were treating similar patients with similar conditions, the differences between those patients doing the best and doing the worst varied widely. Once the behaviors and decision-making processes that separated the high performing doctors from the low performing doctors were identified, those who performed poorly were trained to behave and make decisions like those who performed well. Within one year, the reduction in complications and readmissions saved the hospital close to $14 million.[4]

This type of learning does not happen by accident. Learning organizations often rely on an *after action review* (AAR) to wring out the most information they can from any event.[5] AARs are formal critical inquiries that evaluate past events, both failures and successes, with an eye toward improving future practice. Although this type of practice started in military organizations, it quickly spread to business contexts, where the tradition has been to simply move from one project to another without formally capturing lessons learned. Research has documented that AARs can improve group processes and outcomes.[6] These same practices have also been employed to help individuals improve their leadership skills.[7]

The second primary feature of learning organizations relates to their penchant for experimentation. That is, in addition to critically analyzing their own naturally occurring data in order to practice evidence-based management, learning organizations often create new data by setting up experiments that evaluate the impact of certain interventions or new practices. The results of these experiments can then be used to promote more effective and efficient organizational practices.

For example, although you might consider hand washing a requisite duty for hospital employees, especially for nurses and doctors assigned to treating patients, this requirement is not always practiced. In an effort to find new ways to ensure that its employees routinely washed their hands, Long Island's North Shore University Hospital conducted an experiment. The managers randomly equipped some hospital hand-washing stations with hidden cameras and others with prominently displayed cameras. The compliance rate at the stations with the hidden cameras was a terrible 10 percent, compared to 90 percent at the stations where cameras obviously recorded compliant employees. The results of this experiment were used to justify the use of purchasing and deploying prominently displayed cameras at hand washing stations throughout the hospital.[8]

Third, learning organizations recognize the need to formally capture knowledge that resides within the brains of individual workers and transfer this to written organizational records that can be shared with other workers. This type of "institutionalization" of the employee knowledge base also prevents the organization from losing knowledge when certain workers leave the organization. Learning organizations also try to protect this knowledge base through security provisions that make it difficult for other organizations to steal their knowledge via corporate espionage, especially departing employees who might be tempted to download information onto a flash drive.[9] Indeed, secrecy and retention are so important to some high-tech firms that the very practice of "going public" though initial public offerings (IPOs) has been shown to reduce the innovativeness of firms due to "brain drain."[10]

Fourth, learning organizations constantly look for evidence from the experiences of others and track scientific journals for published studies that might inform their own practices. For example, the New York City school system initiated an incentive system that cost the city over $50 million. However, the program had no effect on student performance or teacher attitudes. The big problem in this case, however, was that the incentive proved ineffective in several independent published studies. Had administers been aware of this research, they could have saved New York City schools the cost of this predictably ineffective program. This case is not unique, and management scholars Jeffrey Pfeffer and Robert Sutton note this happens all the time, stating that "in most workplaces, failure to consider sound evidence repeatedly inflicts unnecessary damage on employee well-being and group performance."[11]

Although many readers of this book will be business majors, one fact that should not be overlooked is that many of the most successful CEOs in history did not hold MBAs. General Electric's Jack Welch, Intel's Andy Grove, Microsoft's Bill Gates and Google's Larry Page were all formally trained in the "hard" sciences. Although the specialized skills learned in an MBA program are useful for gaining entry-level positions, managers who rise to the top of the organization are often those who generate, test, and implement new ideas and discoveries.[12] Indeed, some have begun to question whether the convergent thinking skills associated with a traditional MBA degree are the most relevant in a changing world, and many employers now look in nonbusiness programs for successful leaders.[13]

Learning organizations that employ evidence-based management rely on critical thinking and rigorously analyzed data to gain a long-term sustainable competitive edge relative to other members of their industry.[14] Unfortunately, knowledge-creating organizations remain the exceptions, not the rule. Too many U.S. businesses fall prey to every new management fad promising a painless solution, especially when it is presented in a neat, bright package. Indeed, this tendency has created a veritable cottage industry of non-peer-reviewed, "pop" management books, which rarely reflect serious thinking about the best way to manage in specific companies. Indeed, as one commentator on these books has noted, "No advice is too lame to get a polite, respectful hearing from a business audience."[15] The vague, "one-best-way" recommendations in these books can rarely withstand rigorous scientific scrutiny.[16]

To avoid this "quick-fix" mentality, managers need to take several steps. First, they must keep current with the literature in the field of management and pay particular attention to peer-reviewed journal articles that translate research findings into practical guidelines.

Second, managers must be skeptical when simple solutions are offered and analyze such solutions (and their supposed evidence) thoroughly. Third, they must ensure that the concepts they apply are based on science rather than advocacy, and they should experiment with new solutions themselves whenever possible. In other words, managers need to transform their companies into learning organizations and turn themselves into lifelong learners.

The purpose of this chapter is to help promote the kind of philosophy embodied by learning organizations and evidence-based management. Whereas previous chapters have focused on *content* and learning what is already known about management, this chapter emphasizes the thinking *process*, which will enable you to learn new and innovative approaches to management that will stand the test of time. Being the first to discover and implement innovative management techniques could give your company a sustainable competitive advantage relative to your rivals who are relying on ineffective and widely copied business fads.

The chapter begins by examining the nature of the scientific process, showing you how to successfully conduct your own experiments. It then discusses ways to draw valid causal inferences; this exercise will allow you to maximize your ability to learn from your own experiences and critically evaluate the claims made by others. Next, the chapter considers how to generalize research results to determine whether the results found in one sample and setting are likely to be repeatable in a different sample and setting. Finally, it describes some of the scientific sources to which you can turn when seeking answers to your managerial questions.

Critical Thinking and the Scientific Process

To form a learning organization, all employees—and especially managers—must become more disciplined in their thinking and pay more attention to detail. They must continually ask the question "How do we know that's true?" and push beyond the symptom level to discover underlying causes of problems. How do we come to know things? For example, when we say that we know our solar system contains eight planets, how do we know that this statement is true and under what conditions would we change what we know from one thing to another (e.g., we used to know there were nine planets in our solar system)? When we state that providing workers with specific and difficult goals will lead them to perform better than simply telling them to "do their best," how do we know that this assertion is true? And when we note that an effective organization's structure must match its technology and its environment, how do we know that this claim is true?

Ways of Knowing

Philosophers of science have explored many ways of arriving at knowledge.[17] The most common source of knowledge for most of us is *personal experience*. Most people tend to believe information they acquire by interacting with other people and the world at large and to conclude that their experience reflects truth. Our personal experiences might not always be a reliable source of truth, however, for several reasons. First, different people might have different experiences that point to different truths. Second, as we saw in Chapter 4, people's perceptions and memories of their experiences are often biased, inaccurate, or distorted over time. Finally, even if we disregard inaccuracies of perception or memory, the fact remains that any one person can experience only a tiny fraction of all possible situations, and thus the knowledge acquired by personal experience is extremely limited.

Despite these shortcomings, a reflective and critical approach to one's past experience can lead to enhanced understanding. This case is especially relevant for "productive failures" that, when critically analyzed, lead to insight, understanding, and ultimately future success. For example, IBM's 360 computer series, one of the most popular and profitable lines ever built, was based on the technology of the failed Stretch computer that preceded it.[18] Productive failures can be even more important to an organization's long-term viability than "unproductive successes," where something goes well but no one understands why.

Earlier, we noted that many managers tend to seek quick-fix remedies to their problems. Sustainable competitive advantage does not come from simple solutions to complex problems. Instead, managers need a method for helping them generate and test new methods of competing. Although critically examined personal experience can be a source of knowledge, several problems and pitfalls arise from simply using personal experience as a means of discerning what is true. In fact, the limits of personal experience in this regard led to the development of the **scientific method**. As Charles Sanders Peirce has stated, "To satisfy our doubts . . . it is necessary that a method should be found by which our beliefs may be determined by nothing human, but by some external permanency. . . . The method must be such that the ultimate conclusion of every man shall be the same. Such is the method of science."[19]

Objectivity, or the degree to which scientific findings are independent of any one person's opinion about them, represents the major difference between the scientific approach to knowledge and the other approaches described so far. For example, as the recent scandals made clear, many who conducted so-called research for Wall Street investment firms and banks were anything but objective in their analyses. Conflict of interest came about because the analysts in the research arm of the companies were pressured by those in the investment banking arm of the companies to rate certain firms as good investments despite the problems the researchers uncovered. As one analyst noted, "It's hard enough to be right about stocks, even harder to build customer relationships when all your companies blow up, you knew they were going to, and you couldn't say anything."[20]

Science as an enterprise is *public* in the sense that the methods and results obtained by one scientist are shared with others. It is *self-correcting* in the sense that erroneous findings can be isolated through the replication of one scientist's work by another scientist. In today's competitive and fast-paced environment, however, the manner in which many scientists go public has in some respects changed, and this has impacted the self-correcting nature of applied research. Traditionally, scientists who came upon an important discovery would write about their research and submit it for peer review in a professional journal, where it would be carefully vetted and edited to ensure accuracy—a process that could take up to two years. The process was slow but sure in the sense that irresponsible or erroneous claims were kept out of the public's attention. For example, recently there was a controversy about whether or not the herbal remedy echinacea was able to prevent people from catching the common cold. Two different studies came to the exact opposite conclusions. Because the methods employed by each study were fully reported, however, other researchers could identify the precise differences between the two studies. This allowed future researchers to control for these differences and thus clarify when and why echinacea was effective.[21]

Increasingly, however, researchers are bypassing this process and going straight to an unprofessionally reviewed news release when they think they have made an important discovery. For example, Advanced Cell Technologies, a biotechnology firm, announced in a news release that it had created a human clone embryo. This was a major scientific breakthrough; unfortunately, when other scientists tried to replicate the results it became clear that there were serious flaws in the experiments run by Advanced Cell's scientists, and the claim was essentially bogus. Philip Campbell, editor of *Nature*, the scientific journal where the study should have been submitted first, noted, "It undermines public trust in science if key results are released without peer review."[22]

The public and self-correcting nature of this process, when successfully practiced, means that the results that are eventually accepted are *cumulative*, in the sense that one scientist's experiment often builds on another's work. These features of the scientific method make it ideal as a means of generating reliable knowledge, and it is no coincidence that the physical, natural, and social sciences receive so much emphasis in today's colleges and universities. For these reasons, we will explore the nature of the scientific process more closely. We look first at the major goals or purposes of science and then consider how the scientific method is structured to achieve these objectives.

The Purposes of Science

The basic goal of science is to help humans understand the world around us. Science defines the understanding it seeks as the ability to describe, explain, predict, and control the subjects of its inquiry. We examine each of these objectives in turn. The purpose of some research is simply *description*—that is, drawing an accurate picture of a particular phenomenon or event. Chapter 2, for example, presented data from Mintzberg's study of managerial roles. The purpose of Mintzberg's research was to find out what managers actually do on the job on a daily basis. Chapter 3 reviewed research that described the major dimensions of personality. Chapter 7 examined descriptive research that sought to delineate the dimensions best suited to describe the nature of jobs. The development of scientific knowledge usually begins with this kind of descriptive work. The ultimate criterion for evaluating all descriptive research is the fidelity with which it reflects the real world.

For other scientific studies, *predicting*, or stating what will happen in the future, is the primary goal. Prediction requires that we know the relationships between certain conditions and outcomes. For example, Chapter 6 described research that attempted to predict who leaves organizations and who stays. Chapter 10 reviewed studies of leadership that predicted when decisions are best made by groups and when they are best left to individuals. Chapter 14 discussed studies that predicted the effects associated with various kinds of organizational cultures. When we cannot accurately predict what will happen in a given situation, we have generally failed to understand it.

Studies that focus on prediction often lead to further research in which the goal is to *control* the situation. Predictive studies often uncover relationships between causes and effects. If one can manipulate the causes, it might be possible to affect some outcome in a desirable manner, which can be a source of competitive advantage for firms. So, for example, Eli Lilly spends over $5 billion a year on scientific research devoted to finding the cures for certain diseases. The goal of this research is to control the disease or its symptoms and Eli Lilly outspends all of its competitors when it comes to research and development expenditures.[23] In the field of organizational behavior, as we showed in Chapter 5, many studies have been conducted on how manipulation of pay practices let firms change how hard individuals work. Chapter 8 discussed research that shows how group performance can be controlled by manipulating patterns of communication. In Chapter 13, changing the characteristics of organizational design was shown to improve the fit between the firm and its environment. It is in the area of control that the interests of scientists and management practitioners most clearly converge.[24]

As we have seen throughout this book, managers are responsible for controlling the behaviors of others in organizations. Thus, the more information a study provides on ways to achieve this control, the more useful it is to practicing managers. Indeed, research guided by the other objectives is often perceived by managers as merely academic and not worthwhile. In reality, studies dealing with control often represent the by-products of earlier descriptive or predictive studies. Without good descriptive and predictive research, we would probably do little successful research aimed at control.

The ultimate goal of science is *explanation*—stating why some relationship exists. Some might argue that, as long as we can describe, predict, and control things, why go any further? For example, if managers in the insurance business know that people with college degrees sell more life insurance than people with high school degrees, why find out anything else? Why not just hire college graduates for all sales positions? If researchers can uncover the reason for college graduates' greater success, however, managers might bring about the desired outcome (selling more insurance) in a more efficient or cost-effective way.

For example, suppose that college-educated salespeople outperform their counterparts who lack higher education not because they have more years of study per se, but because on average they are more self-confident. This self-confidence increases persistence on sales calls, which leads to higher sales volume. If this explanation holds true, a manager might be able to hire high school graduates and then train them to become more self-confident and persistent. As suggested by this example, if we know the exact reason why something occurs, we can usually explain and control it much more efficiently.

The Interplay of Theory and Data

Having discussed the different ways of arriving at knowledge and the goals, or purposes, of scientific inquiry, we must now consider precisely what the scientific method entails.

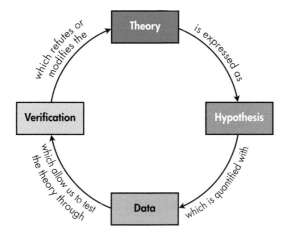

Figure 16.1 The Nature of the Scientific Process

Figure 16.1 represents a conception of scientific inquiry, depicting science as a continuous process that links theory, which resides in the world of abstract ideas, with data, which reside in the world of concrete facts. A theory is translated into real-world terms by the process of creating hypotheses, and real-world data are translated back into the realm of ideas through the process of verification.

Fred Kerlinger, a well-known social scientist, defined a **theory** as "a set of interrelated constructs, definitions, and propositions that presents a systematic view of a phenomenon by specifying relationships among variables."[25] With an understanding of the purposes of science and this definition of theory, it is easy to see why theory plays such a central role in the scientific process. A good theory, through its constructs and definitions, should clearly describe a part of the real world. Moreover, by specifying relations among variables, a theory facilitates both prediction and control. Finally, a theory's systematic nature allows us to explain the relationships described. The preceding chapters of this book were filled with theories intended to help you understand how to manage the behavior of people in organizations.

In some cases, theories can be specified with such precision that they become "quantitative models," where one can enter data at one end of the model and have highly precise predictions about future data come out the other end of the model.[26] For example, at IBM, the company's scientists are trying to build mathematical models that capture the skills and experience of each consultant. Each person's experience is coded as a set of quantitative vectors, and then the company's theories about how to compose teams are converted into mathematical "rules" that allow one to create the optimal team to work on any project, given its requirements.[27]

To have any practical utility, theories must prove themselves in the world of data. Through a process of deduction, researchers generate **hypotheses**, or specific predictions, about the relationships between certain conditions in the real world. These hypotheses are related to the theory in the following way: If the theory is correct, then the predictions made by the hypotheses should be found in the real world. Thus, to truly test IBM's theories about team composition, one would make a prediction that teams formed using the model would outperform teams that were put together via more traditional methods. Elevating a model and treating it as though it is true, without testing its predictions against future, real-world observations, has to be avoided at all costs. Indeed, many attributed the recent financial meltdown to traders who treated untested mathematical models of various financial entities—especially complex mortgage securities called *collateralized debt obligations*—as if they were true. As one modeler noted, "to confuse the model with the world is to embrace a future disaster in the belief that humans obey mathematical principles."[28]

Data enter the scientific process at this point. Once hypotheses are formulated, we can collect data and compare the hypothesized results with the actual results. Through the process of **verification**, we then use this comparison to check the accuracy of the theory and to judge the extent to which it holds true. If very little correspondence exists between the hypothesized results and the actual findings, we must reject the theory. At this point, the process begins again with the generation of a new theory. If the projected and actual findings do correspond somewhat, we might need to change the theory in some way so as to be more consistent with the data. If almost complete correspondence exists between the hypothesized results and the actual findings, we might be tempted to claim that the theory is true. Such a conclusion would not be warranted, however, unless we could establish that all other possible explanations for the results have been eliminated. Because this task is almost never achievable, we usually refer to data that correspond closely with a hypothesis as "supporting" rather than "proving" the theory.

Although we have discussed the scientific method in this section as a very deductive, top-down process that begins with theory and ends with data, in many real-world cases of scientific discovery the flow goes the other way. That is, a scientist's experience with a specific set of data prompts a round of insight and theorizing via a bottom-up inductive process. The key difference, however, between inductive science and data mining is that, in inductive science, the data that are used to generate the theory cannot be used to then verify it.

This might seem like a trivial distinction, but this is what discriminates inductive science from a nonscientific approach that just "selects on the dependent variable." For example, *Good to Great*, by Jim Collins, was one of the best-selling management books of all time.[29] It sold over 3 million copies, topped the *BusinessWeek* bestseller list for years, and was translated into thirty-five different languages. Its author chronicled the success of eleven different companies and distilled five principles that they all shared. The book implied that readers who adopted these principles in their own organization would see similar levels of sustained success over time. The book was well written, supplied a simple formula for success, and gave hope to many managers who were struggling with the complexity of leading large-scale organizations. The only problem with the book was that the advice it offered turned out to be wrong.

As Bruce Niendorf and Kristine Beck showed, the problem with this book (which was not subject to any type of peer review) was that it engaged in data mining and confused correlation with causality. That is, the book started with eleven companies that the author felt had performed well historically and looked at all sorts of data to uncover practices or processes that many of them had in common. Because of the small number of companies, and the fact that the measure of success was taken at the same time as the measures of practices and processes, the results confused sampling error and momentary fluctuations with reliable and predictive differences, as well as cause and effect.

For example, if you were to stand at a roulette wheel for a short time, you would eventually see a group of winners and a group of losers. You could study what the winners did to "learn" the secret of their success, but the true validity of the practices can only be tested by then examining them *in the future* to see if their success is repeated. Since a roulette wheel is by definition random, these "winners" will not be able to systematically win in the future, and their "secrets to success" will be uncovered as fraudulent superstitions. Niendorf and Beck did exactly this with the eleven firms identified as "great" by Jim Collins and they showed that, when one followed these companies into the future, none were truly great. In fact, relative to Fortune 500 firms, few of the eleven had ever made it into the top 200.[30]

To make his study truly scientific, the author could have used the eleven companies that he thought were "great" in the past to build a theory that highlighted key principles of greatness. The key for this to be inductive science, however, would be to apply the principles to a *new set of firms* and then see if the principles derived from the first set of eleven firms based on existing observations *truly predicted future independent observations.* If they did, the theory would have been validated, and any scientists who questioned the validity of the principles could test the theory themselves with their own data. In today's world, with more and more information collected automatically via technology, the temptation to simply mine the data and draw conclusions is a temptation to be avoided.[31]

Characteristics of Good Theories and Good Data

You do not have to be a scientist to create a theory. Indeed, in our daily lives, we routinely develop informal or **implicit theories** about the world around us. We arrive at these theories through our personal experience and are often unaware of their existence. Many of these implicit theories can be lumped together under the general heading of common sense. Thus, although some real-world managers claim to be skeptical of "theories," they often fail to realize that they carry around a large number of implicit theories.

In most cases, scientific theories are developed more formally. We refer to these theories as **explicit theories** to distinguish them from implicit theories. As you have seen, much of this book is intended to persuade managers to replace their implicit theories with explicit theories that have been supported by research. Explicit theories are not always better than implicit theories, however. Moreover, often multiple explicit theories deal with the same subject, and some may be better than others. How do we judge whether a theory is good or bad, or decide which of two competing theories is better?

There are several criteria that are typically employed for judging the worth of theories in organizational behavior.[32] First and foremost, a theory should contribute to the objectives of science. That is, it should be useful in describing, explaining, predicting, or controlling important things. Most theories, whether implicit or explicit, meet this test.

Second, a theory must be logically consistent within itself. Many implicit theories (and some explicit ones) fall short on this criterion. For example, common sense tells us that "Fortune favors the brave." Conversely, common sense also says that "Fools rush in where angels fear to tread," which has the opposite implication. Similarly, common sense tells us that "Two heads are better than one" as well as that "Too many cooks spoil the broth." Clearly, common sense—and many of the implicit theories on which it is based—does not represent good theory because of its self-contradicting nature.

Third, a theory must be consistent with known facts. For example, many people have an implicit theory that men are better leaders than women, but, as we saw in a previous chapter, this is inconsistent with known data that show very weak evidence of sex differences in leadership capacity, which, if anything, supports the superiority of women by a small amount. Thus, any theory that assumed or proposed that men are better than women on this dimension would be a bad theory because it is inconsistent with established facts.

A fourth criterion by which to evaluate a theory is its consistency with respect to future events. The theory must not only predict but also make *testable* predictions. A prediction is considered testable if it can be refuted by data. A theory that predicts all possible outcomes actually says nothing. For example, if a theory states that a particular leadership style can increase, decrease, or leave employee performance unchanged, it has offered nothing of value about the relationship between that leadership style and worker performance.

Finally, simplicity is a desirable characteristic of a theory. Highly complex and involved theories are not only more difficult to test, but also more difficult to apply. A theory that uses only a few concepts to predict and explain some outcome is preferable to one that accomplishes the same goal with more concepts. Simplicity is surprisingly difficult to maintain, however. By their very nature, theories oversimplify the real world. Thus, for a theory to be consistent with real-world data, we must inevitably push it toward increasing complexity over time. A good theory can walk the fine line between being too simple (when it will fail to predict events with any accuracy) and being too complex (when it is no longer testable or useful for any purpose).

Having established the scientific method as the interplay between explicit theories and data, and having covered the characteristics of a good theory, we must next discuss the characteristics of good data. Experienced managers have long known that, "If you can't measure it, you can't manage it." Most data for testing theories are gathered through measurements of the theory's important concepts. Good data are just as important to scientists as is good theory. Several characteristics render some measures—and, therefore, the data they generate— better than others.

First, the measures must possess **reliability**; that is, they must be free of random errors. Suppose, for example, that the person who interviewed you for graduate school was interested in your scholastic aptitude because it predicts success in graduate school. Imagine that, to assess your aptitude, the interviewer handed you two dice and asked you to toss them, suggesting that a high score would mean high aptitude and a low score would indicate low aptitude. At this point, you would probably start wondering about the aptitude of the interviewer. The unreliability of dice as a measure makes them virtually worthless.

Consider the following, less obvious example of a reliability problem. It was once believed that interviewers, after talking to job applicants in an unstructured way for approximately thrity minutes, could provide ratings reflecting the applicants' suitability for many different jobs. Research showed, however, that these ratings were roughly as reliable as the results of tossing dice.[33] An interviewer would rate the same applicant high one day and low another day or two different interviewers would rate the same applicant very differently. As a consequence, in making important decisions like admitting an applicant to graduate school, most institutions rely heavily on scores on tests such as the Graduate Record Exam (GRE), the Graduate Management Admissions Test (GMAT), and the Law School Admissions Test (LSAT). Although these tests are not perfectly reliable (students taking them repeatedly will not get the exact same score each time), they do exhibit a high degree of consistency.

Second, the measures of a theory's concepts must possess **validity**; that is, they must assess what they were meant to assess. To see whether the GMAT is valid, for example, we might seek to determine whether students who perform better on the test actually perform better in graduate school. This means of testing validity is called **criterion-related validation** because it studies whether the measure really predicts the criterion (for example, grade-point average) that it is supposed to be able to predict. Criterion-related validation is based on an objective assessment of a measure's ability to predict future events. Thus, we know that when it comes to predicting success in graduate school, the GMAT shows significantly higher validity relative to a person's prior GPA. Still, many people making selection decisions about graduate school applicants rely on GPA. This hurts applicants who come from schools where grading practices are strict and helps students who come from schools where grade inflation has made obtaining high grades child's play.[34]

Indeed, rampant grade inflation has made some companies turn away from GPA or even college degrees in general as measures of ability or knowledge. Instead of relying on assessments made by colleges, these companies have turned to an SAT-like test that directly measures the kind of business skills employers are looking for. This way, students who learned a great deal, but who have low GPAs because they went to a college with strict grading policies, can prove their superiority to a students who may have learned little, despite a high GPA from a school that practiced grade inflation. Even beyond this, someone who might have developed important skills on-the-job or as part of a Massive Open Online Course (MMOC) can prove themselves even without a college degree. Time will tell if the criterion-related validity for predicting success on-the-job for the "Post-College SAT" is high or low, but the fact that many employers are just looking in this direction speaks volumes about the lack of faith in GPA as a measure of knowledge.[35]

Alternatively, we can assess validity of a measure subjectively by having experts on the concept examine the measure. These experts can determine the extent to which the content embodied in the measure actually reflects the theoretical concept being studied. This approach is called **content validation** because it focuses on whether the content of the test is appropriate according to experts on the subject.

Reliability and validity are closely related. Reliability is necessary for validity, but it is not sufficient for proving it, because we could develop highly reliable measures that might not be valid. For example, we could probably measure people's height reliably, but this measure would have little validity as a measure of scholastic aptitude (that is, it could not predict who would do well in graduate school). Reliability is necessary for validity, however, because an unreliable measure cannot pass any of the tests necessary for establishing validity. An unreliable measure does not relate well even to itself.

A third desirable property of the measures of a theory's concepts is **standardization**, which means that everyone who measures the concepts uses the same instrument in the same way. Because it takes time and effort to develop measures that are reliable and valid, we can achieve a great deal of efficiency by using existing standardized measures.[36] Standardized measures provide two other advantages. First, they are far more likely than other measures to achieve *objectivity*. Because everyone uses the same procedures, the results of measurement are much less likely to be affected by the choice of an investigator. There are many different standardized measures of organizational performance and most of these rely on objective data.[37] The four best recognized dimensions of organizational performance include (1) stock market performance, (2) growth, (3) profitability, and (4) liquidity.[38]

Moreover, when there are changes and improvements in the standard measure, everyone adopts the new measure, resulting in quick, across-the-board diffusion of innovation. For example, when the Bureau of Economic Analysis came up with a new measure of U.S. Gross Domestic Product (GDP), this new and improved measure was quickly adopted by all researchers in that area and, as a result, everyone's research was improved at the same time.[39] There are many different standardized measures of organizational performance.

Finally, standardized measures make it easy to *communicate* and compare results across situations. Although you could construct a scale to measure job satisfaction in your own company, even if you succeeded in developing a reliable and valid measure (a difficult task), you could not compare the satisfaction level in your company to that in other companies. That is because other companies will not have used (and might not be willing to use) your measure. On the other hand, the Job Descriptive Index (JDI) is a standardized measure of job satisfaction that has been used in hundreds of companies. For most standardized measures, the availability of a great deal of existing data allows you to compare your company with other companies that all have been measured on the same criteria in the same way. For these and other reasons, managers should rarely try to develop their own measures for every situation. At worst, the measures would lack reliability and validity. At best, managers would "reinvent the wheel." Of course, on some occasions you might need to test new concepts or develop measures that are unique to your situation. Such cases, however, will be the exception rather than the rule.

Causal Inferences

We can use the scientific method to further our understanding of evidenced-based management. To translate this enhanced understanding into more effective practice, however, we must apply this learning. Knowledge is most applicable when it can be expressed in terms of cause-and-effect relationships. After identifying these relationships, we can often manipulate the causes to bring about the desired effects (such as enhanced productivity or job satisfaction). Good theory and good measures take us a long way toward achieving this objective, but they are not sufficient for identifying cause-and-effect relations (that is, making causal inferences). As noted later in this chapter, making causal inferences depends not only on how the data are obtained, but also on when the data are obtained and what is done with them once collected.

Moreover, even if a manager is not engaging in scientific experimentation but just trying to learn from daily experience, rigorously thinking about cause-and-effect relationships can ensure that he or she does not learn the wrong lesson from past experience. True learning can take place only when a person seriously reflects upon past experience and analyzes it critically. For this reason, we closely examine how to go about making the proper causal inferences.

Criteria for Inferring Cause

One of the foremost authorities on the philosophy of science, John Stuart Mill, argued that to state unequivocally that one thing causes another, we must establish three criteria. First, we must establish *temporal precedence*; that is, the cause must come before—not after—the effect in time. Second, we must document *covariation*; that is, if the cause is varied (for example, turned on or off), the effect must vary as well. Third, we must be able to *eliminate alternative explanations* for the observed results.

The first step in establishing a cause-and-effect relationship is demonstrating **temporal precedence**, which simply means that the cause must precede the effect in time. One common mistake people make in trying to learn from experience is falsely inferring a causal relationship between two variables just because they are related at one point in time. For example, imagine that you tour a factory and observe that work groups with low absenteeism rates have supervisors who give team members a great deal of latitude and allow them to participate in decision making. In contrast, during the same factory tour, you observe that work groups with the highest absenteeism rates are closely monitored by their supervisors at all times and do not participate in decision making. It would be a mistake to jump to the conclusion that close supervision *causes* high absenteeism. It would be an even greater mistake to act on this unproven conclusion by demanding that all managers of the company "loosen up" their supervision.

In fact, the causal order between these two variables might lie in the opposite direction. That is, perhaps all supervisors started out acting the same. High absenteeism in some groups might have caused supervisors to tighten their control, and low absenteeism in other groups might have led their supervisors to give them more latitude. Failing to consider temporal precedence in this case would lead you to learn the wrong lesson from this factory tour. If you then acted on this misinformation and loosened up the supervision of the managers in the plant, absenteeism might actually worsen rather than improve. Instead of solving a problem, you could make the situation worse.

The second criterion for inferring cause is **covariation**, which simply means that the cause and effect are related. For example, if we believe that providing day care for employees' children causes lower absenteeism, then a relationship should exist between company day-care services and low employee absenteeism. Several ways to assess covariation are available, all of which rely on statistical methods. As this text is not a statistics book, and given that most of its readers will likely take courses in statistics, we limit our discussion here to two simple, but widely applicable, statistical techniques. Although not perfect for every situation, they are useful in a wide variety of contexts.

The first means of establishing covariation, known as a *test of mean differences*, compares the average scores of two groups on the outcome we wish to change. For example, Table 16.1 presents data on absenteeism for two groups of workers: ten work in Plant A, which offers an in-house day-care center, and ten work in Plant B, which lacks on-site provisions for day care. As shown in Figure 16.2, the level of absenteeism is much higher for Plant B than for Plant A. This simple analysis of mean differences suggests that day-care provision and absenteeism are, in fact, related.

We might also test for mean differences between numbers of absences at Plant A before and after the establishment of the day-care center and generate data like those listed in Table 16.2 and graphed in Figure 16.3. If the average absenteeism rates were higher before the plant installed the day-care center than they were after it was implemented, we might again conclude (before engaging in more rigorous analyses) that a relationship exists between provided day care and lower absenteeism. Both mean differences described here are easy to comprehend when presented as bar charts like those shown in Figures 16.2 and 16.3.

A second means of establishing covariation is through the use of the **correlation coefficient**. This statistic, a number that ranges from +1.0 to −1.0, expresses the relationship between two things. A +1.0 correlation means that a perfect positive relationship exists between the two measures in question (for example, absenteeism rates and employee age). That is, as the value of one measure increases, the value of the other increases to the same relative degree. A correlation of −1.0 reflects a perfect negative relationship between the two

Table 16.1 **Absence Data at Two Hypothetical Plants**

Employee	Number of absences	
	Plant A (with day care)	Plant B (without day care)
1	10	12
2	11	11
3	8	13
4	11	8
5	3	16
6	4	14
7	3	10
8	2	4
9	1	2
10	5	3
Average	5.8	9.3

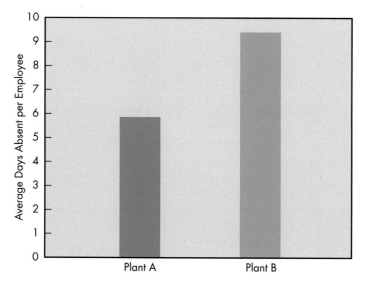

Figure 16.2 **Absenteeism in Two Different Plants Assessed over One Time Period**

Table 16.2 **Absence Data for One Hypothetical Plant at Two Different Times**

Employee	Number of absences at Plant A	
	Before day care	After day care
1	12	10
2	14	11
3	10	8
4	12	11
5	6	3
6	8	4
7	4	3
8	2	2
9	1	1
10	6	5
Average	7.5	5.8

measures. Here, as the value of one variable increases, the value of the other decreases, again to the same relative degree. A correlation of .00 indicates that no relationship links the measures; thus, as the value of one measure increases, the value of the other can be anything—high, medium, or low.

To give you a feeling for other values of the correlation coefficient, Figure 16.4 shows plots of points, where each point represents a person of a given age (specified on the x-axis) and that person's corresponding level of absenteeism (specified on the y-axis). This figure depicts four correlation values: +1.0, +.50, .00, and −.50. The sign of the correlation reveals whether the relationship is positive or negative, and the absolute value of the correlation reveals the magnitude of the relationship.

Returning to our employees at Plants A and B, Table 16.3, in addition to providing data on day care and rates of absenteeism, shows the ages of the workers. We could use the

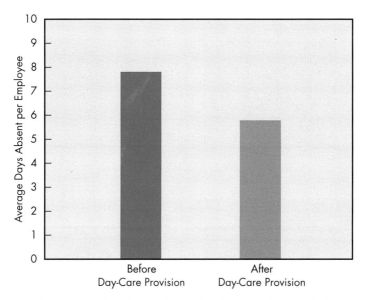

Figure 16.3 Absenteeism at One Plant Assessed over Two Different Time Periods

Table 16.3 Absence and Age Data at Two Hypothetical Plants

Employee	Plant A (day care)		Plant B (no day care)	
	Number of absences	Age	Number of absences	Age
1	10	27	12	27
2	11	31	11	34
3	8	30	13	31
4	11	26	8	25
5	3	40	16	33
6	4	61	14	35
7	3	52	10	25
8	2	47	4	40
9	1	46	2	52
10	5	41	3	46
Average	5.8	40.1	9.3	34.8

correlation coefficient to determine whether a relationship exists between age and absent-eeism. In fact, the correlation between age and absenteeism for these data is –.50, indicating that older workers are absent less often than younger ones. If we plotted these data on a graph, where x is the horizontal axis and y the vertical axis, the result would look like the graph shown in Figure 16.4D. As you can see, graphically depicting the correlation in this fashion makes it easy to understand the strength and nature of the relationship between these two variables.

Once we have established both covariation and temporal precedence, we are only one step away from establishing that something actually caused something else. The *elimination of alternative explanations*, Mill's third criterion for establishing cause, entails a major effort,

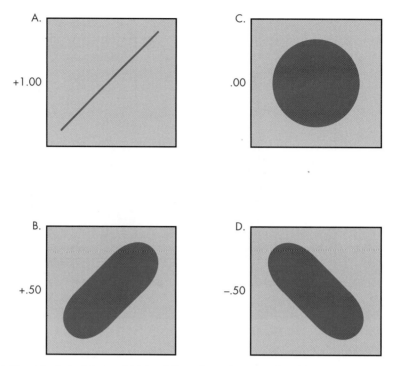

Figure 16.4 Plots Depicting Various Levels of Correlation between Variables

however. In our continuing example, if we are to infer that providing day care caused lower absenteeism, we must show that no other factor caused the low rates. The complexity of most real-world situations makes it very difficult to rule out all other possible explanations. Indeed, this problem, more than any other, complicates the process of conducting research in the applied behavioral social sciences.

In the physical sciences, experimenters can use physical means such as lead shields and vacuum chambers to isolate variables and rule out alternative causes. This kind of tight control is much more difficult to achieve in social science research. In fact, some valid alternative explanations arise so frequently that they have been given special names.

The **selection threat**, for example, involves the danger that the groups we selected for comparison were not the same initially.[40] If we had only the data on absenteeism in the two plants (the data in Table 16.1), the lower mean rate of absenteeism in the plant with day care might have led us to conclude, based on our past experience, that providing day care caused lower absenteeism. Our additional data show that age is negatively related to absenteeism, however, and workers in Plant A are known to be older than those in Plant B. In fact, if we controlled for age by comparing only workers who were the same age, we would find no differences in absenteeism between the plants.

At this point, you might say, "So what? What difference does it make?" It makes a huge difference if your faulty cause-and-effect judgment prompts your company to invest a large sum of money in providing day-care facilities on a corporation-wide basis. Funding of this benefit would be based on your conclusion that day care would pay for itself through lower absenteeism. Because day care is actually irrelevant to absenteeism, this investment would eventually be lost, and many people would be left wondering what happened. The selection threat is the most common threat to studies that compare two different groups at one point in time.

The **history threat** is the most common problem in studies that observe the same group in a "before-and-after" situation. It occurs when the real cause is not the change you made, but rather something else that happened at the same time. In Figure 16.3, when we compared the mean number of absences for Plant A *before* day care with the mean number of absences *after* day care, we found a lower average rate of absenteeism after the day-care program was implemented. We might be tempted to infer that the day-care center caused lower absenteeism. Suppose, however, that we obtained the "before" measure during the summer months and the "after" measure during the winter months. Perhaps people simply found more reasons to be absent in the summer than in the winter. That is, the weather—rather than the day-care center—might have caused the difference in absenteeism rates. If we extended the day-care program throughout the corporation, we would find that it would not reduce absenteeism and would again be left wondering why.

Designing Observations to Infer Cause

The timing and the frequency of data collection affect our ability to make causal interpretations. Deciding on the timing of measurement is an important part of research design. Consider the two *faulty designs* shown in Figure 16.5. In the One Group Before–After design (Figure 16.5A), data are collected both before and after some event or treatment. If the after score differs from the before score, we assume that the change in the situation caused the difference. The flaw in this design relates to the history threat, which is an alternative explanation for the results. In our day-care example, if we collected data from only one plant, once in the summer and once in the winter, we would be using this type of faulty design.

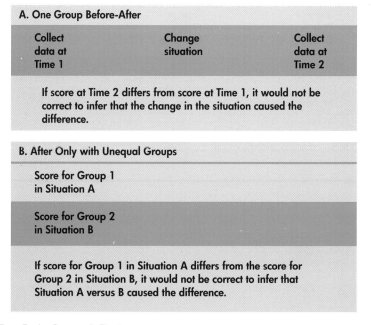

A. One Group Before-After

| Collect data at Time 1 | Change situation | Collect data at Time 2 |

If score at Time 2 differs from score at Time 1, it would not be correct to infer that the change in the situation caused the difference.

B. After Only with Unequal Groups

Score for Group 1 in Situation A

Score for Group 2 in Situation B

If score for Group 1 in Situation A differs from the score for Group 2 in Situation B, it would not be correct to infer that Situation A versus B caused the difference.

Figure 16.5 Two Faulty Research Designs

In the After Only with Unequal Groups design (Figure 16.5B), data are collected from two groups, one of which experiences a situation while the other does not. This design is flawed because we do not know for certain that the groups were equal before the treatment or during the treatment; thus the selection threat might explain the results. In our day-care example, we collected data from both Plant A and Plant B without verifying that the people in those plants were similar (for example, were the same age on average); thus our experiment has this kind of faulty design. Such designs constituted the structure underlying many of our day-to-day past experiences, and, if not analyzed critically, they can lead us to learn the wrong lessons from those past experiences.

We can change designs in several ways to help eliminate some of these threats. Consider the One Group Before–After design, where the history threat poses the major problem. We could improve the situation by adding a control group (that is, a group that does not receive the day-care assistance), thereby turning the design into the Two Groups Before–After design (Figure 16.6A). This design allows us to test whether the two groups were equal initially by comparing scores at Time 1. That is, in our day-care example, was the rate of absenteeism in Plants A and B similar before the treatment—the day-care center—was implemented? This design also allows us to test whether some historical factor other than the day-care center could have caused the results. That is, if the real cause was time of the year (summer versus winter), we could expect a decrease in absenteeism in Plant B as we moved from Time 1 to Time 2, even though no day-care center was established there. This type of design is especially effective in organizational training contexts in order to establish whether or not people actually changed as a result of the training and not some other historical factor.[41]

The Two Groups After Only model becomes even stronger in terms of causal inferences if people are randomly assigned to the groups. **Random assignment** of people to conditions

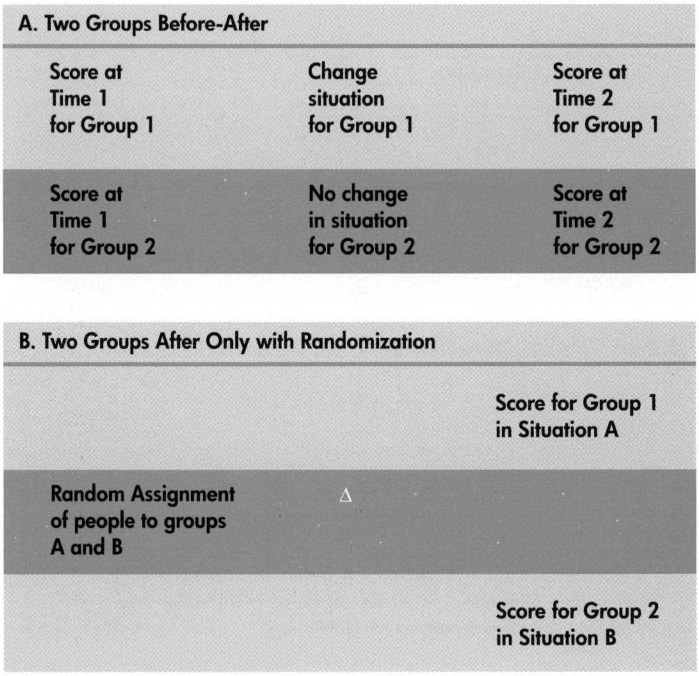

A. Two Groups Before-After		
Score at Time 1 for Group 1	Change situation for Group 1	Score at Time 2 for Group 1
Score at Time 1 for Group 2	No change in situation for Group 2	Score at Time 2 for Group 2

B. Two Groups After Only with Randomization		
		Score for Group 1 in Situation A
Random Assignment of people to groups A and B	Δ	
		Score for Group 2 in Situation B

Figure 16.6 **Two Improved Research Designs**

means that each person has an equal chance of being placed in either the experimental or the control group. We can achieve this random arrangement by flipping coins, tossing dice, or using a random numbers table from a statistics book. In our day-care study, if we could have initially assembled the twenty workers at the two plants and then tossed a coin to see who would get day care and who would not, the odds are that, when we were finished, the two resulting groups would have been equal in age. That is, each group would have included roughly the same number of people of a given age.

In fact, the real value of randomization is that it not only equalizes groups on factors (such as age) expected to influence results, but also equates groups on virtually all factors. Thus, in our day-care study, if we randomized the groups at the outset, we could be fairly confident that they would be equated not only on age, but also on other factors, such as height and weight. You might not think that a person's height or weight would relate to absenteeism, but some research has found such a relationship between absenteeism and weight.[42] Even if we were unaware of this relationship at the outset of the day-care study, it is nice to know that randomization neatly solved a potential problem. In fact, the equalizing effect of random assignment is so powerful that one can often infer cause even in the absence of a before measure. For example, Figure 16.6B shows the Two Groups After Only design, where two groups are established randomly and then exposed to two different situations. Even though there is no before measure that proves the two groups were equal on other potential causal factors, one can safely presume that randomization made them equal (provided there were enough cases), and infer that any differences between the two situations were actually caused by the situation and not some external factor. Because of randomization's ability to rule out both anticipated and unanticipated selection threats, people conducting experiments should randomly assign subjects to treatments whenever possible.

Due to their power for drawing causal inferences, these types of randomized experiments are often conducted by learning organizations. For example, Google runs over 10,000 such experiments every year, and about 10 percent of these result in changes in the business.[43] Most of these randomized experiments are aimed at asking small questions, such as "are pop-up ads more effective if displayed on the right side of the screen or the left?" The answer to this question might be used to justify different rates for posting advertisements or changes in how all advertisements are placed. Clearly, these little experiments are hardly Big Science, but the cumulative effect of all these little changes based upon validated evidence can have a big impact on the bottom line over time.[44]

Because randomization is not always possible, we must often resort to other tools to rule out selection threats. Suppose that, when we start our day-care experiment, we know that workers at the two plants are not evenly distributed in terms of age, and we know that age affects absenteeism. In the real world, we cannot randomly move people from plant to plant; we must work with existing groups.

How, then, can we rule out age as the alternative explanation for our results? We have several choices. First, we could use *homogeneous* groups, or study groups that do not differ in age. For example, we might compare absenteeism in the two plants, but only among workers who are 25 to 35 years old. As you can see from Table 16.3, we would therefore compare Persons 1, 2, 3, and 4 in Plant A with Persons 1, 2, 3, 4, 5, 6, and 7 in Plant B. With this sample, if we still found lower absenteeism in Plant A than in Plant B, we could not attribute the difference to age, because all subjects were roughly the same age.

Alternatively, we could also equate groups by *matching subjects*. For example, we might study only the subjects in Plant A for whom there are corresponding subjects in Plant B, or subjects who are within two years of one another in terms of age. Thus, looking again at

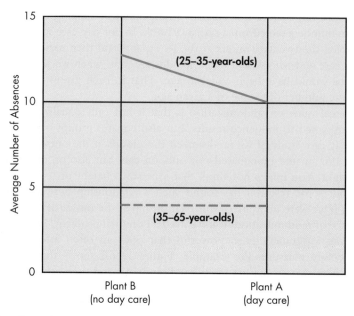

Figure 16.7 The Effect of Age and Day-Care Facilities on Absenteeism

Table 16.3, we could match Subjects 1, 2, 5, 7, and 9 in Plant A with Subjects 1, 3, 8, 9, and 10 in Plant B. If we found lower absenteeism in one plant, we could not attribute this result to age because we equated the groups on this factor.

Finally, we could *build the threat into the design*. That is, we could simply treat age as another possible factor affecting the rate of absenteeism and examine its effect at the same time that we study the effect of day care. One advantage of building alternative explanations into your design is that you can then test for **interactions**. An interaction exists when the relationship between the treatment (the day-care center, in our example) and the outcome (absenteeism) depends on some other variable (age). Figure 16.7 shows a possible result if we built the alternative explanation of age into our day-care study. As you can see, among the younger group of workers, providing day care does lower absenteeism; among the older group, however, it has no effect. Thus the relationship between day care and absenteeism depends on the factor of age.

Clearly, many factors must be considered in designing studies that will allow us to infer causality. The more variables we can control, the tighter our research design, and the more likely that we can rule out alternative explanations for any relationships discovered.

Generalizing Research Results

Research is usually conducted with one sample, in one setting, at one time period. Often, however, we wish to know the generalizability of results, where **generalizability** is defined as the extent to which results obtained in one sample–setting–time configuration can be repeated in a different sample–setting–time configuration. This ability is sometimes of interest when we are conducting research, but always critical when we evaluate research findings to see whether what worked for the investigators can be applied in a real-world setting.

Sample, Setting, and Time

Our day-care example provides a good illustration of how results might not generalize across all samples. Recall that the results of our study eventually showed that provision of day care reduced absenteeism among workers who were 25 to 35 years old but not among members of the older group. Astute managers who studied our results would want to apply these lessons only if their company employed a large number of workers in this age category.

Suppose, however, our design homogenized our subjects on age (that is, used only people in the 25 to 35 bracket). In this case, we would have reported simply that providing day care reduced absenteeism. Managers who read these results, but did not pay enough attention to the details on age, might institute day-care centers in companies where the age of the work-force was not the same as in this original plant, and expect the same results. These managers would soon discover that the results of our work did not generalize to their organizations. Thus a major drawback of making groups homogeneous is that it limits our ability to generalize results across other types of samples.

We might also be concerned about generalizing research results across settings. For example, suppose that both of the plants in our original study were located in rural settings. Assume further that it is more difficult to obtain high-quality day care in rural settings than in urban settings. Someone reading the results of our study who manages a plant in an urban area might establish an in-plant day-care center, only to find that the center has no effect on absenteeism, because childcare is not a problem for workers in urban settings. Here again, our results would not generalize to another setting.

Finally, we might worry about whether our results would generalize across time. For example, suppose that we conducted our study during a time characterized by a huge labor shortage; many more jobs were available than there were people to fill them. At such a time, unemployment rates would be low, both parents might well be working, and many people who might in other circumstances serve as day-care providers would very likely be working at different and perhaps higher-paying jobs. Thus, at the time when we conducted our study, demand for day-care services might have been high but only a small supply was available. By providing our own day-care services, we solved a major problem for our workers with small children, which ultimately led to lower absenteeism rates.

Now move forward ten years, to a time characterized by a labor surplus. Unemployment is high, one parent is likely not working, and anyone capable of setting up a day-care center has opened a business. In this situation, because the demand for day care is small and the supply of day-care services large, company-sponsored day care does not provide a needed service to employees. Consequently, no relationship exists between providing day care and lowering absenteeism. In this case, our results do not generalize across time.

Facilitating Generalization

You might wonder whether any findings are generalizable given the many factors that might differ from one unique sample–setting–time to another. From a researcher's perspective, can we take any steps to increase the ability to generalize? The answer is "yes." Technically, we can safely generalize from one sample to another if the original sample of people we study is *randomly selected* from the larger population of people to which we wish to generalize. For example, you might have noticed that in presidential elections the television networks usually declare a winner long before all the votes have been counted. The key to successfully predicting the final outcome from the initial, partial results is randomly selecting the people polled from the voting population. This procedure ensures that the small percentage of people who are polled are, by all odds, exactly the same as the larger group of voters.

Although random selection is the only way to guarantee the ability to generalize results across samples, from a practical perspective it is often very difficult to achieve. Thus, many organizations like to rely on Web-based surveys where applicants volunteer their opinions for free, as opposed to conducting random sampling from the telephone book, where many of those chosen have to be paid to participate. Although cheaper than the random sampling method, this "convenience-based" sample that might spring from one's website will differ from the population, and most studies suggest it generates younger, more opinionated, less socially active, and less physically active respondents.[45] Any results that are found with this convenience sample will not generalize to groups that are older, less opinionated, or more socially and physically active.

For example, Starbucks routinely polls customers on its website and asks for suggestions about how to improve products or services. If the people who respond to these Web-based surveys differ from the average customer, then the ideas that are suggested might not turn out to work very well for the average customer. In fact, the company found that people who spent a lot of time with their surveys tended to have time on their hands and really loved coffee. They generated many ideas that made taking orders more complex and time consuming, and hence created longer waiting lines. The average customers, who had less time on their hands and were less discerning about how they obtained their caffeine, reacted very negatively to the ideas generated by the Web-based sample. Because of this experience, Starbucks will not adopt any recommendations derived from Web-based samples without a follow-up test with a random sample.[46]

Studies that employ random selection are usually huge in scale, requiring the efforts of many investigators and a great deal of money. More often, in the real world of research, the ability to generalize a finding is achieved not by undertaking one large experiment but, rather, by conducting many small experiments, using the same measures, in which results are replicated in a host of different sample–setting–time configurations. For example, Chapter 5 discussed research results that generalize very well, such as the repeated finding that high performance is more likely to result from setting specific and difficult goals than from offering vague goals like "do your best." The generalizability of this finding comes not from one large study that randomly sampled people, settings, and times but, rather, from many smaller studies, each of which used different samples, settings, and times but obtained the same result.

Although generalizing results is always of interest in evaluating research, the original researchers might not emphasize this issue. Often research is conducted strictly to test or build theories. In such a case, investigators might be less interested in what *does* happen than in what *can* happen.[47] For example, research on biofeedback shows that people can learn to control some of their own physiological processes, such as heart rate and blood pressure, when hooked up to special devices that give them information on these processes. You might think that few real-world situations correspond to the one faced by subjects in this kind of research. That is not the point of this research, however.

Rather, this research is intended to test the theory that humans can voluntarily control supposedly involuntary physiological responses when provided with the appropriate feedback. Nothing inherent in this theory suggests that it would not work with college sophomores in a laboratory setting at some specific time period. Thus, if the results fail to support the theory in this sample–setting–time configuration, we must either reject the theory or modify and retest it. The fact that the subjects, settings, and times were randomly selected is completely irrelevant. With this kind of research, the ultimate aim is not to make the laboratory setting more like the real world but, rather, to make the real world more like the laboratory—that is, to change the real world in ways that benefit us all.

Linking Organizational Behavior Science and Practice

As noted earlier, people in knowledge-creating companies or learning organizations are encouraged to experiment. As a practicing manager, however, you should recognize that a wealth of research conducted by others is just waiting to be discovered. Some studies might deal directly with an issue that is critical to your company or your career or with a problem you are trying to manage. Rather than conducting your own experiment (a choice that is costly in terms of both time and money), you might be able to generalize the findings of these studies to your context. (*Academy of Management Review, Journal of Applied Psychology*, and *Organizational Behavior and Human Decision Processes* are a few of the major scientific journals that publish theory and research related to topics covered in this book.)

A great deal of the research into this area is performed by people working in university settings. Thus you might be able to uncover research on topics of interest by contacting university faculty who publish frequently on aspects of organizational behavior. Faculty and students at local universities can help with management issues, and these people bring fresh perspectives, unique skills, and diverse experiences to the organization. In return, university personnel might provide internships and case studies, or conduct field research in your organization that might result in excellent learning opportunities that promote organizational effectiveness.

For example, FedEx has recently teamed up with researchers at Columbia University to conduct an experiment on the potential for adding electrical vehicles to FedEx's fleet of delivery trucks. FedEx is testing several different vehicles designed by different companies to find the most cost effective and reliable for large-scale use, but one of the biggest questions they have is how to recharge a fleet of electric vehicles as large as this. Leon Wu, a professor at Columbia University's Center for Computational Learning notes that, "If you charged all these vehicles at the same time, you'd overload the system and there would be a blackout." The partnership between FedEx and Columbia is working to solve this problem and is performing several experiments to see how alternative recharging schedules and practices might allow for a less disruptive impact on the power grids of most cities.[48]

Specialized expertise in certain management topics can also be found in some consulting companies. However, one should not count on gaining a sustainable competitive advantage from these types of outside sources. Consulting companies do not always have the answer to your question, and many have their own set of organizational problems that make it difficult for them to truly meet the needs of their clients.

People who teach organizational behavior and executive development often lament the inadequate dialogue that takes place between practicing managers and researchers. This kind of dialogue can develop only when managers and researchers understand each other's work and appreciate its value in guiding their own efforts. Practicing managers need to know what organizational behavior researchers do and why they follow certain paths. Researchers, in turn, need to identify practitioners' most pressing problems so that they can study those issues that managers view as significant. Because it is so important to create and encourage this kind of ongoing practitioner–researcher dialogue, we have included this chapter on research methods in this book.

Although you might never conduct formal research yourself, you will undoubtedly find it invaluable to familiarize yourself with the large body of scientific evidence available on topics that will be crucial to you, your employer, and your employees. Although this research might not provide all the answers you need, it will certainly inspire and intrigue you, perhaps promoting the kind of spirit embodied in some of the learning organizations that rely on evidence-based management described at the outset of this chapter.

Summary

Traditional ways of acquiring knowledge, such as rationalism, personal experience, and reliance on authorities, have many limitations. The advantage of science relative to these more traditional means of knowledge acquisition is its *objectivity*, and science as an enterprise tends to be public, self-correcting, and cumulative. The major goals of science are the description, explanation, prediction, and control of various phenomena. These goals are achieved through an interplay of *theory* and *data*, whereby ideas contained in theories are expressed in testable *hypotheses*, which are then compared with actual data. The correspondence (or lack thereof) between the hypothesized results and the actual results is then used to verify, refute, or modify the theory.

Good theories are characterized by simplicity, self-consistency, and consistency with known facts; they should also contribute to the objectives of science. To be useful, data for testing theories should be *reliable* and *valid*. In obtaining such data, using established *standardized* measures offers many advantages. At the core of many theories lies the idea of establishing causes. Cause can be inferred only when we establish *temporal precedence* and *covariation*, and when we eliminate all *alternative explanations*. The last requirement is often the most troublesome aspect of research in the social sciences, and threats such as *selection* and *history* threats can prove especially problematic. We partially avoid these threats by employing research designs that use control groups and make these controls comparable to experimental groups through *randomization, matching*, or *homogenization*. To *generalize* the findings from one study to another context, it is necessary to randomly select samples, settings, and time periods. This goal is rarely achieved to its fullest extent in the social sciences. Nevertheless, if experimental results are repeatedly confirmed in different samples and settings and at different times, it might be possible to generalize such findings.

Review Questions

1. Many theories seem to follow a similar pattern. They start out simple, grow increasingly complex as empirical tests on the theory proliferate, and then die out or are replaced by new theories. Review the criteria for a good theory and discuss why this pattern occurs so commonly. In your discussion, specify possible conflicts or inconsistencies among the criteria for a good theory.
2. Although objectivity is a hallmark of scientific inquiry, all scientists have their own subjective beliefs and biases surrounding the phenomena they study. Indeed, some scientists are motivated to do their work precisely because they hold passionate beliefs about these phenomena. Discuss whether this kind of passion is an asset or a liability to the scientist. In addition, discuss how science can be an objective exercise even though the people who practice it demonstrate personal biases. What prevents a passionate scientist from cheating or distorting results in favor of his or her personal beliefs?
3. Experiments in organizations usually involve people other than the experimenters—that is, managers or employees. What are some of the ethical responsibilities of an experimenter with respect to these people? Is it ethical, for example, for an experimenter to use one group of employees as a control group when he or she strongly suspects that the treatment given to the experimental group will enhance the members' chances for

success, promotion, or satisfaction? If the experimenter is afraid that explaining the nature of the experiment will cause people to act differently than they would otherwise (and hence ruin the experiment), is it ethical to deceive them about the study's true purpose?

4. Philosopher of science Murray S. Davis once remarked that "The truth of a theory has very little to do with its impact."[49] History, according to Davis, shows that the legacy of a theory depends more on how interesting the theory is perceived to be by practitioners and scientists than on how much truth it holds. Earlier in this chapter, we listed criteria for good theories; now list what you think are criteria for "interesting" theories. Where do these two lists seem to conflict most, and how can scientists and the practitioners they serve generate theories that are both interesting and truthful?

Notes

1 M. Crossan, "Altering Theories of Learning and Action: An Interview with Chris Argyris," *Academy of Management Executive* 17 (2003): 40–46.

2 M. Makarty, "Cause of Death: Medical Error and Overtreatment," *Wall Street Journal*, September 25, 2012, http://blogs.wsj.com/ideas-market/2012/09/25/cause-of-death-medical-error-and-overtreatment/.

3 P. Sellers, "The Liberating Effect of Failure," *CNN Money*, May 29, 2008, http://money.cnn.com/2008/05/29/news/newsmakers/sellers_failure.fortune/.

4 A. W. Mathews, "Hospitals Prescribe Big Data to Track Doctors at Work," *Wall Street Journal*, July 11, 2013, http://online.wsj.com/news/articles/SB1000142412788732355100457844 1154292068308.

5 J. Bersin, "5 Keys to Building a Learning Organization," *Forbes*, January 18, 2012, http://www.forbes.com/sites/joshbersin/2012/01/18/5-keys-to-building-a-learning-organization/.

6 A. J. Villado and A. Winfred, "The Comparative Effect of Subjective and Objective After Action Reviews on Team Performance on a Complex Task," *Journal of Applied Psychology* 98 (2013): 514–528.

7 D. S. DeRue, J. D. Nahrgang, J. R. Hollenbeck, and K. Workman, "A Quasi-Experimental Study of After-Event Reviews and Leadership Development," *Journal of Applied Psychology* 97 (2012): 997–1015.

8 M. Makarty, "How to Stop Hospitals from Killing Us," *Wall Street Journal*, September 21, 2012, http://online.wsj.com/news/articles/SB10000872396390444620104578008263334441352.

9 R. King, "Departing Employees Are Security Horror," *Wall Street Journal*, October 20, 2013, http://online.wsj.com/news/articles/SB10001424052702303442004579123412020578896.

10 L. Kwoh, "Want to Kill Innovation in Your Company? Go Public," *Wall Street Journal*, January 15, 2013, http://blogs.wsj.com/atwork/2013/01/15/want-to-kill-innovation-at-your-company-go-public/.

11 J. Pfeffer and R. Sutton, "Trust the Evidence, Not Your Instincts," *The New York Times*, September 3, 2011, http://www.nytimes.com/2011/09/04/jobs/04pre.html?_r=0.

12 H. Mintzberg, "Ten Ideas Designed to Rile Everyone Who Cares about Management," *Harvard Business Review* 74 (1996): 61–67.

13 D. Jones, "Some Say MBAs No Longer Worth the Extra Cash," *USA Today*, July 22, 2002, http://usatoday30.usatoday.com/money/companies/management/2002-07-21-mbas_x.htm.

14 M. S. Schilling, "Technology Success and Failure in Winner-Take-All Markets: The Impact of Learning Orientation, Timing, and Network Externalities," *Academy of Management Journal* 45 (2002): 387–398.

15 E. Shapiro, *Fad Surfing in the Boardroom: Reclaiming the Courage to Manage in the Age of Instant Answers* (Boston: Addison-Wesley, 1995), 21–22.

16 A. Farnham, "In Search of Suckers," *Fortune*, October 14, 1996, 119–126.

17 E. Nagel, *An Introduction to Logic and the Scientific Method* (New York: Harcourt, 1954).

18 D. Nadler, "Even Failure Can Be Productive," *New York Times*, April 23, 1989, 3.

19 J. Buchler, *Philosophical Writings of Peirce* (New York: Dover, 1955).

20 N. Byrnes, "Rot on the Street: Worse than You Thought," *BusinessWeek*, May 12, 2003, 32–33.

21 J. Carey, "When Medical Studies Collide," *BusinessWeek*, August 6, 2007, 38.

22 G. Naik, "Quick Publishing of Research Breakthroughs Can Lift Stock, but May Undermine Science," *Wall Street Journal*, January 28, 2002, 1–2.

23 P. Loftus, "Eli Lilly, Unlike Rivals, Isn't Pulling Back on R&D," *Wall Street Journal*, October 20, 2013, http://online.wsj.com/news/articles/SB10001424052702304500040457912544 0699770948.

24 J. R. Hollenbeck, "Quasi-Experimentation and Applied Psychology: Introduction to a Special Issue of Personnel Psychology," *Personnel Psychology* 55 (2002): 56–57.

25 F. N. Kerlinger, *Foundations of Behavioral Research* (New York: Holt, Rinehart and Winston, 1986), 9.

26 L. Swedroe, "Trust Models over Instincts," *CBS News Money Watch*, June 17, 2013, http://www.cbsnews.com/news/trust-models-over-instincts/.

27 S. Baker, "Management by the Numbers," *BusinessWeek*, September 8, 2008, 32–38.

28 E. Derman and P. Wilmott, "Perfect Models, Imperfect World," *BusinessWeek*, January 12, 2009, 59–60.

29 J. Collins, *Good to Great: Why Some Companies Make the Leap . . . and Others Don't* (London: Random House, 2001).

30 B. Niendorf and K. Beck, "Good to Great, or Just Good?" *Academy of Management Perspectives* 2 (2008): 13–20.

31 A. Hesseldahl, "A Rich Vein for 'Reality Mining'," *BusinessWeek*, May 5, 2008, 52–53.

32 J. B. Miner, *Theories of Organizational Behavior* (Hinsdale, IL: Dryden Press, 1980).

33 R. Arvey and M. Campion, "The Employment Interview: A Summary and Review of Recent Research," *Personnel Psychology* 34 (1982): 281–322.

34 M. Korn, "M.B.A. Admission Tip: Always Go for an Easy A," *Wall Street Journal*, July 31, 2013, http://online.wsj.com/news/articles/SB10001424127887323997004578640241102477584.

35 D. Belkin, "Are You Ready for the Post-College SAT?" *Wall Street Journal*, August 25, 2013, http://online.wsj.com/news/articles/SB1000142412788732398060457902914395984 3818.

36 J. C. Nunnally, *Psychometric Theory* (New York: McGraw-Hill, 1978), 4.

37 D. J. Ketchen, R. D. Ireland, and L. T. Baker, "The Use of Archival Proxies in Strategic Management Studies: Castles Made of Sand?" *Organizational Research Methods* 16 (2013): 32–42.

38 P. M. Hamann, F. Schiemann, L. Bellora, and T. W. Guenther, "Exploring the Dimensions of Organizational Performance: A Construct Validation Study," *Organizational Research Methods* 16 (2012): 67–87.

39 M. Mandel, "Research Finally Gets Its Due," *BusinessWeek*, October 15, 2007, 12.

40 T. D. Cook and D. T. Campbell, *Quasi-Experimentation: Design Analysis Issues for Field Settings* (Chicago: Rand McNally, 1979), 53.

41 R. E. Silverman, "So Much training, So Little to Show for It," *Wall Street Journal*, October 26, 2012, http://online.wsj.com/news/articles/SB10001424052970204425904578072950518558328.

42 K. R. Parkes, "Relative Weight, Smoking and Mental Health as Predictors of Sickness and Absence from Work," *Journal of Applied Psychology* 72 (1987): 275–287.

43 T. Butterworth, "Taking Ideas on a Test Drive," *Wall Street Journal*, May 7, 2012, http://online.wsj.com/news/articles/SB10001424052702303916904577378443113114400.

44 E. B. King, M. R. Hebl, W. B. Morgan, and A. S. Ahmad, "Field Experiments on Sensitive Organizational Topics," *Organizational Research Methods* 16 (2013): 501–521.

45 B. Helm, "Online Polls: How Good Are They?" *BusinessWeek*, June 16, 2008, 86–87.

46 J. Jarvis, "The Buzz from Starbucks Customers," *BusinessWeek*, April 28, 2008, 37–38.

47 D. G. Mook, "In Defense of External Invalidity," *American Psychologist* 38 (1983): 379–387.

48 C. Suddath, "FedEx's Electric Vehicle Experiment," *Bloomberg Businessweek*, April 5, 2012, http://www.businessweek.com/articles/2012-04-05/fedexs-electric-vehicle-experiment.

49 M. S. Davis, "That's Interesting! Towards a Phenomenology of Sociology and a Sociology of Phenomenology," *Philosophy of the Social Sciences* 1 (1978): 309–344.

Index